Discovering Cape Breton
FOLKLORE

By Richard MacKinnon

To Bnt:

Thanks for all the
support over the years,

Robert MK

Discovering Cape Breton
FOLKLORE

By Richard MacKinnon

CAPE BRETON UNIVERSITY PRESS
SYDNEY, NOVA SCOTIA

Cape Breton University Press recognizes the support of the Province of Nova Scotia, through the Department of Tourism, Culture and Heritage and the support received for it publishing program from the Canada Council's Block Grants Program. We are pleased to work in partnership with these bodies to develop and promote our cultural resources.

Canada Council   Conseil des Arts
for the Arts   du Canada

NOVA SCOTIA
Tourism, Culture and Heritage

Cover art (door): Quarterly Reflections, by Lynn Moore, Howie Centre, NS

Cover design by Cathy MacLean Design, Pleasant Bay, NS

Layout by Gail Jones, Sydney, NS

Printed in Canada by Marquis Book Printing Cap-Saint-Ignace on 100% recycled 100% Post-consumer fiber. Certified EcoLogo and processed chlorine free. Manufactured using biogas energy.

Library and Archives Canada Cataloguing in Publication

MacKinnon, Richard Paul, 1957-
    Discovering Cape Breton folklore / Richard MacKinnon.

Includes bibliographical references.
ISBN 978-1-897009-30-7

    1. Folklore--Nova Scotia--Cape Breton Island. I. Title.

GR113.5.C36M34 2009   398.209716'9   C2009-905876-6

Cape Breton University Press
PO Box 5300
Sydney, NS   B1P 6L2
Canada

Table of Contents

List of Illustrations

Acknowledgements

I have spent the past 25 years or more trying to understand the traditions and culture of Cape Breton, one of the unique places on this planet. Its landscape is beautiful, its climate harsh at times, its people creative and clever. There are many who have assisted while I researched and wrote this book. First, numerous Cape Breton residents allowed me to take up their time by asking them questions and measuring and photographing their homes. Without their cooperation, this book would not be possible. As well, my students over the years have given me lots of ideas and helped me to shape some of those that appear in this book. I have always enjoyed reading their research papers on the distinctive cultural traditions of Cape Breton.

Some of my undergraduate research assistants over the year who have helped with parts of this book include: Karli Bambrick, Michelle Desveaux, Kevin Kearney, Beverly MacDonald, Emily MacLeod, Erin Martell, Sheldon McCormick, Iain Moore, Nicole Morrison, Moira Ross, Bernadine Ryan, Laura Schella, Kim Stockley and Ainslie White. Masters and PhD students who helped along the way include: Erin Columbus, Michael MacDonald, Jodi McDavid and Moira Ross.

My colleagues at CBU have provided discussion, inspiration, collaboration and support over the years. These include: Dr. Rusty Bitterman, Dr. Ian Brodie, Nicole Claener, Dr. Jane Connell, Dr. Bill Davey, Dr. Jim Guy, Dr. Chris MacDonald, Dr. Don MacGillivray, Dr. Terry MacLean, Barry Moore, Dr. Robert Morgan, Dr. Rod Nicholls, Dr. Graham Reynolds, Dr. Michael Robidoux, Dr. Danny Samson, Dr. Heather Sparling, Dr. Arthur Tucker, Dr. Tom Urbaniak and Sheldon MacInnes.

The staff of the CBU library and the Beaton Institute archives would always help me find me what I needed.

Other researchers and scholars who have helped immensely include: Jane Arnold, Archivist, Beaton Institute; Catherine Arsenault, Manager, Beaton Institute; Kinnon Beaton, Celtic Music Interpretive Centre; Kate Currie, former archival assistant, Beaton Institute; Barry Gabriel for drawings and sketches; Mike Hunter, CBU Press; Dr. Kay MacDonald, former Gaelic specialist at the Beaton Institute, Cape Breton University, for translations from Gaelic to English; Doug MacPhee, Order of Canada recipient and former music archivist, Beaton Institute; Dr. Del Muise, Carleton University; Dr. Brian Preston, former Provincial Archaeologist for the province of Nova Scotia; Jim St.Clair for his fieldwork assistance and advice; Dr. Diane Tye, Memorial University of Newfoundland; Don Ward, Cape Breton Regional Library.

Two people who were instrumental in making this book happen: Folklorist and able research assistant, Marie MacSween who manages the production of the scholarly journal, Material Culture Review and soon-to-be-Dr. Jodi McDavid, who was a fine copyeditor as this book came together.

I owe a debt of gratitude to my colleagues at Memorial University of Newfoundland who taught me the joys of fieldwork and ethnographic research. I'll single out Dr. Gerald Pocius, Royal Society of Canada member, Dr. John Mannion, retired Geography professor and expert on the Irish in Atlantic Canada and Dr. Diane Tye, Head of the Folklore Department, MUN. Along the way they and their families have become lifelong friends.

I'd like to thank my parents Pauline and Francis MacKinnon who always encouraged me to learn and to continue studying. I thank my wife Joan Weeks for her unwavering support, encouragement and wise advice and my children Connall, Breagh and Lachlan MacKinnon for being there.

Introduction: Discovering Cape Breton Folklore

There was a Cape Bretoner from Louisbourg who decided to go to the West in search of work. He landed in Vancouver on the waterfront and began searching for employment. He went to the office of the company that manages the ferries running from Vancouver. When he went to the office the manager started asking him questions. First he asked what experience he had with boats.

"I have lots of experience, I've been on boats since I was five years old," was the reply. The manager then asked, "Do you have any experience with navigation?" "Yes," he replied, "I know all about navigation. I don't need any of that new fancy global positioning stuff, as I know all about celestial navigation. I just have to look at the stars and can tell where I am." The manager said, "That's good." He then said, "Do you know anything about knots?" "Yes, I know all about knots, I've been tying knots since I was a young lad." "Well," the manager said, "it looks as if you're the kind of person we need." He said that his company has a literacy policy and that every employee must take a test. The manager asked, "Make me a sentence with the word "great." The Cape Bretoner thought for a minute and replied, "I've got a new shirt and it's just great." The manager replied, "You have the job."

About two weeks later the man's friend phoned from Cape Breton and said, "There's not much work here in Cape Breton; is it difficult finding work in the West?" His friend encouraged him to come out to Vancouver to stay with him while he found work. Sure enough, he landed in Vancouver to visit his friend and he was briefed on how to get a job down at the docks. So he went to see the same manager. The manager asked him some questions. "What experience do you have with boats?" "I have lots of experience, I've been on boats since I was five years old," was the reply. The manager then asked, "Do you have any experience with navigation?" "Yes," he replied, "I know all about navigation. I don't need any of that new fancy global positioning stuff, as I know all about celestial navigation. I just have to look at the stars and can tell where I am." The manager said, "That's good." He then asked, "Do you know anything about knots?" "Yes, I know all about knots, I've been tying knots since I was a young lad." "Well," the manager said, "it looks as if you're the kind of person we need." He said that the company has a literacy policy and that every employee must take a test. The manager said, "Make me a sentence with the word 'fascinate'." Well this stumped the Cape Bretoner because his friend had told him a different word, "great." He thought for a short time and said, "I've got a new shirt and it's just great, it's got nine buttons but I only fasten eight!"

This narrative has a humorous punch line, but there is an unfortunate reality reflected within. Cape Bretoners have had to migrate to other places in search of work for generations. Cape Bretoners are surrounded by the sea; in the centre of the island is a large inland sea—Bras d'Or Lake. Consequently, as one might discern from this narrative, some Cape Bretoners know much about tides, the weather and celestial matters relating to the water. The joke was passed on to me through a conversation with my twin brother Robert who heard it from a Vancouver ferry boat captain who has roots in Cape Breton. It was transmitted orally when Robert was visiting Cape Breton after travelling from Kamloops, British Columbia.

Jokes are simply one of many genres of folklore that can be found in Cape Breton. By passing this joke on to me my brother was engaging in the folklore transmission process: I have continued to tell it in various contexts over the years. As Cape Bretoners, we maintain this joke in our joke-telling repertoire for a variety of reasons—it shows our worldview and issues that are of concern to us, such as outmigration, and it involves language play. Furthermore, we tell it to other Cape Bretoners, who live in a culture that holds verbal acuity and the ability to craft a witty remark or comment as important values. Proficient joke or storytelling has always been an important aspect of Cape Breton's folklore.

What is Folklore?

Folklore is a complicated word. Dictionaries and encyclopedias usually provide enumerative definitions with a listing of items such as jokes, songs, stories, myths, legends, folktales, proverbs, riddles, toasts, blessings, architecture, crafts, customs and beliefs (Leach 1972: 398-403). As David Buchan states, "What basically distinguishes folklore as an academic discipline is its concern with tradition; that is, the area of culture maintained and transmitted by word-of-mouth and by customary practice rather than by the printed or written document." Buchan expands his definition: "Folklore, in operation, concerns itself with both texts and contexts, items and processes and, since traditional learning still permeates modern life, the present as well as the past." The discipline does not concern itself with the quaint; the folklorist addresses "fundamental issues of man and his culture: knowledge, art, thought, feeling and behaviour" (Buchan 1981: 25).

William Thoms first coined the word folklore in 1846 to supply a term for the study of what was previously called "popular antiquities," the antiques or relics of the past. He thought folklore to be the remains of earlier cultures surviving in the present and that by studying these remains one could obtain a sense of what society was once like (Thoms 1965: 5-6). Today, many folklorists are interested in the past but are also fascinated by the role of tradition in our contemporary lives. They continue to debate the boundaries of the discipline and to analyze tradition in a variety of ways (Bascom 1955; Dorson 1982; Dundes 1965; Kirshenblatt-Gimblett 1992).

Michael Taft, head of the American Folklife Centre archives at the Library of Congress, provides a contemporary, simple definition of folklore as "the common creativity of humankind." It is, as Taft points out, "the ways in which you and I are creative, clever and artistic in our everyday lives" (1983: 12). He expands this by saying that folklore is the "kind of creativity which people exhibit when involved in everyday activities of small groups, localities or communities" (19).

Cape Breton Island: A Rich Folklore Context

Cape Breton Island has its own distinct history and a cultural background that creates a dynamic tradition of expression. In the rural and industrial areas of the Island one finds a variety of genres of folklore.

We see this rewarded in the arts: our writers, poets and songmakers win regional, national and international awards for their creativity in language and music. Alistair MacLeod, who writes short stories and novels that draw on Cape Breton's Gaelic and mining culture, won one of the world's most prestigious writing awards in 2001—the International IMPAC Dublin Literary Award; the late Mi'kmaw poet, Rita Joe, received the Order of Canada. Matt Minglewood, a Canadian blues music legend, was given an honorary doctorate by Cape Breton University. He has won numerous music industry awards including the 2004 and 2006 East Coast Music Award's Blues Recording of the Year and the 2005 Maple Blues Award for Entertainer of the Year. Sydney musician, Hubba Paris, was recognized by the East Coast Music Association for his long term commitment to the local music industry when he won the Stompin' Tom Award. Our high school students frequently win awards for their oral skills: Sydney Academy high school is world renowned for its debaters, some of whom, like Sheldon McCormack, have gone on to debate at the university level (McCormack now debates for Queen's University). McCormack is one of Cape Breton's many wordsmiths, having travelled to Harvard University, the University of Connecticut and Oxford University, winning debates against the top debating teams in the world. Furthermore, Cape Breton University has a unique specialty in communication, developed by Dr. Mary Lynch in the 1970s; it is one of the few universities in Canada with this expertise in teaching and research.

Traditional Music

Cape Breton Island is known around the world for its musical folklore and dance traditions. Between 1775 and 1850, more than twenty-five thousand Gaelic-speaking Scots from every region of the Highlands and Islands established communities throughout Cape Breton Island and Eastern Nova Scotia. They brought with them their language and many distinctive oral and musical traditions. Through their interaction with the other established people on the Island (principally the Mi'kmaq, Acadian and Irish populations), a distinctive fiddle and piano style emerged which in turn spawned its own distinct step dance and square dance tradition. These traditions are now receiving international attention and Cape Breton Island performers travel the world bringing this unique form of creativity to others; conversely, visitors flock to the Island to hear these musical traditions. "Celtic Colours," an international Celtic music festival held each October, attracts more than three hundred musicians from all over the Celtic world, including Scotland, Ireland, the United States, Brittany and Canada, to perform at venues across the Island. In 2006, visitors came to Celtic Colours from every province and territory in Canada, forty-five American States and eighteen other countries (Celtic Colours International Festival 2006).

In this collection of essays, I try to provide a sense of the importance of Cape Breton's music tradition with the inclusion of three chapters: "A Brief History of Cape Breton Folksong Collecting," "Protest Song and Verse in Cape Breton" and "Victorian Parlour Instrument Meets the Celtic

Fiddle: The Dynamics of the Cape Breton Piano Style." "A Brief History of Cape Breton Folksong Collecting" takes a historical look at some of the early collectors—most of whom were primarily from outside the region—who came in search of Gaelic folksongs. The chapter looks at the collectors, where the items were collected, and from whom. It provides a rich context not otherwise available, from which to draw resources for future research, as there has yet to be an extensive treatment of the history of folksong collection in the region. "Protest Song and Verse in Cape Breton" explores the rich protest song tradition that had its roots in the industrial region of Cape Breton Island in the 1920s. This chapter examines protest songs and verses from the *Maritime Labour Herald (MLH)* circa 1920 and discusses what previous collectors have used as criterion for authenticating cultural expressions. In "Victorian Parlour Instrument Meets the Celtic Fiddle: The Dynamics of the Cape Breton Piano Style," the features and roots of the distinctive piano accompaniment tradition found in the region are discussed. This chapter looks at the development of the piano from an instrument of accompaniment to a solo instrument, discussing dynamism and conservativism as it pertains to traditional music.

Rituals and Customs

Rituals and customs play a significant role in the ways we celebrate the rites of passage of our lives. Birth, marriage, graduations, promotions and, finally, death all are times when customary behaviour and rituals are enacted. Some rituals are religious, others secular; some are engaged in by a large group and others by smaller groups. Yet all human beings engage in numerous rituals, activities and customary behaviour throughout their lives.

Although rites of passage mark major life-changing events, most communities also have practices and rituals that show creative expression or that help facilitate the customs of day-to-day life, sometimes called folklife.

In this collection, I include one chapter that focuses on the once-customary activity of cockfighting, its meaning and function. This chapter deals with a recreational activity in a mining town, and traces the history of the custom of cockfighting. Cockfighting events are very ritualistic and, due to their illegality, occur at specific times and places and rely highly on informal communication in order to operate.

Another chapter draws attention to folklife and daily practices. "Humorous Nicknames in Cape Breton" highlights the aforementioned importance of oral culture and verbal folklore in Cape Breton, but it also depicts folklife or daily custom by showing the function and form of local naming. It shows how individuals who are creative and clever in their language usage by demonstrating the variety of ways that nicknames are formed in both the rural and industrial regions.

Due to the nature of the material in both of these chapters, my participants asked to be anonymous. Although the quotes in these chapters were collected from community members during the course of fieldwork, their identities are protected as per their request.

Material Culture

Material folklore, or what is referred to as "material culture," is an area of folklore where much of my research has been conducted. At Cape Breton University we publish the *Material Culture Review*, a scholarly journal that is purchased by libraries and archives in more than thirty countries around the world. Material culture includes all the things that humans make and use including houses, barns, clothing, tools, crafts and decorative artifacts of all kinds. Folklorists are not only interested in documenting the material culture in our lives but are interested in exploring deeper questions about the meaning of objects for human beings.

In this collection I have included one chapter from rural Cape Breton and two from the industrial region. "Log Architecture on Cape Breton Island: Cultural Borrowing and Adaptation" examines how this early form of architecture was employed by a diversity of ethnic groups on the Island and postulates a theory of what ethnic group from the Island passed the tradition on to others.

In contrast, two other chapters focus on the architectural traditions of the industrial communities of the Island. "Making a House a Home: Company Housing in Cape Breton," closely examines the houses of one neighbourhood in Sydney, where the houses were built for plant workers of the Sydney steel plant in the early part of the 20th century. "Tompkinsville, Cape Breton Island: Co-operativism and Vernacular Architecture" discusses the first co-operative housing development in Canada in the community of Reserve Mines in the late 1930s. The essay highlights the ways in which some owners have transformed these spaces into meaningful places and homes.

Future Directions

The chapter entitled "Public Image and Private Reality in Cape Breton Folk Traditions" shows that governments and others in positions of authority often use simplistic symbols of tradition, stereotypes if you will, to represent cultural groups. Often these images are inaccurate accounts of the traditional culture of the group. By looking at some of the private traditions of the group one can obtain a more representative understanding of the meaningful traditions of the group being studied.

Around the world, scholars and government officials are now using a phrase other than "folklore" to denote the materials that are found in this collection. The United Nations Educational Scientific and Cultural Organization (UNESCO) now use the phrase "intangible cultural heritage" to refer to folklore—which translates much better throughout the world's different cultures and languages for culture workers, governments and scholars than the word "folklore" (UNESCO 2003).

UNESCO's 2003 *Convention for the Safeguarding of Intangible Cultural Heritage* defines intangible cultural heritage as "the practices, representations, expressions, as well as the knowledge and skills, that communities, groups and, in some cases, individuals recognize as part of their cultural heritage." It is the body of cultural and social expressions that characterize groups and communities and are based on tradition. It can be called "living cultural heritage" or the culture that people practise as part of their daily lives, and include such cultural items as languages and dialects, oral traditions and storytelling, beliefs and customs, traditional knowledge and skills, ways of working and making a living, ways of celebrating that includes music, festivals, rituals, performing arts, traditional foodways and traditional crafts. When this international heritage convention was brought forth in Paris, October 17, 2003, 120 member-states voted for the multilateral treaty; no one voted against it and only a few nations abstained including Australia, the United Kingdom, Switzerland, the United States and Canada (Kurin 2004: 66). For the convention to become international law it was necessary that it be ratified by thirty states. By January 2006, thirty-two states had ratified this agreement, thus making it international law. Canada has still not signed this international heritage convention. If Canada does become a signatory to this convention, I suspect there will be more interest in this important area of Canadian heritage. I chose to title my Canada Research Chair "Intangible Cultural Heritage" in hope that my ongoing research will in some way help to influence heritage policy within, and beyond, our Canadian borders.

At Cape Breton University we have the only program in Nova Scotia and one of the few in the country with a specialty in folklore as well as a specialty in ethnomusicology; we also have a unique focus on Cape Breton Island traditional music. It could be said that our program began in the early 1980s, around the same time I was hired as a lecturer in the departments of Humanities and Community Studies. Around the same time,

Sheldon MacInnes was teaching in the extension program at the university. In those early years we struggled for a foothold in the "core courses" of the university, mainly promoting the discipline through courses that were cross-listed or offered as special topics. Many community members gladly gave of their time and taught as per-course instructors, passing on their skills and knowledge to a new generation. It was difficult to fund courses which did not fit into a major or minor, and many key administrators assisted us at a variety of levels. When I received my Canada Research Chair it enabled the department to grow and flourish, and a fulltime folklorist and ethnomusicologist were hired in quick succession. With the help of these two individuals the department has continued to grow in leaps and bounds and now offers a major in folklore and minor in ethnomusicology.

Although the chapters in this collection focus on music, ritual and custom and material culture, it is not meant to be exhaustive. Other Folklore topic areas that could be added in a future collection could include items of belief, health and illness, foodways, traditional knowledge, festivals and crafts. Other ethnic groups than those explored here could be approached to share their traditional knowledge and practises. As David Buchan points out when discussing the discipline of Folklore, "the subject's involvement with both texts and contexts indicates the close relationship of the discipline to both English and anthropology, but there also exist overlapping areas of concern with medicine, law, religion, language, geography, history, sociology, psychology and music. There are, in fact, very few fields of human activity, and hence intellectual inquiry, that are not touched at some point by tradition" (Buchan 1981: 25).

We stand at an interesting crossroads where much can be achieved. For that reason I have greatly enjoyed compiling some of my previously published work and some new research to provide insights into current issues and future possibilities. I like to think that the essays in *Discovering Cape Breton Folklore* reflect my enthusiasm for the subject and the place, and I hope they will encourage others to become engaged in this complex, fascinating area of human study.

Notes
1. When I use the term Cape Breton, I refer to the whole of the island, and not just the area commonly referred to as industrial Cape Breton. This latter area, largely Cape Breton County is now officially known as the Cape Breton Regional Municipality, which was formed in 1995 from eight former municipalities in Cape Breton County.

Chapter 1
A Brief History of Cape Breton Folksong Collecting

The inspiration for this survey of Cape Breton folksong collecting came early in my graduate studies at Memorial University of Newfoundland. I was fascinated by the history of folksong collection in that province and the descriptions of the early collectors, their education, motivation and research methods. At the time, I examined the types of songs they recorded and thought about comparable songs I was familiar with from Cape Breton. I began to realize that a history of Cape Breton folksong collection had not been documented, despite the fact that the area had a rich folksong tradition. In subsequent research I have been aware of additional collectors and collections and this is by no means a complete history. It is my hope that the information provided here will provide some background for those interested in the fascinating history of folksong collecting and collectors and inspire further research.

An earlier version of this chapter was published in the journal Culture and Tradition *4 (1979): 23-29.*

In the late 18th and early 19th centuries a large group of Scottish Highlanders emigrated from their homeland to Cape Breton Island, located off the northeast coast of Nova Scotia. They brought with them their language, cultural traits and their folksongs. Cape Breton has been viewed as an ideal folksong collecting location and many of its songs have been collected, annotated and published, though few scholars have seriously considered the extent and quality of this material. This chapter examines some of the available published Cape Breton folksong collections and provides bibliographic information and contextual materials for anyone wishing to further investigate this tradition.

One of the first native collectors of Cape Breton Gaelic songs was James D. Gillis from Broad Cove Intervale, Inverness County. He was born on July 11, 1870, to parents of Highland Scottish descent and earned a reputation in Nova Scotia as a poet, piper, fiddler and songmaker. Despite his collecting, he is more well known as a poet and a member of the Atlantic "song fishermen," a group who met to discuss and read their creative writing through the 1920s and 30s. In his varied works of prose and poetry he often intersperses songs and poems. His collections are not thematically categorized and no annotation is attempted. However, they do provide examples of some early 20th-century Gaelic songs native to Cape Breton (see Gillis's two undated collections, as well as publications dated 1915a and b, 1925, 1926, 1936).

In 1929 another Cape Bretoner, Stuart McCawley from Glace Bay, became interested in Cape Breton folksongs. In that year he published *A Book of Songs and "Come All Ye" of Cape Breton and Newfoundland*. McCawley did not categorize any of the songs. Labour songs, Gaelic songs, local love songs, sea songs, ballads, Newfoundland songs, comic ditties and poems are scattered throughout the volume. He does not describe his fieldwork techniques and names only some of the informants. The Cape Breton songs far outnumber those from Newfoundland: "Lukey's Boat," "The Kelligrew's Soiree," "The Newfoundland Fisherman" and "The Spring Maurice Crotty Fought the Old Dog Hood" being the only Newfoundland examples (McCawley 1929: 10, 39, 44, 46).

He provides no bibliographic listing of song variants, no music and in most cases no citation of the communities where the songs were collected. Nevertheless it must be realized that the audience for which this songster was intended would use it solely to obtain the words to these songs unconcerned with scholarly criticism.

In the 1930s, Helen Creighton began collecting folksongs in Cape Breton. She chose Cape Breton because it was considered remote. From the material obtained in the field, she published two compilations of Cape Breton Songs: *Maritime Folksongs* in 1962 and *Gaelic Songs in Nova Scotia* in 1964. In these volumes, excellent annotation is combined with fine translation of texts and tunes. While her collecting trips to Cape Breton can be regarded as successful, they would have been of much more value to folklorists had she provided more data about her informants. She describes the meeting with James D. Gillis as being the "funniest encounter" of one of her trips and comments that while recording Gillis she was "working from the back seat of the car and could crouch low and have [her] chuckle he was so deadly serious" (Creighton 1975: 148-49). No doubt Gillis was eccentric, but if she had viewed him with a different attitude perhaps a better understanding of this songmaker might have been obtained.

A collection of songs quite similar to that of McCawley entitled *Cape Breton Songster: A Book of Favorite English and Gaelic Songs* appeared in 1935. Alphonse MacDonald, the compiler, relies on some of the same informants as both Creighton and McCawley. MacDonald and Creighton collected songs from Malcolm Gillis while both McCawley and MacDonald worked with Harvey MacKenzie and Lauchlin MacNeil. MacDonald's work, like McCawley's, is not intended for an academic audience; there are no annotations. Songs ranging from "Home on the Range," and "Òran Do Cheap Breatainn," to "Our Unspoiled Summerland" and "The Honest Working Man," suggest some of the variety; Scottish Gaelic songs, native Cape Breton songs, cowboy songs, college songs, war songs and labour songs all appear in this collection.

In the autumn of 1937 two non-Nova Scotian collectors appeared in Cape Breton. John Lorne Campbell and his wife Margaret Fay Shaw from Scotland arrived, "with the express purpose of comparing the oral tradition of Barra, in the Outer Hebrides with that of the descendants of immigrants from Barra living in Cape Breton" (Campbell and Shaw 1962: 174). Some of the songs collected on this excursion were published with annotation in *Hebridean Folksongs* by J. L. Campbell and Francis Collinson in 1977. Many of the songs they collected were milling or waulking songs (occupational songs for community wool processing) and from their fieldwork the following conclusion was reached:

> The older people in Cape Breton spoke very good Gaelic, but the tunes of the traditional songs there had been somewhat simplified, very good versions of the words of old waulking songs were extant there, clearly resembling the Hebridean versions. (Campbell and Collinson 1977: 12)

Judging them "somewhat simplified," the Campbells believed that the songs found in Cape Breton had regressed or lost purity in their passage across the ocean. While they were excellent scholars and their collection shows that cultural transfer indeed exists, their methodology was quite limiting because it is the earliest functional study of traditional waulking and milling songs in Cape Breton. Like other collectors of that time, their vision was to collect songs that had made the transatlantic voyage; they did not seem too interested in compositions of Cape Breton origin even though these types of songs would have been readily available.

MacEdward Leach, from Pennsylvania, commenced a Cape Breton folksong collecting expedition in 1950. According to Leach, "Often in the periphery of a culture the most archaic elements are found. It is conceivable that older stories and songs might be found in Cape Breton than in Scotland or Ireland" (Leach 1957: 41). Leach did find a great number of both songs and stories but only published one article about Cape Breton folktales based on his trip. His collected songs are still not in print but have been published on a website produced at Memorial University of Newfoundland, and his collection is housed at its Folklore and Language Archive (www.mun.ca/folklore/leach/).

At about this time Charles Dunn was collecting material for his study *The Highland Settler: A Portrait of the Scottish Gael in Nova Scotia* (1953). In this work fragments of songs sung by descendants of Scottish immigrants are used in descriptions of the settlers' lifestyles. He noted that many of the songs collected were written in Cape Breton and used Cape Breton as a setting, a phenomenon also observed by Creighton. Dunn theorized that the Scottish settlers had undergone a transition in becoming Scottish Cape Bretoners.

Cape Breton's Magazine, another source of folksong texts and material, began publishing in 1972 and was concerned with Acadian, French, English and aboriginal traditions, as well as the Scottish Gaelic presence in Cape Breton. The magazine printed only a few Gaelic Cape Breton songs over the years. However, along with the song texts, the attitudes and perspectives of the singers were described. One singer, Hector Carmichael, gives a better understanding of his repertoire when he says:

> The songs I make is making fun of people. You know. I don't write it down, no I make them. I can't write Gaelic you know. I can read pretty well all the Gaelic but I can't write it. I remember them when I compare them. (Carmichael 1974: 15)

This move toward the study of the singer and the function of his songs differs from the perspective taken by some of the earlier collectors. Folklorists now insist that collecting the *context* of an item of Folklore is just as significant as the item itself. Many early collectors did not think it important to study and interpret this social and cultural context; their discipline did not view this as significant.

Other interested individuals have been collecting songs in this Cape Breton tradition. Ronald MacEachern was an undergraduate folklore student at Memorial University, and a Cape Breton musician and song composer. He obtained a Canada Council grant in 1977 to collect songs in various parts of the Island. His taped song collection has been given to the National Museum of Man, The Miners Museum in Glace Bay, the Beaton Institute in Sydney and Memorial University Folklore Archives in

St. John's. MacEachern did not have the biases of some earlier fieldworkers and collected a wide range of songs; labour songs, love songs, Gaelic songs, mining songs, local ballads and humorous songs. He wrote two reports on his expeditions (1978, 1979a) and some of his songs appear in the publication, *Songs and Stories from Deep Cove* (MacEachern 1979b).

John Shaw has done much Folklore collecting in the Gaelic communities on the island and the fruits of his labour can be found in his landmark publications (MacNeil 1987; MacLellan 2000) and on a web site developed by St. Francis Xavier University (Shaw 2005). Shaw lived in Glendale through the 1970s and 80s and did extensive collecting throughout the region at this time: he is now a professor at Edinburgh University in the School of Scottish Studies. Jim Watson at the Nova Scotia Highland Village in Iona has also conducted fieldwork on the island and the museum has done much work in attempting to preserve and protect Gaelic through its programming, exhibit development and research. Frances McEachern and *Am Braighe* magazine in the early 1990s provided an outlet for those interested in preserving Gaelic tradition and often included articles on song and music in her issues. Effie Rankin has recently brought to light the compositions of the Gaelic Ridge MacDonald bards in a book published by Cape Breton University Press (Rankin 2004).

There are many others who have helped perpetuate the song tradition of the island including Gaelic choirs, bands such as the Rankin Family and the Barra MacNeils and individuals such as Allister MacGillivray, Neil MacPhee and Donnie Campbell to name only a few. There were early radio programs that were interested in Cape Breton music that we do not know much about; much more research needs to be conducted into these early program that broadcast Cape Breton songs as early as the 1930s.

In the years since I was initially interested in this topic, many more collectors and collections have been brought to my attention. Most notable are those of three American women: Laura Boulton, Sidney Cowell and Diane Hamilton. Boulton, an early ethnomusicologist, did research in the area in the early 1940s, the majority of which is now housed at the Columbia University archives. Boulton produced many field recordings and short films during her ethnographic work, and her autobiography entitled *The Music Hunter* (1969) details her international research. Cowell released *Songs from Cape Breton Island* on Folkways (1955). From her obituary in the March 1, 1995, edition of *The New York Times* we learn that she was born in 1903 and later attended Stanford. She and her husband later worked for the United States State Department as "cultural ambassadors." The couple travelled extensively and she made a ten minute film *Gaels of Cape Breton* (1947), which was released by the National Film Board. Her collection is housed at the Library of Congress. Information on Hamilton is also slight; she assumed the name Hamilton (as well as others) to disguise the fact that she was a Guggenheim heiress. She released field recordings entitled *Nova Scotia Folk Music from Cape Breton* (Hamilton 1955), but she also ran Tradition Records in the 1950s.

Although it can certainly be used as a launching point for further research, Appendix 1.1 provides an index of singers of songs in the Scottish tradition in Cape Breton and the collectors who recorded them, while Appendix 1.2 provides a listing of place names where collectors who have published their collections have done fieldwork and the number of singers from each place. It shows that there are a large number of singers in the urban areas of Cape Breton: five from Sydney, six from Glace Bay, one from New Waterford and one from North Sydney. Other areas that have provided numerous informants include places such as Gillisdale (five), Christmas Island (four), Margaree (four) and Southwest Margaree (four). The large number of informants from the industrial region, the Christmas Island region and the Margaree Valley may be as a result of accessibility; these districts are more accessible than the unrepresented Northern Highlands. An index of singers mentioned in the published works shows that the same informants were contacted by several collectors. This suggests that collectors may have used the similar method of finding the "best" singer in each community when conducting fieldwork. These individuals were perceived as the active tradition bearers of the day and were known as authorities by locals as well as outsiders with respect to the island's songs.

Although much collecting has been done throughout the 20th century, further emphasis in the future must be placed on studying, cataloguing, and publishing songs and making them available in new formats for new audiences around the world. As academic programs for the study of folklore have progressed, new techniques and recording technologies have also developed. Today's researcher has many more tools at their disposal and can (and should) provide context to the collected songs. The song-maker, the community in which the song is found, and song annotations and comparisons are now a major part of the field of folksong collection.

APPENDIX 1.1

Index of singers of songs in the Scottish tradition in Cape Breton and the collectors:

Designation	Collector, collection
M	Creighton, *Maritime Folksongs.*
C	Creighton and MacLeod, *Gaelic Songs in Nova Scotia.*
D	Dunn, *The Highland Settler.*
H	Campbell and Collinson, *Hebridean Folksongs.*
G	Gillis, *The Greatest Election.*
L	Leach, "Celtic Tales from Cape Breton."
S	McCawley, *A Book of Songs and "Come All Ye" of Cape Breton.*
B	*Cape Breton's Magazine.*
R	MacEachern, *Songs and Stories from Deep Cove.*
A	MacDonald, *Cape Breton Songster.*
E	Campbell, *Songs Remembered in Exile.*
O	MacLellan, *Brígh An Órain: A Story in Every Song.*
N	Rankin, *As A' Bhràighe Beyond the Braes: The Gaelic Songs of Allan the Ridge MacDonald 1794-1868.*
F	MacDonald, in *The Hebridean Connection.*
I	MacLeod, *An T-Eithireach: Original Gaelic Poems and Melodies.*

Informant, location	*Collection*
Black, Johnny, Sydney	R
Butterworth, Jack, Glace Bay	C
Campbell, Angus, Salmon River	C
Carmichael, Hector, St. Ann's	B
Douglas, William, Sydney	A
Dunbar, J. J., Scotsville	A
Ferguson, Kenneth, Sydney	C, D
Gillis, Angus R., Gillisdale	C
Gillis, Archie A. (Gilleasbuig Aonghuis Alasdair), Broad Cove	O
Gillis, Black Jack, Margaree and Boston	O
Gillis, Christine, Gillisdale	C

Gillis, James D., Mt. Young	C, G
Gillis, John Neil, Gillisdale	C
Gillis, Lachie, Grand Mira	C
Gillis, Malcolm, Margaree	C
Gillis, Mrs. Keogh, MacKinnon's Harbour	D
Gillis, Mrs. Sandy Sheumais, Gillisdale	C, O
Gillis, Neil, Gillisdale	C
Hinkley, Jack Sam, Pleasant Bay	B
Jamieson, J. H., Glace Bay	C
Johnson, Callum and Annie, Barra	O
Johnston, Mrs. J. R., Glace Bay, Beaver Cove	H, E
Kennedy, Mrs. Archie, Gillisdale	C
Larade, Joseph, New Waterford	R
Livingstone, Mrs. Dan, Boulardarie	C
MacArthur, Angus, Broad Cove	O
MacDonald, Allen, South West Margaree	D
MacDonald, Allan the Ridge, Mabou	N
MacDonald, Angus	F
MacDonald, Angus the Ridge, Upper South River, Antigonish County	E
MacDonald, Archibald, New Boston	D
MacDonald, Charles, North River	C
MacDonald, Dan Alex, Framboise	C, D
MacDonald, Donald, South West Margaree	C
MacDonald, Duncan, French Road	D
MacDonald, Francis, South West Margaree	R
MacDonald, Garret, North River Meadow	D
MacDonald, John "The Hunter," Mabou	D
MacDonald, Neill MacLocklainn Bleurs, Albert Bridge	D
MacDonald, Peggy (Peigi Ruairidh Ailein)	O
MacDonald, Rev. Hugh A., Louisburg	C
MacDonald, Rev. J. D. Nelson, Middle River	C
MacDougall, D. J., Christmas Island	E
MacDougall, Mike, Ingonish Beach	R
MacDougall, Mary Ann, Ingonish Beach	R
MacEacharn, Dómhnull, Creignish	O
MacEachern, Archie	A
MacFarlane, Argus Ban, Margaree	D

MacFarlane, D. D., Margaree	D
MacIsaac, Alec John	O
MacIsaac, Angus, Antigonish	E
MacIssac, James, Mira	D
MacKay, D. A., Grand River	C
MacKay, George, North Sydney	B
MacKenzie, Archie J., Christmas Islan	D,M, H, E
MacKenzie, Hugh F., Grand Narrows	C, M
MacKinnon, Captain Donald Joseph, Barra	O
MacKinnon, Hector, Ainslie Glen	E
MacKinnon, Jonathan G., Whycocomagh	D, H, E
MacKinnon, Joseph D., Glace Bay	D
MacKinnon, Neil, Ainslie Glen	E
MacKinnon, Stephen, Big Pond/Sydney	O
MacLean, Alec, Big Baddeck	O
MacLean, Duncan, South West Margaree	D
MacLean, Hugh. Og., Sight Pt.	C
MacLean, Joe Allan, Christmas Island/Sydney	O
MacLean, Mrs. (Catherine Nicholson), Beaver Cove	H
MacLean, Mrs. John A., Albert Bridge	C
MacLean, Margaret, Boisdale	O
MacLean, Mrs. M. B., Beaver Cove	E
MacLean, Peter, Baddeck	M
MacLellan, Archie Dan, Broad Cove	O
MacLellan, Lauchie	O
MacLellan, Neil	O
MacLeod, D. B., Breton Cove	C
MacLeod, D. K., North River	C
MacLeod, Major	C, I, N, I
MacLeod, Malcolm Angus, Birch Plains, (North Shore)	C, O
MacMillan, Mary Ann, Mira	O
MacNeil, Frank, Big Pond	C
MacNeil, Jim, Hughie, Sydney	C
MacNeil, Joe Neil, Big Pond	O
MacNeil, John Dan, Melford	O
MacNeil, John V., Christmas Island	D
MacNeil, Michael, Benacadie Pond	E
MacQueen, Evan, Peter's Brook	D

MacRae, William Dan, Seaview	R
MacVicar, Fred, New Waterford	M
McCawley, Stuart, Glace Bay	S
McInnis, Mrs. Neil (Ann MacDonald), Glace Bay	H, E
McKenzie, Harvey (not given)	S, A
McLellan, Angus, Grand Mira	C
McLellan, Malcolm, Gillisdale	C
McLellan, Vincent A., Sydney	D
McMaster, Mr. and Mrs. Archie, Port Hastings	C
McNeil, Lauchlin, French Road	S, A
Matheson, "Big Norman," Breton Cove	C
Morrison, Murdock, Ferguson's Lake	D
Morrison, Roderick, Drummondville	C
Munro, Kathryn	A
Oliver, James "Nipper," New Waterford	R
Patterson, Mrs. David, Benacadie	C, H, E
Petrie, Hazel, Dingwall	R
Ryan, Mrs. Mary, Sydney	R
Quinn, Allan A., Coxheath	C
Ross, William, Victoria County	S
Shaw, John, North Shore	O
Thomas, Ambrose, Sydney	R
Whittey, Marsella, North Sydney	R
Willams, Johnny, Melford	O
Williams, Sandy, Port Hood	O

APPENDIX 1.2

A listing of known place names where collectors who have published their collections have done field work and the number of singers from each place.

Ainslie Glen, 2

Albert Bridge, 1

Antigonish, 1

Baddeck, 1

Barra, 2

Beaver Cove, 3

Benacadie Pond, 2

Big Baddeck, 1

Big Pond, 3

Birch Plains, 1

Boston, 1

Boisdale, 1

Broad Cove, 3

Breton Cove, 2

Boularderie, 1

Christmas Island, 4

Coxheath, 1

Creignish, 1

Drummondville, 1

Fergusson's Lake, 1

Framboise, 2

French Road, 2

Gillisdale, 5

Glace Bay, 6

Grand Mira, 2

Grand Narrows, 2

Grand River, 1

Louisbourg, 1

Mabou, 1

MacKinnon's Harbour, 1

Margaree, 4

Marion Bridge, 1

Melford, 2

Middle River, 1

Mira, 2

Mount Young, Lake Ainslie, 1

New Boston, 1

New Waterford, 1

North River, 2

North Shore, 2

North Sydney, 1

North River Meadow, 1

Peter's Brook, 1

Pleasant Bay, 1

Port Hood, 1

Salmon River, 1

Skir Dhu, 1

Sight Point, 1

South West Margaree, 4

St. Esprit, 1

Sydney, 5

Upper South River, 1

Whycocomagh, 2

Chapter 2
Victorian Parlour Instrument Meets the Celtic Fiddle:
The Dynamics of the Cape Breton Piano Style

This chapter explores some of the important stylistic features of the Cape Breton piano tradition and looks at how the piano has grown from an instrument of accompaniment to a solo instrument for some influential "star" players.

I argue that the Cape Breton music tradition is a dynamic one, and not as conservative as is sometimes presented. As well, I discuss the most accepted theory as to how the piano tradition developed—from the 19th-century drone, pump organ sound to a piano style marked by aurally-transmitted bass lines and unique chord progressions. By the turn of the 20th century, the Victorian parlour instrument, the piano, grew to be the instrument of choice to accompany the Cape Breton Celtic fiddle. By closely examining some early tune books and by reconstructing some of the history of piano accessibility in early Nova Scotia, I also speculate that aspects of the accompaniment tradition may well be older than contemporary writers suggest.

A version of this research was presented at a joint meeting of the Folklore Studies Association of Canada and the American Folklore Society in Quebec City, October 2007.

Gaelic-speaking Scots from every region of the Highlands and Islands established communities throughout Cape Breton and Eastern Nova Scotia; in the years between 1775 and 1850, more than 25,000 came to these shores. They brought with them their Gaelic language and many of their distinctive oral and musical traditions. Through their interaction with people already established on the island, a distinctive fiddle and piano style emerged that is inextricably connected to its own unique step dance and square dance tradition. There are a few popular publications and some academic works that primarily focus on the Cape Breton fiddle tradition, the most recent being the book *The Cape Breton Fiddle: Making and Maintaining Tradition* by Glenn Graham (2006), but few scholars have chosen to focus on the piano accompaniment tradition (Doherty 1996; Dunlay and Greenberg 1996; Graham 2006; MacGillivray 1981, 1988; MacInnes 1997; MacKinnon 1989).

The driving, rhythmic Cape Breton fiddle tradition with its slow airs, strathspeys, jigs, reels and marches is often presented as a conservative tradition, following closely the patterns of the musicians who came before. It is sometimes presented as retaining the older music of the "Golden Age" of Scottish fiddling in the late 18th century that was forgotten in Scotland but somehow retained in isolated Cape Breton because of the insularity of the people, the geography, the lack of a road system and the close-knit Gaelic communities (Dunlay and Greenberg 1996: 2-3). We know from the work done by folklorists and popular culture scholars that there is often a folklore/popular culture continuum at work with most traditions. Neil Rosenberg's work on country musicians and their markets shows that some country musicians go through various stages from apprentice to journeyman to craftsman to celebrity and can reach local, regional, national or international markets. As Rosenberg says: "There exists within country music a hierarchy of musicians stretching from face-to-face situations which would clearly fit all the defining criteria for folksong, to mass media situations which we generally describe as popular culture (1986: 160). Even in times long past, much oral tradition was influenced extensively by the popular culture of the day whether through broadsides, newspapers, books, radio or television broadcasts. Heather Sparling has recently explored the influence of print collections on the Gaelic song tradition, showing how singers use the print tradition to widen their repertoire and to also ensure the accuracy of song texts being passed on (Sparling 2007).

A close examination of the piano accompaniment tradition that has emerged in Cape Breton calls into question some of these commentaries about the conservative nature of Cape Breton music tradition. Barre Toelken shows us the processes of dynamism and conservatism in folklore and how these twin laws, these dual forces, are constantly at work as any tradition develops and evolves (1979: 34-39). As Toelken says, "conservatism refers to all those processes and forces that result in the retaining of certain information, beliefs, styles, customs and the like, and the attempted passing of those materials, intact, through time and space in all the channels of traditional expression" (35). In contrast, dynamism refers to "all those elements that function to change features, contents, meanings, styles, performance and usage as a particular traditional event takes place repeatedly through space and time" (35). The Cape Breton fiddle tradition is said to have arrived with the Gaelic migrations in the late 18th and early 19th centuries. Much literature on Gaelic Culture in Nova Scotia presents the Gaels as a conservative group often untouched by the popular culture of the day and the outside world beyond their Gaeltacht (Gaelic-speaking territory) (Dunn 1953; MacLellan 2000; MacNeil 1987).

The acceptance of the piano into the Cape Breton fiddle tradition also demonstrates the folklore/popular culture continuum. The Victorian parlour instrument, a product of mass culture of the late 19th century, is incorporated into the Cape Breton fiddle music tradition with its face-to-face interactions in community halls, dances and house parties.

Allister MacGillivray, for example, who conducted a series of interviews with Cape Breton piano players, reveals that many informants talk about pump organs as well as other instruments such as harmonicas, spoons, foot tapping and even knitting needles as early or first accompaniment for fiddlers (MacGillivray 1988). Glenn Graham adds to this body of information by conducting surveys with contemporary players where he asks questions about piano accompaniment (2006: 72-80). Marie MacLellan, a well-known Cape Breton style pianist discusses learning to play the organ in church and going to dances to accompany her sister Theresa first, not on the piano, but on the guitar. As she says, "there were no pianos or organs in the halls then. The guitar was tuned in the Hawaiian styling and played with a bar, but we used to do very well" (qtd. in MacGillivray 1988: 190). Most likely the guitar was put into an open tuning and as she moved up the neck with a bar, the chord would change. Marie's comment raises an interesting question about when guitars first began to be used as instruments of accompaniment and how widespread they were in rural Nova Scotia in the early years of the 20th century. The piano was only one method of accompaniment for fiddle players, but it is the one that seems to have outlasted and superseded other forms as the 20th century unfolded.

Many suggest that the piano tradition emerged from the earlier available pump organ:

> When fiddle music first came to Cape Breton, it remained unaccompanied until the late 19th century, when the pump organ was introduced. By the time of the arrival of upright pianos at the turn of the century, a Cape Breton style of accompaniment had already been developed, with a lift and syncopation that still echoes in today's piano sound. (MacDonald n.d.)

Kate Dunlay and David Greenberg say that:

> Cape Breton music was played without harmonic accompaniment until
> around the turn of the century when pump organs were introduced (a
> second fiddler, foot tapping or step dancing, tapped knitting needles
> or spoons, or occasionally bagpipes or voice did serve as forms of
> accompaniment). By the 1930s the upright piano had taken over.
> (1996: 4)

Indeed they acknowledge that "some Cape Breton pianists have
cultivated a remarkable ability to mimic the fiddle, complete with cuts
and ornamentation, [but] they have also developed their own unique and
very dynamic style of accompaniment" (4). In an exhibit in Cape Breton's
Gaelic College, located in St. Ann's, the history of piano accompaniment is
traced to 1900.

In 1928, as part of its new foray into "ethnic records"[1] Columbia
Records released the first commercial recording of fiddle with piano ac-
companiment which featured Dan Hughie MacEachern and Charlie
MacKinnon playing in what was billed as "The Columbia Scotch Band"
(Ian MacKinnon 1989: 52-53; 223-24). Alick Gillis and his Inverness
Sereneders recorded for Decca Records in Boston in the 1930s with
Elizabeth Maillet on piano and Alcide Aucoin and Alick Gillis on violins
(figure 2.1). Gillis, a native of Southwest Margaree, went to Boston in
the early 1920s where he began playing at the Cape Breton Club. Other
Cape Breton musicians who played with Gillis included Alcide Aucoin
on violin, Betty Maillet and Malcolm Gillis on piano, Jim Aucoin on ac-

Figure 2.1 Alick Gillis and the Inverness Sereneders, 14005A Decca Records, 1936.

Figure 2.2 W. H. Bill Lamey, "Prince Charlie's Welcome to the Isle of Skye," 028-B Celtic, 1943.

cordion, Paul Aucoin on guitar and banjo and Hughie Young on the clappers (MacGillivray 1981: 24; MacKinnon 1989: 53). The Decca catalogue numbers start at 100 and the Cape Breton musicians appear beginning with 12000 and 14000 numbers. Beginning in the late 1920s, they released 33 recordings devoted to Scottish music in their 14000 series.

By the mid-1930s, the Celtic label of Antigonish, Nova Scotia, released recordings of some of the great fiddlers of this period including Angus Allan Gillis, Angus Chisholm, Bill Lamey (figure 2.2) and Winston "Scotty" Fitzgerald (culture.cbu.ca; MacKinnon 1989: 53).

In the early 1900s there were pump organs available for some players either in the churches or in the homes as they were readily available for sale from the Eaton's and Sears-Roebuck catalogues between 1902 and 1915 (*Eaton's* 1910; 1915-1916; *The 1902 Edition of the Sears Roebuck Catalogue* 1969) (figures 2.3 and 2.4). Doug MacPhee mentions playing in halls where only a pump organ was available and having severely cramped legs after playing a music session (MacPhee 1993). One musician talked about placing a vase on some of the lower keys of the pump organ to give it a drone sound similar to a bagpipe. It is certain that by the mid-1930s prominent piano accompanists were learning to play the piano and

Figure 2.3 Eaton's Spring and Summer catalogue, 1901.

beginning to accompany Cape Breton fiddlers. As Lila Hashem notes, she learned to play piano by taking lessons from Jessie Maggie MacLellan: "Then I started picking up piano myself from that book that Jessie Maggie gave me [Scott Skinner]. I had to make up my own left hand because the Skinner book had no bass, just melody lines, and that's how I started the Scottish music." Lila also remembers her first piano:

> When I started taking lessons, we didn't have a piano or organ ourselves but there was a house across the street where I used to go and practice. However when Christmas rolled around here was this big piano for me for a Christmas gift! I can still see it with the big red bow on it. It was a Dorothy piano. "Blind" Collie MacDonald was selling them at that time in Antigonish. (MacGillivray 1981: 185)

Figure 2.4 The Sears Roebuck Catalogue, no. 111. 1902, p 17.

By 1936 Lila had developed her piano playing skills and she had her own radio program in Sydney, sponsored by Brook's grocery store and hosted by Robbie Robertson, where she played Scottish piano solos each week with the theme tune "Road to the Isles" (MacGillivray 1981: 185).

Clearly, the tradition was well developed by the 1920s and 30s. The chording patterns, the distinctive bass runs, the doubling of the melody, and the rhythmic accompaniment on the piano had principally replaced the earlier pump organ accompaniment (Graham 2006: 50; MacGillivray 1981: 269-72).

But is the process of musical development as simple as this? How did the unique style develop and emerge? What factors allowed the piano, a Victorian parlour instrument, to become the foremost instrument of accompaniment for Cape Breton fiddlers? What are the roots of this accompaniment style? At what time were pianos first available in Nova Scotia? I am only scratching the surface in this chapter and raising some unanswered questions. We need to do more research before we fully understand how this distinctive accompaniment tradition has developed.

A primary question that needs to be addressed is: when precisely were pianos and pump organs available in Nova Scotia and on Cape Breton Island? There is no standard history completed on the piano/organ trade in Nova Scotia and indeed there are few studies of the history of Canadian instruments. Frances Roback is one of the few scholars to examine the history of Canadian pianos and organs, through the various forms of advertising developed by the manufacturing companies (Roback 1984: 31-44).[2] An online publication for the Canadian Museum of Civilization on the Making of Musical Instruments in Canada indicates that the earliest Canadian-made organ dates from 1723, by sculptor and cabinetmaker Paul Jourdain for the Quebec Cathedral (Bégin 2003). This exhibit indicates that the first Canadian piano making also began in Quebec "thanks mostly to artisans of German and British origins." By mid-century "there were four piano makers in Toronto, ten in Montreal and three in Quebec" (ibid). Companies that began to make pianos in the mid-19th century included Heintzman, Mason and Risch, R. S. Williams, Willis and Lesage (Ibid; Roback 1984: 31-44); while notable piano makers included Frederick Hund (ca. 1816) and Thomas D. Hood (ca. mid-1800s).

In Nova Scotia, one of the first manufacturers of pianos was H. and J. Philips of Halifax, who went into business in the mid 19th century. The actions for the pianos were imported, but the rest of the work was done in the province. As George MacLaren says:

> Henry J. Philips came to Halifax about 1845 from Hamburg in Germany with pianos to sell, and was so successful that he persuaded

John H. Philips to join him. Together they formed the firm of H. and
J. Philips, and began to manufacture pianofortes in Halifax. (1961: 90)

William Fraser purchased the Philips firm and began manufacturing in
Halifax in 1856; his pianos were exhibited internationally as part of Nova
Scotia's entries for the London and Paris international exhibitions. This
firm was still in business by 1890 (91-92). One of the few Nova Scotian
companies to make both pianos and organs was the Gates Organ and
Piano Co. They began in Annapolis County in 1872, later moving to
Truro. MacLaren says:

> In their first year they only produced twenty five instruments. In 1882,
> however, they reorganized their company with a capital of $60,000 in
> fifty-dollar shares, and removed to larger premises in Truro, a central
> railway junction, where they planned to employ fifty workmen produc-
> ing eight hundred instruments a year. (95)

One organ company, Chute and Hall of Yarmouth, made reed organs
starting around 1883-1893 (Guildford 2007). George MacLaren iden-
tifies thirty-three piano and organ companies existing in Nova Scotia in
the 19th century in places such as Halifax, Dartmouth, Yarmouth, Truro,
Bridgetown, Amherst and Pictou (MacLaren 1961: 138-39).[3]

Pianos were available very early in Nova Scotia, imported long before
they were ever produced in Canada. Indeed, pianos and piano instructors
were part of an early transatlantic trade. As early as May 21, 1817, ads such
as this appear in the Halifax *Royal Gazette*:

> For Sale A New patent piano forte proved to be preferable in tone and
> workmanship to any imported into this province. It can be had on
> trial, if wished, on application, to the master of the 98th band, or at
> this office.

There are numerous advertisements such as this indicating that the precursor to the piano, the pianoforte, was indeed an instrument found in
Halifax, Nova Scotia, in the early years of the 19th century. Along with the
instruments there were pianoforte teachers who advertised their expertise.
For example:

> J Dykes Begs leave very respectfully to return his thanks to the ladies
> and gentlemen of Halifax, who have heretofore humored him with
> their patronage and support and to inform them that he still continues
> to practice his profession as a teacher of music and would be happy to
> tend young persons, who may wish to learn to play on the piano forte,
> either at their own houses, or at his residence opposite the Presbyterian

Meeting House and adjoining the store of Mr. James Smith where they can be accommodated with well-toned pianofortes. He also repairs and tunes musical instruments. (*Royal Gazette* 10 April 1815)

We need to know more about these instruments and teachers in Nova Scotia before we can fully comprehend how the piano accompaniment tradition developed.

But what about Cape Breton? We see many advertisements appearing as early 1873 in the *North Sydney Herald* much like the ones found in Halifax. Ads such as the following regularly appear in the 1870s through to the 1890s:

"Call at Burns's Musical Agency, Sydney, Cape Breton Island if you want a first class piano, organ or melodeon for less money that you can purchase it elsewhere. Sheet music, piano covers, music stools, etc. and furnished at short notice" (*North Sydney Herald,* 10 September 1873).

Through the 1870s to the 1890s W. H. Johnson of Hollis Street, Halifax was advertising many types of pianos such as Knabe, Bell, Wheelock, Dominion, Chickering, Newcomb, Mason and Rich along with Bell and Dominion organs in the Cape Breton newspapers (*North Sydney Herald*, 6 August 1873; 21 April 1886; 19 July 1893; see also figure 2.5). The variety

Figure 2.5 North Sydney Herald, 11 July 1893.

of brand names indicates that piano manufacturing was increasing, making their availability more widespread. Their agent in Sydney was a merchant named H. T. Gayton.

By 1896 the Johnson company moved to larger premises, the former Duffus building on Granville and Buckingham streets in Halifax, indicating that by the turn of the century, pianos had become an important part of the Nova Scotia landscape. At this time a piona factory commenced operations in Amherst, Nova Scotia, not far from the massive Rhodes and Currie woodworking factory in Amherst. By 1900 other companies such as Miller Brothers and MacDonald of Barrington Street, Halifax, were also advertising with local agents in Sydney and North Sydney (*North Sydney Herald*, 5 February 1902). It seems that pianos were indeed available in Nova Scotia and in Cape Breton from at least the mid-19th century, perhaps even earlier; but this still does not help us understand how the distinctive Cape Breton piano tradition emerged. Cape Breton piano players developed their own distinctive runs and chord progressions to accompany the melody lines. As well, they developed their own techniques for imitating triplets and other unique features of the Cape Breton fiddle style.

However, the tune books of Cape Breton compositions produced from the 1940s onward do not include notation for the left hand; the melody line is printed primarily for the fiddler and only secondarily for the accompanist (Beaton 1980; Cranford 1988, 1994, 1997; Dunlay and Greenberg 1996; MacQuarrie 1940). It is understood that the accompanist will have at his or her disposal a whole series of chords, runs and bass lines that provide background, rhythm and lift for the fiddler. In a sense, these are aurally transmitted—learned by ear—while the melody line as printed on the page can be played with the right hand. Simply put, the left hand music follows oral transmission patterns and the right hand follows the melody line of the fiddle as it appears in the written tradition of the tune book.

But what about the earliest tune books that have played a significant role in developing repertoire for Cape Breton fiddlers? Do these provide accompaniment music? Some of the earliest and most influential books for Cape Breton performers do indeed include the bass clef and notes for the left hand along with some advice for accompaniment. For example, *The Beauties of Neil Gow*, a collection revered by many Cape Breton fiddlers, does include music for the left hand (figure 2.6). The title of the collection indicates that all "are adapted for the pianoforte, violin and violoncello." Does this indicate that a form of accompaniment existed in the so-called golden age of Scottish fiddling in the 18th century? If so, was it primarily for the cello and the pianoforte,

Figure 2.6 The Beauties of Niel Gow title page, 1780.

the early precursor to the piano? If a form of accompaniment was in existence, does it have any resemblance to what is now known as the Cape Breton piano accompaniment tradition? Are these different accompaniment traditions? Does the earlier tradition influence the Cape Breton tradition in any way?

J. Scott Skinner, the 19th-century Scottish composer known as the strathspey king offers some insights here. The introduction to the *Harp and the Claymore,* another influential tune book for Cape Breton players, says that Skinner's musical education was in the hands of his brother Sandy "who taught him the violin and the art of vamping accompaniments on the cello" (Skinner 1904: 1). It was his skill at vamping that brought him into contact with Peter Milne who introduced him to strathspeys. Of course, Skinner went on to become the master strathspey composer. Again, his introduction to this collection outlines that "published collections of strathspeys and reels did not begin to appear until after the middle of the 18th century, by which times tunes like 'Tullochgorm' and 'The Reel of Tulloch' were already reckoned old" (Skinner 1904: 5). These two tunes have made their way into the Cape Breton repertoire of Cape Breton fiddlers and accompanists and are favourites of Cape Breton music aficionados.

After a discussion of the unique features of the strathspey, Skinner goes on to comment on the accompaniment tradition of the day:

> In the earlier printed collections of Scottish dance music a very general practice was to give a bass for the cello or harpsichord, the precursor of the modern pianoforte. This is always safe, and, in the case of the older melodies, quite satisfactory. (Skinner 1904: 7)

He even outlines suggestions for how this should be played:

> When strathspeys are rendered on a keyboard, the most satisfactory way, as a rule, is to have simply a bass in octaves. Additional chords may be introduced at times for variety and reinforcement; but the practice of playing thickened chords on the left hand throughout is to be deprecated. The effect is apt to savour a monotonous jingle, the variety of possible chords and their area of distribution being so limited. Still more objectionable is the attempt at elaboration—drowning the air, as Dr. MacDonald puts, with left hand embellishments foreign to the original, even though based upon scientific principles. (Skinner 1904: 7)

He furthermore states that the pianist should avoid playing the melody on the keyboard: "the best results, as a rule, are got by playing the air on the violin, while the piano supplies an accompaniment partaking the nature of a good vamp ... moving in crotchets; firm and well accentuated" (Skinner 1904: 7). A crotchet is an older term for a quarter note. Are there similarities with what Skinner describes and what has become traditional in the Cape Breton piano? While not identical, there does appear to be a similar aesthetic at work here. More research needs to be done on anything similar to what Skinner describes and to what appears in some of the earlier collections.

One important question that needs also to be answered is just when did these 18th and 19th century tune books become available for musicians in Cape Breton and other parts of the Maritimes? The prevailing viewpoint is that this occurred during the late 1930s and early 1940s, during the Second World War. Cape Breton fiddlers such as Dan R. MacDonald were posted to Scotland during the war and, at the time, were introduced to 18th and 19th century tune books. While this may be when Dan R. accessed J. Scott Skinner et al., a close look at newspaper advertisements appearing in Nova Scotia and Cape Breton reveals that tune books were indeed available much earlier than this date throughout Nova Scotia.

As early as 1769 Cuenod Hath was importing fiddle strings and spare bows for violins into Halifax (*Royal Gazette* 31 January 1769). By 1772 a chamber organ, "which may serve very well for a country church" was being sold. In 1773 a variety of tune books were available, such as: Watts's *Psalm and Hymn book*; Wesley's *Hymns*; Diowerth's *Spelling Book*; *Jockey of the Green* (a Scottish ballad sung by Mrs. Hudson of Varshal Gardens); and the *Macaroni's Downfall* sung to the tune of *Babes in the Woods*. Charles Geddes's inventory for 1791 included a complete line of violins, clarinets, German flutes and music books as well as harpsichords, spinets, pianofortes and guitar strings and frets (Hall 1987: 393). By 1798 George Graves was selling items described as violins, music books, music paper, fiddle strings and spare bows at his book shop on the lower side of the parade opposite the church. What were the titles of these books being sold alongside fiddles and bows?

By the 1780s musical magazines were widely available, and *Cheerful Songsters* plus fiddle strings of all kinds were being sold. Clearly this evidence indicates that music books of all kinds including tune books and songsters were making their way across the Atlantic as early as the end of the 18th century in Nova Scotia.

A standard argument that has been raised is that earlier players were not literate in reading music or in writing and thus would not be able to be a part of this publishing world or the print world of late-18th and early-19th century Nova Scotia. The issue of musical literacy of Cape Bretoners has not received much scholarly attention. It is important to keep in mind that by 1852 the *Casket* newspaper was published in Gaelic and in English in Antigonish and, from the beginning, songs and stories were published in both languages. There clearly was a large enough literate population to support a circulation of this size in eastern Nova Scotia. Literacy rates and in particular, the musical literacy of Cape Bretoners in the past, is a topic that warrants more research.

Clearly, my research raises more questions than it provides answers about Cape Breton's piano accompaniment tradition. The conventional wisdom, dating the tradition to the early years of the 20th century provides only part of the picture. Reconstructing the dates of access to tune books, particularly the ones that have become so significant—the Gows, the Marshall Collection, Captain Simon Fraser Collection, the Skinner collection—may well reveal that the accompaniment tradition does have older roots than previously thought (Fraser 1982; Gow 1780, 1799, 1802, 1806, 1817; Marshall 1781, 1822; Skinner 1900, 1904). As well, most of the studies to date talk about the earlier players—those who were born at the turn of the 20th century—Angus Allan Gillis (b. 1897), Dan J. Campbell (b. 1895), Angus Chisholm (b. 1908) and Alick Gillis (b. 1900), but there is very little historical memory of the earlier players. We need to know more about late-18th and early-19th-century tradition bearers and their repertoires. We need to find more out about people such as Alexander J. Beaton (b. 1827), Donald the Tailor Beaton (b. 1856), Donald Campbell (b. 1789), James Campbell (b. 1863) and Malcolm Gillis (b. 1856).

One assumes that the tradition continued to run in families, but more research is required on these earlier players, and questions about their musical literacy should be asked. There has been a commonly held assumption that early piano players were not musically literate; but the evidence of Nova Scotia sheet music which was available as early as the 1750s seems to contradict that assumption.

Notes

1. Several companies started producing "ethnic records" around this time, realizing the diversity of music among various ethnicities and being aware that this would open up more markets to them. Unfortunately, the records had a wide range of production quality as many were quickly and cheaply produced.

2. Some work on the history of Canadian pianos and organs has also been done for the Encyclopedia of Music in Canada (Kalmann, Potvin and Winters 1981: 741).

3. Ethnomusicology researcher Michael MacDonald, at the time a PhD student at the University of Alberta, worked with me exploring early newspaper advertisements for pianos in Nova Scotia, from the 1750s until well into the 19th century.

Chapter 3
Protest Song and Verse in Cape Breton

*In regional enclaves throughout North America where labour and capital
have fought battles over the years, there are many songs and verses about
labour and protest. Folklorist Peter Narváez conducted pioneer research on
the protest song tradition and the use of strike songs in the company town
of Buchans, Newfoundland (2005). Others have examined the songs and
verses of miners and their families, and the diversity of folklore found in
mining communities (Green 1972; Korson 1960, 1964, 1965; Lloyd 1952;
Greenway 1970; O'Donnell 1992a, 1992b). On Cape Breton Island, where
coal mining and steel making were once an essential part of the region's
culture and economy, protest song and verse are found in abundance (Frank
1985, 1986). This chapter explores some previously unexamined protest songs
and verses of Cape Breton, largely culled from the* Maritime Labour Herald
(MLH), *a newspaper of the 1920s that included both locally and internationally composed works. Some earlier folklorists ignored protest songs because
their paradigms did not permit them to view these forms as authentic cultural
expressions, an approach which raises complex issues of how authenticity is
constructed and by whom. My intent is to show that a well-developed protest
song tradition was alive and well and played an important role in the labour
struggles of the 1920s. Indeed, these vernacular materials were used for solidarity during times of upheaval and change in the mid-1920s and were/are
integral to cultural expression.*

An earlier version of this research was published in 2008 in the journal
Ethnologies *30, (2): 33-72.*

Coal was last mined underground in Cape Breton in 2001. But many
continue to find relevance in the repertoire of Canada's only coal mining

choir, the Men of the Deeps, which keeps the songs of the earlier period
alive. Jack O'Donnell, a music professor at St. Francis Xavier University
in Antigonish, Nova Scotia, founded the choir in 1966 in anticipation of
Canada's centennial celebration. With an interest in coal-mining songs,
O'Donnell began a search for material and sponsored a song-making contest. The result was an assemblage of numerous old and new songs about
industrialization and the mining industry. Since then, the choir and its
director have performed throughout the world, made professional recordings and published books on coal mining songs (O'Donnell 1975, 1992a,
1992b). To enable these endeavours, O'Donnell obtained the sanction of
mine management, which included securing wages for missed time when
choir members were practising or travelling around the world.

O'Donnell introduced songs to the choir's repertoire from the
Korson and Greenway mining song collections and ultimately brought the
repertoire out of kitchens and community halls into the more formal setting of the theatre and concert hall. While the notion of a miners' choir
was traditional in some areas of the British Isles, there does not seem to be
a precedent in Cape Breton; here, it was more common for a person with
an untrained voice to sing *a cappella*.[1] It was also customary for individual
miners to sing as they travelled in the man-rake to their work site.[2] This
move from individual to large group singing in three or four part harmo-
nies is a transformation that has kept the songs alive. O'Donnell's choir
has spawned keen interest in songs of this kind and the songs have become
expressive of the culture of the company towns of Cape Breton; now, it is
common to hear material popularized by the Men of the Deeps sung at
house parties and other informal gatherings.

As defined by Narváez, the company town is a single-enterprise community "where major areas of social and cultural life such as food procure-
ment, housing, friendship groups, entertainments and public activities are
either company dominated or at least highly influenced by company policies and concerns" (2005: 300). He points out that these communities are
of interest to folklorists as they possess the characteristics of traditional folk
societies as well as those of complex urban societies.

Folklorists and other scholars refer to protest songs by various
monikers. They have debated the nuances in meanings of terms such
as "labour lore," "industrial lore," "industrial folksong," "protest song,"
"propaganda song," "occupational folklore," "occupational folklife" and
"organizational folklore" (American Folklore Society 1984; Denisoff 1966;
Fowke 1969; Frank 1985: 213; Jones 1985; McCarl 1978: 176). Edith
Fowke claims that, "although Canada is very rich in occupational songs,
we have comparatively few industrial or labour songs" (1969: 34). While

collectors of folksongs throughout Canada have not assiduously searched for material about industry or labour, Canada does in fact possess an abundance of such songs, contrary to Fowke's statement. It is her paradigm as a song collector primarily interested in older folksongs and ballads that prevents her from viewing these kinds of songs as authentic or legitimate traditions that make up a song repertoire in an industrial community (Greenhill 2003). John Greenway's simple definition of protest songs is more useful: "[t]hese are the struggle songs of the people. They are the outbursts of bitterness, of hatred for the oppressor, of determination to endure hardships together and to fight for a better life" (1970: 10). He sees them as promoting unity and communality, togetherness and support for a union.

Before assessing song and verse, I will take a cursory look at the historical context of coal and steel development on Cape Breton Island. Coal was being mined in the region as early as the 18th century to serve as fuel for the fireplaces at the fishing *entrepôt* of Louisbourg. It was not until the early 19th century, however, that the British-owned General Mining Association began to build pitheads, company stores and company housing in the Sydney coal fields. During the latter half of the 19th century, a number of private enterprises operated mines in Cape Breton, but by 1893, some of the smaller companies partnered with off-Island capital interests to form the Dominion Coal Company. This group built piers and discharging plants in Boston and loading facilities in Sydney and Louisbourg. By 1898, this company was transformed into Dominion Iron and Steel Corporation with the intention of constructing a steel plant in Sydney. Labour historian Don MacGillivray points out that by this time Cape Breton Island

> held approximately one-fifth of the total provincial population; two-thirds of the provincial revenue came from the area, as did seventy-five percent of Dominion Steel's coal—in national terms Cape Breton's contribution accounting for forty-five percent of the country's entire coal production. (1973: 50)

There was much industrial activity on Cape Breton Island at the turn of the 20th century. It was this development and the conflicts between labour and capital which followed that sparked the creativity of song and verse makers. The fact that the management team spent no more than a few years in the coal fields and never put down roots on the Island accentuated some of the conflicts. Managers were referred to in Cape Breton as "floaters" having, "no stake in the community and no love for the people" (Frank 1971: 43). On the occasion of Dominion Coal Company's incorporation its president, H. M. Whitney, stated that his work and life would be one with the people. Less than five years later, however, he left Cape Breton and sold his interests to a Montreal consortium—the British Empire Steel and Coal Corporation (BESCO)—led by Roy Wolvin, a Great Lakes shipping entrepreneur (MacGillivray 1979). Under Wolvin's leadership, BESCO's treatment of the Cape Breton worker was ruthless and hard-hearted. Social and living conditions were deplorable, wages in the steel mill and coal mines were low under his management, and labour/management conflict was common (MacGillivray 1973, 1978, 1979).

The Cape Breton songs I explore here come out of this working-class tradition: many were composed and published in the 1920s when miners battled foreign owned companies and struggled to form unions. The songs closely follow Greenway's definition of protest songs; they express the attitudes of coal miners and their families, many discuss oppression, exploitation, hardship and successful struggle through solidarity. They are often accompanied by large doses of humour, satire, sarcasm and wit, attesting to the vibrant oral tradition of the day.

I am not, however, the first to appreciate that these songs are a valuable source for the interpretation and study of Cape Breton's cultural traditions (Frank 1985, 1986; O'Donnell 1992a, 1992b). Looking at a previously unexamined corpus of song and verse that originally appeared throughout the 1920s in *The Maritime Labour Herald* (*MLH*)—a Glace Bay newspaper—allows me to understand who they are, where the compos-

, N. S. — **Dec. 29, 1923**

LABOR HERALD

Better That!

(Dedicated to J. B. McLachlan, jailed because he fought for the Miners and Steelworkers.)

The judge's words
   May pound my ears
Like a devil dancing
   On a drum;
But better that
   Than woman's tears
For children starved,
   And I stay dumb!

The prison bars
   May sear my soul
Like a gridiron in
   The heat of Hell:
But better that
   Than men dig coal
For a cutthroat crew
   And not rebel!

My family faces
   Haunt my dreams,
We may not meet
   This side the grave:
But better that
   Than further schemes
To keep my fellow
   Man a slave!

—J. S. WALLACE

Figure 3.1 An example from the MLH, 29 December 1932, 4.

ers are from, the date of composition and the tune or air, if mentioned (figure 3.1).

One hundred and twenty-four songs and verse appeared in the newspaper between 1921 and 1926 (see appendix 3.1). Almost half of the songs and verses (fifty-five) are of Cape Breton composition. Other places of origin include industrial centres such as Glasgow, Germany, Florence, the Republic of Ireland and England. American regions such as West Virginia, New England and Memphis are represented, as are Canadian cities such as Ottawa and Montreal and smaller Nova Scotia mine districts such as Springhill and Westville. This geographical representation speaks volumes about the Glace Bay newspaper's wide appeal in labour circles of the 1920s. "Canada Free" is one of only five of the songs presented with its air or music; it is said to be sung to "The Maple Leaf" and the musical notation is provided with the lyrics (*MLH*, 10 December 1922: 5). Other tunes for songs include "Yankee Doodle Dandy," "Oh Canada," "My Mayland, My Mayland" and "Maryland" (*MLH*, 3 December 1921: 5; 7 October 1922: 7; 28 April 1923: 8; 15 May 1926: 4).

The songs I am exploring can be called protest songs, notwithstanding that Fowke limits her definition of industrial songs to "those describing any form of work" (1969: 34). Archie Green extends this idea when he notes that, "[a]n industrial folksong describes work itself and portrays the life, diversions and struggles of men [*sic*] on the job" (1972: 8). But as I will show, song and verse of industrial protest can also refer to activities beyond the domain of work and can include references to important individuals and events in communities at times of struggle, strife or strike. In the body of material examined here, satire and humour also play a significant role.

As is shown by, for example, George Korson's deletion of a large quantity of songs from his study due to personal political convictions, individuals who research songs of industrial protest are often selective about the kinds of songs designated under that rubric.[3] Korson describes his criteria for selection in a letter to Archie Green:

> When I found that [a ballad] had been written by an outsider I didn't use it.... I had to be especially careful because in the 1920s and 30s the communists were making a determined effort to capture the United Mine Workers of America, and some of their songs were composed by their organizers. When I was sure of this source—and I had ways of finding out—I just didn't use the song in my collection. (1972: 18)

This practice of designating a song based on the affiliation or political persuasion of the composer is open to question. While many of the songs analyzed here were indeed composed by members of the Communist Party of

Canada, I contend that the more important concerns ought to be whether or not the song entered oral tradition, how long it was part of oral tradition and whether or not the song held meaning for people.

Addressing these concerns can be complex; in many cases our only record of the so-called songs are newspaper accounts or songbooks that offer the lyrics without the accompanying music. Often, the contemporary reader is not provided with a composer's name and pseudonyms are commonly employed to protect her or his identity. Furthermore, as Greenway and Narváez have shown, protest song and verses do not often acquire the trait of persistence and sometimes do not last long beyond the event or incident for which they are created (Greenway 1953: 3; Narváez 2005).

One song and verse maker from Cape Breton Island who Korson would not have acknowledged because of his left-wing, Communist political perspective is Donald "Dawn" Fraser. Born on July 1, 1888, in Oxford, Nova Scotia, he moved with his family to Glace Bay in 1901 when the Cape Breton industrial communities were booming with coal and steel development. After travelling through the eastern United States and serving a short stint in the army, he returned to Cape Breton in 1919 to begin writing song and verse about the discontent among the labouring classes (Frank and MacGillivray 1976: 10). One scholar argues that the intense class conflict that emerged in Cape Breton in the 1920s

> grew out of the intersection of *two historical cycles*: the coal miners' embrace of the heightened aspirations and class consciousness that swept the European and North American working class following the Bolshevik revolution and the end of World War I; and the arrival of BESCO, a new and particularly aggressive industrial landlord eager to exploit coal holdings that formed the most profitable part of its operations but which were becoming increasingly vulnerable to extra-provincial competitive pressures" (Manley 1992: 66). Fraser entered the fray of labour's wars by composing poems and songs that represent the feelings and attitudes of working class people in this era; he became a vocal critic of BESCO.

Described as "Cape Breton's nearest equivalent to Joe Hill,"[4] Fraser was not a coal miner but a newspaper reporter who frequently contributed to the *MLH* (Frank and MacGillivray 1976: 10). This newspaper became significant in the class struggles of the early 1920s and was one of the "key institutions" to support the Communist Party of Canada, along with the Workers Educational Clubs and the Communist Party headquarters in Glace Bay (Manley 1992: 85). The first edition of the paper was published in Glace Bay in late October 1921, with James B. McLachlan as the "dominant spirit," and William Ulric Cotton as the first editor (MacEwan 1976: 74). Silby Barrett was President, A. S. MacIntyre, Vice President and A. S. McKillop, Secretary-Treasurer (*MLH*, 1 April 1922: 3).[5] It was published every Saturday and was "devoted to the interests of Labour" (*MLH*, 1 April 1922: 3). The majority of the shares in the paper were held by unions of the day and, "until it folded in 1926 ... it was to all intents a Party paper, described on one occasion by Tim Buck as a Maritimes version of Lenin's 'collective organizer'" (Manley 1992: 86). The reference to the newspaper as a collective organizer derives from a quotation of Lenin's:

> The role of a newspaper, however, is not limited solely to the dissemina-
> tion of ideas, to political education, and to the enlistment of political
> allies. A newspaper is not only a collective propagandist and a collective
> agitator, it is also a collective organizer. (Lenin 1903)

The three editors, W. U. Cotton (1921-23), Tom Bell (1923-1924) and J. B. McLachlan (1924-1926), were all Communist Party of Canada members and as John Manley points out:

> [r]eaders were exposed not only to coverage of local and national
> events, but also to reports on Party life abroad, numerous vignettes
> of socialist construction in the USSR (some of them from the pen of
> Roscoe Fillmore, the celebrated Nova Scotia Marxist who placed his
> horticultural expertise at the disposal of the USSR in 1923) and items
> of political analysis by leading Comintern figures. (Manley 1992: 86)

It is clear that Dawn Fraser had a major influence on the *MLH*; in the years between 1921 and 1926, thirty-four of his verses were published in it. David Frank points out that many of his compositions were designed for recitation:

> [h]e appeared frequently at homes and parties, on streetcorners and in
> bar-rooms, at labour gatherings at the moviehouses, and on one memo-
> rable occasion he read his longest epic to a summer crowd of several
> thousand people on the Lingan and Dominion beach. (1985: 214)

Some of the longer poems were serialized and some also reappeared months or weeks after the initial publication date. In addition to his work in newspaper and pamphlet form, Fraser published four volumes of rhyme that are known by few today (Fraser 1924; 1926; 1944; n.d.). Fraser, it seems, would first publish his work in the newspaper and then gather the composed verses together for a publication. Sometimes a poem would be accompanied by an advertisement for his upcoming book. For example, following the publication of "The Widow in the Ward" Fraser writes, "[f]rom Fraser's new book, *Songs of Siberia and Rhymes of the Road*, second edition. The only book published of the late War that the public demanded a second edition of" (*MLH*, 30 June 1923: 4).

Much of Fraser's work depicts the mining corporation's cold, callous and uncompromising treatment of workers. For example, "The Case of Jim O'Coughlan," is a thinly veiled description of the sentencing and jailing of James Bryson McLachlan, one of the most vocal Cape Breton labour leaders of the 1920s. In 1923, McLachlan was arrested for "publishing false information likely to prejudice the public interest," but the charge was later changed to "publishing misleading information and imparting communist literature into Glace Bay" (MacEwan 1976: 111). When neither charge could be substantiated, a third charge of "seditious libel" was brought forth by the Crown; on this McLachlan was found guilty and sentenced to two years in Dorchester penitentiary. He served three months (MacEwan 1976: 111).

In "The Case of Jim O'Coughlan" Fraser provides a short history of the days leading up to McLachlan's jailing. Moreover, he satirizes and criticizes the management and supervisory personnel of the large conglomerate BESCO. He is particularly scathing in his criticism of one BESCO leader, Roy Wolvin:

> Now of all the bosses that e'er was cursed,
> ROY THE WOLFE[6] was called the worst,
> He was the leading parasite
> That fed on the workers day and night;
> Greedy, growling wolf for more,
> He stole the bread from the workers door,
> Grew fat on starving children's cries
> And filled the papers with foolish lies -
> That his company couldn't afford to pay -
> Yet he got three hundred dollars a day.
> For doing nothing but looking wise,
> Starving kids and telling lies;
> Thus he promoted the capitalist game
> 'Til babies were taught to curse his name,
> And Roy the Wolf and his thieving band
> Spread distress throughout the land,
> 'Til Jim O'Coughlan and other men
> Started one of the many fights

For Labour's cause and workers' rights.
And they called on ROY THE WOLFE to give
More of the gold that they might live,
More of the gold they had to pay
To meet the prices from day to day....
(*MLH*, 1 March 1924: 2)

As will be seen in chapter four, the use of nicknaming was a common tradition among miners. Fraser captures the sly and untrustworthy nature of manager Roy Wolvin by calling him the "Wolf," a name by which he was known in the mining communities (Davey and MacKinnon 2001). The poem was serialized each Saturday throughout the months of February and March, 1924. On February 16, 1924, Fraser says, "[w]orkers, cut this out and save it carefully along with your 'Pluck-Me' slips [pay stubs]. Next week we will tell you of a great Capitalist called 'Roy the Wolf' who lived many years ago" (*MLH*, 16 February 1924: 2). This direction gives an indication of how this verse was passed on. People cut texts out of the newspaper, saved them at home, pasted them on wash house walls at the pit and most importantly, discussed the content with friends and family. While initially using the mass-mediated form of the newspaper, the content of the poems was passed on via oral or face-to-face means.

Many of the ills and difficulties of this period of labour/management strife and class struggle are described in this and other verses by Fraser. In addition to "The Case of Jim O'Coughlan," two other poems are devoted to this union leader: "Away False Teachings of My Youth," and "Honest Bell What Did Bruce Say" (*MLH*, 27 October 1923: 4; 2 June 1923: 4).

One other Communist Party of Canada member and labour leader, "Red" Malcolm Bruce, appears as a main figure in some of Fraser's work. Originally from Ontario, Bruce spent much time during the 1920s fighting labour's struggles in the Cape Breton coal fields. "Honest Bell What did Bruce Say?" "The Hair Breadth Escape of Red Malcolm Bruce" and "Tell My Friend the Prison Warden I Hadn't Time to Call" all focus on events during Bruce's stay in the Cape Breton area, including a charge of libel while fighting labour's cause. Fraser points out that "Tell My Friend the Prison Warden I Hadn't Time to Call" was sung by Bruce himself (*MLH*, 2 June 1923: 4; 9 June 1923: 4; 23 June 1923: 4).

While Fraser was a gifted social commentator and poet, it is extremely difficult to assess whether or not his work entered oral tradition. If so, one would expect to find versions being sung by traditional or professional singers of the time or recorded in song collections or LP recordings. Yet, a close examination of two collections of the 1920s and 30s which provided the general public with easy access to the lyrics of some of the most popular songs on the island reveals none of Fraser's work (McCawley 1929; MacDonald 1935). Only one, "Hard Winter at the Mines," was noted by a song collector (Ronald MacEachern).[7] David Frank sees Fraser's work as a recitation tradition not unlike the poems of Robert Service, rather than a song tradition (1986: 37). According to Frank, "[w]ith Dawn Fraser... we enter into the area where the oral emphasis and the spontaneity of the folk tradition seem to give way to a more conscious effort to construct a local working-class culture" (1986: 37). Yet the traditions of verse-making or folk poetry and song-making are similar, in that identical attitudes and feelings are expressed in both forms. While a song moves to the level of performance, a verse remains on the page unless it is performed as a recitation. Yet both song and verse express the widespread feelings and attitudes of working people and their families.

One possible reason that so few of Fraser's lyrics seem to have entered oral tradition lies in the fact that many of his lyrics reflect particularly harsh times and events in the history of the Cape Breton labour movement. There may be a conscious forgetting of these particular kinds of songs and verse. Fraser's verse may be too strong a reminder of a painful period for the songs to enter the lasting oral tradition. The songs composed during labour struggles, strikes or particularly difficult times may lose their meaning for the people when the events surrounding their composition are forgotten.

Much of Fraser's work is a part of the broadside tradition. As the editors of a reprinted volume of his poetry attest,

> [h]is writings appeared in pamphlets, books, magazines, and newspaper.... Sometimes his outpourings were simply posted on a bulletin board at the main intersection at Glace Bay.... He read his verse on the streets, at union meetings, at parties, and at massive labour and political meetings at the Savoy and Russell Theatres in Glace Bay. (Frank and MacGillivray 1976: 10).

Much of the industrial protest verse and song appearing in the newspaper criticizes the mining and steel corporations and their representatives, while chastising "blacklegs" or scab workers and praising some of the well-known union leaders at home and abroad. For example, a verse criticizing BESCO for its exploitation of labour appears in the April 26, 1924, edition of the *MLH* entitled, "Cape Breton Miner and BESCO":

You will go into the mines and toil all day,
And work like a slave to keep hunger away,

You're slaving all day to provide us with coal:
But you don't get enough to keep body and soul.

BESCO can drive in a big motor car,
For he gets the profits, whatever they are:
But you must exist there in shacks I am told,
For BESCO, that chap, has to pile up the gold.
You see what he did down in old Newfoundland:
He placed thousands of dollars in Sir Richard's hand,
In order he might that rich country control:
For BESCO, that chap, hasn't got any soul.

A nice little trip to Cape Breton he planned:
He invited the members all down to a man:
But dark clouds started rising, the weather turned cold,
So they postponed that picnic and saved BESCO's gold.
(*MLH*, 26 April 1924: 5)

Using the quatrain format common in folksong and folk poetry, this verse hints at political connections between BESCO and Newfoundland Prime Minister Richard Squires (1919-1923, 1928-1932) while characterizing BESCO as an exploitative company.

Other verses in this newspaper follow the "Come-All-Ye" format, common with the broadside tradition in both the British Isles and North America. In December 1924, "Dirty Danny" appears. Written from the point of view of the captured worker, it describes how the company policeman "Dirty Danny" catches the worker stealing wood from company property and the consequences of this offence:

Come All You honest workers and listen to me,
When you hear my story with me you'll agree,
Arrested for nothing, and glad to admit,
One evening last week when coming from the pit.

Now a Company policeman, a man I know well,
And for to expose him the truth I must tell,
Wherever you see him you hear people say:
"There goes Dirty Danny – belongs to East Bay."

One evening of late, coming home from the mine,
As I walked along, some wood I did find,
It being my intention – the truth I must say –
To use it to kindle a fire the next day.
I had not gone far when I heard someone shout:
"You're taking great chances, you better look out.
I will have you arrested and a fine make you pay."
Remarked Dirty Danny – belongs to East Bay.

Without hesitation I threw the wood down,
And quickly departing for home I was bound;
But two evenings later I'll have you to know,
McAuley came afrer [*sic*] me and I had to go.

Now when I did appear, His Honor did say:
"Now you're charged with stealing, what have you to say?"
I pleaded not guilty, but this was no good –
Dirty Danny, he swore I was caught with the wood.

I tried to explain, but I saw it was no use
His honor remarked, "Sir I want no excuse,
You will pay $7.50 or else put up bail,
Or the rest of this night you will spend in the jail."

Now, times being hard and my dollars but few,
I had to consider just what I could do:
To pay $7.50 was sure hard on me –
I will never forgive him, His Honor, A. B.

Now Dirty Danny, your friends are but few,
And what I hear men say if you only knew,
You'd be so ashamed you'd decide on a cruise
And go back to East Bay and hide in the spruce.

Now one thing I'll mention, I almost forgot,
I hope, Dirty Danny, hard luck is your lot,
And everyone slight you wherever you be
Just to remind you of what you did to me.

Now to conclude, and to finish my song;
The truth I have stated, you'll find it's not wrong
I hope to get even – if I live some day
With my "friend" Dirty Danny belongs to East Bay.

This verse uses many of the standard characteristics of the broadside tradition: opening formula, quatrain form, repetition of particular phrases ("Dirty Danny – belongs to East Bay"), dialogue, personal testimonial and a closing formula. Structurally, the song is very similar to many that have entered oral tradition throughout the British Isles and North America. Nevertheless, we are told nothing about the tune of the song, nor if it has ever had a life apart from this printing.

A famous saying in Cape Breton, "They Can't Stand the Gaff," was first uttered in 1925. It is attributed to J. E. McClurg, then Vice-President of BESCO, who suggested that miners could not take the pressure that BESCO was putting on them and that their strike would fold.[8] It appears as the title to a verse in the newspaper attributed to "E.E.R." in 1925:

They Can't Stand the Gaff
Seated round the table in the Council room of Hell
Sat the secret service agents of the Pit.
'Twas the regular weekly meeting when they gathered there to tell
Of the things of Earth that with them made a "hit."
They told of wars and strife and hate in every land and clime,
Of pestilence and murder and despair,
They told of orgies gluttonous in palaces sublime,
And of slums where children lived on scanty fare.

They reported on the grafter and the gambler and the sneak,
Of birds of prey who feast on human kind.
They told of slimy hypocrites with countenance so meek,
And of moral perverts tainting children's minds
But the Prince of Darkness answered that their tales were small and
    boring,
There was nothing new in wickedness to hear;
And he showed his grave displeasure by their indolence deploring,
Till each imp began to shrink with timid fear.

Then spoke a lively demon from a land of ice and snow,
And said, "I think I have a good report,

For in Canada I've BESCO, Sir, to help me as you know,
And to them oft in sin I must resort.
Their work has been most excellent in many years gone by,
They've bee [sic] loyal to Your Majesty, I know;
They've made little children suffer and afflicted mother's cry,
And o'er the land have scattered pain and woe.

They've starved and crushed and broken the lives of many men,
They're as merciless as Hell could have them be;
And though their slaves are starving they cut their wage again,
And laughed aloud their agony to see.

Then spoke their chief official (who would grace our service here)
As he mocked the suffering children with a laugh;
"From these angry, cursing miners we have nothing now to fear,
For I'm positive they cannot stand the gaff."
Then Satan's brow grew gribhter (sic) and loud he laughed and long;
"That's a joke," he said, "at which all hell can laugh!
And my blessing rests eternal on the man so brave and strong,
Who mocks at pain and anguish with, 'They cannot stand the gaff'."
(*MLH*, 14 April 1925: 4)

The composer of "They Can't Stand the Gaff" is listed as "E.E.R." to protect his or her identity. It was common for composers to include only their initials. The composer criticizes BESCO's leaders and places them in hell with support from the devil himself for making callous statements against working people. Prompted by the phrase "they can't stand the gaff," the poem castigates the company for its treatment of its workers. The poem is a visceral reaction to the company statement and represents attitudes held by many in the mining towns in the midst of the long, bitter strike of 1925. It is difficult, however, to know if this verse was ever sung or indeed if it entered oral tradition. It was most likely talked about and discussed on the streets of New Waterford and Glace Bay after it appeared on April 14, 1925. We do know that the phrase, "standing the gaff"—meaning to "stay the course on a picket line" or to "stand up against injustice"—has indeed entered oral tradition and still survives in Cape Breton Island. It can sometimes be heard during a strike; media reports of a recent long, bitter strike at the multinational Stora Enso pulp and paper mill in Port Hawkesbury used this phrase in headlines and in stories about the strikers ("Standing the Gaff at Stora": 14).

Many verses of this nature appeared between 1921 and 1926 in the *MLH*, some with known composers, some with anonymous authors and some with pseudonyms. "The Empty, Raggedy Stocking," published on Christmas Eve, 1921 with an anonymous composer, paints an image of children who will not receive gifts in their stockings on Christmas Eve:

> What of the empty, raggedy stockings
> That will hang by the chimney on Christmas Eve
> With their mute appeals from the poor little owners
> To the dear old Santa in whom they believe?
>
> For their share of his presents they ask such a little,
> "Just a dolly to hold in my arms while I sleep,
> A little tin auto that runs when you wind it
> A sounding red drum or a wooly white sheep."
>
> The only light in their dim dark existence
> Is that wonderful day when old Santa will come
> With his treasure filled pack that he brings on his back
> From his fairyland, snowyland, toyland home.
>
> What beautiful dream will come to them sleeping
> Under the coverlet shabby and worn.
> But what of the empty, raggedy stockings
> That will hang by the chimney on Christmas morn.
> (*MLH*, 24 December 1921: 1)

Another significant composer of the time is J. S. (Joe) Wallace, Secretary of the Nova Scotia branch of the Canadian Labour Party in 1925. At least five songs attributed to him appeared in the *MLH* between 1921 and 1926. One is "Voice of the Workers," composed in 1923:

> Corn beef and sauerkraut
> Or pig's feet and tripe
> Plaster pie and cold tea
> A drag on my pipe
> That's my fare, for my tastes ain't fine
> And I got to count the gulps from my grub when I dine.
>
> Dollar lid, Woolworth tie
> And blue cotton shirt

> Grey sock and shoddy shirt
> Brown beneath the dirt—
> That's my style for my tastes ain't fine
> And I got to stretch my dough double when I'm buyin'.
> Lean to or tenement
> Paper shingled shack
> Drafty doors, choked flues
> Outhouses at the back.
> That's my home for my tastes ain't fine
> The box I get when livin' like the box I get when dyin'!
>
> What's my work you ask?
> I dig coal a spell
> Sheer sheep and skin steers
> Lumberjack as well—
> That's my job I hump it all the time
> Making heaven from half the world, getting half for mine.
> (*MLH*, 6 October 1923: 4)

Wallace's poem discusses food, clothing, housing and the diversity of work that a miner had to become accustomed to in order to survive. Other of his poems are listed in appendix 3.1), and they clearly indicate his political stripe: along with being a poet he was an active member of the Communist party. Joe S. Wallace (1880-1975) was also a member of the group of Atlantic Canadian poets known as "The Song Fishermen" that included Stuart McCawley, James D. Gillis, Andrew Merkel, Charles Bruce, Kenneth and Robert Leslie, Molly Beresford, Ethel Butler and others. Alexander Kizuk says that Wallace achieved, "a degree of notoriety as a Communist poet published in the Soviet Union and Canada" (1993: 178). Gwendolyn Davies points out that the Song Fishermen "were to represent a Nova Scotia voice in poetry at the very time rural values and the oral tradition were being eroded by out-migration, a changing economy and the impact of modern media" (Davies 1987: 138).

The *MLH* gives the names of the following Nova Scotian composers: George Strattmen, originally from Westville; Dannie Boutilier, Springhill; A. I. McNiven, Sydney; and Gordon Robertson, Glace Bay. Pseudonyms include: "Wage Slave," "William Waterford," "The Mixer" and "Big Guy" from Glace Bay. Other composers are listed as "student" or with abbreviations such as "F.T.R.," "P.E.P.," "R.E.F.," "E.E.R.," and "G.C.S." No doubt residents of the Cape Breton mining communities from 1921-1926 knew

the identities of the composers in their midst despite the use of pseudonyms; all were supporters of the *MLH* and many were members of the
Communist Party of Canada.

It is difficult to trace the origins of some of the composers of songs
in the *MLH* from outside the region. Ralph Chaplin, the writer of "The
Industrial Heretics" and "Heretics," was an IWW organizer (Industrial
Workers of the World, whose slogan was "One Big Union"). According
to R. Serge Denisoff, he "wrote militant lyrics to the "Battle Hymn of
the Republic" and produced "Solidarity Forever," the official anthem of
the American labour movement" (1969: 427). The poetry of the famous
English socialist and writer, William Morris, commonly appeared in newspapers, particularly the labour presses, in the 1880s and 90s (Foner 1975:
321-22). Thomas Hood's poem, "The Song of the Shirt" was published in
1923 in *MLH*. Foner says that this poem was the "most popular British
verse in the pre-Civil War labour press in the United States" (1975: 76). It
originally appeared in *Punch* in 1843 and "was an instant success. It was
first reprinted in the United States in the *Fall River Mechanic* of December
7, 1844, and was widely published in an 1851 newspaper story concerned
with efforts of women seamstresses in New York to form the Shirt Sewers
Cooperative Union" (Foner 1975: 76). E. C. Tyler's "The Scab's Hereafter,"
is one of numerous anti-scab songs to be found in the labour presses of the
19th century. One common theme is evident in Tyler's work: the scab ar-
rives at the gates of heaven, enters, and then is exiled to hell. Foner points
out that this theme is found in some of Joe Hill's songs of the late 19th
century (1975: 247-48.)

One local composer identified only by "G.C.S." composed "That
Grand and Glorious Day," which was meant to be sung during a May Day
parade:

> In our humble home we sit,
> Are we broken-hearted? NIT.
> We are happy and cheerful as can be,
> For we know that every Red
> Will be up and out of bed,
> On that Grand and Glorious Day
> The First of May.
>
> Tramp, tramp, tramp, the boys are marching,
> Cheer up, comrades, and be gay,

For you know we're out to fight,
To fight, with all our might.
On that Grand and Glorious Day
The First of May.

From dawn till dark at night,
We will carry on the fight,
The fight for our freedom and our cause,
Though it may be hard and long,
We will sing the same old song,
On that Grand and Glorious Day
The First of May

Tramp, tramp, tramp, the boys are marching,
Cheer up, comrades, and be gay,
We are in this fight to win,
We will never sink but swim
On that Grand and Glorious Day
The First of May

Now that we have BESCO scared,
And the miners are prepared,
We will raise the Scarlet Banner to the sky
And we'll sing the same old hymn,
To our dear beloved Jim,
On that Grand and Glorious Day,
The First of May.

Tramp, tramp, tramp the boys are marching,
Marching on to victory
We have BESCO up a tree
And forever there they'll be
On that Grand and Glorious Day
The First of May.

We had BESCO on the bank
But our district officers sank,
When one might [*sic*] push would our
Greatest victory win.

But their hearts were far too small.
When they heard BESCO call,
For God's sake come to work,
Or we will fail.

Tramp, tramp, tramp, the boys are marching
Cheer up, children, and be gay,
For soon will come the day,
When your dad will draw a pay,
On the Grand and Glorious Day
The First of May.
(*MLH* 24 April 1926: 1)

This song of local composition, as with many others, makes reference to "dear beloved Jim" (*MLH* editor J. B. McLachlan) and to the numerous battles with BESCO. While May Day is not celebrated today in Cape Breton Island, in the 1920s marches and parades would have been organized on that date of international labour celebration. As Craig Heron and Steve Penfold say, "In Glace Bay, Montreal, Timmins and a few western Canadian cities, May Day parades became significant local events in the 1920s that could draw as many as 3-4,000 marchers" (2005: 172). John Manley cites a May Day celebration in Glace Bay in 1923 "where some 5,000 miners and their families marched behind the 'biggest red flag in Canada' emblazoned with the legend, 'Long Live Communism'" (1992: 75).

Some of the verses and songs that clearly entered oral tradition were first printed in 1929 in *A Book of Come All Ye's From Cape Breton and Newfoundland* by Glace Bay native Stuart McCawley. This songster contains lyrics with no music. Two industrial songs, "The Yahie Miners" and "The Honest Working Man" appear in this collection amidst a potpourri of war songs, cowboy songs, Gaelic songs, broadside ballads (published in broadsheet periodicals) and popular songs (McCawley 1929: 25, 26). This collection provides a sense of the diversity of songs prevalent in the Island at this period of industrial strife. Indeed, we are only now starting to understand the diversity of music and song of this period of Cape Breton's history.[9]

Stuart McCawley describes "The Honest Working Man" as:

the national anthem of the Cape Breton worker many years ago and a popular song with the troops in war. It was written as a piece of irony aimed at the importation of additional labour in the summer months. Anyone not porridge-bred and Gaelic was a "foreigner." (1929: 7)

Although it is difficult to assess its popularity, the song seems to have been widespread in Cape Breton mining communities. Helen Creighton and Margaret Sargent collected versions of this song and as recently as 1978, Ron MacEachern recorded a version sung by Charlie MacKinnon, a well known performer who has cut a number of recordings of Cape Breton music (MacEachern 1978). After I delivered a presentation in 1982 to the Old Sydney Historical Society an older man greeted me and proceeded to sing a version of "The Honest Working Man." He claimed he had not heard the song in many years. Although evidence of its origins is sparse, it has had a long life in the Cape Breton industrial communities. As David Frank says:

> it is difficult to date this song, but it again appears to be associated with the late 19th century period of development in the industry, when coal mining was almost entirely seasonal and the chief competition for local labour came from Acadians and Newfoundlanders rather than European immigrants. (1986: 29)

The song is concerned with the importing of Newfoundlanders and "foreign labourers" into Cape Breton, a common practice in many North American industrial frontiers.

Chorus

'Way down in East Cape Breton, where they knit the sock and mitten,
Chezzetcookers represented by the dusky black and tan;
May they never be selected, and home rule be protected,
And never be connected with the honest working man.

But raises high my dander, next door lives a Newfoundlander,
Whose wife you cannot stand her, since high living she began,
Along with the railroad rackers,[10] also the codfish packers,
Who steal the cheese and crackers from the honest working man.

When leaves fall in the autumn and fish freeze to the bottom,
They take a 3 ton schooner and go round the Western shore;
They load her with provisions, hard tack and codfish mizzens,
The like I never heard of since the downfall of Bras d'Or.

The man who mixes mortar, gets a dollar and a quarter,
The sugar factory worker he gets a dollar ten,

While there's my next door neighbor, who subsists on outside labour,
In the winter scarcely earns enough to feed a sickly hen.

They cross the Bay of Fundy, they reach her on a Monday,
Did you see my brother Angus? Now tell me if you can;
He was once a soapbox greaseman, but now he is a policeman,
Because he could not earn a living as an honest working man.
(McCawley 1929: 7)

Although in McCawley's printed version no tune is included, Edith Fowke states it is Irish, from the Tipperary song, "The Hills of Mallabon," composed in 1840 (1969: 40). Charlie MacKinnon changed the words of the first verse, so he would not offend his Newfoundland friends (O'Donnell 1992a: 114):

I think I'll go meander with my friend the Newfoundlander;
He is the finest fellow to ever grace the land
His name is John Allie; he's from the Codroy Valley.
He works in the coal mines with the honest working man.
(O'Donnell 1992a: 113)

This change reflects a reversal of the original verse's intention of criticizing Newfoundlanders. MacKinnon indicates that a good relationship existed with the Codroy Valley Newfoundlanders who came to the coal mining towns in the winter months to supplement their farm incomes. Many had roots in the Cape Breton Island Gaeltacht and Acadian fishing communities (MacKinnon 2002). Essentially the song is about scab labour and, as Jack O'Donnell notes, these types of songs "are common in mining communities throughout the world" (1992a: 114). As David Frank illustrates, the variations in versions show that its original connotations had begun to change by the early years of the 20th century.

By the 1920s, the song appeared to have lost much of its original meaning. "It is sung at picnics and parties," wrote Stuart McCawley in a newspaper column in 1926, "and goes best after a few shots of strong rum. The swing of the song is good and the local touches are laugh provoking" (1986: 30).

Another verse was added by 1935, again changing the original meaning of the song:

Way down in East Cape Breton
Where you get a welcome fitting,
In Sydney you will meet them
They are loyal to a man,

From the farmer to the miner
There isn't any finer,
He will show you how to treat them
As no other body can. (MacDonald 1935: 10, 11)

As Frank suggests, the ethnic rivalries, once common in the industrial setting, were "being superseded by a local sense of identity as Cape Bretoners" (1986: 30).

"The Yahie Miners" is also concerned with the attitudes held by established coal miners toward migrants who threaten their jobs. David Frank argues that the term "Yahie," derived from "Dhachaich," the Gaelic word for home, may describe the Gaelic workers who flocked to the industrial communities from Cape Breton's rural districts (1986: 28). The song, however, mentions Yahies from "Rocky Boston," suggesting that these workers may have been coming from beyond the shores of Cape Breton. The composer may be making a reference to the many Newfoundlanders travelling to and from what was referred to as "the Boston States." Many stayed to find permanent employment in the steel mill and coal mines. This song not only seems to have been widespread in the Cape Breton industrial area, but is internationally known, with variants throughout the British Isles and North America. The Cape Breton variants seem to be derived from the British song, "The Blackleg Miners" which can be dated to a lockout in the north England community of Durham in 1844 (Frank 1986: 27). McCawley states, "This Come-All-Ye is sixty years old and still sung in District 26" (1929: 21).[11] The version appearing in McCawley's book does not offer the name of a performer, nor does it include the music of the tune:

Early in the month of May
When all the ice is gone away.
The Yahies, they come down to work
With their white bags and dirty shirts,
The dirty Yahie miners.

Chorus
Bonnie boys, Oh won't you gang,
Bonnie boys, Oh won't you gang,
Bonnie boys, Oh won't you gang,
To beat the Yahie miners.

They take their picks and they go down
A-digging coal on underground,
For board and lodging can't be found
For dirty Yahie miners.

Into Mitchell's they do deal,
Nothing there but Injun meal.
Sour molasses will make them squeal,
The dirty Yahie miners.

Join the Union right away,
Don't you wait until after pay,
Join the Union right away,
You dirty Yahie miners.

Mrs. McNabb, she keeps the Hall
Where the Yahies they do call,
You'll see them flock around the Hall,
The dirty Yahie miners.

Don't go near MacDonald's door,
Else the bully will have you sure;
For he goes 'round from door to door
Converting Yahie miners.

Jimmie Brinick he jumped in,
Caught MacKeigan by the chin,
Give me Maggie though she's thin,
For I'm no Yahie miner.

From Rocky Boston they do come,
The damndest Yahies ever found,
Around the office they do crowd,
The dirty Yahie miners.

The Lorway road is now clear,
There are no Yahies on the beer,
The reason why there are none here,
They're frightened of the miners. (1929: 20-21)

The version published by Jack O'Donnell was collected by Alphonse MacDonald to the tune of "Blackleg Miners" (O'Donnell 1992a: 115-16). The topics mentioned in the song include: the difficulty faced by workers trying to find lodging in a booming industrial town; dealings with a merchant who, it seems, is only able to provide the newcomers with subsistence food; the pressures to join the union; and fighting and drinking. In a sense, the song offers an ethnographic description of the kinds of difficulties faced in any booming industrial town in North America.[12]

It is interesting to note that one of the most prolific song collectors of the 20th century in the Maritimes, Helen Creighton, failed to record examples of these kinds of songs on her two recording expeditions to Cape Breton Island.[13] Nevertheless, judging by a comment in her biography, she was aware that such a song and verse tradition existed:

> There were miners at Inverness, and I felt they too would have songs. When we saw one walking home with his lunch box we offered him a ride. I said, "Have you miner's songs down here?" and was delighted when he said, "Yes, we have a lot of them." I said, "What are they like?" He looked so surprised that I said, "How do they go?" To this he answered, "Mine are here." That seemed a strange remark so I said, "Who sings them?" Then he began to laugh. "Did you say songs? I thought you said sons." (Creighton 1975: 145)

Despite the confusion, it is clear that Creighton assumes that male coal miners should know some mining songs.

Of the 124 songs in the collection analyzed here, at least six were composed by women. Ella Wheeler Wilcox published "Here and Now" and her work appeared in the American presses and was associated with the early American Federation of Labor (Foner 1975: 168-69, 186). Other women composers include Celia Baldwin, Rebecca Buhay, Elma Ehelich Levinger and unnamed female Glace Bay students. There may well be other women composers amongst those who chose to use abbreviations or pseudonyms to disguise their identities. The actions and roles of non-waged working-class women have been largely ignored in some of the early Cape Breton labour history scholarship. Steven Penfold's seminal work in this area indicates that "the dominant historical view of women in Canadian coal-mining communities has placed them at home and dependant on men, if they are mentioned at all" (1994: 21). Women played active roles during strikes, organized crowd actions and were often the financial controllers and budgeters of households who made a little money stretch as far as possible (Frank 1983: 137-43).

Women's voices were indeed heard in protest songs within the *MLH* even though it appears that the majority of composers were men. Steven Penfold has outlined the way in which symbols of gender were employed in this period and how women's domestic labour "constituted an important, but hidden, support mechanism for the union movement in Cape Breton" (Penfold: 43). It is in songs such as those composed by Buhay that we get a glimpse of the 1920s quest for equal rights for women, and of the role that women played in the class struggles of the 1920s.

We know about Rebecca (Becky) Buhay because of Joan Sangster's work on the history of women on the left in Canada in the 20th century (1989). Buhay, a pivotal leader in the Communist Party of Canada in the 1920s and 1930s, was from a working-class Jewish family who emigrated to Montreal from London's east end. She worked as a photo finisher, tobacco worker and garment industry worker (65). She helped organize the Amalgamated Clothing Workers Union of America, went to New York City toward the end of the First World War and became involved in American socialist politics. Sangster says, "Buhay's high profile led to government surveillance and her hasty return to Montreal in late 1919" (66). On her return to Canada she helped organize the Montreal Labour College and by 1922 was "deeply involved in the [Communist] Party [of Canada]" (ibid.). She moved to Toronto to Communist Party headquarters by 1929 and became secretary of the Canadian Labour Defence League and head of the women's department (ibid.).

Cape Bretoners would have been aware of her compositions, as three of Buhay's songs appeared in MLH in 1924: "The Machine Awakes," "Daughters Awake" and "The Song of the Street." "Daughters Awake" provides a clear example of her position on equality for women in society; she asks women to be forceful in advocating change:

Too long you've been the thralls of men,
In kitchen, factory and den,
Too long you've paid the price for all
Without a voice—unheard; your call;
You've borne the children of each age,
Yet never a word in history's page.
Demand the right to have your say

In the making and building of the day!...
(*MLH*, 16 August 1924: 3)

Her songs ask workers to rise up and change the capitalist society in which they are ensnared. In "The Machine Awakens" she says:

The roar of the machines breaks into song:
"Revolt!" It cries "Revolt," "revolt"!
Awaken to action these automatons of flesh and blood,
Gather together the bundle herders,
Stop the rhythm of their feet and hands,
"End this hell!" "End this hell!"
And the dreamer into action is stirred.
(*MLH*, 19 July 1924: 3)

It is clear from these short excerpts that women's voices were indeed heard in protest songs within the *MLH* even though it appears that the major-ity of composers were men. Steven Penfold has outlined the way in which symbols of gender were employed in this period and how women's domes-tic labour "constituted an important, but hidden, support mechanism for the union movement in Cape Breton" (Penfold: 43). It is in songs such as those composed by Buhay that we get a glimpse of the 1920s quest for equal rights for women, and of the role that women played in the class struggles of the 1920s.

This chapter, exploring a small corpus of protest songs composed during the 1920s that appeared in the *MLH*, shows the diversity of music and verse in Canadian industrial communities in the early years of the 20th century. These compositions played a significant role in helping to develop a working-class ideology within the community throughout the 1920s. Dawn Fraser's radical compositions were a prominent feature of the newspaper, a host of other self-identified composers were frequent contributors, and a select group of song and verse writers used pseudonyms and abbreviations to partially conceal their identities. Some of the songs included here have a life in tradition, while others do not. Whether or not they were sung, however, the fact of their publication helps define the state of social discontent in this period of Cape Breton's history. One scholar points out that songs or verses like this are, "less likely to be taken seriously, and thus censored or repressed, than more rational and literal forms of communication, such as speeches or pamphlets" (Lewis 1985: 155). This work also shows that the pressures of the working-class community were clearly articulated in these compositions. As well, the songs and verses helped to promote solidarity among miners and their families in their struggle against mine managers and BESCO during the various strikes and work stoppages of the time. Many of them are oppositional and offer an alternative vision of the kind of society working-class families would like to have. This constructive dissent is similar to what Greenhill has found in her study of Ontario folk poetry: "[t]hey present—and usually actively advocate—alternatives to the status quo, to mainstream culture, to 'progress,' or even to change" (1989: 214).

There are currently no operating coal mines in Cape Breton. Nevertheless, every June 11th, coalmining communities observe a holiday called Davis Day to commemorate the killing of coal miner William Davis by company police on the picket line during the 1925 New Waterford strike. A number of songs re-narrating the events of that day have been composed. The Davis Day celebration begins with an ecumenical church service followed by one-minute of silence for departed brothers and sisters, and the placing of wreaths at a miners' monument by municipal officials, individuals and unions. The day also includes speeches by union leaders, closing prayers and songs sung by the Men of the Deeps choir. The choir always keeps June 11th free to perform at this event.

Long after the mines, the coal miners and their descendants are gone, the song and verse of the day will continue to provide a useful framework for understanding the complexities of daily life and the expressive culture and attitudes of working people living in industrial towns throughout the world.

Notes

1. For a discussion of the choral singing tradition of Welsh miners see Williams (1998). At the end of the 19th century, choral singing was an important aspect of many Welsh mining villages and song competitions were part of the tradition (Rhos Male Voice Choir n.d.).

2. A man-rake is the conveyance system that takes men in and out of the coal mines, a small train of open cars running on rails that in the past were made of wood and later of steel.

3. George Korson, one of the most prolific American collectors of mining songs and lore, did not formally conduct fieldwork in Cape Breton. However, at a union conference in the United States he met Bob Stewart, a coal miner from Glace Bay, and collected some of his songs. Korson recorded songs such as "Jolly Wee Miner Man," "The Bumps," "The Yahie Miners" and "Arise Ye Nova Scotia Slaves" (Korson 1965: 103-04, 236, 334, 424).

4. Industrial Workers of the World (IWW) organizer Joe Hill was well known for his songs about labour and class consciousness before his execution in 1915.

5. According to David Frank,

> "Silby Barrett was a young Newfoundlander who had gone from the fishing boats to the coal mines as a young man. After working in Ohio he had been converted to the union cause, and by the time he settled in Glace Bay in 1908 he was a strong UMW supporter. Unschooled but possessed of a flamboy-

ant personality and a salty wit, Barrett came under McLachlan's influence..."
(1999: 120-21).

William Ulric Cotton was a "young Eastern townships lawyer" who had previous experience as editor of Cotton's Weekly, "Canada's most popular socialist newspaper" in 1912
(Frank 1999: 112). Alex S. McIntyre was a "radical from the hotbed of the Phalen local"
(264).
6. Fraser sometimes uses "Wolfe" and at others "Wolf" throughout the poem.
7. MacEachern collected the song from a New Aberdeen singer in 1977. It is now in the
collection of the Beaton Institute, Cape Breton University. MacEachern is also discussed
in chapter 1.
8. McClurg explained to a newspaper reporter during the 1925 strike that conditions were
"getting better every day they stayed out.... Poker game nothing. We have all the cards....
Let them stay out two months or six months, it matters not; eventually they will have to
come to us.... They can't stand the gaff." Frank calls this "one of the most memorable statements in Cape Breton labour history," and "the remark was regarded as an offensive slur." In
turn, "Standing the Gaff" became "a rallying cry of the strike" (Frank 1999: 374).
9. A colleague recently asked me if the Centre for Cape Breton Studies at Cape Breton
University was interested in early 78 rpm recording of Lebanese songs brought to the Island
with Lebanese settlers who came to work in the steel mill in early 20th century Sydney. The
collection was slated for disposal. As more of this kind of material is gathered we will obtain
a better understanding of the diversity of song brought to the Island by numerous ethnic
and cultural groups.
10. A railroad racker is a labourer whose occupations "are not specifically identified who
perform unskilled, simple duties, primarily manual, that may be learned within a short period of time and that require little or no independent judgment" (Bureau of Labor Statistics
2001).
11. District 26 is the number given to the Cape Breton Island coal miners' local of the
United Mine Workers of America.
12. David Frank mentions that a Cape Breton Island song contest in 1966 elicited a song,
"Kelly's Cove" that appears to be a version of "The Yahie Miners" (1986: 29).
13. It might have been particularly difficult for a single female collector in the 1920s and
1930s to establish sufficient rapport with miners and their families, though numerous examples existed on the Island at the time of her extensive collecting expeditions. This ab-
sence of mining songs in Creighton's collection serves as a reminder for folksong analyzers
to exercise caution when making cultural generalizations from early song collections. The
biases and limitations of collectors and collections are seldom discussed in interpretations
of early song collections.

Appendix 3.1

Title	Composer / Author	Date	Place	Music / Air / Sung By	MLH
I. S. Henri's Manual of the Heritage of Canada and the United States				Lucy Locket Lost her Pocket (also known as Yankee Doodle Dandy)	December 3, 1921, 5.
The Empty, Raggedy Stocking					December 24, 1921, 1.
Creed of Big Business	Wage Slave				February 25, 1922, 5.
Good Times	H. Gay				March 18, 1922, 6.
The Soldiers Bonus	A. I. McNiven		Sydney, NS		March 18, 1922, 6.
The Striker					April 29, 1922, 7.
Help the Children	John F. Waddington				May 6, 1922, 5.
The Parasites	Dawn Fraser	1922	North Sydney, NS		June 3, 1922, 6.
Last Post	I. S. Henri and Sir Adolphe Routhier	Circa WWI		O Canada	October 7, 1922, 7.
Canada Free				The Maple Leaf	December 10, 1922, 5.
I Go Upon a Quest	George D. Herron	March 1, 1915	Florence, Italy		December 16, 1922, 5.
Sydney's Jaundiced Chief	J. P. McNeil				March 10, 1923, 3.
The Red Flag				My Mayland, My Mayland	April 28, 1923, 8.

The Parasites	Dawn Fraser	May 1, 1923			May 12, 1923, 5.
Honest Bell, What Did Bruce Say?	Dawn Fraser				June 2, 1923, 4.
The Hair Breath Escape of Red Malcolm Bruce	Dawn Fraser				June 9, 1923, 4.
Make Room for Life	Porte Wood Taylor				June 9, 1923, 4.
The Song of the Shirt	Thomas Hood				June 9, 1923, 5.
The Tale of the Tom Cat or The Jewells of Nick Czar	Dawn Fraser		Cape Breton, NS		June 14, 1923, 2.
Awake	J. Wallace		Cape Breton, NS		June 23, 1923, 4.
Tell My Friend, the Prison Warden, that I Hadn't Time to Call	Dawn Fraser		Cape Breton, NS	As sung by Malcolm Bruce	June 23, 1923, 4.
The Widow in the Ward	Dawn Fraser		Cape Breton, NS		June 30, 1923, 4.
District 26	S. Major		Montreal, QC		July 7, 1923, 4.
Mr. Recruiting Officer Didn't You Take My Name	Dawn Fraser		Cape Breton, NS		July 7, 1923, 4.
The Scab's Hereafter	E. C. Turner				August 11, 1923, 4.
Henry Doubb on Judgment Day: A Vision SATIRIC	John S. Clarke		Glasgow, Scotland		September 1, 1923

The World for the Worker	S. Sharp	Republic, Ireland	September 22, 1923
Prayer of the Employer	J. S. Wallace	Cape Breton, NS	September 29, 1923, 4
Voice of the Workers	J. S. Wallace	Cape Breton, NS	October 6, 1923
Away False Teachings of My Youth	Dawn Fraser		October 27, 1923, 4.
Better That	J. S. Wallace	Cape Breton, NS	December 29, 1923, 4.
Away False Teachings My Youth	Dawn Fraser		December 29, 1923, 5.
Is it Peace			January 5, 1924, 4.
The Shoppers Saturday Night			January 5, 1924, 4.
The Strikebreaker		West Virginia	January 19, 1924, 4.
The Case of Jim O'Coughlin	Dawn Fraser	Cape Breton, NS	February 16, 1924, 2
The Case of Jim O'Coughlin Chapter 2-- Roy The Wolfe	Dawn Fraser	Cape Breton, NS	March 1, 1924, 2.
The Case of Jim O'Coughlin (continued)	Dawn Fraser	Cape Breton, NS	March 8, 1924, 2.

Title	Author	Date Written	Location	Publication
Vote it Down	Stringhm Mine			March 8, 1924, 3.
The Case of Jim O'Coughlin (continued)	Dawn Fraser			March 15, 1924, 4.
The Day of Days	William Morris		England	March 22, 1924, 4.
The Commune	Simon Felshin	March 18, 1871		March 22, 1924, 4.
You Have Nothing To Lose But Your Chains	Henry Roenne			March 29, 1924, 8.
A Fair Trial				April 5, 1924, 4.
Dalyrimple and Barrett	William Waterford		Cape Breton, NS	April 26, 1924, 4.
CB Miner and BESCO	F. T. R.		Cape Breton, NS	April 26, 1924, 5.
The Rise of the Red River	J. S. Wallace		Cape Breton, NS	May 3, 1924, 4.
The Parasites Exposed	Dawn Fraser		Cape Breton, NS	May 3, 1924, 6.
Wearing of the Red	Dawn Fraser	May 1, 1924 (written 2:00 - 2:05)	Cape Breton, NS	May 3, 1924, 8.

Title	Author	Year	Place	Date
War	Henry George Weiss			May 10, 1924, 4.
The Wearing of the Red	Dawn Fraser		Cape Breton, NS	May 10, 1924, 4.
The Reward	Dawn Fraser	1924	Cape Breton, NS	May 17, 1924, 2.
Mother When the Whistles Blow	George Strattmen		Westville, NS	May 17, 1924, 3.
The Red Flag	Celia Baldwin			May 17, 1924, 8.
The Industrial Heretics	Ralph Chaplin			May 31, 1924, 1.
O Liberty the One I Mean	George Strattmen		Westville, NS	May 31, 1924, 7.
To Edith	Ralph Chaplin			June 7, 1924, 1.
Song of Separation	Ralph Chaplin			June 21, 19204, 1.
Blame it On the Reds				June 21, 1924, 5.
The Last Signal	George Strattmen		Florence, CB, NS	June 21, 1924, 7.
SALAAM	Ralph Chaplin			June 28, 1924, 1, 4.

Title	Author	Location	Date
The Red Brotherhood	Joe Wallace		July 5, 1924, 8.
The Machine Awakes	Rebecca Buhay		July 19, 1924, 3.
Here and Now	Ella Wheeler Wilcox		July 26, 1924, 4.
The Crime of Johnny Kyle Part One	Dawn Fraser	Cape Breton, NS	July 26, 1924, 6.
Send the Bill to BESCO	Dawn Fraser	Cape Breton, NS	August 9, 1924, 1.
The Crime of Johnny Kyle Part Two	Dawn Fraser	Cape Breton, NS	August 9, 1924, 6.
The Crime of Johnny Kyle Part Three	Dawn Fraser	Cape Breton, NS	August 9, 1924, 6.
Yes, What's da Use		Cape Breton, NS	August 9, 1924, 6.
The Perfect Day	George Strattmen	Florence, CB, NS	August 9, 1924, 7.
The Crime of Johnny Kyle Part Four	Dawn Fraser	Cape Breton, NS	August 16, 1924, 6.
The Old Song Resung	Elma Ehelich Levinger		August 16, 1924, 3.
Daughters Awake	Rebecca Buhay		August 16, 1924, 3.

The Crime of Johnny Kyle Part Five			August 23, 1924, 6.
The Shutdown			August 30, 1924, 3.
The Song of the Street	Rebecca Buhay		August 30, 1924
I Was a Stranger and they Took Me In	Dawn Fraser	Cape Breton, NS	August. 30, 1924, 6.
I Was a Stranger and they Took Me In	Dawn Fraser	Cape Breton, NS	September 6, 1924, 6.
Lord Loves Ya Lewis			September 13, 1924, 1.
I Was a Stranger and they Took Me In (continued)	Dawn Fraser	Cape Breton, NS	September 20, 1924, 6.
I Walked Right In and He Turned Around and He Walked Right Out Again		Cape Breton, NS	September 27, 1924, 1.
I Was A Stranger and Took Me In (continued)	Dawn Fraser	Cape Breton, NS	October 11, 1924, 6.
Wayfarers			October 11, 1924, 8.

A Nurse	Wordsworth		October 18, 1924, 2.
The Christians	Dawn Fraser	Cape Breton, NS	October 18, 1924, 6.
Greetings! Little Labour Herald. What? Three Years Old Today.	Dawn Fraser	Cape Breton, NS	October 25, 1924, 4.
Overheard at Caledonia		Cape Breton, NS	October 25, 1924, 6.
The Christians (continued)	Dawn Fraser	Cape Breton, NS	October 25, 1924, 6.
The Christians (continued)	Dawn Fraser	Cape Breton, NS	November 1, 1924, .6
The Christians (continued)	Dawn Fraser	Cape Breton, NS	November 8, 1924, 6.
Revolution	Ferdinand Freiligrath	Germany	November 15, 1924, 1.
The Christians (continued)	Dawn Fraser	Cape Breton, NS	November 15, 1924, 6.
To the Poets	"The Mixer"		December 6, 1924, 4.
Dirty Danny	"P.E.P."	Cape Breton, NS	December 13, 1924, 6.
The Vampire II	Bert Leach		December 20, 1924, 1, 4.

Title	Author	Place	Date
To the Public	Donnie W. Boutilier	Springhill, NS	January 3, 1925, 3.
God of the fighting Clan	John Niehardt		January 17, 1925, 2.
Sons of a Nation	Thomas Campbell	Nova Scotia	February 14, 1925, 3.
What is Slavery	Shelley		February 21, 1925, 1.
The Worm and the Vulture		Glasgow, Scotland	February 28, 1925, 1.
In Pastures Bare He Leadeth Us	"R.E.F."	New Waterford, CB, NS	March 21, 1925, 3.
The Five Point Star	J. S. Wallace	Halifax, NS	March 28, 1925, 1.
The Workers Child	Thomas Campbell	Nova Scotia	March 28, 1925, 1.
Bread and Roses	Joseph Oppenheim	New England	March 28, 1925, 1.
The Battle of Glace Bay	Lloyd Roberts	Ottawa, ON	April 4, 1925, 3.
Can You Stand the Gaff	Patrick Owney	Memphis, TN	April 14, 1925, 4.
They Can't Stand the Gaff	"E.E.R."	Cape Breton, NS	April 14, 1925, 4.
The Workers Cry	John C. Nechardt		April 11, 1925, 1.
The Gaff	Gordon Robertson	New Aberdeen, CB, NS	April 11, 1925, 2.
No More Deaf, No More Dumb, No More Blind	J. S. Wallace	Cape Breton	January 30, 1926, 3.
The Dauntless Three	"Big Guy"	Glace Bay, CB, NS	February 27, 1926, 3.

The Scab				March 20, 1926, 3.
The May Day Call		Glace Bay, CB, NS		April 10, 1926, 1.
Saturday's Child	Countee P. Cullen			
The Factory Child				April 17, 1926, 1.
I Charge You, British Workers	Dawn Fraser	Cape Breton, NS		April 17, 1926, 3.
That Grand and Glorious Day	G.C.S.	Cape Breton, NS		April 24, 1926, 1.
Stand Up for Justice	Student	Cape Breton, NS		April 24, 1926, 2.
The Heretics	Ralph Chaplin			May 8, 1926, 3.
The Red Flag	James Connell		Maryland	May 15, 1926, 4.
We'll Never Let the Red Flag Fall	Student	Glace Bay, CB, NS		May 22, 1926, 3.
A Most Unfriendly Act	Dawn Fraser	Cape Breton, NS		June 26, 1926, 1.
Cape Breton's Curse Adieu, Adieu	Dawn Fraser	Cape Breton, NS		July 10, 1926, 1.
The Red Flag	James Connell		Maryland	July 10, 1926, 3.

Chapter 4
Humorous Nicknames in Cape Breton

Nicknames are a widespread feature of Cape Breton's contemporary oral tradition. In this chapter I discuss Cape Breton nicknames in general and then focus on some specific humorous names from what was once referred to as Industrial Cape Breton. This essay was written when the Sydney Steel Plant and the coal fields surrounding Sydney were operating.

By examining how these names were generated I hope to demonstrate a sense of the function of these small but pithy items in contemporary Cape Breton folk culture.

An earlier version of this chapter was originally published in the book Northeast Folklore: Essays in Honour of Edward D. Ives, *edited by Pauleena MacDougall and David Taylor, 353-62. Orono, ME: University of Maine.*

In the foreword to *Nicknames: Past and Present*, Eric Partridge (1976) offers a descriptive definition of nicknames:

> A nickname is not, as some would be wit suggested, a name bestowed in the nick of time, but an additional name, an also name, an eke name; late Middle English, nekename. To the sense "additional," we have to subjoin the derivative "substituted" especially if bestowed in ridicule or irony. (ix)

In many Cape Breton cases, the nickname is the only name by which a community member is known; though an additional name, it often substitutes for, or replaces, the Christian name.

A broad survey of Cape Breton names from a variety of communities and ethnic groups reveals that there are two major categories of Cape

Breton nicknames: those generated by features of language such as phonetics, alliteration, contraction and substitution, and those created by external or social factors (Davey and MacKinnon 1988: 4-5). The most common phonetic feature used in the first category is the y/ie suffix. Names such as Tommy Peggie, Big Hughie and Big Johnny abound. Added or substituted names such as Scratchie, Birdie, Sharky, Slimy, Porky, Pinky and Buddy are also common in many communities. Alliteration is yet another characteristic feature, shown in names such as Billy the Brat, Dynamite Dan, Dangerous Dan and Beer Bottle.

The second category, names generated by external and social factors, seems to represent the larger number of names. Physical characteristics, habitual actions, events of local importance, character traits, popular culture, occupations and humour are all sources for this group of names (5-10). In this chapter, I focus precisely on a few specific events that cause the creation of nicknames. Due to the nature of some of the material, those that I interviewed wished to remain anonymous, but all quotes come from fieldwork.

The small communities and hamlets that hugged the banks of the Atlantic Ocean throughout the 19th century were transformed into coal towns by the early years of the 20th century. The work force for this booming industry consisted of Gaelic Scots, French Acadian and Irish, many of whom migrated from the rural communities of Cape Breton. A large number of Europeans—Italian, Polish, Hungarian and Czechoslovakian—were also attracted by the employment opportunities of Cape Breton's coal fields. Before long, coal mines and company-owned housing were predominant features of Cape Breton Island's physical landscape.

While mining is no longer the core of these communities, nicknames are still commonly used. The first name I examine is that of Mira Dan MacDonald. In the words of one informant:

> Say, Mira Dan, Yea. That was Mira Dan MacDonald.... I think he was born in Antigonish, but ah, followed the mining.... But ah, apparently he was quite a scrapper in his younger days, and ah, he attended one of the outdoor Scottish picnics out in Grand Mira. And ah, he got into a fight and I guess ah, he was known to be a pretty good scrapper, and I guess there was some chap from Mira.... Yea, Mira Dan got into a fight in Mira at this picnic with some boxer that was supposed to be pretty tough from the Mira area and of course, he beat him, and then, the name Mira Dan, that's where the name came from, it stuck to him.[1]

The narrative describing this name formation is interesting in that it requires contextual insider information to fully understand the subtleties of the name's meaning. While one might think that Dan came from Mira—as was the case with Johnny Washabuct, Angus Lingan or John Caledonia who were named for their communities of origin—that is not the case with Mira Dan. As opposed to offering insight into Dan MacDonald's home town, this name represents a play on the traditional form of nickname formation in that a particular event in the life of this individual led to the creation of the nickname, after Dan seized the opportunity to demonstrate his physical attributes in the community of Mira. To arrive at an understanding of the creation of this name, it is important to appreciate the value of physical strength in mining communities. A strong body was needed to perform the arduous tasks required of coal miners. Although not officially condoned, fighting was common in the industrial communities. In fact, competitive strength sports, including track-and-field, hockey, baseball and harness racing were popular throughout industrial Cape Breton. Indeed, numerous Canadian champions of the boxing ring were born in the industrial Cape Breton area.

Another name that requires some local knowledge to fully comprehend is Johnny Slut. *The Oxford English Dictionary* defines the term "slut" as a slovenly woman, a slattern or a hussy. The obvious interpretation one has upon hearing the name is that it may describe the slovenly behaviour of an individual. The informant describes the derivation of this name:

> Like John MacNeil's, I think at one point somebody said there were seven or eight John MacNeils.... There was Jack MacNeil, Long Jack MacNeil, Black Jack MacNeil because he was dark complected [*sic*], you know, and then there was another fellow they called Johnny Slut MacNeil and ah, how that name stuck to him, that was his favourite word when he worked in the mines you know, everything was a slut, ah you slut, so the name stuck to John and it continued on, it stuck to the family....

This name makes sense only when one realizes that there is a distinct form of language in mining communities known locally as "pit talk" (Colls 1977). Pit talk is marked by much use of scatological language and curse words of which "slut" is a mild expression. Such language may serve as a mechanism whereby workers contend with the fear associated with their work in the dark, dusty and dangerous environment of a coal mine. This form of speech is predominantly used in the mines although some individuals carry this speaking habit into their everyday discourse within the wider community. Consequently, it is not uncommon to see this kind of language usage spill over into community nicknames.

What is interesting here, however, is that Johnny's nickname is passed on to other family members—the encountering of which is, again, not unusual with nicknames throughout Cape Breton Island. A name can pass to a sister, brother and even to children who are sometimes completely unaware of the name's origin. Another example from the participant illustrates how these names can pass from one family member to another:

Ah, Jelly Beans or Jelly MacKinnon, Jelly Beans.... And ah, how he got that name, um, there was Father Raymond Campbell who was parish priest.... for many many years. He ah, "christened" him with that. Ah Jelly used to deliver the *Cape Breton Post* or the *Sydney Post Record* at that time to that area and on payday when he'd get his money, he used to stop at ... a little store and he was very fond of jelly beans, And Father Campbell was in there a couple of times so he christened him "Here comes Jelly Beans" and that name stuck to him.... It was even passed on to his sister Theresa, yea they call her Theresa Jelly, But that's where the name came from.

Yet another instance of how a nickname is passed on in families:

Well Shorty Angus MacDonald, that's obvious, he was a short man, there were several Angus MacDonalds, Shorty Angus and he has a son Hughie, and he goes by Hughie Shorty, meaning Hughie, son of Shorty, and he has a daughter ... and she's Lizzie Shorty, they refer to her as Lizzie Shorty.

While some names derive from events in one's life such as Mira Dan's fight, an individual's common saying such as Johnny the Slut, a brother's penchant for jelly beans or the diminutive size of a father, nicknames are generally generated out of humour. At times the humour is based on irony. Hairy John describes a balding man and Tiny describes a very large woman. Other humorous names are created by a desire to ridicule a particular trait of an individual. Radio Jim describes a mouthy person. Bif refers to someone who always has a beef about something. Looking Glass Joe describes a man who has a habit of looking at his reflection in windows and mirrors. The Stumps are a family whose physical characteristics can be described as short and squat. In contrast, the Bull Oxes are a family who are big, husky and strong. In fact, calling someone, or a family, after a particular animal is one of the more common nickname forms, particularly when the individuals involved are believed to possess some of the stereotypical traits of the animal mentioned. Skunk, Tiger, Snake, Rat, Silverfox, Mouse, Roddie the Bear, Rannie the Moose, Cat, Kittens, Rooster and Piggy are only a few of the more common appellations made from animal names.

Food is yet another source for names with examples such as Beef, Ham, Cookie, Biscuits, Crackers and Johnny Pudding coming readily to mind. A chubby person could be called Ham whereas a young child who had a liking for certain foods, such as cookies or biscuits, might be given that nickname for life.

Occupations are yet another name-generating source. Joe the Wrangler worked with horses; the Doughboys ran a bakery; my grandfather, Soldier Alex, was a sergeant in the Second World War and an overman in the mines; Danny Cage worked in a shaft mine lowering the cage into the pit and Butcher Boy and his family ran a meat business. Occupations no longer common in contemporary society such as tailors, saddlers, coopers and weavers are also represented in the nicknames.

Other names are given for peculiar attributes or characteristics. Dan Sticking it Out is a man who walks in such a way that his *derrière* protrudes when he walks. Gumeye has a habit of squinting and Scratchie Itchie Archie Alex is accustomed to scratching himself. Skinhead is bald-headed, Saucy Flossie is impudent and Thirty Days spent a lot of time in the local lockup. Some names such as Hairy Hole and Baloney Joe derive from the washhouse of the mine where men shower together and note any unique anatomical features through nicknames.

One of the important functions that these small, pithy items serve in communities is the role they play in identifying individuals. In locales where the same surname is common—as it often is in Cape Breton—the use of a moniker or nickname is often necessary to decipher the various MacDonalds, MacKinnons or McIsaacs in one community. For example, a friend of mine is called Neil Johnny John McIsaac after his father and grandfather. Being a MacKinnon, I am sometimes asked whether my people are the Beaver Cove MacKinnons, or the MacKinnon Brook MacKinnons; both families have relatives in my home community. In some of the rural areas of Cape Breton, particularly in some of the Scottish Gaelic areas, there are nicknames which can reveal information going back three or four generations. A study of nicknames in the Scottish Highlands by Nancy Dorian aptly called these nicknames "genealogical names" (1970: 306-307).

One study of Cape Breton nicknames concluded that there is little evidence of the use of nicknames in Cape Breton as reflections of ethnic tensions: "It may be that nicknames drawn from the new industrial culture functioned more in the cause of solidarity than division within the industrial community and formed one of the ingredients in the development of new local or regional identity" (Frank 1988: 61). When moving beyond the archive and into the field, however, one finds there is more to nicknames than meets the eye or the ear; there is more to these names than group solidarity. For example, derogatory or derisive names are often applied to individuals as a form of social control (McDavid 2002). The names serve to stigmatize the bearers for behaviour that is not condoned. For example, my research uncovered one man who was always referred to as Bonnie the Racer. On the surface it does not seem offensive, but Bonnie did not want people to use this name in his presence. As the story goes, when Bonnie was a young man he drove a snowplough for the municipality. Apparently after drinking at a tavern during a notable winter storm, Bonnie proceeded to drive the snowplough very fast along the main street. The outcome was that he scratched and damaged a number of vehicles in the process. Youngsters, most of whom did not know this story, had great fun yelling this nickname out to Bonnie as they walked past his house on their way to school. He, of course, was offended by this and at times would chase the young students, which, in turn, helped to perpetuate the name's usage.

Many nicknames highlight characteristics that make the recipient of the name different from the majority of the community. They can be derisive and offensive, often citing ethnic characteristics that are not actually present (for example, racial slurs may be employed in the nicknames of Caucasian individuals, linking them to other ethnic groups with characteristics that are less desirable by community standards). Other unfortunate nicknames draw attention to qualities that the community would find offensive. These frequently have to do with Carnivalesque ideas: excrement, sex, cleanliness, etc. These names often involve adding a term like "Shitty," "Smelly," or "Whore" to the given name, and are all derisive names rather than those of solidarity. Hazlitt had it right when he said "a nickname is the heaviest stone that the devil can throw at a man" (1852: 174).

A third function of this form of language usage is to commemorate or immortalize minor events in the history of a place or in the life of a person. The anecdote or story continues to exist and the short nickname usually brings to mind a much longer story. In some cases it is a story that the individual would prefer to forget; in others it becomes begrudgingly accepted by both the community and the person bestowed with the name. For example, my grand-uncle was always known as Suey. Apparently the newspaper he worked for as a young boy held an annual contest at a local theatre wherein their newspaper boys read and yelled out the headlines. The most articulate headline reader would receive a large prize. When it was my grand-uncle's turn to read, he became nervous and instead of reading the headline "SUICIDE IN GLACE BAY," he called out "SUEYCIDE IN GLACE BAY" and was promptly assigned the name Suey for the remainder of his life. For those who know the origin of the name, it offers a chance to jokingly deride the man for his mispronunciation at a young age.

But more importantly, the name brings to mind a minor incident in this man's life as well as a long-past community activity, and allows the story to go into wider circulation.

While some people have argued that Cape Breton nicknames seldom enter into official culture, a quick glance at official records reveals this not to be the case. An examination of archival daybooks and account books at the Beaton Institute, Cape Breton University, reveals that nicknames are often used to distinguish one person from another in Cape Breton. The 1886 Account Book of John MacKeen of Clayton Farm, Mabou reveals names such as Neil Red Sandy MacDonald, James Saddler Murphy, Allan the Ridge MacDonald, Donald Ban Beaton (Ban means pale, white or fair-haired in Gaelic), Angus Big Sandy the Ridge MacDonald, Dave Colorado Smith, James the Post MacDougall and Archy the Saddler MacDonald.[2] An 1865 ledger from the same farm offers names such as Isabelle Red, Archy MacDonald and Alex Thresher Beaton.[3] Throughout the 19th century, the daybooks and ledgers of the General Mining Association reveal that nicknames were regularly used to distinguish the various employees with similar last names.[4]

In truth, nicknames are more than just humorous names. Their brevity, sound, allusiveness and symbolism make them important community metaphors. While they are usually short, they are often full of meaning for those who understand the story behind the name. In his study of West Indies nicknames, Frank Manning uses Geertz's phrase to term them "symbolic orders of person definition." He thinks "they serve to individuate persons and to suggest something further about them that is culturally significant" (Manning 1974: 13). For Cape Breton communities, this may be one of the chief reasons they have existed in the past and why they continue to play an important role in the life and culture of the region.

In conclusion, nicknames serve a number of important functions including identification, entertainment, social control and increasing trust and solidarity. They may also reflect community or ethnic tensions, and allude to important minor events in an individual's or community's past. Nicknames are extremely important but under-examined aspects of Cape Breton's oral tradition. Future research could perhaps focus precisely on the scatological nicknames found within the mines which might be related to the practical joking behaviour commonly found among miners. Moreover, there seems to be a vibrant nicknaming tradition among Cape Breton school children that represents another area that warrants more work. Another possible avenue to explore is the prevalence of nickname usage in official documents such as census records, ledgers, account books and diaries. This fascinating naming tradition serves as a valuable tool for understanding past and contemporary community relations, language usage and the role of humour in small communities.

Notes

1. Quotes in this article are from a single, unnamed informant.
2. Beaton Institute, Account Book of John MacKeen, son of Honorable William MacKeen, Clayton Farm, MG 12, 109, A 8 doc. 1866.
3. Ibid.
4. The General Mining Association account books, daybooks and ledgers are located at the Beaton Institute.

Chapter 5
Cockfighting in Cape Breton:
Its Meaning and Function

A scorching summer sun glares off the roofs of pickup trucks and station wagons parked near a red barn on the outskirts of a small mining community. From outside one hears the occasional crowing of roosters and the yelling and clapping of the men within. Inside, silver and steel spurs snugly attached to roosters' claws slash violently through the air as twenty-dollar bills exchange hands. It's a Sunday afternoon in 1975, and I am about to witness a clandestine, and illegal, cockfight. Inside the modern barn, twenty or so men, young and old, stand around the recently constructed cockpit in the middle of the threshing floor. Some joke with their friends, others pay up the money just lost in a bet, but all focus their attention on the red, orange and blue birds being caressed and fondled by their owners. These birds and the ones strutting pompously in wooden cages scattered throughout the room contrast sharply with the defeated warrior who lies in a tangled heap in a bloody pool in the corne; one eye is gone and his brightly coloured feathers are spattered with his own blood. One cockfight has ended and another is about to begin.

An earlier version of this chapter was presented at a Folklore Studies Association of Canada conference in the 1980s.[1]

Cockfighting is found in the Maritimes as well as many other regional enclaves throughout the world. In Canada, the matches are cloaked in secrecy because of the illegality of the activity; the criminal code considers cockfighting to be such a heinous crime that even watching a match is punishable by six months in jail, a five-hundred dollar fine, or both (Criminal Code 1973: 400-04). A conviction can result from merely keeping a cockpit: "Everyone who builds, makes, maintains or keeps a cockpit on premises that he owns or occupies, or allows a cockpit to be built, made or maintained, or kept on such premises is guilty of an offence punishable on summary conviction" (Criminal Code 1973: 403).[2] Like it or not, like drinking during prohibition, or smoking marijuana, cockfights existed as an underground activity. This chapter provides an ethnographic description of cockfighting in one industrial community and tries to explain some of the reasons it continued for so long. For obvious reasons the participants in this fieldwork are not identified.

The sport of fighting well-trained, muscular roosters can be traced to antiquity (Brand 1888: 59; Strutt 1834: 281-83). One writer points out that "it is indeed so old that we hardly know from whence to derive its origin" (Blaine 1852: 1209).[3] Another writer claims:

> the history of our noble game cock is more or less obscure. That he existed before the coming of Christ and the Christian era is well established. Just how long before that time game cocks were fought no one can even surmise. (Rupert 1949: 1)

Cockfighting is a culturally important hobby, sport, leisure activity and ritual in Asia, Europe, South, Central and North America (Fitz-Barnard 1921; Pridgen 1938; Finterbusch 1929; Smith 1919; Bryant and Capel 1974; Del Sento 1975; Blake 1984).

Despite its usual positioning outside the law—there have been numerous attempts to outlaw this activity over the centuries—its popularity was widespread geographically and temporally (Strutt 1834: 281-82). In 1366 cockfighting was prohibited by a public proclamation in Britain but the sport maintained its popularity and was publicly condoned and supported by the aristocracy and royalty (Strutt 1834: 281-82). By 1654 the activity was still extremely popular in England but Oliver Cromwell proclaimed an ordinance against the sport. He did not oppose the notion of cockfighting *per se*, but the activities of the large assemblies of people who gather to watch the matches (figure 5.1). These public meetings, according to the proclamation:

> are by experience found to tend many times to the disturbance of the publique peace, and are commonly accompanied with gaming, drinking, swearing, quarreling and other dissolute practises to the dishonor of God, and do often produce the ruine of persons and their families. (Fitz-Barnard 1921: 8)[4]

Still cockfighting flourished and by 1833 William IV was forced to pass an Act of Parliament outlawing the activity.

Fryday March 31. 1654.

ORdered by *His Highness the Lord Protector,* and *his* Council, *That* this Ordinance *be forthwith printed and published.*

HENRY SCROBELL *Clerk of the Council*

London, **Printed by** *William du-Gard* **and** *Henry Hills,* **Printers to His Highness the Lord Protector,** 1654.

AN
ORDINANCE

Prohibiting

Cock-Matches

Whereas the Publique meetings and Assemblies of People together in diverse parts of this Nation, under pretence of Matches for Cock-fighting, are by experience found to tend many times to the disturbance of the public Peace, and are commonly accompanied with Gaming, Drinking, Swearing, Quarrelling, and other dissolute practices, to the dishonor of God, and do often produce the ruine of Persons and their Families. For prevention thereof, be it Ordained by his Highness the Lord Protector, by and with the advice and consent of his Council, That from henceforth there shall be no publique or set meetings or assemblies of any persons within England or Wales, upon Matches made for Cock-fighting; And that every such meeting, and assemblies of people for the end and purposes aforesaid, is hereby declared to be an unlawful Assembly, and shall be so adjudged, deemed, and taken to be, and punished; And all Sheriffs, Justices of the Peace, Maiors, Bayliffs, Constables and Head-boroughs, within their several Counties, Cities, Limits, and Jurisdictions, are hereby required to suppress, hinder, and disperse all such meetings and assemblies.

Figure 5.1 Cromwell Proclamation. Khattar Collection, Cape Breton University.

There are hints that in the late 18th and early 19th centuries, when New England United Empire Loyalists, Gaelic Scots and Irish migrants were coming to the Maritimes, cockfighting was a popular activity in this region. Advertisements for cockfights appear in Halifax newspapers at the end of the 18th century. On March 6, 1792, James Fraser of the New Brunswick Fusiliers announced he "will engage to fight a main of five battles on the twenty-third of April next being St. George's day," using "birds of last spring from two pounds, ten ounces to four pounds, give and take two ounces"(*Royal Gazette* [Halifax] 6 March 1792, advertisement). Cockfights regularly occurred at Halifax taverns throughout the 19th century and some were held as late as 1917 (Nova Scotia Provincial Museum 1934-1935: 67). One reference indicates that in some rural Cape Breton schools, there was a tradition of school boys bringing cocks to school for fighting during the Lenten season (Thomson 1906: 219-21). This tradition closely parallels an 18th century Scottish custom cited by Joseph Strutt (1834: 281). One study points out that it was 18th-century British Isles settlers who brought the tradition of blood sports such as cockfighting to the Appalachians (Herzog 1985: 114-26). A letter concerning activities on the Isle of Harris, Scotland written to relatives in Cape Breton in the 1950s mentions cockfighting was once a popular activity:

> ...there is also a tradition that the people of the neighboring parish of North Uist used to bring creels full of cocks to fight on the Earram with the Berneray cocks. Cockfights were the rage at the time. It seems that the Uist people did not take their visitor cocks home with them in Berneray, whereas the spectators had a good feast made from the game cocks. (Kenneth Morrison Papers)

These references suggest Scottish antecedents for Cape Breton Island's cockfighting and documents its continuing popularity well into the 20th century. However a thorough examination of the possible Highland Scottish roots of cockfighting as it is practised in the Maritimes is sorely needed as the sport will not be fully understood until more research is undertaken. It is clear that cockfighting has been a common activity in the Maritime region and particularly in the former coal mining communities of Cape Breton Island since at least the turn of the 20th century (Cameron 1991: 191-94). In more modern times it is difficult to assess the number of participants who engaged in this activity because of its illegality. One study indicates there are more than 500,000 participants in the United States (McCaghy and Neal 1974: 557-69).

A set of rules for cockfighting in North America was compiled in the 1950s by Henry Wortham: "Modern Tournament and Derby Rules."[5] One

Figure 5.2 Pen and ink sketch, 1949. Khattar Collection, Cape Breton University.

Figure 5.3 Cape Breton cockfight, 1950. Khattar Collection, Cape Breton University.

Cape Breton cock owner said that fights were organized over the telephone or through the mail: "I give my pals a day or two notice and then it spreads by word of mouth" ("Cockfighter" 1975).[6] After notifying participants, a cockpit must be constructed. In this instance, a pit is merely a circle approximately 15 feet in diameter (4.5 m) surrounded by a discarded conveyor belt propped in a vertical position with wooden pegs to encase the circle. Most pits are set up inside barns, but some are built in open fields (figure 5.2).

Participants mingle and socialize around the pit prior to the commencement of a fight; the majority are men although sometimes women and children also attend. A drink of rum or moonshine sometimes accompanies the jokes and latest gossip. If there are spectators or visitors from outside the community, they are introduced to everyone at the fight.

Two cock owners then challenge each other to the first match, a nonpartisan referee is chosen to ensure a fair fight and bets are recorded (figure 5.3). The money is collected, the two birds are weighed to make sure there is no weight advantage, and gaffs are strapped to the cocks' natural claws. A gaff is a polished steel prong about two or three inches in length which is curved, closely resembling the natural spur of a cock (figure 5.4). One gaff is fixed on each spur of the fighting cock; as a result, gaffs are sometimes called "spurs." It is up to the owner to decide what type of fighting tool to strap to his bird. One owner describes putting gaffs or spurs on his rooster:

> You cut his natural spurs with about half inch long. And these steel spurs, they fit right over. You just put tape on till it fits tight. Then tape it all, and wrap it, and tie it. And they have the steel spur instead of the natural spur.... Most of the spurs in Cape Breton, they run from an inch-and-a-half and three-quarters to three inches. I always use two-and-a half. (Wilson 1990: 58)

The owners bring their respective cocks to the centre of the pit for preliminary pecking to allow birds to sniff each other's scent. They are then brought to opposite sides of the pit, the owner sets them down, and the fight begins. The cocks stalk each other like prize boxers, and with amazing speed they attempt to land lethal blows. Each rooster has his own fighting style: "Some are shufflers and others are strikers," says a cock owner.

Sometimes a match will take more than an hour, at other times, only a matter of seconds: "Sometimes a bird will go up in the air and go down dead, his heart or something. Same as a fighter may get hit in the brain...." On some occasions one cock will spring out of the pit and, although the owner repeatedly tries to bring him back, the cock will just not fight. In other cases, a stalemate occurs when neither bird shows any interest, or

Figure 5.4 Khattar Collection, Cape Breton University. Photo by Barry Gabriel.

when one cock plunges a spur or gaff so deep it must be removed by the owner. A cock owner explains the rules at this stage of the match:

> You fight till the birds get hooked. What happens: one bird will maybe drive his spur in a wing or something and get in too far. And he can't get it out. So then they're tied up. So when they're hooked, the referee will call for a break. So you'll break.... You handle your bird. The two men—each guy grabs his own bird, very gently and you sort out any spurs that are hooked or stuck. Then you go back to your own side of the pit.... And there's a line—probably about three feet from the wall. And you stand on that line or behind that line. And the referee counts

to 21. And you drop your bird again. And they go again. Till they're hooked again. (Wilson 1990: 59)

At the end of a fight, injured birds are doctored by owners, dead birds are given away and bets are paid to the winners. One breeder of fighting roosters explains:

> ...nine times out of ten (a bird that loses) he's dead. Or he's so close to dead—there's no life left in him, actually that's worthwhile keeping. But you have the option—it's the bet—all fights are on a bet. And if you really like your bird, and he gets a crippling blow, like accidentally, sometimes they'll break a leg sometimes. They'll hit the ground. Or break a wing. Well, once he's disabled, you're pretty sure he's going to get cut down before too long. He's not going to last long. So, if you like the bird you could save him. All you've got to do is call him out—pay the bets off and take your bird out.... (Wilson 1990: 54)

This sport is an expensive activity for owners. Top-of-the-line fowl imported from the southern United States, Ireland, Mexico, Spain and El Salvador cost between one thousand and twenty-five hundred dollars, while local birds can cost anywhere from two to five hundred dollars. Feed is another major expense. For one cock owner who owned more than one hundred birds, feed costs over fifty dollars a week. In addition to scratch feed, birds are sometimes fed eggs, raw hamburger and even apples. Birds are often advertised for sale in trade magazines such as *Grit and Steel,* which has been in circulation for more than one hundred years (figure 5.5).

Betting is the most expensive side of cockfighting. There are two kinds: main bets and side bets. The owners of the two cocks matched against each other usually engage in main betting; these are often for large sums of money. Side betting is for spectators. As the cockfighter says: "I seen one bet in the States fought for ten thousand dollars with a side bet for one thousand dollars."

Figure 5.5 Grit and Steel magazine. The Gamecock, December 1953.

Figure 5.6 Muffs or mutts. Khattar Collection, Cape Breton University.

In addition to the high costs of keeping and betting on cocks, it is time-consuming and arduous to train fighting roosters. Just as boxers rigorously train for championship bouts, cocks must be in top physical condition for their fights. Owners construct treadmills for cocks to strengthen their legs. Food is often dangled just out of their reach to force them to run around man-made tracks. Wing and leg exercises and even sparring matches are an essential part of the training procedure. Sparring matches are accomplished with the aid of what look like boxing gloves, or pads (locally referred to as "muffs" or "mutts") attached to the cocks' natural claws, so the birds will not be injured during practice sessions (figure 5.6).

Throughout training, birds are kept in separate quarters: small, 1 m by 1.5 m (5 by 3 ft) wooden boxes that look like overturned, reused packing or fish crates. The reason for this is that cocks are bred to be temperamental, pugnacious and scrappy. "It's not as bad as people think," says the cockfighter. "It's born in them to fight. If you put a rooster in front of a mirror he'll kill himself fighting with it [his reflection]."

While the sport is illegal in the Maritimes, individuals are seldom charged with this activity. The only notable raid on a cockfight was in 1974 when RCMP became concerned about a match being billed as, "the Nova Scotia Finals" (*Time* 1974: 7). The RCMP rounded up thirty-nine men and attempted to confiscate and kill thirty-two flapping roosters.

According to one participant, the constables had difficulty rounding up the birds amidst the pandemonium. One participant said, "Finally a couple of the boys [both rooster owners] step in and say, 'for the love of God,' and do the job themselves" (Bruce 1974: 74).[7] Each man was charged twenty-eight dollars and the man owning the cockpit was charged two hundred dollars. Owners also had their fighting paraphernalia, such as muffs, spurs and gaffs, confiscated (Cockfighters 1974: 17). This raid caused a lot of controversy in Nova Scotia and a local MLA even publicly asked for an amendment against the cockfighting legislation and openly supported the sport (*Cape Breton Post* 1974a 1974). This MLA stated:

> Let's see something done to relieve the cruelty to people before we start worrying about roosters.... Let's start worrying about willful exploitation and cruelty by one human being to another before we start shedding crocodile tears over a few fighting roosters who are only following instinct. (Bruce 1974: 74)

He acknowledged, "the sport of cockfighting is a widely accepted practice in the community and the time has come to adjust the law in the face of long accepted practice" (ibid.).

There have been no raids since 1974 and officials do not consider cockfighting to be a priority crime. One RCMP official said that some people have been caught transporting cocks and paraphernalia such as spurs, gaffs and muffs, but no arrests have been made. He stated, in 1984, "I suspect there is just as much fighting now as there ever was, it's just more secretive, almost like a private club."[8] The cockfighter concurred; "We don't tell anybody where a fight will be or when it is. We keep it amongst ourselves."

After exploring the origins and manners of this old but clandestine activity, I would suggest a number of reasons this sport has continued to exist at the "hidden" level of culture in Cape Breton. There are important reasons that individuals, mainly men, choose to continue to perpetuate an underground, clandestine tradition such as cockfighting. First, the activity thrives in an industrial region, an area where coal mining has been occurring on a large scale since the early years of the 19th century. Coal mining is a dangerous activity, particularly in the Nova Scotia coal fields which extend up to five miles underneath the Atlantic Ocean. Miners work in a hostile environment where courage, valour and strength are necessary and important values for everyday living and survival. The cockfight may be viewed as a metaphor for the kind of work values that are required by men who work in the deeps. The cockfight may be didactic, teaching men that courage, hard work, resilience and toughness—all qualities possessed by the best cocks—are necessary in the world of work in the subterranean, submarine coal mine where "winning" the coal is a daily battle. So, the cockfight may be viewed as an expressive cultural text, an occasion where certain necessary values are expressed and reified. Clifford Geertz, in his influential study of Balinese cockfighting, says that participants at Balinese cockfights experience "a kind of sentimental education. What he learns there is what his culture's ethos and his private sensibility (or anyway certain aspects of them) look like when spelled out externally in a collective text" (Geertz 1974: 27). The sporting event or game of the cockfight teaches much about some of the important aspects of the world view held by people who live and work in this industrial community.

It is important to point out that although cockfighting is illegal, it is tacitly accepted and tolerated by Cape Breton Island community members as well as the police. Seldom are individuals charged under the Canadian Criminal Code. One participant tells a story to substantiate this point:

> About three years, four years ago, and a bunch of us—I took three or four young fellows from here with me. We had my old green wagon. I had four roosters, going over to a fight. Sunday night. And didn't the damn Mounties stop us on the highway. So there's two Mounties. So there's one guy, you know, he said, "What have you got in those boxes there?" "Oh," I said, "that"s roosters." "Where you going with the roosters?" I said, "I'm selling them." I opened the crate and he looked at them, yeah saw them. And they started to walk away. And I guess he got telling the other fellow. The other fellow stopped and he came right back again. "Mind if I have a look at them?" So I opened one up. He reached in the box and he picked this one out. You know, good, safe, already to fight, all primed up. "Yeah," he said, "boys having a little fight tonight, are they?" I said, "What are you talking about?" He said, "I can see by the look of your birds. These are nice-looking birds you got there. Don't need to fool me," he said. "I know all about those fellows." He said, "You wouldn't have the spurs on you, by any chance?" I said, "no, no." "Well, that's all right," he said. (Wilson 1990: 58)

Local law enforcement officers seem to recognize that this activity has been "traditionalized" or viewed as "a tradition" in the community. In a sense, it is a form of customary behaviour that has been passed on via informal learning from one person to another and has meaning for those who participate. As one cockfighting enthusiast describes:

> But all the people that are in it that I know today—they're all men that were in it when I was a kid. None of them ever got rich at it, none of them ever made money at it. Matter of fact, a lot of them go in the

hole some winters. But they do it more as a tradition.... It's just like a habit—they've been at it all their life. You know some of these guys really love it.... To them, it's a part of their tradition, part of their life-style.... (Wilson 1990: 63)

This acceptance of the sport as "tradition" further supports its importance in the fabric of the industrial community.

On one level, the cockfight teaches the values necessary for surviving in a difficult work place; on another, it provides a socially sanctioned way for men who work in a high risk environment to relieve tension and anxiety. The winning, losing, yelling and debating which occur at a cockfight help to diffuse personal animosities among men who need to rely on each other in their daily underground work in the coal mine. Pent-up emotions and feelings can be released in a socially sanctioned way while attending the cockfight. The pitting of animal against animal in a gruesome fight, with the humans observing and participating by betting, allows humans to safely displace their own aggressive feelings.

On another level, it is a way to pass the time, an entertainment, where violence is played out before an interested crowd. In some ways, this is not so different from much mass-mediated violence presented to the consuming television public who are "entertained" by violent acts on their television screens. One major difference is that with cockfighting, the audience is at the scene, closely observing, smelling and experiencing the fighting match between cocks. With television, the audience is distanced by mass-mediated technology; viewers are entertained by watching violent acts that originate many miles away. The prevalence of mass-mediated television violence highlight the entertainment value of violence in contemporary society, like cockfighting.

The entertainment appeal of cockfighting is similar to the lure of boxing. In fact, in the communities where cockfighting prevails, boxing is also a popular sport and many of the individuals who are cockfighting enthusiasts are also avid boxing fans. One reason why cockfighting and boxing are of interest to people is that by watching these kinds of events, viewers are openly and explicitly violating the societal taboo against violence. One scholar, Timothy Mitchell, discusses the voyeuristic nature of blood sports and calls this activity "transgressive seeing" (Mitchell 1991: 170). In his study of bullfighting he compares watching blood sports to pornography and says:

it is extremely difficult for human beings to gaze upon transgression without being aroused in some way.... Physiological arousal, whether of a gratifying or guilty variety, is an automatic result of viewing bull-

fights, since they are transgressive by definition and fully participate in
the erotic dynamics of violence. (Mitchell 1991: 171)

Joyce Carol Oates, in writing about boxing, agrees with Mitchell. She says,
"boxing as a public spectacle is akin to pornography; in each case the spec-
tator is made a voyeur, distanced, yet presumably intimately involved in
an event that is not supposed to be happening as it is happening" (Oates
1987: 105-106). This theory of "transgressive seeing" helps to explain why
people from industrial communities find cockfighting to be a tradition, a
sport and a past time.

    I have shown in this work that cockfighting, a form of "hidden cul-
ture"[9] and sport, has existed in one area of the Maritimes for at least one
hundred years. There are distinctive cultural reasons that cockfights have
existed for so long and to hold meaning for people, particularly in industrial communities. Clearly hidden elements of culture such as cockfighting
are extremely important for our understanding of present and past human
values. Moreover, the kinds of traditional customary activities we engage
in can teach us much about our notions of masculinity, gender, the transmission of values, how we are entertained, our world view and our fears
and concerns. Serious attention needs to be given to our various customary activities and rituals whether legal or illegal, public or private, open or
clandestine, which play significant roles in the lives of Canadians.

Notes
1. I would like to thank the following people for providing comments and assistance while
working on this chapter: Joan Weeks, Dr. Diane Tye, Dr. Bill Davey, Dr. Don MacGillivray,
Dr. Danny Samson, Dr. Michael Robidoux and the unidentified reviewers of this essay. I
would also like to thank the librarians at Cape Breton University for giving me access to the
Thomas Khattar special collection of books and materials on cockfighting.
2. In the United States, cockfighting is illegal in all but four states: Arizona, New Mexico,
Oklahoma and Louisiana (Herzog 1985: 114).
3. There are numerous books that examine cockfighting in the historical past. See Markham
(1654: 81-92); *Hoyle's Improved Edition* (1830: 284-88); Sketchley (1814); Atkinson
(1938); Scott (1957).
4. A framed copy of Cromwell's proclamation is found in the Thomas Khattar Collection
of the Cape Breton University library.
5. For a discussion of these rules see Harris (1987: 100-11).
6. All interview quotes in this article come from an interview with an anonymous participant, "Cockfighter," and were conducted in 1975.
7. For a more detailed description of this raid see *Cape Breton Post* (1974b); *Halifax
Chronicle Herald* (1974).
8. Interview with RCMP constable by Joan Weeks and Richard MacKinnon, tape recorded
interview.

9. I have borrowed this term from Graham Seal's work on Australian folklore. Seal calls folklore "hidden culture" for three reasons: he sees folklore as such a commonplace factor in our lives that many people rarely notice it; when it is noticed by writers or researchers it is considered mundane and ordinary and perhaps trivial; because it is informally generated and transmitted, it is essentially an unofficial mode of activity (1989: 16-17).

Chapter 6
Log Architecture on Cape Breton Island:
Cultural Borrowing and Adaptation

This chapter was originally one part of a larger study of the vernacular architecture of the Codroy Valley, southwestern Newfoundland (MacKinnon 1991, 2002). In order to understand fully some of the origins of the architectural patterns in the Codroy Valley, I examined the buildings of one of the antecedent regions, the area where most Codroy Valley Scottish settlers came from—Cape Breton Island. In my initial archival research I found many mentions of log buildings. However, in my field survey of Cape Breton architecture I could not find any extant examples of this form of dwelling or outbuilding except for a reconstruction at the Nova Scotia Highland Village in Iona, an open air museum devoted to Scottish Nova Scotian folklife. In the 1980s, two log buildings came to light and in this chapter I have closely examined these structures: one from Marble Mountain, and the other from Alba, communities situated along Bras d'Or Lake in the centre of the island. I am primarily interested in exploring what these buildings tell us about peoples' attitude and thoughts, and following this, about the borrowing and adapting of architectural ideas. First, I will examine some of the available archival and published literature on Cape Breton Island log buildings, setting the context for my examination of the two houses.

Originally published in Material Culture *24 (1992) 1-18.1*

Various writers indicate that a particular form of log construction was a predominant feature in the 19th-century landscape of Cape Breton Island. One of the questions Robert G. Haliburton asks in his 1861 survey of the region is "What can a farm of 200 acres, with a log house and barn and 40 acres cleared, be purchased for per acre?" (1958: 158). He adds, according to one farmer's reply, "a farm of that description could be purchased for from £20 to £40 per acre." A second respondent states, "from £10 to £20" (160). It is difficult to determine Haliburton's definition of log house and barn; he may be referring to buildings constructed of logs left in the round, or to ones built from logs squared with an adze or hewing axe. Haliburton is not alone in his use of this word to describe 19th-century vernacular dwellings of Cape Breton; many travellers—from the early 19th century to the local historians of the 20th century—also use the word "log" to describe buildings of their communities (figure 6.1). For example, John F. Hart, a local historian from the Margaree Valley, states that "hardy pioneers" erected "log cabins" as temporary dwellings which were eventually replaced by frame dwellings when settlers were more firmly established in the region (Hart 1962: 12). Hart, like other local historians, believes that

Figure 6.1

log dwellings were the first form of temporary dwellings and that other more advanced forms developed as people became more settled.

One of the more reliable descriptions is a late 19th century personal experience account published in the Gaelic newspaper *MacTalla*:

> River Denys runs into Malagawatch Lake and when we came in 1821, there wasn't a white man living there. We started to cut down the forest where we intended establishing everyone near a neighbor and after that, everyone began building little log houses, thatched between the logs and narrow sticks, hewn with an axe or adze put down for a floor. (1894: 1)

This description, published seventy years after the time of settlement, outlines the building of log structures. We are not told, however, whether the logs are placed in a vertical or a horizontal position, or if the logs are earthfast or are on sills. We learn that interstices between logs are filled or "thatched," that floors are made from hewn logs and that neighbours chose to build houses close to each other in the landscape. While the details in this account suggest our author is not romanticizing about the settlement period, the contemporary reader must be wary because of the long delay between the actual settlement experience and its recording.

Others have written about their perceptions more immediately after encountering Cape Breton log structures. Augustes Wallet DesBarres, the Solicitor General of Nova Scotia (and son of J. F. W. DesBarres) who received his appointment shortly after Cape Breton was annexed to Nova Scotia in 1820, describes an 1818 visit to a farm owned by a Scottish immigrant on Bras d'Or Lake:

> The farm lot where I was, consisted of 200 acres of land, 15 of which were cut down and cleared away in the form of a square; about nine acres of this was sown and planted, the remainder being used as meadow ground: in the centre of the clearing stood the dwelling house, constructed of square logs dovetailed into each other, and covered over at the top with shingles; in the inside a cleanliness and neatness of arrangement seemed to bespeak peculiar comfort and content.... (Tennyson 1986: 82-83)

In addition to providing a sense of the size of the pioneer farmstead, Desbarres describes the end-notching as being dovetailed—a form of cornering used in horizontal log dwellings throughout North America. There is no agreement upon the origin of this kind of horizontal log construction. Some argue it was brought to America by Pennsylvania Germans and then diffused to other parts of North America (Gowans 1962: 6; Kniffen and Glassie 1986: 177). Others see it as a form brought to America by the

Swedish settlers of the Delaware Valley in the late 1630s (Hutslar 1977: 1; Jordan 1978: 23; Jordan and Kaups 1989: 135-78; Noble 1984: 41).

Nevertheless, there are numerous accounts of log structures on Cape Breton. Haliburton provides a detailed description of this form of horizontal log construction:

> The log-house or cottage is a rough but rather picturesque construction; and when first erected is not uncomfortable. The logs of pine or hemlock are laid one upon another with their ends let into notches, and the interstices filled with moss and clay. The chimney is of stone built with mud or clay. Rough boards form the roof, which is sometimes constructed of poles and layers of thick bark. Nails and glass are the only materials for which money is needed. There are many degrees of comfort and improvement in these log houses. In the winter—if in bleak situations, they are often protected from the cold by spruce trees cut down and placed in an upright position against the walls most exposed to the winds. (1958: 65)

The birchbark Haliburton refers to was commonly used underneath the shingles or clapboard for insulation in many 19th-century Cape Breton houses. He also usefully provides a description of how cut-down spruce trees are employed as a form of insulation. Although we are not given a description of the kind of end-notching used in this building which would provide the degree of detail necessary to compare this type with other documented forms, it is evident that the observer here is referring to a horizontal log structure with end notching along with some form of a stone chimney.

Although settlers of Scottish descent predominate, Cape Breton Island is peopled by a number of other ethnic groups including the aboriginal Mi'kmaq, English, Irish and Acadian French. Other settlers employed log technology in their buildings as well. Anselme Chiasson provides a detailed description of the interior of an Acadian log house in Cheticamp on the northwest coast of the island:

> The house isn't finished inside. The floor itself is of squared wood, sometimes even of small, round logs or "rollons." The furniture is very rustic, a dining table made of planks, no chairs, just benches for seats. Against the wall there is a "dorsué" (sideboard or shelving) for the dishes.

> Wooden beds, simple sleeping couches, but with one peculiarity, there are no bedroom or partition walls.... In the ceiling, at the edge of the wall, there is an opening, and attached to the wall is a ladder to climb up. This leads to the attic where all supplies are stored (wool, clothing,

Figure 6.2 Nova Scotia Highland Village, Iona, Cape Breton.

beans, et cetera) and where, often, boys sleep on straw mattresses on the
floor. (Chiasson 1986: 39)

The floor plan of this Spartan house seems to consist of one large *salle com-
mune* where all of the family's daily activities occurred. Studies in other
regions show that log buildings were not only constructed with this one-
room plan, but were built with a multitude of floor plans ranging from the
simple one room type to the complex multi-room plan (Rempel 1980: 46;
Stanley 1983: 22-23).

While the documentary evidence of log construction on the Island is
extensive, until recently there has been little physical evidence to support
the published accounts. Neither in my initial survey of Cape Breton Island
nor in the records of the Canadian Inventory of Historic Buildings devoted
to the area are there examples of log buildings. The Nova Scotia Highland
Village, an open-air living museum devoted to Scottish Cape Breton culture in Iona, Cape Breton, constructed a horizontal log building in the
1960s to represent the "first" house of the Scottish immigrants (figure 6.2).
The building's design is based on research conducted by museum staff on
the relict remains of two horizontal log dwellings which are no longer extant, and upon the memories of older, local carpenters who remembered
seeing log buildings in the region (Highland Village Society 1986).

In October 1987, two horizontal log houses were discovered in the
communities of Marble Mountain and Alba; one building dates from the

Figure 6.3 McEachern-MacRitchie house, Alba, Cape Breton.

first generation of Scottish Cape Breton settlement in the early 19th century, and the other from the mid-century (*Cape Breton's Magazine* 1988). Both buildings had substantial alterations at the end of the 19th century. I have recorded by photographing, documenting and measuring both the McEachern-MacRitchie house in West Alba and the Keough house in Marble Mountain.

Situated on Bras d'Or Lake and 300 feet (91 m) from the road, the McEachern-MacRitchie house is now 30 by 18 feet (9 x 5.5) in size with a kitchen, pantry, parlour and two small bedrooms (figures 6.3 and 6.4). However, this layout dates from the latter part of the 19th century when major renovations occurred in the house, including the addition of wainscoting and a pantry in the kitchen, the removal of a large, stone, end chimney, and the addition of a large extension for bedrooms and a parlour. Originally, the house was 21 by 18 feet (6.4 x 5.5 m) in size containing one room with a large, stone, end chimney; sleeping quarters were in the loft reached by a ladder in a corner by the chimney. The original size of the building can be determined by examining the loft where one can see pieces of the original end wall still in place above the first floor ceiling. Each wall of the original log pen 18 by 21 feet (5.5 x 6.4 m) is made of twelve rounded logs, V-notched in the corners, with a squared 6 by 10 inch (15 x 25 cm) log on the top serving as a foundation plate for the roof and its rafters (figure 6.5). There were originally five trusses of rafters with dovetailed

Figure 6.4 McEachern-MacRitchie floor plan. By Barry Gabriel.

collar beams and no purlins placed on average 3.5 feet (1 m) apart. These trusses are made of squared, hand-hewn logs held together by wooden pins; two more were added when the house was extensively altered at the end of the 19th century. The roof is sheathed with 9 inch (23 cm) wide pine boards and covered with wooden shingles. The logs are not exposed but rather are covered with vertically laid laths and eighteen layers of shingles with a 6 inch (15 cm) face. Judging by the spacing between the logs, which are chinked with local moss, it does not seem that the bare logs were ever left exposed to the weather. I suspect that from the date of its original construction, the house was always sheathed with shingles or clapboard.

Figure 6.5 V Notching, McEachern-MacRitchie house, Alba, Cape Breton.

Houses such as the McEachern-MacRitchie house were probably more common in Cape Breton than we are led to believe by the few extant examples. These kinds of buildings were most likely expanded or attached to the larger frame houses, which became more popular as the 19th century progressed. Local tradition says that Margaret MacPhail, a writer who bases her work on experiences in rural Cape Breton, describes the Cassell-MacEachern house in the novel, *Loch Bras d'Or*:

> As he looked about the warm cozy kitchen he noted though it was a log house the walls were ceiled with wide pine boards with heavy open beams overhead, the large stone chimney was in the centre of the side wall. At one end of this room was a curtained built-in bed for the parents, under it a trundle bed that was pulled out at night for Kirsty. The weaving loom took quite a space at the other end of the kitchen with the spinning wheel and jackreel. On the wall beside the loom pegs formed a warping frame. It was all familiar to Hamish.

As he climbed the steep stairway to the loft, he saw four beds built in along the eaves. Two were on either side of the chimney which were cozy from the well heated stones. From the rafters hung dried herbs such as tansy, burdock, calendula, mint, blackberry roots all of which Mrs. McNabb prepared skillfully for various ailments, huge branches of goldenrod for bright yellow dye. (1970: 9-10)

It is difficult to date this dwelling, but the property is referred to in some public documents by the mid-19th century. The original grantee, Alexander McEachern, purchased 100 acres (40.4 ha) from the government by 1859 and received grants of 200 acres (81 ha) of adjacent land in 1867 and 1868. The date the land was granted does not provide a clear indication of first settlement, as grants of land in Cape Breton Island were often applied for only after the settler had resided on the property for a number of years. Born in 1818 in Scotland, Alexander was a son of Hugh McEachern (1744-1842), one of the pioneer settlers in Alba who migrated to Cape Breton in 1828. By 1864 Alexander was a weigh office keeper, by 1871 a Justice of the Peace, and by 1881, the operator of the post office, resigning in 1896. The Cassell family, consisting of Alexander, Lockhart and Mary (all unmarried) succeeded to the property in 1901. An adopted daughter of the Cassell family married Lauchlan MacRitchie, and subsequently, the MacRitchies succeeded in the occupancy of the property. By the 1940s Mary had died and the property was abandoned in 1970

Figure 6.6 Keough house, Marble Mountain, Cape Breton.

Figure 6.7 Keough house floor plan. By Barry Gabriel.

when Lauchlan MacRitchie entered a senior's home. George MacRitchie, Lauchlan's adopted son, the non-resident owner when the research was undertaken.[1]

While the McEachern-MacRitchie house dates from the first half of the 19th century, the pioneer period of settlement, the Keough house near Marble Mountain dates from the second half of the 19th century when stoves became more commonly used throughout Cape Breton (figures 6.6 and 6.7). Situated on Bras d'Or Lake, 200 yards from the road and 300 yards (183 m) from the lake; almost square, it measures 21 ft by 22 ft (approx. 6.4 m by 6.7 m). The kitchen takes up most of the dwelling space, measuring 16 ft by 13 ft (approx. 5 m by 4 m). Unlike the McEachern-MacRitchie house, the kitchen does not seem to have ever possessed a stone chimney. Rather, two stoves heated the house, one in the kitchen, and the other in the small parlour. Off the kitchen are two small pantries each being 6 by 6 feet (2 m by 2 m). A door from the kitchen leads to a parlour and a small bedroom, measuring 16 by 7 ft and 7 by 7 ft (4.9 by 2.1 m, and 2.1 by 2.1 m) respectively; a hatch door in the kitchen floor leads to the root cellar constructed of double-walled field stones. A dogleg stairwell in one corner of the kitchen leads to the open loft.

Like the McEachern-MacRitchie house, each wall of the log pen 21 by 22 feet (6.4 x 6.7 m) is made of twelve squared logs, V notched in the corners, with a larger, squared 6 by 10 inch (15 cm x 25 cm) log on the top serving as a foundation plate for the roof and its rafters. These large, squared top plates are very long; on three walls they run the entire length of the house. There are two end plates with eight supporting 4 by 5 inch (10 cm x 13 cm) studs. Like the McEachern-MacRitchie house, there are five trusses of rafters with dovetailed collar beams (no purlins) placed on average 3.5 feet (1 m) apart. These trusses are made of squared, hand hewn logs held together by wooden pins and are dovetailed into the large, squared top plate. Like the McEachern-MacRitchie house, the roof is sheathed with wide pine boards and covered with wooden shingles. Likewise, the logs are not exposed; the spacing between the logs indicates it must have always been covered with clapboard.

What does this examination of log dwellings in 19th-century Cape Breton tell us? First, it lays to rest the debate about whether or not log buildings were prevalent in this pioneer district of eastern North America. Some scholars have argued that log houses have become romantic symbols and that people wrongly assume their forebears lived in houses such as these. I am not suggesting that this form was the only one available to Cape Breton builders, but that it was one of the possible choices available in the early-to-late 19th century. Research on buildings of this kind in other areas indicates that many structures built in this way were not temporary—as is often suggested—but were meant to be permanent dwellings. In Ontario and in the United States, for example, log houses were still being constructed in the latter part of the 19th century, a time when there were ample building materials available other than log (Rempel 1980; Roberts 1984, 1988). The two houses examined in this chapter indicate that these were permanent dwellings, always sheathed over with boards and shingles to disguise the logs and built from a similar template.

The evidence presented here indicates that early Scottish settlers of Cape Breton Island used horizontal log architecture. These Scots did not have a tradition of log building upon arriving in the new world; their homeland architectural tradition was one of stone, clay or peat (Allen 1979; Fenton 1968; Fenton and Walker 1981; Noble 1983-84; Sinclair 1953). Research to date indicates that neither the English nor the Irish who settled Cape Breton Island at this same period had a homeland tradition of using log construction (Gailey 1984; Harrison and Hutton 1984; Mannion 1974).

One might argue that independent invention could account for the existence of this technology in the repertoires of Cape Breton Island builders, but there are more plausible explanations. Terry Jordan and Matti Kaups argue that the diagnostic feature of the V-notch in horizontal log construction was introduced to the new world via 17th-century Finnish and Swedish settlers in the Delaware Valley. Through their extensive fieldwork, they show that the V-notch was a well-established construction feature of both pioneer midland America and Scandinavia and that its ancestor is found in medieval Norway (Jordan and Kaups 1989: 141-51). Its use by Cape Breton Scots may indicate that pioneer ideas, worked out by early settlers of the Delaware Valley, had diffused far to the northeast by the early years of the 19th century. An architectural trait such as V-notching may have made its way to Cape Breton where builders readily borrowed ideas from those who had already faced the wilderness and perfected the use of any technology.

On Cape Breton Island and around the Maritimes, the one ethnic group already well-established in the region were the Acadian settlers who had been on new world soil since the mid-17th century. These people had a widespread knowledge of woodlore and an extensive understanding of log construction. Only with further fieldwork into the log building tradition of Maritime Acadians will we able to discover whether or not Acadian settlers helped to diffuse this architectural trait to other ethnic groups of the region, such as Cape Breton's Scots.

Another hypothesis follows from Warren Roberts's speculations that there may be another unexplored source for some of the North American log building traditions—the British Isles or Scottish Highlands. Roberts postulated the idea that a "special type of log construction flourished in New England as early as 1650" (1984: 33). He sees this form as having possible roots in Great Britain and surmises that it may have been Scottish settlers in areas as far afield as Virginia, Maryland and Nova Scotia who brought this form of construction to the New World (Roberts 1984: 33-34). Roberts suggests: "Unless more information should come to light from England and Scotland, it may never be possible to be more precise about the British origins of log construction" (1984: 34).

While northern Scotland was largely deforested by the time of migrations to North America, older patterns of building may have remained vestigial in the minds of emigrants. Research into Scottish Gaelic oral traditions indicates that older patterns of storytelling, singing and genealogy—spanning a number of generations—continued in the new world and particularly on Cape Breton Island (Dunn 1953; MacNeil 1987). Older oral patterns continued to thrive among these people even when they moved from Cape Breton Island to southwestern Newfoundland between 1840 and 1860 (Bennett 1989; Ommer 1977). Gaelic singing and storytelling persisted in Newfoundland; so too did the use of horizontal logs in the construction of barns and outbuildings (MacKinnon 1991: 46-57). Further architectural fieldwork in outpost regions where Scottish settlers migrated may add credence to Roberts's speculations on the origins of new world log construction.

A close examination of the modifications on the McEachern-MacRitchie house and an analysis of the Keough house reveal that the early pattern of the one-room log house was transformed by the end of the 19th century. At this stage, more rooms were constructed; a parlour, pantries and a bedroom on the ground floor were added to the original one-room plan. This indicates there may have been cultural borrowing from the New England architectural tradition where many of Nova Scotia's architectural ideas have their roots (Ennals and Holdsworth 1981; Gowans 1962). Jordan and Kaups, Roberts and others have shown that cultural borrowing is one of the essential features of the North American log building tradition, which accounts for its widespread popularity in pioneer districts (Hutslar 1977; Jordan and Kaups 1989; Roberts 1988: 274-88). But while the builders and owners of the McEachern-MacRitchie and Keough houses were preserving an older pattern of log technology, they were also borrowing modern ideas about the layout and design of houses. At the end of the 19th century, when the Cassells bought the house from Alexander

McEachern, they modified the building to suit their own needs. No longer did the open hearth suit them; instead they wanted a more modern dwelling complete with Douglas fir wainscotting on the walls and ceiling, a separate parlour, bedrooms on the ground floor, and a stove rather than a hearth. Likewise when the Keough house was constructed, the walls were made of log but the use of stoves and the interior plan (comparable to the modified McEachern-MacRitchie plan) speaks to modernity, not a conservative clinging to older ways. The newer ideas were possibly deriving from the New England region where many Cape Bretoners were travelling to and from at the end of the 19th century.

The latter-day existence of log houses in Cape Breton demonstrates that vernacular patterns are often stable and tenacious, lasting much longer than many architectural fads or fashions. The changes in these structures also show that vernacular builders of this region readily adapted to new ideas about spatial usage at the end of the 19th century. Whatever explanation eventually proves to be more plausible for the origin of log buildings in Nova Scotia, these extant houses raise many unanswered questions about diffusion of architectural traits, ethnic group interaction and cultural borrowing in the pioneer landscape.

Notes

I am indebted to Dr. Gerald Pocius, Memorial University of Newfoundland, who supervised the PhD thesis from which this chapter emerged; Jim St.Clair for his fieldwork assistance and advice; Dr. Brian Preston, former Provincial Archaeologist for Nova Scotia; and to Kay MacDonald, former Gaelic specialist at the Beaton Institute, Cape Breton University, for translations from Gaelic to English. Earlier versions of this chapter were presented at the Folklore Studies Association of Canada Annual Conference, Université de Moncton (May 1991) and the Society for the Study of Architecture in Canada Conference, Baddeck, Cape Breton Island, June (1991).

1. Brian Preston, former Provincial Archaeologist for the province of Nova Scotia, provided the history of the property.

Chapter 7
Making a House a Home:
Company Housing in Cape Breton

*Much work needs to be done to record and analyze the company housing of
Cape Breton Island. This chapter examines only one small part of the process: focusing on the way in which individuals transformed their company-
built houses into "homes." This exploration can give us an understanding of
individual and community aesthetics. It helps to explain the way in which
people renovate, personalize and transform their living spaces into meaningful places. As architect Alice Gray Read states: "The house is anonymous and
mute. Only when it is touched by an owner, lived in and made over inside
and out does it begin to bear the identity of its occupants" (1986: 192). In
attempting to understand the individual and community aesthetics at work, I
have examined one neighbourhood where company-built housing is predominant: the Richmond Street and Victoria Road area of Sydney, near the area of
Sydney known as "Ashby."[1] In this discussion I hope to provide a clearer sense
of how this row housing, built on a grid pattern next to the Sydney Steel Mill,
has been personalized and transformed over time.*

This chapter was originally published in Material History Review *48
(1998).*

Alistair MacLeod, who sets many of his short stories in Cape Breton mining towns, describes a fictional community in "The Return":

> Then there is the mine silhouetted against it all, looking like a toy from
> a mecanno set; yet its bells ring as the coal-laden cars fly up out of the
> deep, grumble as they are unloaded, and flee with thundering power
> down the slopes they leave behind. Then the blackened houses begin

and march row and row up the hill to where we stand and beyond to where we go. (MacLeod 1976: 103-104)

When writers or journalists describe mining or industrial towns, the houses of the workers inevitably appear as bleak, blackened abodes where life is eked out in the shadow of the mine. Even though housing for industrial workers is an important part of Atlantic Canada's material landscape, little scholarly attention has been given to these structures. The buildings tell a story about the working people who made this region what it is today, a story sometimes ignored by history books, that seem to prefer glorifying captains of industry and our military and political leaders.

In the late 19th century, Canadian federal government national policy encouraged industrialization. The resulting boom in the Atlantic region radically changed the built landscape of many Nova Scotia communities (Acheson 1985; Latta and Tye 1989; Muise 1980). Entire neighbourhoods of workers' housing emerged in towns and cities, their housing patterns very different from the region's traditional vernacular styles. Some were built by private individuals and contractors. Most were developed by the coal and steel companies or by the owners of mills, factories and lumber woods operations. They flourished in towns such as Amherst and Stellarton, Nova Scotia, Wabana and Aguathuna, Newfoundland, and Marysville and Grand Falls, New Brunswick (Holdsworth 1984; Latremouille 1986; MacKinnon 1982; Miller and Sharpless 1985; Mulrooney 1991; Soloman 1985; Wynn 1981).

With the establishment of the Sydney Steel Plant by Dominion Iron and Steel Corporation (DISCO) in 1899, and Sydney's concomitant economic boom, construction of workers' housing began in earnest. Sydney's population grew from 3,200 in 1899; to 9,900 in 1901; and 22,000 in 1913 (Black n.d.: 1). Between 1896 and 1900 more than 3,600 immigrants from all over the world (Italian, Polish, Ukrainian, Lithuanian and other peoples) came to Cape Breton seeking work in the coal and steel industries (Forbes and Muise 1993: 167). The establishment of the Sydney Steel works followed the vast expansion in the Cape Breton coal industry. Henry Melville Whitney of Boston formed the Dominion Coal Company in 1893 by purchasing several smaller private coal mines, which had been in operation since mid 19th century. In this year he also obtained a ninety-nine year lease of the unworked resources of the coal fields (Crawley 1990: 145).

Rapid industrialization of Cape Breton Island brought about many changes to Sydney. One author has said that in this transition, wage earners displaced the small independent producer: "Sydney had become predominantly a community of wage labourers" (Crawley 1990: 150). Problems facing the city at this period included a lack of housing to meet demand, insufficient water and sewage infrastructure, and abysmal streets and roads. The working classes had a difficult life. Low wages, poor working conditions, thirteen-hour night shifts, eleven-hour day shifts (with no pay for overtime) was the lot of the Sydney steel worker of the day (Crawley 1990: 154).

In a talk to the Canadian Political Science Association in 1913, Bryce Stewart described Sydney's company housing. To summarize his study, there were too few houses to meet the needs of the incoming population. In 1909 the Dominion Iron and Steel Company, for example, owned 142 houses; yet there were 303 applications on file with the company for housing (Stewart 1913: 13). Most of these applications were from families; single men made their homes in large boarding houses, in "shacks," or in other working-class homes as boarders. Around the steel plant and coke ovens a variety of ethnic groups lived in company-owned housing including Austrians, Russians, Poles, Italians and West Indians (from Barbados), as well as the predominant Newfoundlanders and native Cape Bretoners.

In my study area of this one Sydney neighbourhood, fifty-five duplexes were constructed between 1903 and 1913, twenty on Richmond Street and thirty-five on Victoria Road (figures 7.1, 7.2 and 7.3). The streets of the area are named for the four counties of Cape Breton Island– Inverness, Richmond, Victoria and Cape Breton. The Victoria Road row is located adjacent to the former steel plant's coke ovens (dismantled in the recent remediation of the Sydney steel plant site, but still posing industrial hazards).[2] The Richmond Street rows, likewise, are close to the former bar mill of the steel plant and a short distance from one of the plant's main entry gates.

Richmond Street Houses

The plan of the twenty Richmond Street duplexes originally included a front room (15 ft 9 in by 11 ft 3 in/ 4.8 m by 3.4 m) with a coal burning fireplace, a small dining room (10 ft by 12 ft 9 in/ 3 m by 3.8 m) and a kitchen (12 ft 9 in/ 3.8 m square) to the rear (figure 7.4). The upstairs contained four small bedrooms, two being eleven feet four and one-half inches by eleven feet three inches (3.5 x 3.4 m) in size and two being eleven feet four and one-half inches by nine feet six inches (3.5 m x 2.8 m)in size. A veranda (6 by 20 ft/ 2 m by 6 m) was built at the time the houses were constructed.

Each kitchen contained a sink and a trap door leading to an unfinished cellar. A built-in corner cupboard resembled the ubiquitous British

Figure 7.1 Courtesy GIS Laboratory, Cape Breton University.

Figure 7.2 Richmond Street, Sydney

Figure 7.3 Victoria Road, Sydney.

Figure 7.4 Richmond Street houses, 1912. Dominion Coal Company. Plan 1744. Beaton Institute, Cape Breton University.

Figure 7.5 Kitchen of a Richmond Street house.

Figure 7.6 Front room of a Richmond Street house showing fireplace.

Isles "sideboard" of old world communities of Scots, English and Irish settlers (Fenton and Walker 1981: 153; Gailey 1966: 18-34; Mannion 1974: 142-43, 254). John Mannion points out that large wooden dressers with bottom drawers and shelving on top were the most outstanding feature of Irish peasant furniture at the time of migration to North America (142). This built-in cupboard with two enclosed lower cupboards and four exposed upper shelves was roughly 4 ft wide and 8 ft (1.2 m by 2.4 m) high. The lower cupboards were 3 ft in height and 3 ft wide (approx. 1 metre square); the upper shelves were spaced 15 in (0.38 m) apart and equally wide. Sigurd Erixon points out that this form of kitchen furniture in Europe had descended from the court sideboards of an earlier aristocracy (1938: 137-72).

Each front room had a coal fireplace 19.75 in wide by 26 in high (50 cm by 66 cm) with an iron fender in front (figure 7.6). Homes sat on a concrete foundation, a concrete wall laid in a dug-out trench provided the foundation on the front and rear. Present-day concrete end walls were put in by owners of the homes after 1948, when these homes were purchased from the steel company. A concrete pier provides support in the centre of the house. Joists are 2-by-8 in (5 by 20 cm) in 5-ft (1.5 m) lengths, while upright studs are 2-by-4 in (5 by 10 cm); a 1-by-6 in (2.54 by 15 cm) wall plate separates the ground floor wall from the upper storey wall. Rafters (2-by-6/ 5 by 15 cm) are joined at the peak and are supported by a 2-by-4 (5 by 10 cm) tie beam. Rough sheathing of 1-inch (2.54 cm) board covers the entire structure. On the roof there were originally two layers of tarpaper covered with wooden shingles, but asphalt shingles replaced these in the 1940s. The rest of the outer walls have one layer of wallpaper followed by 1-inch (2.54 cm) sheathing and a layer of wooden shingles.

The backyard was fenced in by the owner and contained an outhouse, a coal and coke shed, and a back service lane, which is still evident in the landscape (figure 7.7). A resident recalls one use for this landscape feature:

> In the old days like that before the city started garbage disposal, garbage collection, we used to just take our garbage and throw it over the back fence there all winter. And then in the spring of the year the company would send probably six or eight men from the general yard and a truck and shovels and they would clean her from one end to the other. Sometimes it would take weeks, but they would clean here from one end to the other, and when you'd have her clean you'd start it over again for next year....[3]

Ashes from stoves were also deposited in back alleys for collection every year. Today the alley is used mainly as a walking path for many of the

Figure 7.7 Back service lane, Richmond Street.

neighbourhoods' residents, a place to pitch horseshoes in the summer, or a place for various children's games.

Many of the men who worked in the heavy mills (including the blooming mill, the bar mill, the nail mill and the plate mill) resided in the Richmond Street houses. While the houses were originally built by the company in 1913, they were purchased from DOSCO (Dominion Steel and Coal Corporation) by employees in the late 1940s, for $17-18,000. This is a significant time, for it is after this date that a number of transformations in the houses occurred.

When the houses were still owned by the company, a crew of company employees maintained the houses. According to one informant, they were spray painted with oil and oakum twice between 1913 and 1948, giving the houses either a green hue or a dark brown hue. There were no full cellars in these company-built houses; residents began to dig their own basements only after purchasing the homes from the steel company.

A coal fireplace originally heated the front room. A cast iron stove (locally referred to as a "Quebec" heater after its place of manufacture) warmed the small hallway downstairs. For fuel, the hall stove regularly used "coke" while the large kitchen stove used coal. In some houses, a small "coke" heater was also used in the upstairs bedrooms. In the 1940s, hot air coal furnaces began to appear and by the 1950s a coal stove called a "Warm Morning" became commonly used in these homes (MacLaren

1972). Residents fondly remember these stoves: when conducting field-work I have often heard residents' mention how well they worked and how much heat they could generate. In the late 1940s and early 1950s, oil furnaces also began to appear on Richmond Street. One informant remembers that oil furnaces began to appear particularly after the 1947 strike. Many of the cellars were dug out, by hand in most cases, to provide a space to locate the coal and oil-fired furnaces.

The interior walls of the houses were originally surfaced with plaster and lath. Today, most are covered with numerous layers of paint and wall paper. In some, panel board (a popular form of interior walling which began to be used in Cape Breton in the late 1960s) has replaced the plaster and lath. Originally the houses had no insulation; at present, most are insulated with fibreglass and are covered by vinyl or aluminum siding, introduced to the neighbourhood in this same period.

Between the steel plant and the twenty duplexes on Richmond Street is a large field once owned by the company. Here, residents grew gardens or kept cows and horses. As one resident states:

> There was an old gentleman, Malcolm MacNeil who kept cows, he and my father shared the same pasture; they did the fencing. They never used fancy wire or anything; they always got old used cable or something they used for fencing. And, oh, in them days there was some hairy days too and cows would get out and get roaming around the city. They had an old pound keeper by the name of Hillman and you'd have to go over and pay four dollars to get your cow out of the pound, and it never pleased my father too much; he used to stretch the English language when he'd have to go for his cow....

Many steel-worker families found it necessary to keep a small kitchen garden, a cow and a few hens to supply fresh produce, milk and eggs. Neighbours shared the product of their toil with each other; whatever produce was not used in a household was given away to nearby residents. The materials used for fencing the gardens were often discarded materials from work sites at the Sydney Steel Plant.

This squatting on company-owned land for their own use is one way in which original settlers of the row transformed the company-created environment into a meaningful place. The company tolerated the workers fencing off company-owned gardening areas. Some of the original residents came from rural backgrounds where farming, planting and animal husbandry were common. In this way, older residual, agricultural patterns continued in the industrial community. This pattern of small-scale gardening and subsistence farming continued into the 1960s when it largely disappeared. Today, more recent houses have been constructed on that side of the street, and the field between the plant and the houses lies unused.

Victoria Road Houses: Exteriors

These duplexes are similar in size and shape to the Richmond Street homes (figure 7.8). One difference is the use of a central dormer: this form has a gable roof with the large, central dormer cutting the roofline. This shallow-pitched central dormer hints at the gothic revival style, which began to appear in the Maritimes in the early years of the 19th century, becoming extremely popular toward the end of the century. This particular architectural feature was popular in other Cape Breton company towns including New Waterford, Glace Bay, Reserve Mines and Inverness (Ennals and Holdsworth 1981: 86-102; Penny 1989: 69).

These homes (consisting of one-half the duplex) are 24 by 24 feet (7.3 by 7.3 m) in size and possess a front room with a fireplace (called a living room in the original plan), a kitchen and a pantry on the ground floor, plus four small bedrooms on the second floor (figure 7.9). They were built without foundations and, as with their counterparts on Richmond Street, had an outhouse and coal shed to the rear of the dwelling.

On both Richmond Street and Victoria Road, original plans did not call for a bathroom or any indoor plumbing. A drain from the kitchen sink

Figure 7.8 Victoria Road, Sydney.

Figure 7.9 Victoria Road houses, 1906. Dominion Coal Company. Plan 917. Beaton Institute, Cape Breton University.

led to the back yard; water was obtained from wells in the neighbourhood. Plumbing was not installed in many of these houses until the 1930s. An unpublished paper explains the living conditions:

> [...] frequently during winter we arose to find the water frozen and kids were compelled to huddle around the fireplace until the pipes were thawed. Fires were usually banked but morning found us rising to cold kitchens, cold furniture and bread that had lost all courage to rise. Even after the plumbing and hot water burners were installed it was not uncommon to find that the hot water front in the old coal stove had frozen solid during the night. (McCormack, n.d.:1)

Numerous reports about the poor conditions of the company houses in the first thirty years of the 20th century are verified in a Royal Commission of the time prompted by labour-management strife occurring in the region (Duncan 1926).

Mike McCormack provides a sense of some of the activities inside Victoria Road company houses in his narrative about growing up in such a house:

> But growing up on Victoria Road wasn't all bad. I made my friends I still cherish 60 years later. Only the very affluent had telephones and radio was in its infancy. Gramophones were quite the thing and television had not even been contemplated.... We got to be pretty good 45 players and in the neighborhood regular games were played for groceries and small cash prizes. Some of us couldn't carry a tune in a bucket but those with musical inclinations were forever exchanging the words and music of popular songs.... As for sports, we had no proper equipment but we managed to field a pretty fair baseball team playing a series every year with the boys from the Coke Oven district. (McCormack n.d.: 2)

There was much interaction between the Richmond Street rows and the Victoria Road rows: people worked together in the mill's departments, they went to the same churches, drank in the nearby Whitney Pier clubs or local Legion, and played baseball and other games on the streets and nearby fields.

The exteriors tell us that people made a number of cosmetic modifications on the company houses only after the houses were purchased from the company in the late 1940s. Some of the changes made after this date include: enclosing verandas, painting shingles and trim, siding the homes with aluminium and vinyl, insulating, digging out the basements to install central heating and reconstructing the end walls of the foundations. The verandas speak of people communicating with each other. It was a place for resting, doing household chores, relaxing and observing each other's behaviour.[4] Residents say that much time was spent on the verandas before the widespread popularity of radio and television. A development in the neighbourhood is the use of decorative iron work on the verandas. A local blacksmith repaired one veranda with iron railings made in his Whitney Pier shop and neighbours borrowed the idea and have begun to copy this decorative technique for their own verandas.

While the front yard consists of a few feet of grass with some shrubs, bushes and trees, the use of the backyard was for a coal and coke storage shed, an outhouse and a garden. Like the Richmond Street houses, the back alley behind the houses was a service lane, a pathway for children, a place for keeping garbage and ashes and a place to have a horseshoe pitch.

Interiors

While the exteriors of houses and the landscape reveal some of the patterns of the lifestyle of steel-worker families, the interiors provide clues to the way in which people assert their individuality. For example, each house has its collection of family photographs and other mementos in the front room either on the bureau, on top of the mantle over the fireplace or on the piano or, in the early years of the 20th century, the pipe organ. One interviewee's front room showcased wedding photographs and portraits of family members alongside autographed baseball cards, clearly showing values and his interests. It is the front room, sometimes called, "the parlour" of the house, where this form of display is most prevalent. Sometimes used when guests came to visit, it was often employed for other purposes:

> It was just another room; we never could afford fancy furniture. My poor mother and father they also used to, like, lay in a little extra in the larder for the winter and there's always be a barrel of apples in there and a half a barrel of pork and whatever you could get, meats. And you stored it in the front room, yea. We didn't have Duncan Fife, we didn't know who he was then, we don't care either. Fancy furniture was never part of the decor around here.

Other informants say that the front room sometimes doubled as a bedroom, especially if the household kept boarders, a common practice in the neighbourhood in the first half of the 20th century. This working class variation deviates from the standard image of the front room presented in many 19th-century pattern books as, "the repository for the most elegant and artistic objects" and the most formal room of the house (Wright 1985: 32). Indeed, it functioned as an area of display, a storage room and a bedroom when required.

While the front room or parlour contains images of the family, the living room's walls include plaques received upon retirement, photographs of horse races and winners, photographs of grandchildren and a crucifix. The small livingroom is an extensively used room: it is the place where the television is kept and where the large, floor-model radio was once situated. Comfortable chairs and small couches are the furniture of this room. One must walk through the living room from the front entry of the house before entering the kitchen, making this a heavily travelled thoroughfare in the house. In the bedrooms (the more private areas) the only decorative items of ornamentation, besides the paper or paint over the plaster and lath and the furniture, are items such as holy pictures and crucifixes. In a sense, the walls of this house are like a life encyclopedia, offering a visual expression of some of the life experiences and significant events of this family.

Some of these interior objects tell us that for many residents of this area, family is important. Many of the significant objects centre around family members: children, grandchildren, brothers, sisters and more distant relatives. Various sports activities are also significant: baseball, hockey and darts trophies abound in many homes. Some are placed on display in windows so fellow citizens can view these achievements. Images of rural beauty also abound, particularly images of places such as the Margaree Valley and the Mira River regions of Cape Breton. This is an important point, for many steel working and mining families originally came to the industrial towns from rural areas of Cape Breton Island and many retained a connection to these areas through the building of summer cabins. Work is also significant: plaques on walls refer to work situations and events such as retirement. The message inherent in these objects is that while family and sporting events are extremely important, steel workers also take great pride in their arduous and difficult work.

While the walls of houses tell us about many aspects of the daily lives of a steel family, there are other issues about which the objects are silent. Interviews reveal that sharing among neighbours was an important feature of the neighbourhood. For example, one resident says:

> And then my poor father he used to go to Sydney River and he'd come home in the spring of the year with a wagon full of gaspereaux, and, it was just like a, well, hard to describe, but he'd be coming down the street and he'd be dishing them out by the pan full as he goes along, almost every other door, to whoever wanted them. It'd be the same way, near the ice in the fall and he'd be out getting eels, he used to get eels. As soon as he'd come home he'd deliver them from door to door....

Sharing of gaspereaux and eels—a special food for many—was a way of connecting the community. Indeed sharing in various ways—from helping to build a fence to providing food for neighbours at wakes and funerals—was a common feature of this neighbourhood.

But all neighbours were not treated with the same respect. Old hurts take a long time to heal and some go back for generations. For example, I asked one informant if there was much rivalry in the neighbourhood between the two streets—Victoria Road and Richmond Street. The reply:

> I don't think there was rivalry, but this is a hard thing to talk about....
> Some of the houses were occupied by, well, people who scabbed during
> the strike in 1923 and some of the residents here in these houses were
> blacklisted by the company and put out of some of these houses. [...]
> Well I know when I was a kid I used to hear them talk about them you
> know that there was certain families put out of these houses because of
> that strike. And some of their famous scabs moved into them. Now I
> don't have to tell you Richard that there was animosity between these
> people and you know, like my poor father used to say, if the milk goes
> sour, send it to so and so, and don't give them anything else.... And it
> lived with them until it went to their grave, and you know the stigma
> is still there on some of their families.

Old wounds, particularly ones created during strikes; take a long time to heal. In this strong union neighbourhood, scabs—people who cross picket lines during strikes—are treated with little respect. The animosity directed at particular families has passed from one generation to another.[5]

These houses and this neighbourhood tell us something about how houses are transformed into homes in this industrial community (figure 7.10). One generalization is that it takes much more than a coat of paint to transform their prefabricated spaces into meaningful places or homes where life is lived.[6] Continuing the rural pattern of gardening and animal husbandry was an important feature of the neighbourhood in the early years of the 20th century. Some minor structural changes in the 1940s—constructing foundation end walls and digging out basements, adding insulation, bricking up fireplaces and adding vinyl and aluminium siding—made these houses more comfortable for the residents. The work was usually done by the owners of the homes, or with the assistance from neighbours, only after the dwellings were purchased from the company. A whole underground economy was at work as well: services were regularly exchanged and reciprocal arrangements were the norm.

The ways in which houses are furnished and decorated also adds much to the creation of homes. Photographs, plaques, paintings, wall hangings and wall papers are ways in which rooms are personalized and individual-

Figure 7.10 Richmond Street, Sydney.

ized, telling much about family history, life's experiences and some of the important moments of a mill family. Oral narratives about past events of significance to the community such as strikes and strike breakers also help to create a neighbourhood and sense of belonging in this community.

In the past, every neighbourhood family worked in the mill. Today, while many residents are retired from the plant and others terminated when it closed once-an-for-all, the neighbourhood includes people with no connection.[7] One resident quipped, "When I grew up here they were company houses, now they're [called] duplexes; and now I don't live near the steel plant any more, I live in Grecoville," referring to a national pizza franchise established in the neighbourhood. Even though the neighbourhood changed, the buildings, yards and artifacts continue to provide insights into some of the important values which lie at the heart of industrial communities: hard work, competition in sports and pastimes, loyalty to family and neighbours and sharing of resources and time. By looking at some of the ways houses are transformed into homes in this neighbourhood, we begin to see some of the sinew, which connects people in our world, as the powerful forces of industrialization shape it.

Notes

1. The name Ashby derives from a farm of this same name once situated in this area owned by Henry Davenport in the mid 19th century. Thanks to Dr. Robert Morgan, former Director of Research and Development and Archivist, Cape Breton University, for providing this information.

2. For a video presentation of the steel plant showing the coke ovens in operation see Elizabeth Beaton's *Making Steel* (1992).

3. All unattributed quotes in this article come from interviews conducted with company housing residents in the summer of 1992.

4. Gwendolyn Wright, writing in a different context, discusses the advent of the verandah:

> In the last quarter of the 19th century, spacious porches of various shapes and sizes appeared around the house. These were entrance porticos and simple back service porches, open verandahs (galleries along the side of the building), piazzas (Americanism for verandah) and upper floor balconies. These porches had specific uses: resting, dining or doing household chores, watching the afternoon sun, or relaxing in the evening breeze of summer. Ornamentation became more elaborate by the 1880s: support posts were rounded rather than squared off, and were heavy with detailing. (Wright 1985: 24)

5. For a discussion of some of the strikes during this period see: Forbes and Muise (1993: 233-71).

6. Many company houses in this area were prefabricated by Rhodes and Curry of Amherst for on-site construction (Tye 1986).

7. At the time this article was originally written, a Chinese company, MinMetals, had purchased the Sydney Steel Plant from the Province of Nova Scotia. The plant was finally closed and dismantled in 2000.

Chapter 8
Tompkinsville:
Co-operativism and Vernacular Architecture

Joining with one's neighbours to aid in a construction project or communal work activity was once an essential part of the fabric of Atlantic Canadian communities. Outside activities such as barn and house raisings or wood-chopping frolics to gather wood for a widowed member of the community or local clergy are frequently mentioned in the region's autobiographies and oral histories; interior activities such as spinning bees, quilting bees and milling frolics played essential roles in the transmission of work patterns and oral traditions inside homes (Bennett 1989; MacKinnon 1991). Even though the issue of co-operativism is important for understanding the way in which communities and neighbourhoods are formed and maintained, this process has been largely unexplored in much of the literature on vernacular architecture.[1] In this chapter I examine one neighbourhood of eleven homes in Tompkinsville, Cape Breton Island—a co-operative housing development begun in 1938 in the former coal mining town of Reserve Mines—to help unravel some of the complexities of this issue. I am thoroughly indebted to the late Mary Laben, who at the time I was studying Tompkinsville, was the last surviving pioneer of this neighbourhood; her voice can be heard throughout this chapter. She thoughtfully and carefully answered my endless questions about the development of the neighborhood and allowed me to take measured sketches and photographs of her home. Mary and her husband Joe, both now deceased, were two of the prime forces behind this housing development.[2]

An earlier version of this research was published in Material History Review *44 (1996), 45-63.*

The term "vernacular" has been used interchangeably with the terms "folk," "common," "native" or "non-academic" architecture. It is usually placed at the other end of the spectrum from professionally designed architecture or what is sometimes termed "high style" architecture. Vernacular buildings are often owner built; that is, the owner takes an active hands-on role in the entire process of designing and constructing the building, from deciding upon the size and shape of interior spaces, to obtaining the materials. One scholar, Kingston Heath, uses the analogy of a filter to define the vernacular in architecture. He argues that a fixed locale or region, with its unique character, cultural mix, values, materials, climate and topography "filter" conventional ideas about architecture, whether they be folk, popular or high style. What results from this filtering process is vernacular architecture—"product of a place, of a people, by a people" (1988: 5).

A region or neighbourhood's vernacular architecture is an expression of the community's personality. While not common in Canada, studying regional personality is a familiar idea to European folklife scholars and ethnologists. J. Geraint Jenkins, a Welsh ethnologist and museum curator, describes the domain of this field: "in folklife studies we are concerned primarily with the recording and study of regional personality and features which distinguish one community from the other, whether they be social, oral or material should be our concern" (Jenkins 1960: 260). A region's needs, tastes and cultural expressions are shown in the way people design, build and use their homes and outbuildings; these are fine expressions of regional personality. Some features which make a neighbourhood a distinct region include the public spaces, the religious buildings and the local culture, but the houses people choose to build are extremely important in the shaping of a distinct, vernacular district.

Vernacular architecture has been studied in Europe for many years, but only in the past twenty or thirty years have North American scholars viewed it as an acceptable field of research (Addy 1898; Deetz 1977; Fox 1942: 307-19; Fox and Raglan 1951-1954; Glassie 1968, 1975; Herman 1987; Kniffen 1965: 549-77; Kniffen and Glassie 1986: 159-81; Peate 1946; Williams 1991).[3] Folklorists, geographers, architectural historians and archaeologists are interested in vernacular buildings because they are said to provide a more democratic view of the remote and recent past than do the kinds of buildings traditionally studied in architectural histories. As Henry Glassie says: "historians study not the past but the literary remains of the past. Nevertheless, most of the world's societies have been non-literate. They left no literary remains..." (Glassie 1977: 30). In contrast, "the landscape is the product of the divine average" (30). Vernacular buildings in the landscape are a rich source for those trying to understand the inter-action of human beings and the built environment.

While few academic studies of Atlantic Canada's vernacular archi-tecture exist, a number of popular studies of the region's buildings have recently been published and a few predominant themes appear in both academic and popular literature. Most popular studies, for example, are guided by the social history of a community; these publications are pri-marily pen and ink sketchbooks or photograph collections with a discus-sion of the history associated with the building owners. Historical societies, provincial government departments, municipalities and local museums are often responsible for these kinds of publications (Heritage Trust of Nova Scotia 1967, 1972; Jenson 1972; McNabb and Parker 1986; Nova Scotia Association of Architects 1976; St.Clair and MacLeod 1992; Sunderland 1980). One popular work deviates from this approach and attempts to survey the various types of Nova Scotia's working class housing from the 18th century to the present (Latremouille 1986). While this is a valuable first attempt to examine the province's vernacular dwellings, the work suf-fers from the author's nostalgic view that only building choices in the past were creative and intelligent, while more recent vernacular buildings are seen as uninspiring, government-sponsored imitations, lacking beauty and meaning (1986: 83-90).

In the academic world, cultural geographers and folklorists have dominated Atlantic Canadian vernacular architecture scholarship. Geographers have addressed themes such as architectural transfer, adaptation and change and have been interested in the shape and location of buildings in the wider cultural landscape. For example, Peter Ennals and Deryk Holdsworth propose an overall typology of buildings for the region, outlining some of the major architectural forms evident in the Maritime landscape (1981: 86-102). Peter Ennals has also assessed Acadian architecture, documenting both the earliest known forms and the recent Acadian interest in replicating 18th-century Québécois buildings (1982; 1983; 1992). John Mannion and David B. Mills have explored the persistence, modification and alteration of Irish architecture and material culture in Atlantic Canada (Mannion 1974; Mills 1977).

Folklorists have provided vernacular architecture micro-studies of some specific sub-regions within Atlantic Canada exploring issues such as architectural transfer and change, the contrast between tradition and modernity, gender and spatial usage and the patterns of modification (MacKinnon 1991; Pocius 1982, 1987, 1992; Tye 1986). One of the most important studies of Atlantic Canadian vernacular architecture and landscape is an analysis of the homes, outbuildings and spatial usage in the Newfoundland outport of Calvert (Pocius 1992). This work is the first of its kind in Atlantic Canada to employ current methodological and theoretical approaches from the fields of material culture and folklife to interpret the shaping of the built environment of a coastal community. In Newfoundland, there are both academic and popular works devoted to vernacular architecture. In Cape Breton, some preliminary work has been completed, but much remains to be done before a thorough understanding of the Island's building traditions can be obtained.

Architects, archaeologists and architectural historians have also been interested in the vernacular architecture of the region. Alan Penny, affiliated with Dalhousie University, published a style guide to Nova Scotia's architecture entitled *Houses of Nova Scotia*, which included many examples of the region's vernacular forms (1989). André Crépeau and David Christianson, archaeologists at the Fortress of Louisbourg National Historic Site, have explored pre-expulsion Acadian vernacular architecture in their fieldwork (1995). H. M. Scott Smith's two works on Prince Edward Island architecture, one focusing on the region's churches, and the other on its domestic housing, likewise provide the reader with photographs, floor plans and fine descriptions of the Island's many distinctive architectural features (1989; 1990).[4]

This does not mean that only old and rural architecture is vernacular, although many vernacular architecture studies to date focus on older rural forms. Many urban houses such as those in Tompkinsville described in this chapter also exhibit vernacular features. Only recently have scholars begun to explore the vernacular aspects of contemporary housing. As Dell Upton and John Michael Vlach state: "Clearly more investigation of contemporary buildings, including commercial as well as residential structures, is needed" (1986: xvi).[5]

This study of a housing development in Reserve Mines, Cape Breton, known as Tompkinsville, employs a methodological approach developed by vernacular architecture scholars which includes the recording of buildings through photographs, measured drawings, interviews with residents and reliance upon fieldwork and research to understand the architectural patterns in the landscape (cf. Glassie 1968; 1975).

Reserve Mines, Cape Breton

In deciding to work co-operatively to build their homes, Tompkinsville pioneers were following the co-operative philosophy expounded by what is now known as the Antigonish Movement. This was a social and economic reform movement begun by priests at St. Francis Xavier University, in Antigonish. Two of the founders, Father Jimmy Tompkins and Father Moses M. Coady, led the movement to local, regional, national and international significance. The founders and leaders believed that individuals could raise themselves from economic plight and become better physical, moral and spiritual beings through adult education and cooperation. They envisioned that individuals in small study clubs could solve their own difficult problems through cooperative study and work. Through cooperatives, libraries, credit unions, grocery stores, gasoline stations and housing, groups developed in Atlantic Canada following the tenets of this philosophy.

Moses M. Coady points out that the Antigonish Movement faced opposition in attempting to promote education and cooperation in the early 1930s, a time of great hardship in Cape Breton:

> By 1933 ... the Extension workers had been making excursions from time to time into the industrial areas of Cape Breton Island. Mass meetings were held at which the value of education and the possibilities of economic and social improvement were set forth. It was difficult to get a hearing. Large numbers of the industrial workers had been flirting with left wing theories and in some cases they were beginning to be pronounced revolutionaries. The Communist propaganda was doing its work. (1939: 56)

These feelings of discontent in the 1930s were provoked by the struggles of the previous decade, a hard, bitter time of great unrest amongst workers of Cape Breton. That decade saw numerous strikes in the coal industry and sharp class conflict; a culture of resistance amongst coal miners resulted from the workers' struggles with industrial capitalists.[6] One scholar notes there were at least fifty-eight strikes in the Sydney coal field between 1920 and 1925, "most of them over not wage issues but such matters as work assignments, fines and suspensions, and the role of the pit committees and the union within the workplace" (Frank 1993: 245).

Workers were also unhappy about their living conditions. Some of Cape Breton's coal miners and their families were housed in poorly maintained, dilapidated duplexes built by mining companies at the end of the 19th century. A Royal Commission on Coal in 1925 interviewed a number of Cape Breton miners about their homes and one mentions to the commissioner:

> there was three rooms downstairs: kitchen, dining room and front room. Upstairs there was two bedrooms, but there is other two holes in the wall. I would not exactly like to call them bedrooms, they are too small, one you cannot get a bed in at all unless you saw it off." (82).

Three-room and two-room plans were the norm for early 20th-century company housing in the Cape Breton Industrial region. Mary Arnold, a New York housing reformer who played a significant role in the Tompkinsville housing development, outlines conditions in the 1930s:

> It is difficult to tell one house from another. If you are a comparative stranger in Reserve and wish to visit a friend, you take the nearest telegraph pole and count down from it two, three or four houses as the case may be. All the houses are painted a dark green or brown.... (Arnold n.d.: 10-11)[7]

While similar in style, some houses were also in poor condition with no cellars, rotted sills and badly constructed windows and doors:

> It is hard to keep damp and dirt from seeping up through the cracks. As in all old houses, the wind finds an easy way inside around doors and windows. Planning fifty or sixty years ago took little account of the work which must be done by a miner's wife and the sink is often in a dark corner behind a door. The yards are small and only the braver spirits find a way to grass and flowers. (Arnold n.d.: 11)

These duplexes were more than seventy-five years old with shingles painted dark green or with unpainted clapboards. There were no indoor toilets, and the front and back yards were dusty and dirty. The rent charged by the mining company in 1938 was ten dollars per month (Skillen 1939: 388).

The *Housing Survey of Reserve Mines*, a report of housing conditions in the early 1940s, was done with the assistance of a representative of the United Mine Workers of America District 26 and the local municipality. The survey of 320 dwellings in Reserve Mines showed that 1,799 people lived in these houses and that 88 per cent had no bathroom or indoor toilet; no sewer system was developed in the community. Forty-seven per cent of the houses were more than 50 years old, verifying the poor conditions faced by miners and their families. Of the 320 houses, 159—or 49 per cent—were considered overcrowded and there were at least 30 "shacks," temporary houses found around mine sites at the development stage, which were deemed "uninhabitable." The report concluded that 125-150 new housing units were required for the community, that a sewage system must be installed and that the community must plan to provide for individual ownership, co-operative ownership and subsidized low rental limited dividend corporation projects (1945: 2-6).

Moreover, the report petitioned the Premier and Minister of Highways of Nova Scotia, Angus L. MacDonald, about the deplorable conditions of roads in the community. The worst conditions were said to be in the neighbourhood where many of the Tompkinsville pioneers originally lived:

> Bad as these conditions are, the greatest evils [are] on the so-called Company Streets. These serve Belgiumtown and Lorway, both very populous areas. These roads are low and soft and wholly lacking in adequate drainage.... In the Belgiumtown ... waste from the houses drains directly in the roadway. This adds up to a very nasty, unsanitary condition.... (1945: 6)

This survey indicates that available housing and conditions were inadequate for miners and their families. The poor conditions helped to bolster the resolve of miners to search for solutions to their housing problems. The co-operative experiment at Tompkinsville was one innovative approach to solving this fundamental human problem.

Tompkins and Coady

This was the social context the leaders of the co-operative movement faced when attempting to persuade coal miners and their families to work co-operatively. Father Jimmy Tompkins, born in Margaree, Cape Breton, on September 7, 1870, is the foremost founder of the Antigonish Movement. Dr. Moses M. Coady, co-founder of the Antigonish Movement, was twelve years younger than Tompkins; the two were also cousins. Coady has been called, "a devoted priest, a zealous apostle of the social order—a magnetic leader ... "who showed thousands of people throughout the world ... how to become masters of their own destiny" (McKean n.d., n.p.).

Father Jimmy attended Margaree Forks School and St. Francis Xavier University in Antigonish. In 1896 was invited to join the teaching staff at the university, where he taught Greek and Math. He attended the Urban College in Rome, became a priest, and upon his return to Nova Scotia, again taught at St. FX. He was a fine orator and writer, displayed an excellent knowledge of rhetoric and was asked to help conduct fundraising for the university. He was successful in procuring funds from American businessmen to construct needed buildings on the campus. Tompkins agreed fully with the Sills-Learned Report calling for a Maritime Federation of Universities, published by the Carnegie foundation in 1922 and, as a supporter of these views, was at odds with the board of St. FX and with Bishop Morrison of Antigonish who were not in favour of federation. They wanted St. Francis Xavier University to remain a Roman Catholic institution. Tompkins was ordered by his bishop to go to Canso, Nova Scotia in 1923, and it was in Canso he was able to see firsthand the plight of Nova Scotia's working people and the need for adult education and more co-operative enterprises. In 1935 he moved to St. Joseph's Parish in the mining community of Reserve Mines where he began to inspire others to follow his co-operative ideals (Boyle 1953).

Coady was born in Northeast Margaree, Cape Breton, on January 3, 1882, and worked on his family's farm as a young boy. As he says, "We were carpenters, coopers, woodsmen, fishermen, farmers all in one. I was doing a man's work when I was ten." In his biography he reveals that he did not go to school regularly until he was fifteen years old: "I went a few weeks after planting in the spring and a little longer time after digging in the fall. I was fortunate, however, that my parents taught me at home...." He attended school in Margaree, Normal College in Truro and St. FX. He also was offered a position at St. Francis Xavier in 1910 and, like his cousin Jimmy Tompkins, he entered the Urban College in Rome where he obtained, "the best in theological and philosophical training of the time." He did postgraduate studies in education in Washington, DC. In the early 1920s he helped to organize the Nova Scotia Teacher's Union and founded and edited their *Bulletin*. When a leader was needed for the newly established Extension Department at St. FX in 1928, Coady was the logical choice. His first attempts at adult education brought him back to his home community of Margaree where, when considering offering courses in music and art, he developed the idea of forming small study clubs. One of his first tasks as the director of the Extension Department was to organize the many fishermen of the province into a union. By 1930, he brought together in Halifax 208 delegates from the many Nova Scotia fishing villages to form the United Maritime Fishermen (McKean n.d., n.p.).

Coady continued to work with co-operative enterprises throughout his life. He died in 1959 and is buried in Antigonish; Tompkins died in 1953 and buried in Reserve Mines, St. Joseph's Parish, not far from the present-day Tompkinsville housing development.

The Development of Tompkinsville

The neighbourhood of Tompkinsville, in the heart of the Cape Breton mining district, exhibits many aspects of local, vernacular architecture (figure 8.1). This neighbourhood development was begun in 1938 by miners and their families who were dissatisfied with the inadequate housing provided by the resident mining companies. Following the co-operative philosophy of the Antigonish Movement, the miners and their families formed study

Figure 8.1 Map of Cape Breton Island showing Tompkinsville.

groups and taught themselves to build houses suited to their specific needs. It was the first co-operative housing group in Canada and was used as a model for the construction of numerous housing developments throughout eastern Nova Scotia until the 1960s. Much of the architectural landscape of Cape Breton's industrial communities in the 1940s, 1950s and 1960s was shaped by co-operative housing groups following the pattern worked out by the early Tompkinsville residents.

While the Tompkinsville houses were built in 1938, preparation actually began a few years before. Establishing a Credit Union in the community was the first experience some of the miners had with the co-operative philosophy.

A Credit Union study club was organized in October 1932, with Joe Laben taking a leadership role (figure 8.2). After much reading, thinking and discussion, the first credit union was started on March 2, 1933 with forty-three members and a share capital of thirty-seven dollars (History of

Arnold Credit Union). It was difficult at first
to get some miners interested in the study
groups. As Mary Arnold says: "You couldn't
do anything with some fellows. They never read anything or seem to care. They
don't even know what Father Tompkins
or Father Coady are talking about. And as
for a study club, just try to get them into
one..." (Arnold, n.d.: 6). By the mid 1930s
a number of Reserve Mines residents were
gradually accepting the ideas being presented by Father Tompkins. Mary Laben
describes Father Tompkins' influence on the
community:

Figure 8.2 Joe Laben (courtesy Mary Laben).

> So, Dr. Tompkins came to Reserve in 1935. And of course the first
> thing that he did, he gave one look around and saw everybody standing
> around the corners and going to the taverns and drinking and every-
> thing else, and I guess he said, I guess I better start doing something. So
> he got a library. Organized with the help of the Carnegie foundation,
> you know.
>
> So they, he'd pinhole every boy or girl that he'd meet in the street to go
> to the library to read. So Joe went to the library with Father Jimmy and
> he'd start reading his books. And start what we, at that time we were, we
> were after organizing the Credit Union. And there was talks of a store.
> And there was talks of fish plants and one thing or another.

In 1935, as Mary Laben points out, the first community library was
established with the assistance of Fr. Tompkins. As Tompkins said: "Read.
Books are the university of the people. Ideas have hands and feet. Choose
your ideas. They will work for you. You must study" (Arnold, n.d.: 8).[8] In
this Reserve Mines library, the team of co-operators were introduced to
many texts on co-operativism, self-worth and the industrial revolution.
Mary Laben explains:

> So they, we had, they organized study clubs, in Reserve at that time
> they had organized twenty-three study clubs, meeting in people's hous-
> es. So every Sunday evening after Mass there'd be nine or ten or eleven
> arrive at my little house in Belgiumtown. And I'd go to another house
> where there was a bunch of women holding a meeting. [...] Joe in the
> library had read Warbasse's book [1917]. They had a question box, and
> everybody as asked to put a question in the box. Something, and if
> they couldn't answer it among themselves they got Dr. Tompkins to
> answer it.

Figure 8.3 Site plan of Reserve Mines. By Barry Gabriel.

By the fall of 1936, a small group was working on the establishment of a co-operative store. On November 8, 1937, the store, for miners and their families, was opened in the community of Reserve Mines, located across the street from the church and convent. It provided an alternative to the company stores that dominated mining communities.[9]

A land study was started by a group of men who met every Sunday at Joe Laben's company house in a neighbourhood called Belgiumtown, where many immigrant families resided (figure 8.3). Mary Laben describes her house in Belgiumtown: "When we were married, sixty-one years ago we went to live in Belgiumtown. In a little house, two rooms downstairs and two rooms upstairs and an outdoor toilet... (figure 8.4)."

The notes from the group's meeting say, "At first it was hard to get a crowd to stick" (History of the Arnold Credit Union n.d.). Five miners attended the first meeting: Joe Laben, the president; Ray McNabb, treasurer; Ed Kelly, secretary; and John Smith and Mick Gardner. This club studied pamphlets such as the *Industrial Revolution, Consumers Co-op* and *Why Workers should be Co-operators*, published by American co-operative agencies. Each member had to make a speech at an appointed time of each

Figure 8.4 Typical of two-room company houses built at the turn of the century in the Belgiumtown area of Reserve Mines, 1906. Dominion Coal Company. Plan 919. Beaton Institute, Cape Breton University.

meeting. Their notes indicate that "the questions were very interesting and helpful to keep crowd together" and that "speech making was well liked" by the assembled group. Books were being circulated from the community library and individuals enjoyed discussing their contents and learned much about co-operative principles and values.

It was not until the group had established a credit union, a co-operative store and a community library, that a housing project was considered. A housing study club was organized in the spring of 1937 with the following officers being appointed: Joe Laben, President; Jonathan Steele, vice-president; Duncan Curry, secretary; and Ray McNabb, treasurer. Following the same tried format used with their previous co-operative successes, the study club examined many issues relating to housing. Duncan Curry, Alex McIntyre and Jonathan Steele were taken into the club to replace Mick Gardner, Mick Young and Jonathan Aucoin who had resigned. Mary Laben explains what happened:

> [...] And in Warbasse's book it said, that everybody that paid rent to a landlord donated the house back every twenty years to the person. So everybody was living in the Coal Company's house. So every twenty years it was donated back to the Coal Company. So somebody said, "why can't we build houses?" They were all miners none of them ever had a hammer in their hand in their life. So they went to Dr. Jimmy

with a proposition. And Dr. Jimmy was tickled to death talking about it. So then they decided, "well, where could we get a piece of land?" That. So Dr. Jimmy, all this land here belonged to a old fellow out the road. So he had turned around ... he had died ... he had willed the whole thing to our Parish. St. Joseph's Parish, Reserve. So Dr. Jimmy said ... use that land and instead of putting the dead on it, let's put the living on it. So we each paid fifty dollars a piece, which was hard to get at that time.

One of their first tasks was to make a careful study of the *Housing Act* of Nova Scotia. At this stage of the project, two outsiders, Mary Arnold and Mabel Reed, co-operative organizers from the United States, came to assist them in their proposed endeavour. Connected to the St. FX Extension Department, these social reformers offered to help the group. The group accepted the two women as manager and assistant manager, respectively, because of their previous experience with co-operative housing developments. Mary Laben describes how Mary Arnold came to Tompkinsville:

> They used to have seminars in Antigonish. And Joe went up to the seminar and he gave a talk on what they'd like to do. Build some homes for themselves and that. And this lady from New York happened to be at the seminar. Her name was Mary Arnold. So she went to Dr. Jimmy and she, after the meeting, and she said, I'd like to go to Reserve and help those men. I have just finished building a co-operative apartment in New York. So Dr. Jimmy invited her down. She had a place to stay.

At once, they began to plan for their proposed homes and to bring their wives together with Mary Arnold and Mabel Reed to plan for the interior layouts.[10] Mary Arnold stayed in Reserve Mines for more than one year during construction and helped with planning, organizing, bookkeeping and building cardboard models of the homes.[11] Reformer, builder, co-operator and manager of apartments, Ms. Arnold assisted in numerous ways in the completion of this housing group. The group decided to use a contractor to build one house, to allow them to observe the building process and to assess construction time, costs and materials. As she says in her book:

> Let the contract for a budget house to a reliable builder, got the total cost of such a house built under contract conditions, made it similar in every way to the houses which the men planned to build, and then cost accounted every joist and every sill of the budget house as well as every hour of work by skilled men.... We could obtain accurate figures against which we could check labour and materials in the houses built by the men...." (Arnold n.d.: 23)

This first house in the neighbourhood was where Mary Arnold lived during her stay in Reserve Mines.

Joe Laben, the president of the housing co-operative, took a leadership role in this housing development; he was smitten with the co-operative philosophy, especially after Father Jimmy Tompkins became the parish priest in St. Joseph's Parish in 1935. Joe Laben was born in Rhineland, Germany, on March 19, 1907, came to Canada in 1910. He married Mary Steele of Reserve Mines in 1931. As a youth, Joe attended school until grade three and then began a life of work like many other Cape Breton youths of the time. In 1920, he began his career in the coal mines at the age of thirteen and continued to work in the deeps and on the surface until 1947.

After two years of weekly studies of carpentry, plumbing, electricity and general house construction, Joe, Mary and each of the men and their families had completed a small, cardboard scale model of the houses to be built (figure 8.5). As Mary Laben describes, the women played a key role in the whole process:

> The women, the women decided, they all built little, little cardboard homes like is in that picture. Exactly the same, you know, and they even pictured in it, well, what I got you know why, I could put it there, or I could put it here. Katie, uh, Mrs. McNabb she did her whole kitchen around because she had eight. And so she put, she had a window in the

Figure 8.5 Tompkinsville planning using cardboard models of houses.

middle on both sides. She put the whole cupboards because she'd need them you know. And then when room for her table and room for her stove and that went in her kitchen.

Men and women jointly helped to construct the houses, Ms. Laben continues:

> Yes, the women, the, there's more shingles went on those houses with women then there were with men. Oh yes they helped put up the gyprock and everything. But they, but we also had women study clubs that ah, that somebody from uh, Truro. The Government sent somebody down from Truro that taught us with a loom. To weave, you know. We did quite a bit of that, and we did, we knit, and crocheted. And then the, when it came, when it came the fall they sent down someone that helped us can. We all had a garden. We got settled ... and they sent us down ah, ah woman to show us what to do with canning and the canning machine, and what we had in the garden, and what to do with it and everything else....

On April 1, 1938, group members started digging the first basements by hand and the co-operative housing experiment was become a physical reality (figure 8.6). The members aimed to build their homes for five hundred dollars; at the time a comparable house, built by a private contractor, cost approximately ten thousand dollars.

Figure 8.6 Housing group members digging basements by hand, in 1938. Mary Arnold is in the centre of the photograph with a pick in her hand (courtesy Catharine MacNeil, resident of Reserve Mines).

A travel writer, Clara Dennis, stumbled across the Tompkinsville housing group in her travels throughout Cape Breton Island in 1938. She met one of the Tompkinsville pioneers at work on his home and she quotes him describing how the group was formed:

> "We're all coal miners—shooters, bottommers, loaders and so on," he said. "We work in the coal mines here in Reserve. If anyone had told me a year ago that I would build a house!—well, I wouldn't have believed him, that's all. When the co-operative movement struck Reserve, I joined one of the study groups that were formed. We studied different things in our group. One of our members found a law about housing on the Statute Books of Nova Scotia. He sprung it on our meeting. We found we could borrow from the government seventy-five per cent of the cost of a house. We would only have to pay two and a half per cent interest and would have twenty-five years to repay the loan. We decided to take advantage of the law and build homes for ourselves." (1940: 108)

After examining the law for almost two years, the group studied housing, planning and all aspects of building; in a sense, they taught themselves the whole process of planning, designing and building houses, from making forms and concrete foundations to framing and roofing houses. As George Clarke says:

> An expert showed us how to mix the cement for the first foundation and we went ahead and did the rest. We worked in gangs of three. Three would put up the frame, the next three would come along and board it in, three would lay the floors and so on. We went from house to house, till all were finished—co-operation you see, co-operators. (Dennis 1940: 109)

Juggling difficult shift work schedules, the miners proceeded to complete the project within one year. Finally, on November 27, 1938, the group's dreams were realized when the housing development was completed. The terms of the mortgage were simple; one quarter of the total project's value was needed for the down payment. The group used their donated land as collateral, the government loan was rated at 3.5 per cent per year and their local credit union put up the bal-

Figure 8.7 Father Jimmy Tompkins.

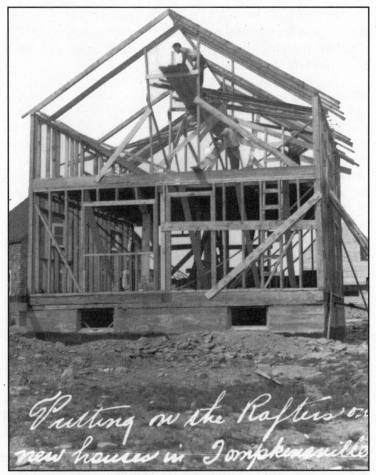

Figure 8.8 1938 (courtesy Catharine MacNeil, resident of Reserve Mines).

ance of 1.0 per cent. The initial term was for twenty-five years but the group paid off their mortgage within twenty. In 1958 the Tompkinsville mortgage was burned at a ceremony at the Silver Rail, a popular Cape Breton Island dance club in the 1950s and 1960s. A song entitled "Hurrah to Tompkinsville!!" was composed for the occasion by Agnes and Eldie Gallant to the tune of the "Battle Hymn of the Republic."[12]

I   Mary Arnold came to town to see what she could do.
        Along with Doctor Jimmy and Doctor Coady too.
        They all got together, to help the working man
        To build a home of his own.

Chorus

Come and let us sing together, come and let us sing together

Come and let us sing together, Hurrah to Tompkinsville![13]

While the project was progressing, Joe Laben was invited to assist other co-operative housing developments in communities throughout Nova Scotia.[14] For more than three years he travelled the province assisting in co-operative projects. While Laben continued to teach others about the benefits of co-operative housing, his wife Mary worked at the Sydney airport managing the food services for Cara Enterprises. Because of his knowledge and wisdom, Joe was asked by St. FX to assist in their extension work and to lecture at the Coady International Institute on the issue of co-operative housing. Mary Laben discusses some of the groups Joe helped:

> There's two in Dominion that he built. There's two in Glace Bay that he built. One, one right by St. John's church, the hill. There's one over in [New] Waterford, there's one in Sydney Mines. There's three in Newfoundland. He went over to Newfoundland. [...] And in Sydney, in Sydney there must be, oh easy, there must be about two hundred. And New Glasgow and Springhill. Canso ah, he went right clean to PEI. Went right, travelled right. He even, he even ... went to Ottawa to the House [of Commons] and, spoke to them in the House about what they were doing....

There was much interest in Nova Scotia in this innovative project begun by this group of reserve mines coal miners. A survey entitled Co-op Housing Nova Scotia indicates that between March 11, 1938, when the Tompkinsville experiment began, and July 16, 1952, there were 35 housing groups developed in the province (*Public Archives of Nova Scotia* n.d.: 37). Cape Breton communities such as Glace Bay, New Waterford, Inverness and Sydney built co-operative housing. On the mainland, communities such as Stellarton followed in the co-operative spirit. From 1953 to 1973, there were 982 co-operative housing projects developed in Nova Scotia (37-58).

Joe and Mary Laben's house in Tompkinsville became a visiting site for Coady International students and for anyone interested in co-operative housing. Over the years, Joe received a number of awards for his contribution to the well-being of his community and of Canada including: the Centennial Medal in recognition of valuable service to the nation in 1967, an Antigonish Movement service award in 1974, a visit from the Governor General of Canada, Ed Schreyer and his wife in 1982, and the Order of Canada in 1985.[15]

Tompkinsville Houses

The eleven houses in this neighbourhood were laid out in a block of land originally designated for the parish graveyard and situated approximately three hundred yards from the centre of Reserve Mines where the church, convent, library, credit union, company houses and store are located (figure 8.9). Tompkinsville Road was driven in at a diagonal off the highway that runs between Reserve Mines and Sydney, and the land was divided in a grid. Each house was situated on a piece of land on average 100 by 165 ft (30 by 50 m). Nine of the eleven builders placed their houses close to the road, leaving room behind for gardens; only one house on the northwestern side deviated from this arrangement, situating the home in the centre of the lot. Another house on the southeastern side of the neighbourhood was situated in a different manner from the rest, being rotated forty-five degrees and placed closer to the centre of the lot.

Ten of the eleven builders chose to construct gable roofs; only one used a half-hipped form, known locally as the Cheticamp style, because of its popularity in the rural Acadian community of Cheticamp on the western side of the Island (Latremouille 1986: 37).[16] Each Tompkinsville house was two stories in height and had a bathroom and six rooms, including a kitchen, dining room and living room on the ground floor and three bedrooms upstairs (figures 8.10 and 8.11). Each house was unique—no two houses exactly alike in floor plan or decoration—although all chose the three-room ground floor plan for their living space. One of the pioneers succinctly summed up the minor variations:

> [...] one has no hall, another has an extra window, another has the bathroom downstairs, and so on. I liked a fireplace more than anything else, so I saved on my floors (they're not all hardwood) and put the money in the fireplace. One man put his extra money on a ceiling. He saw a fancy ceiling in a church and liked it. So, in one of his rooms he has a fancy diamond ceiling—very pretty—where I have only a plain ceiling. (Qtd. in Dennis: 109-10)

Although the process of construction was communal and the floor plans were similar, individual builders were innovative in their use of cosmetic details and interior arrangements. The owners were proud of their accomplishments and allowed many visitors from Cape Breton and beyond to see the fruits of their labour. The interiors of houses were brightly coloured, causing one traveller in 1938 to focus on the cosmetic details of the visited house:

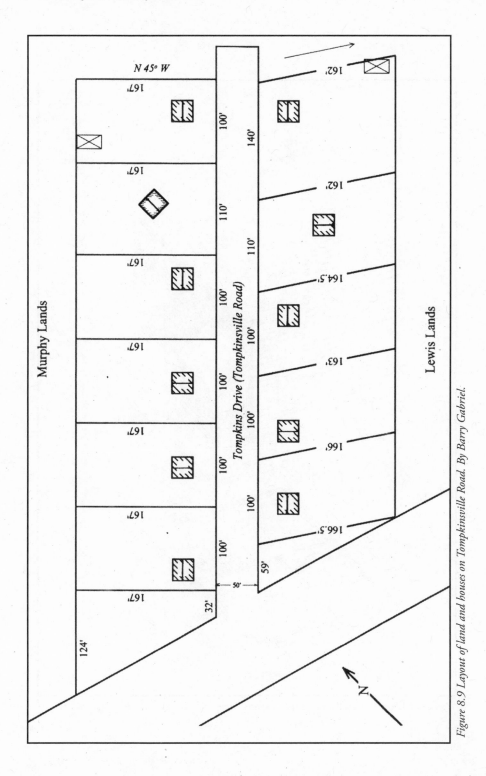

Figure 8.9 Layout of land and houses on Tompkinsville Road. By Barry Gabriel.

Figure 8.10 First floor and front façade, Joe and Mary Laben's house. By Barry Gabriel.

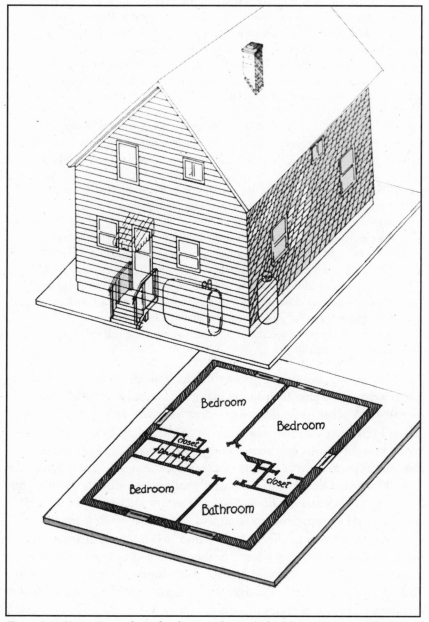

Figure 8.11 Upper story and rear façade, Joe and Mary Laben's house. By Barry Gabriel.

The floor of one room was a royal blue. The walls had light blue paper and the woodwork was white. In another room the floor was pink. White curtains at the windows had dainty frills of pink. "This is our guest room," said one housewife, as she opened the door of a most attractive room. Floor of a delicate yellow, mauve walls and a ceiling of pastel green blended together and gave a most pleasing effect. "We got the color scheme from a magazine," the housewife said. "See the nice big clothes closet," she continued. "We never had such a thing as a closet in a room before. The last house we lived in had no bathtub or no hot water—very awkward that was." (Dennis 1940: 110)

While both men and women helped construct the homes, women made the primary decisions on the cosmetic details of the interiors. Travel writer Clara Dennis describes the spacious and well laid out kitchens:

There were most adorable little kitchens in the houses—kitchens that would delight the heart of any housewife. To the miner's wife they were a special joy for with different members of her family working perhaps different shifts in the mine, she might have to prepare as many as seven or eight different meals a day instead of the regulation three. One kitchen had a window built over the sink, and the miner's wife looked out on a beautiful view as she worked. A built-in flour bin and four closets with four closet doors, was an original idea in another kitchen. One kitchen was red and grey, with red and grey linoleum on the floor. Another had black linoleum and the chairs were Spanish red and Royal blue.... (Dennis: 111)

This passage points out the way in which the members of the housing group were able to alter their individual spatial layouts in this all important room—the kitchen—the place where much activity occurred.

On my first visit to Tompkinsville to visit Mary Laben, the last surviving pioneer of this neighbourhood, I was welcomed into her comfortable, sun-filled kitchen at the rear of the house (figures 8.12 and 8.13). She said, "I love my kitchen" and she proudly showed me around, pointing out its many features and details including a sunny kitchen nook with table and chairs, a large space for cooking and a wall of cupboards for storage.

While the rear kitchen is sunny and inviting, "the front room" or living room is where the many photographs of daughters, nieces, their friends and acquaintances and Mary Laben's husband, Joe, are displayed. This "personal museum" displayed the various rites of passage of family members and the various awards offered to Joe Laben for his contribution to co-operativism and housing (figure 8.13). It is here that special guests are brought and where Mary Laben spent much of her time. The influence of the Roman Catholic faith of Mary and her husband is also demonstrated

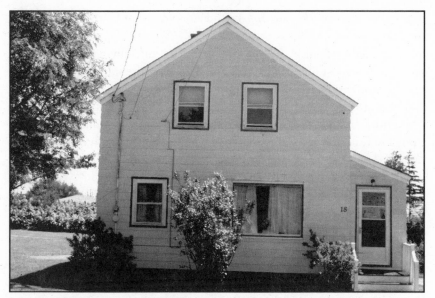

Figure 8.12 Exterior, Joe and Mary Laben's house, 1993.

Figure 8.13 Living room or "front room," Joe and Mary Laben's house, 1993.

by a large image of *The Last Supper* and a depiction of Christ that overlook the living room.

The Laben floor plan has a kitchen to the rear, a living room or "front room" as it is most often called in Cape Breton, at the side of the house facing the road, and a small dining room transformed into a small bedroom. A small bathroom was built off the dining room for Joe Laben when illness made it increasingly difficult to climb the stairway. The dining room continued to function as a bedroom when Mary Laben found it difficult to get up and down the stairs later in life. The upstairs has three bedrooms with small closets along with a small bathroom.

While Joe and Mary Laben's house and those of their neighbours were built co-operatively as a response to company domination of housing, it is ironic that residents chose familiar spatial patterns when deciding to construct their own houses. A variation on the grid pattern was used to lay out the neighbourhood, a common town plan used in the many coal mining towns of Cape Breton and in other areas of North America.[17] Even though their motivation for building co-operatively was to move away from the company housing owned and managed by the Dominion Steel and Coal Company, they chose the basic three-room plan with a front room, dining room and rear kitchen when selecting suitable spaces for their new houses. This plan made its appearance throughout the Island in the various company houses which were built as early as the 1830s with the arrival of the British-owned General Mining Association. While some two-room plans were used in Cape Breton's company housing, by 1900, the standard plan in company duplexes built by the Dominion Steel and Coal Company was the three-room form; homes of this type can be found in communities such as Dominion, Glace Bay, New Waterford, New Victoria, Sydney Mines and Inverness as well as in Reserve Mines. Even though company houses were considered to be drafty and sub-standard, the builders of Tompkinsville demonstrated conservatism in selecting these floor plans for their new homes.

Moreover, Mary and Joe Laben also chose to build a home with the gable facing the road. While many of the early and mid-19th century company houses were attached rows, copying British mining housing, the early-20th-century single family company homes were gable-entry-to-the-road homes. The gable front house, with a main entrance off to one side on an end gable, is said to have emerged in North America by the 1830s (Glassie 1968: 54-56; Noble 1984: 107-109). The house type grew largely from the late 18th-century interest in classical forms, which promoted the architectural style called classical revival, so popular in religious, public and domestic buildings from the 1820s until the 1860s (Hamlin 1964;

Latremouille 1986: 30; Maitland 1984; Young 1982).[18] Allen Noble points out that orienting the gable to the street allowed narrower and less expensive urban town lots to be used by builders; more buildings could be placed in smaller geographic spaces (1984: 107). Thomas Hubka (1985: 38-39) points out that New England farmers readily accepted this form into their building repertoire after the 1830s, at a time when there was considerable reorganization of space on new England farms. Moreover, he argues the primary appeal to Americans of the classical movement was nationalistic; this architectural style became a symbol of the new American republic, which was attempting to build a nation based on classical ideals: "the image of Greece and Rome became a symbol of progress…" (196). This house type, without the classical details, appeared in Cape Breton mining communities at the turn of the 20th century; and it was this form that Joe and Mary chose when deciding on a suitable home in the Tompkinsville neighbourhood.

While following a familiar local pattern of interior spatial design, Tompkinsville residents also followed familiar land-use patterns in their exterior yards. They planned for and planted gardens to help supply their families with fresh produce and root crops. The garden was not a hobby but a necessity for many, especially at times when the mines were reduced to one or two shifts a week, a common occurrence throughout the 1930s. Many of Tompkinsville's and industrial Cape Breton's residents have rural roots; their forebears came from rural Inverness, Victoria and Richmond Counties of Cape Breton in droves at the turn of the 20th century when coal mining was booming on the Island. The Tompkinsville residents grew root crops and vegetables in the 1930s to help feed their families in difficult times. Mary Laben points out that in addition to beans, peas, carrots, squash, turnip and potatoes, their garden also contained a large patch of strawberries, which supplied more than twenty five baskets each year.

Numerous changes have happened in this neighbourhood in the last seven decades. Many of the original residents have died and younger citizens have purchased the homes of the Tompkinsville pioneers. Many of the houses have had aluminium siding applied in the 1960s and 1970s in an attempt to cut heating costs in time of rising oil prices.

Innovation and Conservatism

The Tompkinsville houses tell a story of innovation and conservatism. The co-operative nature of the planning and construction of the neighbourhood was a response to domination of housing by a mining corporation in a company town. This group of Reserve Mines coal miners were the first to apply some of the co-operative ideas of Tompkins and Coady to the building of homes. While innovative, these builders were also conservative in choosing familiar spatial patterns for their homes and yards.

The Tompkinsville housing co-operative suits our definition of vernacular architecture. For example, the builders controlled the entire building process in the neighbourhood. Despite the poor economic climate, the owners saw that by working together to construct homes they were able to afford suitable, comfortable houses. This whole co-operative enterprise allowed mining families to break away from the confines of the company-owned housing so prevalent in the community at the time, yet they used the spatial patterns with which they had become accustomed. Their co-operative building process was, in itself, an older conventional vernacular pattern. Barns, outbuildings and houses were once "raised" in many communities in a communal fashion with entire neighbourhoods of men, women and children assisting in some way. While neighbourhood residents were limited by costs and size, they also adjusted and altered their architecture to suit their own needs, modifying each unit to match the particular aesthetics of the family. The architecture of this neighbourhood is clearly, "product of a place, of a people, by a people" (Heath 1988: 5).

Joe Laben and his wife Mary played an integral role in the development of the Tompkinsville architectural experiment. They nurtured the idea of co-operative housing through many discussions and study clubs, through readings, conversations, arguments and debates. As Alex Laidlaw says, "Co-operation is not an easier way of doing things. It is a harder way by reason of its democratic methods. It is worthwhile not only on the grounds of ease, but because of its humanism and because it is fair and equitable."[19] Tompkinsville residents moved from theory to practice as they constructed their own homes, following co-operative ideals. Their tenacious drive has transformed many working class neighbourhoods in Atlantic Canada who have followed their example. The Laben's home remains a place to visit when one wants to find out about the development of co-operative housing in the Maritimes.

Architecturally, the Tompkinsville houses would not fare well if one evaluated them according to criteria developed by governments to assess the significant historical buildings in our communities.[20] These houses are not extremely old, they are not designed by a well-known architect, they don't represent a unique architectural style and they are not directly associated with a prestigious merchant or industrialist. Moreover, they are now often sheathed in aluminum or vinyl siding, a renovation made by many working-class people throughout Nova Scotia in the late 20th century. Nevertheless, the process of construction and the influence of this housing development at the local, regional, national, and indeed international levels, would suggest that the neighbourhood should be recognized as a significant part of Nova Scotia's built heritage. Vernacular dwellings like those found in Tompkinsville deserve to be represented more extensively in our historic building inventories and in our designated Canadian historic properties for they offer us a more realistic portrayal of the lives of working class Canadians.

Notes

1. One exception is the fine study by Dolores Hayden that explores some of the late 19th- and early 20th-century co-operative experiments in housing advocated by a group of women she calls "material feminists." These women argued that a "complete transformation of the spatial design and material culture of American homes, neighbourhoods and cities" was needed to change the exploitation of women in society (Hayden 1981: 3).

2. Interview quotes in this chapter are from Mary Laben (1993). The archival material for this chapter derives from the Beaton Institute archives, Cape Breton University, and the Public Archives of Nova Scotia. An early version of this article was also submitted to the Nova Scotia Department of Culture for their Heritage Unit, and presented at the Folklore Studies Association of Canada annual conference at Carleton University, Ottawa (June 2-6, 1993).

3. North American scholars such as Fred Kniffen, Henry Glassie and James Deetz have been extremely influential in the study of folk architecture and material culture. One of the better bibliographic sources for North American vernacular architecture is the Vernacular Architecture Forum, a newsletter published by the society of the same name which includes notes, reviews and an extensive bibliography in each issue.

4. In Newfoundland, some work has been completed, but much remains to be done before a complete understanding of the island's vernacular building tradition can be understood. The academic study of Newfoundland's vernacular architecture has been dominated by four individuals: Gerald Pocius, Shane O'Dea, John Mannion and David Mills. For some of their studies not already cited see O'Dea (1973, 1982a, 1982b). For examples of popular works see: Newfoundland Historic Trust (1975, 1978). Shane O'Dea has completed a survey of some of the popular studies of Atlantic Canadian architecture in O'Dea (1980).

5. For a study of housing built in industrial communities which have many vernacular influences see Carter (1991). For a popular novel which explores the vernacular influences on contemporary housing see Kidder (1985).

6. For a sense of the times see Frank (1985, 1986); Fraser (1992); MacGillivray (1991).

7. In working on this project I uncovered a first draft of a book by Mary Arnold in the attic of a co-operative house in New Waterford. A copy of this typescript has been deposited in the Beaton Institute archives, Cape Breton University. See a later version in Arnold (1940).

8. The present-day Cape Breton Regional Library developed from this first Reserve Mines library; today there are thirteen branches and two bookmobiles to service the island of Cape Breton.

9. On Cape Breton Island company stores were referred to as "Pluck-Me's" because the stores were viewed by miners and their families as part of an exploitative system. The bill at the "Pluck-Me" store was taken directly off the paycheck before the miner was able to collect his pay. During the bitter strikes in the 1920s, some "Pluck-Me" stores were burned

because of their symbolic associations (Frank 1985: 203-18).

10. At this stage the housing group consisted of: Mary Arnold, manager; Joe Laben, president; Duncan Curry, secretary; Ray McNabb, treasurer; Allan McMullin, director; Angus Curry, director; Ed Kelly, director; Jonathan Steele, vice-president; A. S. McIntyre; director; John Smith, director; George Clark, director and Mabel Reed, assistant manager (History of Arnold Credit Union).

11. See Mary Arnold's book, *The Story of Tompkinsville* (1940) for her version of how this neighborhood came into being. Mary Arnold was involved in co-operative development in New York City where she was manager of a group called Consumer Co-operative Services. The notes in her book, *Father Jimmy of Nova Scotia* (1958), state that she produced a film, *The Turn of The Tide* (1943), about lobster fishermen along the coast of Maine and a book, *In the Land of the Grasshopper Song* (1957).

12. Songmaking is an important aspect of Cape Breton's oral culture. Important events in communities, whether humorous incidents, tragic mine accidents or happy occasions are recorded in many songs of local composition. Thanks are offered to Elizabeth Beaton, Cape Breton University for bringing this song to my attention.

13. The song in its entirety:

I   Mary Arnold came to town to see what she could do.
        Along with Doctor Jimmy and Doctor Coady too.
        They all got together, to help the working man
        To build a home of his own.

Chorus

        Come and let us sing together, come and let us sing together
        Come and let us sing together, Hurrah to Tompkinsville!

II   They called the men together to form a study group
        They studied hard to get a plan the working man to suit.
        They called on Doctors, Priest and Prince to see what they could do.
        Among them all they worked a plan, to see their dreams come true.

III   In nineteen hundred and thirty eight, we started to turn the sod.
        The work was hard, the money scarce. We were a determined squad.
        The blisters were big, our backs were sore, foundations were dug by hand,
        But the project went right along.

IV   Big Allie used to sing to us to get us all in trim
        And Hooker used to join him which would make it twice as grim.
        John Allen watched while Kelly worked his garden every day
        But he never grew a dad-blamed thing!

V   Folks from all around the world, have traveled far to see
        The benefits of group action here in this community
        We've got our homes, a Credit Union and a Co-op Store
        And a handsome Library.

VI   Tompkinsville is gathered here to sing and celebrate
        The burning of the MORTGAGE, every cent is paid to date.
        We did it all together, to help each other out.
        And it only took us twenty years!

14. Forbes (1993) points out, "by late 1938, spokesmen for the Antigonish Movement claimed direct involvement by approximately 50,000 in activities including 42 cooperative stores, 17 cooperative lobster canneries, 10 fish-processing plants, 140 credit unions, and 2,390 study clubs—1500 in Nova Scotia, 500 in New Brunswick, and 390 in Prince Edward Island" (294).

15. This material was obtained from Mrs. Mary Laben. Much of this biographical material is found in an unpublished manuscript in her possession which was compiled by members of the community when Joe Laben was nominated for the Order of Canada.

16. Latremouille points out that the high winds in the Cheticamp area led to the choice of this roof form: "The builders around Cheticamp oriented their houses to face the hipped gables into the prevailing southeast winter wind." Even though the wind conditions were different in the industrial communities on the eastern end of the island, people from Cheticamp brought this roof style with them when they went to work in the mines (1986: 37).

17. For an article examining the vernacular nature of grid iron plans see Marshall (1986: 81-88). For a description of the layout of Cape Breton coal mining town in 1928 see McNabb (1990: Plate 37).

18. Many Cape Breton Island churches are constructed in the classical revival style.

19. Quotation from Alex Laidlaw on poster: "Father of the Canadian Cooperative Movement: Alex Laidlaw," designed by Blair Kerrigan Glyphics for the Cooperative Housing Foundation Canada, 1988. B and G Horizontal File no. 8, Beaton Institute, Cape Breton University.

20. Some of these criteria are derived from the Federal Heritage Building Review Office Evaluation Sheet.

Postscript
Public Image and Private Reality in Cape Breton Folk Traditions

In this final chapter I will examine some of the public images of a few selected items of the region's folklore and folklife as it is often presented to outsiders. I will show that cultural intervention has happened at a number of levels and that the images presented and created by this process are not exactly accurate descriptions of Cape Breton Island's traditional culture. Furthermore, I will provide examples of some of the more private traditions that are still important to people, but are not the kinds of selective images chosen by interveners to present to the world at large. I hope in this way to offer a better understanding of the role folklore plays in the lives of people from this part of Canada and to offer some new directions for research and public presentation.

An earlier version of this paper was published in Forerunner *3.1 (1990): 28-31.*

Concluding an essay entitled "Images and Impressions of Glace Bay," Cape Breton labour historian Don MacGillivray writes:

> To understand and appreciate the mining community of Glace Bay, or the other mining areas, or Cape Bretoners in general, it is necessary to penetrate the fog formulated by politicians, journalists, tourists, industrial relations experts, novelists and, yes, academics, and to concentrate on the traditions and on the culture. That is why they have survived. (1983: 188)

In a sense, what I hope to do in this discussion is to penetrate the fog to some degree by focusing on some of the specific aspects of tradition or cultural activities of the region. Folklore is often used to present an image of this region's culture to both outsiders and local residents alike. Governments choose folkloric symbols for tourism brochures, museums select representative items of culture for display, and novelists choose particular aspects of culture to incorporate into their plots, thereby giving reverence and importance to selected folkloric items. Like a sculptor shaping a piece of clay, an image is created in this process; sometimes it is accurate, other times, it is a shallow simulation of the realities of the everyday life in a district.

One American scholar, David Whisnant, calls this entire process of shaping an image of tradition a "cultural intervention." "An intervener," says Whisnant,

> by virtue of his or her status, power and established credibility, is frequently able to define what the culture is, to normalize and legitimize that definition in the larger society, and even to feed it back into the culture itself, where it may be internalized as "real," "traditional" or "authentic".... (1983: 260)

Whisnant shows how cultural institutions such as the White Top folk festival, the Hindman Settlement School and the work of one individual—Olive Dame Campbell—have shaped an image of the folklife of the Southern Appalachians that was not entirely accurate. At best, the interveners of this district hopelessly romanticized the past; at worst, they offered a past to the resident and general public that never existed in the first place, and even tried to bury certain traditions which did not meet their middle-class, genteel approval. Items of Folklore such as imported ballads never originally sung in the region, dances never stepped to and crafts never created in the region were promoted as authentic, while locally composed materials were seen as somehow inferior and not worthy of perpetuation or preservation. This process of selecting and arranging images of tradition, or "intervening" within a culture, is indeed a complicated one and has occurred within many cultural groups and communities, whether Appalachian mountaineers, North American Indians, Georgia Blacks, Scottish Highlanders or Cape Bretoners.

Cape Breton Island is populated by numerous ethnic groups ranging from Irish, Scottish, Mi'kmaq and French Acadian, to American, English, West Indian, Ukrainian, Polish and Italian, to name a few. It would be impossible to analyze each of these groups and the public presentation of some of their traditions; thus, in this chapter, I will select only a few examples to show the differences between the public image and the private reality.

First, I will focus on the Gaelic Scots, many of whom migrated to Nova Scotia during the Highland clearances of the late 18th and early 19th centuries. Their Gaelic language, with its oral literature of songs, poetry, legends and folktales, were brought with them across the Atlantic Ocean along with their customs, beliefs and material culture. But if one takes a close look at the image of Scottish culture often presented, one can readily see a loving emphasis on specific stereotypes (McKay 1992). For example, the kilted bagpiper in all his regalia or young dancers doing the Highland fling to create the image of Scottishness are often used by government to make this part of the world unique and attractive to visitors. While bag-piping was indeed a common instrument for dance music among Nova Scotian Scots from the time of initial settlement to the fairly recent past, players were seldom dressed in the elaborate costumes used by government promotions. Rather, old photographs in archives reveal pipers playing for friends dressed in Sunday best clothes, rather than in colourful kilts, tams and sporrans (Gibson 1998: xiv-xvi). Likewise, people often danced, but preferred step dancing and square dancing in kitchens and community halls to the imported competitive Highland flings.

If this image itself is somewhat inaccurate, where and how did this image emerge? A study by British social historians traces the origin of this image to the Victorian, romantic love for all things Scottish promoted and perpetuated by royalty and aristocracy (Hobsbawm and Ranger 1983). Even though the Highlands and Islands had been cleared by landlords, aristocratic culture in England and the Lowlands revelled in the concocted symbols of this past. One study that examines postcards and the images of Highland culture contained in these ephemeral but influential portraits concluded that "almost all popular portrayals of highlanders are humorous or at least 'good-humored'." "Highlanders," as they are presented in these popular images "seem to have all the sartorial, physical, emotional and intellectual qualities (and the oomph) of garden gnomes" (MacLean and Carrell 1986: 88).

But what about Cape Breton Island? In Nova Scotia one can trace the use of these kinds of images to at least the First World War period and into the 1930s when a College of Celtic Arts and Crafts was estab-lished. Arts and crafts revivalists arrived in the region, and the music hall Harry Lauder image of Scottish culture first began to appear. The College of Celtic Arts and Crafts, based on the principles of the Scandinavian folk school movement, was established in the late 1930s in St. Ann's by Angus William Rudd MacKenzie a Presbyterian minister from Portree, Isle of Skye, and his wife Angela Alice Brownell (Lamb 1992: 9). Inspired by William Morris's view of craft revivalism, they brought in outside teachers

Figure 9.1 Gaelic College Pipe Band, Baddeck, NS. Photo by Richard MacKinnon.

to teach their highly romanticized version of arts and crafts. The celtic arts and crafts taught at this school, however, were not primarily the kinds of activities local Cape Bretoners regularly engaged in. Little emphasis was placed on the Gaelic language and the concomitant traditions surrounding this once common language in Cape Breton. Rather, competitive highland dancing, bagpiping with all its regalia, drumming and the production of kilts for a burgeoning North American market were its main concerns (figure 9.1).

Some local Gaelic speakers found it difficult to understand the kind of "culture" being presented at this school. My grandfather, for example, a fluent Gaelic speaker who grew up on a rural Cape Breton farm and moved away to work in the coal mines of industrial Cape Breton as a young man, could never understand the kind of Scottish culture presented at a school. For a man who had never worn a kilt, never danced a sword dance and did not understand the vogue for tartan, this image of Scottish culture was indeed puzzling. His image of Cape Breton Scottish culture was instead one of working the land with a team of horses, getting the winter wood out of the woods, going into the mine at 4:30 in the morning to work the dayshift and coming home tired, dancing at the community hall to well-known fiddlers, and using his Gaelic only when conversing with his older mother, who did not understand much English, or when attempting to conceal meanings of certain words or stories from his inquisitive grandchildren. While he was puzzled by this image, he would have been aware that the image was also appearing elsewhere in his community.

Following Lauder's first American broadcast in 1929, a number of Lauder imitators began to visit the Maritimes, bringing their concocted image of Highland culture to a region with a vibrant Gaelic culture (MacDonald 1988: 133-34). From the late 1920s, through to the 1940s, Lauder clones brought Lowland Scottish dialect, colourful tartans and a simplistic public stereotype of culture to Cape Breton Island and Nova Scotia.

Other public displays of culture became more prevalent by the 1960s including summertime events aimed at both a local and a visiting tourist market, largely from the Eastern United States. These kinds of events included large summertime festivals, cultural shows and outdoor concerts that attempted to typify the kind of music enjoyed by a local audience. Indeed many of the performers were the same ones who played at local pubs and community dances, but the repertoires at the outdoor galas are inevitably different in the two settings. Following in the footsteps of some of the American festivals, the usual structure of performance was (and continues to be) an outdoor venue with a stage for performers and the audience sitting in a large field, only after they've managed to battle a traffic jam to get to their spot in the field. Up to five thousand people sometimes come out for such events to hear performances of fiddle music and singing and to see some of the step dancers, highland dancers and dance troupes of various kinds display aspects of their culture to the waiting audience. An audience of this size enjoys fast reels and jigs; slow airs and waltzes do not inspire a crowd of this magnitude, which may ultimately lead to the demise of certain musical forms from performer's repertoires. For many, these touristic events become the government-sanctioned stereotype of local culture.

In Cape Breton, concerts have become annual events in small communities, sponsored and organized by local clergy and parish councils, and often bringing some financial rewards. For example, the Nova Scotia Highland Village in Iona has a Highland Village Day once each summer, when hundreds of tourists and locals come to the open-air museum to hear performers from all over the Island dance, play and sing. In past years profits from such events were in the thousands of dollars; however, some of the museum's workers have quietly worried about possible damage to the village's fields and the museum itself where the audience often camps for the weekend of the event. Moreover, they have had to contend with minor vandalism, but they are more worried about the possibility of major damage in the form of fire to some of the buildings and artifacts on the museum's site.

This kind of public display is not only found on the festival stage, but also within other established cultural institutions of the region. The Gaelic word, *ceilidh*, is used in a completely new sense by many contemporary cultural promoters. In the 19th century Scottish Highlands and in Cape Breton until the last twenty years or so, the word "ceilidh" referred to a small gathering of friends and neighbours for conversation, news, gossip and stories—a ritual of cultural transmission. A ceilidh was an intimate occasion, a time for friends and neighbours to renew the sinew and connecting tissue that binds a community together. It was a way for people to connect in a face-to-face situation, where people learned to tolerate each other's idiosyncrasies, and to respect each other's talents. However, with the recent transformation of the word, it has become synonymous with a large, touristic gathering. One local highway in Cape Breton Island is referred to as "the Ceilidh Trail" and government ad campaigns welcome visitors to "come for the ceilidh" in Nova Scotia. In the late 1980s, a local theatre sponsored what they called a summertime weekly "ceilidh" in Glace Bay, a mining community in the heart of Cape Breton's industrial district. A researcher who assessed this performance states that it was financially supported by provincial and federal governments, and "the stage was awash with tartan for a musical performance of a 'Traditional Highland Wedding'" (MacDonald 1988: 134). It was billed as emphasizing the cultural fabric that is Cape Breton Island and the Celtic communities throughout the Island, yet it "uneasily fitted round waltzes and pianos into an 18th-century setting, set the largely 19th-century Highland clearances as though in the 16th and 17th centuries, and continuously romanticized the image of Cape Breton Scottish culture." The author concludes by saying, "a corresponding distortion of Canadian history would have Confederation in the 17th century, Toronto in the Yukon, and Louis Riel negotiating the Free Trade pact with Ronald Reagan" (MacDonald 1988: 134-35).

What we can see in these examples is a public image of a cultural group, and that this image can be manipulated, distorted or altered to suit the needs of whoever is shaping it. The folkways and traditions in many communities are often quite different from these public displays, but that reality is unfortunately seldom viewed by a tourist audience. The audience, to use an idea of Erving Goffman's, is kept in the front area of culture, never to get even a glimpse of the back region where the most vital and meaningful cultural events occur (1959: 107).

To provide an example of local folkways not influenced by governmental or institutional intervention I will describe a house raising in Pleasant Bay, Cape Breton Island. In April 1988, a woman's house burned to the ground, injuring her severely and destroying all her possessions. After spending months recuperating in a hospital burn unit in Nova Scotia's capital, Halifax, the owner returned to find a new house constructed by the local men of the community (figures 9.2, 9.3, 9.4). The basement was poured in one day and on another day in the following week the house was almost entirely completed. The house itself was a one-story bungalow, a modern, common house-type found throughout Cape Breton Island.

On this and similar occasions, women of the community provided lunch and refreshments for the workers. By working in this way, this community is following one of its older folkway patterns—a communal gathering for the common good. Barn raisings, church raisings, wood frolics, spinning bees, milling frolics and the like were once very common in many rural areas of Cape Breton Island. In this way, a community is connecting with its past while also living in the modern world. While a house raising is a little unusual at the present, other forms of folkways which help to bind a community together are still common. For example, benefit concerts and dances for individuals who have suffered losses are still held; when an individual dies, neighbours and friends still bring food, drink and condolences even though many of the activities surrounding wakes and death now occur at a funeral parlour rather than in the family home as in the past. Likewise, a visiting tradition is still very common in both industrial and rural communities which offer a chance for people to share food, drink, conversation and hospitality. When a young couple decides to marry in some communities, elaborate wedding showers occur, where friends of the bride and groom, and friends and neighbours of the couple's parents and grandparents meet face-to-face for fun and ritual. Speeches are made, special foods are consumed and expensive gifts are given to the young couple. Frequently enough gifts are given to supply the young couple with many of the necessary appliances, linen, blankets and decorations for establishing a household. Likewise, when a baby is to be born, family and relatives organize another communal gathering to supply needed materials for the future member of the community. Besides providing material goods, and offering afternoons and evenings of entertainment, conversation and gossip, these kinds of activities reconnect members of families and communities, and welcome new members to the group. One could spend hours analyzing each of these events, but the important point of it all is that values are transmitted on these occasions; they teach the members of the community the unwritten rules common in the area: sharing, aiding others, showing respect for the elderly, for example.

This book has explored other local folkways, important to Cape Breton Island communities, such as music traditions, custom and ritual,

Figure 9.2 House raising, Pleasant Bay, NS. Photo by Richard MacKinnon.

Figure 9.3 House raising, Pleasant Bay, NS. Photo by Richard MacKinnon.

Figure 9.4 House raising, Pleasant Bay, NS. Photo by Richard MacKinnon.

and material culture. As examined in chapter 4, "Humorous Nicknames in Industrial Cape Breton," the use of proverbs, riddles and even nicknaming are still important aspects of community life—in English, Acadian and Mi'kmaq groups, and in rural as well as industrial communities (Davey and MacKinnon 1996: 2001).

Verbal folklore and oral tradition often contrast sharply with the master narrative of standard history presented by the state in many of our formal institutions such as schools and museums; the oral tradition offers a different view of the world from what is presented in formal documents. When one closely examines Mi'kmaw oral tradition, for example, the precise date of the earliest occupation of Cape Breton Island is debatable. Mi'kmaw narratives, however, can tell us a great deal about the earliest people and their land, their values and their attitudes. Memories of an early landscape are embedded in the consciousness of the Mi'kmaq through the many stories and legends that have been passed down from generation to generation. These stories tell how mountains, rivers and lakes assumed their present form and express attitudes toward nature and wildlife that cannot be discovered in other sources.

Some stories have passed into the safekeeping of a particular family. Historian Stephen Augustine received the Mi'kmaw creation story from his great grandmother, Isabel. She, in turn, had received it from her grandfather, a hereditary chief of the Mi'kmaq Grand Council and a Keeper of the Story. In this version, Glooscap was created by a series of lightning bolts. Later, he spoke with the bald eagle, sent from the heavens as a guardian of the Mi'kmaq. As the bird soared overhead, Glooscap caught and held one of the feathers that drifted to the ground. Since that day, the Mi'kmaq have revered the eagle feather as a symbol of their connection with the Great Spirit (Augustine 1997: 3). This, to a folklorist, is an explanatory story or etiological legend—a legend that helps to explain people's belief systems, worldviews and values. In all cultures, these kinds of legends and myths are important. Surprisingly, there has been very little study and collection of the various oral narrative genres in much of Cape Breton. Personal experience narratives, myths, epics, folktales, jokes or tall tales are only some of the various genres of oral folklore that still need to be collected and interpreted.

As with the Mi'kmaq, there are many stories within the other cultural groups that contribute to Cape Breton culture and much work is required to document and preserve these traditions. A necessary first step would be the creation of an inventory of threatened Cape Breton Island oral traditions, be it the traditions of Eastern European settlers, African Nova Scotians or Gaels. Within Cape Breton's Gaelic culture, for example, it is paramount that the older tradition bearers be recorded before the threatened Gaelic language is forever lost.

The work of scholar John Shaw represents an important step in this regard. In his edited collections *Tales Until Dawn* (MacNeil 1987) and *A Story in Every Song: The Songs and Tales of Lauchie MacLellan* (MacLellan 2000), Shaw brings to a wide audience the creative genius of two of Cape Breton's Gaelic tradition bearers—Joe Neil MacNeil and Lauchie MacLellan. In addition to including the Gaelic and English texts of a wide variety of stories and songs, Shaw has collaborated with these tradition bearers to produce their life histories. The stories, songs and life histories of Cape Breton Island tradition bearers have also been told in such publications as *Cape Breton's Magazine* and *Am Braighe,* but in reality, more research needs to be done in this whole topic area.

In both Mi'kmaw and Gaelic culture, stories abound about the interactions between the Gaels and the Mi'kmaq. For example, Lauchie MacLellan tells about going to work in the lumber woods in Musquodoboit, Nova Scotia, injuring his foot with an axe and being brought to the home of a Mi'kmaq family to convalesce for eight weeks. There, an elder used folk remedies to help heal the injury. The story reveals that Lauchie learned much about Mi'kmaw values regarding hospitality, medicine, food and cooking through this process (MacLellan 2000: 86-93). Another story from Gaelic tradition, told by D. D. MacFarlane of Southwest Margaree, is about Archie Cameron who came from Strathglass to settle in Margaree. Cameron and his sons were clearing land, preparing it for cultivation and building their homes when they were confronted by a Mi'kmaw man who gestured that he wanted the white man to leave the land immediately. Each day the Mi'kmaq returned while the Gaels continued with their work. Finally the Mi'kmaq offered a solution, "Let's wrestle. If you remain on top, I will leave the land to you, but if I remain on top, you will have to depart." They agreed to this solution and settled on the time and location. Both men were strong and courageous and they both tried every trick they knew. For a long time it was difficult to say who would be the winner. In a while, the Mi'kmaq's back was seen to yield under the hard back of the Gael. "The Mi'kmaq got up, clasped the hand of the Gael, said goodbye to him and in a short time he departed from Margaree" (Creighton and MacLeod 1964: 274-75). Like many legends, this one presents a story whose truth is debatable. True or not, the story demonstrates the confrontation of cultures in a pioneer landscape and how, in one way or another, European settlers drove the Mi'kmaq off their lands. An article written by Rusty Bitterman discusses the influx of settler populations into indigenous landscapes in the Middle River district of Cape Breton Island and the conflicts that ensued (71-87).

Verbal folklore and traditional stories are not meant to separate fact from fiction, although that is the way they are often interpreted. Oral stories clearly differ from the detailed facts of history. It is important, however, that we collect, record, study and interpret them, and look for the truths embedded in them with a view to achieving another perspective—perhaps even a more balanced perspective—on the past. The myths and legends passed down through oral tradition tell us about the values and beliefs of a culture. They convey deeply spiritual meaning about the underlying relationship between human beings and all of creation. They express a distinctive worldview and deal with feelings, beliefs and attitudes. For these reasons all oral traditions are important.

Balancing the Public and the Private

Are public displays of culture able to incorporate some of these private traditions into their performances (such as the rich labour song movement presented in chapter 2 or the piano music accompaniment tradition explored in chapter 3)? Or do they create cultures of their own with little relevance to the needs and culture of the local community? There is no simple answer to these questions. A recent conference on tourism in Nova Scotia was warned by one of the speakers that organizers should be careful not to alienate the local population when organizing and planning festivals and concerts, for when the local community is not involved and actively participating on the event, the affair becomes an imposition the community can do without. This was duly noted by a number of local organizers because the organizing of festivals is supported by the provincial government as a way to increase tourist visitation to the island.

But what of the traditional culture itself? Is there an effect on the actual cultural performances? Some argue that the increase in open-air festivals and concerts is a positive development, for they provide many younger musicians and entertainers an outlet, or a forum for their music to meet a wider audience. It has been shown that the television documentary, *Vanishing Cape Breton Fiddler*, nurtured and promoted the playing of violins by young players in Cape Breton Island (1971). In a sense, the show caused younger musicians to re-examine the fiddle and to begin to look at the roots of this tradition. Young musicians were able to contact older musicians at concerts, public events and open-air festivals, learning some of the older fiddle styles. But the image of a young fiddler learning at the knee of the master is not entirely accurate, for a recent study found that many of the younger musicians have learned their style from recordings which began to be produced largely by outside American companies such as Decca and Rounder records, beginning in the 1930s and extending to the 40s and 50s (Garrison 1985; MacKinnon 1989).

Festivals are not the only way in which the visitor is presented an image of Cape Breton culture. Our museums also offer a very selective presentation of the region. Like many districts of North America, the Maritimes has its fair share of historic houses devoted mainly to wealthy, famous, aggressive men, the captains of politics and industry during the 18th and 19th centuries. In these houses, furniture, art and collectible antiques become icons, preserved and conserved to educate the public about the lives of the rich and famous, the statesmen and captains of industrial capitalism. For example, the Ranna Cossitt house in Sydney is a symmetrical Georgian style house dating from the first period of the city's development in the 1780s (figure 9.5). Minister Cosset was an influential citizen of late 18th century, the first Anglican minister to live and work in Sydney and a member of Cape Breton's Executive Council. He arrived in Sydney on June 2, 1786, and built his house and parsonage in 1787; it is purported to be one of the oldest houses in the city. Its age and connection to an important citizen was one of the motivations for restoring and converting the former residence into a museum. In contrast, in Sydney there is no historic house museum devoted to the black workers from the Caribbean who came to work in the steel plant at the turn of the 20th century, bringing their various cultural traditions with them. At the Fortress of Louisbourg, a world-class tourist destination, little attention was paid until very recently to interpreting black culture, even though research indicated that most families in 18th-century Louisbourg had slaves as part of their households (Donovan 1995; Weeks 2007: 7-9).

Our open-air, folk museums offer a more democratic view of history than do the historic homes, focusing on the lives of ordinary citizens, their work habits and local folkways. Demonstrations of the older folkways such as spinning, weaving, hooked rug making, ploughing fields and gathering the harvest are the public displays of these kinds of institutions. The Nova Scotia Highland Village in Iona is an open-air museum devoted to the Scottish Gaelic culture of Nova Scotia (figure 9.6). The idea for the establishment of this museum can be traced to as early as 1938, the year of the British Empire Exhibition in Glasgow Scotland. A Scottish *clachan* or village was reconstructed as one of the exhibits that year and the premier of Nova Scotia, Angus L. MacDonald, happened to see this reconstruction. Upon returning, he and his companions began to examine the possibility

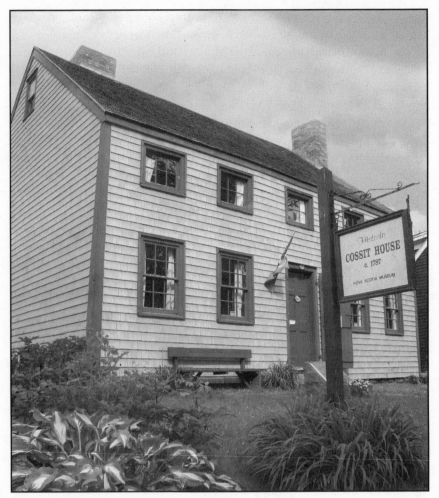

Figure 9.5 Ranna Cossett house, Sydney. Photo by Carol Kennedy.

of reconstructing a Scottish village on Nova Scotia soil but were interrupted by the start of the Second World War.

    Following the war and a failed attempt to begin the museum by the
Association of Scottish Societies in Nova Scotia, the local community of
Iona and its Board of Trade became involved, and museum construction
commenced in 1962. Today, the Highland Village is a living history museum and cultural centre that celebrates the Gaelic experience in Nova
Scotia. The museum contains buildings ranging from a blacksmith's forge,
houses from different historical periods, a store, church, barns, a replica
of a Hebridean stone house, or *taigh dubh* (black house) in Gaelic. Most
buildings were taken from other communities, disassembled and moved to

Figure 9.6 MacDonald House, Nova Scotia Highland Village. Photo by Richard MacKinnon.

the site. Two of the museum's buildings, a late-19th-century house and a church, were moved from their original locations to the museum on barges through the St. Peter's Canal and along Bras d'Or Lake to Iona (figure 9.7). These buildings were moved more than fifty miles. What is interesting here is that the museum took on this entire task not only to provide the folk museum with needed buildings, but as an experiment. There is a historical tradition of "movings" as they are called in the Maritime region: houses, barns, churches and outbuildings were and still are regularly moved short and long distances in the landscape. The museum wanted this building for its site, but also wanted to see how a moving was carried out, in an at-

Figure 9.7 House moving, Nova Scotia Highland Village. Photo by Richard MacKinnon.

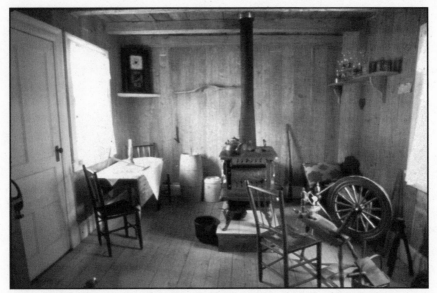

Figure 9.8 1890s house, Nova Scotia Highland Village. Photo by Richard MacKinnon.

tempt to understand how and why these kinds of activities occurred in the past (MacKinnon 1995). Other activities occurring at the museum include Gaelic language classes for museum workers, a Gaelic preschool for local children and a genealogy computer system for visitors interested in tracing their roots.

While this museum tries to offer a more accurate reflection of the life of Scottish settlers in Nova Scotia than do some of the other public images previously mentioned, there are also some minor problems. First, Gaelic settlers in the 19th century seldom settled in a village. Rather farms of Scottish settlers were often miles apart, strung along river valleys, the Atlantic Ocean, situated on upland plateaus, or nestled at the base of mountains. In fact, the land upon which this museum was situated originally comprised only one farm of a Scottish settler. While the buildings and artifacts within are indeed reflective of Cape Breton's material traditions, and the buildings themselves offer the visitor a cross section of the kinds of architecture once common at various times in the region, the geographic layout is stereotypical (figure 9.8). It offers a clearer view of the attitude and aesthetics of the original cultural interveners—from the provincial premier of the time to the original board of directors—than an accurate reflection of Scottish settlement pattern found on the Island.

While I have focused in this chapter on images of Scottish culture, other ethnic groups in the Maritimes have similar difficulties with the public presentation of their folkways. In Cape Breton, the Mi'kmaq have no open-air or folk museum devoted to their folkways. In fact, there is almost a complete avoidance of their presence in many museums and in much of our tourist literature, even though there are numerous settlements on the Island and throughout the Maritime region. This in itself is a powerful political statement being made by even contemporary cultural interveners, the historical societies who decide on what aspects of our past to glorify and display and the agencies of government who decide what museums are most appropriate to fund. If Mi'kmaq people are included in tourism literature, their prowess as basketmakers or craftsmen is usually how they are presented. Little is told of their complex storytelling and singing traditions, community funeral customs and traditional beliefs, their hunting, trapping and work practices, and their attitudes toward nature and conservation.

As an example of a private tradition seldom discussed in the tourist literature I will spend a few moments describing one very old but still popularly practised calendar custom in Mi'kmaq society. On or about July 26 every year, the Mi'kmaq have a devotion to St. Anne on Chapel Island, Cape Breton, calling it the "mission to St. Anne." It is an annual sacred occasion, a pilgrimage, when friends and relatives gather from all over the Maritimes and even the eastern United States. The site itself is sacred to Mi'kmaw culture, a gathering place for Mi'kmaq and their Grand Council long before Mi'kmaq were converted to Christianity in the early years of the 17th century. Originally this occasion was the time for sanctioned courting customs, marriages, settling of disputes and baptisms, and it lasted for four or five days. Today it lasts three days and combines a religious procession and church services with political speeches, visiting friends and other leisure activities. There have been many changes and alterations within this tradition over the years, and numerous interveners in the tradition from clergy to anthropologists and even a few tourists. Nevertheless, the tradition is still meaningful to Mi'kmaq; it is not primarily a touristic performance, but rather, an occasion for young and old to connect with their past and present, to worship and to entertain themselves.

Conclusion

Most of the formal institutions in Western society place a higher value on the written word than oral culture and tradition. From my viewpoint, this is problematic; I believe we should be asking, "What are the conditions that promote the continued development of oral traditions?" For example, I believe that government funding should assist the involvement of our museums and other cultural institutions in oral history, life history and folklore collection projects in the communities they serve. The funded organizations could do this by working with the many cultural groups who are interested in passing on the knowledge of their traditions to another generation and providing a means to share their customs and traditions with the wider community, as well as facilitating access to methods of collection and documentation. Language programming, increased research and more publications are required. Some of this occurs—a good example can be found at the aforementioned Nova Scotia Highland Village where the museum sponsors research projects and is actively engaged in attempts to preserve and revive the Gaelic language. More could be done, indeed, more needs to be done, to emphasize the importance of oral culture in our society.

One of the big problems with all this is how to reconcile the private reality with the public image. It is also a question of ethics. If the interveners, whomever they may be—governments, festival organizers, historical societies, tourism leaders, or museum directors—become more aware of their own influences, biases and impact on local traditional cultures, then perhaps more sensitive public portrayals of culture will prevail. If the shapers of our public images do not want to become aware of important local or private aspects of culture and instead are intentionally or unintentionally manipulating images for profit or gain, there is indeed a grave danger that the images will outlive and eventually usurp the reality. As one commentator from Scotland observed:

> There is so much of this stuff.... It has been distributed so widely for so many generations that descendants of Highlanders in other countries hang their Scottish Highland identity on the peg it provides. Not only descendants of Highland exiles are affected. Gradually the material and the perception of us it represents filters its way back and is absorbed into our lives, eventually being proudly possessed by us, traditionalized, believed. (MacLean and Carrell 1986: 91)

I hope that Cape Bretoners will begin to understand these public images and that tourists and visitors will demand more accurate realities when wanting to experience aspects of a local culture. More culturally sensitive tourism strategies are needed, along with more complex analyses of Maritime culture. The tourism department logo asks a visitor to "Put Yourself in the Picture" but the tourist and local alike, I hope, will begin to ask "what kind of picture are you offering?" and "how accurate is this picture?" before deciding whether or not to become a part of the Maritime masterpiece.

References

Acheson, T. W. 1985. The National Policy and the Industrialization of the Maritimes, 1880-1910. In *The Acadiensis Reader, Volume Two: Atlantic Canada After Confederation*, edited by P. A. Buckner and David Frank, 171-201. Fredericton: Acadiensis Press.

Addy, Sidney Oldall. 1898. *The Evolution of the English House*. London: Swan Sonenschein.

Allen, N. G. 1979. Walling Materials in the Eighteenth Century Highlands. *Vernacular Building, Scottish Vernacular Buildings Working Group Newsletter* 5:1-7.

American Folklore Society. 1984. *Folklore/Folklife*. Washington, DC: American Folklore Society.

Arnold, Mary. N.d. *The Story of Tompkinsville*. Unpublished paper. Beaton Institute, Cape Breton University.

———. 1940. The Story of Tompkinsville. New York: The Co-operative League.

———. 1958. *Father Jimmy of Nova Scotia*. Chicago: Co-operative League of the USA.

Arnold, Mary (writer) and James MacPherson (producer). 1943. *The Turn of the Tide*. Film. Continuity.

Arnold, Mary and Mabel Reed. 1957. *In the Land of the Grasshopper Song*. New York: Vantage Press.

Atkinson, Herbert. 1938. *Cockfighting and Game Fowl from the Notebooks of Herbert Atkinson of Ewelme together with the Life and Letters of John Harris, the Cornish Cocker*. Bath: George Bagntun.

Augustine, Stephen J. 1997. The Mi'Kmaq Creation Story: Lessons to Learn. Paper presented at Mi'kmawey 97, An Intertribal-International Conference, 10-12 October. Sydney, NS.

Bascom, William R. 1955. Verbal Art. *Journal of American Folklore* 68 (269): 245-52.

Beaton, Elizabeth, Tamara Lynch and Stephan Steinhouse (producers). 1992. *Making Steel*. Film. Beaton Institute, University College of Cape Breton and The National Film Board of Canada.

Beaton, Joseph. 1980. *Mabou Music*. Antigonish: Casket Printing.

Bégin, Carmelle. 2003. Opus: The Making of Musical Instruments in Canada. *Civilization.ca*. Online exhibition. http://www.civilization.ca/cmc/exhibitions/arts/opus/opuse.shtml. Accessed 7 November 2007.

Bennett, Margaret. 1989. *The Last Stronghold: Scottish Gaelic Traditions in Newfoundland*. Canada's Atlantic Folklore and Folklife Series 13. St. John's, NL: Breakwater Books.

Bitterman, Rusty. 1990. Economic Stratification and Agrarian Settlement: Middle River in the Early Nineteenth Century. In *The Island: New Perspectives on Cape Breton History 1713-1990*, edited by Kenneth Donovan, 71-87. Fredericton, NB, and Sydney, NS: Acadiensis Press and University College of Cape Breton Press.

Black, Joe. N.d. Hunkey Town: The Immigrant Family and Its Company Home. Unpublished paper. Beaton Institute, Cape Breton University

Blaine, Delabore P. 1852. *An Encyclopedia of Rural Sports*. London: Longman, Brown, Green.

Blake, Nick. 1984. Blood and Feathers on Sunday. *The Globe and Mail*, 13 October.

Boulton, Laura. 1947. *Gaels of Cape Breton*. Film. National Film Board of Canada.

———. 1969. *The Music Hunter*. Garden City, NY: Doubleday.

Boyle, George. 1953. *Father Tompkins of Nova Scotia*. New York: P. T. Kennedy and Sons.

Brand, John. 1888. *Observations on the Popular Antiquities of Great Britain*. London: George Bell and Sons.

Bruce, Harry. 1974. The Politics of Cape Breton Cockfighting. *Maclean's*, July.

Bryant Clifton D. and William C. Capel. 1974. Profiles of the American Cocker. *Grit and Steel* 65(6): 27-28.

Buchan, David. 1981. MUN's Folklore Department: the Newfoundland Dimension. *Bulletin of the Folklore Studies Association of Canada* 5(3-4): 25-29.

Bureau of Labor Statistics. 2001. Occupational Classification System Manual *United States Department of Labor*. http://www.bls.gov/ncs/ocs/ocsm/comH889.htm. Accessed 23 July 2009.

Cameron, Silver Donald. 1991. *Wind, Whales and Whiskey: A Cape Breton Voyage*. Toronto: Macmillan.

Campbell, John L. 1990. *Songs Remembered in Exile*. Aberdeen: Aberdeen University Press.

Campbell, John L. and Francis Collinson. 1969. *Hebridean Folksongs* vol. 1. Oxford: Clarendon Press.

———. 1977. *Hebridean Folksongs* vol. 2. Oxford: Clarendon Press.

Campbell, John L. and Margaret F. Shaw. 1962. Letters to the Editor: Canadian Folksong Collections. *Journal of the International Folk Music Council* 14:174.

Cape Breton Post. 1974a. Law Against Rooster Fighting Should be Amended. 16 February.

———. 1974b. 39 persons fined total of $1150.00 in City Court. 21 February.

Cape Breton's Magazine. 1988. Searching for the Pioneer Log House. 48(June): 69-74.

Carmichael, Hector. 1974. Hector Carmichael: A Maker of Songs. *Cape Breton's Magazine* 7(March): 15-17.

Carter, Tom. 1991. Traditional Design in an Industrial Age: Vernacular Domestic Architecture in Victorian Utah. *Journal of American Folklore* 104(414): 419-42.

Celtic Colours International Festival. 2006. Welcome to Celtic Colours International Festival. *Celtic Colours*. http://www.celtic-colours.com. Accessed 16 July 2006.

Chiasson, Father Anselme. 1986. *History and Acadian Traditions of Cheticamp*. St. John's, NL: Breakwater Books.

Coady, Moses. 1939. *Masters of their Own Destiny*. New York: Harper and Brothers Publishers.

Cockfighter. 1975. Interviewed by Richard MacKinnon.

Colls, Robert. 1977. *The Collier's Rant: Songs and Culture in the Industrial Village*. London: Croom Helm.

Cowell, Sidney Robertson (producer). 1955a. *Songs from Cape Breton Island*. LP recording. Folkways.

Cranford, Paul Stewart. 1988. *Jerry Holland's Collection of Fiddle Tunes*. Englishtown, NS: Cranford Publications.

———. 1994. *Brenda Stubbert's Collection of Fiddle Tunes*. Englishtown, NS: Cranford Publications.

———. 1997. *Winston Fitzgerald: A Collection of Fiddle Tunes*. Englishtown, NS: Cranford Publications.

Crawley, Ron. 1990. Class Conflict and the Establishment of the Sydney Steel Industry, 1899-1904. In *The Island*, edited by Ken Donovan, 145-64. Sydney, NS: Cape Breton University Press.

Creighton, Helen. 1962. *Maritime Folksongs*. Toronto: Ryerson Press.

———. 1975. *A Life in Folklore*. Toronto: McGraw-Hill Press.

Creighton, Helen and Calum MacLeod. 1964. *Gaelic Songs in Nova Scotia*. National Museum of Canada, Bulletin No. 198. Anthropological Series, No. 66. Ottawa: Department of the Secretary of State.

Crépeau, Andrée and David Christianson. 1995. Home and Hearth: An Archaeological Perspective on Acadian Domestic Architecture. *Canadian Folklore canadien* 17(2): 93-109.

Criminal Code and Selected Statutes. 1973. Ottawa: Information Canada.

Davey, William and Richard MacKinnon. 1988. Personal Nicknames in Cape Breton. Paper presented at the Canadian Society for the Study of Names, Windsor, ON, 2 June.

———. 1996. The Use of Nicknames in Cape Breton. In *The Centre of the World at the Edge of a Continent: Cultural Studies of Cape Breton*, edited by Carol Corbin and Judith A. Rolls, 197-220. Sydney, NS: University College of Cape Breton Press.

———. 2001. Nicknaming Patterns and Traditions among Cape Breton Coal Miners. *Acadiensis* 30(2): 71-83.

Davies, Gwendolyn. 1987. The Song Fishermen: A Regional Poetry Celebration. In *People and Place: Studies of Small Town Life in the Maritimes*, edited by Larry McCann, 137-50. Fredericton: Acadiensis Press.

Deetz, James. 1977. *In Small Things Forgotten: The Archaeology of Early American Life*. Garden City, NY: Doubleday.

Del Sento, Steven L. 1975. Roles, Rules and Organization: A Descriptive Account of Cockfighting in Rural Louisiana. *Southern Folklore Quarterly* 39(1): 1-14.

Denisoff, R. Serge. 1966. Songs of Persuasion: A Sociological Analysis of Urban Propaganda Songs. *Journal of American Folklore* 79(314): 581-89.

———. 1969. Folk Music and the American Left: A Generational-Ideological Comparison. *British Journal of Sociology* 20(4): 427-42.

Dennis, Clara. 1940. *Cape Breton Over*. Toronto: Ryerson Press.

Doherty, Elizabeth A. 1996. *The Paradox of the Periphery: Evolution of the Cape Breton Fiddle Tradition*, 1928-1995. PhD diss., University of Limerick.

Donovan, Kenneth, ed. 1990. *The Island: New Perspectives on Cape Breton History, 1713-1990*. Fredericton, NB, and Sydney, NS: Acadiensis Press and University College of Cape Breton Press.

Donovan, Kenneth. 1995. Slaves and Their Owners in Ile Royale, 1713-1760. *Acadiensis* 25:3-32.

Dorian, Nancy. 1970. A Substitute Name System in the Scottish Highlands. *American Anthropologist* 72:303-19.

Dorson, Richard, ed. 1982. *Folklore and Folklife: An Introduction*. Chicago, IL: University of Chicago Press.

Duncan, Sir Andrew Rae. 1926. *Report of Provincial Royal Commission on Coal Mining Industry in Nova Scotia*. Halifax, NS: Government of Nova Scotia.

Dundes, Alan, ed. 1965. *The Study of Folklore*. Englewood Cliffs, New Jersey: Prentice-Hall.

Dunlay, Kate and David Greenberg. 1996. *Traditional Celtic Violin Music of Cape Breton*. Toronto: Dungreen Music.

Dunn, Charles W. 1953. *Highland Settler: A Portrait of the Scottish Gael in Nova Scotia*. Toronto: University of Toronto Press.

Eaton's Fall & Winter Catalogue. 1915-1916. Toronto: T. Eaton and Co.

Eaton's Spring & Summer Catalogue. 1910. Toronto: T. Eaton and Co.

Ennals, Peter. 1982. The Yankee Origins of Bluenose Vernacular Architecture. *American Review of Canadian Studies* 12(2): 5-21.

————. 1983. The Folk Legacy in Acadian Domestic Architecture: A Study in Mislaid Self-Images. In *Dimensions of Canadian Architecture: Society for the Study of Architecture in Canada: Selected Papers*, edited by Shane O'Dea and Gerald L. Pocius, 8-12. Ottawa: Society for the Study of Architecture in Canada.

————. 1992. Acadians in Maritime Canada. In *To Build in a New Land: Ethnic Landscapes in North America*, edited by Allen G. Noble, 8-12. Baltimore, MD: Johns Hopkins University Press.

Ennals, Peter and Deryck Holdsworth. 1981. Vernacular Architecture and the Cultural Landscape of the Maritime Provinces: A Reconnaissance. *Acadiensis* 10:86-106.

Erixon, Sigurd. 1938. West European Connections and Culture Relations. *Folkliv* 2:137-72.

Fenton, Alexander. 1968. Alternating Stone and Turf: An Obsolete Building Practice. *Folk Life* 6:94-103.

Fenton, Alexander and Bruce Walker. 1981. *The Rural Architecture of Scotland*. Edinburgh: John Donald.

Finterbusch, C. A. 1929. *Cockfighting All Over the World*. Graffney, SC: Grit and Steel.

Fitz-Barnard, Captain L. 1921. *Fighting Sports*. London: Odham's Press.

Foner, Philip S. 1975. *American Labour Songs of the Nineteenth Century*. Urbana, IL: University of Illinois Press.

Forbes, Ernest R. 1993. The 1930s: Depression and Retrenchment. In *The Atlantic Provinces in Confederation*, edited by Ernest R. Forbes and Del A. Muise, 272-305. Toronto: University of Toronto Press.

Forbes, Ernest R. and Del A. Muise, eds. 1993. *The Atlantic Provinces in Confederation*. Toronto: University of Toronto Press.

Fowke, Edith. 1969. Labour and Industrial Protest Songs in Canada. *Journal of American Folklore* 82(323): 34-50.

Fox, Sir Cyril. 1942. Some South Pembrokeshire Cottages. *Antiquity* 16:307-19.

Fox, Sir Cyril and Lord Raglan. 1951-1954. *Monmouthshire Houses: A Study of Building Techniques and Smaller House Plans in the 15th to 17th Centuries*. 3 vols. Cardiff: National Museum of Wales.

Frank, David. 1971. Coal Masters and Coal Miners: Strikes and Roots of Class Conflict in the Cape Breton Coal Industry. MA thesis, Dalhousie University.

————. 1983. The Miner's Financier: Women in the Cape Breton Coal Towns, 1917. *Atlantis* 8(2): 137-43.

————. 1985. Tradition and Culture in the Cape Breton Mining Community in the Early Twentieth Century. In *The Island*, edited by Ken Donovan, 203-18. Sydney, NS: Cape Breton University Press.

————. 1986. The Industrial Folksong in Cape Breton. *Canadian Folklore Canadien* 8(1-2): 21-42.

————. 1988. A Note on Cape Breton Nicknames. *Journal of the Association of the Atlantic Provinces Linguistics Association* 10:54-63.

————. 1993. Class and Region, Resistance and Accommodation. In *The Atlantic Provinces in Confederation*, edited by Ernest R. Forbes and Del A. Muise, 233-71. Toronto: University of Toronto Press.

————. 1999. *J. B. McLachlan: A Biography*. Toronto: James Lorimer.

Frank, David and Don MacGillivray. 1976. Introduction to *Echoes from Labour's War: Industrial Cape Breton in the 1920s*, by Dawn Fraser, 1-16. Toronto: New Hogtown Press.

Fraser, Dawn. N.d. *Great War Story: The Crime of Johnny Kyle and Other Stuff*. Glace Bay, NS: Eastern Publishing.

————. 1924. *Songs of Siberia and Rhymes of the Road*. Glace Bay, NS: Eastern Publishing.

————. 1926. *Echoes From Labour's War*. N.p.

————. 1944. Narrative Verse and Comments including Songs of Siberia, Echoes from Labour's War, Fraser's Filosophies all the Old Stuff and a lot of new ones. Glace Bay NS: Eastern Publishing.

Fraser, Simon, ed. 1982. *The Airs and Melodies Peculiar to the Highlands of Scotland and the Isles*. Sydney, NS: Paul S. Cranford.

Frazer, Alexander. 1903. The Gaelic Folksongs of Canada. A paper at the Royal Society of Canada. Montreal, 20 May. Toronto: Hope.

Gailey, Alan. 1966. Kitchen Furniture. *Ulster Folklife* 12:18-34.

————. 1984. *Rural Houses of the North of Ireland*. Edinburgh: John Donald.

Garrison, Virginia Hope. 1985. Traditional and Non-Traditional Teaching and Learning Practices in Folk Music: An Ethnographic Field Study of Cape Breton Fiddling. PhD diss., University of Wisconsin-Madison.

Geertz, Clifford, ed. 1974. Deep Play: Notes on the Balinese Cockfight. In *Myth, Symbol and Culture*, 1-37. New York: Norton and Company.

General Mining Association. N.d. Account books, daybooks and ledgers. Beaton Institute, Cape Breton University.

Gibson, John G. 1998. *Traditional Gaelic Bagpiping, 1745-1945*. Montreal and Kingston: McGill-Queen's University Press.

Gillis, James D. N.d.a *A Maritime Life: A Romance, The Life of Kalby MacKee*. North Sydney, NS: Herald Print.

————. N.d.b. *The Pie Social: A Modern Romance*. North Sydney, NS: The Herald Print.

————. 1915a. *A Little Sketch of My Life*. Halifax, NS: T.C. Allen.

————. 1915b. *The Greatest Election*. Halifax, NS: T.C. Allen.

————. 1925. *Modern English: Leave the Old to the Old*. Halifax, NS: T.C. Allen.

————. 1926. *The Cape Breton Giant: A Truthful Memoir*. Halifax, NS: T.C. Allen.

————. 1936. *My Palestine Pilgrimage*. North Sydney, NS: Herald Print.

Glassie, Henry. 1968. *Pattern in the Material Folk Culture of the Eastern United States*. University of Pennsylvania Monographs in Folklore and Folklife 1. Philadelphia: University of Pennsylvania Press.

————. 1975. *Folk Housing in Middle Virginia: A Structural Analysis of Historic Artifacts*. Knoxville, TN: University of Tennessee Press.

————. 1977. Meaningful Things and Appropriate Myths: The Artifact's Place in American Studies. In *Prospects: An Annual of American Studies*, edited by Jack Salzman, 111-30. New York: Burt Franklin.

Goffman, Erving. 1959. *The Presentation of Self in Everyday Life*. Garden City, NY: Doubleday Anchor Books.

Gow, Niel. 1780. *The Beauties of Niel Gow*. Edinburgh: Robert Purdie.

Gow, Niel and Sons. 1799. *Part First of the Complete Repository of Original Scots Tunes; Slow Strathspeys and Dances*. Edinburgh: Robert Purdie.

————. 1802. *Part Second of the Complete Repository of Original Scots Tunes; Strathspeys, Jigs and Dances*. Edinburgh: Robert Purdie.

————. 1806. *Part Third of the Complete Repository of Original Scots Tunes; Strathspeys, Jigs and Dances*. Edinburgh: Robert Purdie.

————. 1817. *Part Fourth of the Complete Repository of Original Scots Tunes; Strathspeys, Jigs and Dances*. Edinburgh: Niel Gow and Sons.

Gowans, Alan. 1962. New England Architecture in Nova Scotia. *Detroit Institute of Arts, Art Quarterly* 25:6-33.

Graham, Glenn. 2006. *The Cape Breton Fiddle: Making and Maintaining Tradition.* Sydney, NS: Cape Breton University Press.

Green, Archie. 1972. *Only a Miner: Studies in Recorded Coal-Mining Songs.* Urbana, IL: University of Illinois Press.

Greenhill, Pauline. 1989. *True Poetry: Traditional and Popular Verse in Ontario.* Montreal and Kingston: McGill-Queen's University Press.

———. 2003. Radical? Feminist? Nationalist? The Canadian Paradox of Edith Fowke. *The Folklore Historian* 20:22-33.

Greenway, John. 1970. *American Folksongs of Protest.* New York: Octagon Books.

Guildford, Mary. 2007. Personal correspondence. Nova Scotia Museum, 6 September.

Haliburton, Robert G. 1958. Appendix H: Inverness County, 1861. In *Uniacke's Sketches of Cape Breton*, edited by C. Bruce Fergusson. Halifax, NS: Public Archives of Nova Scotia.

Halifax Chronicle Herald. 1974. Cockfighters draw minimal fines due to precedent, 21 February.

Hall, Frederick A. 1987. Musical Yankees and Tories in Maritime Settlements of Eighteenth-Century Canada. *American Music* 5(4): 391-402.

Hamilton, Diane (producer). 1955. *Nova Scotia Folk Music from Cape Breton.* LP recording. Elektra.

Hamlin, Talbot. 1964. *Greek Revival Architecture in America.* New York: Dover.

Harris, Jim. 1987. The Rules of Cockfighting. In *Hoein 'in the Short Rows*, edited by Francis Edward Abernathy, 100-111. Dallas: Southern Methodist University Press.

Harrison, Barry and Barbara Hutton. 1984. *Vernacular Houses in North Yorkshire and Cleveland.* Edinburgh: John Donald.

Hart, John F. 1962. *History of Northeast Margaree.* Margaree Centre, NS: Privately published.

Hayden, Dolores. 1981. *The Grand Domestic Revolution: A History of Feminist Designs for American Homes.* Cambridge: MIT Press.

Hazlitt, William. 1852. *Men and Manners: Sketches and Essays.* London: Office of the Illustrated London Library.

Heath, Kingston William. 1988. Defining the Nature of Vernacular. *Material Culture* 20(2): 1-8.

Heritage Trust of Nova Scotia. 1967. *Founded Upon a Rock: Historic Buildings of Halifax and Vicinity Standing in 1967.* Halifax, NS: Heritage Trust of Nova Scotia.

———. 1972. *Seasoned Timbers: A Sampling of Historic Buildings Unique to Western Nova Scotia.* Halifax, NS: Heritage Trust of Nova Scotia.

Herman, Bernard L. 1987. *Architecture and Rural Life in Central Delaware, 1700-1900.* Knoxville, TN: University of Tennessee Press.

Heron, Craig and Steve Penfold. 2005. *The Workers' Festival: A History of Labour Day.* Toronto: University of Toronto Press.

Herzog, Harold A. 1985. Hackfights and Derbies. *Appalachian Journal: A Regional Studies Review* 12:114.

Highland Village Day: 1962-1986. 1986. Pamphlet. Highland Village Society, Iona.

History of Arnold Credit Union. N.d. Working Paper, People's Library. MG 14-184-B. Beaton Institute, Cape Breton University.

Hobsbawm, Eric and Terence Ranger. eds. 1983. *The Invention of Tradition.* Cambridge: Cambridge University Press.

Holdsworth, Deryck. 1984. Housing the Industrial Worker: Early Canadian Examples. Unpublished paper presented at the History of Industrial Housing Conference, Ironbridge, England.

Housing Survey of Reserve Mines. 1945. MG14-184-E.B. Beaton Institute, Cape Breton University.

Hoyle's Improved Edition of the Rules for Playing Fashionable Games. 1830. New York: W. C. Borradaile.

Hubka, Thomas. 1985. *Big House, Little House, Back House, Barn: The Connected Farm Buildings of New England*. Hanover: University Press of New England.

Hutslar, Donald A. 1977. *The Log Architecture of Ohio*. Columbus, OH: Ohio Historical Society.

Jenkins, J. Geraint. 1960. Fieldwork and Documentation in Folk-life Studies. *Journal of the Royal Anthropological Institute of Great Britain and Ireland* 90(2): 259-71.

Jenson, L. B. 1972. *Wood and Stone*. Halifax, NS: Petheric Press.

Jones, Michael Owen. 1985. On Folklorists Studying Organizations: A Reply to Robert S. McCarl. *American Folklore Society Newsletter* 14(2): 54-56, 58.

Jordan, Terry G. 1978. *Texas Log Buildings: A Folk Architecture*. Austin, TX: University of Texas Press.

Jordan, Terry G. and Matti Kaupps. 1989. T*he American Backwoods Frontier: An Ethnic and Ecological Interpretation*. Baltimore and London: The Johns Hopkins University Press.

Kallmann, Helmut, Gilles Potvin and Kenneth Winters, eds. 1981. *Encyclopedia of Music in Canada*. Toronto: University of Toronto Press.

Kidder, Tracy. 1985. *House*. New York: Avon Books.

Kirshenblatt-Gimblett, Barbara. 1992. Mistaken Dichotomies. In *Public Folklore*, edited by Robert Baron and Nicholas R. Spitzer, 29-48. Washington and London: Smithsonian Institution Press.

Kizuk, R. Alexander.1993. Molly Beresford and the Song Fishermen of Halifax: Cultural Production, Canon and Desire in 1920s Canadian Poetry. In *Myth and Milieu: Atlantic Literature and Culture 1918-1939*, edited by Gwendolyn Davies, 175-94. Fredericton, NB: Acadiensis Press.

Kniffen, Fred. 1965. Folk Housing: Key to Diffusion. *Annals of the Association of American Geographers* 55:549-77.

Kniffen, Fred and Henry Glassie. 1986. Building in Wood in the Eastern United States: A Time-Place Perspective. In *Common Places: Readings in Vernacular Architecture*, edited by Dell Upton and John Michael Vlach, 159-81. Athens, GA: University of Georgia Press.

Korson, George. 1960. *Black Rock: Mining Folklore of the Pennsylvania Dutch*. Baltimore, MD: Johns Hopkins Press.

———. 1964. *Minstrels of the Mine Patch*. Hatboro, PA: Folklore Associates.

———. 1965. *Coal Dust on the Fiddle*. Hatboro, PA: Folklore Associates.

Kurin, Richard. 2004. Safeguarding Intangible Cultural Heritage in the 2003 UNESCO Convention: A Critical Appraisal. *Museum International* 56(1-2): 66-77.

Laben, Mary. 1993. Interviewed by Richard MacKinnon, Tompskinsville, Reserve Mines, NS, 7 January.

Lamb, James B. 1992. The Celtic Crusader: *The Story of A. W. R. MacKenzie and the Gaelic College*. Halifax, NS: Lancelot Press.

Latremouille, JoAnn. 1986. *Pride of Home: The Working Class Housing Tradition in Nova Scotia 1749-1949*. Hantsport, NS: Lancelot Press.

Latta, Peter and Diane Tye. 1989. Symbols of Change: The Legacy of Two Early Twentieth-Century Nova Scotian Builders. *Nova Scotia Historical Review* 9(2): 18-34.

Leach, MacEdward. 1957. Celtic Tales from Cape Breton. In *Studies in Folklore*, edited by W. Edson Richmond, 40-54. Bloomington, IN: Indiana University Press.

Leach, Maria, ed. 1972. *Funk and Wagnalls Standard Dictionary of Folklore, Mythology and Legend*. San Francisco: Harper.

Lenin. 1903. Where to Begin. *SocialistWorker.org*. http://www.socialistworker.org/2004-2/500Supp/500Supp_WhereToBegin.shtml. Accessed 22 July 2009.

Lewis, George H. 1985. The Role of Music in Popular Social Movements: A Theory and Case Study of the Island of Hawaii, USA. *International Review of the Aesthetics and Sociology of Music* 16(2): 153-62.

Lloyd, A. L. 1952. *Come All Ye Bold Miners*. London: Lawrence and Wishart.

MacDonald, Alphonse. 1935. *Cape Breton Songster*. Sydney, NS: Privately published.

Macdonald, Angus John. 1984. *The Hebridean Connection: Eachdruidhean agus Sgeulachdan bho Sheanachaidhean Uidhist; Accounts and Stories of the Uist Sennachies*, edited by Donald A. Fergusson. Halifax, NS: Donald A. Fergusson.

MacDonald, Norman. 1988. Putting on the Kilt: The Scottish Stereotype and Ethnic Community Survival in Cape Breton. *Canadian Ethnic Studies* 20(3): 132-46.

MacDonald, Paul. N.d. The Cape Breton Piano Style. *Cranford Publications*. http://www.cranfordpub.com/articles/cape_breton_piano.htm. Accessed 15 September 2007.

MacEachern, Ron. 1978. Collecting on Cape Breton Island. *Canadian Folk Music Society Newsletter* 13(3): 7-10.

———. 1979a. Report from Cape Breton. *Canadian Folk Music Society Bulletin* 14(1): 10-11.

———. 1979b. *Songs and Stories from Deep Cove Cape Breton as Remembered by Amby Thomas*. Sydney, NS: College of Cape Breton Press.

MacEwan, Paul. 1976. *Miners and Steelworkers*. Toronto: Hakkert and Company.

MacGillivray, Allister. 1981. *The Cape Breton Fiddler*. Sydney, NS: City Printers.

———. 1988. *A Cape Breton Ceilidh*. Sydney, NS: Sea Cape Music.

MacGillivray, Don. 1973. Cape Breton in the 1920s: A Community Besieged. In *Essays in Cape Breton History*, edited by Don MacGillivray and Brian Tennyson, 49-67. Windsor, NS: Lancelot Press.

———. 1983. Glace Bay: Images and Impressions. In *Mining Photographs and Other Pictures, 1948–1968. A Selection from the Negative Archives of Shedden Studio, Glace Bay, Cape Breton*, edited by H. D. Bullock and Robert Wilkie, 171-91. Halifax and Sydney, NS: NSCAD University Press and University College of Cape Breton Press.

———. 1991. Work Poetry/Poésie De Travail. The Industrial Verse of Slim McInnis. *Labour/Le Travail* 28:271-84.

MacInnes, Sheldon. 1997. *A Journey in Celtic Music: Cape Breton Style*. Sydney, NS: University College of Cape Breton Press.

MacKeen, John. 1865. Farm ledger. MG 12-109-A. Beaton Institute, Cape Breton University.

———. 1866. Account book. MG 12-109-A. Beaton Institute, Cape Breton University.

MacKinnon, Ian. 1989. Fiddling to Fortune: The Role of Commercial Recordings Made by Cape Breton Fiddlers in the Fiddle Tradition of Cape Breton Island. MA thesis, Memorial University of Newfoundland.

MacKinnon, Richard. 1979. Cape Breton Scottish Folksong Collections. *Culture & Tradition* 4:23-29.

———. 1982. Workers' Housing in Wabana, Bell Island, Newfoundland. *Material History Bulletin* 14:67-72.

———. 1990. Cape Breton Tradition: Public Image and Private Reality. *Forerunner* 3(1): 28-31.

———. 1991. Vernacular Architecture in the Codroy Valley: Local and External Influences on the Development of a Building Tradition. PhD diss., Memorial University of Newfoundland.

———. 1992. Log Architecture on Cape Breton Island: Cultural Borrowing and Adaptation. *Material Culture* 24:1-18.

———. 1995. House Movings and Alterations: Stability and Change in the Codroy Valley Landscape. *Canadian Folklore canadien* 17(2): 31-50.

———. 1996. Tompkinsville, Cape Breton Island: Co-operativism and Vernacular Architecture. *Material History Review* 44:45-63.

———. 1998. Making a House a Home: Company Housing in Cape Breton Island. *Material History Review* 47:46-56.

———. 2000. Humorous Nicknames in Cape Breton. In *Northeast Folklore: Essays in Honour of Edward D. Ives*, edited by Pauleena MacDougall and David Taylor, 353-62. Orono, ME: University of Maine Press and the Maine Folklife Centre.

———. 2002. *Vernacular Architecture in the Codroy Valley*. Ottawa: National Museum of Civilization.

———. 2008. Protest Song and Verse in Cape Breton Island. *Ethnologies* 30(2): 33-72.

MacLaren, George. 1961. *Antique Furniture by Nova Scotian Craftsmen*. Toronto: Ryerson Press.

———. 1972. *The Romance of the Heating Stove*. Halifax, NS: Nova Scotia Museum.

MacLean, Malcolm and Christopher Carrell, eds. 1986. *As an Fhearann (From the Land): Clearance, Conflict and Crofting A Century of Images of the Scottish Highlands*. Edinburgh: Mainstream Publishing.

MacLellan, Lauchie. 2000. *Brigh an òrain A Story in Every Song: The Songs and Tales of Lauchie MacLellan*, edited and translated by John Shaw. Montreal and Kingston: McGill-Queen's University Press.

MacLeod, Alistair. 1976. *The Lost Salt Gift of Blood*. Toronto: McClelland and Stewart.

MacLeod, C. I. N. 1952. *An T-Eilthireach: Original Gaelic Poems and Melodies*. Glace Bay, NS: Brodie Printing Service Ltd.

MacNeil, Joe Neil. 1987. *Tales Until Dawn: The World of a Cape Breton Gaelic Story-Teller*, edited and translated by John Shaw. Montreal and Kingston: McGill-Queen's University Press.

MacPhail, Margaret. 1970. *Loch Bras D' Or*. Windsor, NS: Lancelot Press.

MacPhee, Doug. 1993. Interviewed by Richard MacKinnon, 21 January.

MacQuarrie, Gordon F. 1975. *The Cape Breton Collection of Scottish Melodies for the Violin*. Medford, MA: J. Beaton.

MacTalla. 1894. Eachdraidh Bhartimeuis. 3(1): 1.

Maitland, Leslie. 1984. *Neoclassical Architecture in Canada*. Studies in Archaeology, Architecture and History. Ottawa: National Historic Parks and Site Branches, Parks Canada, Environment Canada.

Manley, John. 1992. Preaching the Red Stuff: J. B. McLachlan, Communism and the Cape Breton Miners, 1922-1935. *Labour/Le Travail* 30:65-114.

Manning, Frank. 1974. Nicknames and Number Plates in the British West Indies. *Journal of American Folklore* 87(344): 123-32.

Mannion, John J. 1974. *Irish Settlements in Eastern Canada: A Study of Cultural Transfer and Adaptation*. University of Toronto Geography Research Publications 12. Toronto, Ontario: Published for the University of Toronto, Department of Geography by the University of Toronto Press.

Mannion, John J., ed. 1977. *The Peopling of Newfoundland: Essays in Historical Geography*. Social and Economic Papers of Memorial University of Newfoundland 8. St. John's, NL: Institute of Social and Economic Research.

Markham, Gervase. 1654. *Country Contentments or, the Husbandman's Recreations*. London: W. Wilson for E. Brewster and George Sawbridge.

Marshall, Howard Wight. 1986. A Good Grid-Iron: The Vernacular Design of a Western Cow Town. In *Perspectives in Vernacular Architecture II*, edited by Camille Wells, 81-88. Columbia, MO: University of Missouri Press.

Marshall, William. 1781. *A Collection of Strathspey Reels with a Bass for the Violoncello or Harpsichord*. Edinburgh: Neil Stewart.

———. 1822. *Marshall's Scottish Airs, Melodies, Strathspeys, Reels, &c. for the Piano Forte, Harp, Violin & Violoncello*. Edinburgh: Alexander Robertson.

Marvan, Garry. 1984. The Cockfight in Andalusia, Spain: Images of the Truly Male. *Anthropological Quarterly* 57:68.

McCaghy, C. H. and A. C. Neal. 1974. The Fraternity of Cockfighters: Ethical Embellishments of an Illegal Sport. *Journal of Popular Culture* 8:557-69.

McCarl, Robert S. Jr. 1978. Occupational Folklife: A Theoretical Hypothesis. *Western Folklore* 37(3): 145-60.

McCawley, Stuart. 1929a. *A Book of Songs and "Come-All-Ye" of Cape Breton and Newfoundland*. Glace Bay, NS: Brodie Printing Service.

———. 1929b. *Cape Breton Humor*. Glace Bay: Brodie Printing Service.

McCormack, Mike. N.d. Reminiscences of Life in the Company Houses on Victoria Road. Unpublished paper. Beaton Institute, Cape Breton University.

McDavid, Sara Jodi. 2002. "We're Dirty Sons of Bitches": Residence Rites of Passage at a Small Maritime University. MA thesis, Memorial University of Newfoundland.

McKay, Ian. 1992. Tartanism Triumphant: The Construction of Scottishness in Nova Scotia, 1933-1954. *Acadiensis* 21(2): 5-48.

McKean, R. N.d. *A Great Man Dies and Lives in the Antigonish Movement Abroad*. Antigonish, NS: Coady Institute.

McNabb, Debra and Lewis Parker. 1986. *Old Sydney Town: Historic Buildings of the North End*. Sydney, NS: Old Sydney Society.

Miller, Donald L. and Richard E. Sharpless. 1985. *The Kingdom of Coal: Work, Enterprise, and Ethnic Communities in the Mine Fields*. Philadelphia, PA: University of Pennsylvania Press.

Mills, David B. 1977. The Development of Folk Architecture in Trinity Bay, Newfoundland. In *The Peopling of Newfoundland: Essays in Historical Geography*, edited by John J. Mannion, 77-101. Social and Economic Papers of Memorial University of Newfoundland 8. St. John's, NL: Institute of Social and Economic Research.

Mitchell, Timothy. 1991. *Blood Sport: A Social History of Spanish Bullfighting*. Philadelphia, PA: University of Pennsylvania Press.

Morrison, Kenneth. 1953. Letter. December 12. Kenneth Morrison Papers, MG 6-65. Beaton Institute, Cape Breton University.

Muise, Del. 1980. The Making of an Industrial Community: Cape Breton Coal Towns, 1867-1900. In *Cape Breton Historical Essays*, edited by Don MacGillivray and Brian Tennyson, 76-94. Sydney, NS: College of Cape Breton Press.

Mulrooney, Margaret M. 1991. A Legacy of Coal: The Coal Company Towns of Southwestern Pennsylvania. In *Perspectives in Vernacular Architecture, IV*, edited by Thomas Carter and Bernard L. Herman, 130-37. Columbia and London: University of Missouri Press for the Vernacular Architecture Forum.

Narváez. Peter. 2005. Tradition and Labour: The Strike Songs of a Newfoundland Company Town. In *Bean Blossom to Bannerman: Odyssey of a Folklorist: A Festschrift for Neil Rosenberg*, edited by Martin Lovelace, Peter Narváez and Diane Tye, 299-342. St. John's, NL: Memorial University of Newfoundland Folklore and Language Publications.

Newfoundland Historic Trust. 1975. *A Gift of Heritage.* St. John's, NL: Newfoundland Historic Trust.

————. 1978. *Ten Historic Towns.* St. John's, NL: Newfoundland Historic Trust.

The 1902 Edition of the Sears Roebuck Catalogue. 1969. New York: Bounty Books.

Noble, Allen G. 1984. *Wood, Brick and Stone: The North American Settlement Landscape.* 2 Vols. Amherst, MA: University of Massachusetts Press.

Noble, R. Ross. 1983-84. Turf-Walled Houses of the Central Highlands: An Experiment in Reconstruction. *Folk Life* 22:68-83.

Nova Scotia Association of Architects. 1976. *Exploring Halifax.* Toronto: Greey De Pencier.

Nova Scotia Provincial Museum. 1934-1935. *Report on the Provincial Museum for 1934-1935.* Halifax, NS: King's Printer.

O'Dea, Shane. 1973. *The Domestic Architecture of Old St. John's.* St. John's, NL: Newfoundland Historical Society.

————. 1980. Architecture and Building History in Atlantic Canada. *Acadiensis* 10:158-63.

————. 1982a. Simplicity and Survival: Vernacular Response in Newfoundland Architecture. *Newfoundland Quarterly* 13:19-31.

————. 1982b. The Development of Cooking and Heating Technology in the Newfoundland House. *Material History Bulletin* 15:11-18.

O'Donnell, John C. 1975. *The Men of the Deeps.* LP recording. Waterloo, ON: Waterloo Music Company.

————. 1992a. *And Now the Fields are Green: A Collection of Coal Mining Songs in Canada.* Sydney, NS: University College of Cape Breton Press.

————. 1992b. "Join the Union or You'll Die": Songs Relating to the Labour Union Movement in Canada's Coal Mining Communities. *Canadian Folklore canadien* 14(2): 113-36.

Oates, Joyce Carol. 1987. *On Boxing.* New York: Dolphin/Doubleday.

Ommer, Rosemary E. 1977. Highland Scots Migration to Southwestern Newfoundland: A Study of Kinship. In *The Peopling of Newfoundland: Essays in Historical Geography,* edited by John J. Mannion, 212-233. Social and Economic Papers of Memorial University of Newfoundland 8. St. John's, NL: Institute of Social and Economic Research.

Partridge, Eric. 1976. Foreword. In *Nicknames: Past and Present,* edited by Vernon Noble. London: Hamilton.

Peate, Iowerth. 1946. *The Welsh House: A Study in Folk Culture.* Liverpool: Brython Press.

Penfold, Steven. 1994. Have You No Manhood in You?: Gender and Class in the Cape Breton Coal Towns, 1920-1926. *Acadiensis* 23(2): 21-44.

Penny, Alan. 1989. *Houses of Nova Scotia.* Halifax, NS: Formac Press.

Pocius, Gerald L. 1982. Architecture on Newfoundland's Southern Shore: Diversity and the Emergence of New World Forms. In *Perspectives in Vernacular Architecture,* ed. Camille Wells, 217-32. Annapolis, MD: Vernacular Architecture Forum.

————. 1987. Raised Roofs and High Hopes: Rebuildings on Newfoundland's Southern Shore. *Material Culture* 19:67-84.

————. 1992. *A Place To Belong: Community Order and Everyday Space in Calvert, Newfoundland.* Montreal and Kingston; Athens, GA: McGill Queen's University Press; University of Georgia Press.

Pridgen, Tim. 1938. *Courage: The Story of Modern Cockfighting.* London: Little Brown and Co.

Public Archives of Nova Scotia. N.d. Co-op Housing Nova Scotia. VF, V, 186, 3.

Rankin, Effie. 2004. *As A' Bhràighe Beyond The Braes: The Gaelic Songs of Allan The Ridge MacDonald 1794-1868.* Sydney, NS: Cape Breton University Press.

RCMP Constable. 1984. Interviewed by Richard MacKinnon and Joan Weeks.

Reed, Alice Gray. 1986. Making a House a Home in a Philadelphia Neighborhood. In *Perspectives in Vernacular Architecture II,* edited by Camille Wells, 192-99. Columbia, MO: University of Missouri Press.

Rempel, John I. 1980. *Building With Wood and Other Aspects of Nineteenth-Century Building in Central Canada.* Toronto: University of Toronto Press.

Resident. 1992. Interviewed by Richard MacKinnon. 21 May.

Reynolds, Charles (director) 1972. *The Vanishing Cape Breton Fiddler.* Film. Canadian Broadcasting Corporation.

Rhos Male Voice Choir. N.d. *BBC Wales.* http://www.bbc.co.uk/wales/music/sites/genres_artists/choirs_brass/rhos_male_voice_choir.shtml. Accessed 23 July 2009.

Roback, Frances. 1984. Advertising Canadian Pianos, 1850-1914. *Material History Bulletin* 20:31-44.

Roberts, Warren E. 1984. *Log Buildings of Southern Indiana.* Bloomington: Trickster Press.

———. 1988. *Viewpoints on Folklife: Looking at the Overlooked.* American Material Culture and Folklife: Masters of Material Culture (series). Ann Arbour: UMI Research Press.

Rosenberg, Neil V. 1986. Big Fish, Small Pond: Country Musicians and their Market. In *Media Sense: the Folklore-Popular Culture Continuum,* edited by Peter Narváez and Martin Laba, 149-66. Bowling Green, KY: Bowling Green State University Press.

Rupert, Arch. 1949. *The Art of Cockfighting: A Handbook for Beginners and Old-timers.* New York: The Devin-Adair Press.

Sangster, Joan. 1989. *Dreams of Equality: Women on the Canadian Left, 1920-1950.* Toronto: McClelland and Stewart.

Scott, G. R. 1957. *The History of Cockfighting.* London: Charles Skilton.

Seal, Graham. 1989. *The Hidden Culture: Folklore in Australian Society.* Melbourne: Oxford University Press.

Shaw, John, ed. 2005. *Gael Stream / Struth nan Gaidheal.* http://gaelstream.stfx.ca/. Accessed 23 July 2009.

Shunpiking. 2006. Standing the Gaff at Stora – An Election Challenge. May.

Sinclair, Colin. 1953. *The Thatched Houses of the Old Highlands.* London: Oliver and Boyd.

Sketchley, W. 1814. *The Cocker Containing Every Information to the Breeders and Amateurs of that Noble Bird, the Game Cock.* London: Burton on Trent.

Skillen, Edward, Jr. 1939. New Houses and New Men: Nova Scotia Miners Raise Themselves Nearer Security Through Co-operation. *Commonwealth* 18:388-90.

Skinner, J. Scott. 1900. *The Scottish Violinist.* Glasgow: Bayley and Ferguson.

———. 1904. *The Harp and the Claymore.* Glasgow: Bayley and Ferguson.

Smith, H. M. Scott. 1989. *The Historic Churches of Prince Edward Island.* Erin, ON: Boston Mills Press.

———. 1990. *The Historic Houses of Prince Edward Island.* Erin, ON: Boston Mills Press.

Smith, Harrison W. 1919. Sarawak: the Land of the White Rajahs. *National Geographic Magazine.* 35(2): 110-67.

Soloman, Nancy. 1985. Folk Housing in a Company Town: The Case of Kitzmiller, Maryland. MA thesis, George Washington University.

Sparling, Heather. 2007. Transmission Processes in Cape Breton Gaelic Song Culture. In *Folk Music, Traditional Music, Ethnomusicology: Canadian Perspectives, Past and Present,* edited by Anna Hoefnagels and Gordon E. Smith, 13-26. Newcastle: Cambridge Scholars Publishing.

St.Clair, James O., and Mary Kay MacLeod. 1992. *No Place Like Home: The Life and Times of Cape Breton Heritage Buildings*. Sydney, NS: University College of Cape Breton Press.

Stanley, Laurie. 1983. *The Well-Watered Garden: The Presbyterian Church in Cape Breton, 1798-1860*. Sydney, NS: University College of Cape Breton Press.

Stewart, Bryce. 1913. Social Survey of Sydney. Paper presented at First Annual Conference of the Canadian Political Science Association, Ottawa, 4-6 September. Beaton Institute, Cape Breton University.

Strutt, Joseph. 1834. *The Sports and Pastimes of the People of England*. London: Thomas Tegg and Son.

Sunderland, Terry. 1980. *Still Standing: Cape Breton Buildings from Days Gone By*. Sydney, NS: College of Cape Breton Press.

Taft, Michael. 1983. *Discovering Saskatchewan Folklore: Three Case Studies*. Edmonton, AB: NeWest Press.

Tennyson, Brian, ed. 1986. *Impressions of Cape Breton*. Sydney, NS: University College of Cape Breton Press.

Thoms, William. 1965. Folklore. In *The Study of Folklore*, edited by Alan Dundes, 4-6. Englewood Cliffs, NJ: Prentice Hall.

Thomson, A. F. 1906. A Nova Scotia Cockfight. *The Canadian Magazine* 27(3): 219-21.

Time. 1974. Nova Scotia Finals. Canadian Edition. 18 February, 7.

Toelken, Barre. 1979. *The Dynamics of Folklore*. Boston: Houghton Mifflin.

Tye, Diane. 1986. The Housing of a Work Force: Workers' Housing in Amherst, Nova Scotia, 1900-1914. *Society for the Study of Architecture in Canada Bulletin* 11:14-16.

UNESCO. 2003. UNESCO International Convention for the Safeguarding of the Intangible Cultural Heritage, Paris, 17 October.

Upton, Dell and John Michael Vlach, eds. 1986. *Common Places: Readings in American Vernacular Architecture*. Athens, GA: University of Georgia Press.

Warbasse, J. P. 1917. *What is Co-operation?* New York: Vanguard Press.

Weeks, Joan and the Glace Bay Universal Negro Improvement Association. 2007. *One God One Aim One Destiny: African Nova Scotians in Cape Breton*. Sydney, NS: Centre for Cape Breton Studies.

Wells, Camille, ed. 1986. *Perspectives in Vernacular Architecture II*. Columbia, MO: University of Missouri Press.

Whisnant, David. 1983. *All That is Native and Fine*. Chapel Hill, NC: University of North Carolina Press.

Williams, Gareth. 1998. *Valleys of Song: Music and Society in Wales, 1840-1914*. Oxford: Clarendon Press.

Williams, Michael Ann. 1991. *Home Place: The Social Use and Meaning of the Folk Dwelling in Southwestern North Carolina*. Athens, GA: University of Georgia Press.

Wilson, Jim. 1990. Cockfighting: An Introduction from conversations with Jim Wilson. *Cape Breton's Magazine* 55(August): 53-65.

Wright, Gwendolyn. 1985. *Moralism and the Model Home: Domestic Architecture and Cultural Conflict in Chicago, 1873-1913*. Chicago, IL: University of Chicago Press.

Wynn, Graeme. 1981. *Timber Colony: A Historical Geography of Early Nineteenth Century New Brunswick*. Toronto: University of Toronto Press.

Young, C., ed. 1982. *Fredericton Heritage Handbook*. Fredericton, NB: Fredericton Heritage Trust.

KEVIN PHILLIPS

BOILING
POINT

□ □ □

Democrats,
Republicans,
and the Decline of
Middle-Class Prosperity

HarperPerennial
A Division of HarperCollins*Publishers*

A hardcover edition of this book was originally published in 1993 by Random House, Inc. It is here reprinted by arrangement with Random House, Inc.

HarperCollins books may be purchased for educational, business, or sales promotional use. For information, please write: Special Markets Department, HarperCollins Publishers, Inc., 10 East 53rd Street, New York, NY 10022.

First HarperPerennial edition published 1994.

Library of Congress Cataloging-in-Publication Data

Phillips, Kevin P.
    Boiling point : Democrats, Republicans, and the decline of middle-class prosperity / Kevin Phillips. — 1st HarperPerennial ed.
      p. cm.
    Originally published: New York : Random House, c1993.
    Includes bibliographical references and index.
    ISBN 0-06-097582-2 (paper)
      1. Middle classes—United States.   2. Middle classes—United States—
Political activity.   3. Cost and standard of living—United States.   4. United States—
Economic policy.   I. Title.
    [HT690.U6P48   1994]
    305.5'5—dc20   93-34373

---

98 97 96 95   RRD(H) 10 9 8 7 6 5 4 3 2

*To Brent, Emily
and Andrew*

Contents

Preface to the HarperPerennial Edition

Now that we are in the mid-1990s, the problems of the middle class are no longer quite what they were in the 1992 presidential election year when I completed the first version of this book.

In important ways, unfortunately, they are *worse*. Middle-class Americans have even more reasons to be worried.

The economy got slightly better in late 1992 and 1993, but with little resemblance to past recoveries from economic downturns. Jobs are not coming back as usual; hopes are not brightening. The presidential candidate who claimed that the Republican incumbent was destroying the middle class and that he would rescue it is now himself in the White House. But the middle class knows it is still in trouble, and the new administration has even added some new problems. Now Republican politicians are charging the new man in the White House—correctly, I think—with breaking his own promises to Middle America. The political part of the equation is less hopeful. Republican-versus-Democratic politics may no longer offer a solution.

Bill Clinton has read this book. The press reported in early February that he had taken it to Camp David on his first weekend in office. Then he was spotted with *Boiling Point* tucked under his arm, and then, in late March, when Dan Rather went to interview him for the program "48 Hours," he had the book in the Oval Office. What is less clear is *why* he read it: to help middle-class Americans roll back the problems the book describes? or to get more sense of the frustration politics that was abroad in the land, and what it might mean if or when he failed to deliver? I am not sure, but I lean toward the cynical interpretation.

Let us jump back two years. For a contest that pivoted on middle-class anger and fear of the economic future—emotions that victor Clinton tapped better than any Democrat since Franklin D. Roosevelt and that Ross Perot rode to a stronger showing than any other third party candidate since Theodore Roosevelt—the presidential election of 1992 produced surprisingly little discussion of what had gone wrong with the economy and what changes the new president would make. As the voters firmed against George Bush and his administration, there was less need for Clinton to explain his purpose in detail, and as the campaign concluded, he was suitably vague in most of his discussions.

Yet the evidence of widespread fears was so pronounced, raising the prospect of a watershed change in national politics, economics, and culture, that it seems worthwhile to spell out, as I shall do in this book, some of what was happening to produce these concerns. Sixty-two percent of Americans voted to replace the president, with some of the most striking shifts coming in suburbia, confirming that the economic damage to middle-class America was real enough. One purpose of this book is simply to describe this damage—to tell middle-class householders and voters just what happened to them over the two decades, what happened to their disposable income, their taxes, their home values, their earnings, their job prospects, their services from government, their assets and net worth, their safety net of pensions, health care, and insurance, and their children's prospects of enjoying the same upward mobility and living standard as they themselves had enjoyed. I believe that it is also important to explain a critical change in national political fashion: how opinion molders and officials who, from the New Deal to the Nixon years, had spoken up for the common people and fought for the "little guy" transformed their outlooks, so that by the 1980s, the country's leaders were embracing or flirting with an elitist philosophy that celebrated investors, entrepreneurs, and the rich while neglecting the interests of a middle class that found itself increasingly threatened. The Democrats successfully raised these charges against George Bush in 1992, but now they are having to answer a new set of charges and criticisms raised against them—to which we shall turn momentarily.

The politics and political volatility of the middle class is an old fascination of mine. Back in late 1967, I finished a book whose analyses would be used in the 1968 Republican campaign. The book was then released in 1969 as *The Emerging Republican Majority*. Coming years would confirm its thesis—that the worn-out New Deal Democratic coalition was breaking up in favor of a new Republican presidential majority based on a new middle-class populism and a new Southern-Western alignment that I called the Sun Belt. One newsmagazine labeled the book "the political bible of the Nixon Era," and its arguments influenced Republican strategy not only in 1972 but right through 1980.

Two decades later, *The Politics of Rich and Poor*, which I began to write in 1987 but published in 1990, crystallized issues that Michael Dukakis touched only hesitantly in the 1988 campaign. However, its message fell on fertile ground in June 1990, and its portrait of the rich as the major beneficaries of the Reagan and Bush eras quickly became a pivot of the 1990 congressional elections and grew from there. In 1992, as the presidential campaign began, *Newsweek* described *The Politics of Rich and Poor* as a "founding document." The *New York Times* noted that Democratic strategists "revere" the book's thesis that the 1990s are marked by a populist reaction to the economic excesses of the 1980s.

Most of the Democratic presidential hopefuls and contenders of 1991–92—from Bill Clinton to Mario Cuomo, Lloyd Bentsen, Dick Gephardt, Tom Harkin, Douglas Wilder, and Jerry Brown—had read *The Politics of Rich and Poor* or drawn on its theses. So had Pat Buchanan on the Republican side; and in December 1991, well before Ross Perot went public, I received an unexpected telephone call from the *Dallas Morning News*. The Texas billionaire was supposedly blue-printing a 1992 presidential campaign based in part on *The Politics of Rich and Poor*. Was I involved, the reporter asked? I was not.

The most famous of cloth-coat Republicans, Richard Nixon, had given me a laudatory comment for the dust jacket of *The Politics of Rich and Poor*, but George Bush and his political advisers chose to ignore the analysis. There is no longer much need to dwell on the Bush administration; even some of its own former participants have been writing books dismissing its domestic policies. Clearly, many of its officials had no interest in the swing voters from the small-town South, blue-collar Peoria, Levittown, or the ends of Northern urban subway lines who had rallied first to Nixon and then later to Reagan—constituencies and shifts I had discussed in *The Emerging Republican Majority*. As Pat Buchanan and Ross Perot insisted in their own blunt language, Skull and Bones and the prep schools and country clubs were once again in charge. When Bush lost an Iowa straw poll in 1987, he suggested that his absent supporters were too busy on the golf course or at air shows or debutante parties to come out and vote. It was a revealing glimpse—and a revealing prophecy—of Bush economic loyalties to come. Nixon's cloth-coat coalition of earlier years was abandoned during the Bush years; in a sense, it was also betrayed.

For many Americans, including significant numbers of Republicans, the sense that ordinary Americans had been abandoned played a significant role in Bush's defeat. Favoritism to the rich and imploding speculative bubbles had been devastating to Republican national coalitions before, in the late nineteenth-century Gilded Age and in the early 1930s, and in 1992 it happened again. Large chunks of the GOP coalition, especially those recruited in the Nixon and Reagan years, abandoned Bush for Perot and even for Clinton. Network exit polls on November 3 showed more than one-quarter of self-identified Republicans voting against their incumbent president.

In 1990, I had written that Bush was vulnerable to losing the support of the Middle American swing constituencies that had backed Nixon and Reagan. I felt this even more strongly in 1991 and 1992 as I worked on this present book and saw the severe damage that the circumstances and policies since 1973 had inflicted on middle-class voters. Small wonder that U.S. politics turned sour in 1990–92 just as it had following previous periods of excessive debt and speculation and subsequent downturns. Herbert Hoover's share of the total presidential vote plummeted eighteen points from 1928 to 1932; Bush's percentage dropped a nearly comparable sixteen points between 1988 and 1992.

In examining this explosion, where it came from and where it's going, *Boiling Point* picks up where *The Politics of Rich and Poor* left off. It explains how and why much of the middle class stagnated economically (or worse) while those at the top did so well, why this was politically disastrous for the GOP, and why remedial policies have now become the key to the 1996 elections. Many of the gruesome details are drawn from the nation's major metropolitan areas: New York, Los Angeles, Chicago, Philadelphia, Boston, Dallas–Fort Worth, the San Francisco Bay area, and south Florida. To read of this quiet devastation is to understand what undercut Bush, fueled Perot's populist insurgency, and gave Bill Clinton his winning appeal to a middle class whose interests had, in fact, been forgotten much as Clinton said they were. Yet this same populist thrust that brought Clinton to the White House also set the new Democratic presidency on a razor's edge.

The introduction to the hardcover version of this book was written immediately after the 1992 election, at which point—presumably like most other Americans—I still judged Bill Clinton by his campaign promises and expressions of strong commitment to middle-class voters. For a Democrat, they were extraordinary. On July 16, he went before the Democratic National Convention and promised to write a new chapter in U.S. political and economic life:

In the name of all the people who do the work, pay the taxes, raise the kids and play by the rules—the hardworking Americans who make up our forgotten middle class—I accept your nomination for the presidency of the United States of America. I am a product of the middle class. And when I am your president you will be forgotten no more.

He had campaigned on the idea of a middle-class tax cut, putting it in his New Hampshire primary television ads. Then in the autumn, he said that he planned to raise the top tax bracket from 31 percent to 36 percent for people making more than $200,000 annually and to put a 10 percent surtax on people making more than $1 million annually. The middle class would not be touched. But then some confusion arose, and on "Meet the Press" on October 25, moderator Tim Russert pressured Clinton campaign chairman Mickey Kantor: "Yesterday, the campaign spokesman for your candidate defined the middle class as $50,000. Bill Clinton had said previously that he wouldn't raise taxes on anyone making less than $200,000—any family. Can we expect that people making between $50,000 and $200,000 are eligible for taxation?" Kantor took the bait: "He is only going to raise taxes marginally on those folks making $200,000 a year or more....There will be no taxes on the middle class."

Clinton should not have taken these commitments so lightly. George Bush had broken tax promises—and he paid the price in an election that undermined the old Republican presidential coalition in pivotal major metropolitan areas from New York to Los Angeles and drove Bush's share of the total vote to just 37.5 percent, two points below Herbert Hoover. So it was surprising that the new president, too, reneged, first on his campaign commitment to give the middle class a tax cut and then on his assurance that taxes would be raised only on the rich, and not on those making less than $200,000 a year. The taxes he proposed in February were much broader in sweep and reached far lower on the income ladder. By the time of Clinton's first hundred days in office in late April, he had the lowest job approval rating of any president since the pre–World War II invention of polling.

Fiscal policy was not the only offense. Voters were displeased by his choice of allowing gays into the military as his first order of post-inaugural business and by nominations like that of Zoë Baird, proposed for U.S. Attorney General even though she had hired an illegal immigrant as a housekeeper and had failed to pay Social Security taxes for her. Besides which, Washington insiders were everywhere, causing even the *New York Times* to editorialize that Clinton's pledge to break the grip of special interests had been "broken from day one."

Never before had middle-class voters turned on a newly elected president so quickly. They sensed a breach of faith, although some of the debate hinges on definitions. Without saying so publicly, Clinton seems to be defining the middle class as the $35,000-to-$50,000-a-year electrician, fast-food store manager, teacher, or junior government employee. This may be a good definition from the standpoint of Democratic politics—recovering these voters is an important key to the party's future—but it is much more debatable in real-world economics. Some experts are now saying that only about 45 to 50 percent of Americans still enjoy a middle-class standard of living. Probably so, and this would mean that the "middle class" is no longer really in the demographic middle. Instead, it may reach from annual incomes in the $40,000 to $45,000 range, depending on where one lives, up to $150,000 to $200,000 in annual earnings in the major metropolitan areas (say, a midlevel corporate manager in the New York suburbs and his high school teacher wife). And that would put the true *lifestyle* middle class (including the upper middle class) in the forty-fifth to ninety-eighth percentiles nationally.

During the 1992 presidential campaign, Bill Clinton seemed to accept the implications of this same definition: that the $100,000-to-$200,000-a-year American families were by no means rich and that an overwhelming majority were part of the middle class. But, in all likelihood, that definition became inconvenient for him once the campaign was over and prosperous suburbia had cast its votes. As president, he wanted their money—the taxes he would take—more than he wanted supportive impressions given to Gallup polltakers. Certainly the income tax increases he proposed and Congress narrowly passed were a clear breach of promise to the upper middle class. The top tax rate of 36 percent, instead of being confined to incomes over $200,000, was imposed on families with incomes over $140,000 and individuals with incomes over $115,000. The 10 percent surtax, supposed to be limited to millionaires, was imposed on those with incomes over $250,000. And the Medicare tax, previously not levied above $135,000 of income, was uncapped so that the self-employed paid an additional 2.9 percent (beyond income tax) on all earned income. And because of the quirks in the federal tax code, as various exemptions and deductions were phased out, accountants calculated that many families in the $250,000 to $400,000 range would be facing marginal federal rates on income of 44 to 46 percent, which could rise to well over 50 percent when state income taxes were added in. Some families in the $175,000 range would find themselves facing 40 to 42 percent marginal federal rates. So-called wealthy retirees with annual incomes over $44,000, for whom 85 percent of their Social Security receipts would now be taxed, also faced wicked marginal rates. It was, as economists acknowledged, the largest increase in marginal tax rates since the 1930s.

While middle-class families in the $50,000 to $85,000 range escaped, they also knew that that had not been the administration's intention. Clinton had proposed a broad-based energy tax, specifically targeted to consumers, but had to abandon it when Congress refused to agree. The tax on Social Security also hit the middle class. And the air in Washington hummed with the president's mention of other taxes in which he was interested: levies on payrolls, on tobacco, on hospitals, and even on broad national consumption through the sort of value-added tax found all over Europe. In short, the Clinton of the 1992 campaign, who claimed to simply seek revenue from the top 1 percent of Americans, principally millionaires, in the name of fairness and recapturing the loot of the 1980s, was not the real Clinton. The real one, the events of 1993 made clear, wanted a lot more revenue from ordinary Americans, not just the richest Americans, in order to pay for the agenda of a more activist government.

Moreover, although the lower-middle and middle-middle class had escaped most of the new taxes imposed in 1993, other aspects of the Clinton agenda gave them pause. America's large corporations, out to maximize their profits, were cutting their workforces left and right—3,000 workers here, 8,000 there. The Clinton administration was doing no more to try to stop them than had the Bush administration, despite Clinton's earlier criticism. Also to the point, Clinton picked up where Bush had left off in supporting the North American Free Trade Agreement, which organized labor feared would not only move U.S. blue-collar jobs to Mexico but increase the leverage by which business could keep workers' real wage levels in the United States on the same downcurve so evident during the 1980s. Not only union leaders were aroused. Ross Perot charged that NAFTA would "destroy the middle class in this country," and his criticism of the Clinton administration was mirrored by the Democratic chairman of the Senate Commerce Committee, Fritz Hollings of South Carolina. "The crowd that came to town on behalf of the middle class is going to destroy the middle class," said Hollings. From the steel mills of Pennsylvania to the farm machinery plants of the Midwest, workers who might cheer Clinton's raising income taxes on upper-middle-class suburbia simultaneously worried that Perot and Hollings might be right about the fate of the former blue-collar middle class.

For middle-class America, the message in Clinton's bold but deceptively financed 1993 health reform program was also mixed. The idea of universal health care coverage and security was widely applauded. But on the other hand, the 75 to 90 percent of middle-class Americans who already had health insurance also shared genuine concerns that for them, the costs of health care were almost certainly going to rise, through higher premiums or taxes, while the crush of more Americans enjoying full access to an inadequate number of family physicians almost certainly would mean a deterioration of quality care for a large number of those hitherto satisfied. Another part of the American Dream would be sagging along with wages, pension prices, home values, and the prospect of children getting a good job after graduation from high school or college.

As if that wasn't enough, still another threat was on the horizon: the possibility that Clinton would break an additional set of pledges and give into deficit-reduction advocates who urged him to cut middle-class entitlements.

No one should doubt that deficit pressures will be powerful over the remaining Clinton years. The major deficit-reduction groups, funded by Wall Street and the business community, share a common policy goal: to push the budget deficit to much lower levels principally by means-testing Social Security and slashing middle-class entitlements at the same time as they quietly pursue a backstage agenda of seeking tax changes favorable to the nation's top investors. However, the history of government debt and deficits in previous great powers suggests that the prospects of long-term debt reduction are slim and that calling on the middle class to sacrifice toward that end is the fiscal and historical equivalent of a con job.

The bad news of 1994, unknowable in 1992, comes in several different parts. The first is that the economy's failure to bounce back strongly from the downturn of 1990–92 probably means a watershed change in which America's economic decline from its postwar peak will involve ongoing middle-class job losses even amid alleged prosperity as well as in recession. Magazine stories and newspaper headlines for 1993, unfortunately, have continued to profile more of what chapters 5, 6, and 7 of this book already lay out: unraveling employee fringe benefits, mounting mortgage defaults in suburbia, corporate white-collar purges, growing ranks of unemployed couples, tripling water bills, and property tax rises for ordinary homeowners forced by the drop in commercial real estate values.

The second piece of bad news is political: the middle class has less and less reason to believe in the promises of presidents and presidential candidates. The Republicans may deliver, upon occasion and on some issues, for the $100,000-to-$200,000-a-year upper middle class. And the Democrats, in turn, may from time to time produce results for the lower middle class. But neither has anything resembling an across-the-board commitment to the $50,000-to-$100,000-a-year families who are at the heart of the middle class—and who now confront an unnerving, discouraging one-two punch from deceptive politicians and tightening economies.

So almost all of the trends and circumstances described two years ago are still present, although a few circumstances have eased. What is harder to see is the prospect for a reversal.

Kevin P. Phillips
Bethesda, Maryland
October 1993

Introduction: The Legitimacy of
Middle-Class Frustration

The rich get the gold mine and the middle class gets the shaft. It's wrong and it's going to ruin the country.

—Democratic presidential nominee Bill Clinton, 1992

I want a revolution where the working class and the middle class take back control of the Republican Party.

—Republican presidential candidate Patrick Buchanan, 1992

The American people can't afford it themselves, so I'm buying the country back for them.

—Independent presidential candidate Ross Perot, 1992

The ruling class has lost touch with the American people. They have lost touch because they swim in a world of privilege, power and wealth.

—Democratic presidential candidate Jerry Brown, 1992

Statements like these defined the 1992 presidential race as a watershed, spurred unexpected millions to go to the polls and made George Bush the first popularly chosen Republican president to be defeated for reelection since 1932. Voters told survey-takers there was "no chance" that things could get better in the United States if Bush was reelected—and he was not. For six weeks in late spring and early summer, Ross Perot, the independent presidential contender, moved ahead of the Democratic and Republican contenders in national polls though he had not yet announced his candidacy. Nobody had seen anything like it before.

Americans had reached their boiling point. In 1964 a mere 29 percent had told polltakers that government was run for the benefit of a few big interests. Following Watergate, that surged to 66 percent, and climbed to 70 percent in 1980 after disenchantment with the Carter presidency. By 1992 the proportion of Americans who felt that government favored the rich and powerful had reached 80 percent. Unprecedented numbers of citizens also believed that "quite a few" of the people running the government were crooked. A mere 24 percent had said so in 1958, 45 percent in 1976 and 49 percent in 1980. No *majority* had said so, though—until 1992, when the percentage soared to 65 percent. Political analyst William Schneider combined these measures of indignation along with three others into what he called a "P.O. Index." The conclusion, Schneider argued, was unmistakable: postwar Americans had never been so angry.

By condemning the Reagan-Bush administrations for favoritism to the rich and neglect of the middle class, Clinton tapped a historic Republican vulnerability and took a strong lead over Bush from July onward. True, many voters still doubted the Arkansas governor's trustworthiness. His last rival for the Democratic nomination, former California governor Jerry Brown, had insisted that Clinton couldn't be believed because he was financed by the same elites he purported to deplore. Many voters, however, felt they had no choice. The Iran-Contra and Iraqgate scandals had called the president's own good faith into question, and no independent candidate had cracked the Democratic-Republican monopoly of the presidency in one hundred thirty-six years. By November 3 many Americans were applauding Perot, and a surprising 19 percent voted for him. But of the candidates demanding change, only one was electable.

When the dust settled, an angry and frustrated middle class, displaying marked populist tendencies, had defeated one president and chosen another, making Clinton the first Democrat since Franklin D. Roosevelt to enter the White House propelled by a major election victory instead of a close race or by succession to the presidency from the vice presidency. Hopeful Democrats saluted a watershed and predicted that a new era was beginning. Yet America's economic and fiscal difficulties were in some ways the worst since the 1930s, which meant that the frustration politics that brought down George Bush would not abate until the challenge was met. Besides, middle-class Americans were just beginning to realize how much they had to be unhappy about. They would hold the new president—and his campaign promises, vague as they were—to account.

Because this book is about the dynamics and, yes, the *legitimacy* of middle-class frustration, I will not revisit—except in scattered pages and footnotes—the account of the concentration of wealth that I set forth in *The Politics of Rich and Poor* three years ago. With each year, fewer doubted that upper-income Americans had hugely profited in the previous decade. The allegations bitterly disputed when *The Politics of Rich and Poor* was published had become almost common wisdom by 1992, even though the trend toward even greater concentration was finally slackening. Clinton himself waved copies of *America: What Went Wrong,* a compilation of newspaper articles detailing how the decade had favored the rich at the expense of the middle class, and brandished a parallel *New York Times* analysis suggesting that the top 1 percent had received over half of the additional income generated in the United States from 1977 to 1989. Voters were not the only ones aroused; even skeptical economists were starting to pay attention. After reading the Federal Reserve Board's own survey research, Fed chairman Alan Greenspan told several meetings in early 1992 what had been obvious to millions of his fellow Americans: that growing weakness in family income distribution might help explain low consumer confidence. Then came spring's Los Angeles riots, reflecting economic as well as racial tensions, which further illustrated the destructive effects of declining economic expectations.

Republicans had been indignant over earlier Congressional Budget Office calculations, derived from federal income tax returns, that the wealthiest 1 percent had received roughly 60 percent of the after-tax income gains realized by all U.S. families from 1977 to 1989. But the Federal Reserve Board's studies provided nonpartisan but similar documentation for the 1983–89 period, which coincided with the Reagan boom years. Between 1962 and 1983 the share of total private net worth held by the top 1 percent had barely budged. From 1983 to 1989, it surged from 31 percent to 37 percent, reaching heights unseen since 1929! Economist Paul Krugman noted "a big unprecedented jump in inequality to Great Gatsby levels," while Harvard economic historian Claudia Goldin found "inequality at its highest since the great leveling of wages and wealth during the New Deal and World War Two."

So much for the rich. The middle class, in the meantime, had stalled. The Fed found that the average pretax family income, adjusted for inflation, did indeed rise from $33,400 in 1983 to $35,700 in 1989, but this was an *average* inflated by huge gains at the top. *Median* family income—a more revealing measurement of the yearly receipts of the family smack in the middle—increased by only 0.4 percent on an inflation-adjusted basis during those six years. In the face of such evidence, defensive commentators began falling back to a new line of ideological trenches: Yes, America's rich *were* amassing a disproportionate share of wealth and income; however, the pattern was worldwide, reflecting a global economic shift that concentrated rewards among those with capital, skills and education, so that government biases were not important.

Whatever the general trends might have been, willful governmental actions—direct and indirect—probably accounted for 30 to 50 percent of this upward shift. It is true that inequality and polarization had begun intensifying in the 1970s, years in which Democratic, Liberal and Labour regimes governed the United States, Canada and Britain, so that Ronald Reagan and Margaret Thatcher were not the initial or sole perpetrators. And during the 1980s, even socialist-run nations, from Scandinavia to New Zealand, produced somewhat similar economic behavior. Nevertheless, the key, which too many observers ignore—and which we shall examine in more depth in Chapter 2—is that economics, politics and ideology run in broadly similar patterns, and that during the 1980s the broad pattern of government and politics in the prosperous Western nations was conservative. The result was to intensify favoritism to the upper brackets.

Most of the global economic effects that emerged in the mid-1970s—inflation, the increasing unpopularity of big government, the growing competitive weakness of old-line industry, anger at labor unions—had aided this political change by strengthening conservative critiques and the opposition parties that promoted them. The victories of Thatcher and Reagan in 1979–80 in the West's two leading financial centers launched what conservatives excitedly called "revolutions"—transformations that were supposed to unleash capitalist energies and market economies on a grand scale. By 1986–87 the Group of Seven leading economic nations had undergone startling political realignments: aggressive free-market conservatism was in style, more so than at any other time since World War I. The ensuing policy changes, ranging from tax reductions to financial deregulation, regulatory permissiveness, strict treatment of labor and glorification of the rich, proved to be an elixir for global stock markets, property values and business opportunities, just as supply-side economists had predicted. The drawback in the United States, however, was that as the 1980s boom crested, rising taxes and other costs were gobbling up much of the nominal income gain of the middle class, while public services and the government safety net were starting to deteriorate. By the end of the decade, these economic effects were producing political unrest.

In addition to the Federal Reserve Board's analysis that middle incomes stagnated from 1983 to 1989, the Joint Economic Committee of Congress pointed out that for the nation's two-parent families, on average, the relatively meager gains of the 1980s came from the paychecks of working wives. Two thirds of the increase came from more hours worked, *not* from higher real wages earned. While there is no clear cause-and-effect, we shall see repeatedly in future chapters that the wider the gates of opportunity opened for the top 1 percent of Americans, the more they seemed to shut for the average household.

Such trends were new in the American experience. So a critical question arises: Did the 1980s represent the first U.S. boom in which the interests of the middle class—not those of subordinate groups like farmers or labor-union members, but America's powerful and idealized middle-class majority—were pushed aside for the interests of the nation's several hundred thousand richest families?

No one, including Ronald Reagan, had intended this. However, the 1983–89 boom itself was far from uniform; all too frequently, one sector's gain was another's loss. As the Dow-Jones industrial average soared between 1980 and 1986, the value of U.S. farmland simultaneously dropped from $712 billion to $392 billion as collapsing commodity prices put more farmers out of business. Corporate chief executives' compensation set new records as workers' real hourly wages declined. Young workers watched their inflation-adjusted wages and net worth fall behind what their fathers had at a similar age. And while financial assets like stocks and bonds were surging, the value of family homes in roughly half of the nation's metropolitan areas shrank during the 1980s on an inflation-adjusted basis. It was not an equal-opportunity decade.

Middle-class householders found themselves sitting down more and more often with a figurative pencil and piece of paper. *Somebody* had profited enormously in the 1980s, with all that whipped cream and meringue in the financial markets, boardrooms and lawyers' offices, and now *somebody* else—a lot of somebodies—would lose their jobs, pay higher taxes on incomes with lower real purchasing power and otherwise foot the bills for the decline that followed (as declines usually do) the debt-and-speculative boom. What made the 1990s hangover even worse, though, was that the United States was losing its postwar global economic advantage so critical to earlier middle-class prosperity and expansion. Voters were worried, and began to ask whom to blame for the unequal gains and losses.

The new conservatism, which shaped the political economies of the major industrial nations, began as a move to limit big government, but by the late 1980s had revealed a less popular aspect: a developing inattentiveness to public-sector functions, economic fairness and jobs. Voters now saw this threatening the interests of the middle class, not just the poor. By 1992, as we shall see, many of these changes had further weakened the economy and helped produce a populist counter-tide among frustrated individuals.

Glorification of the unfettered marketplace soon came to include a permissiveness toward securities markets, real estate speculation and corporate reorganizations that helped bring about a level of specula-tive tremors and financial jitters unseen since the 1930s. But while speculators and corporate raiders took home huge sums, the average American family wound up fearing for the safety of its bank accounts, insurance coverage, home values and pension coverage.

Meanwhile, the postwar middle-class "social contract" broke down. The most successful Americans—baseball players, money managers, entertainers and corporate executives—negotiated huge salaries or compensation packages that increasingly dwarfed what other Ameri-cans received, distantly echoing late-nineteenth-century "survival of the fittest" excesses. By 1990 corporate chief executives, whose 1980 compensation had been 30 to 40 times higher than that of their average worker, were being paid sums 130 to 140 times greater. In this climate, top executives lost compunctions about terminating blue-collar and middle-class jobs in order to make their companies "competitive." They moved production to Taiwan and Mexico, liquidated company pension plans and reduced other employee benefits. Upper-middle-class professionals and vendors of private services were also able to charge rapidly escalating prices for health care, legal costs, banking services, college tuition, entertainment tickets, cable television charges and the like.

Securities markets also moved ahead as ordinary folk lost ground. After 1929, Wall Street and Main Street had crashed together. In 1991–92, when unprecedented numbers of Americans went on public assistance and personal bankruptcies set an all-time record, the Dow-Jones Industrial Average reached new highs. As corporations purged their white-collar staffs and cut their costs, they often bolstered their stock prices.

Financial booms that produce the great new fortunes inevitably bring record levels of debt, leverage and speculation. At the crest, captains of industry give way to financial manipulators and paper plunderers—as in the late 1980s, when the Horatio Alger figures of American industry were overshadowed by the Charles Keatings, Mi-chael Milkens and Ivan Boeskys. Then the boom disappears in an implosion of assets—crumbling savings and loan institutions, banks and commercial rent estate—and pain spreads to the real economy, where ordinary families live and work. Popular bitterness grows.

Long before the presidential election, it was clear that the economy had become stagnant, producing the weakest growth since the Hoover years. Unfortunately, as we shall see in later chapters, previous world economic powers as they begin to ebb have shown the same pattern: stagnation develops as wealth and income bunch at the top while rising taxes, ballooning debt and declining purchasing power weigh down the middle. In the United States, merely to service the $4 trillion national debt of 1992—up fourfold from $1 trillion in 1980—required some $235 billion a year in net interest payments, most of which went to high-income bondholders (and some went abroad) while the money to make the payments was raised from broad-based taxes.

Even as the middle class was shrinking, the "top 1 percent economy" marshaled its own well-funded intellectual champions, ever ready to contend that critical studies or statistics were wrong, that America's true weakness lay in eroded family values or a pernicious politics of "envy," or to argue that the rich hadn't really done that well (or that if they had, it made no difference because the ranks of "the rich" were always changing). Some of these champions were in Congress, but many hung their hats at conservative foundations— the Heritage Foundation, the Hudson Institute, the American Enterprise Institute and the Manhattan Institute, as well as other lesser centers.

The aim of this book, by contrast, is to focus on the factors and predicaments that many defenders of the status quo have tried to sidestep—middle-class decline as a national danger signal, rising economic polarization, the irony of tax rates that hit record highs for average families and record lows for millionaires, the inadequacy and even misrepresentation of government statistics, and the citizenry's worry over endangered pensions, home values and future living standards, deteriorating public services and the rapidly increasing cost of private services, including health care. Taken together, these issues and the public's legitimate complaints about them go a long way to explain yet another symptom—*the dangerous rise of middle-class frustration politics.*

Kindred attitudes were also visible in other G-7 nations, but the United States of the 1990s was unique in one important dimension— the special discomfort and trauma that overtakes a fading great economic power, less and less able to sustain the unique affluence once bestowed on its ordinary middle-rank citizenry. In 1992 major policy changes to deal with that future finally began to weigh in the national debate. But that is for the final chapter. Let us now begin at the beginning: Within just two generations after the triumph of 1945, what had happened to middle-class America—to its taxes and purchasing power, pensions and neighborhoods, hopes and dreams—and how had it come to pass?

PART ONE

THE MIDDLE CLASS
IN PERIL

CHAPTER 1

America's Crisis—The Decline
of the Middle Class

Whatever the promise of higher incomes in the mid-80's, it is gone now. Instead of continuing to rise, real incomes—that is, wages and salaries adjusted for inflation—have declined over the last three years, with the decline becoming particularly noticeable this fall, as the national economy slowed. The upshot is that most Americans are entering the 1990's worse off than they were in the early 1970's. Only those Americans whose incomes are in the top 20 percent have escaped stagnation; their incomes have grown significantly.

—*The New York Times*, December 1990

Any substantial decline of the middle class—even if it is partially psychological—would be ominous for the U.S. as a whole. It is the middle class whose values and ambitions set the tone for the country. Without it the U.S. could become a house divided in which middle Americans would no longer serve as a powerful voice for political compromise. . . . Virtually everyone agrees that America needs to maintain its middle class.

—*Time* magazine, November 1986

The middle class in this country is in far worse shape than most people really have any idea. That's the big casino, and that's what's going to change the course of this country.

—Former Democratic national chairman Robert Strauss, 1991

As the American middle class shrank in the early 1990s, its members had reason to be nervous. Survey after survey showed that middle-income ranks, while not precisely definable by dollars or purchasing power, had thinned by 8 to 15 percentage points of the nation's population from the days of John F. Kennedy, Lyndon Johnson and Richard Nixon, an unprecedented decline.[1] Each year, especially in the late 1980s, a little more of what citizens perceived as the legacy of America's postwar zenith—great corporations, downtown office towers, famous landmarks and even colleges—was being deeded over to investors in London, Paris, Frankfurt and Tokyo, cities the average

American tourist, in turn, couldn't afford to visit because the U.S. dollar bought so little. Meanwhile, the blue-collar middle class, once large, was receding with disturbing rapidity from the old steel, rubber and auto towns that had earlier symbolized U.S. industrial prowess—places like Detroit, Pittsburgh, Youngstown, Akron and Flint, now themselves fading. Some of these workers could remember, from their own long-ago military service in postwar Germany and Austria, when U.S. captains and corporals had barracked in Bavarian castles, when the dollar was king and when a pack of American cigarettes brought even more than dollars could buy. Only a little more than a generation later, families of U.S. enlisted personnel stationed locally were poor enough to qualify for public assistance in some parts of the booming German Federal Republic.

Even in the United States, the median U.S. family income, $35,000 in 1990, no longer assured the middle-class status and life-style that median earnings had brought ordinary households twenty or thirty years earlier. The end of American exceptionalism—of the unique advantages of being American—was closing in on more and more of those without capital, skills or education who still dreamed yesteryear's dream. Household purchasing power was eroding more than federal inflation statistics acknowledged. For more and more families, educational and medical costs were climbing faster than incomes, and together with rising federal, state and local taxes, they ravaged nominal earnings figures and turned the middle-class "squeeze" into something worse: a slow, economic retreat that most of its victims could not comprehend. Worry about this slippage and what it might foreshadow for future prosperity was unfocused, although discussion began to intensify during the 1992 elections. Optimists pointed out that America had survived crises before—it would survive this one, too.

Besides, many middle-class Americans were not entirely comfortable with the idea that their problems had become the nation's new bellwether. Images from television and Hollywood—and even the 1980s reassurances of a Hollywood president—reinforced this uncertainty. So did the renewed concern about the poor focused by 1992's urban riots. For most of the twentieth century, the middle class had grown larger and stronger; the conventional images of economic hardship and need were mostly low-income cityscapes—immigrants packed nine to a room, women dead in Manhattan's 1911 Triangle fire clutching $10-a-week pay envelopes, four-generation families in the rat-and-cockroach-infested galleries of the South Bronx. Since the Depression, to be sure, rural portraits also qualified: California agricultural labor camps overcrowded with migrants from the Oklahoma dust bowl, Kentucky's coal-seamed Cumberland Mountains, and the flat, heat-shimmered poverty of the Mississippi Delta. Fear in Mall City didn't really count. No one ever repossessed the future on Maplewood Terrace. Tree-lined suburban streets were a land of plenty.

Yet the 1980s and 1990s began to produce some surprisingly different pictures. Across broad swaths of charcoal-grill and lawnmower America, the middle class was in trouble. Decay and even poverty were expanding into new precincts. Suburbia, now home for the first time to a majority of the national population, was exactly where the American Dream was increasingly at risk. In late 1989 and 1990, real family income and purchasing power began to decline. By the end of 1992 it was clear that the economic stagnation of the Bush years had wiped out the small gains of the 1980s; median household income fell 3.5 percent in 1991, after adjustment for inflation, leaving the average family worse off than it was when George Bush took office in January 1989. The statistics of middle-class erosion were startling, as we shall see. Welfare, food stamps and unemployment lines soon came to suburbs and high-tech centers, where a few years earlier such pain had seemed impossible.

The unlucky Bush administration presided over the lowest economic growth rate of any four-year regime since Herbert Hoover's. In February 1992 the California State Department of Finance contended that the state's 1990–91 job decline, the worst since the 1930s, had been misrepresented by federal authorities, who said only 160,000 jobs had been lost. State records showed that the true loss had been over 500,000 jobs. Similar figures in New York showed 400,000 jobs lost in 1990–91 beyond what had been acknowledged by Washington.[2] During the 1992 presidential election, real unemployment in these states was probably in double digits, though official calculations remained artificially low. Wall Street economists were predicting the nineties would have the lowest overall expansion rate since the Depression thirties. Citizens heard experts repeatedly warn that many of the jobs were lost forever, even with nominal recovery. Economic polarization and discomfort were seeping further into the life of the average American family, and as the future of the middle class slowly became a political issue, warnings abounded.

Fear in the Urbanoid Village

Economists, urbanologists, demographers and sociologists all added their voices. Dire forecasts of some Cassandras would prove premature or wrong, but they were not implausible. Something new *was* in the wind.

As the post-1989 economy stagnated, with the recession deepening into what some described as the longest downturn since the 1930s, polltakers reported an extraordinary degree of popular concern about America's prospects. In late 1991, 63 percent told NBC sample-takers that the United States was in decline. Survey after survey reported citizens' concern that the next generation—their own children—would not live as well as theirs. Then in 1992 another sampling reported a more immediate disquiet: 55 percent of Americans said that children in America now were worse off than when the person asked was growing up.[3]

Economically or technologically, that simply wasn't true. But there were other measurements by which it *was* true, which fanned the concerns of parents and social scientists alike. Marc Miringoff, director of New York's Fordham University Institute for Innovation in Social Policy, announced in 1992 that his national Index of Social Health—a monitor of seventeen problems ranging from child abuse to the percentage of Americans without health insurance—had dropped to record lows. On a scale of 100, it had fallen from 68 when the numbers were first compiled in 1970 to 39 in 1988 and 33 in 1989. Five problems, said Miringoff, had never been worse: child abuse, teen suicide, the chasm between rich and poor, the percentage of people who have no health insurance and the portion of their own money that people over sixty-five were obliged to spend on doctors' bills.[4] A month later, Berry Brazelton, professor emeritus of pediatrics at the Harvard School of Medicine, told the World Congress on Child Health that society in the United States was breaking down, with children in poorer communities becoming infected with a sense of self-destruction while middle-class two-earner families were pushed beyond their capacities to function.[5]

Consumer specialists, in turn, had begun predicting an end to the Age of Consumption that had begun around 1900 in favor of a new, subdued spending ethic. Increased dependence on proliferating discount stores would be an important hallmark of the new frugality. Pawnshops were also booming, as chains like Texas-based Cash America Investments set up facilities in middle- and lower-middle-class shopping centers across the no-longer-buoyant Sun Belt.

More and more people, experts said, would be bunking in and commuting from remote stucco dormitories like Moreno Valley, California, seventy miles east of Los Angeles along a clogged freeway. One local urbanologist called Moreno Valley "the cruelest suburb of them all."[6] Between 1980 and 1990 its population had soared from 28,000 to 119,000, lured by comparatively cheap (and adequate) family housing. But the amenities in such places were so limited—mostly food markets, fast-food emporia, auto-parts and hardware stores—that Mayor Barbara Sigmund of affluent Princeton, New Jersey, called them "urbanoid villages." The young breadwinners, just twenty-eight years old on average and with $35,000–$50,000 family incomes, spent so much travel time in their cars that some child-care centers were open from 4:00 A.M. to midnight to accommodate the estimated 71 percent of the work force who were commuters. "People come to Moreno Valley for the American Dream, but for a lot of them it becomes the American nightmare," said Theresa Canady, vice chair of the city Planning Commission. "A lot of people hardly get to spend any time with their families."[7]

Established, close-in suburbia—the big, roomy houses on cheery tree-lined streets—was becoming unaffordable, especially for young families. In some of the most fashionable areas, from New York to California, the 1990 Census found the populations aging—and declining. Frank Levy, the incomes demographer, reported in 1991 that Americans aged thirty-five to forty-four, moving into middle age, were only half as wealthy, on an inflation-adjusted basis, as their parents had been at the same age. That disparity in assets, he predicted, would *worsen* as the United States moved into the twenty-first century.[8]

Many economists predicted that family income data for the early- to mid-1990s would extend the polarization of the 1980s, when the prime beneficiaries, the top 1 percent of Americans, a million families, increased their inflation-adjusted income by a whopping 50 to 75 percent. The next 4 percent gained a respectable 25 percent, but below that, gains tapered toward stagnation. Worse still, these were *nominal* gains; gains that had been further reduced—or turned into losses—by state and federal taxes and other increased costs exceeding the official calculations.

The erosion of the middle class cataloged during the 1980s was projected to continue. In early 1992 the Joint Economic Committee of Congress reported that while two-parent families on average had made slight gains from 1979 to 1989, "fully 80% of these families are on a treadmill—they saw their net family income decline over the past decade, or grow by a smaller percentage than did their hours of work."[9] The Congressional Budget Office calculated that middle-income families with children would have lower inflation-adjusted after-tax incomes in 1992—$29,500—than they had in 1980 ($30,900).[10] And the University of Michigan's Survey Research Center Panel Study of Income Dynamics forecast continued middle-class slippage: "The probability of falling from middle-income to lower-income status increased significantly after 1980. . . . The middle-class decline documented in our study may well continue into the 1990s. The recession of 1990–92 should further retard upward mobility for lower-income adults, while causing many borderline cases to fall into poverty."[11]

State-level analyses produced more negative results. From New York and Massachusetts to Illinois and California, official tax compilations published in 1991 and 1992 showed that in the 1980s the share of income going to the top 1 percent, 5 percent or 10 percent ballooned while what went to the middle 40 percent or 60 percent shrank. And as these statistics built up, concern about the disparities grew, and so did local demand for more progressive state income taxes.*

According to a study by three Census Bureau economists, the United States by the mid-1980s had the largest gap between rich and poor among the major Western nations.[12] Still another survey found that the United States had a much smaller middle-income group than countries like Sweden, Norway, Germany, Switzerland and Holland.[13] The irony was heavy: Was the once-egalitarian United States becoming more stratified and polarized than Europe—and what would it mean?

Housing analysts, in turn, warned that home ownership was losing its half-century meaning as a piggy bank for the American dream. In many parts of the country, single-family homes, the principal repository of middle-class net worth, were either (a) continuing to lose value in absolute terms or (b) gaining nominal value but lagging behind the rate of inflation. The Mortgage Bankers Association reported that in 1990 the amount borrowed against the average American home rose to 57.5 percent of its value, possibly the highest ever, reducing homeowners' equity by $300 billion or 16 percent—the biggest drop on record.[14] Price declines were also steep in some areas—in places like Southern California home values fell 20 to 40 percent from their 1989 peaks to 1992, especially when adjusted for inflation.

Large, aging chunks of suburbia were forecast to rot. Urbanologists like Roosevelt University's Pierre DeVise predicted that more older,

*See Chapter 5.

declining locales would swell the list of 500 suburban jurisdictions (out of 6,500) characterized as poor in 1989. This could expand the 9.5 million suburbanites already below the poverty line, a majority of them white and 36 percent of them children.[15]

Residents of even affluent suburbs began to see a new uncertainty and risk. In late 1990, 23 percent of the unemployment claims in Massachusetts were being filed by workers with a college education and a technical or professional background; and in the high-tech corridor along once-fabled Route 128, 37 percent of the jobless were such workers—a rate officials said they had never seen before.[16] In greater Phoenix, Arizona, 54 percent of new welfare applicants had never received assistance before.[17] Laid-off executives in high-tech Salem, New Hampshire, forced to borrow money to pay their real estate taxes from the town welfare officers, found themselves repaying the loans with blue-collar municipal labor. As winter set in in late 1991, Philadelphia authorities reported thousands of middle-class families they'd never seen before applying for public assistance to pay their heating bills. In the warmer suburbs of Southern California, mortgage foreclosures set all-time records. "This is the worst I've ever seen it in Southern California," said James Cornwall, president of a trustee firm that handles foreclosures for Home Savings of America. "Even during the recessions of the early '70s and '80s, we never saw this many homes going under."[18] In early 1992 greater Chicago suburban homeless shelters reported 50 percent increases in use over the previous year. The director of the Illinois Coalition to End Homelessness said, "Homelessness has finally caught up with the suburbs. All indications say that the problem has only begun its cycle stages."[19] In the suburbs of Atlanta the Horseshoe Bend Country Club launched a job-hunting program to aid unemployed members.[20]

Circumstances like these, unseen in prior post–World War II recessions, created a sense of foreboding. Suburbia was no longer economic high ground, relatively safe from the cyclical storms that moved through factory and farm districts; this time, in some metropolitan areas, suburbia—which now, after all, housed a majority of the nation's population—was bearing the brunt. Local analyses by *The Philadelphia Inquirer* made just that case. Between January 1990 and January 1992, unemployment rose by 39.6 percent in the city but grew by over 50 percent in suburban Bucks, Delaware and Montgomery counties. Meanwhile, 1991 applications for state mortgage assistance rose by 16 percent in Philadelphia versus 58 percent to 107 percent in the three suburban counties. Sheriff's foreclosures in Philadelphia were up 13 percent from the last quarter of 1990 to the last quarter of 1991; in suburban counties, the increase ranged from 48 percent to 146 percent.[21]

Times were tougher in suburbia, experts said, for three reasons: the greater vulnerability of companies and jobs there than in the already weakened cities, the indebtedness and financial precariousness of the mobile middle class after the expansion of the 1980s, and the perils of owning houses bought at peak prices just as values began to sink. Timothy Smeeding, author of *Whither the Middle Class?*, suggested that "the blow may have fallen hardest in the suburbs because white-collar professionals who live in the city 'are much more likely to be working for governments, or businesses closely related to govern-ments, like bankruptcy lawyers or lawyers helping people refinance their house, or in the health-care sector, which is the only growing set of jobs.' "[22]

In metropolitan Chicago, the biggest proportionate surge in aid to families with dependent children and medical assistance came in the suburbs. During 1991 AFDC payments rose an average of 16.4 percent in Chicago's so-called collar counties compared with 7.8 percent in Cook County, which includes the city itself. "It's more than humilia-tion. It's close to devastation," said Nanci Vanderwell, president of the board of directors of Northwest Community Services in Elk Grove Village. "This is the thing that could not happen. They think 'we're out in the suburbs, we have a home or a condo or a nice apartment, this isn't supposed to happen to us.' "[23] Polling in suburban Maricopa County, Arizona, encompassing Phoenix, found that by early 1992 the highest ratio of complaints about job losses or income declines were coming among the affluent upper-middle class.[24] And in Texas, as a middle-class wave expanded the state's welfare, food stamp and Med-icaid rolls, some of the biggest 1991 increases came in the Dallas area, with suburban counties like Denton and Rockwall leading the way. "What we're seeing is a lot of previously middle-class people coming to our offices," said Jerome Lindsay, regional administrator for the Human Services Department. "They considered themselves taxpayers and didn't think they would ever need our services."[25]

Other suburban areas worried about turning into prosperous but embarrassed Du Page County, Illinois, where stunned officials in late 1990 counted 363 homeless young people between the ages of sixteen and twenty.[26] And then there was suburban Jefferson County, Colo-rado, outside Denver, where emergency shelters and food banks were swamped in the winter of 1990–91: "People are living in homes they can't sell," said Nancy Osborne, Jeffco Action Center director. "They have no furniture. They have no food."[27]

Food itself was increasingly becoming a mainstay of public assistance. By November 1991, 24.56 million Americans—virtually one in ten—were receiving federal food stamps. "This litany of need," said the chairman of the House of Representatives Select Committee on Hunger, "continues to document the erosion of the American middle class."[28] In many prosperous suburbs of Boston, unprecedented numbers of unemployed engineers and executives found themselves turning for assistance to charitable food pantries—some of which set up hidden side entrances for those humiliated and embarrassed.[29] Outside Washington, D.C., rich suburban Fairfax County charted the area's largest 1991 rise in free hot lunches and in applications to qualify for them. The county's food-services director said, "Some of the people coming in today are people who never thought they would end up in this situation. They probably had a good job and were laid off. The first thing they try to take care of is their children."[30]

Many restaurateurs, especially fast-food purveyors, announced plans to move downscale during the nineties, tailoring lower-priced menus to families needing cheap food but having no time to prepare it themselves. Marketers warned their corporate clients: The stereotyped middle class is shrinking; the sub-middle class is growing. Marissa Piesman, coauthor of *The Yuppie Handbook,* predicted the emergence of the "schleppy"—a person off the fast track who is "living with less grandiose expectations and accepting limitations."[31]

Demographers offered yet another warning. Millions of women—mothers, wives and sisters—had entered the work force during the 1980s, sacrificing leisure time within the family and accepting a reduced quality of life in order to provide additional paychecks essential to keeping their families afloat. The problem in the 1990s, the experts said, was that few families still had nonworking women available to bolster purchasing power for another weak decade.

Personnel experts had their own dire predictions. Even before General Motors announced that 15,000 of its 99,000 salaried positions would be eliminated between 1991 and 1993, placement firms calculated that millions more white-collar workers, professionals and managers in companies all across the country would lose their jobs during the 1990s, following the 1.5 million discharged in the 1980s. Moreover, worsening international competitiveness pressures meant most of the jobs lost would never come back. As the corporate hemorrhage accelerated, the authoritative newsletter *Workplace Trends* reported that, on average, 2,700 permanent jobs had been cut each day in the third quarter of 1991.[32] Editor Dan Lacey prophesied that corporate downsizing would continue through the decade: "This is not just a recession. This is the end of a 40-year boom. Everything we consider to be a normal workplace relationship is not—it is a postwar boom relationship."[33] He predicted that by the year 2000 the nation's top 500 companies would reduce their payrolls by an additional several million workers. Fortune 500 corporations would be lopping off assistant vice presidents and marketing coordinators as cold-bloodedly as they had discharged highly paid blue-collar and production-line workers in the early 1980s.

Young people, in particular, would face a new and harsher employment world, experts said. Pay and prospects for high school graduates had been eroding for over a decade, and wages for white-collar workers were beginning to follow blue-collar wages in decline. In 1992 the Economic Policy Institute reported that wages of college graduates fell 3.1 percent in real terms between 1987 and 1991. "Having a college degree," the institute said, "no longer affords protection against falling wage trends."[34] Against the competition of so many unemployed older persons competing for jobs, Samuel Ehrenhalt, regional director of the Bureau of Labor Statistics, warned in 1992 that "College graduates are facing the toughest job market in a half-century in the New York region."[35]

There were plenty of upbeat counterassertions as well. The overall U.S. economy and per capita incomes were certain to expand, economists said. The improved productivity painfully achieved in manufacturing could spread to services. It wouldn't be hard for the decade's growth rate to exceed low expectations, and even some relative pessimists predicted a boom in the second half of the nineties. Most Americans still believed they had greater opportunities than their parents had. Polls made that clear. And even declining housing prices had a silver lining; they would make home ownership more affordable.

But the near-term picture was definitely a shade of gray. For almost three decades after World War II a rising tide had lifted virtually all boats. However, from the late 1970s to the early 1990s, a more discriminatory international economic realignment occurred, one that favored persons with capital, education and skills at the expense of those less well endowed. And with two thirds of Americans psychologically self-enlisted in the middle class, a significant minority faced a real threat of downward mobility. Jobs and Maplewood Terrace were at stake together. Yet the traumas of economic slippage cataloged by authors like Barbara Ehrenreich and Katherine Newman were only starting to translate into politics.[36] At first, people affected didn't know which party or ideology to blame, just as those losing ground in the boom years of 1927 or 1928—and there were many—hadn't known until the battering of the Great Depression provided the answer.

The new decade's first confrontation over emergent wealth issues came in October 1990, when the Bush administration, having agreed to higher taxes, found itself on the defensive over *whose* taxes were going to go up. Republicans found themselves labeled protectors of the rich, fell into temporary disrepute with some of those who were not rich, and lost ten points in some party-identification surveys.* That image, an old Republican weakness, angered voters until it was superseded by the excitement over the Persian Gulf.

But autumn's budget acrimony had raised questions that would persist and grow in the larger political debate of the 1990s. Was the unfolding crisis of the middle class unavoidable, the relentless corollary of global economic and technological change, or was it aggravated by Republican favoritism to the top 1 percent of the population? Were Americans suffering the effects of a historic shift in wealth and its distribution, or were their politicians to blame for mishandling national assets? When the middle class finally decided, the political implications would not end in Washington (or Albany and Sacramento); they would echo around the world.

That was because the middle classes of great economic powers have a special significance. A generation earlier, the size and wealth of the postwar American middle class had matched and then surpassed those of history's two previous bourgeois zeniths—seventeenth-century Holland and late-nineteenth-century England. At its peak, back in the "happy days" of the 1950s and the early 1960s, the American middle class was hardly an expression of high culture, but neither was the Holland of smug, pipe-smoking Calvinist burghers nor the England of Victorian frumpery and humming new machinery whose beneficiaries, in the title of R. F. Delderfield's famous novel, assumed that "God is an Englishman." The suburbs of Detroit and Kansas City, equally sure in 1954 that He was an American, played a similar historical role. All three middle-class societies were world-class successes, and just as important, the weakening and polarization of the earlier two had been ill omens for their countries' international as well as domestic effec-

*The damage was severe enough that from roughly October 15 to October 25, when Congress finished the budget agreement and left town, media reports had begun to speak of Republican candidates being in "free fall."

tiveness. Against this backdrop, the erosion and deepening frustration of the U.S. middle class as the 1990s began suggested a national trend that also had global importance.

The Post–World War II Heyday
of the U.S. Middle Class

Nearly a half century earlier the American middle class of the late 1940s was the economic wonder of a still-war-ravaged world and dwarfed any predecessors, even the boom-fed U.S. middle class of the 1920s. Victory in World War II had been its crucible. The upbeat Americans flooding into such new postwar suburbs as Levittown, New York, and Oak Lawn, Illinois, celebrating a victory over Adolf Hitler, imperial Japan *and* the Great Depression, represented a milestone: the most broadly based middle class that the world had ever seen. Its emergence and America's zenith went together.

In his mid-century best-seller *The Big Change: 1900–1950,* social historian Frederick Lewis Allen looked back on the prosperity of the Roaring Twenties and dismissed it, by comparison, as small potatoes. For most Americans in the 1920s the money for stocks, refrigerators and new Dodge cars really hadn't been there. Compilations by the Brookings Institution showed a mere 2.3 percent of American families with incomes over $10,000 a year in 1929, and only 8 percent in the broader but still-comfortable category of those earning over $5,000. On the dark side, 71 percent had family incomes below $2,500, 60 percent under $2,000, 42 percent below $1,500 and 21 percent under $1,000.[37] What made this inadequate, Brookings researchers emphasized, was that "at 1929 prices, a family income of $2,000 may be regarded as sufficient to supply only basic necessities."[38] This estimate exaggerated cash requirements for the many Americans still living on farms, but the purchasing-power caveat was valid: the America of flappers, bathtub gin and Pierce-Arrows had been more middle-class in its dreams than in its disposable dollars. Too large a percentage of households was still poor. Middle-class incomes were a small minority.

By 1950 this was no longer true. Data published by the Joint Economic Committee of Congress for 1948, when prices were only a third above 1929 levels, found that the percentage of families with annual incomes below $1,000 had dropped by half to 10.6 percent. Those subsisting in the $1,000–$2,000 yearly range shrank from just under 40 percent to 14.5 percent. Upward movement was everywhere. Some 20.6 percent of 1948 families had yearly receipts between $2,000 and

$3,000, and a much larger 33.6 percent earned $3,000 to $5,000.[39] The latter group, growing rapidly, from 1.2 million in 1928 to 14 million in 1948, was the foundation of an incipient middle-class majority.[40]

At the top, families making over $5,000 a year nearly tripled from 8 percent to 20.8 percent. Within that category, though, the surprising revelation was that the upper-middle and upper-class component, the Packard-and-country-club group making over $10,000, had remained almost constant—2.3 percent in 1929, 2.9 percent in 1948. The real explosion—the one that would redefine America and affect the entire world—occurred among the solid, stereotypical middle-class families with $5,000 to $10,000 a year. From just 5.7 percent in 1929, they swelled to 17.9 percent in 1948.[41]

Social chronicler Allen called this new alignment "the central fact of prosperity [in 1952] . . . Millions of families in our industrial cities and towns, and on the farms, have been lifted from poverty or near poverty to a status where they can enjoy what has traditionally been considered a middle-class way of life."[42] The National Bureau of Economic Research called it "one of the great social revolutions of history."[43] Fleshing out over another two decades, it would carry hundreds of millions of children and grandchildren of Alabama sharecroppers, Montana copper miners, Boston Irish policemen and Hungarian-American steelworkers in Pittsburgh to scarcely imagined affluence. By 1973 inflation-adjusted U.S. median family incomes had doubled those of 1948. Not even the richest European countries could come close. America's middle-class Golden Era was under way.

While no single factor explains this phenomenon, America's all-powerful postwar economy—the massive industrial, financial and trade supremacy that followed America's success in arms—was the decisive prerequisite. From mid-Depression 1932 to 1950, the U.S. share of world manufacturing ballooned from 31.8 percent to 44.7 percent, and trade followed suit. Such lopsided international economic preeminence, whether Britain's global trade and industrial dominance of the 1850s and the 1860s or Holland's trade leadership two centuries earlier (when New York was still New Amsterdam), is an unmistakable dynamo of middle-class expansion.* The achievement of the U.S. mid-

*Chapter 8 describes the peak years of U.S., British and Dutch economic, industrial and commercial power and how these golden eras overlapped with middle-class values and prosperity. Books like Paul Kennedy's *The Rise and Fall of the Great Powers* have singled out the precedents of Holland and Britain, along with (sixteenth-century) Hapsburg Spain, from a strategic, military and fiscal standpoint. But the vital importance of the zenith and then erosion of the middle class as great powers rise and fall deserves more attention. Even dle class in the late 1940s was a wonder, but it wasn't unique. Neither was the vulnerability that would be so apparent by the 1990s.

The Central Role of the Middle Class in Great-Power Zeniths

Not only has the global success of a great economic power been a catalyst for the expansion of its middle class, but the reverse also has been true. Outbursts of bourgeois spirit and inventiveness, the triumph of middle-class values over those of established elites, have often prodded countries toward peaks of economic and political achievement. When these same nations have later turned away from these values, when the elites have again triumphed over the middle classes, the results have been inauspicious.

The rise of the Dutch republic of the early seventeenth century reflected the revolution a generation earlier that had liberated Holland's Protestant merchants, traders and sea captains from Catholic, aristocratic Hapsburg Spain. In *The Embarrassment of Riches,* historian Simon Schama explains Holland's golden-era culture as "shared, in large measure, by that very broad stratum of the populations between artisans and trading merchants that in England would have been known as 'the middling sort'; in Holland the *brede middenstand.*"[44] "The Republic was an island of plenty in an ocean of want. Its artisans, even its unskilled workers and its farmers (for it seems a misnomer to call them peasants) enjoyed higher real incomes, better diets and safer livelihoods than [people] anywhere else on the continent."[45] Another scholar, noting that the "neatness, order, cleanliness of their urban life and its physical sophistication entranced and amazed Europe," credited the "prudent, self-satisfied, unostentatious" Calvinist merchants and burgomasters for indelibly stamping the persona of their class on Dutch society.[46]

A triumphant middle class also characterized mid-nineteenth-century Britain. By 1860, "with 2% of the world's population and 10 percent of Europe's, the United Kingdom . . . had a capacity in modern industries equal to 40–45 percent of the world's potential and 55–60 percent of that in Europe."[47] Industrial workers naturally predominated, so that one 1867 estimate identified just one citizen in five as middle-class (and even this calculus included all artisans, officeworkers

---

Spain was starting to generate a significant middle class in its early- to mid-sixteenth-century zenith, but soon lost it—at great long-term cost.

and supervisory workers).[48] But in spirit, mid-century Britain was indisputably Europe's preeminent middle-class country. Not only was its middle-class population proportionately larger than elsewhere in Europe, but, more important, the values of this class dominated British government and opinion. Continental visitors had long characterized Britain as a "nation of shopkeepers" or marveled at the importance of "the honest middle class, that precious portion of nations."[49] And this tendency increased in the 1840s and 1850s after Sir Robert Peel, son of a Lancashire cotton master, and William E. Gladstone, son of a Liverpool merchant, became prime ministers.

A painful reconfirmation of the cultural and economic stimulus provided by the Dutch of the "golden era" and the British middle class of the mid-nineteenth century came years later when entrepreneurs in both countries gave way to speculators, rentiers and other passive investors who lived off capital, not enterprise. Whether in Holland circa 1700 or Britain circa 1900, this class was not reluctant to invest its guilders and pounds sterling abroad when more money could be made from the industry of a rival nation. As I shall show in Chapter 8, such transitions in a nation's history often foreshadow trouble—declining manufacturing competitiveness, stagnant real wages, increased economic polarization and early worries over declining world-power status.

In the United States of the Reagan boom years, the analogy was self-evident yet broadly dismissed. Too few policymakers, caught up in the new enthusiasm for wealth, investment and financial elites, wanted to remember that America's own golden era, spanning the "good war" of 1941–45, the "best years" of 1945–50, and the "happy days" of 1950–60 had been marked by an aggressive, even egalitarian middle-class culture. Once the 1929 Crash had soured the reputation of Republican politicians, speculative finance, established wealth and what would later be called "trickle-down" economics, more assertive democratic values took hold in the 1930s, and they continued to dominate U.S. politics and society for a quarter century after the war.

In short, the crucial transformation of the United States, which made it possible for Americans to overcome the Depression and then secure the benefits of World War II, was political and social as well as economic. We have seen how the income gap between rich and poor narrowed between 1929 and 1948 as some 20 to 30 percent of the U.S. population climbed into the middle class, roughly doubling its ranks. By 1950, class differences were also declining in clothing, automobiles, food and even personal hygiene. Revealingly, and despite the postwar boom, the great rich (with incomes over $1 million a year), estimated at 600 in 1929, declined to approximately 130 by 1948.[50] The rich were now Hollywood's villains, while the heroes were usually honest middle-class achievers. Popular culture in the United States, Frederick Lewis Allen wrote, had learned to express popular recriminations over the Crash and the Depression:

> Among the sons and daughters of the rich there is a vague, surviving guilt complex: an embarrassed consciousness that during the Depression great numbers of people were resentful of their way of life and suspicious of the origin of the funds that made it possible. This guilt complex takes many forms, and one of them is a preference for the sort of entertainment which won't seem to involve putting on airs. The same is true in some degree of people in the upper echelons of a business organization: so aware are they of the distrust of them which unionism fosters that they go out of their way at a company party to show that they have no princely delusions.[51]

Such anti-elite attitudes held the maximum U.S. personal income tax bracket at or near 91 percent from World War II until 1964, and partly as a result, between 1929 and 1945, the share of U.S. national income going to the top 1 percent of Americans—over $16,000 a year—shrank from 13 percent to 7 percent, and that of the top 5 percent—over $8,000—dipped from 28 percent to 17 percent.[52] As the rich were squeezed, the middle class advanced.* Egalitarianism and economic growth seem to have gone together. Meanwhile, the puritanical emphasis introduced into politics by the Depression also helped keep down both interest rates and financial speculation. And even when the Republicans captured Congress and the presidency in 1952, White House strategists declined to seek reduction of the 91 percent top personal income tax rate. The United States, at the heart of the mid-twentieth-century world, was militantly middle-class, bourgeois, burgerlijk, in the style of early Victorian Britain and seventeenth-century Holland. Few people wanted to bring back the well-remembered extremes—either the undertaxed, overspeculating millionaires of the 1920s or the lines of unemployed waiting at the soup kitchens of the 1930s. A generation later, as these values eroded, as the middle class lost ground and stratification returned, the United States began to lose a vital national force.

---

*By 1990, conversely, as the middle class declined, the top 1 percent of Americans *regained* the 13 percent of national income they had in 1929.

First Whiffs of "Middle-Class Decline"

The 1950s were the last indisputably "good decade" for the American middle class. Economically, the middle class continued to expand in the 1960s, particularly in the rapidly urbanizing South and Sun Belt. But the culture of the new decade was propelled by a reemerging national desire for excitement, by youthful rebellion against smug middle-class mores, by the civil rights revolution and by a rekindling fascination with elites, sparked by the new president, John F. Kennedy, his Vassar-educated, Social Register wife, and a White House full of Harvard's best and brightest. Sophisticates dismissed the Eisenhower 1950s for suburban dullness and stagnation.

The excitability of the 1960s spread even to Wall Street. The stock market was one institution the Eisenhower years had energized, and speculation crept back with go-go money managers, men like Jim Ling and the conglomerate movement, accelerating as the Dow-Jones Industrial Average touched the 1000 mark for the first time in 1966. Poverty became a chic social cause (and less of a chastening family memory), and by the end of the sixties Southampton and Manhattan millionaires were holding cocktail parties for grape pickers and Black Panthers. Cosmopolitan secret agent James Bond, with his insistence on shaken, not stirred, martinis, had displaced beer-drinking private eye Mike Hammer. *The Saturday Evening Post*—with its Norman Rockwell covers of quilt-robed, hair-curlered wives in station wagons dropping husbands at suburban railroad stations—went out of business.

But if the middle class of the 1960s had gone out of fashion, if it was under siege by the Vietnam War protesters and the other youthful rebels, it was still prosperous, still getting richer and bigger. Yet here, too, important storm clouds were gathering. Inflation resulting from the war in Vietnam and other federal borrowing and the consequent budget deficits was about to bring the steady postwar economic gains to a halt. In 1973 petroleum producers from Arabia to Latin America, unwilling to watch 5–6 percent annual inflation erode the $4 per barrel they were being paid for their oil, doubled their price over the next two years and helped throw the United States into a severe recession.

We now know that the resulting stagflation brought real family income growth more or less to an end. Figure 1, a picture worth a page of technical explanations, shows how median family income, climbing since the end of World War II, began to flatten in 1973. And with some ups and downs, family and household income has remained on that

Figure 1. *The Stagnation of American Prosperity Since 1973*

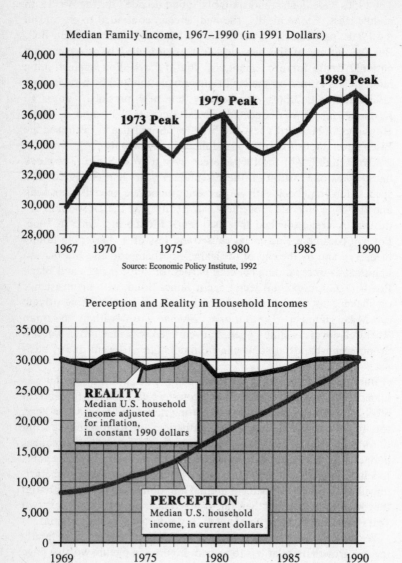

Median Family Income, 1967–1990 (in 1991 Dollars)

1973 Peak

1979 Peak

1989 Peak

Source: Economic Policy Institute, 1992

Perception and Reality in Household Incomes

REALITY
Median U.S. household
income adjusted
for inflation,
in constant 1990 dollars

PERCEPTION
Median U.S. household
income, in current dollars

Source: *The New York Times*, November 17, 1991

Figure 1. (continued)

Private-Production Workers' Average Weekly Earnings, 1947–1989
(in 1982 Dollars)

Source: *Christian Science Monitor*, April 29, 1991

plateau ever since.* Calculations of after-tax income were even more dismaying, as we shall see. Other yardsticks—such as real manufacturing wages—began showing outright decline. Moreover, stagflation fed social disruption, so that by the late 1960s and early 1970s, divorces, drug use and hemlines were rising alongside inflation, interest rates and debt. To a sizable minority of Americans, middle-class values were something to be mocked, although the Republican party was starting to discover and build a contrary-minded presidential "new majority" determined to hold fast to the values under siege.

Unfortunately, 1960s America was turning down a familiar pathway. Great prosperity and the cosmopolitanism that accompanied it had undercut middle-class values and initiative before: certainly in Holland's eighteenth-century "periwig" era, then again in luxury-craving Edwardian England, weary of Victorian pieties. The precedents for the United States were all too relevant, as Chapter 8 will show.

*Median family income does have shortcomings as a measurement, which are discussed in Chapter 4. Unfortunately, as that discussion will amplify, the alternative measurements also have weaknesses.

By the late 1980s some concerned Americans had begun to invoke the warnings made in the early twentieth century by former British colonial secretary Joseph Chamberlain, who had judged his own country at risk for reorienting itself toward finance, distribution and other services instead of manufacturing, and for becoming more divided between rich and poor and less self-sufficient.[53] Nor, he said, could a great power avoid competitive deterioration simply because its people had new leisure-time opportunities and conveniences and were richer. Spain and Holland, he added, were richer in the early twentieth century than they had been during their great years, but had lost their once-unique importance.[54]

Many of the new pressures that Americans were feeling in their household accounts were related to a somewhat similar transformation and relative decline of the United States as a great economic power. While no one could directly blame the decade's "middle-class squeeze"—from tax revolts in Massachusetts to the pain of automobile insurance rates in New Jersey, runaway college tuition and health-care costs everywhere and a federal income tax system that put suburban lawyers and dentists in a higher marginal bracket than millionaires—on America's loss of mid-century economic omnipotence, on its declining egalitarian commitment or on its rising tolerance of debt and speculation, there *was* a link.

The Two-Decade Middle-Class Plateau

By the 1990s, as it became unmistakable that recurrent slow growth was in its third decade, a broader apprehension began taking shape. The American dream had rarely, if ever, languished for so long without a clear sign of revitalization.

At first, to be sure, diminished middle-class headway in the United States after Vietnam and the oil shock had seemed merely temporary. But oil prices and inflation ratcheted up again in 1978–80, raising interest rates and spurring two recessions in 1980 and 1981–82. Real household incomes stagnated. Then, even as business recovered in 1983 and thereafter, economists noticed an unanticipated corollary: wage levels were not rebounding at their usual rate. From the rubber plants of Akron, Ohio, to the copper smelters of Montana, more and more of manufacturing's regional emergency wards began to look like graveyards. More mothers, wives and sisters were obliged to enter the work force to keep their families afloat (or to maintain their halves of broken families). By the mid-1980s, statisticians were mapping another significant negative: this was the first postwar recovery period in which economic inequality continued to worsen.

By several other measures, the 1970s marked the onset of a weakness that continued into the 1980s despite the apparent boom. Productivity, one key determinant of prosperity, decelerated in the 1970s, then grew during the 1980s at only one third the improvement rate reached in the 1960s. Unemployment, too, had spiked higher in the seventies than in the sixties; then in the 1980s, the *average* unemployment rate—more than 7 percent—exceeded the annual U.S. rate in all but two of the years between 1950 and 1979. Back in the sixties, 5 percent unemployment had meant recession; the jobless rates of the eighties never dropped that low, even at the peak of the boom.[55] Capacity utilization, the government's yardstick of how fully U.S. factories and facilities are working, fell on a decade-to-decade basis in the seventies and then again in the eighties. As for decade-to-decade growth in real average annual GNP, that had ebbed and flowed as follows: 1940s—4.3 percent; 1950s—3.2 percent; 1960s—3.9 percent; 1970s—2.8 percent; 1980s—2.6 percent.[56] Measured against strong growth periods, the 1980s were substandard, as the 1970s had been. Merrill Lynch's early forecast for the entire 1990s anticipated even more sluggishness—a weak real GNP growth rate in the 2.0 percent range, lowest since the Depression-troubled 1930s.

By late 1990, with a new recession starting to bite, *The New York Times* observed that "for a brief moment in the mid-1980s, it looked as if Americans would again know how it feels to get ahead." Instead, wage and income gains proved short-lived, and in the early 1990s real incomes dropped again.[57] The median family incomes for 1990 and 1991 fell back to late-1970s levels when adjusted for inflation and taxes. According to other measurements, households were losing headway not only in terms of income but in *wealth*—this even before the real estate and financial-assets implosion of 1990–92. In a 1991 study entitled *The Economic Future of American Families,* incomes experts Frank Levy and Richard Michel calculated that during the 1970s and 1980s, real new wealth per family had expanded at only a 0.4 percent average annual rate, with gains concentrated among mature home-owning and stock-owning upper-bracket families.[58] The Federal Reserve Board study published in 1992 made the same point. As we have seen, members of the thirty-five–forty-four age group, collectively, were little more than half as wealthy (in constant dollars) as their parents—postwar America's prime beneficiaries—had been at the same age. Those younger were worse off. And Levy and Michel predicted the disparity would widen as the "baby boomers" approached retirement age in 2020 or 2025. For the 1984–88 period alone, the Census Bureau reported that the median net worth of all households—assets minus debts—declined by 4 percent.[59] Rising household debt was an important negative. The most prosperous Americans, of course, greatly increased their net worth during this period.*

Levy and other scholars have taken 1973 as the year when family and household income began to flatten, giving the stagnation process a generally accepted starting point. The weakness of the 1970s is little disputed; the economic circumstances of the 1980s, however, are far more complex, the stuff from which long debates and intense statistical disputes flow. For example, the small 1980–89 increase in inflation-adjusted middle-class incomes, at first much emphasized by the Bush administration, required discounting in two ways: first, because further adjustments for federal, state and local taxes combined to produce a *decline*, and second, because the *overall* nationwide increase, especially in averages, disguised important variations among component income groups. Growth in after-tax disposable family income was concentrated in a way that made the decade difficult for people in the middle. As we shall later see in more detail, for the 1980s as a whole, those near the top prospered (and the top 1 percent soared), the 40th to 80th percentiles ran in place, and the bottom two fifths lost ground.

On the other hand, too much can be made of how real weekly wages for production and nonsupervisory workers, the principal sustenance of ordinary families, fell slightly in the 1980s, according to data from the federal Bureau of Labor Statistics. Not only were supervisors excluded, but BLS data failed to recognize that many individuals worked second jobs or put in longer hours to avoid economic losses. In circumstance after circumstance, leisure was sacrificed to maintain purchasing power. In 1987 the average U.S. worker put in ninety-five more hours of work per year than in 1979—the equivalent of three and a half extra weeks.[60] Some extended their regular job hours; others moonlighted. To keep ahead, more households needed two workers, and not all had them. Wage earners obviously were not the decade's gainers; that reward went to upper-bracket families who transcended wage or salary dependence with financial and real estate assets that brought in rents, interest, dividends and capital gains.

A high percentage of individual U.S. households simply lost ground. Researchers at the University of Michigan, who had begun tracking

---

*A little bit of math makes the point. Between 1984 and 1988, the net worth of the Forbes 400 richest Americans roughly *doubled,* while the median net worth of the overall population stagnated or declined.

the fortunes of a representative cross section of five thousand American families in 1968, tabulated an ever-larger share that reported a creeping deterioration in purchasing power. Between 1968 and 1972, the earnings of 39 percent of these families fell behind inflation, a share that rose to 43 percent in the period from 1973 to 1977. Then in the tougher years from 1978 to 1982, fully 56 percent of the population fell behind.[61] By the end of the 1980s, according to the Michigan researchers, middle-income ranks were shrinking rapidly. Timothy Smeeding, one of the economists involved in the study, said that "what we are looking at is a permanent decline in the size of the middle class."[62]

Because the rich, in the meantime, were steadily boosting their income and assets, official tabulations revealed an extraordinary trend: the collective income of the elite top 1 percent of Americans was overtaking the combined income of the entire middle 20 percent of the population! In 1977, according to the Congressional Budget Office, the top 1 percent had enjoyed 8.3 percent of national pretax family income versus 16.3 percent for the entire middle quintile. Then by 1980 the top 1 percent commanded 9.2 percent and the middle quintile 16.0 percent. In 1985 the two figures were 11.6 percent and 15.1 percent, and by 1989 the split was 13.0 percent and 14.7 percent.[63] Other tabulations emphasizing capital gains put the share of the top 1 percent in the 14 percent range. For these shares nearly to converge was striking. (Full details appear in Appendix A.)

Explanations of why the top 1 percent had so greatly outpaced the middle ranged from the effect of federal tax cuts favoring the rich to the buoyant influence of conservative economics on financial markets and the inevitable effect of worldwide demand for capital, education and skills. Labor leaders, not surprisingly, emphasized the loss of America's postwar concentration of highly paid manufacturing jobs— the shut doors and shrinking employment in western Pennsylvania steel mills, St. Louis auto plants and Louisiana petrochemical producers as foreign producers invaded one market after another. The loss may or may not have been inevitable, but it surely influenced income distribution. During the postwar quarter century, and even into the 1980s, major unionized manufacturing areas, with their mid-range wage scales, enjoyed less economic inequality than other parts of the country.[64] By contrast, from Miami to Los Angeles, many wealthy service-industry areas—whose economies were based on finance, data processing, communications and retirement—registered local rich-poor gaps approaching those of India and other Third World countries.[65] Services and finance meant polarization, a pattern that Chapter 8 will amplify.

Still other economists tied middle-class stagnation to America's excessive borrowing in the 1980s, when household, corporate and national debt soared. This, too, was a factor. The weight of U.S. family indebtedness, and the consequent reduction of disposable income, will be examined in Chapter 7. As for *national* indebtedness, the combination of heavy U.S. international borrowing, high real interest rates, the overvalued dollar and the rising trade deficit of the early 1980s undercut U.S. manufacturing and blue-collar employment—and this was merely an early effect. The burden that future repayment of debt would have on U.S. living standards was still years from its peak. After calculating that U.S. international indebtedness would reach nearly a trillion dollars by the mid-1990s, Harvard economist Benjamin Friedman indicated that to pay down those obligations, Americans would have to divert overseas 1 to 2 percentage points of national income otherwise spendable at home.[66] Parents found themselves confiding worries to pollsters about a decline in the next generation's living standard, something unprecedented for Americans. To many worried Americans, the economic plateau was starting to look like a downslope.

Admittedly, public economic fears have not been a reliable *long-term* barometer. Historians participating in the debates of the 1970s and 1980s pointed out that America had undergone crises of confidence almost from the start, although there *was* an economic logic to the ebb and flow: pessimism deepened in the 1840s and 1850s, following the economic crash of 1837; it intensified again during the years from 1893 to 1914, and once more in the decade after 1929. David Donald, chairman of Harvard's graduate program on the history of American civilization, summed up the frustrations of 1893–97 and thereafter: "Those in the middle felt threatened, and not just financially, either. There was a sense of squeezed opportunities and expectations, a sense that the rules of the game had changed. The flood of immigrants were Eastern European and Mediterranean, many Jews, and they threatened to be unassimilable. The big gas and oil interests were growing. People had a sense of no longer feeling at home, of not having control."[67] Somewhat similar frustrations returned during the hard times of the 1930s.* For the short term, then, public frustrations have been revealing; it is in the long term that they have been misleading. Bernard Bailyn, a Harvard expert on the colonial period, pointed out that even the Pilgrims thought the American dream was unraveling thirty years after they landed on Plymouth Rock![68]

---

*Chapter 9 will discuss the frustration politics of the 1890s and 1930s—and how many of those same themes and issues recurred in the early 1990s.

Nevertheless, the apprehension that began in the mid-1970s is probably modern America's most enduring; it surged again at the end of the decade, and then again in 1983–84 following the recession and a series of attention-getting books and articles by such liberal economists as Lester Thurow and Robert Kuttner. To be sure, serious debate during the 1988 presidential campaign was inhibited by the income gains of 1983–87, as well as by Democratic nominee Michael Dukakis's naive self-congratulation for an already imploding Massachusetts Miracle. But by 1990–92 another recession brought new real-income declines and the plight of the middle class became a central if only superficially discussed ingredient of the 1992 presidential contest. America's uncertain global economic status added to public nervousness. Nations *do* peak. Ebbing hegemonies *do* bring stagnation. So let us now turn to the shaky American middle class of the early 1990s: just who belonged to it—and, in addition, who had already slid from its ranks or was about to slide.

The Eroding Middle Class of the Early 1990s

How convenient if neat government statistics could tell political or market researchers that the middle-class population of Illinois had dropped from 54 percent in 1980 to 45 percent in 1990, or that Collier County, Florida, had the nation's highest ratio of middle-class residents—or that middle-class percentages for the United States were falling well below those for Norway (after being higher in 1950). But such data don't exist, partly because middle-class status—especially in the late-twentieth-century United States—depends at least as much on one's state of mind as on one's bank balance.

Most attempts to calculate the historical emergence of the middle class have built their guesswork on vocational or income categories. Such broad estimates have described the middle class as growing from 10 to 20 percent of the population after the Civil War to 20 to 30 percent in 1940. Public opinion polls have also been a source, beginning in the 1930s, and since the 1970s these samplings have generally shown 55 to 75 percent of Americans categorizing themselves as middle-class, although results vary with the phrasing of the questions.[69]

Imprecision is unavoidable. Surveys in the late 1940s, still swayed by class consciousness and lingering economic insecurity, found only 37 percent of Americans who identified themselves as middle-class; even among many of those with obvious upward mobility, working-class self-identification still prevailed. By the 1990s the problem was the opposite: too many people called themselves middle-class because belonging had become almost obligatory in the national culture. More and more of them were being unrealistic. A look at the changing dollar incomes of the various U.S. economic strata in the late 1970s and 1980s—the top 1 percent, top 5 percent, top 10 percent and the remaining deciles—not only confirms stagnation below the top, but suggests that, for a growing minority of Americans, middle-class self-assessments were becoming illusions.

During the 1980s, as Table 1 shows, the 1 million households in the top 1 percent roared ahead, becoming an increasingly distant "upper," especially in statistical series that included capital gains income, thereby increasing the advantage of the rich.* This is Upper America— or, as one phrasemaker called it, the nation's "overclass." The "class" status of the next 9 percent is harder to call; its upper portions gained substantially, in some ways transcending "the middle class" during the 1980s. But for most Americans in this $80,000–$200,000 category, their incomes were too small to be upper-class compared with the top 1 percent. "Upper-middle class" is a better description.

Table 1. Average Income Level and Effective Federal Tax Rates in Each Family Decile by Year
[Corporate income tax allocated to capital income]

					Percent Change		
					1977–90	1980–90	1985–90
Decile	1977	1980	1985	1990			
	Average income level (in 1988 dollars)						
First	4,277	3,852	3,568	3,805	−11.0	1.2	6.7
Second	8,663	7,982	7,717	8,251	−4.8	3.4	6.9
Third	13,510	12,530	12,230	13,110	−3.7	4.6	7.2
Fourth	18,980	17,240	17,010	18,200	−4.1	5.6	7.0
Fifth	24,520	22,380	22,070	23,580	−3.8	5.4	6.9
Sixth	30,430	28,100	27,620	29,490	−3.1	5.0	6.8
Seventh	36,880	34,370	34,620	36,890	0.0	7.3	6.5
Eighth	44,820	42,050	43,370	46,280	3.3	10.1	6.7
Ninth	56,360	53,660	56,190	59,860	6.2	11.6	6.5
Tenth	111,100	107,900	123,200	133,200	19.9	23.4	8.2
Top 5 percent	149,500	146,000	172,100	187,400	25.4	28.3	8.9
Top 1 percent	319,100	321,400	415,700	463,800	45.4	44.3	11.6
All deciles	34,830	32,850	34,480	37,050	6.4	12.8	7.4

Source: Congressional Budget Office, House Ways and Means Committee, 1992 Green Book.

*Capital gains were not included in the standard calculations of income made by the Census Bureau.

The next 10 percentiles (80th to 89th), spanning 1990 incomes in the $60,000–$80,000 range, constituted the upper reaches of the traditional middle class (especially for residents of metropolitan New York, Washington, Los Angeles or San Francisco, where such incomes did not support upper-middle-class status). Incomes in the lower reaches of this group were precarious for a family with children in Manhattan, but qualified for the solid Oldsmobile-and-charcoal-grill middle class in burgeoning new Sun Belt suburbia. The 60th to 79th percentiles, further down the income ladder at $40,000 to $60,000 a year, could be called "middle-middle class," although such families found it hard to live in affluent locales where housing costs and taxes were punitive.*

As the 1990s got under way, the mid-rank 40th to 59th percentiles posed the most obvious problem of slow attrition: had the median family with its median income actually lost middle-class status and purchasing power? In Nampa, Idaho, or Spartanburg, South Carolina, probably not. But in the richer metropolitan areas, a family of four with an income in the $28,000–$40,000 range simply didn't command the local equivalent of a middle-class life-style. As early as the mid-1980s, incomes experts like Frank Levy were concluding that "being in the middle of the distribution *no longer guaranteed a middle-class income*," which he calculated was enjoyed by only 45 percent of Americans.[70] In the 20th to 39th deciles, middle-class status was rare; incomes here were stagnating while the costs of maintaining a middle-class life-style were rising. Chapter 7 will further pursue the evidence that the true U.S. middle class has been shrinking, as incomes polarized toward either end of the scale, and as many families at and below the median-income range slipped from middle-class ranks.

Critics do have a point, as we will see, in calling family-income statistics misleading because declining family size has, to a limited extent, enabled these units to make the same money go further. They are likewise correct in contending that median family-income numbers "lose" some of the growth shown in faster-rising per capita income calculations for the same period. Profiles by private marketing firms of the top 20 percent to 25 percent of U.S. households, those enjoying most of the nation's disposable income, unmistakably confirmed the increased buying power so visible circa 1987 in the aisles of Neiman-Marcus, Bloomingdale's and luxury-car dealerships. But very little of this benefited people in the middle. Income growth at the top was big

*According to one study, for a 1990 family to match the standard of living $100,000 brought in Minneapolis would have required $112,700 in New York City, $111,600 in San Francisco, $110,000 in Los Angeles and $106,200 in Boston, but only $93,300 in Miami or $90,000 in New Orleans ("How Rich Is Rich? Locale Plays Big Role," *USA Today,* October 22, 1990).

enough to boost economic averages, but had much less effect on actual average *families.*

Meanwhile, some of the same calculations that revealed the income surge for the top 1 percent and the moderate gains for the upper-middle class concurred that further down, unusual numbers of Americans *were* dropping out of the lower-middle class. The University of Michigan study provided the best documentation—and by cultural and historical yardsticks, this widespread slippage was more significant than the ongoing upward mobility of a small elite. Polarization, as we shall see, has generally meant bad news for nations, and worriers began to ponder a new question: Was the bottom starting to fall out of Middle America?

Demographers were already explaining who was slipping—and why. Several million highly paid, unionized blue-collar production workers had lost their jobs in manufacturing in the early and mid-1980s, especially in the Great Lakes industrial heartland, and many of the jobs remaining were paying less. For a brief moment—a historical crest— America in the quarter century after the war was rich enough for steel-mill or production-line workers in Flint, Michigan, or south St. Louis to enjoy higher incomes and better living standards than branch bank managers in London or shop supervisors in Stuttgart. Policy changes aggravated their decline, but part of the blue-collar Middle America of the 1960s and early 1970s *was* living higher on the international scale than the U.S. economy could sustain once world prosperity resumed a more normal distribution.

Withering farm areas and dying small towns also became impossible to ignore during the 1980s, especially in the Midwest and Rocky Mountains. In a dozen states, areas covering ten and fifteen counties lost at least 10 percent of their population between 1980 and 1990. In five entire states—Montana, Wisconsin, Louisiana, West Virginia and Wyoming—real median family income *declined* by 11 to 20 percent from the 1980 to the 1990 Census. The rural and small-town component of the middle class shrank (or migrated) as farms were sold or foreclosed and merchants gave in and boarded up their stores.

Even family acrimony and dissolution added to middle-class erosion. Although divorce rates started coming down in the eighties, they remained high enough to make divorced women (and the children in their custody) another group of losers, falling out of the middle class as so many others did. Sudden, steep income drops could make 1990's affluent Elizabeth Arden customer a surprise 1991 statistic in the "feminization of poverty."

Young families, in addition, were whipsawed by low starting salaries, by declining career prospects and wealth opportunities relative to
those their parents had enjoyed and by the inability to afford a home
(or even to afford marriage as opposed to cohabitation).* Incomes-
watcher Frank Levy had no doubt that "it is much harder for a male
high school graduate to be in 'the Middle Class' now than it was ten
years ago."[71]

And, finally, the 1990s counted millions of middle managers from
business and the professions, who had already lost jobs or were fearful
that they would, caught in the white-collar, suburban aftermath of
corporate America's bloody early 1980s downsizing of blue-collar employment in response to foreign competition and changed world circumstances. The postwar social contract was being breached; major
U.S. corporations were giving up their earlier roles as providers of a
uniquely American prosperity. Now their horizons and loyalties were
increasingly global. Even the downsizing of U.S. military defenses
became a factor, as chills spread across the Sun Belt when hundreds of
thousands of aerospace engineers, defense workers and military personnel lost their jobs.

By 1992, the nation's most painful income declines were coming in
a *new* set of states—service, financial, aerospace and high-technology
centers racked by the economic downturn. In Massachusetts and Connecticut, median household incomes had dropped almost 10 percent
from 1989 to 1991. In California, the UCLA Business Forecasting
Project confirmed the worst economic downturn since the 1930s, and
editorialists pondered the hitherto unthinkable: the end of middle-class
optimism.

A few years into the decade, then, the middle class was approximately 45 percent of the population, including perhaps half the 40th to
59th percentiles, and virtually everyone in the 60th to 98th percentiles,
below the "upper" 1 percent. But despite unprecedented prosperity at
the top, the proportion of people whose purchasing power or defined
incomes made them "middle-class" was certainly 5 to 10 percentage
points smaller than it had been ten or twenty years earlier. Americans
on the margin were more nervous, more harried and more politically
volatile. And they had reason to be, because during the 1980s many
policymakers in Washington and state capitals and county seats had
adopted a very different philosophy from the middle-class commitment that had underpinned America's mid-century rise.

*Chapter 7 will provide more detail.

CHAPTER 2

The New Political Economics of the 1980s: "Soaking the Middle Class"

In the '30s we had the New Deal. In the '40s and '50s we had the Fair Deal. And in the '80s, middle-income Americans got the raw deal.

—U.S. Senate Budget Committee Chairman James Sasser, 1991

Those people in Washington who write the complex tangle of rules by which the economy operates have, over the last 20 years, rigged the game—by design and default—to favor the privileged, the powerful and the influential. At the expense of everyone else.

—"America: What Went Wrong," *The Philadelphia Inquirer,* 1991

Americans' surrender of the ideal of equal sacrifice has occurred without much public debate or even awareness that we were doing it. It has come rather as a byproduct of discrete policies that seemed otherwise perfectly sensible.

—Political economist Robert Reich, 1986

To some extent, the erosion of the U.S. middle class in the 1980s and early 1990s reflected technological change and global economic upheaval. But politics was also involved. The Reagan administration introduced new philosophies, tentative and little understood at first, to justify policies of redistributing tax burdens, exalting markets, overre-warding the rich and the manipulations of finance, cutting back public services and then pointing with a cynical shrug toward exchequers emptied by selective tax cuts and tax expenditures to favored groups. As these trends intensified, to the great benefit of the financial markets, so did economic polarization—and so did the pressure on families in the humdrum middle and lower middle, as well as those at the bottom.

This national transformation was no accident. Economic circum-stances had begun souring for Americans in the 1970s, and in 1980 the U.S. electorate had embraced new leaders who, as we shall see, un-leashed the third of America's Republican-led capitalist booms in which income and wealth were realigned upward.* Some of these same economic forces worked to the detriment of ordinary Americans by encouraging speculation, shifting tax burdens and redistributing income in ways that eventually became controversial in the nineties. In retrospect, what would become "Soak the middle" policies that led to rising Social Security taxes, as well as an income tax system that imposed higher marginal rates on middle managers than on corporate CEOs, had been nobody's 1980 political platform—obviously—and most swing voters that year, preoccupied with liberal social and economic failures, took at face value conservatism's renewed emphasis on tax reduction, markets and incentive economics. Not until the mid- to late 1980s was it clear that a more ambitious new ideology was developing—in Europe as well as the United States—to shift economic burdens *toward* society's low- and middle-income users of products and services and *away* from capitalism's investors and other lions of the corporate veldt. At first, of course, the objective had been a familiar, broad renewal of American enterprise, and policy components like lower taxes and less regulation were eminently sensible.

Meanwhile, the conservatives who held up Washington's free-market banners in the early 1980s had relatively few questions to answer. American voters were frazzled by bracket creep and resentful of big government. For them, economic redistribution involved "Tax and spend," the liberal Democratic politics that had recycled upper- and middle-class tax revenues downward from Franklin D. Roosevelt's 1930s New Deal to Lyndon Johnson's 1960s Great Society. Opposition to more such welfare statism—some of which was linked to racial fear—stoked Middle America's fiscal conservatism and spurred its preference for a Republican president in 1980.

Equally to the point, rival political memories of conservatives using government policy to transfer wealth *upward* had grown dim, becoming little more than storybook plots of twelfth-century sheriffs of Nottingham and arrogant French Bourbon kings. This, after all, was not *American* practice—unless one recalled how U.S. Treasury Secretary Alexander Hamilton, in 1794, sent troops to force western Pennsylvania farmers to pay new taxes on corn liquor, partly so that the federal government could fund the Revolutionary War debt held by speculators. Or how the federal government, in the quarter century after the Civil War, used the gold standard as a vehicle to impose nationwide money-supply deflation, rewarding bondholders while

*The details of this process are described in *The Politics of Rich and Poor*.

commodity prices collapsed and farmers lost their lands. Even as recently as the 1930s, sour memories of the pro-wealth Republican policies of the Roaring Twenties were immediate enough that when Hollywood released its spectacular 1939 version of *Robin Hood,* starring dashing Errol Flynn as Robin and Basil Rathbone as the arrogant sheriff of Nottingham, few doubted that the hero of Sherwood Forest was the good guy, the Franklin D. Roosevelt of medieval England. By the mid-1980s, however, Robin Hood had become a negative symbol, an ideological villain to *Wall Street Journal* editorialists *and* their avid readers in the White House. Philosophically, the drawbridge of Nottingham Castle was creaking down. The sheriff was ready to ride again.

The Significance of America's Third Capitalist Heyday

To the average American family of 1980, cultural issues were important, but economics were probably a greater preoccupation. Too much regulation and a sense of excessive, heavy-handed government placed near the top of the list, polls showed. Labor unions, many people felt, were pushing the costs of U.S. products too high. Taxes had to come down, especially because inflation, people's top concern, was lifting middle-income people into ever-steeper brackets. And inflation itself had to be stopped.

When disdain for expanding bureaucracy converges with worry about overregulation and dislike of labor unions, inflation and higher taxes, the middle class usually opts for strongly conservative politics. This was the voters' response during the 1980s to the excesses of the late 1970s, just as it had been the reaction in the 1920s to the price rises and expanded regulation accompanying World War I, and, before that, to the explosion of prices and bureaucracy brought about by the Civil War. Beyond any coincidence, all three countertides of anti-tax, antigovernment and anti-inflation sentiment produced strong enough ideological currents—and corollary financial booms—to suggest that the Gilded Age (from the mid-1870s to the mid-1890s), the Roaring Twenties and the 1980s were what I have called "capitalist heydays."

These three heydays, described at some length in *The Politics of Rich and Poor,* each involved ten common elements.

Shared "Capitalist Heyday" Circumstances of the 1980s,
1920s and the Gilded Age

1. Republican presidents and dominant conservative politics;
2. Popular and elite belief that government had previously become too big and that there should be less of it;
3. Exaltation of business, with philosophic emphasis on the *private* sector rather than the *public* sector;
4. Low national regard for organized labor;
5. Major restructuring of the U.S. economy, accompanied by merger waves and innovations in business reorganization;
6. Tax reduction, especially high-bracket income taxes;
7. Pursuit of disinflation in response to prior inflation;
8. Economic weakness in the commodity-producing U.S. heartland, with stronger prosperity in the coastal areas;
9. Concentration of wealth and increasing inequality of income;
10. Rising and increasingly precarious levels of speculation, leverage and debt.

Collectively, it was not the sort of rising tide that lifted all boats. This mix of conservatism, skepticism about government, enthusiasm for business, deregulation, tax cuts, disinflation and leveraged corporate restructuring has always concentrated its high yields on the top 1 percent of Americans. But despite this inherent bias toward the rich, much of the middle class—smaller and more elite back then—also shared in the boom of the Gilded Age and the Roaring Twenties, albeit often marginally.* The downside was that, after 1893 and 1929—and then again during 1987–91—middle-class Americans suffered in the inevitable subsequent collapse of banks, credit and asset values. However, in the first two periods, no long-term slippage resulted, because after the boom and bust, the middle class, along with the country itself, bounced back more strongly than ever.

Skeptics like MIT's Lester Thurow and Harvard professor Benjamin Friedman argued that the 1980s, by contrast, threatened a *lasting* decline, that the unique recklessness of public finance in the 1980s posed a critical difference. Whereas during the Gilded Age and the 1920s a careful federal government had maintained regular budget

---

*Federal economic data for these periods are minimal. The principal benefits went to the rich, and the 10 to 20 percent of Americans in the middle class also improved their income and wealth. Below these levels, the boom petered out. Part Two of this book opens with a look at the "squeezes" on Middle America and its income in the two previous heydays.

surpluses, the several administrations of the 1980s ran up huge deficits that tripled the national debt yet simultaneously provoked new budgetary processes that kept forcing revenue increases. Worse still, the two previous boom-bust periods had come when American economic power was still ascending internationally. The boom of the 1980s, by contrast, was staged as U.S. global economic decline took hold, but under the premise that the go-go policies and attitudes involved were a revitalization process. This time some of the huge new debt load and intensifying economic polarization did have longer-term implications.

These pages will argue that America's heyday practices of the 1980s were, for the first time, those of a weakening great economic power, risking its credit and its future and abusing its middle-class citizenry for the benefit of elites and special interests. But "Soak the middle" practices were not unique to the United States. Similar patterns were also apparent in other major nations that had shifted to the right during the 1980s and chosen governments philosophically akin to the Reagan administration. The interests of Middle Britain, Middle Japan and Middle Canada were also being subordinated to those of economic elites—or so local critics would be charging as the 1980s ended.

The International Supremacy of Conservative Political Economics: From Exuberance to Excess?

Squeezing the ordinary people is one of history's oldest fiscal practices. Sixteenth-century Spain and eighteenth-century France, for example, largely excused the nobility from taxes, levying them principally or the peasants and middle classes, provoking some of the anger that ultimately led to revolution and its philosophical rationalization by Karl Marx. Socialism in Europe temporarily created a reverse set of abuses in the middle third of the twentieth century, but, all the while, conservative preference for cutting government programs and shifting taxes back to the average citizen smoldered in still-warm embers, ready to reignite. This happened in the 1980s as conservative tax and deregulation philosophies spread, and as the political right took control of most governments in the Group of Seven nations—the United States, Japan, Canada, Britain, France, Germany and Italy. Moreover, the conservatism involved was far more crusading and aggressive than at any other time in the previous fifty years. In Europe, as in the United States, tax cuts and deregulation were at first energizing. More controversial policies that burdened the middle—for the sake of unburdening those at the top—were to come later, when conservative governments were surer of their power and ideology.

This militant new conservatism was ideologically powerful enough to spread far beyond the major financial powers, swaying even nominally Labor or Socialist governments in nations like Australia, New Zealand and Spain. Upward redistribution of wealth became global, and the rich became objects of emulation almost everywhere. Nevertheless, the most aggressive ideology and results seem to have come in the United States and Britain, the principal seedbeds of the new free-market religion. A survey conducted by three U.S. Census Bureau economists, which compared early- and mid-1980s household earnings for the United States, Canada, Sweden, Australia and West Germany, found that the gap between rich and poor was the greatest in the United States. The highest percentage of income was going to the top 10 percent of households, and they had also enjoyed the greatest increase in their share. Canada was second. Socialist Sweden was at the low end, with the upper-income quintile holding roughly constant in its share of income during 1981–87.[1]

But if ideology was a brake in Sweden, it was an accelerator in Margaret Thatcher's Britain. In 1991 the Central Statistical Office of the British Treasury released new income data documenting a sharp rise in household income inequality. In 1979 the poorest fifth had accounted for 9.5 percent of after-tax income; by 1988 that dropped to 6.9 percent. Meanwhile the share of the top fifth rose from 37 percent to 44 percent.[2]

The reign of uninhibited conservative economics within the Group of Seven probably peaked in 1987–88, when the ruling governments of Britain, Canada and the United States scored strong—and somewhat unexpected—reelection victories. By 1988 and 1989 conservative British, Japanese and Canadian regimes had begun pursuing regressive tax policies that would soon arouse middle-class anger, with predictable political consequences.

British prime minister Margaret Thatcher had overcome familiar charges of favoring the rich to win a third straight Conservative party victory in 1987. However, she quickly followed up in 1988 by proposing bold new reductions in the popular national health service, urging further cuts in Britain's top income tax rate (trimming it from 60 percent to 40 percent) and then topping both with a fiscal stunner: the replacement of property taxes at the local government level by a "community service charge" or head tax levied equally on each individual, rich or poor. Tory stalwarts hoped the per capita charge would force a tax-aroused citizenry to take pruning shears to local government, but debate soon came to pivot on unfairness—on how a cleaning woman in a low-income council house would now pay the same as the belted earl down the lane in his Jacobean manor. Critics enjoyed pointing out how Thatcher herself would pay $3,600 a year less in poll taxes than she currently paid in property taxes on her retirement home in Dulwich.[3]

Tory economic self-interest notwithstanding, Thatcher's boldness represented historical bravado. The last time a British government imposed a uniform poll tax on its people—back in 1381—a mob forced its way into the Tower of London, seized royal ministers and beheaded the chancellor of the exchequer.[4] And sure enough, by the time the poll tax went into effect on April 1, 1990, London's streets once again echoed to riots and marching feet. The prime minister herself was never threatened physically, but the political peril was consuming. No sooner had Conservatives been drubbed in May's local elections, thanks to the poll tax and a spreading recession, than opposition Labourites went ahead by 12 to 15 points in trial heats for a future general election. To save the party, many back-bench Conservative parliamentarians said both Thatcher and the poll tax would have to go. A November insurrection forced the embattled prime minister to step down, then the second decision—whether and how to replace the poll tax—hung fire until March 1991, when the Conservatives lost a hitherto safe seat in a by-election in northwest England's Ribble Valley. The winning candidate, Michael Carr of the small third-party Liberal Democrats, boasted that "When the poll tax is finally put to rest in its grave, its epitaph will read: 'Here lies the poll tax. Killed in Ribble Valley!' "[5]

The execution was announced a few days later by John Major, the new prime minister who had replaced Thatcher. But the party continued to disagree over how to replace the tax until substitute measures were spelled out in April—a hybrid of a seven-bracket property tax, an adjustment for family size and a further 2-percentage-point increase in the regressive value-added (consumption) tax. It was not a popular solution, but with Thatcher gone, the poll tax repudiated and John Major, whose origins were lower-middle class, forsaking Thatcher-type rhetoric, escalating public spending on services and promising a "classless" society, the Conservatives lost forty seats but kept a narrow majority in the 1992 national elections.

Canada's ruling Conservatives made their own fiscal miscalculation in 1988 after winning lopsided control of Parliament for five more years. That year, the top individual tax rate had been cut from 34 percent to 29 percent and the top corporate rate from 36 percent to 28 percent. Then in April 1989, reflecting the general Western ideological movement toward taxing consumption rather than income, Prime Minister Brian Mulroney proposed a new 9 percent "goods and services tax" (GST), quickly labeled the cribs-to-coffins tax, which applied to just about all goods except food—and also to piano lessons, lawyer fees and even sending a fax. In part, the GST was to replace a sixty-five-year-old manufacturers' sales tax, then levied at a rate of 12 percent on only about a third of goods and services purchased by Canadians. But the basis of vulnerability was obvious. Ed Broadbent, leader of the opposition New Democratic party, quickly attacked the proposal as "extraordinarily regressive," because the "poor pay the same rate as the rich."[6]

Polls taken when Parliament reconvened in autumn showed 75 percent of the electorate opposed to the GST, and by December, when the government backtracked by reducing its proposed 9 percent rate to 7 percent, public support for the Conservatives had dropped to just 21 percent in Canada's Gallup Poll. A year later, when after an energetic filibuster Canada's Senate finally approved the GST for January 1991 start-up, support for Mulroney and the Conservatives had sunk to a rock-bottom 15 percent! Before the final vote, opposition Liberals blew kazoos and waved polls that showed 80 percent of Canadians didn't want the tax, and the *Toronto Star* ran an editorial cartoon showing the prime minister as a menacing, fanged vampire and a caption that read: "I want to suck your wallet."[7]

The unfairness theme continued, with critics saying it would be better to return the corporate tax rate to 36 percent, or at least to set up a corporate minimum tax (to get $8 billion a year from 60,000 concerns that managed to pay no federal tax at all).[8] Middle-class Canadians agreed. Voters in the $30,000–$50,000 bracket condemned the new GST (after it had gone into effect) by 76 percent to 23 percent in 1991 polls.[9] In September 1990, influenced by recession, the GST controversy and threats to the country's social safety net, a surprising number of middle-class voters had joined in electing Ontario's first-ever socialist provincial government.

In Japan, anger at Japan's (conservative) Liberal Democratic party for pairing a new 3 percent consumption tax with top-income-tax-bracket reduction had already come to a head in 1989. Over the previous two years, soaring stock and real estate prices had, perversely, begun to shred Japan's self-image as a broadly middle-class society.

The record real estate prices were making property owners rich while people without property found themselves in a hole, unable to buy homes or to keep up with the Japanese equivalent of the Joneses. In response to a 1988 survey by the Government Economy Planning Agency, 74 percent of Japanese went so far as to call their country's economic system basically unfair.[10] And to add to voters' disenchantment, the governing LDP was embroiled in the infamous Recruit Corporation scandal, which caught leading politicians in a web of bribes, greed and easy-money stock deals.

So when the government proposed a new 3 percent tax on consumption, while lowering the top income-tax rate from 60 percent to 50 percent and cutting the top corporate rate from 42 percent to 37.5 percent, public indignation crystallized. Japan's Socialists won a surprise victory in the July 1989 elections for the upper house of parliament, making big gains among housewives and the elderly after attacking the unpopular consumption levy and suggesting that the revenues would be better raised by taxing stock market and real estate profits.*

LDP leaders understood that some changes were necessary. Modifications in the consumption tax were set forth in time for the early 1990 elections to parliament's lower house, and the LDP easily retained power despite gains by the Socialist minority. However, as the speculative bubble in the Japanese real estate and stock markets— Japan's even frothier equivalent of the Reagan boom—fell apart in 1991–92, with new scandals adding to government woes, LDP fortunes remained uncertain and the opposition maintained its control of the upper house of parliament in mid-1992 elections.

The common denominator was obvious: conservative governments, consistent in their capitalist and free-market assertiveness, were trying to manage markets and raise revenues in ways that would least interfere with business, investment, property and the rich, a goal that frequently involved increasing the burden on those who were not rich. In Britain, where Conservative free-market ideology was purest, the infuriating poll tax was a logical extension of the dismantling of the public sector and enlargement of the private sector already under way

---

*Voter concern was justified. Economists at S. G. Warburg in Tokyo calculated in 1992 that since tax "reform" in April 1989 the amount a Japanese paid in income tax had grown, on average, by 14.5 percent a year, while the average household income had risen only 7.7 percent a year. Worse still, because Social Security contributions had also climbed an average of 11.7 percent a year, total household income was also lower in mid-1992 than it would have been without tax reform ("So Rich, So Poor," *The Economist*, June 20, 1992, p. 32).

through privatization, deregulation, taxation of consumption (to reduce taxes on income that might become investment), cuts in social services and attempts to finance public services by narrow user fees instead of broad general revenues. The problem, simply, was that it angered ordinary Britons. The British middle class never opposed selling off stale socialist enterprises or restoring economic incentive. But by 1989–90, following the Thatcher regime's announcement of the poll tax and plans to curb the National Health Service, opinion surveys showed the average middle-class voter increasingly concerned about where this new ideology might lead: to the rich getting richer, to more uncertainty for the middle class and to cutbacks in services for the average family (not just the poor). In the major financial capitals of the West, the 1980s ended as economic conservatism overplayed its political hand and voters began to look to the center.

"Soak the Middle" Economics in the United States

Many of the same philosophies also guided Washington, although not to the extent of such a huge symbolic error as Britain's poll tax. Following Ronald Reagan's election in 1980, the ultraconservative Heritage Foundation had presented incoming Republican office-holders with a blueprint (*Mandate for Leadership*) for greatly reducing the cost and size of the federal government, including abolition of several government departments and functions and large-scale privatization. However, if only a few agencies were actually shuttered (such as the Civil Aeronautics Board and the Office of Economic Opportunity), and if relatively little was privatized beyond Conrail and the Federal National Mortgage Association, that was in part because the Reagan administration, from the beginning, was preoccupied elsewhere: with tax cuts and what quickly became the Economic Recovery Tax Act of 1981.

Hostility to progressive income taxation was a mainstay of the Reagan wing of the Republican party. The new president's personal appetite for switching to a flat-rate personal income tax and abolishing the corporate income tax, whetted by the punitive 91 percent top rate of his movie-star years, told only part of the story. For two centuries of American fiscal history, the GOP and its antecedent upper-bracket parties, the eighteenth-century Federalists and nineteenth-century Whigs, had usually been reluctant to tax income or wealth; they generally preferred to tax production or consumption.

Under Federalist and Whig governance, the early United States raised most of its national revenue from excise taxes and import tariffs. The new Republican party continued this tilt, after its formation in the mid-1850s, despite inaugurating a temporary income tax to fight the Civil War (and then ending it in 1872). The *permanent* progressive income tax was not enacted until 1913 under Democratic president Woodrow Wilson, although reform-minded GOP president Theodore Roosevelt had also urged it. The conservative Republican presidents of the 1920s were less sympathetic. Income tax rates had soared (to a top rate of 77 percent) during World War I, but Presidents Harding and Coolidge brought the top rate down to 25 percent by 1925. In 1920 income taxes had produced 66 percent of federal government revenues versus 15 percent for excise taxes and tariffs; by 1928 that proportion had shifted to 56 percent versus 27 percent. Because the average American family was not rich enough to have to pay income taxes in the 1920s, in some ways it was better off when they predominated.

When Franklin D. Roosevelt, the New Deal and World War II restored the primacy of the income tax, Republicans were unhappy—and especially unhappy with a top rate that briefly reached 94 percent in 1944. However, after GOP-led attempts to reduce the upper-rate structure backfired politically in the 1948 elections, the Republicans made no real effort to rewrite the rate tables during the 1950s. Nor did Richard Nixon, after his 1969 inauguration, respond to conservative arguments for bracket reduction that would go beyond the cuts made by Democrats in 1964. Once inflation rekindled in the mid-1970s, though, so did Republican sentiment for reducing income taxes again and increasing the burden on wages and consumption. One spur was the persuasive argument of lobbyists for capital formation and investment that U.S. entrepreneurialism was being diminished; a second was the extent to which price rises were souring Middle America on income taxation. Bracket creep had long since forced average families to become income tax payers; now it was relentlessly saddling ordinary householders with rates once reserved for the top 5 percent of earners. For all these reasons, the Reagan years would become the first period since the 1920s when Republicans could think about displacing the old *progressive* income tax with *regressive* revenue devices, such as (1) a minimally progressive or even flat income tax; (2) a broadened, higher-rate flat tax on employees (FICA); and (3) user fees, excise taxes and consumption taxes.

In retrospect, conservative economic strategists would fail only with the boldest of their new ideas—a flat-rate, single-bracket income tax and a national consumption tax. Otherwise, by the end of the 1980s, renascent U.S. conservatism had all but dismantled the progressive rate structure of the New Deal, creating a system that applied virtually the same top rates to Los Angeles high school principals as to millionaires. Back in 1950 a salaried $100,000-a-year family in the top 1 percent income group would have paid combined federal taxes at an approximately 50 percent rate that was eight times the 5 to 6 percent effective rate paid by a $3,000-a-year median-income family.* But by 1990 a $500,000-a-year family paid an effective overall federal tax rate of about 29 percent, only slightly higher than the 28 percent paid by the $50,000-a-year two-earner household identified as the "average family" by the Tax Foundation.

Following the first Reagan-era tax cuts in 1981, middle-class families, pleased that their own income taxes were being reduced by 25 percent (over three years) and simultaneously indexed against inflation, scarcely worried that much bigger reductions were going to corporations and upper-bracket taxpayers. By 1986, however, alert voters could identify a half-dozen instances in which the decade's emerging theology leaned hardest on middle-class taxpayers. In Chapter 5, I will lay out these matters in detail; here I simply want to document the importance of the *political* and *ideological* upheaval.

A good place to begin is the overhaul of the Social Security retirement system following the 1983 recommendations of a bipartisan commission headed by former Republican Council of Economic Advisers chairman Alan Greenspan. The commission was spurred by fears of insufficient revenues to finance the expected huge costs of baby-boomer retirement after 2010. As a solution, it recommended—and Congress accepted—a rapid escalation of the single-rate Social Security (FICA) tax. Back in 1980, earnings up to $25,000 had been taxable at a rate of 6.13 percent, for a maximum yearly individual contribution of $1,588. The new plan, by contrast, expanded planned FICA increases to make earnings up to $51,300 taxable as of 1990 at an annual rate of 7.65 percent, requiring a maximum individual contribution of $3,924. With so many more wives working, this represented—as we shall see—a very large federal tax increase on two-earner couples in the middle and upper-middle class. For the top 1 percent of taxpayers, with over $200,000 a year, FICA increases were proportionately minor; what often became a $2,000–$4,000 additional annual burden fell hardest in the middle.

In ideological terms, Washington was raising *regressive* Social Secu-

*See page 1112 of *The Statistical History of the United States* (New York: Basic Books, 1976) for the effective income tax rates that year—47 percent on the $100,000 family, 3.5 percent on the $3,000 family. My increases are to allow for FICA taxes (1 percent each from employer and employee on $3,000) and excise taxes.

rity taxes even as *progressive* income taxes were being cut—especially for those at the top. Quietly but steadily, the federal revenue-raising burden was shifting away from the income tax (corporate and individual), which had produced 60 percent of total receipts in 1980 but just 55 percent in 1990, and toward FICA levies, which had brought in 31 percent of the total in 1980 but a larger 37 percent in 1990. Table 2 suggests that for families in the middle quintile, by the end of the decade the net easing of federal income tax burdens was canceled out by increased Social Security taxes.

In addition, a slick use of surplus Social Security dollars—*not* legally required to be set aside for future retirees—served to reduce pressures for a higher top income tax rate. In 1985 the architects of the Gramm-Rudman deficit-reduction act succeeded in specifying that any annual Social Security tax surplus—by 1991, it was $75 billion—could be used to reduce the official federal deficit calculation. This jeopardized the original purpose of the 1983 FICA tax increase, and when one member of the U.S. Senate Finance Committee, Daniel P. Moynihan of New York, later referred to it as "robbery," a second member, John Heinz of Pennsylvania, was more precise: No, he pointed out, it was closer to embezzlement.[11] One of Reagan's Social Security commissioners, Dorcas Hardy, would later write a book making the same point.*

Then in 1986, the president and Congress agreed on yet another far-reaching federal tax overhaul in the name of "fairness and simplification." These changes further reduced income tax rates, but while taking away many tax shelters important to the rich, also took away popular deductions and credits long cherished by the middle class. Opinion surveys found voters skeptical: the newest reform, they thought, only made the federal income tax more complex and less fair.

Table 2. Federal Effective Tax Rates for All of
the Middle Quintile (combined) Families

	1977	1980	1985	1988	1993 (est.)
Individual Income Tax	6.9%	7.9%	6.7%	6.4%	6.2%
Social Security Tax (FICA)	8.1%	8.6%	9.7%	10.1%	10.1%

Source: Congressional Budget Office tax simulation model, cited in U.S. House Ways and Means Committee 1992 Green Book, p. 1529.

Note: A second computation by several CBO economists found combined federal income Social Security and excise taxes as a percentage of average family income rising from 20.4% in 1980 to 20.9% in 1990 (*New York Times*, October 1, 1992).

*See p. 184.

Before long, one unusual legislative wrinkle would become particularly infamous. In addition to the two statutory rates of 15 percent and 28 percent, which was the new top bracket (reduced from 50 percent), Washington legislative draftsmen introduced "the bubble," a special 33 percent marginal rate that applied not to the *richest* taxpayers but to the *upper-middle class* in the $70,000–$170,000 bracket.* Although supporters insisted that this made the new tax structure more progressive, the effect on the upper-middle class and on the truly rich was just the opposite: the 33 percent marginal rate imposed on a $125,000 corporate middle manager *dropped* to 28 percent for David Rockefeller, Sam Walton and even those with mere million-dollar incomes. The explanation was that the multibillion-dollar revenues gained from putting upper-middle-class taxpayers in a special 33 percent bubble were critical to avoiding a third bracket with a top rate in the mid-thirties that would have applied to genuinely high incomes. Bubbles exist in other parts of the tax code, but the imposition of the highest marginal rate on the upper-middle class, not the rich, had no parallel in any other major nation's late-twentieth-century income tax chart. As progressivity eroded, the income tax was managing to develop a few *regressive* twists.

Meanwhile, the outline of a major new "user fee" emerged in 1988, when Congress and the president enacted a program of health insurance against catastrophic illness for those over sixty-five. Instead of being financed out of general revenues (or even out of Social Security levies on the overall work force), "catastrophic" was to be funded by what was demonstrably a surtax confined to senior citizens, but which politicians preferred to call an "income-based premium." On their regular income tax, the elderly were to pay a 15 percent surcharge, which was capped at $800 per individual and $1,600 per couple in 1989, but rising to $2,100 per couple by 1993. As a percentage of income, the surcharge would have hit hardest those individuals and couples in the $25,000–$45,000 range. In the autumn of 1989, however, senior citizens in the $25,000-and-over range—the "rich" elderly, some reports called them—mobilized in such anger that a trembling Congress repealed the legislation. Despite this retreat under fire, the fiscal philosophy involved remained largely unchanged until 1990.†

By the late 1980s, some senior citizens also faced other marginal

---

*The 1986 bubble and its successor, the slightly different 1991 bubble, will be explained in Chapter 5.

†In 1990, that year's budget agreement raised the true top rate from 28 percent to 31 percent.

rates far above the 28 percent maximum by then applied to the highest incomes. Two cross-effects were involved: first, the 1983 reforms had included a decision to tax Social Security benefits for single persons with incomes above $25,000 and for couples above $32,000; and second, there was a long-standing limitation on *other* income, under which Social Security recipients aged sixty-five to sixty-nine lost $1 in benefits for every $3 of income above roughly $10,000 a year. As pointed out relentlessly in publications for retired persons, the effective tax rate on additional earnings—by the time penalties and federal and state taxes were applied—could reach 80 percent.[12]

Meanwhile, spending responsibilities for programs from Medicaid to transportation were increasingly turned back by Washington to states and localities, often accompanied by proportionately lower federal contributions. This reduced the tax revenues that federal authorities would otherwise have needed, and as we shall see in more detail later, helped make it possible to ease federal taxation of high incomes. However, it also meant much more regressive taxes at lower levels of government: state sales; alcohol, tobacco and gasoline levies; local property taxes; and a host of charges and user fees. Some states and localities did raise their income tax brackets during the 1980s, but the biggest states—New York and California—implemented top-rate reductions paralleling the federal cuts and reflecting Washington's philosophy. In states like Illinois and Massachusetts, among others, incomes were taxed at only one rate. Florida, Connecticut, Texas and seven other jurisdictions didn't even have state income levies.

Like Social Security, state and local levies were generally regressive—and regressive taxes were a fiscal growth area of the 1980s. In 1982 Washington had collected $298 billion in federal income taxes while state and local taxes totaled $266 billion.[13] In 1990 federal income levies produced $493 billion while the state and local tax receipts had jumped to $540 billion, with much of the increment coming from sales and property taxes and user fees.[14] The distributional economics were a far cry from those of the federal income tax—especially the old, pre-Reagan rate structure. Compilations for 1990 showed that combined state and local taxes took 14.8 percent of the annual income of the poor, about 10 percent of that of the middle classes and a much lower 7.6 percent from the top 1 percent.

In 1990 there were even attempts to take back the existing federal day-care tax credit from a large portion of the middle class, prompting Colorado congresswoman Pat Schroeder to complain, "This is not like restricting deductions for a Rolls-Royce or a Mercedes. In many urban areas, you're talking about taking away the benefits for families with two teachers or a fireman and a teacher."[15]

That same year, Congress and the Bush administration increased federal excise taxes on alcohol, tobacco and gasoline, as well as user fees. Some 4.1 million owners of recreational boats were outraged to find they would have to start paying fees of $25 to $100 a year for Coast Guard decals in order to operate in navigable U.S. waters. What had been free to ordinary Americans now, in more and more cases, required access charges. At the state level, the proliferation of user fees and nuisance taxes was even worse, exemplified by Florida's new surtax on speeding tickets and Maryland's fees on burial lots.

Alongside their new emphasis on charging fees for services, some administration strategists proposed to reduce or eliminate middle-class eligibility for federal aid programs by means testing, pursuing earlier hints given when middle-income Social Security pensions were exposed to taxation in 1983. In 1991, federal budget director Richard Darman recommended income-eligibility ceilings for federal agricultural payments, Medicare premium subsidies, college aid and school lunches. The idea of cutting off federal grants to hundreds of thousands of college students with family incomes over $20,000 prompted some educators to complain about hurting the middle and lower-middle classes to help the poor. Darman, however, had even more sweeping transformations in mind, urging Congress and the administration to agree on some income level "higher than $20,000 and lower than $125,000" and then "apply it uniformly across the board" as the cutoff point for "a whole range of mandatory [benefit] programs aside from Social Security."[16] His aim was less to maximize benefits for the poor than to reduce the deficit by curbing middle-class entitlements—even if this meant reducing net income to the middle class—while protecting the reductions in top income tax rates that had been achieved during the 1980s.

Even tax-collection directives were targeted on the middle class instead of the rich. In March 1991 Internal Revenue commissioner Fred Goldberg told the House Ways and Means Oversight Subcommittee about the request he had rejected from the federal Office of Management and Budget. Officials at that agency had wanted to step up tax audits against lower- and middle-income taxpayers, whose wages, receipts and transactions could be easily monitored, and to de-emphasize audits of high-income individuals and businesses, whose financial holdings and maneuvers were much harder to trace.

Taken together, these changes added up to a striking new ideology of favoring the investing class at the expense of the middle class—a considerable turnabout. As we have seen, the new bias also extended to banks, financial markets and corporate mergers. In political terms, though, the future pivot would be whether the policy revolution of the 1980s had quietly decreased the after-tax purchasing power of most families in the mid-section of the U.S. population—and the answer seems to be "yes." Contemporary calculations varied, however, blurred by the tendency of most national organizations to measure only the impact of federal taxes while omitting state and local levies because of the wide variations between jurisdictions.

The effect of federal tax changes alone is spelled out in Tables 3A and 3B, prepared by the conservative Tax Foundation (co-chaired in the early 1990s by former Reagan budget director James C. Miller III). Note that Table 3A showed a 1977–87 *decline* in median family income after adjusting for inflation and changes in direct federal taxes. Within this table, the 1982–87 figures show a gain, but of only 5 percent. For all the 1980s talk about tax cuts, *after-tax* median family income never

Table 3. Changes in Family After-Tax Income, 1977–1990

A) Median Family Income Before and After Direct Federal Taxes and Inflation, 1977–1987

Year	Median Family Income[a]	Direct Federal Taxes			After-tax Income	
		Income Tax[b]	Social Security	Total	Current Dollars	1987 Dollars[c]
1977	15,949	1,466	933	2,399	13,550	25,518
1978	17,318	1,717	1,048	2,765	14,553	25,442
1979	19,048	1,881	1,168	3,049	15,999	25,116
1980	20,586	2,143	1,262	3,405	17,181	23,763
1981	21,462	2,267	1,427	3,694	17,768	22,266
1982	23,036	2,342	1,543	3,885	19,151	22,610
1983	23,943	2,277	1,604	3,881	20,062	22,854
1984	25,415	2,395	1,703	4,098	21,317	23,374
1985	25,992	2,466	1,832	4,298	21,694	23,005
1986[d]	27,144	2,865	1,941	4,806	22,338	23,220
1987[d]	28,230	2,704	2,018	4,722	23,508	23,508

[a]Median income for all families with one earner employed full-time, year-round.

[b]Married couple filing joint return, two dependent children.

[c]Adjusted by Consumer Price Index of the Bureau of Labor Statistics. Assumes 4% inflation in 1987.

[d]Estimated by Tax Foundation.

Sources: U.S. Department of Commerce, Bureau of the Census; U.S. Department of Labor, Bureau of Labor Statistics; Treasury Department, Internal Revenue Service.

Source: *Tax Features*, July/August 1987.

B) Median Family Income Before and After Direct Federal Taxes and Inflation
1980–1990

Year	Two-Earner Median Family Income[a]	Direct Federal Taxes			After-Tax Income	
		Income Tax[b]	Social Security	Total	Current Dollars	1990 Dollars[c]
1980	$29,627	$4,050	$1,816	$5,866	$23,761	$37,902
1981	32,224	4,386	2,143	6,529	25,695	37,155
1982	34,515	4,450	2,313	6,763	27,752	37,800
1983	36,106	4,300	2,419	6,719	29,387	38,781
1984	38,713	4,634	2,710	7,344	31,369	39,684
1985	40,593	4,787	2,862	7,649	32,944	40,243
1986	42,492	5,158	3,038	8,196	34,298	41,130
1987	44,536	5,291	3,184	8,475	36,061	41,724
1988	46,658	5,618	3,504	9,122	37,538	41,705
1989	49,000	6,022	3,687	9,709	39,381	41,744
1990[d]	51,421	6,357	3,934	10,291	41,130	41,130

[a]Median income for household with two earners employed full-time, year round.

[b]Married couple filing joint return, two dependent children.

[c]Adjusted by consumer price index, estimated 6% inflation in 1990.

[d]Estimate.

Source: Tax Foundation; U.S. Department of Commerce, Bureau of the Census; U.S. Department of Labor, Bureau of Labor Statistics; U.S. Treasury Department, Internal Revenue Service.

did recover its late 1970s levels. In 1988, however, the foundation abandoned the official federal yardstick of a median family with one earner to redefine "the median family as two earners working fulltime the year round with two dependents."[17] Such families were doing better. But despite this new formula the 1987–90 data for the average family yielded an after-tax net income *decline*—and even before the 1991–92 data worsened the trend, the overall result for the period from 1977 to 1990 was relative stagnation. Moreover, once state and local tax increases were added, the impact on the average family's after-tax income is even more pronounced, as the state-level details in Chapter 5 show.

In short, for the typical family, the combined tax reforms, rearrangements and user fees of the 1980s, coming on top of inflation, meant no gain in purchasing power. The rich were no longer being soaked, but those in the middle were. Behind the façade of shared prosperity and tax cuts for everyone, the average American family was no longer advancing.

Middle-Class Interests and the Breach of the
Postwar "Social Contract"

Few developments of the 1980s were less expected (or debated) than the breakdown of the broad political consensus, effective from World War II through the 1970s, that government's duty was to the great mass of citizens, not to a small elite. Yet this breakdown was probably inevitable in the 1980s, once heyday capitalism was ready to move beyond its broadly supported first stage of imposing curbs on bureaucracy and regulatory excesses, encouraging entrepreneurial incentive and framing general tax reduction. Successful movements tend to succumb to their own appetites, spurning restraint, and as we have seen, that became a particular pitfall of tax policy in the late 1980s. This chapter will argue that capitalist-conservative theology eventually trespassed on middle-class psychology in several counterproductive ways: (1) by reducing not just unpopular, overbearing bureaucratic usurpations of government but familiar, comforting services and roles; (2) by an intense, overly ideological emphasis on markets and marketplace functions at the expense of some community values and traditions; (3) by "one-world" capitalist approaches to trade and markets that sometimes subordinated national economic interests and sacrificed salvageable industries; (4) by downgrading the principle of shared sacrifice and disproportionate burden-bearing by the rich; and (5) by development of theories of economic efficiency and globalization that either lionized financiers and investors or opposed interference with their interests.

The 1980s, to repeat, began with government fairly in disrepute for its swollen size and record of aggravating rather than solving problems. And for all that conservatism's boldest ambitions failed—such as Britain's poll tax and proposals in the United States to abolish the departments of Energy and Education—the ruling politicians in both countries took advantage of the new climate to achieve much more than simply impugning excessive government and government services. In the United States, for example, programs ranging from revenue-sharing to Urban Development Action Grants were terminated or sharply reduced. By the late 1980s the hostility to government put into overdrive by the rapprochement of neoconservatives and traditional laissez-faire Republicans in the late 1970s had helped achieve a substantial reduction in discretionary nondefense federal spending as a percentage of both outlays and the GNP. Entitlement programs were untouchable, but discretionary domestic spending declined from about 22 percent of federal outlays in 1980 to under 15 percent in 1989.

Moreover, although foreign visitors to the United States might be struck by the decay, the crumbling infrastructure, the "Brazilianization" of old cities like New York, the Reagan and Bush administrations continued to transfer program responsibility back to the states with inadequate financial support. Then, because of the severe recession that began in 1990, state and local governments from New York and Massachusetts to California confronted enormous fiscal deficits that promised to persist well into the decade—and reduced public outlays signaled further "Brazilianization."

Some of the same price was paid in Britain, where the Thatcher government unenthusiastically administered an already aging transportation system, worsening matters by abolishing the Greater London Council with its central planning authority for local buses, underground rail service, roads and traffic. Soon London started seizing up for large parts of the day. Public services in Britain had been so trimmed by the end of the decade that observers despaired at the erosion of public education, British Railways and the once-respected health service. Conditions on London's Underground had deteriorated to such a point that its chief executive described the system as "an appalling shambles."[18] British doctors even talked briefly about organizing a new party to fight the next election on the issue of a better health service.[19]

The changed political economics were the same on both sides of the Atlantic. The rich, with mushrooming after-tax income, were free to buy any service they desired, from helicopters, well-protected townhouses and Harley Street medical specialists to access to Harvard and Eton; it was the middle-class majorities in both countries that needed good publicly provided services—and so they duly reminded officials in opinion polls. In California or New York, Lewisham or Hertfordshire, declining services meant declining quality of life.

As the economic downturn of the early 1990s dragged on, some reductions became painful. In New York, where an $8 billion budget deficit for the 1992 fiscal year obliged the state to make deep spending cuts, suburban communities faced huge reductions in the unrestricted state-aid dollars used to patrol streets, fight fires, shovel snow and maintain parks and libraries.[20] In California the results of cutting services so as to eliminate half of a $14.6 billion state deficit ranged from a crippling effect on the state university system to a sharp reduction in firefighting crews and cuts in food safety and water-quality programs.[21] The next round of cuts in fiscal 1993 raised fears about the end of the California dream: already staggering under the burden of high unemployment, slumping revenues and the Los Angeles riots, the state was forced to slash education, health and welfare and support for city and county governments, as well as raising charges and fees. Moving companies began to report that record numbers of residents were packing and leaving the Golden State.

High-income persons did not suffer, but middle-class voters usually worried when federal and state reductions went too far. They opposed the welfare state in theory and favored rolling it back, but when the Reagan administration made its heaviest assault on middle-class federal programs in 1985, targeting school-lunch assistance, college aid, mass transit, general revenue sharing and others, even GOP voters protested. To the top 1 percent of Americans, government transfer payments were a negligible part of their own income (four tenths of 1 percent in 1988), while the payments Washington made to others merely aggravated federal tax demands. By contrast, citizens in the mid-range 40th to 59th percentiles received almost 10 percent of their total 1988 income from transfer payments, and enjoyed other substantial benefits from government loans, subsidies, aid programs and facilities ranging from national parks to intercoastal waterways. So although no precise data existed, many middle-class families believed themselves net gainers and worried that reduced or privatized services or a new system of means tests, charges and user fees would take money from their pockets. Conservative columnist Warren Brookes complained in 1990 that the broad middle class saw a "bigger stake" in federal spending (being its biggest beneficiary) than in keeping income taxes at their 1990 levels, and polls supported him.[22] As the economic downturn worsened, forcing cutbacks at the state and local levels, voter support for federal-program outlays and activist government grew.

Conservatism's occasional extreme exaltation of economic markets represented another breach with the beliefs that guided America's successful years after 1945. While liberals like to invoke societal and "community" values at the expense of incentive, markets and human acquisitiveness, the failing of the political right—amply indulged in the 1980s and into the 1990s—is to deify "markets" and "incentive" to the detriment of social and community interests. The more extreme mid-1980s examples, such as the Law and Economics movement, verged on self-caricature. One of its leaders, federal appeals court judge Richard A. Posner, proclaimed that the law should emphasize markets, efficiency and "wealth-maximization," not elusive concepts like society or fairness; and in a moment of particular enthusiasm, he even suggested making a market in babies so that it would be easier for couples to adopt.[23] Other market conservatives, such as the editorial writers of the *Wall Street Journal,* thought that "civil rights" should be increasingly defined economically, and President Reagan himself on July 3, 1987, proposed an Economic Bill of Rights in a ceremony at Washington's Jefferson Memorial. In sharp contrast to Franklin D. Roosevelt, who promoted a different Four Freedoms, Reagan invoked *commercial* liberties:

> The freedom to work and pursue a livelihood in one's own way, free from excessive government regulation and subsidized government competition; freedom to enjoy the fruits of one's labor without excessive taxing, spending and borrowing by the government; the freedom to own and control one's own property free from coercive or confiscatory regulation; and freedom to participate in a free market, to contract freely for goods and services and to achieve one's full potential without government limits on opportunity.[24]

Earlier Reagan-era hymns to economic individualism, together with conservatism's seeming abandonment of the egalitarianism of the New Deal and Fair Deal periods, prompted sociologist Robert N. Bellah to complain in mid-decade that rugged self-reliance had become "cancerous," sapping the middle class's sense of community and institutional commitment.[25] In addition to permissiveness toward finance and mergers, the politics of economic individualism, liberals charged, had shortchanged community interests like public schools, public roads, public parks, public health, public transport and public libraries. The supreme American public spaces of the Reagan era were not learning centers but economic arenas—the omnipresent marketplace, from office buildings and suburban malls to gentrified downtown shopping concourses.[26] For Middle America, the new preoccupation with enterprise and markets to the detriment of public services did have a downside: as public outlays on roads, schools and health came under pressure, the predictable results—worsened commuter gridlock, crowded classrooms and shortchanged hospitals and clinics—confronted ordinary families with either accepting lost services or paying new taxes or fees or higher bills, and as Chapter 6 shows, these losses and pressures became an ingredient of the middle-class squeeze.

The international aspect of 1980s worship of markets also broke with the past in a way that affected many average families. Some conservatives became "capitalist one-worlders," scoffing at national boundaries and even the concept of the nation-state. In the words of

The Wall Street Journal, they were "the economists and academics who believe that in a global economy, with goods and especially capital surging across political borders, the economic fortunes of individual countries aren't important anymore. The U.S. trade deficit and other statistics, they argue, are only artificial figures in what has become a multinational corporate economy in which political distinctions matter little. It's all one big market, they contend, so why worry about it?"[27] Workers who lost jobs in embattled U.S. industries were less able to shrug, and federal policymakers' responsiveness to boundaryless economics in the 1980s—including openness to lobbyists who promoted foreign interests—almost certainly abetted the decade's decline in real manufacturing wages. Perhaps America's older manufacturing industries, unimportant to adherents of the global market, truly had been a prop of the broader U.S. postwar affluence, so that their decline pulled America's short-lived blue-collar middle class down with them. Perhaps finance and services could not make up the loss. Views of this sort clashed with prevailing opinion, but we will see in Chapter 8 that previous similar transitions in Holland and Britain had signaled economic polarization and trouble, *not* revival, for the middle class.

Inroads on the principles of egalitarianism and disproportionate burden-bearing by the rich were widespread enough by the end of the 1980s that tax policy was just one ingredient. In the United States, calls for states' rights or "local decision-making" sometimes involved pushing federal programs and activities down to levels of government where the program would be abandoned, where money was unavailable or where funding would be too onerous for those who controlled local policy. While Washington could not openly discriminate against areas with greater needs than resources, pushing burdens back to state and local government often had the same effect. Yet it was striking how few politicians spoke up for the national "commonweal"—the general good or shared prosperity of the community. To America's Founding Fathers of 1776, attention to the commonweal was essential to national well-being. Private property, while important and valuable, was never an end in itself.

In Margaret Thatcher's Britain and Ronald Reagan's United States, however, a contrary philosophic shift became unmistakable. The willingness of America's elite to make economic sacrifice or serve in the military, to cite two conspicuous examples, had begun to erode during the 1960s, and widening urban racial gaps reinforced even liberal doubt about government's usefulness in promoting equality. Lyndon Johnson's ambitious Great Society had been much less successful than

Franklin Roosevelt's New Deal. By the 1980s many public-policy experts openly acknowledged being disheartened by government's failures during the 1960s, and sociologists like Seymour Martin Lipset allowed that increased acceptance of inequality in the West had "even socialist parties . . . acknowledging that for the economy to work you have to have unequal rewards."[28] During the 1980s the economic gap between people at the top and everyone else widened in virtually every arena—from sports and entertainment to business and finance. Inequality began to run amok.

To some extent, America was caught up in a two-part social myth: on the one hand an update of Horatio Alger and the anybody-can-make-it thesis, and on the other what Professor Benjamin DeMott called "the myth of classlessness"—the insistence that there were no classes in America, and that everyone, rich and poor, had common interests.[29] Conservatives were the self-serving propagators, he said, citing George Bush's insistence that class is "for European democracies or something else—it isn't for the United States of America. We are not going to be divided by class."[30] Yet many upper-middle-class cultural liberals shared the conservative desire to suppress any resurgent national discussion of economic class or of the quiet decline of egalitarian culture. Economist Robert Kuttner, a self-confessed populist, stood out from the prevalent elite opinion in being appalled "that the standard line on the declining middle has gone straight from 'It isn't happening' to 'We can't do anything about it.' "[31]

The Emerging Populist Protest

Yet the irony, just as in the 1960s, was that voters were ahead of the nation's opinion-molders in perceiving the failure and self-interest of an elite—this time, one premised on wealth and the glories of the marketplace. Writers and scholars might discuss rising acceptance of inequality and the fashionable admiration of the rich, but polls suggest that the electorate had started to become disenchanted in 1987 and 1988. By early 1990 *The New York Times* noted that Wall Street found an unnerving whiff of populism in the public's anger over junk-bond pioneer Michael Milken's $550-million-a-year salary, coupled with enthusiastic national response to books like *Bonfire of the Vanities* and *Barbarians at the Gates*.[32] Another measurement of popular disenchantment was apparent in the ratings slide of once-hot television glitz operas like *Dallas, Dynasty* and *Falconcrest*.

Then, in the autumn of 1990, when the issues of concentrated wealth and higher taxes for the rich suddenly took center stage in Washington's federal budget debate, public opinion polls in the United States surprised politicians with their populist intensity. Further detail will be set forth in Chapter 3, but *Fortune* magazine's survey right after the November elections found three quarters of respondents indicating that they had supported candidates in the election partly because of promises to spread the tax burden more fairly (from the middle class to the rich). December polling for NBC News and *The Wall Street Journal* found 84 percent of the public backing the Democrats' proposed surtax on millionaires—and that included 80 percent of the Republicans! Then in March 1991 the Roper Poll reported six out of ten Americans calling the federal tax system unfair and emphasizing increased fairness (higher corporate income taxes and a "millionaires' tax"). And an April national survey by the *Los Angeles Times* found a similar resentment of the federal tax system's unfairness, coupled with agreement by three quarters of respondents that "the wealthy should pay a higher tax rate than they do now."[33] There was good reason that by 1992, in what was by then an obvious populist surge, two of the three presidential candidates—Democrat Clinton and independent Perot—favored increasing taxes on the rich.

Nor was resentment of official favoritism to wealth confined to America. As we have seen, surveys were measuring related unhappiness among average voters in Britain, Canada and Japan. In all three countries, voters told polltakers that conservatism or conservative governments favored the rich and paid too little attention to the middle class, although voters had other complaints about the liberal or left alternatives.[34] The belief among some opinion-molders that the public accepted the economic philosophy of the 1980s and opposed raising taxes on the top 1 percent because of belief they themselves would be rich one day simply did not square with the evidence.

Indeed, as the 1992 elections made clear, something vaguely resembling the populist spirit that elected Andrew Jackson and Harry Truman was alive and well in the U.S. political system, and not just in obvious locales like Ohio steel towns and Missouri farm-foreclosure centers but to a significant extent also in raw new subdivisions at the ends of California freeways and on winding lanes in overtaxed suburban Long Island. Clinton's plurality of even the suburban vote should not have been a surprise. Sixty years earlier, under the New Deal, egalitarianism and government economic activism had replaced the conservatism of the 1920s because many in the middle class thought that they, too, might be in jeopardy and people looked to Washington for help. Some of those same concerns and fears were taking shape again in the early 1990s, even though voter doubts about the Democrats lingered, suspicions of government was still strong and the role electoral politics itself could play was unclear: could voters bring about another national watershed from the grass roots, or was Washington, divided for so long between the parties and encrusted with special interests, so paralyzed and self-protective that Americans could no longer expect politics and voting to be a solution?

The Middle-Class Political Response of the 1990s: Populism or Stalemate?

The great political upheaval of the 1960s is not that of Senator Eugene McCarthy's relatively small group of upper-middle-class intellectual supporters, but a populist revolt of the American masses who have been elevated by prosperity to middle-class status and conservatism. *Their* revolt is against the caste, policies and taxation of the mandarins of Establishment liberalism.

—Kevin P. Phillips, *The Emerging Republican Majority*, 1969

Anti-establishment populism has been the most important force in our politics for the last twenty years. It is neither liberal nor conservative. Politicians on both sides have used it effectively. American populism has three important characteristics. It is ideologically ambivalent. And it has displaced progressivism as the dominant motif of American politics. Elites tend to be rich and well-educated, hence, economically conservative and culturally sophisticated. Populism is anti-elitist and therefore just the reverse—left-wing on economic issues and right-wing on social and cultural issues.

—Political analyst William Schneider, 1986

In 1990 and 1991, as disenchanted Americans started telling pollsters—sometimes by 65 percent and even 75 percent majorities—that the United States was "seriously off on the wrong track," the anti-establishment populism so recurrent in U.S. political history roared once again. As I shall discuss in Chapter 9, angry outsiders like Vermont Socialist Bernard Sanders and Louisiana neo-fascist David Duke surprised observers by their political success, which foreshadowed the further populist waves of 1992. Columnist David Broder, a pillar of establishment thinking, muttered about "populist chic," and to an extent, his skepticism was appropriate: the capital's political class, worried about grass-roots anger, began the 1992 presidential election year weighing appeals to the frustrated middle class. Middle-class populism became a cliché—until Ross Perot's independent populist presidential candidacy pulled into a temporary lead in late-spring polls, and fear spread that middle-class frustration might be out of control.

Much of this was predictable. Populism in the United States has been more strident than almost anywhere else.[1] Yet the American style has been not to indulge in dangerous radicalism but over the last two centuries to harness and contain it: recurrent populism has been a periodic restorative of the unique genius of an American political process that, ultimately, has been orderly and centrist.

In contrast to continental Europe, where many capital cities have laid out broad boulevards to let the artillery suppress revolutionary mobs, the United States has achieved its revolutions through the ballot box, changing long-term control of the White House once every generation or so, usually all but expelling the party in power. And because the United States has no hereditary aristocracy to get in the way, these watersheds have also served to reshuffle the nation's elites.

This is what happened in 1800, 1828, 1860, 1932 and, most recently, 1968. After the 1966 elections, my sense that the conservative tide was producing another of these great waves prompted me to undertake my book *The Emerging Republican Majority.* Although very few political scientists agreed with its theses when it was published in 1969, by 1993 the Republicans had held the White House for twenty of the previous twenty-four years, clearly confirming my prediction.

The economics of the 1980s suggested that another tide would soon wash in. In *The Politics of Rich and Poor,* published in 1990, I suggested that many of the prerequisites of such a transition were in place—excessive wealth concentration (the traditional Republican Achilles' heel) and the rising anger of middle-class voters, along with other populist symptoms that ranged from intensifying public frustration with Washington to proliferating ballot initiatives and support for limiting officeholders' terms. The political calendar certainly suggested that another watershed could come in the 1990s, but in *Rich and Poor* I declined to predict that it would take the traditional electoral form.

In Chapters 1 and 2, I have tried to illustrate the rising plight of the middle class since 1973 and how it was made worse by the new economic philosophies of the 1980s. Here, in this chapter, I hope to frame the political importance of that deterioration. On the one hand, the possibility for upheaval could be seen in the economic vulnerability of the Republican middle-class, "populist-conservative" national majority that had been stitched together a quarter century earlier, a vulnerability that was evident in opinion polls revealing fears about future living standards and complaints about the economic unfairness of the 1980s and overtaxation of the middle class alongside inadequate taxation of the rich. Disbelievers, however, pointed to Washington's comfortable and unprecedented division of power between a Republican executive branch and a Democratic legislature, cemented by special interests. Fringe candidates and unexpectedly successful populist presidential contenders might cross the 1991–92 political sky like comets, but a broad national success for outsider politics would not easily be achieved—and even winning the election would only be the beginning. Polls taken for Ohio's Kettering Foundation, which became a touchstone for anti-Washington candidates in 1992, showed voters concerned that Washington had become an iron triangle beyond the reach of effective electoral correction.

The Late-Twentieth-Century Reemergence of U.S. Populism

The populism that had helped conservatives win the White House in 1968 remained wary of government over the next quarter century or so, and these suspicions flamed up again in the early 1990s. The economy had weakened and Washington seemed captive to special interests. Partly because of Watergate but also for other reasons, the Republican dominance of the presidency that had begun in 1968 never became more than a limited Washington beachhead; the Democrats usually controlled Congress, producing a divided government that shared power with a "moderate establishment," bipartisan in its makeup, interest-group in its economics, replacing the prior liberal Democratic one. The result was that populist forces bubbled on the right *and* left, although usually without much serious effect.*

From the standpoint of alienation and institutional disenchantment, however, the electorate of the early 1990s was seething. The average voter's increasing frustration with the domination by special interests of representative government—the constitutional system tailored to the Founding Fathers' insistence that elected legislators and executives make decisions, not voters themselves—had aroused sentiment for popular direct rule or plebiscitary government. By the late 1980s, voters were ready to take matters into their own hands by supporting record numbers of ballot initiatives, drives to limit the number of terms elected officials could serve and crusades to recall governors or oust unpopular judges at the ballot box (as with California chief justice

---

*As an example of the typical marginalization of splinter-party populism, David Duke— later to be the subject of enormous press coverage—ran for president in 1988 on a third-party Populist ticket, receiving only 48,000 votes and almost no media coverage.

Rose Bird), as well as demands that some economic regulators (such as state insurance commissioners) be elected rather than appointed. Disgruntled citizens also reveled in statewide ballot victories that forced legislatures to cut their staffs and budgets (as in California Proposition 140 of 1990) and compelled state officials to detail their contacts with and payments from lobbyists. The support Perot commanded in 1992 for ideas like a national "electronic town hall" and enacting new federal tax changes by nationwide popular referendum drew on this same mood.

Appropriately, it had been during the first populist/progressive reform wave in 1900–1914 that such tools as initiatives, referenda and recalls were first introduced at the state level. Together with nonpartisan or unicameral legislatures and direct popular election of U.S. senators (who had previously been elected by state legislatures), these expedients were a response to the corruption of the Gilded Age, and were advanced by such politicians as Senators Hiram Johnson of California, George Norris of Nebraska and Robert LaFollette of Wisconsin to take power away from elected politicians, who were too easily bought, and give it to the people. California, in particular, inserted the right of popular initiative into the state constitution in 1911 as a specific device for the electorate to diffuse the power of special interests and monopolies.

By the late 1980s, popular concern had regained a similar intensity. As reported by the National Conference of State Legislatures, the number of initiatives on state ballots set records. There were 54 in 1982, then 55 in 1988, 64 in 1990 and finally 75 in 1992.[2] Attempts to limit the number of terms that state legislators and officials could serve also mushroomed from three states in 1990 (California, Colorado and Oklahoma) to 14 in 1992. National polls showed two-to-one majorities in favor of slapping similar limitations on members of Congress.

The Republicans, because they controlled few state legislatures, were particularly active proponents of limitations on terms and prerogatives that they believed would cripple rival Democrats. The American electorate, however, trusted neither party. Mid-1991 polling showed that, by 61 percent to 28 percent, voters thought it better that Congress and the White House be controlled by different parties. The result in early 1992 was still essentially the same: 61 percent to 32 percent.[3] That changed in the summer, to Clinton's benefit, but these suspicions of concentrated power were classic populism: Divide power, let them watch each other. Polls also showed a majority of Americans favoring a third major party.[4]

In the early 1980s, the plebiscitary thrust of U.S. populism had been predominantly conservative, set forth in votes to limit taxes and government and to reject cultural liberalism (the defeat, for example, of state constitutional amendments for equal rights for women, even in ostensibly liberal New York and New Jersey). By the end of the decade, however, some changing economic resentments were apparent in initiatives related to insurance, consumer protection and taxes. In 1991 fully 75 percent of Californians, including a majority of self-identified Republicans, told polltakers they favored increasing the top state income tax rate from 9.3 percent to 11 percent for family incomes over $200,000, in order to restore levels that had existed through 1987. Thus, when Republican governor Pete Wilson reluctantly acquiesced during the state's 1991 budget crisis, a spokesman for the California Tax Reform Association boasted that Wilson gave in because "they knew we were going to the 1992 ballot with an initiative to tax the rich, and they knew we were going to win."[5] A dozen other states also raised top income tax rates in 1991–92.

It was a revealing symptom. As party strategists on both sides turned their attention to the 1992 election, they noted that the U.S. electorate now wanted federal tax fairness and some form of national health insurance. We have seen how polls published in *The Wall Street Journal* and elsewhere showed that 84 percent of Americans favored a surtax on millionaires, 81 percent backed the Democrats' Gore-Downey tax increase on the rich and 67 percent backed a federal health insurance program. A new common wisdom was in the wind.

Less well understood, though, was Americans' gathering anger at the rich and at the speculative practices so widespread in business and finance in the 1980s. In its poll taken right after the 1990 election, *Fortune* magazine found that one out of three Americans felt the United States would be better off without any millionaires at all, up from one out of four a decade earlier, while 55 percent of respondents agreed that "millionaires have gotten where they are by exploiting others."[6] A Democratic party survey by Mellman and Lazarus in 1991 claimed that instead of thinking that the economy improved under Reagan and Bush, more voters believed that "the rich have gotten richer while the middle class got stuck paying the bill."[7] That autumn a Gallup-CNN poll found voters, by two-to-one, tagging the Republicans as the party of "political favoritism and corruption," while three out of four said the GOP favored the wealthy and business.[8] Results like these bespoke a resentment of what had happened in the 1980s, as well as an important mood change: conservative economics and economic elites were beginning to displace liberal social policies and cultural elites as the prime target of populist voters. Seeds that would flower in late 1991 and 1992 were already beginning to germinate.

Corporate America had added to the provocation, as even sympathetic publications like *Business Week* condemned the soaring pay of chief executive officers. Experts told U.S. Senate hearings that in 1990, the average CEO of a major U.S. corporation had received 113 times the compensation of an average worker, up from 29 a decade earlier. Japanese and German CEOs, by contrast, received on average just 20 to 35 times the pay of one of their average workers.[9] The vast size of top-executive salaries and golden parachutes, awarded while so many workers and middle-level managers were being laid off, helped sour even upper-bracket Americans on the workings of heyday capitalism. One early 1992 NBC/Wall Street Journal poll found rank-and-file Republicans just as lopsidedly angry as Democrats at excessive CEO salaries. In 1991 the Roper polling organization showed a startling decline since 1982 in citizens who believed in the worthiness of business profits. The biggest slippage came among the most active and well-informed tenth of the public, some themselves corporate executives. For the first time, favorable statements about the profit motive and profit system drew less than majority support, with 52 percent of "influentials" agreeing that "most [business] profits go to make rich people richer."[10]

Survey-takers were also reporting a broader frustration, in which large majorities of Americans indicated that instead of "going in the right direction," things in the United States had gotten "seriously off on the wrong track." In late 1990, as the recession was deepening and the United States was debating whether to drive Iraq out of Kuwait, Americans had chosen "seriously off on the wrong track" by ratios of over two-to-one. In February and March 1991, as the war ended favorably, optimism flared again for a few weeks. But by summertime pessimism once again led by solid majorities. By 1992 belief that things had gone wrong had returned to the fearful levels of 1979–80.

This wasn't 1894, when Ohio currency reformer and Populist spokesman Jacob Coxey marched his disgruntled "army" on Washington. And it was even less like the 25 percent unemployment of mid-Depression 1933. However, as the 1992 presidential campaign began, the smugness of the 1980s was giving way to that unique mix of populism, frustration and incipient reformism that has been present in most U.S. political upheavals.

Middle-Class Populism and
the Vulnerable Republican Coalition

The extent to which the post-1968 Republican presidential coalition would become restive in the K-Marts and bitter in the subdivisions reflected its origins: as the product of the *previous* wave of middle-class populism—the wave that replaced the old New Deal elites with Nixon's cloth-coat Republicanism—it was particularly sensitive to a redefinition in the 1990s of middle-class priorities. By late 1991, as the recession-trapped U.S. economy weakened again, a national survey by the Times-Mirror Corporation revealed what threatened to become the cleavage line. "The potential for division within the ranks of the Republican party along socioeconomic lines is very strong," Times-Mirror polltakers said, because low-middle- and middle-income Republicans of a populist or "disaffected" stripe were being drawn toward a directional change in Washington in favor of national health insurance, protection of American jobs, higher taxes on the wealthy and more federal government help for the middle class.[11]

The lesson of U.S. history has been that such qualms rarely remain abstract. Nowhere is the populist mode in American politics more pronounced than in its record of inciting once-a-generation national upheavals in which some new regional supremacy, economic ascendancy or demographic majority pushes to the fore, putting a new party in the White House and in the process debunking some existing elite, be it Philadelphia financiers in 1828, slave owners in 1860, economic royalists in 1932 or liberal intelligentsia and bureaucrats in 1968.

Historians date the nation's first watershed from 1800, when Thomas Jefferson, penman of the Declaration of Independence, triumphed over the commercially and financially attuned Federalists of America's coastal strip and went on to build a generation of Jeffersonian presidential dominance. By 1824 this first loose party system had become meaningless and was ready for a new definition. That came in 1828, when Andrew Jackson's presidential victory turned another egalitarian political wave into a watershed for the new Democratic party. The Jacksonian coalition, in turn, lasted until the 1850s, when slavery tore it apart. Then in 1860 the antislavery issue, together with the expansion of the frontier westward, tipped the national power balance and helped elect antislavery Northerner Abraham Lincoln as president. The war followed, and ultimately there arose a new Civil War–based Republican majority, including substantial elements of the old Jacksonian Coalition. *The critical point, to which we will return shortly, is that in each of these upheavals, the values of the common man were front-and-center.*

The next watershed, 1896, worked differently. National politics had been stalemated for twenty years, as neither party was able to win more than a plurality in presidential elections. But in 1896, the industrial and financial captains of the Republican party narrowly beat back the fusion of the Democratic and Populist parties behind William Jennings Bryan of Nebraska. The Bryan movement couldn't reach beyond its agrarian origins to speak for workers in manufacturing—a fatal weakness because, in 1890, manufacturing for the first time represented a larger share of GNP than agriculture. A relatively united Northeast and Great Lakes defeated the fiery Nebraskan, giving industrial Republicanism a second-wave supremacy based in the populous, urbanizing states of the North. The year 1896 was a watershed in which populism defined its common-man constituency too narrowly to succeed.

The political transformation of 1932 produced the more usual egalitarian pattern, as the Depression enabled a new hard-times coalition to fuse the populist South and West with the blue-collar industrial North. This combination included America's decisive new demographic force, urbanization, and what would prove to be the zenith of the immigrant-filled, labor-leaning great cities of the North from Boston, New York and Philadelphia to Cleveland, Detroit and Chicago. Once again, common-man economics had the political muscle.

Which brings us to the next watershed, 1968, and the socioeconomic factors that a quarter century later made the Republican establishment vulnerable to middle-class populism. Before the Nixon coalition came together in 1968, a considerable minority of experts was predicting a progressive or leftish politics, along the lines of what Charles Reich talked about in his 1970 best-seller, *The Greening of America.* Indeed, many political scientists who had grown up under the New Deal concluded that watershed politics in the United States always reflected the interests of the common man, whether the "free soil, free labor" followers of Abraham Lincoln or Franklin D. Roosevelt's "forgotten Americans" of 1932. Any new major change, they said, would have to come from the same direction.

What they missed was that by 1968 the "common man" was driving a two-year-old Pontiac, grumbling about welfare chiselers and pondering a move to suburbia to get away from high crime rates and enroll his children in better schools. Meanwhile the national Democrats were forsaking their old New Deal meat-and-potatoes liberalism to identify with minorities and counterculture forces. This gave Republicans another chance to speak for "average American" interests as the Democrats veered off on parochial tangents. The Republicans had such an opportunity twice before: first in 1860, when Democrats divided over the narrow, unsustainable cause of Southern slave owners and secession, then again in 1896 when that year's Democratic convention, in turning to Bryan, embraced what proved to be parochial images of Farm Belt radicalism and evangelism. It would work again in 1968–72.

In 1968 Richard Nixon and Alabama governor George Wallace, the third-party candidate, together captured 57 percent of the total presidential vote. Without Wallace in 1972, Nixon won by a 61 percent landslide and launched still another of America's "common man" revolutions, this one the most affluent ever. Its swing voters came from what pundit Joseph Kraft called Middle America—the people in the middle whose incomes, relatively traditional culture and flag-waving support of America were generally under siege by civil rights activists, inflation, riots and the worsening mess in Vietnam.[12] Its new bastions were suburbia and the Sun Belt—a combination of lower-middle-class Archie Bunker country at the end of the big-city subway lines, commuter country and small towns almost anywhere, and new look-alike suburbs backhoed and bulldozed out of red Georgia clay, Florida mangrove swamp, East Texas piney woods and the fringe of the California desert.

This fit the common-man watershed model, albeit with lower-middle-class tailoring. Prior to World War II, the much smaller U.S. "middle class"—politically divided by Civil War geography, economically far above the median and culturally closer to establishment values—was split between Northern and Southern regional parties but dominated neither. The New Majority, by contrast, was Northern *and* Southern, conservative *and* populist, middle-class *and* arriviste, an unprecedented and volatile combination to store and handle.

Conservatives confirmed the transition with a new rhetoric. Richard Nixon's outreach was no surprise; his famous 1952 Checkers speech, invoking the Nixon family's less-than-affluent middle-class status and his wife's "good Republican cloth coat"—expensive minks were for "the rich"—resonated in Levittown and Oak Lawn. But the more revealing approach was that of the *other* major standard-bearer of 1964–72 presidential insurgency, Alabama's Wallace. As a boy, Wallace had chopped cotton, and as a World War II enlisted man, he and his wife had lived in a converted New Mexico chicken coop. As a presidential candidate, he aimed his campaign at the "truck driver, the beautician and the barber," and only one broad class appeal was possible. George Wallace was for the "folks"—and in the 1960s, the folks (like the Alabama governor himself) mostly thought of themselves as the "great American middle class."

In short, the Middle America of the Nixon era represented a whole new chapter in political sociology: the self-perceived middle class now took in a vast population whose parents and grandparents had cheered the establishment-baiting insurgencies of Franklin D. Roosevelt, Al Smith, Robert La Follette and William Jennings Bryan. By the end of the 1960s, the typical more or less median-income U.S. voters considered themselves "middle-class," but with enough uncertainties, inelegancies and outsider sentiments to introduce entirely new meaning to the term.

Appropriately enough, 1968 and 1969 saw the emergence of a sweeping new lexicon of politics, producing in two years—just as in 1932 and 1933—the slogans and labels of an electoral revolution. During the 1968 campaign, Richard Nixon talked about the "forgotten middle-class Americans," the "silent center" and the "quiet majority." Then on May 9, 1969, Vice President Spiro Agnew said, "It's time for America's silent majority to stand up for its rights," putting another major phrase in the political dictionary. "Joe Sixpack," beer-drinking symbol of the administration's hoped-for appeal to the blue-collar lower-middle class, made his figurative appearance as the 1970s began.[13] Even middle-of-the-country geography became a repository of implied wisdom when Nixon White House aide John Ehrlichman, resurrecting an old vaudeville cliché, recommended that GOP politics "play in Peoria."

Language like this was profoundly *un*conservative and much disliked by Republicanism's old upper-class elites. The new GOP mindset emphasized the *middle* part of the country in virtually every way—economically, culturally and even geographically—but with enough anti-establishment rhetoric to raise the ghost of William Jennings Bryan. The 1964–72 speeches of Barry Goldwater, Ronald Reagan, George Wallace and Richard Nixon sizzled with caustic references to bankrupt elites, arrogant establishments, "limousine" liberals, Harvard intellectuals, know-it-all judges, Ivy League "pointy-head" experts, the Liberal Establishment and the Eastern Seaboard. Goldwater, the 1964 Republican presidential nominee, had even joked about sawing off the East Coast.

Those were the formative years, because the coalition that elected Ronald Reagan continued to follow most of the same regional, ethnic and religious patterns laid down in 1968–72. Reagan's forty-nine-state landslide of 1984, in which he captured 59 percent of the popular vote, was very similar to Nixon's forty-nine-state and 61 percent popular-vote landslide of 1972, although Reagan was stronger among young voters whereas Nixon had done better among Southerners. However, it was the new circumstances of the late 1980s and George Bush's candidacy in 1988 that revealed the potential instability of a coalition with populist swing voters and elite leaders and forced attention to fall on Middle America's essential schizophrenia: cultural conservatism and traditionalism at loggerheads with decidedly unconservative economic resentments.

The Two Faces of Middle-Class Populism

The populist constituencies of the old New Majority had mixed reactions to the emerging Republican economics of the 1980s. Wall Street Republicanism has never appealed in places like northern Alabama, south Boston and panhandle Idaho. Ronald Reagan, with his innate populist, anti-establishment appeal, could keep this incipient dissent in check, as he did easily in 1984. Not so Bush, the Andover- and Yale-educated scion of a prominent investment banking family. In early summer 1988 polls, in which he trailed several Democratic rivals by 5 to 10 points, GOP strategists perceived that Bush provoked cleavages typical of less happy Republican eras. Voters saw Bush as too friendly to the rich rather than committed to ordinary people. Advisers told him to stay away from his sprawling million-dollar vacation "cottage" in Kennebunkport, Maine, where the aura of old money was as evident as salt spray and lobster pots. Surveys in June and July showed him facing close races even in safe Republican states like Indiana and Nebraska.

Recognizing the coalition's vulnerability, Republican strategists sought to keep anti-elite economic sentiment among swing voters from dominating the election dialogue, so they put forward the New Majority populism's *other* face—cultural, religious, racial and nationalist— another politics with a long history. Its postwar success began in the early 1950s, when reporters shorthanded the key themes of the 1952 Eisenhower presidential campaign as K-1, C-2—"Korea, Communism and Corruption." Then, as we have seen, two successive Nixon campaigns sounded a clarion call against central-city riots, soaring crime rates, permissive judges, antiwar demonstrators and flag burners, campus radicalism, busing for racial balance and racial quotas. One of

1972's most memorable GOP alliterations portrayed Democratic presidential nominee George McGovern as the candidate of "acid, amnesty and abortion."

Resurrecting this demonology proved to be a powerful GOP tactic in 1988. These cutting-edge issues from the social cockpit of the late 1960s and early 1970s had played the same long-term coalition-building role for post-1968 Republicans that slavery, the war between the states and Northern Yankee–versus–Irish Catholic tensions had contributed to the Civil War–based Republican national majority a century earlier. So in 1988, as the Republicans came under criticism for resurgent upper-bracket economics and preferences, it was logical to return to the old symbols—the flags, the battles, the cultural tensions, the disdain for liberal elites and racial fears—around which their coalition had originally gathered so many millions of ordinary people in 1968–72.

Indeed, the Gilded Age provided a direct strategic precedent for the use of cultural themes to suppress economic populism. In the 1870s and 1880s, as Granger, Greenback and Populist splinter candidacies siphoned off Republican voters, especially in the deflation-racked Farm Belt, the GOP countered by "waving the bloody shirt" of Civil War politics. The objective was to make Iowa farmers and Indiana mill workers remember their comrades at Shiloh's Hornet's Nest and Gettysburg's Cemetery Ridge, and forget the railroad owners in Minneapolis and the bankers in New York.

Finally, during the great economic confrontation of 1896 with William Jennings Bryan, the GOP cast presidential nominee William McKinley as the nation's "patriotic leader." In his classic history *The Populist Movement,* Lawrence Goodwyn recalled how the Republican National Committee distributed carloads of flags throughout the country and Mark Hanna "conceived the idea of a public 'flag day' in the nation's leading cities—a day specifically in honor of McKinley. 'Sound Money clubs' of New York and San Francisco were put in charge of enormous flag day spectacles. . . . In the critical Midwestern states, Civil War veterans known as 'Patriotic Heroes' toured with buglers and a cannon mounted on a flatcar."[14]

It worked. On economic issues alone, Bryan might have reduced the GOP coalition fatally, notwithstanding his prairie parochialism. Even with that albatross, he ran a close race in swing states like California, Ohio and Indiana. But with the help of flags and lopsided financial resources, the Republicans won, albeit narrowly. The threat was over, even though Bryan made another reasonably strong (46 percent) race in 1900, when the Republicans introduced still another tactic that would reemerge in the 1990s: parades of U.S. soldiers returning from their overseas victory in the Spanish-American war.

In the 1988 election, campaigners for George Bush not only won but rolled back a large midsummer Democratic lead by waving their own "bloody shirt" and reintroducing the social themes and hostilities of the GOP's 1968–72 crucible years. In 1987 Bush had made a half-hour program for broadcast in Florida describing his Christian experience of being born again; during the election year itself, he paid his famous campaign visit to a New Jersey flag factory. Then there was the campaign's even more famous television commercial attacking Massachusetts' furloughs for convicted killers and featuring Willie Horton, the black escapee who raped a white woman in Maryland. The Horton advertisements renewed America's ongoing racial sensitivities. The Yale-educated Republican nominee even managed to pin the fatal "elitist" label on the Democratic donkey by linking opponent Dukakis to "Harvard boutiques." One Democratic adviser complained to bemused journalists that "They're running a class war against us, saying we're a bunch of Cambridge-Brookline eccentric literature professors. We've got to fight back and say that they're the party of privilege, the party of the rich folks."

But they did not, so what the election showed was that Republicans still understood the two faces of American populism—an enmity toward establishment economics mixed with a distaste for cultural liberalism—far better than the Democrats. Two decades of winning populist constituencies had been instructive. To let capitalist-conservative heyday economics and concentrated wealth become the principal debate could have been fatal. Two years later, as we shall see, the Democrats *did* make economics dominate the 1990 midterm elections, slashing at the Republicans as the "party of the rich" for weeks before a stunned GOP could counterattack. Republican voter identification plummeted, and for the first time since the Reagan era began, the favoritism-to-wealth issue was centrally framed.

As 1991 began, the Republicans knew what they wanted in 1992: an election context in which powerful cultural and patriotic themes suppressed debate over weak economic growth, bias toward the rich and middle-class frustration. And for a few months they had it—thanks to a successful war in the Persian Gulf that sent George Bush's ratings soaring toward 90 percent and whetted party hopes of a 1992 landslide with all-powerful coattails. But by late spring the public had come to believe that Bush stopped the fighting too soon, leaving Saddam Hussein in power, so that voters rated the Gulf war as only a partial victory, diluting its political resonance. Even so, knowing that the war was a plus for the president, Republican strategists envisioned a campaign that combined the flags, patriotism and military parades used to combat populism in 1896 with a rekindled attention to the racial and cultural themes of 1968–72. By early summer, pundits were describing the putative strategy as "KCQ"—Kuwait, crime and quotas.

Law-and-order sympathies were exploited by issues like the death penalty and insistence on conservative judges. Racial concerns were touched by a series of White House attacks on racial quotas and on Democratic civil rights legislation for requiring them. The president's attack on "political correctness" invoked yet another genuine tension of the Nixon era—fear of campus radicalism. Flag-burning, too, had angered many Americans two decades earlier, and in 1990 Bush had proposed an anti–flag desecration constitutional amendment. Nevertheless 1992 opened with much of this renewed social-issue strategy in jeopardy. A weak economy was crowding the Persian Gulf war into the background; the administration's civil rights compromise with the Democrats had helped stimulate the rise of two combative Republican presidential primary challengers, David Duke, who quickly faded, and Patrick Buchanan, who, as we shall see in Chapter 9, wound up turning part of the issue of racial tension and quotas back against the Bush administration; and even the anti-crime drumbeat was losing credibility as violence soared in city after city. In the spring of 1992, following the racially triggered riots in Los Angeles, polls showed Bush losing ground for want of domestic-policy credibility despite law-and-order rhetoric. Democrat Clinton gained little for his higher marks for handling racial problems. The big gains after Los Angeles went to the man in the middle—independent Perot. The 1980s schizophrenia of middle-class populism was breaking down.

Hard times also shifted the balance from cultural to economic populism. Economic discontents dominated the opinion polls. With rising anxiety, the 1992 Republican presidential campaign sought to overcome the new anti-Washington and populist economic challenges—from a former Republican-turned-independent as well as a Democrat—with cultural, law-and-order, patriotic and foreign policy themes combined under one description: values. But one after another, these tactics failed, culminating in the disastrous August GOP convention in which "family values" appeared to be increasingly synonymous with the controversial agenda of the Religious Right. Fewer and fewer offsets existed to a politics in which voter unhappiness was increasingly economic.

Uncertain Trumpet: The Democrats
and Economic Populism

From mid-1991 through most of 1992, the Democrats moved toward the presidential election with growing attention to middle-class-squeeze issues and economic populism. However, for most of the 1980s, and again in the first half of 1991, they had been ambivalent, more inclined to work with the Republican architects of the era's conservative economics than to criticize them. That left them with a credibility problem when they rose, belatedly, to the attack.

Not that there was anything unusual in this. In the Gilded Age and then again in the 1920s, large numbers of Democrats were drumbeaters for boom-era capitalism. Grover Cleveland, the conservative Democrat unlucky enough to be president when the Panic of 1893 signaled the beginning of the end of the Gilded Age, was as conservative as Chester Arthur and Benjamin Harrison, the Republicans who had preceded him. And during the 1920s, not only did congressional Democrats collaborate with the GOP on federal income tax changes, but all three Democratic presidential nominees of the decade—James Cox (1920), John W. Davis (1924) and Alfred E. Smith (1928)—wound up by 1936 joining the conservative Liberty League to oppose Franklin D. Roosevelt and the New Deal.

Loyalty to the economics of the common man, not those of the elite, may be the hallmark of history's great Democrats, the Jacksons and Roosevelts, but not of the second-tier Democrats who tend to come to the fore during capitalist-conservative heydays.* These Democrats tend to cooperate with the Republicans in reducing government and cutting taxes, following the broad preference of voters during economic expansions. As a result, party politics in the aftermath of capitalist-conservative heydays and during the subsequent implosion of their debt-and-speculative bubbles has not been a simple story. In the Gilded Age, when Democrats had narrowly elected a president just before the Panic of 1893 hit, they were incumbent *losers,* not out-of-power *beneficiaries* of the embarrassment of conservative economics. Voters were resentful enough in 1894 to give the Republicans an extraordinary 117-seat gain in the House of Representatives. Moreover, fierce 1893–96 economic policy disagreements ripped the hapless Democratic party down the middle, so that when the majority ultimately radicalized to fuse with the Populists and nominate Bryan, many party conservatives bolted, voting for Republican McKinley or backing the

*For a more detailed discussion, see *The Politics of Rich and Poor,* pp. 46–51.

short-lived pro–gold standard National Democratic party. By contrast, had the financial unraveling that followed the Panic of 1893 come with a Republican president in office, a mildly populist Democratic presidential nominee would almost certainly have won in 1896, and the unfolding early-twentieth-century progressive era would have been run by Democrats instead of by its *Republican* White House hero, Theodore Roosevelt.

When the bubble of the 1920s popped in 1929, however, the Democrats were lucky. Republican Herbert Hoover was president, and it hardly mattered that Democrats were, in Arthur Schlesinger's words, "all over the place" philosophically or that their unprophetic 1932 presidential campaign had indicted the GOP for, of all things, excessive federal spending. All that counted electorally was that hapless Republican Hoover was in the White House, getting the blame, as the economy got worse—and worse.

Though "Democrats swooned," according to one pundit, when I laid out in *The Politics of Rich and Poor* the parallels between the 1980s, the 1920s and the Gilded Age, they did not necessarily have cause. The *opportunity* was there; the history of seizing it successfully was something else. Nor was leading a middle-class "populist" reaction something their liberal biases in the years since 1968 had conditioned them for. George Bush in the White House as real estate sagged and marble-halled financial institutions shuddered provided a Democratic advantage, but not a guarantee.

Indeed, during the 1980s economic populism was only an intermittent Democratic tactic. In 1982, when unemployment was about to reach double digits at election time, they could sound populist trumpets. "It's not fair, it's Republican," contended one clever television advertisement. And Democratic strategists attributed their recapture of fourteen Southern U.S. House seats to populist economic themes, so much so that a Populist Caucus was launched in the House of Representatives in February 1983. Populist and economic nationalist rhetoric was also a factor in 1986, when Democrats recaptured the U.S. Senate.

Democratic presidential nominees, however, were less inclined to such approaches. Following Walter Mondale's 41 percent–59 percent loss to Ronald Reagan in 1984, Washington's liberal-funded Economic Policy Institute commissioned a poll by Fingerhut-Granados Opinion Research, which found pro-Reagan "swing" Democrats lopsidedly citing Mondale's green-eyeshade emphasis on deficit reduction and tax increases as one reason they did not vote for him.[15] According to the polltakers, Mondale would have done better with populist positions on themes like Social Security, tax fairness and trade policy because "swing" voters favored them, supporting the Democratic party for its commitment to "working people," "the average person" and "fairness."[16] In those days, though, many marginal voters were also suspicious of "fairness" because they associated the word with redistribution from the middle class to the welfare poor.

Four years later, even harsher criticisms of an insufficient populist approach were directed at Michael Dukakis. We have seen how the Republicans, mindful of popular psychologies, equated Dukakis with Harvard and "boutique liberalism," but, for most of the general election campaign, Dukakis, for his part, rejected economic populist counterthemes. The pre-nomination opportunity had certainly been there. In July 1988 Democratic strategist Robert Beckel brandished a new party poll of 601 "swing" Democrats and explained how the Democrats' ten-point lead over George Bush was largely the product of economic disillusionment: "Ronald Reagan convinced these voters that their interests were with the wealthy. They bought into trickle-down theory." But since then, Beckel added, they have become convinced that "where they are losing out is not to poor people but to wealthy people. They believe that the dollars they have lost have gone up, not down."[17]

What Dukakis preferred to talk about, however, was "competence, not ideology," seeking to claim credit as governor of Massachusetts for a local economic "miracle"—one that was already coming undone. After a brief flirtation with populist language around Labor Day, he returned to it only in late October, when all was almost lost. The irony, as Bush campaign manager Lee Atwater admitted after the election, was that he had been worried in early September because "the way to win a presidential race against the Republicans is to develop the class warfare issue, as Dukakis did at the end. To divide up the haves and have nots and to try to invigorate the New Deal coalition and to attack."[18] Vincent Breglio, director of the Republican presidential campaign's polling division, later disclosed that even Dukakis's half-hearted last-minute populist rhetoric had made Bush survey-takers nervous: "Going into the last week of the campaign, we clearly saw that the populist message of Dukakis was having an impact. It was cutting."[19]

Surveys by Democrats outside the Dukakis campaign showed the same thing. One immediate preelection sampling by the Analysis Group recorded voters giving their "highest priority to a populist agenda: making sure the 'wealthy and big corporations pay their fair share of taxes.' "[20] In addition, pollsters Stanley Greenberg and Celinda Lake pointed out, "had the swing segments of the national electorate focused on the policy agenda, Dukakis would have run much more strongly. These [swing] voters, conventionally seen as conservative, are even more populist than the electorate as a whole. Over 70 percent of Reagan Democrats, moderate conservative Democrats, and undecided [on the eve of election] voters gave fair taxes for the rich and corporations the highest score as a goal for the next president."[21]

The October 1987 stock market crash lingered in voters' minds, but the 1988 economy was reasonably strong. Real disposable income was increasing. By autumn 1990 economic circumstances were much worse, helping Democrats drive home populist issues in the midterm congressional elections, especially after Bush had retracted his promise of "No new taxes." Then the question became *whose* new taxes, and Republicans wriggled with embarrassment for three brutal weeks in October as the media hung on the president's insistence on cutting capital gains rates for the rich along with his refusal to back a new 33 percent top rate or 10 percent surtax on millionaires.

Neo-populism was beginning to find a rhythm. Swing voters moved away from the GOP in droves and, in parts of the country, Republican candidates went into what reporters started calling "free fall." In Iowa not just Democrats but even half the self-identified *Republicans* characterized the GOP as the party of the rich, and populist Tom Harkin became the state's first Democratic U.S. senator to be elected to two full terms. George Bush's own national approval ratings slid from the 70s in September to a low of 48 percent in late-October ABC polls.

It was a brief few weeks of mild populist triumph, though, because public attention soon shifted back to the Persian Gulf—and although the country continued to slide into recession, Democrats, cowed by Bush's success in the Gulf, also found themselves, even for ten to twelve weeks after the war's end in March, holding their tongues on the weak state of the economy. Bush had been calling it "Saddam Hussein's recession," although arbiters from the National Bureau of Economic Research determined that the downturn had begun in July, just *before* Iraq's invasion of Kuwait. The war's end, the president promised, would bring a strong economic resurgence.

For the Democrats the hopes of the prior autumn seemed to have collapsed. By many measures that ranged from the largest collapse of U.S. financial institutions since the 1930s to the record number of Americans drawing public assistance, the U.S. economy was hitting bumps not experienced since the Great Depression, which should have made it easy for Democrats to indict the mistakes of the 1980s. Nevertheless, spring 1991 opinion polls on which party was better able to keep America prosperous found the Democrats falling below the GOP, partly because of the halo Republicans still enjoyed from the Gulf war, but also because Democrats, relentless in attacking prior Republican recessions and their hardships, this time restrained themselves.

However, as the recession lingered into summer and public restiveness resurged, Democratic blood started stirring. Clearly it had not been Saddam's recession, and was probably George Bush's after all. In late June potential presidential candidates were given details from the party poll that, as we have seen, found voters believing that under Reagan and Bush "the rich have gotten richer, while the middle class got stuck paying the bill." The most surprising and intriguing result, though, came from four hypothetical matchups between President Bush and "imaginary Democratic candidate Jones."[22] Designed to test different economic populist themes, all four trial heats showed Bush actually *losing* whenever these issues came into play.

By autumn, as the economy slid into the second stage of what was becoming America's longest postwar slump, June's hypothetical matchups had been replaced by actual elections, important ones, in which Bush-supported Republicans lost to populist-sounding outsider candidates in what the press began interpreting as middle-class revolts. On October 19 former Ku Klux Klan leader and ex–American Nazi David Duke, now a Republican state representative from suburban New Orleans but still well beyond the pale of respectability, defeated the sitting GOP governor of Louisiana in an open primary. Four weeks later, he met Democratic former governor Edwin Edwards in a mid-November runoff, winning two fifths of the total vote and getting a surprising 60 percent support from the white middle class.

On November 5, in a special Pennsylvania U.S. Senate election, little-known Democrat Harris Wofford, running on a platform the press capsuled as "middle-class populism," electrified the country by turning an early 44-point Republican lead into a 10-point Democratic victory over Richard Thornburgh, the former Pennsylvania governor and U.S. attorney general who had left Bush's cabinet to make the race. A few days before the election, Wofford campaign strategist James Carville—described as a Svengali by Thornburgh and characterized by *The Wall Street Journal* as "dripping with contempt for Washington"—had said, "This kind of climate is where political tornadoes come from, and maybe we can show the party not to be enthralled with the dominant elite wing of the party and to talk about real economic issues."[23]

After Wofford's landslide, more national Democrats were ready to agree. Back in late summer, when Bush was strong, the Democrats emerging to seek their party's presidential nomination were mostly populists and outsiders—Senator Tom Harkin of Iowa, Senator Bob Kerrey of Nebraska, Governor Bill Clinton of Arkansas, Governor Douglas Wilder of Virginia and ex-governor Jerry Brown of California. Though former senator Paul Tsongas of Massachusetts was a nonpopulist, he was also an outsider. As Bush's ratings fell with the economy in November and December, their decisions to run began to look prescient—and so-called first-tier candidates like House Majority Leader Richard Gephardt and Senator Lloyd Bentsen began to regret their decisions not to run. Clinton, who developed a strong message about 1980s favoritism to the top 1 percent and unfairness to the middle class, quickly became the Democratic front-runner. His ability to blend concern for the middle class with ability to create a biracial coalition increased his strength, although he suffered from alleged sexual scandals, draft avoidance and other questions of personal integrity that followed him from Arkansas.

The most surprising trumpet of anti-Washington outsiderism and economic populism in 1992 came from the emergence of the first billionaire populist in U.S. political history—independent presidential contender Ross Perot of Texas, who had moved ahead of both Bush and Clinton in public opinion polls in June before he withdrew in July. Perot, who openly labeled Bush and Secretary of State James A. Baker III as "country clubbers" and "preppies," came from a moderate Republican background and generally sidestepped the vulnerability of Democratic nominees to charges of social liberalism, which made him more powerful a voice for populist reforms of the federal tax code and what amounted to an outsider revolt against Washington. Perot's July withdrawal made Clinton the only populist in the race, and after a successful acceptance speech to the Democratic convention, he surged to a large and unexpected lead. Perot's reentry in October made Democrats nervous, but on November 3 the Texan drew his 19 percent of the vote about equally from Clinton and Bush in one of the most populist-flavored outcomes in U.S. electoral history.

The Stalemate of American Politics

Political watersheds in the United States depend on the ability to affect institutions as well as grass-roots restiveness. Even as unhappy middle-class voters found themselves cross-pressured between Democratic *economic* populism, Republican *cultural* populism, and a powerful independent with a revolutionary message, national politics circa 1992 also faced unusual, even unprecedented blockages in its circulatory system. The Republican takeover of the presidency that began in 1968, by failing to change Congress as in previous realignments, provided evidence that perhaps politics was no longer fluid enough to produce old-style, top-to-bottom national political upheavals. Two decades later the institutional clogging was even worse. This was part of what made voters so responsive to Perot for several months—the sense that an institutional revolution might be necessary to make the system work again.

Divided government and the interest groups that proliferated around it were at the root of the problem. By the 1980s the pattern of mostly Republican presidents facing Democrats in one or both houses of Congress had a three-decade history reaching back to the Eisenhower years. Indeed, once the Republicans lost their six-year control of the U.S. Senate in 1986, the two parties seemed at times to have partitioned Washington. Capitol Hill and the legislative branch were the Democratic sphere of influence; the broad downtown boulevards, with the White House and executive branch, were Republican. In previous eras, divided power had been a temporary complication; during the Reagan-Bush era it fast became a de facto principle of national governance. At the same time, the effectiveness of government degenerated; economic interest groups fattened on the fragmentation of power and achieved leverage unmatched since the Gilded Age.

From a historical standpoint, what was missing in the U.S. political process was a full-fledged opposition—a party with an outsider's mentality, minimally rooted in Washington and forced back to the grass roots for revitalization by its relative weakness at both ends of Pennsylvania Avenue. For two thirds of the 1932–68 New Deal cycle, the Republicans controlled no elected Washington power base. In the 1960s, as a result, they easily took up an outsidership role. The Democrats, for their part, had been outsiders most of the time from 1896 to 1932. By comparison, what followed after 1968 slowly made split control of government not a fluke but an *assumption*. From 1968 to 1976, congressionally based Democrats schemed to get the White

House back; but the election of Jimmy Carter in 1976 proved so disruptive—politically, even counterproductive—that they were almost relieved when the GOP recaptured the White House in 1980. Loss of the Senate to the Republicans in that same election was a dislocation, but when Democrats recaptured the Senate in 1986, congressional leaders resumed a familiar and comfortable position: control of a co-equal branch of government; partnership (of a sort) in national policymaking.

National political self-renewal processes suffered, and both parties had activists who chafed. However, because the nation's agenda was set more from the electronic bully pulpit of the presidency than by the confusion of Congress, Democrats paid a greater political price. Time after time during the 1980s, they found themselves drawn as collaborators into what were basically *conservative* rescriptings of U.S. economic policy: the tax overhauls of 1981 and 1986, the Social Security tax expansion of 1983, the Gramm-Rudman budget reform, the 1989 Republican-Democratic deal over increased congressional pay (both sides agreed not to attack each other for pay-raise support), the 1990 bipartisan budget (which essentially blocked any anti-cyclical fiscal response to that year's unfolding recession) and so on.

Some collusion was to be expected. During previous GOP conservative-capitalist heydays, as we have seen, leading Democratic politicians had abandoned their "little guy" moorings to join in what were essentially "establishment" economics. However, the institutional cohabitation of a Democratic Congress with two successive Republican presidents in the 1980s was a boom-era first, unseen in previous heydays, and it inhibited Democrats from developing either an opposition mind-set or an effective critique of the 1980s political economy. Belaboring what many of their own senior congressional leaders had joined in shaping wasn't easy.

In the November 1990 congressional elections, when favoritism to the rich became an issue, Republicans drew most of the blame, losing one seat in the Senate and eight in the House. But Democrats paid an unusual penalty for their policy collaboration. Normally, when the party in the White House loses congressional seats in U.S. midterm elections, by way of reaction the other party's incumbents gain on average. Not so in 1990, according to tabulations by Democratic analysts Alan Baron and William Schneider. Granted that Republican incumbents fell further, but on average, Democratic incumbents, many of them prominent participants in bipartisan Washington decision-making, also weakened. Results like these reinforced doubt that the two-party system could still provide a once-a-generation, outsider and reformist broom to sweep out Washington.

What made it worse, ordinary citizens felt, was official Washington's apparent capture by special-interest groups. America's traditional, broad separation of powers set forth in the U.S. Constitution—from the requirement that tax legislation must originate in the House of Representatives to the president's veto power—was a familiar restraint; the mechanics had often been cumbersome in Jefferson's day or Roosevelt's. But interest-group proliferation and Balkanization grew worse during the 1980s, and the talk that lobbies had become a fourth branch of government was less and less facetious.

No other national capital had anything comparable; the District of Columbia was the political equivalent of a coral atoll, with new domestic and foreign special-pleading organisms attaching themselves daily. During the decade following Reagan's inauguration, lobbying firms and consulting groups more than doubled in personnel and billings. The role of lobbyists for foreign interests grew even more rapidly. Worse, as high-tech and multi-media election campaigns grew more expensive, politicians had to pay increased attention to special-interest money, ranging from political action committee donations to the personal contributions of GOP millionaires and the phone banks and in-kind donations of Democratic labor unions. Previous cyclical upheaval had not confronted this kind of entrenchment.

Stymied by such influence, the average person was beginning to conclude that his or her opinion and vote were all but powerless, as the Ohio-based Kettering Foundation discovered in its preelection opinion survey. On the one hand, this perceived institutional unresponsiveness complicated the prospect for an upheaval in Washington, but it simultaneously fed the hopes of an angry public to achieve exactly that—and the extraordinary grass-roots responsiveness to the Draft Perot movement was the most vivid result. "People point their fingers at politicians, at powerful lobbyists and at people in the media," said Kettering president David Mathews, a former U.S. secretary of health, education and welfare. "They see these three groups as a political class, the rulers of an oligarchy that has replaced democracy." Citizens "know that the political system is now designed to respond to interest groups rather than individual citizens and they are hopping mad about it."[24]

That was not unprecedented, especially for those who could recall the corruption of the Gilded Age a century earlier, but the 1990s did raise a new dimension of challenge. Like the fear of middle-class decline, concern over national atrophy and oligarchy also had a ring of plausibility. Pessimists like Professor Mancur Olson in his book *The Rise and Decline of Nations* couched their worry in historical terms, concluding that the United States might be bogging down in the same interest-group paralysis that earlier afflicted previous great empires, including Britain.[25]

In the past, as America had approached its political watersheds, radicalizing and disaffected portions of the electorate had made the system work by, in effect, creating a new political coalition to occupy the political center, which then dealt with the nation's problems. As the 1990s began, the institutional and interest-group barriers to another successful grass-roots revolt and Washington purge seemed enormous. To optimists, Clinton's victory, building on an outsider image of promises to reform Washington and represent the middle class rather than the rich, promised a new common-man loyalty and revitalization of government. Yet Clinton had close ties to party contributors and interest groups, and middle-class radicalization in support of Perot's powerful insurgency was a historical trouble sign, as Chapter 9 will pursue further. Moreover, public dissatisfaction with Washington policy favoritism to the rich and well connected showed little likelihood of subsiding, and the too softly named "middle-class squeeze"—to which we now turn in Part II—was coming into focus as something potentially more ominous.

PART TWO

THE MIDDLE-CLASS SQUEEZE: A PORTRAIT

CHAPTER 4

Middle America and the "Unfairness" of Conservative-Capitalist Boom Periods

I want to recall our attention to what our economy is really all about: not money, but people. The original Greek word "economy" meant "the management of a household or family." . . . We must let the Greeks remind us that the fundamental purpose of our complicated and technical economy is the well-being of our families. This is why I'm so disturbed about what I see going on on Wall Street these days. Corporations have become chips in a casino game, played for high stakes by people who produce nothing, invent nothing, grow nothing and service nothing. The market is now a game itself.

—House Democratic whip Richard Gephardt, 1987

Unemployment in large cities appears to be far more severe than official government numbers indicate. . . . Employment statistics released recently from the 1990 census show huge differences between the number of people who consider themselves jobless and the numbers reflected in estimated local unemployment rates issued monthly by the Bureau of Labor Statistics.

—*The Philadelphia Inquirer,* 1992

Despite its widespread currency, the term "squeeze" failed to describe what was overtaking middle-class Americans in the 1990s because the term had arrived in the late 1980s as a quibble with the Reagan boom: that despite the surge of billionaires and the glitter of high finance, ordinary families were under pressure and many were losing ground. But there was no crisis, merely a discomfort. Three or four years later, as the circumstances of the average household worsened and as middle-class populism elbowed its way into 1991–92 politics, angrier terminology was appropriate. The principal provocations of this anger, from corporate job cutbacks, declining public services and unfair taxes to inflationary stresses underestimated by government statisticians, are what these next chapters will examine.

By 1990 the beginning of a debate over wealth and income shifts and their effects on the middle class had become unavoidable. Evidence was falling into place. A decade and a half of upward redistribution, which gave the top 1 percent of the population of Britain and the United States an additional 3 to 6 percentage points of their respective national incomes, had obliged former British prime minister Margaret Thatcher and a number of conservative politicians and pundits in the United States to acknowledge that, yes, the rich had reaped the greatest benefit. Yet for the next several years, through the 1992 elections, conservatives insisted on a politically essential corollary: that while people in the middle had indeed profited less, they had still gained ground, which made the 1980s better than the 1970s, when most people had *lost* purchasing power.

In the coming chapters, we will look at what happened to incomes, taxes and the cost of services middle-class Americans had to buy. It is a discouraging picture. But from the start, another part of the case for 1980s economic policy also rested on a dubious premise. The broadly indicted 1970s had not been uniformly difficult for Middle America. The early stages of inflation often are not. Many Americans who would lose ground in the 1980s had profited during the late 1970s: farmers crowing over high commodity prices, independents and wildcatters in the oil business, a fair proportion of unionized production-line workers whose wages and fringe benefits kept climbing, and even some suburbanites whose fast-inflating home values would soon stall. It was relevant that many who had been angriest about the 1970s—notably, investors whose stocks and bonds took a beating from accelerating stagflation—emerged as the big winners of the eighties, and glorified them accordingly. For many people in the middle, however, the 1980s showed that one relatively stagnant decade was replacing another.

The 1990s also began with doubts, but of a new variety. The 1980s had included a number of boom years, even if their benefits went disproportionately to the rich. The nineties, by contrast, quickly emerged as the era of the hangover after the debt party. For many low-middle- and middle-income Americans, what had been stagnation in the 1980s became economic regression in the early 1990s, and the mistakes of the 1980s began to sink in. Democratic politicians started charging the 1989–92 Bush administration with the weakest economic growth since Herbert Hoover. Claims of economic progress that had been believable in 1987 and 1988 rang increasingly hollow in 1991 and 1992. Perceptions of a "squeeze" darkened into something more.

The crux was how it occurred: that the economic circumstances of many Americans in the 40th to 85th percentiles during the Reagan-Bush years were undercut by deliberate philosophies, even if their eventual results were unsought. Indeed, by emphasizing tax cuts, deregulation, disinflation, finance and the growth of financial assets, all three of America's capitalist heydays have been geared to the investing and capital-forming top 1 percent of the population, benefiting the great economic middle much less and for the most part only indirectly (through achievements in technology and modernization of the overall economy). Capitalism has revitalized itself, but such periods are not easy for the average citizen.

Nor should this have been surprising. From the "survival of the fittest" theories of late-nineteenth-century Social Darwinists led by William Graham Sumner to the "help the poor by cutting the taxes of the rich" claims of supply-side thinkers a century later, conservative heyday philosophy has repeatedly favored the strong and the successful.* As we have seen, theology in such periods regularly abandons the average American for a favored group at the top. The preoccupation with the middle class so characteristic of Jacksonian democracy or the Nixon years fades away in the glorification of wealth. During the late-nineteenth-century Gilded Age and then again in the Roaring Twenties, the top 1 percent of Americans were also the principal beneficiaries of income and wealth, while portions of Middle America lost ground, as in the late-twentieth-century's squeeze. Later in this chapter I will show how these pressures have occurred.

Yet the Reagan-Bush heyday also differed from the previous booms because of confusing and difficult-to-measure circumstances that transformed a nominal 1980–89 improvement of 5 to 10 percent in the average American family's income into a frequent decline in real purchasing power. The various stresses that produced this result are broadly framed in this chapter and then detailed in subsequent ones. They were the undiscussed, even hidden, dark sides of the boom.

One such circumstance was the increasingly dense barrage of federal, state and local taxes that assailed the median American family by 1992. A century earlier, by contrast, comparatively few taxes had affected the typical citizen—they were mostly import duties, property taxes and excise taxes on liquor and certain manufactures. Not so by the early 1990s. Though official statistics on the tax burden and its shifts were piecemeal and never combined federal, state *and* local

*In addition to the shared heyday characteristics profiled in Chapter 2, more detail on the philosophic origins of these periods can be found in Chapter 3 of my 1990 book, *The Politics of Rich and Poor.*

effects, the average family could sense that combined tax pressures were greater than officially acknowledged.

A second source of confusion was ongoing stagflation involving a change of 4 percent or 5 percent a year in the price index. In previous heydays, inflation had been broken or reversed before the boom got under way, so that with prices stable or declining, voters in the 1890s and 1920s didn't have to adjust nominal gains into inflation-adjusted reality. In the Reagan-Bush years, they did.

Then there was the confusion of what was happening to the United States in terms of international indebtedness. *Private* financiers and businessmen a century earlier had borrowed heavily overseas, but the U.S. Treasury itself ran a surplus from 1867 to 1893—and again during the 1920s. In the 1980s, however, Washington pyramided federal budget deficits at an unprecedented rate; and as both private- and public-sector America borrowed around the world, the dollar eventually plummeted, which brought unusual, disconcerting side effects. By the late eighties, well-heeled foreigners could buy U.S. corporations and "trophy" buildings cheaply while middle-class Americans could no longer afford to stay in London, Zurich, Frankfurt or Tokyo. The Japanese were the world's new "rich" tourists. Ordinary U.S. citizens knew something had been lost, but weren't quite sure what.

Moreover, not only did the uneasy middle class of the computer era have to sort out unprecedented complexities, but tricky and unreliable official U.S. statistics added to the problem. Although federal data showed average family incomes up somewhat during the 1980s, even after adjustment for inflation, middle-class families told pollsters that official price-index adjustments underestimated the reduction in their purchasing power. Several new nongovernmental indexes painted the erosion from taxes and inflation in vivid, even shocking colors (see pages 94 and 96). Inadequate and contradictory reports and indexes added to national confusion, as we will also examine.

Yet despite these new complications, it is useful to begin with how the two previous heydays also buffeted Middle America. There is a common thread. And so before I examine such *specific* squeezes as rising taxes, eroding private and government benefits, declining public services and increasingly high-cost private services like schools, banks, insurance and health care, it's appropriate to look at the recurring ideological and historical backdrop—at how previous capitalist-conservative go-go periods affected the ordinary American.

Middle America in the Gilded Age and the Roaring Twenties

By their nature, heydays tend to bypass the everyday citizen. In January 1928, as the great stock market boom of the 1920s roared toward its speculative mountaintop, the editors of *The Nation* complained of "a pyramiding of wealth beyond all the dreams of Solomon and Croesus" following disclosure by the Internal Revenue Service that the number of Americans with million-dollar-a-year incomes in 1927 "broke all records with 228, while the number of $5,000,000 incomes doubled."[1] But the editors were also indignant that the percentage of Americans with middle-class incomes in the $2,000 to $5,000 range simultaneously fell from 2.17 million in 1926 to 2.09 million in 1927, with "a corresponding decline in the income reported by all these classes." "Prosperity," the magazine complained, "can hardly be called healthy unless well spread out, and these figures would seem to indicate that there is something radically wrong with our distribution system."[2]

The twenties, like the eighties, were, as we have seen, a boom for only a minority of the U.S. population. If no economist or pundit found a "middle-class squeeze" in an era captivated by Wall Street speculators, fast automobiles and short skirts, that, as we have also seen, was partly because the middle class of those days was too small and—at 15 to 20 percent of the population—too elite. The real "squeeze" was on the decade's true "Middle America": farmers, clerical and blue-collar workers. The rural families being pushed off their farms in Minnesota or Kansas had been America's turn-of-the-century yeomanry. The embattled United Mine Workers and railroad brotherhoods, in turn, were the country's biggest unions and their members had been among its best-paid workers, and yet membership was shrinking relentlessly well before the Great Depression.* Textiles, shoes and shipbuilding joined railroads and coal in decline. As many as two hundred thousand workers a year were being replaced by automatic and semiautomatic machinery, giving the dictionary of boom-era economics a new phrase that would recur in the 1980s—"technological unemployment." In 1928, near prosperity's peak, the

---

*Farm families' share of U.S. national income dropped from 15 percent in 1920 to just 9 percent in 1928, and the number of farmers shrank from 31.6 million to 29.6 million. Thirty percent of coal miners were unemployed during the decade, and the United Mine Workers Union saw its membership drop from half a million in 1920 to barely 75,000 in 1928 (Geoffrey Perrett, *America in the Twenties* [New York: Simon and Schuster, 1982], p. 325).

AFL-CIO counted 18 percent of union members out of work, a sharp contrast with more reassuring government estimates.³ "Forgotten Americans" abounded in ballyhoo years like 1927 and 1928, long before Franklin D. Roosevelt gave them a name in mid-Depression 1932. And in other statistics akin to those of the Reagan era, most of the middle third of Americans seem to have run in place or even lost ground economically during the Great Gatsby period when Charles Lindbergh was soaring across the Atlantic and Radio Corporation of America stock was jumping over the Dow-Jones moon.

Contemporary surveys, in fact, recorded much more erosion of incomes among ordinary Americans of the late 1920s than one would guess from the decade's excited worship of new technology and unchained stock markets. As joblessness cut unexpected swaths, many breadwinners solved their problems—as they would again in the 1970s and 1980s—by sending wives and daughters to work. The official percentage of the work force constituted by women jumped from 20.7 in 1920 to 22.0 in 1930, which probably understates the change. But it did not overcome purchasing-power weakness, even if one is slightly skeptical of the Brookings Institution assertion that the three fifths of American families with late 1920s earnings below $2,000 dollars a year had less than they needed to buy basic necessities. Stuart Chase, the popular economics writer, voiced much the same concern in a prophetic book entitled *Prosperity: Fact or Myth,* published in 1929. Behind the image of new two-lane highways full of automobiles, the first talking movies and the quadrupled ranks of millionairedom, most Americans hadn't really gained during the decade, including many who wore white collars. Here is Chase citing a famous American historian on the frustrations of the upper-middle class:

> For this reason, James Truslow Adams believes that the professional man is worse off than he used to be. His income has not increased as fast as the new demands upon it—leaving a more slender margin than a generation ago, or even than a decade ago. He calls it "prosperity without peace of mind." To bring Mr. Adams into the world cost $100. To bring a baby into the same social stratum today costs $1,500. His family when he was a boy rented a dignified, spacious New York house for $1,200 a year. Today one must pay that sum for a 11 x 14 room with a folding wall-bed and a cooking shelf, in a "good" apartment house. Sunshine, air, quiet, spaciousness, dignity, privacy—where are they to be found in apartment living? One used to get them, together with food, clothing, and all other expenses, for $3,000 a year.⁴

Despite a paucity of government data, analysts have tried to supply specifics about who was hurting. One economist contended that the lower 93 percent of the nonfarm population actually experienced a 4 percent decline in real disposable per capita income between 1923 and 1929![5] Farmers, of course, suffered much steeper declines, but agrarian problems were familiar and widely acknowledged. And looking back in the early 1930s, Marriner Eccles, the New Deal chairman of the Federal Reserve Board, joined in calling 1920s income maldistribution an important reason for prosperity's unsustainability:

> While national income rose to high levels, it was so distributed that the incomes of a majority of families were entirely inadequate and business activity was sustained only by a rapid and unsound increase in the private debt structure, including ever-increasing installment-buying of consumption.[6]

The parallel is hardly perfect, but no one can miss the similarity to the 1980s and early 1990s. Net worths in Roaring Twenties Middle America were affected as well as income, and between 1920 and 1929, years of presumed national prosperity, the U.S. Agriculture Department recorded that the value of farmland fell by 30 to 40 percent in the nation's breadbasket from Indiana to the Dakotas, a little less than the decline registered in the same areas from 1981 to 1987. Farmers' equity also fell sharply.

Things had actually been worse a generation earlier, in the first of the boom-era "squeezes," when the financial backwash of the Gilded Age pounded less at *economic* Middle America—the income midsection of the population—than at *geographic* Middle America, the rural heartland of the nation from the Appalachians west to the Rocky Mountains. In a word, Farm Belt America was devastated. Few late-twentieth-century suburbanites in Ventura County, California, or Rockland County, New York, grumbling about high college tuitions, suburban traffic gridlock or Social Security deductions, could imagine the agonies rural Texans, Missourians or Nebraskans suffered from Washington's restoration of pro-creditor, gold standard policies in the 1870s and the ensuing deflation of the money supply, a shrinkage that reduced commodity prices and farm income while simultaneously tightening farmers' debt and mortgage burdens for a full generation before the 1893 crash. Because 74 percent of Americans lived in rural areas in the 1870s and agriculture constituted the main component of U.S. GNP, huge numbers of livelihoods were ruined, and the Farmers'

Alliance convened massive protest meetings of farm families who stood under giant banners, swatting horseflies in the Texas or Iowa breeze as they heard populist speakers plead for the late-nineteenth-century equivalent of "fairness." But as farm prices collapsed, so did an important early version of the American Dream. Here is William Greider in his history of U.S. monetary policy:

> Millions of humble farm families were forced into deeper poverty. Many were compelled to surrender what they thought was their American birthright—ownership of their own modest plot of land, a tangible asset that meant self-sufficiency and freedom to the hardworking yeomanry. Every growing season, as prices fell, their land and labor became worth less. To begin again at the next planting, they must borrow more at punishing rates to buy seed and supplies, but by harvesttime, prices had fallen further and they were unable to pay off their obligations. To continue farming, they must borrow still more. Eventually, when the debt became overwhelming, they would forfeit the land to their creditors, just as the *rentier* accumulated larger and larger holdings, when the French peasantry failed. The process—liquidation and consolidation—was as old as capitalism.[7]

In sum, all three of America's conservative-capitalist heydays have involved processes of Darwinian renewal and economic redistribution *away* from weak or fading midportions of the population and *toward* the top 1 percent of Americans, along with educationally or technologically advanced portions of the middle and upper-middle classes. The very rich flourish because they have capitalism's all-important lever—capital—and the three heydays have been the country's preeminent periods of expanding millionairedom. As a broad calculus, during these periods of purgation and modernization, some 10 to 20 percent of Americans, mostly those with capital, skills and direction, have made significant, direct gains in real income. On the other side of the ledger, however, and even before the booms ended, another 30 to 50 percent with less capital, skill or education, typically suffered from the harsh effects on humdrum or declining sectors of the economy and on people of average or below-average circumstances. So it was again in the 1980s and early 1990s; cutting-edge portions of the middle class profited along with the top 1 percent, but the general midsection of the population—our hapless median family—once again stagnated or lost economic ground amid circumstances biased toward skilled achievers. In *direct* income effects, at least, ordinary Americans near or below the

50th percentile appear to have been losers during capitalist heydays more often than beneficiaries. And none of the squeezes have been accidents.

Confusing Taxes and Stagflation:
The Economic Uniqueness of the Reagan-Bush Heyday

The average family did not get overall tax relief in the 1980s; claims that it did were false. Nor were changes in the cost of living as mild for middle-class Americans as the official data suggested. Indeed, in late 1991, one prominent New York economist, Edward Hyman of the ISI Group, put together a measure of the ferocious interaction of the two trends by combining the rise in taxes, medical payments, Social Security and interest payments as a percentage of personal income and calling it "the New Misery Index." Figure 2 shows how the four categories took 24 percent of personal income in 1960; by 1990 the total had risen to 40 percent—with the largest increase coming during the eighties.

In particular, the gap between the promise of lower tax burdens and the reality of rising ones was new to this boom era. Whatever the problems of the average Middle American breadwinner of the 1880s or 1890s, direct federal taxes were unimportant because Gilded Age Washington raised most of its money in a roundabout way from tariffs and excise levies. Once the temporary Civil War income tax was removed in the 1870s, the federal government did not tax income again until 1913. Even in the 1920s, the income tax affected relatively few Americans. Only 15 percent of U.S. families filed returns in 1927, and for a family of four with $5,000 per year, falling in the economic top 8 percent, the income tax owed was negligible—just $8 a year, according to the U.S. Census Bureau.[8] As for state and local taxes, during the Gilded Age and Roaring Twenties they fell mostly on property, principally farms and other real estate, and when ordinary householders were sorely pressed, commonly farm owners caught between declining incomes and outdated high assessments, they had no problem identifying what was happening.

Income taxes remained a minor burden until World War II, when earnings of many Americans began to rise. A family of four with a median income of $3,000 a year in 1948 paid hardly any income taxes, but in time, more and more households were forced to file returns by the prosperity of the 1950s and the inflationary Vietnam boom of the 1960s. By the 1970s not only had most families started paying signifi-

Figure 2. The New Misery Index?

Taxes + Interest payments + medical + Social Security payments
as a % of personal income

Source: *Barron's*, October 14, 1991
Based on data from Ed Hyman, ISI Group Inc.

cant income levies to federal and state authorities, but inflation was pushing a considerable minority into brackets hitherto reserved for senior executives and professionals. For median families, federal income taxes grew from near irrelevance to obnoxiousness in just one generation. Then in the 1980s, when Washington finally lowered income tax brackets, increases during the decade in all kinds of other taxes—federal excise, federal Social Security, state sales, local property and miscellaneous fees and charges—more than offset the reduction. Ultimately, the reshuffling of the 1980s provided something the 1920s had not: an opportunity for various levels of officialdom to *increase* the total federal, state and local tax burden even while the Reagan administration, in particular, claimed to be *reducing* taxes because of the changes made in federal rates. Rank-and-file voters might not be sure what was happening, but in 1991 the Tax Foundation calculated that Tax Freedom Day, the date when Americans finished paying their yearly federal, state and local tax burden and started working for themselves, had moved ahead to May 8, the latest ever.

Although the Republicans are rarely the proponents of tax increases, the escalation of overall revenue-raising from one GOP heyday to the next was relentless: combined federal, state and local revenues represented only 7 to 8 percent of total U.S. personal income in the 1890s, about 15 percent by 1927 and 42 to 43 percent by 1990. More to the point, during the previous heydays, as noted, the process of reallocating tax burdens had not been a major means of income and wealth redistribution. By the 1980s, however, it had become just that—and the extent to which policymakers significantly restructured the tax burden is part of the discussion in Chapter 5.

Chapter 6, in turn, will examine the unique impact, for a heyday, of steep 1980s inflation in services from health care to college costs and bank fees. By contrast, the 1870s through the mid-1890s had been *deflationary,* because once the paper-money buildup generated by the Civil War ended in the late 1860s, Washington continued to rein in the money supply, dropping prices to lows unseen since Lincoln's election. Price trends in the 1920s were also relatively stable because once the inflation caused by World War I was reversed by the deep recession of 1920–21, the Consumer Price Index stayed within a narrow band.* There was no ongoing deflation as in the late nineteenth century, except in commodity and farmland prices, but overall inflation was not a problem either.

In both heydays, the result favored stock and bond markets because disinflation is good for creditors and financial assets. At the same time, disinflation and especially deflation are painful traps for debtors and commodity producers—and farmers, encouraged to borrow money to buy more land and expand production during flush times, are often both. This was the familiar kind of squeeze, which staggered rural and small-town America during both previous heydays.

What made the 1980s and early 1990s both confusing and different, then, was that they combined the familiar disinflationary boom—surging stocks and bonds as inflation tumbled from 13 percent in 1980 to one third as much three years later—with a lingering inflation that soon stabilized in the 4–5 percent range. Slumping commodity prices put miners, oil producers and farmers through the usual deflationary wringer, at its worst in 1986. However, for the average American, who was neither a crushed farmer nor an exuberant Wall Streeter, a major impact of the Reagan-Bush era was not so much disinflation as ongoing price increases, especially for services, that often seemed to be

*Between 1923 and 1929, it ranged from 51 to 53, based on the year 1967 representing 100.

larger than government yardsticks acknowledged. This time, more of the squeeze would be in understated *inflation,* not *deflation.*

Back in the Roaring Twenties, successful middle-class Americans, such as novelist Sinclair Lewis's stereotypical Midwestern supersalesman George Babbitt, had found themselves trying to keep up with the Joneses in pursuit of luxuries and services that hadn't been available before—autos, radios, toasters, refrigerators, movie tickets and even airplane rides. Undoubtedly this had its frustrations, but the prices of basic goods and services were relatively stable. Movements were small. During the 1980s, by contrast, the middle class was hurt by several offsets to purchasing power that were rising much faster than the ostensibly mild inflation of the Consumer Price Index. The first involved virtually unregulated inflation in the cost of private services—health care, automobile insurance, legal and financial services, bank fees and college tuition. A second reflected how the prices of small, niggling middle-class items from weekly newsmagazines and shoeshines to contact lens solution and per-hour charges at parking garages were soaring at three to four times the CPI rate.* The third represented the onrush of governmental charges ranging from federal taxes, Social Security hikes and state and local taxes to an explosion of miscellaneous governmental fees. The federal government's reassuring calculations of inflation simply did not adequately measure the greater concentrated impact of these costs on people in the middle. The extent of the erosion, detailed in Chapter 6, was critical to whether the middle class was gaining or losing.

While experts generally agreed that the inflationary effects of rising service costs and tax burdens were harder to chart than the inflation of commodity prices during the 1970s, consumers were more blunt, telling pollsters and reporters that federal measurements understated inflation's new burden. In 1991, consumer survey-taker Albert Sindlinger explained that beginning in mid-1990, the three thousand Americans in his monthly sample had reported their perception that the rate of increase in the cost of living (including taxes) had returned to double

---

*The Consumer Price Index gave relatively little weight to miscellaneous items—shoeshines, haircuts, parking and the like—but beginning in 1983 their prices rose sharply. In 1985–86, the Manufacturers Hanover Bank Nuisance Index rose by 15 percent a year, more than four times the CPI rate. Legg Mason's kindred Trivia Index—forty-five items ranging from an ice cream cone to a birthday card—rose three to four times faster than the CPI. In the words of the Manufacturers Hanover chief economist, "Consumers have a gnawing suspicion that there is more inflation out there than is captured in official government statistics—and the skepticism is justified" ("Prices of Small Items, Services, Rise Rapidly," *Wall Street Journal,* April 24, 1987).

digits.* The likelihood that government understated these pressures was important, because recalculating inflation at a level even one or two points above official estimates would force a major reworking of the economic statistics of the late 1980s and early 1990s. Growth estimates would shrivel. Real median-family or average-family income would have been weaker. So would the typical household's purchasing power. And the gap between the huge gains of the rich and the disarray of the middle class would have threatened even more political danger.

Yet, as more and more economists were recognizing, federal statistics *were* becoming unreliable, and sometimes unusable.

The Late-Twentieth-Century Hazard
of U.S. Economic Statistics

By the early 1990s economists, money managers and even journalists had begun to throw up their hands. Horror stories abounded, like the 1991 admission that the Commerce Department had missed $73 billion in U.S. trade accounts or the major revisions later made in 1990 GNP figures. In early 1992 the Commerce and Labor departments released new data revealing that the growth in U.S. manufacturing from 1977 to 1989 was one third below previous estimates. Part of the collective weakness of federal statistics resulted from inadequate government funding, part from conceptual obsolescence and part from simple inaccuracy.

In 1992, after Census Bureau officials held up for four months the release of a study showing that nearly one out of five Americans who worked full time were not paid enough to keep a family of four above the poverty line, critics went further, calling it the third such political manipulation in a year—the first being the refusal by Commerce Secretary Robert Mosbacher to adjust the 1990 Census figures for undercounting, especially of poor people in urban areas, and the second being claims by a Census demographer that her superiors had tried to fire her because she released estimates of Iraqi deaths during the Gulf war that were higher than official calculations and embarrassed the White House.[9] Just before the 1992 presidential election *The Christian Science Monitor* reported widespread suspicion inside and outside the government that the Bush administration had manipulated the government spending process to produce a brighter picture of the U.S. econ-

*By December 1991, as official data pegged U.S. annual inflation in the 3–4 percent range and the Federal Reserve pushed short-term interest rates down to that level, Sindlinger reported a much higher estimate of the annual increase in the cost of living—14 percent!

omy in the third-quarter GDP (gross domestic product) statistics released on October 27.

What seems indisputable is that during the 1980s Reagan administration budget cuts forced staff reductions at the various federal agencies that kept statistics while also undercutting the research needed to keep sampling techniques abreast of economic changes. Robert Ortner, the Commerce Department under secretary in charge, later acknowledged that budget pressures had sidetracked an effort to modernize U.S. statistics and make them more comparable to bookkeeping done in other countries.[10]

By the Bush years, disgruntlement over poor data was abundant. One broad charge was that U.S. statistics were out of date because they had been designed to measure the vanished economy of the 1940s and 1950s. Baltimore economist Ben Laden, who studied the statistics problem for the National Association of Business Economists, complained about inadequate attention to regionalism: "Within the past decade, we have had much greater diversity in regional performance than we ever had before, starting with the farm depression and the manufacturing depression in the early 1980s and then the drop in oil prices, which killed Texas. But the federal government is doing very little to track regional differences."[11]

Small sampling bases also contributed to unreliability. "History is being rewritten on a monthly basis," said Allen Sinai, chief economist of the Boston Company. "It makes it very hard for private-sector analysts and public policymakers to come to correct conclusions."[12] Several years into the new decade, Congress and the Bush administration started discussing proposals to increase funding for data collection, stung by reminders like that from James Smith, a former president of the National Association of Business Economists: "The United States spends more money subsidizing the production of honey-bee wax than it does collecting federal statistics. That's a fact."[13]

Specific complaints piled up about the government's unemployment and inflation measurements. In contrast to many European countries, the United States in compiling jobless data excluded persons without employment who had stopped looking for work, while part-time workers who wanted full-time jobs were nevertheless counted as entirely employed. In the spring of 1991, when the official unemployment rate was 6.8 percent, Lawrence Mishel of Washington's liberal-tilting Economic Policy Institute argued that "What you really have is a total unemployment and underemployment rate of 12.4 percent."[14]

Commissioner of Labor Statistics Janet Norwood, after declining reappointment in 1991, began speaking out on the inadequacies of government data. Not only did she acknowledge that the unemployment numbers were misleading, but she said, "I am very worried, extraordinarily concerned, about the polarization I see going on in our country."[15] Shortly thereafter, the California Department of Finance issued an analysis suggesting that in 1991 the federal government had seriously underestimated the effect of the recession in California and some other major states, undercounting job losses nationwide by more than 2 million. The decline in California employment was the worst since the 1930s, and Washington was alleged to have underestimated the plunge by more than 350,000 jobs in that state alone. The department's principal economist, Ted Gibson, said, "To me, it's very obvious that the recession is far, far deeper than the [Labor Department] figures are indicating."[16] In 1992, Labor Department record-keepers all but conceded, admitting that 600,000 more jobs than previously acknowledged had been lost in 1991. For the nation as a whole, roughly a quarter of U.S. families seem to have been affected by 1990–92 unemployment.*

In Philadelphia, where official Labor Department sampling found only 6 percent unemployment in April 1990, the official U.S. Census—conducted that same month with a lot more thoroughness—found 9.7 percent joblessness. Then two years later, with the official rate up to 7.7 percent, *The Philadelphia Inquirer* projected that the city's actual unemployment rate had probably climbed into double digits. The Census counts of unemployment in other cities as of April 1990 were also much higher than the Labor Department's numbers. In Detroit the Labor Department estimated 9.8 percent versus the Census's 19.7 percent; in New York, 5.9 percent versus the Census's 9.0 percent; in Los Angeles, 6.1 percent versus 8.4 percent, and in Chicago, 7.9 percent versus 11.3 percent.[17]

The government's pivotal Consumer Price Index also had critics. First, said some, the CPI had not adequately reflected the 1980s surge in medical and educational costs. Second, the Index understated the effect of inflation on important demographic subgroups like baby boomers, homeowners and the middle class. Moreover, the formula used for the CPI had been updated last in 1987, using 1980 Census data

---

*According to an early 1992 Time/CNN poll, 23 percent of those surveyed said they had been unemployed, not by their own choice, at some time during 1991. In February 1992, New Jersey's Newark Star-Ledger/Eagleton Institute poll reported that more than a third of New Jerseyans said an adult in their household had been out of work and actively seeking a job in 1991.

and consumer spending patterns from 1982–84, and the next update was not scheduled until 1995.[18]

A corporal's guard led by consumer pollster Sindlinger further contended that the CPI greatly understated 1990–91 inflation by its inadequate treatment of taxes. Property, sales and excise levies were included in whole or in part because of their effect on the cost of goods and services, but income taxes, Social Security taxes and many federal, state and local taxes and fees were excluded. "Conceptually, he [Sindlinger] is right," Irwin Kellner, chief economist for Manufacturers Hanover Bank, told *The New York Times,* but "I wouldn't want to be pinned down to his specific number."[19]

Cost-of-living measurements in other nations, however, *did* pay more attention to taxes, especially after the spread of consumption taxes during the 1970s and 1980s obliged governments to incorporate the various new levies into consumer price indexes to increase their accuracy for wage negotiation and other purposes. For example, it was routine in June 1992, when John Dawkins, the treasurer of Australia, announced that increased charges and taxes in Australia's two biggest states would add 0.5 percentage point to the nation's inflation rate in the next fiscal year. Years earlier, U.S. researchers had also toyed with an expanded tax-and-price index, and according to former Labor Department officials involved in the project, combined price *and* tax index inflation averaged 6.9 percent for the period between 1967 and 1985, seven tenths of a point over the 6.2 percent increase actually recorded in the CPI.[20] But official yardsticks were not revised.

Few doubted that important aspects of 1980s and 1990s economic behavior were being poorly measured, not least for categories of Middle America. Blurry statistics might complicate national decision-making, but they also helped confuse—and possibly mislead—voters who otherwise could have been angered.

Misleading Statistics and Political Misperceptions

Those who control definitions and statistics often control policy, a lesson well understood by those who wanted to shape or rebut what Americans thought of 1980s economics. The otherwise confusing multiple series and forms of "government data" were a boon to liberal and conservative economists, activists and commentators who packaged their preferred numbers to serve their partisan purposes. Income trends and tax burdens, in particular, were the favorite clay of ideological sculptors, so for those who would judge the Reagan and Bush eras, a short guide is in order.

Proponents of 1980s economic policies preferred to emphasize gains in real per capita income, which rose from $12,351 in 1980 to $14,387 in 1990, as proof of the administration's success. Yet even before the decline of 1991, the growth in per capita income during the 1980s was deceptive. Some of it reflected gains highly concentrated among America's top earners. Then, as we shall see in more detail in Chapter 6, another substantial part of the 1980s increase, far from representing added productivity, reflected the expansion of the labor force from 58 percent of adults to 63 percent as more women took jobs to keep their households above water. As this happened, family expenses surged, not least child care, but per capita income growth statistics were not adjusted accordingly. So they greatly overstated growth in genuinely disposable real income during the decade.

Across the ideological aisle, liberal foes of GOP economics often strained their argument by uncritical preoccupation with median family income data. True, weaknesses in the broader economy were the principal reason that U.S. median family incomes plateaued after 1973, but as conservatives pointed out, changes in family size also played a role. As the average family shrank from 3.29 persons in 1980 to 3.18 persons in 1990, somewhat less money in constant dollars was needed to sustain its prior living standard. By not making that adjustment, regular Census Bureau data overstated the stagnation.*

A second complaint about median family income data—that by assuming one breadwinner, it misrepresented the "average" family, which by now had *two* earners—prompted some organizations (such as the Tax Foundation) to redefine the "average" family to include two workers and a higher income. These families, however, while more upwardly mobile during the 1980s, were also a minority, and their earnings *overstated* the decade's progress. Yet even their incomes stagnated, as we have seen, once adjusted for changes in the federal tax burden. Definitional hopscotch couldn't dispel the troubling reality.

Liberals, for their part, were correct in emphasizing how hourly manufacturing wages *declined* during the 1980s, yet wrong in insisting

*Conservative detractors of the significance of the median-income trend also contended that the Census Bureau's surveys relied on inaccurate estimates and missed about 10 percent of the earnings assumable from tax returns and W-2 forms. Another complaint was that the median-income calculations involved only *money* income and ignored the growing role of employee benefits and government transfer payments. On the other hand, others counterargued that by the late 1980s and early 1990s, the median income's year-to-year change was being abnormally fattened by a demographic bulge of families in the forty-five- to fifty-four-year-old bracket, where income maximizes. Questions about the exactitude of the year-to-year data, however, don't negate the trend from the mid-1970s to the early 1990s. Relative stagnation is still a fair description.

that the average weekly wage also fell, despite the confirming data published by the Bureau of Labor Statistics. Rival statistics from the Social Security Administration, which showed weekly wages rising, were better because these numbers reflected overall work-force hours and earnings, not just select sampling. The catch, as amplified on pages 157 to 159, was that the principal reason for rising work-force earnings—a sharp increase in men and women working overtime or moonlighting with second jobs—reflected the worries of a *squeezed* work force, not a *contented* one. Household fears were the spur, not economic growth, as conservatives contended.

In short, most of the available income, cost and wage measurements involve some distortion. However, now that some of these biases have been noted, the next two chapters will use the different yardsticks as necessary, while concentrating on the important larger circumstances: inflation's greater-than-acknowledged erosion of middle-class purchasing power and, just as important, the underappreciated burden of federal, state and local tax changes and increases. The tax rearrangements, to which we turn first, were more than simply another economic ingredient in the third and latest squeeze on Middle America. Much like the great deflation visited on the rural United States in the post–Civil War era, they, too, were also a sign that the political establishment of the 1980s was willing to shift fiscal priorities that once favored the broad mass of Americans to serve the interests of a relatively small elite.

CHAPTER 5

The Great Tax Misrepresentation of the 1980s

True marginal tax rates in the United States are at their peak for two-earner couples making between $50,000 and $100,000 a year—precisely the middle-income people who would best respond to the incentive of lower rates. America has one of the world's least progressive tax structures . . . the payroll tax wreaks havoc with marginal tax rates. The average proportion of income paid in tax by the poorest 50% of families rose in the 1980s by 6%, while for the richest 10% it fell by 10%.

—*The Economist,* January 20, 1990

There are many people who believe that the only way we can get this country turned around is to tax the middle class more and punish them more, but the truth is that middle-class Americans are basically the only group of Americans who've been taxed more in the 1980s and during the last 12 years, even though their incomes have gone down. The wealthiest Americans have been taxed much less, even though their incomes have gone up.

—Democratic presidential nominee Bill Clinton, 1992

Compared with the relatively straightforward tax reductions of previous eras, those of the 1980s could be said to represent an era of tax *deception,* especially where the average American family was concerned. Rhetoric about new efficiency, simplification and fairness in revenue-raising, though often sincere, was misleading. While lower income taxes did become a pleasing reality for billionaires, whose numbers multiplied tenfold as the top rate on unearned income fell from 70 percent in 1981 to 28 percent in 1988 and the stock market soared, *ordinary* households soon found themselves facing their highest overall tax rates in the history of the republic.

In 1992, Thomas Block, president of H&R Block, the tax preparers with seven thousand offices across the nation, explaining that he had commissioned a university research project in response to the growing "perception among middle-income taxpayers that they pay too much tax in relation to high-income earners," announced that was just what his experts had found: between 1977 and 1990, the tax bill for a taxpayer earning $50,000 a year had increased 7.75 percent, while the bill for taxpayers with incomes of $200,000 a year had dropped 27.75 percent. Block allowed that he had hoped President Bush would sign congressional Democrats' middle-class tax cut legislation—which Bush instead vetoed—because boosting the top tax rate on the wealthy "would have gone a long way in restoring equity."[1]

Months earlier, the Washington-based Tax Foundation had determined that for the year 1990, direct and indirect federal, state and local taxes had become an unprecedented weight on the typical U.S. family, taking a record 37.3 cents of every dollar.[2] Data also supported an ironic corollary: that the average wealthy family with a million-dollar income paid a *lower* rate, probably 35 or 36 cents on every dollar—and probably their lowest in sixty years.

Computing the relative burdens was not difficult. The average family, by the Foundation's calculus, would have paid 28 cents of every dollar in all kinds of federal taxes and 9 cents in state and local taxes.* The millionaire's family, using other estimates, would have paid about 28 to 29 cents on every dollar in federal taxes, but probably only about 7 cents in state taxes.† Wealthy households' total dollar payments were much higher than the typical family's, to be sure, yet their relative burden as a percentage of income was lighter, a striking reversal of mid-twentieth-century political and fiscal equity.

In some jurisdictions, moreover, regressive state tax structures made the surprising disparity even larger. In Pennsylvania, for example, the average family would have paid 38 cents on every dollar (28.2 cents in federal taxes, 9.8 cents to states and courthouses) versus approximately 34 cents for the rich; in Texas, the relative combined tax burdens were 37 cents for the middle class, 32 cents for the rich; in Illinois, the ratio was 40 cents per dollar for the average family, 34 cents per dollar for millionaire taxpayers; in Florida, the difference was between 36 cents and 31 cents.[3]

This is hardly what middle-income Americans could have expected from the promises of supply-side economists of the early 1980s or from

---

*The Tax Foundation, like most other analysts, used a methodology that included both the employee's *and* employer's FICA payments as being attributed to the employee's federal tax burden.

†The estimate of a 28–29 percent effective federal rate for million-dollar incomes is based on Urban Institute and Congressional Budget Office estimates for the top 1 percent, while the estimate of a 7 percent effective state tax rate comes from the 1991 study *A Far Cry from Fair* by Citizens for Tax Justice.

the speeches of administration and congressional tax reform architects circa 1986. The reality, however, was that as Washington lowered federal tax burdens on high incomes, the overall effects of federal fiscal policy wound up boosting other federal, state and local assessments on people in the middle enough to make the nation's collective tax burden of the early 1990s set records as a percentage of peacetime GNP and national income. In Chapters 2 and 4, I described the evolution of this philosophy and how the exactions heaped upon the middle-income family and even the upper-middle-income family came from all directions: federal income tax "bubbles" through which the upper-middle class paid higher marginal rates than millionaires, relentless expansion of Social Security rates and taxable income bases, soaring local property taxes (especially in the Northeast) and state tax increases and fees often targeted on ordinary purchases and breadwinners. Citizens for Tax Justice, a union-funded group, threw its critical spotlight on how Texas, in the late 1980s, raised its sales tax rate from 4.125 percent to 6.25 percent, boosted cigarette taxes by 21.2 cents per pack and increased the gasoline tax by 5 cents. These changes, the group calculated, cost poor Texas families 3.1 percent more of their annual incomes, took 1.6 percent from middle-income earnings and tapped wealthy households for a mere 0.4 percent.[4]

State-level raids on new revenue sources were sometimes comical in their desperation. Wisconsin, for example, in November 1990, began trying to collect sales tax on drinks served on airplanes that were flying over the state until the practice was overturned by the Wisconsin Court of Appeals.[5] But even serious revenue efforts were extending in unusual and provocative directions. New York City, unsatisfied with registering only dogs, decided to charge license fees for cats, too, and began requiring animal-grooming salons to provide names and addresses of pet owners.[6] In 1991 California not only increased the sales tax to 7.25 percent, but became the first state to extend it to snack foods after an angry debate over what was included and what wasn't.* Ritz Crackers were taxed, saltines weren't. On July 16, as the $200-million-a-year snack tax went into effect, the *Los Angeles Times* published what must be one of the more extraordinary charts in the annals of state tax policy.

State Board of Equalization member Brad Sherman, a prominent

*A few months later, Pennsylvania applied its sales tax to snack foods and set off a debate about whether bagels were taxable—they were if baked on the store's premises but they were not if prepackaged. In California, however, the debate ended on November 3, 1992, when citizens voted by two to one to repeal the snack tax even though it would cost the state hundreds of millions of dollars in revenue that would have to be made up elsewhere.

Figure 3. Taxing Your Snack

Now Taxed	Remaining Exempt
■ All forms of candy	★ Baking chocolate
■ Rice cakes	★ Baking confections
■ Cupcakes	★ Glazed fruit sold for baking
■ Twinkies	(but not when sold as candy)
■ Granola bars	★ Cereals
■ Screaming Yellow Zonkers	★ Muffins
■ Cracker Jack	★ Doughnuts, pastry sold
■ Fig Newtons	as bakery products
■ Ritz Crackers	★ Slice of pie purchased from a deli
■ Carnation breakfast bars	(but not as prepackaged snack)
■ Pringles chips	★ Saltine crackers
■ Cheese puffs	★ Nuts
■ Doritos	★ Seeds
■ Cheez-It crackers	★ Dried fruit
■ Ding Dongs	

Source: State Board of Equalization

opponent, had complained before enactment that the "definition of snack foods says nothing about caviar or brie. But it does tax cookies, potato chips, corn chips, popcorn and pretzels. In other words, the country club spread or lobbyists' reception menu of brie, caviar and French bread will be untaxed, but the average person's party of chips, cookies and pretzels will be taxed."[7] After enactment, most critics began emphasizing the technical difficulty of distinguishing, as the law required, between foods and snacks. Ding Dongs were foods for federal food stamp purposes but taxable snacks within the boundaries of California. Weeks after the tax went into effect, the Board of Equalization was still debating the revenue status of chocolate chips, marshmallows—and Ninja Turtle Snack Pies!

As the fiscal crises worsened in 1992 the states began enacting more fees and charges in lieu of overt taxes. New York imposed tough new penalties on unpaid parking tickets, where fines and penalties already brought in nearly a half billion dollars a year. In California, where state officials purported to avoid any new taxes, another $530 million a year in fees were imposed on persons who wanted to take college courses, register pleasure boats, enroll children for treatment of leukemia or file lawsuits, while the state also cut $1.3 billion of aid to local governments and special districts, forcing them to raise taxes and utility rates.[7A]

U.S. fiscal history has had its share of revolts against provocative taxes, from the Boston Tea Party and the Whiskey Rebellion of 1794 to California's famous Proposition 13 of 1978. By the early 1990s the provocations were again reaching that level—or worse. The paradox of the 1980s, however, lay in how the tax revolt of the late 1970s, which began as a middle-class or even populist insurgency against rising property taxes in California, was transformed into a dismantling of the progressive income tax and a re-attuning of the federal tax system to concerns about markets and efficiency, not fairness, with the results we have just seen.

To be sure, reforms included in 1986 and 1990 federal tax legislation helped America's poor by cutting millions off the income tax rolls (1986) and by increasing the value of the low-income tax credit (1990). For those at the economic bottom, these modifications mitigated the FICA increases and other regressive changes. But otherwise, as we have seen, the thrust of federal and state tax policy in the 1980s and early 1990s was toward expanding the sort of taxes that took their highest ratios of household income from the poor and middle classes: Social Security, sales, property and excise. Because the average family did not receive new exclusions or credits, the rise of its combined federal, state and local tax burden to record levels by the early 1990s became a central ingredient in the reduction of middle-class real disposable income.

The Downward Redistribution of the Federal Tax Burden

A succinct, one-paragraph history of federal taxation of the ordinary U.S. family since World War II, if penned by angry progressives, might read this way: During these years, the top income tax rate on the richest Americans fell from 91 percent to 31 percent while the burden on the average household soared because of bracket creep, FICA increases and the eroding value of family exemptions. Back in 1948 a family of four earning the median income would have owed little or no federal income tax while paying a mere 1 percent of its income to Social Security. By 1955 that same family would have been laying out 9 percent for Social Security and income tax together, and by 1990, according to tax expert Eugene Steuerle of the Urban Institute, a median-income family faced a combined federal tax rate of almost 25 percent, while other estimates set it at 26 percent to 28 percent.

Traditional families with two or more children were particular losers. Economist Steuerle, who put much of the blame on the declining inflation-adjusted value of family exemptions, emphasized that "taxes on households with dependents have increased at a faster rate than for most other households."[8] Congresswoman Patricia Schroeder of Colorado, chair of the House Select Committee on Children, Youth and Families, said that: "People are just beginning to realize that taxes on families have never been this high in the history of the Republic."[9]

Conservatism's one-paragraph synopsis, by contrast, was cheery, even boastful. Reduction of tax rates on the rich, by stripping economic disincentives from the tax code, culminated in the investment, entrepreneurialism, stock market boom and capitalist bow wave of the Reagan years. As a result, the share of total federal income taxes paid by the flush top 1 percent of Americans kept increasing, especially in the crescendo of the 1980s when it rose from 18 percent to 27 percent. According to supply-side chroniclers, this showed that the U.S. income tax was actually getting *more* progressive—taking more from the rich and gathering less from everyone else.

A foreign visitor asked to arbitrate might assume that one of these analyses had to be false. In fact, *both* sequences of *facts* were correct, which helps explain the debate that arose in the 1990s between partisans of contrary interpretations.

It helps to proceed by laying out basic undisputed circumstances. For a $1-million-a-year earner, the top federal income tax rate fell from 91 percent in 1955 to 70 percent in 1964, 50 percent in 1981, 28 percent in 1988 and 31 percent in 1991. No one suggests otherwise. Meanwhile, for a median-income family of four, it is also beyond debate that the sheltering effect of the federal income tax personal or dependent exemption shrank relentlessly after World War II, whittled by inflation to a fraction of its former value. In 1948, when the exemption was $600 and the median family took in $3,000, a family of four with these earnings, as we have seen, was largely shielded against federal income taxes.* Through the 1950s, the exemption could still minimize median-family federal tax burdens. That ended as rising inflation weakened the benefit of dependent exemptions in the 1960s and shrank them further in the 1970s. By 1990, despite an increase in the exemption to $2,050, the effect was just a shadow of yesteryear's. As Appendix B details, to shelter the same percentage of per capita income as the $600 figure did in 1948 would have required a $7,781 exemption!

Besides doubling exemptions, the federal tax policy of the 1980s cut income tax rates for ordinary families. This, too, was a solid fact. As

*The $3,000-a-year family of 1948 would have had a $600 adjusted income after exemptions, to which the lowest rate of 16 percent applied, for an estimated federal income tax of $100.

a result, the effective income tax rate of 11.4 percent paid by the median family in 1981 dropped to 10.5 percent in 1982 and 9.1 percent in 1988.[10] Middle America would have benefited more from rate reductions if they hadn't been partly offset in the late 1980s by the loss of hitherto significant deductions—for state sales taxes, for interest paid on personal loans and credit cards and (in many cases) for individual retirement accounts.

The larger reality, though, was that the shrinkage of dependent exemption benefits from 1950 to 1990 had cost ordinary families many, many more dollars than 1980s bracket reductions could recoup. In addition, Social Security taxes were a fast-rising burden in the Reagan and Bush years, and excise taxes on alcohol, tobacco and gasoline were also climbing. So by the early 1990s, according to Brookings Institution calculations, the median or average family in the $30,000–$50,000 range was laying out a slightly higher percentage of earnings in *combined* federal income, excise and FICA taxes than it had been at the beginning of the 1980s. Table 4 pairs the 1948–90 decline of the effective federal tax rate on the rich with the rise during the same period of the effective tax rate on the median family.

The Tax Foundation, as noted, also reported that the overall tax burden for the average family set a record in 1990 and that median family income was stagnant, after adjustment for federal taxes. Calculations by the Urban Institute, in turn, show that the median family paid out the following percentages of its earnings in federal income and Social Security taxes: 23.08 percent in 1980, 25.09 percent in 1981, 23.78 percent in 1983, 24.44 percent in 1985, 24.63 percent in 1990.[11] Excise taxes, not included in the institute's calculation, further increased the weight. Overall, expanding tax pressures were part of a declining purchasing power. As we have seen, the Congressional Budget Office calculated that in constant 1990 dollars, a typical middle-income family's earnings after federal income tax dropped from $30,900 in 1980 to $29,500 in 1992.

Net federal tax reduction for the 1980s, then, was largely an illusion. Despite politicians' contrary pretenses, federal revenue needs made it impossible to let the middle class off the fiscal hook. The decision in 1983 to boost Social Security taxes even as income tax rates were coming down had been a bellwether. What Washington gave $40,000 households with its income tax hand it largely took back with its FICA hand. Appendix B shows the relentless 1980s rise of the FICA tax rate and the even more sweeping enlargement of the earnings base to which that taxation applied.

The fairness complaint was that while the overall tax changes of the

Table 4. The Great Tax-Rate Turnaround, 1948–90
Median Families versus Millionaires or the Top 1 Percent

	Median Family's Effective Federal Tax Rate (Income and FICA)*	Millionaire or Top 1% Family's Effective Federal Tax Rate (Income and FICA)†
1948	5.30%	76.9%
1955	9.06	85.5
1960	12.35	85.5
1965	11.55	66.9
1970	16.06	68.6
1975	20.03	
1977		35.5
1980	23.68	31.7
1981	25.09	
1982	24.46	
1983	23.78	
1984	24.25	
1985	24.44	24.9
1986	24.77	
1987	23.21	
1988	24.30	26.9
1989	24.37	26.7
1990	24.63	

*The data in this column originates as follows: the 1948 figure comes from *The Statistical History of the United States, 1976;* the figures for 1955 to 1983 come from Alan Lerman of the U.S. Department of the Treasury Office of Tax Analysis. The calculations after 1983 come from Eugene Steuerle and Jon Bakija, *Right Ways and Wrong Ways to Reform Social Security* (Washington, D.C.: Urban Institute Press, 1993).

†The figures for 1948 to 1970 represent the effective tax rates for those earning $1 million a year and come from U.S. Treasury Department unpublished data set forth on p. 1112 of *The Statistical History of the United States, 1976.* FICA is not included, but the rates would not even be affected by a percentage point. The rates from 1977 onward are for the top 1% of families as computed by the Congressional Budget Office tax simulation model and include all federal taxes. Source: the 1992 Green Book of the House Ways and Means Committee, p. 1510. The effective rate on millionaires would be close to the rate on the top 1 percent.

1980s slightly raised rather than reduced the total federal tax burdens of the average or median family, these same revisions did reduce—*significantly*—the tax burdens of the richest Americans, continuing a pattern of relief that began in the mid-1950s. Back in 1948 or 1955, when the average American family was paying only 1 to 2 percent of its income for Social Security and little or no federal income tax, a senior corporate executive making $200,000 in yearly salary, admittedly rare in those days, would have paid 65 to 75 percent or so. One profile of Charles Wilson, the chairman of General Motors, estimated that he would have kept only $164,000 from a 1950 salary of $626,-000.[12] Wealthy salaried people generally paid high federal income taxes during the Truman and early Eisenhower years, although oilmen had lucrative depletion allowances and other shelters and entrepreneurs enjoyed the advantage of low capital gains taxes. The pyramiding deductions, credits and gimmicks of the 1960s and 1970s, which President Jimmy Carter would call a disgrace, were still largely a gleam in the eye of Washington lobbyists and congressional tax-writers.

Meanwhile, over the next three decades, the broad funding strategies on which Washington depended to support federal expenditures slowly shifted away from a reliance on taxes that burdened the upper brackets (the personal and corporate income taxes, along with estate taxes) toward borrowing and levies that fell elsewhere. In the 1950s, as Table 5 shows, the personal income tax, corporate income tax and estate tax provided over three quarters of all funds. By the 1980s that had fallen to roughly half. As the burden on those at the top fell, a greater proportion of money was raised by taxing those in the middle or borrowing against future living standards.

By its late-1980s zenith, the philosophic reversal involved had far-reaching practical effects. In the early 1950s, when $600,000-a-year salaried executives faced an effective tax rate that official estimates placed near 75 percent, a median-family breadwinner, as we have seen, virtually escaped the Internal Revenue Service with an effective income tax rate of just 5 percent. Federal income tax tables back then applied twenty-three successive brackets eventually reaching 91 percent. This made tax progressivity obvious on its face. Thirty-five years later, an extraordinary convergence was taking place: the effective combined rate of federal taxes (income, excise and FICA) on median or average families had climbed to the 25–28 percent range, depending on the calculation, while the rate on households with $500,000 incomes had

Table 5. Source of Funds for Federal Spending
(Average Annual Shares)

Decade	Personal Income Tax	Corporate Income Tax	Payroll Tax	Excise/ Estate	Borrowing
1950s	42.0%	26.9%	11.5%	17.2%	2.5%
1960s	42.0%	20.4%	18.4%	14.9%	4.4%
1970s	40.3%	13.3%	27.7%	11.3%	11.1%
1980s	38.0%	7.7%	29.2%	8.2%	17.7%

Source: Robert J. Shapiro, "Paying for Progress," Progressive Policy Institute, February 1991. Calculations derived by the author from *Budget of the United States Government,* fiscal year 1991, "Historical Tables," Tables 1.1 and 2.2.

declined to roughly 28 percent. There, in a sentence, was the fiscal revolution.

We have already examined the philosophic transition that supported the tax changes of the sixties, the seventies and (especially) the eighties and how they reduced the bite on the rich and increased it on the average family. In less than a generation, the average American went from being a political icon to being a fiscal milch cow. As Chapter 8 will show, historically this has been a dangerous transformation for great nations. Yet the contrary insistences marshaled by conservatives require some further clarification: After all, the share of federal income taxes paid by the top 1 percent did rise sharply from 1980 to the end of the decade. Wasn't this proof that everyone else actually got off more easily, paying a *shrinking* share of the federal tax burden?

Not really. During the 1980s the portion of overall federal income tax revenues that were collected from the richest 1 percent increased by about 50 percent (from 18 percent to 27 percent) because that group's share of national income grew by roughly that same ratio—from about 8 percent to 12–13 percent. Actually, because the tax rates of the rich were significantly higher than those of others during most of the decade, their share of taxes paid should have increased even more sharply than their share of income, but that is where the rate cuts came in.

The role of tax policy in upper-bracket gains was both direct and indirect. The indirect role, all too often ignored, was the more important. From 1979 to 1982, as the maximum tax rate on capital gains fell from 49 percent to 20 percent while the maximum income tax rate on unearned income dropped from 70 percent to 50 percent, the effect on the financial markets—once they were also reassured by disinflation—was to fuel a massive boom. In a nutshell, the lower tax rates raised the return on and thus the value of financial assets like stocks and bonds, just as many supply-siders had predicted. Economist Robert Shapiro of the Progressive Policy Institute later summarized how the 90 percent growth in incomes for the top 1 percent of Americans during the 1980s came about because "the top 1 percent own vast capital assets, the value of which increased when tax incentives artificially raised their rate of return."[13] As the Dow-Jones Industrial Average soared during the 1980s, so did its ability to turn new stock issues and financial deals into wealth for affluent Americans. From 1978 to 1988 the number of persons with million-dollar annual incomes skyrocketed from 2,041 to 65,303. Even allowing for inflation, that was an eightfold increase.[14]

Moreover, when the owners of financial assets—the top 1 percent

Figure 4. The Comparative Benefits of the Tax Reform Act of 1986

Income Bracket	Size of Tax Cut	Average 1989 Tax Savings per Return
Up to $10,000	11%	$37
$10,000–$20,000	6%	$69
$20,000–$30,000	11%	$300
$30,000–$40,000	11%	$467
$40,000–$50,000	16%	$1,000
$50,000–$75,000	16%	$1,523
$75,000–$100,000	18%	$3,034
$100,000–$200,000	22%	$7,203
$200,000–$500,000	27%	$24,603
$500,000–$1,000,000	34%	$86,084
$1,000,000 or more	31%	$281,033

Source: Internal Revenue Service, *Philadelphia Inquirer*, October 21, 1991

Fewer people pay the minimum tax . . . And they pay less

Income bracket	Taxpayers In 1986	Taxpayers in 1989	down	Income bracket	Avg. tax paid in 1986	Avg. tax paid in 1989	down
$100,000–$200,000	126,127	29,195	77%	$100,000–$200,000	$10,295	$4,561	56%
$200,00–$500,000	46,874	14,112	70%	$200,000–$500,000	$23,237	$9,037	61%
$500,000–$1,000,000	10,428	4,176	60%	$500,000–$1,000,000	$45,218	$20,694	54%
$1,000,000 or more	15,259	2,361	85%	$1,000,000 or more	$116,395	$54,758	53%

Source: Internal Revenue Service, *Philadelphia Inquirer*, October 21, 1991

owned half of the privately owned corporate stock in the United States—received their dividends, rents or interests, those, too, were taxed at new low levels. As noted earlier, the top tax rate on unearned income dropped from 70 percent in 1980 to 50 percent in 1982 and 28 percent in 1988—the biggest decline since the 1920s. Changes in the alternative minimum tax also quietly reduced its effect on America's richest individuals, and as Figure 4 shows, by 1989 the top 1 percent of Americans had collected large and lopsided benefits from the supposedly reformist Tax Reform Act of 1986. Thus, while it was the *indirect* effect of the several tax cuts that produced the explosion of pretax income as the rich took profits from the stock market, there was also a smaller *direct* effect felt in the greater amount of income that was left after income and capital gains taxes were paid. Before the Reagan cuts, the collective rich had kept their effective rates in the 33–40 percent range through tax shelters. After the rate cuts, some new income came as money was taken out of shelters, although a much larger amount came from rising business and stock market profits. As the income of the top 1 percent soared, so did the share of total income tax receipts they paid.

As for the percentage of federal taxes paid by the huge block of Americans in the anonymous and often stagnating middle, that went down because their share of national income dropped. They were running in place as those at the top soared. The burden of their taxation increased, however, because the effective federal tax rate—the portion of their income taken by FICA, excise and income taxes combined—*rose* for median- and average-income families during the 1980s. The top 1 percent and (to a lesser extent) the top 5 percent were the only groups for whom the effective federal rate *fell* significantly. The details of these shifts can be found in Appendix B.

Federal tax trends poignantly illustrate how, in three or four decades, the mid-century fiscal tilt to the middle class was reversed. During the buoyant 1950s, increased middle-class taxes were largely a product of prosperity, growing as the average family's real income grew. By 1960 the annual income tax of $700 for a family of four at the median income just under $6,000 was not oppressive.[15] But then came inflation. The 1970s hit the middle class hard, as stagflation eroded real median-family income while bracket creep pushed taxes up anyway. Then in the 1980s, the realignment of federal, state and local taxes became more ideological and complex.

In short, as America's mid-century hegemony faded, the average middle-class or working-class family stopped being the economic favorite of federal policymakers, yielding that place to a much smaller group of top-bracket investors and wealth creators, for whom all sorts of vital roles were proclaimed. Until late 1990, when the rich became a target again, the top 1 percent of Americans of the 1980s had reassumed the place they had held in the 1880s and 1920s in a restored conservative fiscal theology. Meanwhile, at the state and local level, to which we now turn, regressivity was even more pronounced—and so were the effects of tax changes on the typical household.

State and Local Taxes—The Rising Weight of Regressivity

From the 1870s to the early 1940s, save for the years of World War I, state and local revenues—the resource for building roads and running schools—*exceeded* those of the federal government. Governments closer to the people raised and spent most of the money. Then the cost of World War II quickly centralized fiscal power in Washington, and over the next half century, federal taxation, led by the income tax, remained substantially larger than state and local levies, thereby dominating the attention of lobbyists, economists and reformers.

However, as the return of program responsibility from Washington to the states accelerated in the 1980s, the increase produced in state and local taxes became an essential component in the broad rearrangement of the national tax burden that worked to squeeze the middle class. By 1991 state and local taxes had risen to 44 percent of the national tax revenue total (exclusive of FICA), up from 32 percent in 1960, according to the New York–based Center for the Study of the States.[16] Not only was the progressive income tax being weakened as a linchpin of the U.S. revenue system; the state and local levies moving to the fore were often regressive.

For American families in the median- or average-income range, we have already seen how rising FICA and excise taxes ate up most or all of the 1980s reduction in federal income taxes. State and local levies and charges, which also fell most heavily on low and middle incomes, were climbing as fast as FICA. Between 1980 and 1989, per capita state taxes almost doubled, growing from $658 to $1,150.[17] To supply yet another measure, as of 1990 state and local revenues had climbed to 22.1 percent of U.S. personal income, up from 20.5 percent in 1982 and 16.5 percent in 1967, while federal revenues oscillated in a steady band from 23 percent to 26 percent. Yet because state and local levies varied from jurisdiction to jurisdiction, computations of trends in disposable income generally sidestepped their impact, thereby missing a growing source of damage to the average household.

For 1990, as already noted, the Tax Foundation showed that the average family with $46,000 a year, two earners and two children, suffered a direct and indirect federal tax bite totaling 28.2 percent of income. State and local taxes took another 9.1 percent.[18] Citizens for Tax Justice, in its own exhaustive survey, set the 1990 figure for the state and local tax burden on the average family slightly higher at 10.0 percent, and simultaneously detailed the wide range between the *lowest* state and local combined burden (Alaska at 2.9 percent) and the *highest* (Michigan, with 13.1 percent).[19]

As a matter of course, state and local governments varied in how much they had enlarged their activities and outlays during the go-go years. Some jurisdictions had recklessly expanded programs, personnel and pay, and by the late 1980s needed new revenues accordingly.

However, another important reason for the new upward pressure on state taxes lay in how Washington had reduced federal aid to states and localities, specifically eliminating federal revenue-sharing with local governments launched a decade earlier by Richard Nixon, while Congress and the executive branch also required state and local authorities to absorb significantly more of the total cost of Medicaid, transportation, housing and education. The result, computed in constant dollars, was that federal aid to states and cities *dropped* by an eighth from 1978 to 1989, according to the Advisory Council on Intergovernmental Relations, and by the end of the decade, Washington provided just 17 percent of state and municipal budgets.[20] To add to local troubles, legislative and executive branch officials in Washington frequently compensated for their own difficulty in funding new domestic programs by mandating specific instructions and duties upon the states as a condition of getting the federal aid that still flowed.* All of these factors put states in the same painful situation: needing to raise more revenues.

Municipal, county and local governments also found themselves grasping for revenues, all the more so after the 1990–91 downturn thrust many states into their greatest fiscal crises since the 1930s. New York governor Mario Cuomo voiced the complaint of the hard-pressed urban Northeast: "In effect, the middle class and the working poor of our cities have been called upon to pay for the huge income tax cuts at the federal level. Prosperity never trickled down in the 1980s, only the tax burden did. And no one noticed it."[21]

The same governors and state legislators quick to protest how "shift and shaft" federalism had passed the fiscal buck stateward during the 1980s were, in turn, often just as ready to cut assistance to lesser units of local government, forcing *them* to consider tax increases. By 1991 Hal Hovey, editor of *State Policy Reports,* indicated that cuts in state aid to counties, cities and towns were being discussed in half of the fifty states.[22] Meanwhile, counties and municipalities were also being dogged by federal cuts, and the U.S. Conference of Mayors released a study saying that Washington's contribution to U.S. cities dropped 64

*Over one quarter of all the federal acts preempting state and local laws in favor of federal standards and mandates since 1789 were passed between 1981 and 1989, most of them dealing with health, safety and education—and representing a growing load on the states. Even against the background of recession, *The New York Times* reported in 1992 that federal authorities continued to create or expand domestic spending programs with little or no review of the financial burdens then placed on state and local government ("U.S. Adds Programs with Little Review of Local Burdens," *New York Times,* March 24, 1992).

percent between 1980 and 1990.[23] As both higher-level funding sources dried up, cities and villages in New York State began the 1990s with only 25 percent of their budgets from federal and state aid, down from 40 percent a decade earlier.[24] Fiscal weakness was aggravating fiscal weakness. The dominoes were falling.

Cuomo and others were correct in that one reason taxes were going up in Hempstead, Riverside and Bangor was that they had gone down on Washington's Form 1040. Some of the cost of the federal income tax reductions, federally mandated programs and other federal responsibilities shifted to the states would be billed through thousands of legislatures, county councils, city halls, town assessors' offices and special tax districts from Maine to California. In 1991, the *Chicago Tribune*'s Jon Margolis offered a wry summation:

> So if your property taxes have gone up, if there are too many other kids in your child's class, if it takes two minutes for the "911" dispatcher to answer, if you're waiting longer for the bus and if the nearby lake is getting dirtier, please understand that this is the cost of cutting [federal] taxes, somebody's if not yours. You are paying for the tax cut that had to go to that guy in the Lincoln Town Car who just zoomed by taking his kid from their privately guarded subdivision to a private school.[25]

Moreover, even though the burden would increase more rapidly in the 1990s, the rise in state and local taxes during the 1980s had *already* affected Middle America, adding a further offset to nominal income gains. Table 6 illustrates how combined state and local taxes constituted a rising burden on an average family of four during the 1980s:

Besides the obvious problem—that fast-rising state and local taxes

Table 6. The Rising State and Local Tax Burden, 1980–1991
Percentage of Average Families' Incomes Spent on State and Local Taxes, 1985–90

	1985	1990
Lowest 20%	12.6%	13.8%
Second 20%	10.0	10.9
Middle 20%	9.1	10.0
Fourth 20%	8.6	9.5
Next 15%	8.4	9.2
Next 4%	8.2	8.7
Top 1%	7.1	7.6
Average Family	9.1	10.0

Source: *A Far Cry from Fair*, Citizens for Tax Justice, April 1991, p. 18.

weighed heaviest on low and middle incomes—the effects of this changing tax load on consumer purchasing power and inflation were difficult to calculate. *Some* state and local taxes are included in federal inflation (CPI) measurements, so that part of their escalation found its way into CPI as an offset to family purchasing power, but part of it went unmeasured. From federal bailouts to local taxes and fees, the cost of government was soaring, which should have found its way into the cost of living, but by and large did not.

Many important increases in state taxes occurred unannounced following the 1986 federal tax revisions, when the large majority of states using the federal definition of adjusted gross income took advantage of Washington's elimination of some federal credits and deductions. These automatically increased the taxable income of middle- and upper-bracket taxpayers, thus enlarging state revenue bases. However, in circumstances where states passed legislation for new taxes, they usually opted for regressive-type levies. For example, after tabulating 22 separate increases in state sales-tax rates between 1985 and 1990, 92 separate increases in state motor-fuels taxes, and 62 separate increases in state cigarette taxes, Citizens for Tax Justice, a labor-oriented group, said the impact would be hardest on the little guy. Middle-income families paid on average 4.2 percent of their incomes in sales and excise taxes while those in the top 1 percent paid just 1.3 percent.[26] The new increases would follow a similar distribution.

Federal levies on alcohol, tobacco and gasoline also rose in 1990. They, too, were regressive. The combined results of federal and state excise taxes, especially the gasoline tax, were particularly painful to rural areas.[27]

State levies were also becoming increasingly ingenious. California had its snack tax, and the list of new taxes passed by New York in 1990, to cite an egregious example, included a new container tax of 2 cents on soda, a 5 percent surcharge on hotel rooms costing over $100 a night, a 5 percent surcharge on car rentals, a 4 percent tax on cleaning and security services and parking garages and a 4 percent sales tax on telephone services using 800 and 900 numbers.[28] And as we have seen with Florida's taxes on speeding tickets and Wisconsin's attempt to tax drinks on airplanes, innovation was a 1991–92 byword in state taxation—and often concentrating its maximum impact on the middle class.

Fees and penalties began substituting for visible additional taxes. Those for auto licenses, mortgage filings and park visits were familiar. But in some jurisdictions, particularly California, fees were becoming a major preoccupation of state fiscal authorities. Back in 1953 California had started levying penalty assessments or surcharges on motorists' fines. As budget problems worsened in the 1980s and early 1990s, the surcharges soared, so that 1991's basic assessment for the state was $17 for every $10 of fine—enough to turn a $100 infraction into a $270 violation and earn $480 million a year for the state treasury.[29] "The basic problem here is that the state is in financial trouble," said Richard Stanford, presiding judge of the Orange County Municipal Court. "They're looking to the courts as a revenue source. And that's not what the courts are meant to be."[30]

In California, after the passage of Proposition 13 in 1978 curbed property taxes, other kinds of fees also soared. Business license fees, for example, increased by 229 percent from 1979 to 1990.[31] New York State imposed a broad range of new "fees"—including such items as a "laundromat inspection fee," based on a state employee visiting a laundromat, counting the washers and dryers, multiplying the total by $12 and presenting the owner with a bill in that amount.[32] In Dallas, Texas, where property taxes had risen by 67.8 percent in five years, the City Council decided to avoid a tax increase in 1991, opting instead to approve higher charges for water, gas, electricity, garbage pickup and the 911 emergency telephone system.[33] In a trend closely linked to the rise of user fees, utility charges, especially water bills, were increasing sharply in many jurisdictions, not least Boston, where water and sewer rates for the sixty cities and towns served by the Massachusetts Water Resources Authority rose 420 percent between 1985 and 1992, and were expected to double again by 1995, putting the average annual bill for a family of four at more than $1,000.[34] In New York's Long Island, rates soared so much that some senior citizens complained about paying more for water than for heat.

Local property taxes, curbed in many other states besides California after Proposition 13, were themselves again on the rise. In 1982 property taxes had averaged $3.26 for every $100 of personal income, *down* from the 1970s. But by 1988 the average was back up to $3.51 for each $100 of income.[35] Upward pressure was greatest in the Northeast, which had four of the nation's five highest-property-tax states, and where many suburban townships (and even a few counties) taxed homeowners steeply enough that a family of four with an average income and a midsized house paid $2,500 to $5,000 a year in real estate taxes. Appendix B shows the ten counties charging the highest per capita property taxes in the nation. It also shows how property taxes in New Jersey, a cockpit of voter revolt, expanded during the 1980s at a rate far exceeding the Consumer Price Index.

In February 1991, *The New York Times* profiled Angelo Verduci, a seventy-four-year-old retiree in the fast-growing suburb of Edison, New Jersey, whose income was $13,000 a year and who was paying $2,654 a year in property taxes on a small cement house that he built himself thirty years earlier when the Raritan Valley was still rural.[36] Each tax increase, he said, cut into his budget for food, clothing and medical care. Lower-middle-class families in Long Island, New York, and retirees in the Washington suburbs with $28,000-a-year pensions made the same complaint: local property taxes, not income taxes, had become their greatest fiscal burden.

In Maryland and Virginia, counties, not cities, provided most municipal services and set countywide burdens on homeowners. But the usual pattern elsewhere was for taxes to vary from town to town, which also involved inequities. In Illinois's Cook County (metropolitan Chicago), countywide averages camouflaged a wide variation. Suburbs blessed with crowded shopping malls, corporate plants and office buildings billed homeowners only about one third as much as poor jurisdictions without these lucrative revenue sources. In north suburban Niles, police officers got new Oldsmobile 88s each year and residents enjoyed free bus service, yet owners paid taxes of only $1,500 or so a year on houses worth $150,000. By contrast, in south suburban Harvey, $1,400 a year represented the taxes on a mere $50,000 house, and the cash-starved city of 36,000 left abandoned cars on the streets for months and removed snow mostly by letting it melt.[37]

In some areas, the collapsed real estate boom of the early 1990s made property taxes politically incendiary. Jurisdictions happily feeding on higher tax revenues from inflated real estate values went into fiscal shock as the boom went bust: as values plummeted, angry ratepayers demanded that their own assessments be marked down to reflect how 1989's $300,000 home had become 1991's $220,000 white elephant, and then the problems began. Local authorities sometimes had to wait (Connecticut towns, for example, could revalue only once every ten years). Yet even where revisions were feasible, reduced *assessments* often simply forced jurisdictions to raise *rates* to maintain revenues. Many cities and suburbs faced a glum prospect: rising property taxes *and* declining services in the years ahead.

In some jurisdictions, fees on builders had become a device for sidestepping property tax increases. Beginning in the 1980s, revenue-strained local governments had started requiring developers of residential subdivisions, shopping malls or office parks to agree to absorb many of the expenses hitherto financed by tax dollars. Municipal politicians liked levying "impact fees" to reduce upward pressure on homeowner taxes because their constituents felt the fees only indirectly, through higher home prices and rents. One pioneering county, Anne Arundel, in Maryland, collected—up front—$2,629 for roads and schools and $3,000 for sewers for each new home, and in 1990 fully thirty-nine states allowed their municipalities to tax builders in this way.[38]

The effect on housing prices was inflationary enough to help launch a federal Advisory Commission on Regulatory Barriers to Affordable Housing, whose chairman pointed to an unnamed builder whose costs had jumped 126 percent in six years because of fees and deplored how Southern California home buyers paid $20,000 extra for houses.[39] However, if the fees hadn't been levied, real estate taxes necessarily would have been somewhat higher, although as a trade-off the initial price tag of new homes would have been somewhat lower.

Some areas divided their property levies, tailoring them to particular community services and needs through a multitude of special-purpose taxing districts—sewer, flood control, elementary school, high school, even library. Duplicative and confusing it might be, but ratepayers did have more sense of exactly where their money was going. Of the fifty states, Illinois led with the most taxing bodies in the nation, an extraordinary 6,500.[40]

User fees and special taxes, like real estate impact fees, also mushroomed during the late 1980s as states, counties and municipalities became increasingly desperate to charge citizens for services previously funded by federal aid or broad-based taxes. Here, too, some efforts were innovative. In 1990, Fort Collins, Colorado, on the historic Overland Trail, tried to redefine its local streets as public utilities so that revenues for repairs could be raised by charging residents fees for road use.[41] To pay for a beach park in Port Hueneme, California, city fathers levied an unprecedented "view tax" on residents based on how much of the Pacific Ocean could be seen from each home.[42]

In November 1990 the nearly bankrupt city of Philadelphia agreed to levy a special higher real estate tax requested by—and, indeed, to be paid solely by—property owners in an eighty-block downtown area. Special guards and private street cleaners were to be hired to obtain levels of security and sanitation not provided to other neighborhoods. Kindred customized arrangements were also worked out in parts of New York, Denver and New Orleans. John J. DiIulio, director of Princeton University's Center of Domestic Policy Studies, saw Philadelphia's arrangement as an ominous trend: "We're moving away from a system that monitors a concern for general equity in the distribution of government services, toward a market where citizens are treated very differently within the same jurisdiction based on their ability to pay special-purpose taxes."[43]

The rise in state and local taxes at record rates, even as services declined, underscored the economic polarization taking hold in the eighties. For the upper-middle class, the over-$100,000-a-year families in the top 5 percent but not in the top 1 percent or 2 percent, the increase in state and local taxes was annoying, but affordable. Inadequate services could be paid for privately, albeit with grumbling. To average-income families, however, the accelerating state and local taxes, as well as the escalating user fees and special charges—frequently imposed, as Chapter 6 will discuss, to pay for access and services that had been free back in 1955 or 1962—contributed to a fading real purchasing power. America's return to localism added new fiscal pressures to the middle-class squeeze.

The Gathering Threat to the Upper-Middle Class

The upper-middle-class family with an income of $100,000 or $150,000 finished the decade with significant advantages over the $45,000-a-year average family. Its bracket cuts during the 1980s had been bigger, and a fair part of its earnings still escaped rising FICA taxes. Yet it's also fair to say that by the 1990s those edges were beginning to erode. Partly to keep rates low at the very top, federal and state policymakers were nibbling more and more at the upper middle: those families who were in the top 10 percent (over $80,000 a year) but below the $250,000-a-year households of the top 1 percent. Although Bill Clinton had pledged in 1992 that his plans to increase the rates paid by the rich would not affect families with annual incomes under $200,000, for many reasons these strata were beginning to look like the next revenue target of government at most levels.

As we have seen, one of the most striking changes in federal tax treatment of the upper-middle class during the Reagan era was that even though their income tax rates declined, their gains were less than those of the rich, so that the two groups wound up paying roughly the same effective overall federal tax rate (25 to 28 percent). This was an enormous change from, say, 1928, when upper-middle-class taxpayers just inside the top 3 percent of incomes had paid an effective rate of 1 percent, less than a twentieth of the rate that applied to millionaires. Even in the mid-1950s, a taxpayer just inside the top 3 percent would have paid about a third of the rate that applied to million-dollar-a-year earners.

After the 1986 tax revisions, however, not only did the effective rates converge, but as we saw in Chapter 2, federal tax-writers came up with an unusual income tax device—the "bubble," in which a 33 percent marginal rate applied to households in the $70,000–$170,000 bracket, thereafter falling to 28 percent for those with higher earnings. There is no great mystery about its origins. Attempts to shrink the bracket structure down to just two rates—15 percent and then 28 percent (which kicked in at more or less the average family income)—didn't raise quite enough money in the computer projections. To meet their needs, policymakers seemingly had three choices: to lower the income threshold at which the 28 percent rate began, or to keep just two rates but raise the 28 percent bracket to something like 29 percent, or to create a third bracket of 33 percent kicking in at roughly $200,000. Legislators in both parties, led by Oregon Republican Bob Packwood, opposed a third rate that would single out the top 1 percent and chose instead to raise the needed several billion by a complicated bubble-cum-surcharge that would take the same money principally from the upper-middle class, giving *them* a higher marginal rate (33 percent) than a billionaire.

In the 1950s or 1960s, such a proposal would have been shouted down. In the 1980s, however, it was enacted, and a large bipartisan group of politicians and tax experts thereafter insisted that the bubble didn't undercut progressivity because millionaires wound up paying a slightly higher *effective* rate on their overall incomes even though the upper-middle class paid a higher *marginal* rate on their highest earnings. Never mind that the bubble manifestly did undercut progressivity because its revenues were used to avoid a higher rate on the richest Americans. What was striking was how drastically former values had been transformed. A Mellon or Rockefeller or Milken probably paid a slightly higher effective rate than a Los Angeles police captain, but hardly anyone cited the vivid contrast with 1929, 1950 or even 1960 to make an indisputable historical point: *that the progressivity of the U.S. income tax system had been largely lost.*

In 1990, because of what tax expert Emil Sunley of the accounting firm Deloitte & Touche called George Bush's "passion for subterfuge," a new bubble was created.[44] Bush refused to accept a new third rate any higher than 31 percent, which by itself would not bring in enough new revenue to match the billions being collected from the 2 million upper-middle-class taxpayers in the existing bubble or surcharge zone. As a result, the new 31 percent rate was teamed with a *second* bubble-cum-surcharge arrangement, prompting one former Treasury economist to tell a Washington tax conference that "Like a bad nightmare, the bubble is back, only in a more insidious form."[45] This time, the distortion involved a phaseout of family exemptions and a rising offset against itemized deductions that combined to create a surcharge for incomes above $150,000 but less than $275,000.

While this second bubble affected fewer people, critics pointed out that it introduced a new bias: unfair treatment of large families. That was because as households in the $150,000–$275,000 range saw their individual family-member exemptions phased out, the de facto surcharge was greatest on the largest households. John G. Wilkins of Coopers & Lybrand explained that the effective marginal rate for 1991 in that bracket varied from 33 percent for a married couple with no children to 37.3 percent for a family with eight children. For incomes above $275,000, the marginal rate dropped back to 31 percent. Figure 5 shows the structure and marginal-rate effects of both the "old" (1988–90) and "new" (post-1991) bubbles.

Figure 5. The New Tax Rate Bubble

Figures are based on average gross income for a family of six under the old and new tax laws

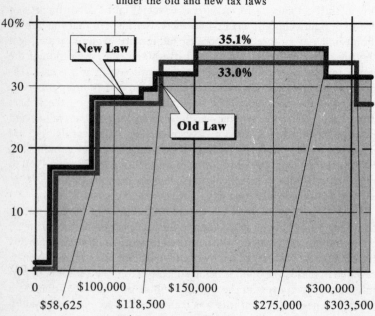

Investor's Daily, 11/21/90   Source: Coopers & Lybrand

There was also a broader basis to the rising burden of the upper-middle class. Former deputy assistant treasury secretary Steven Entin pointed out that "Federal marginal rates of 33 percent to 34 percent put taxpayers who face state and local income taxes and payroll taxes on earned income in fairly high tax brackets easily exceeding 35 percent to 45 percent."[46] He had in mind the additional effect of state and local income tax, but the 1990 budget act also expanded the reach of the 1.45 percent Medicare component of the Social Security tax, increasing the taxable income base to which it applied in 1991 from $53,400 to $125,000. Self-employed doctors, lawyers and others would also have to pay the employer's share, for a total tax of 2.9 percent on the more-than-doubled income base.

Worse still, from the upper-middle-class standpoint, the income base to which the Social Security portion of the FICA tax applied was predicted by some to climb toward $100,000. No serious moves were made in the 1992 election year, but forecasts of subsequent increases were commonplace. Movement toward taxing $100,000 or $125,000 families at 7.65 percent for Social Security and Medicare would push their *effective,* and not just *marginal,* rates of income-type taxation well above those of million-dollar earners.

In the meantime, tax experts also foresaw a threat to the federal deductions for state and local income taxes, as well as for property taxes and mortgage interest paid on homes. Indeed, following a provision in the 1990 budget act, a taxpayer's itemized deductions were reduced in 1991 by $300 for every $10,000 of adjusted gross income above $100,000. That meant that a $150,000-a-year family would lose $1,500 in deductions and, based on their new 31 percent rate, pay an additional $465 a year. In its first year, only a small, prosperous portion of the middle class was affected, and not very burdensomely. Skeptics, however, pointed out that during the 1990 debate, legislators from New York and other high-tax states had predicted that deduction limits, once established, would expand and possibly lead to no further deductibility for state and local income taxes.[47]

A second federal tax change was also bearing down on middle-class Americans—subjecting employee fringe benefits, now largely untaxed, to the federal income tax. Health and Human Services Secretary Louis Sullivan announced in 1991 that the Bush administration was considering that beyond a certain "cap" level, employees would have to pay taxes on employer-provided health benefits. If a cap were set at $1,200, for example, then a worker whose employer paid $2,000 in health insurance premiums would be taxed on the additional $800.[48]

A third gleam in the eye of federal fiscal policymakers involved eliminating or reducing middle-class—and especially *upper-middle-*class—eligibility for federal income tax credits and federal program benefits. Millionaires would not care, but $75,000 or $125,000 families were angry at being called "rich." There was also interest in restricting the federal day-care credit, still claimable on April 15 tax returns by prosperous families (despite being capped for them at $480 a year for each child), to stop affluent households from qualifying.

State governments, too, were intensifying the pressure. In 1990, 1991 and 1992, enormous projected budget deficits obliged many states to reverse the tides of the 1980s and start raising top income tax brackets again, almost always hitting the upper-middle class as well as the rich. The changes in 1990 had been minor; those enacted in 1991 were much more significant. In California the top rate was raised from 9.3 percent to 10 percent on incomes over $200,000, and 11 percent on incomes over $400,000, restoring the old top rate that had been in place through 1987. In New York, Governor Mario Cuomo opposed a rate increase but gave in on a computation change that increased the take from New Yorkers with six-figure incomes. Vermont, which had previously claimed 28 percent of federal income taxes owed as its state tax, hiked that assessment to 34 percent of federal taxes over $13,100, raising the effective top rate to 11.56 percent, from 9.52 percent, of taxable income. Minnesota established a new top rate of 8.5 percent, up from 8 percent, for families with taxable incomes exceeding $173,000. In Maine, GOP governor John McKernan proposed raising the top rate from 8.5 percent to 10 percent for couples with incomes of more than $75,000.[49] North Carolina raised its top rate from 7 percent to 8 percent, but only for joint returns with income of at least $100,000. Steven Gold, director of the New York–based Center for the Study of the States, suggested that the pattern was following the projection in *The Politics of Rich and Poor*: "Concern about 'fairness' is in, and tax rates on the wealthy are more likely to rise than fall."[50]

State taxes on services and service professions also gained momentum in 1991 and 1992, despite prior embarrassments in Florida and Massachusetts (two states that found themselves repealing service taxes only months after they had been enacted). What made such levies inevitable, supporters argued, was the economy's slow shift from manufacturing to services, which obliged revenue-raising methodologies to follow suit. And they pointed to New York's quiet success with a piecemeal strategy of minimizing powerful opposition by targeting just a few additional services at a time—in 1990, for example, adding taxes on cleaning and security services to previous existing taxes on auto repairs and appliance installation. In 1992, Connecticut legislators targeted groups ranging from podiatrists to fur breeders, while Ohio raised registration fees on such professionals as licensed nursing home administrators to asbestos hazard evaluation specialists.[51] "They [the states] are going to go after groups one by one instead," predicted Fred Ferguson, director of state tax policy at Price Waterhouse. "They'll start with landscape gardeners, architects, people who don't have much political pull. Then they'll gradually expand it to everyone else."[52]

Finally, as the 1990s unfolded, state and local politicians showed a growing disposition not just to tax upper-middle-class services and professions, but to target items principally consumed by moderately affluent households. Evanston, Illinois, seat of Northwestern University, seriously considered slapping an 0.5 percent tuition tax on Northwestern's 10,500 students, as well as others at three smaller local colleges.[53] By 1991 almost fifty cities in California had enacted local taxes on cable television, and, on a national basis, travelers began to notice more and more taxes on airline flights, car rentals and hotel rooms. In 1991, airline ticket taxes and user fees rose by $2.5 billion. Some eighty airports hit renters with a 5–10 percent "off-airport car-rental fee." And local taxes on hotel rooms, many well into double digits—21 percent in New York City, 15 percent in Houston, 12 percent in Chicago—expanded by $500 million over three years.[54]

If the 1980s were the decade in which the average $45,000-a-year household was stuck between a rock and a hard place, the 1990s began with a similar prospect—worsened by accelerating white-collar-job cutbacks—for many of the $85,000-, $115,000- and $150,000-a-year Americans whose earnings put them within the top 6, 4 or even 2 percent on the national charts. To think of them as wealthy was an illusion.

Deceptive Discussions of Taxing the Wealthy

One significant contrast between the 1980s and previous conservative-capitalist heydays of U.S. history resulted from inflation's role in nurturing deceptive notions of who was rich, setting the scene for an unappreciated favoritism to those whose level of wealth was beyond the ken of even most college graduates. For the typical American forty-five, fifty or sixty years old who had grown up in the 1940s, 1950s or early 1960s thinking that a millionaire was really rich and that $50,000 a year was a high income, the impressions of childhood lingered. Debate after debate in Congress took place as unrich politicians, who knew *they* could not keep homes in two cities on $125,000 a year, nevertheless orated about burdening the "rich" by phasing out itemized deductions for families in the over-$100,000 bracket or curbing federal Medicare subsidies at the $125,000 level.

That kind of income had fallen short of truly "rich" even in the early years of the century, although ordinary Americans getting by on $2,000 a year could plausibly miss the distinction. Then the enormous inflation since World War II gave a well-off professional of the early 1990s a nominal $150,000-a-year income, which seemed more affluent than it was—in after-tax purchasing power, it was no greater than the earnings of a $10,000-a-year lawyer of 1927 or the $6,000-a-year man of 1900. These bourgeois worthies of the McKinley and Coolidge eras had been prosperous, yes, but nobody would have taken seriously the idea that revenue measures aimed at them were hitting the rich. In 1990 or 1992, however, people *were* fooled that way about $150,000-a-year professionals, and those with truly large incomes took shelter in the confusion.

Actual "riches" in the 1990s began much higher—maybe at $1 million a year and $8 million to $10 million in assets. The number of billionaires had increased tenfold during the 1980s from six to sixty; investment banker Michael Milken took home $550 million in 1987 alone; for baseball shortstops and second-echelon rock stars, $2 million a year was common; and portraits of corporate chief executives paid hundreds of times as much as their average worker typically cited $8 million or $18 million compensation packages. Yet the who-was-really-rich implications of these new numbers lagged so much that ostensibly serious journalists, economists and public servants talked about taxing "wealthy" retirees with $50,000, targeting the itemized deductions and fringe benefits of "rich" $150,000-a-year households and fulfilling "progressivity" with a federal income tax bubble that imposed higher marginal rates on $165,000-a-year orthodontists than on multimillionaires. Misperception was rife, and the upper-middle class was starting to pay the price.

For all these reasons, from new philosophic values to statistical numbness, tax policy in the 1980s rode a wave of deception. The ultimate fiscal truth of the early 1990s was that for America's two or three hundred thousand somewhat rich or genuinely rich families, combined taxes as a share of income were probably at their lowest point in more than sixty years, whereas for middle-class families, combined federal, state and local taxes took a higher portion of income than ever before and were rising steadily.

CHAPTER 6

Services, Quality of Life and the Middle-Class Squeeze

If you're a typical American, the car you'll drive to work tomorrow and the road you'll take to get there will be older and shoddier than the ones you were using one decade ago or even two. Your children's school will have more pupils per teacher; your paycheck precious few more dollars per hour.

—*The Boston Globe*, 1992

To appreciate the magnitude of the economy's deterioration in the last two decades, imagine what the living standards of the typical middle-class family would be like if it had as many wage earners (just one)—and as many children—as its parents had and also was responsible for subsidizing its parents' retirement, including medical bills.

—David Vogel, editor, *California Management Review*, 1987

Government and the market, joined with Points of Light, will overwhelm our social problems.

—President George Bush, June 12, 1991

Middle classes do not rise or fall on tax burdens alone. For many U.S. families in the 1980s and early 1990s, a broader range of economic circumstances was also worsening. Public services were declining in quality and availability across much of the nation, especially in the big cities. Private services vital to the middle class like health care, higher education and insurance were becoming less affordable. Employee benefits and retirement options were beginning to erode. So was family leisure time. And middle-class net worth was starting to slip—especially for younger Americans unlikely to achieve the wealth of the previous generation.

These fears, along with the unprecedented tax bite, were what made the middle-class squeeze of the 1980s and 1990s unique. The foreclosure notices tacked by sheriff's deputies to the doors of late-nineteenth-century Nebraska and Texas farmhouses had been harsher, but the broad middle class was not eroding back then—it was growing. Nor is there much parallel to the consumer complaints of the 1920s. Local gentry, with their diminishing fortunes scaled to the prior century's economy, might complain that $3,000 or $4,000 a year no longer provided much if any social status, while the new middle class— George Babbitt and his confreres—might grouse that they didn't have enough money for all the new household gadgetry available. Yet the cost of basic, vital middle-class services like education and health care was not climbing out of sight. Public services were improving rather than failing. Suburbia was not apprehensive even amid prosperity, as in 1987–88. There was nothing remotely equivalent to a $4 trillion national debt. Foreign visitors to Henry Cabot Lodge's Boston or Babe Ruth's New York City did not pen sorrowful commentaries on incipient "Brazilianization."

In short, previous cyclical troughs for the U.S. middle class had been mere hiccups in the historical expansion that reached a late-twentieth-century zenith at some point in the 1960s or 1970s when 50 to 55 percent of Americans belonged to an economic middle class without any foreign or historical equivalent and another 10 to 15 percent loosely felt that they did. The potentially critical change by the 1980s and 1990s was that the middle class was no longer expanding but declining—even in intervals of economic recovery like the mid-eighties—under the ongoing pressures of global economic realignment, polarization and income stratification.

Defenders of the Reagan and Bush years had a partially plausible rebuttal: that an important part of the middle-class shrinkage reflected that millions of people were climbing toward *higher* economic status, witness the expansion of Americans with constant-dollar incomes over $50,000 a year from 24.8 percent in 1980 to 30.5 percent in 1990. This *was* happening. But as we shall see, the middle-class pressures described in this chapter justify skepticism, suggesting that many such income gains took on a phantom quality after further adjustment for taxes and fees, declining public services, increasingly unaffordable private services, shrinking employee benefits and retirement prospects, lost leisure time and quality of life, and even declining net worth. If much of the gain for those climbing over $50,000 (or in some areas, over $100,000) was an illusion, how much more important were the difficulties of the millions simultaneously falling from the vulnerable portions of the middle class—the downwardly mobile victims of the collapsing blue-collar wage structure of Fort Wayne, Indiana, or the nervous members of the Roswell, Georgia, country club that began offering unemployed executives seminars on joblessness.

Declining Public Services

As the 1980s boom ended, the public sector, far from being a counter-cyclical safety cushion as in the New Deal years, was more like a domino. Many federal outlays were contracting, but the most visible cutbacks would be at the local level. "All the way across the country, the fabric of local government is being shredded," the president of the National Association of Counties said as the recession unfolded in early 1991. The message from the federal government in the 1980s had been "You locals, you need to have the federal government off your back. But what it really meant was 'fend for yourself.' "[1]

If a potential state and local financial crisis had been gathering on the horizon, the early 1990s downturn brought it to a head. Henry Aaron, director of economic studies at Washington's Brookings Institution, said gloomily, "I think you would have to go back to the Great Depression to find similar anguish, in terms of the number of states that are facing an unprecedented cutback in services or significant increases in taxes," and from New England to California the cold surgery of budget-cutting knives bore him out.[2] Mayors, managers and town supervisors up and down New York State found themselves stunned by Governor Mario Cuomo's 1991–92 proposed budget reductions of 50 percent in the unrestricted aid used by their localities to police streets, remove snow and keep parks and libraries operating, of 60 percent or more in state money for road and highway maintenance, and of an average of 10 percent in state aid to local school districts.[3] Final cuts were lower, but in Suffolk County, where suburbs thrown up nearly overnight in Long Island potato fields had been a symbol of the post–World War II housing boom, the county government began furloughing most of its twelve thousand employees every Friday, reducing public services.* Next door, Nassau County's vaunted Republican machine had ruled for three quarters of a century and employed the highest ratio of park workers of any major U.S. suburban jurisdiction, with amenities ranging from public beaches, pools and golf courses to free concerts at the Eisenhower Park bandshell. Budget pressures brought these good times to an end in 1992.[4]

In California, where two dozen school districts were flirting with bankruptcy, one district superintendent said he had cut as much as he could: "There's not much more I can do here without closing the doors, handing over the keys to the state, and saying 'You guys run

---

*In September 1992, local authorities announced that for the first time in memory, the assessed value of property on Long Island was going down—meaning that tax revenues would erode without rate increases, adding to the pressure to reduce public services.

it.' "[5] By 1992 Los Angeles could not afford to fill vacancies opening up in the police department, and across Massachusetts, small towns were fighting big-city problems with shrinking police forces. Especially on both coasts, state and local government was starting to deliver less.

In spring 1992, as the National Association of State Budget officers released its annual *Fiscal Survey of the States,* executive director Brian Roherty predicted that as those states badly hit by the recession emerged from its shadow after several more years, there would be less assistance to the middle class and poor alike: "What we will see are downsized state governments with smaller work forces, new ways of doing business and new priorities. There isn't enough money any more, so states will have to find long-term solutions and make some grim choices."[6] Raymond C. Scheppach, executive director of the National Governors' Association, predicted a permanent reduction in state government that would force attention to restructuring major state services such as education, welfare and health."[7]

This gathering constriction of public services, more severe than recession statistics alone would have suggested, was also worsened by several 1980s public-policy legacies. Many state and local governments had expanded their payrolls and ambitions with thinly disguised recklessness, while Washington had reduced and transformed the nature of its own important financial help. Federal matching grants to the states did roughly double for a group of burdensome entitlement programs over which the states had no control and where enlarged assistance was an ill omen—Medicaid, for one, and also Aid to Families with Dependent Children. On the helpful side of the ledger, however, the flexible federal grants hitherto popular for giving states money to meet local needs—revenue-sharing was the prime example—fell by more than half.[8] In the late 1970s, Washington had provided 25 percent of state and local budgets; by 1990, as we have seen, that had dipped to 17 percent.

The federal government's own resources were strained, to be sure, both by the money lost in income tax reduction and even more by the galloping 1980s expansion of Social Security, Medicare, defense outlays and interest payments on the national debt. So it was the category of Washington assistance called "discretionary" that had to shrivel. So-called domestic discretionary outlays fell from 22.6 percent of federal outlays to 14.7 percent in 1987 and stabilized at less than 15 percent through 1991. Revenue-sharing and other state and local aid programs were prominent among the losers. As federal support was withdrawn from states and localities, one trigger of the early 1990s public-services crisis was already being cocked.

Too many states had overexpanded during the 1980s, naively assuming that revenues would keep rising. Not only did state and local government employment expand by 15 percent during the decade, but wages outpaced inflation by increasing 82 percent during the ten years ending in June 1991.[9] That was faster than the wage growth of private-sector workers. So as prosperity wound down in New England in 1989 and then across much of the rest of the country in 1990–91, what should have been a merely painful readjustment verged on fiscal calamity, raising a choice between large-scale cuts in services, payroll reductions and increases in state and local taxes—or, as it turned out, all three.

Not that public services slumped overnight. Diminishing commitment in Washington harked back a decade to the Reagan administration's new emphasis on privatization and the marketplace. But the early 1990s downturn brought the budget issue front and center—and on a painfully broad front.

The "three R's" were especially quick to suffer. Public libraries, which got 81 percent of their financing from local government, began cutting back hours and even closing across much of the country, in some hard-pressed communities because lending books could not compete with maintaining police and fire protection. In rural West Virginia, in small towns like Poca, Eleanor and Buffalo, 1991 revenue pressures shut one-room libraries that served as community centers and classroom auxiliaries. One third of the libraries in Massachusetts reported reduced hours, and in New Bedford, all but one of the branch libraries closed in July to save money for the rest of the fiscal year.[10] Demonstrators in Brooklyn, New York, draped library doors with black cloth to protest layoffs and service cuts.

When librarians and their supporters from around the United States converged on Washington in July 1991 to demonstrate for more financial help, officials of the American Library Association drew a surprising contrast: The plight of public libraries, they said, was worse than during the Great Depression. Back then, government authorities had placed great emphasis on keeping the libraries open. In the early 1990s, priorities were different. The Bush administration's fiscal 1992 budget recommended a 73 percent *decline* in the annual federal allotment for public libraries—to just $35 million.[11]

Public education, a traditional middle-class preoccupation, was in fiscal trouble from primary and secondary levels right up to community colleges and state universities. Even in prosperous 1987, spending by all levels of government on public and private education had totaled just 5.1 percent of the U.S. Gross National Product, putting the United

States a weak tenth among fifteen advanced nations, far behind leaders like Denmark (7.6 percent), Sweden (7.2 percent), Canada (7.1 percent) and the Netherlands (6.8 percent), albeit on a rough par with Japan and Britain (5.0 percent).[12] Then the pressures of the new decade forced states and localities to apply their budget scalpels, and spring 1991 saw cash-strapped school districts, especially in Massachusetts, New York, Florida and California, send dismissal notices to tens of thousands of teachers, a grim ritual signaling the worst school layoffs in a decade. No national records were kept, but thousands of teachers were eventually discharged that year, notwithstanding burgeoning school attendance in states like Florida and California, where teacher-pupil ratios worsened.[13] Nineteen ninety-two brought more of the same. For many states, ongoing weak revenues meant an ongoing crisis in financing local public education.

In many hard-pressed school districts, where two or three years of cumulating cuts had undercut teacher-pupil ratios and curriculum enrichment, more and more middle-class parents scrimped to afford private schools. At the end of 1991 the National Association of Independent Schools announced that at elementary- and secondary-school levels, private school applications were up as much as 33 percent from 1990, despite tuitions averaging $6,400 a year, because parents wanted to avoid the overcrowded classes, violence and drugs that plagued so many public schools. Thirty-six percent of these parents sent children to private schools on incomes of less than $50,000 a year.[14] But in a growing percentage of districts, government-provided primary and secondary education was becoming a bare-bones service, unacceptable to those who could somehow afford something better.

The squeeze on the middle class took slightly different form at the higher-education level, where state colleges and universities were chalking up some of the nation's steepest price hikes—tuition increases that the American Council on Education calculated at an average 10 to 12 percent in 1991.[15] Despite the rise, a simultaneous decline in education budgets in many states still required staff to be slashed, class sizes to be increased and courses to be consolidated. In California's state university system, about one thousand full-time instructors were laid off and another two thousand part-time lecturers were not replaced before classes opened for the 1991–92 school year.[16] In many places, particularly California and the Northeastern states, the 1992–93 school year brought further glum tuition and layoff notices, but in several others, tuition increases eased because of declining inflation and voter anger. The chairman of the California Assembly's higher education policy committee estimated that with student fees having increased 65 percent in the past two years in the University of California system, 60 percent in the California State University system and 100 percent at community colleges, 200,000 students could be pushed out of higher education. Peter Magrath, president of the National Association of State Universities and Land Grant Colleges, summed up what was happening: "All public four-year universities, with some limited exceptions, like Utah and Alaska, are under the worst fiscal stress since the Great Depression."[16A]

The burden of rising tuition, observers agreed, would fall on middle-class parents, including many whose deteriorating financial condition made it impossible to keep children in expensive private colleges and universities. Applications at many of the better public institutions were up by 15 percent, because although the cost of tuition, room and board at the average four-year institution rose to $4,970 for in-state students in 1990, it remained well below the $13,544 price tag at the average private institution.[17] Nevertheless, between 1980 and 1987, the average tuition at public four-year universities increased from 3.8 percent to 4.8 percent of median family income.[18] By the early 1990s it was over 5 percent.

Until they bowed to political pressure in 1992, Bush administration officials were surprisingly unsympathetic. In pursuit of its blueprint for curbing federal aid to middle-class and working-class families, the White House announced in May 1991 that it would ask Congress to slash federal tuition grants to college students whose families had incomes above the poverty level, disqualifying some four hundred thousand.* Across the country, at little-known schools serving hum-drum communities, local officials told the press that the plan could devastate student aid and further tighten the squeeze on middle-income and working-class students, obliging more of them to take out loans, use up a bigger chunk of family savings, find jobs, go to college only part time or simply drop out.[19] Other governmental and private student aid was already shrinking.

In some places, student reaction to the state-level cutbacks in public education had turned violent. State university students in New York joined in a demonstration in which thousands of irate protesters smashed the glass doors outside the governor's office. In September 1991 thousands of incensed Texas high schoolers laid siege to school

---

*In 1992, as the elections got under way, the Bush administration partly reversed itself and helped arrange a new loan program.

administration headquarters in Dallas, throwing bottles and rocks and facing police in riot gear to protest the layoffs of some three hundred teachers and cutbacks that put as many as seventy-two students in classrooms designed for thirty-five.[20]

Class differences colored Washington perceptions. In response to the Bush administration's proposal to cut college loans for the middle class, Democratic U.S. senator Bill Bradley called for *expanding* loan assistance to the middle class and funding it with a 10 percent income tax surcharge on million-dollar-a-year incomes.[21] Meanwhile, neoconservative James Q. Wilson, with a blithe indifference to middle-class economic frustration, proposed a program of federal assistance to "enable families in underclass neighborhoods to enroll their children, at an early age, in boarding schools" for uplift.[22] It was the sort of cavalier sociology that conservatives a generation earlier had attributed to liberals.

Public hospitals across the country, admittedly more important to lower-income groups than to the middle class, were also failing or running unsustainable operating deficits. In their 1991 annual report, New York City's Hospital Visiting Committee described municipal hospital care as the worst "in recent memory."[23] The same was true from Boston to Los Angeles. In Illinois, the *Chicago Tribune* worried over the incipient breakdown of the state's mental health system.[24]

The unfortunate overlap of declining services with rising charges and costs also came to the fore in another important sector: transportation in general and urban/suburban mass transit in particular. In the early 1980s, an ideological lack of interest in public mass transit, whetted by a desire to shift transportation ownership and finance into private hands, had been almost as pervasive in Ronald Reagan's Washington as in Margaret Thatcher's Britain.

For politicians, the repair and finance of the U.S. transportation infrastructure posed an extraordinary post-1981 challenge. The nation's aging roads and bridges, railroad systems, mass transit facilities, airports, waterways and water treatment systems were deteriorating—in some places, massively. Back in 1952, even before the launching of the interstate highway system, 6.9 percent of the nonmilitary portion of the federal budget went to "infrastructure"; by 1990 that had fallen to 1.2 percent.[25] The result was poor maintenance and cumulative structural neglect. State and local governments, of course, had to concentrate a much higher ratio of their revenues on these priorities, yet even so, whereas back in 1960 public works had accounted for 19 percent of combined government spending at all levels, by 1984 it represented only 7 percent.[26] Too many needs were competing for too few dollars. Motorists and travelers found potholed highways, trembling bridges, crime-ridden subway stations and overcrowded airports, especially in the Northeast, which had the highest ratio of worn-out and unsafe facilities. More than just annoyance was involved; Pat Choate, author of *America in Ruins,* estimated that nationally, wear and tear from poor road surfaces increased the costs of car ownership, on average, by about 30 percent.[27]

Inadequate "infrastructure"—could technocrats ever have chosen a less appealing label?—gained recognition as a full-fledged crisis in the 1980s, but the financial alarms sounded by the nation's inventory of crumbling concrete and sagging steel came at an almost impossible time for federal policymakers committed to a new philosophy of reducing taxes, cutting domestic spending and privatizing government functions. Rebuilding was incompatible with economizing and privatizing. Within a few years, a Republican-run Transportation Department estimated that it would cost about $50 billion to replace or repair the nation's 240,000 deficient bridges and another $315 billion to maintain highways through the year 2000 in the condition they were in in 1983.[28] And that was just a down payment, because by the end of the eighties, officials were estimating the nation's overall infrastructural needs at as much as $3 trillion.

Deficit-conscious Washington could not even contemplate this kind of investment. The Reagan administration's contrary leanings, unfolded during the 1980s, were to deregulate the bus industry, sell off the government-run railroad systems (Amtrak and Conrail), propose elimination of federal mass transit subsidies and decline to release the $17 billion sitting in the federal highway and airport trust funds (because spending the money on hand would have made the federal budget deficit look worse). Privatization, deregulation and localization would be the Republican answer to any crisis. As federal support ebbed, TRIP (The Railroad Information Program), a Washington transportation research group, calculated that as federal support ebbed, the share of highway-improvement costs borne by state and local governments had risen to 77.6 percent of the total in 1988, up from 74 percent in 1980.[29] So after the Bush administration's announcement in 1990 of a national transportation policy, which proposed a further proportional rise in the burden borne by the states, TRIP prepared and released its data to document that such a shift had *already* taken place.

Shrinking transportation services were becoming commonplace in different parts of America. As the forces of the market took over from

politics and government regulation, many small cities lost airline service, railroad service, bus service—or some combination. Riders of
urban mass transit systems also suffered as the federal share of operating expenses slid from 28 percent in 1981 to 17 percent in 1991.[30]
Shrinking federal support and the recession's impact on state and local
revenues brought cutbacks in local public transit services and fare
hikes. "What we've been seeing is a spate of fare increases over the past
six months or so," a spokesman for the American Public Transit
Association said in 1991. "Many systems have found themselves with
no choice."[31]

Meanwhile, for the average breadwinner in the suburbs, with their
new majority of the nation's population, the mounting inadequacy of
the U.S. transportation system was felt most in traffic gridlock, the
ten-mile-long snails of steel, glass and rubber that crawled through
most major U.S. metropolitan areas twice a day. In California, which
had the most cars and the worst gridlock, the state Chamber of Commerce indicated that delays in 1988 cost each motorist $135 in lost time
and $97 in fuel and maintenance, and later official estimates were far
higher.[32] The Texas Transportation Institute had calculated in 1986
that the state's per capita traffic congestion cost was $400, while the
Federal Highway Administration estimated the national cost of traffic
congestion that same year at $9 billion and about 750 million worker
hours.[33]

Congestion had worsened by 1991, when California officials estimated the cost to each state motorist at $1,200 a year, including 1.2
billion hours per year sitting in traffic, or 10.5 workdays per driver.[34]
Sky-high housing costs in Los Angeles and San Francisco had been
forcing more and more median-income families out to affordable but
distant new suburbs—places like Moreno Valley, Simi Valley and
Santa Clarita, with three- or three-and-a-half-hour round-trips to the
office. Commuters from these hinterlands spent 15 to 20 percent of
their waking hours in cars. Statewide, the average driver might face
only 6 to 7 hours a month of congestion and gridlock; commuters on
the San Bernardino and Riverside expressways, however, could match
that in a bad week. Time spent in traffic was a rapidly emerging
nonmonetary tax on leisure time and quality of life.

Around Los Angeles, moreover, gridlock was moving off the freeways and spreading into backup roads and residential neighborhoods.
The average ten-mile commute in 1990 took thirty to forty minutes, ten
to fifteen minutes longer than it had two years earlier.[35] Commuters
eagerly awaited new handbooks detailing shortcuts from community
to community that avoided main routes. "I can regularly count 100

cars lined up down a shortcut that two years ago was completely vacant," said Neele Mayer, a Sherman Oaks resident who used six different routes to get to work. "It's a real nightmare."[36]

Tightened budget pressures, however, were only one reason that government was delivering poorer services by the early 1990s. The inefficient public sector, as conservatives complained, was character-ized by entrenched bureaucracies, obsolescent programs and greedy public-employee unions. The proof could be stark. In 1986, to deal with the working-class municipality of Ecorse, Michigan, which was some $6 million in debt and in violation of a court order to balance its budget, a tough-minded local judge decided to put the city into receiv-ership under a municipal-bond expert whose solution was to "privatize just about everything, holding the line on taxes, slashing the municipal work force almost by half and signing up private firms to provide most services."[37] This ice-bath worked where politics as usual would have failed; Ecorse learned how to operate within a reasonable budget. The crunch on state and local finances in the early 1990s, the worst since the 1930s, had some of the same effect nationally. Bankruptcies, receiv-erships and privatization became chilling but often effective solutions for bloated municipal pay scales and labor contracts, all frequent by-products of Democratic politics or union alliances.

Consolidating or sharing services also made sense. Nyack, New York, dissolved its police force in 1991, paying to be patrolled by officers from nearby Orangetown and Clarktown. In northern New Jersey, two neighboring school boards agreed to negotiate a joint arrangement with a private food company, saving $40,000 annually. Civic leaders of Westchester County, New York, began debating a report called *Government at the Crossroads,* which, besides proposing a central school board to oversee the existing fifty-six districts, went so far as to suggest that some of the country's smaller towns and villages be combined.[38] New York State listed some ten thousand governmen-tal entities, from counties down to sewer districts, and as revenue pressures tightened, voters began to wonder: Just how many of their tax dollars went to support four or five partially duplicative layers of local authority? Declining assistance from larger jurisdictions was only part of the cash squeeze on state and local services; an important part also came from excess bureaucracy and top-heavy payrolls relative to the changing 1990s revenue base.*

But conservative enthusiasm for reducing federal support for many

*Pressures to reduce the size and staffing of state and local government had a mixed impact on the middle-class squeeze. On the one hand, they did limit tax increases, but on the other hand, widespread public-employee discharges also undercut the middle class.

public services, in the name of localism and privatization, often had less admirable motives than increasing competition and improving efficiency. As we have seen, fiscal burdens were also redistributed by localizing government services and shifting their funding from Washington back to cash-strapped grass roots. As federal aid to states and localities and federal income tax rates both shrank in the 1980s, the increasing demands on local revenue to support local services required not just higher taxes but also higher tolls on New York bridges and steeper state university and community college tuition in California. Services once virtually free for average-income families were now increasingly expensive. Users, not taxpayers, should bear more charges, conservative philosophers argued. "From each according to his degree of use" was to replace the mid-century credo of "From each according to his ability to pay." Then there were the situations, like central Philadelphia's special police protection, where a service formerly free to the general public became available only to a limited group for an extra fee. So, too, with high-priced private tollroads that let affluent commuters buy their way out of the traffic jams of a public transportation infrastructure inadequately maintained out of general revenues.

Similarly, where public schools became underfunded, prosperous middle-class families didn't always shift their children to private schools; some raised private money to turn their local schools into public-private hybrids. In Los Angeles, where most public schools were choking in a budget noose, relatively affluent parents, principally Westside residents, developed a subsidy system of carnivals, bake sales, raffles and booster clubs to raise the tens (or hundreds) of thousands of dollars for what local school authorities had once routinely provided—music teachers, art instructors and supplies, librarians and physical education instructors. "As bad as it is, and it is bad, it is going to get worse," Los Angeles School Board president Jackie Goldberg said in 1991. "I don't want to see people trying to make up the losses of hundreds of millions of dollars with fundraisers . . . but I do think this is going to be the wave of the future."[39]

Crime prevention and personal security, meanwhile, offered the most striking metropolitan-area example of the same phenomenon. It was only during the nineteenth century that large-scale publicly supported police forces took over urban security functions, but by the 1980s and 1990s there were signs that this public role was declining. Safety, too, was being privatized. After the city of Philadelphia and downtown businessmen negotiated their 1990 arrangement whereby special taxes would buy special police services, a survey by *The Phila-*

delphia Inquirer came to a sweeping national conclusion: "Americans who can afford it have stopped relying on the government to protect them from crime. They are hiring their own police."[40]

There were about 1.5 million private security personnel by 1990, in fact—from security guards to armored-car drivers and private investigators. As late as 1975, combined federal, state and local government spending on police protection, approximately $30 billion, had been roughly twice the money spent on *private* security. By 1980, however, private security outlays had gone ahead, and by the early 1990s, they had roughly doubled the expenditures for public police protection, while private security payrolls were twice as large. James K. Stewart, former head of the National Institute of Justice, the federal Justice Department's think tank, summed up the metamorphosis: "Something has really changed in this country. I'd say we are moving from a system of justice to a system where people are purchasing security, which is different from justice, because justice is a value that benefits all of society. Private security partitions off security to just a few."[41] Lawrence W. Sherman, president of Washington's Crime Control Institute, agreed that special taxes like Philadelphia's (and other special-purpose levies in New York, Michigan and Kansas City) could warp the system: "The logical place for this to wind up is that every crime will have its own tax, except for the unpopular offenses that involve the poor or are not important to middle-class voters."[42]

Families with merely average income, though, rarely profited from such arrangements. This embattled tier of the middle class could not afford the expensive apartment buildings, exclusive neighborhoods or walled-in clusters of golf villas with state-of-the-art private security and guards. For those with ordinary earnings in major metropolitan areas, danger was just a street or a staircase away. Buy-it-yourself police protection was beginning to make personal security in parts of the United States into an Anglicized, high-tech version of Italy or Brazil: generally reliable, even cushioned, for the top 1 to 5 percent of the population, increasingly thin not just for the poor but for significant layers of the middle class.

With even less debate than in the reorientation of tax policy, many public services in the United States were slowly undergoing a gradual transformation in their availability and financing, reflecting a polarizing, stratifying nation in which people in the middle were slowly losing not just services but the solicitude of government that their forebears of 1948 and 1962 had taken for granted. For more and more Americans, lost or reduced public services in schools, universities, parks, libraries, transportation and family safety meant increased household outlays, which subtracted from what officialdom called real disposable income and represented a de facto tax levied by the inadequacy of government in the early 1990s relative to the regimes of twenty to thirty years earlier.

The In-Between Sector—Charitable Services

Charity—which provides services coming between the public and private sectors—also became a burden that fell disproportionately on the average American during the 1980s. If liberals have been overenthusiastic about the services of the welfare state, U.S. conservatives have been naive about how charitable or nonprofit organizations can partially replace the role of the state. Back in the 1920s, Herbert Hoover's emphasis on the role of voluntary organizations—charitable and business—in lieu of government regulation foreshadowed what would emerge again in the 1980s.*

Ronald Reagan had crystallized the new mood in October 1981 with a speech to the National Alliance of Business proclaiming volunteerism "an essential part of our plan to give government back to the people" and calling for $100 billion a year in individual, foundation and corporate contributions. The hopeful theory was that charity would take over welfare functions from government, while Reaganomics would give middle-class and rich potential donors more surplus income to contribute to organizations assisting the truly needy, who alone would require and receive help.[43]

This view of government, carried into the 1990s in more moderate form through George Bush's Thousand Points of Light program, included the belief that services should not be provided to the middle class, which was prosperous enough to take care of itself. There was a catch, however—in fact, several catches: first, this philosophy fur-

---

*In 1931, as the Great Depression deepened, Hoover renewed his emphasis on voluntarism by recruiting Walter S. Gifford, president of the American Telephone and Telegraph Company, to head the President's Organization on Unemployment Relief. Hoover theorized that traditional American altruism would feed the hungry in place of a government role that was to be avoided. Gifford promised that " 'America will feel the thrill of a great spiritual experience,' but he and his colleagues could only raise $100 million of a hoped-for $175 million budget, and in any event, the task was far too great" (Milton Goldin, "Sweet Charity," *History Today,* September 1991, p. 10). Fund-raising consultant Goldin pointed out that "given these developments, philanthropy's critics during the 1930s and 1940s considered private-sector giving not only a bankrupt tradition but a contemptible device used by the rich to escape taxes."

thered conservative plans to reduce or end middle-class eligibility for federal aid programs; second, the middle class did *not,* as we have seen, make notable economic progress; and third, funding assistance to low-income Americans through charity and volunteerism turned out to be yet another surprising chapter in the burdening of the middle class and the working poor.

Throughout history, Americans have always dug deeper into their pockets to help redress hard times, and they did so in 1981–82, then again in the mid-1980s when the regional recession rolled across the commodity states, and then once again in the downturn of the early 1990s. Ironically, however, the people who dug deeper were mostly poor and average-income individuals and families—people who could see the hardship around them. A survey by the Gallup Organization and Independent Sector found that in 1990 contributors with incomes under $10,000 gave away 5.5 percent to charity, more than any other group.[44] And Internal Revenue Service data indicated that among taxpayers itemizing deductions, those who had adjusted gross incomes of $25,000 to $30,000—median-income families, in short—raised their average donations by 62 percent between 1980 and 1988 ((from $665 to $1,075) despite tax changes that made giving more costly.[45]

Conversely, as the top bracket shrank from 70 percent in 1980 to just 28 percent in 1988, taxpayers with incomes over $1 million slashed their charitable donations from $207,089 to $72,784, while taxpayers in the $500,000–$1 million group cut their average charitable outlays from $47,432 to $16,602.[46] "We're seeing a new spirit of giving and caring across the nation," Brian O'Connell, the president of Independent Sector, said in 1991, "but the sad thing is that most of the truly wealthy are proving to be downright stingy."[47] In short, the extent to which charitable services filled growing gaps left by declining government services became a charge to ordinary Americans, not to those at the top whose incomes were soaring.

By the end of the 1980s, just as the weight of the tax system had been shifted to fall on Middle America, so had the weight of giving for charitable services.

The High Cost of Private Services

If deflation on the farm and in the oil patch kept the prices of commodities under control after 1981, thereby reducing the overall national inflation rate, that was not true of services, where costs rose in the early 1990s just as they had in the 1980s, even while, in many everyday services, quality continued to deteriorate. In 1987, at the peak of the hurry-up, go-go mood of the Reagan years, *Time* magazine captured a powerful frustration bothering Americans in a cover story on the collapse of personal service in the U.S. marketplace, whether by flight attendants, repairmen, bank clerks, salespeople or hospital assistants.[48] The heyday of personal services, historians said, had probably come in the postwar era, when labor was reasonably paid and prices fairly stable. Businesses could afford to lavish service on customers—for example, music stores provided record players for those who wanted to listen to disks before buying them, and drugstores offered free delivery. That changed in the 1970s and 1980s, when inflation forced businesses to slash services to cut costs and deregulation fostered price wars and further cutbacks in service.[49]

By the end of the 1980s, real service with a genuine smile was mostly a memory. The movie *Back to the Future* entertained audiences with the scene in which the time-traveler played by Michael J. Fox walked past a 1950s-style filling station and was stunned to see four cheery, neat attendants run up to a car that had just pulled in in order to fill its gas tank, check the oil, wipe the chrome and do the windows. In late-1980s Japan, by contrast, service station attendants not only still did that, but they also doffed their hats, shouted their thanks and they stopped traffic so the customer could drive away.[50]

Yet annoying as the change in quality of service was, price changes were even more painful during the 1980s, especially for services important to the middle class. When the Conference Board, a business-sponsored research group, sampled the consumer satisfaction of seven thousand families in early 1990, they identified a number of services that were perceived to give the poorest value: hospital and health costs, auto insurance, bank service charges, college tuition, lawyers' fees, cable television and admission to sports events.[51]

Not only did costs for these services outpace inflation during the 1980s, but they consumed an oversized chunk of the average middle-class family's outlays. The rich and most of the poor were proportionately less affected. Economists disagreed whether these kinds of fast-climbing service costs were fully reflected in the overall national Consumer Price Index. However, had there been a CPI specifically for middle-class consumption patterns, it was indisputable that these categories of increases would have been more heavily weighted.

Regulation—or often its lack—was a recurrent culprit. High bank charges and soaring cable television rates followed 1980s deregulation. Insurance and health care, in turn, were important unfolding regulatory challenges of the 1990s. Indeed, many of the fastest-rising costs for private services owed part of their momentum to nonregulation. Government, it was starting to appear, could be inflationary not simply through excessive bureaucracies, extravagance, overregulation and wage settlements, but also through permissiveness toward professions and industries.

If tuition at public universities and colleges outpaced inflation during the 1980s, as we have seen, the increase at private colleges and universities was even steeper. From 1980 to 1988, incomes in the United States rose only 53 percent, compared with a 68 percent increase in the cost of public colleges and a doubling of costs at private ones.[52] Appendix C shows the change. Ivy League schools were greening themselves the most rapidly. The result, said Williams College economist Morton Schapiro, was a loss of middle-class enrollment. The costlier private colleges and public universities alike lost a disproportion of students from families in the badly squeezed $40,000- to $60,000-a-year range; some transferred to lower-cost private schools; others left for community colleges, where tuition was comparatively cheap.[53] Meanwhile, the proportion of low-income students at the more expensive schools remained stable because of financial aid, and the spaces opened by the middle-class exodus were generally filled by higher-income students whose families could afford the tuition.*

The percentage of freshmen who chose colleges because of low tuition or financial aid or because they could live near home and save money reached an all-time high in 1991, according to the Higher Education Research Institute at the University of California at Los Angeles.[54] At a number of the country's most prestigious private universities, financial pressures were so bad that administrators began to talk about prospective annual deficits akin to those of major suburban counties—$40 million to $50 million at schools like Stanford, Columbia and Yale—unless major cutbacks could be made in faculty and administrative costs.[55] Not only fewer middle-class Americans but also fewer Americans of any kind would be able to attend these schools because more top schools were stepping up pursuit of affluent foreign students. At the University of Pennsylvania, for example, international students made up 11 percent of the entering class in autumn 1991, up from just 2 percent ten years earlier. Only 8 percent of the foreigners at Penn required financial assistance versus 45 percent of the overall student body.[56]

Entertainment was another area where the middle class was paying

---

*In 1991 the Bush administration negotiated a consent decree under which the seven Ivy League universities agreed not to collude in setting tuition, salaries and financial aid—as they by and large had since 1986.

much more. In July 1991 the federal General Accounting Office released a study showing that in the four years following deregulation of cable television in 1986, the cost of basic service had risen 56 percent—twice the rate of inflation—while the more expensive "second tier" service (channels like CNN, TBS and TNT) rose 61 percent.[57] In Los Angeles the increase was much worse—107 percent in four and a half years.[58] Many companies also began charging for what had previously been free, such as converter boxes. To keep costs under control, squeezed subscribers dumped expensive premium channels and pay-per-view services. Economists unsympathetic to the cable companies charged that subscribers were being forced to underwrite the huge buyout costs that the larger surviving cable firms found themselves left with after absorbing smaller rivals, although industry officials blamed rate increases on skyrocketing program costs, especially in sports and entertainment.

That prices for concerts and sports events were going skyward was also obvious to consumers. In 1991 the *Los Angeles Times* showed how the laissez-faire economics of ticket sales had been running amok in Southern California, supporting so many promoters and middlemen that "tickets to many events can no longer be purchased anywhere at face value."[59] The price of a $17.50 concert ticket, for example, would, in reality, be anywhere from $19.50 to $26.05—$19.50, if bought at the box office, which added a $2.00 "facility fee"; $22.75, if bought through a neighborhood Ticketmaster outlet, which added a $3.25 "convenience" charge to the $2.00 facility fee; and $26.05 when a single ticket was bought by telephone (the $2.00 facility fee, plus a $5.00 phone convenience fee and a $1.55 processing fee). Admittedly, the high basic charges principally reflected the enormous compensation paid to both sports figures and entertainers—$10 million a year to heavyweight boxing champions and $2 million to right fielders, for example, and the forty highest-paid entertainers listed by *Forbes* magazine in 1991 all made at least $18 million over a two-year period.[60] But packagers and promoters further swelled the ticket price to consumers.

Complaints about Ticketmaster's various charges had already convinced New York's State Consumer Protection Board that it should ask the legislature for a 10 percent cap on service fees: "I have serious concerns about the excessively high level of service fees that ticket agencies like Ticketmaster sometimes charge," said executive director Richard Kessel in 1991. "And now, due to the proposed merger of Ticketmaster and Ticketron, there will be less competition in the field, which in turn could lead to even higher service fees."[61] Some state regulators and legislators asked the Bush administration to disapprove the merger, but it declined.

Legal fees also surged during the 1980s, at a cost to consumers but also to the broader economy. In the process, the average earnings of a law-firm partner ballooned from $74,000 a year in 1979 to just under $150,000 a year in 1990. By 1989–90 some state and federal judges, themselves among the lower-paid U.S. lawyers, became so outraged at swollen legal fees that they started to disallow the charges that came before them. In scaling back one bloated billing, Chief Judge Donald D. Alsop of the U.S. District Court in Minnesota observed that "it is no wonder that the average business person or citizen can no longer afford to resort to the courts and engage in litigation to resolve private disputes."[62] The press even found itself starting to pay attention to HALT—Help Abolish Legal Tyranny, a consumer rights watchdog founded in 1978 by two Rhodes scholars—despite the naive, even utopian cast to HALT's proposed remedies: that lawyers, like auto mechanics and other service providers, would have to give prospective clients written estimates, would have to give clients refunds for over-charging or incompetence, and would have to let non-lawyers share in handling out-of-court legal matters.[63]

Beyond its up-front charges to consumers, however, the American legal system—lawyers in general and trial lawyers in particular, as well as many plaintiffs, some judges and many jurors—was imposing an even greater burden on the American economy through what foes cataloged as unprecedented litigiousness, overexpansion of rights and liabilities, extremism in jury awards and clogged courts.* Critics also deplored the negative impact of excess legalism on the international competitiveness of U.S. business, on new-product development, and (as this chapter will pursue) on the rocketing costs of health care and insurance, especially automobile insurance.

As for banks, many trembling on the precipice of insolvency in the early 1990s, the surge in their charges, like the rise in cable television fees, was partly a consequence of deregulation. The permissiveness of the early 1980s had helped lure commercial banks and savings and loan institutions into unsound speculative practices that eventually left sur-

---

*In 1991, Vice President Dan Quayle, in his role as chairman of the President's Council on Competitiveness, pointedly asked the annual convention of the American Bar Association, "Does America really need 70% of the world's lawyers? Is it healthy for our economy to have 18 million new lawsuits coursing through the system annually? Is it right that people with disputes come up against staggering expense and delay?" (Time, "Do We Have Too Many Lawyers?" August 26, 1991, p. 54).

vivors grasping for every possible way to increase income. To many large banks small customers were an inconvenience, given the broader vistas of deregulation, so in 1990 and thereafter, once defaulting real estate loans and rising federal deposit insurance premiums started biting, institutions began to announce a wide range of additional requirements, minimum balances, charges and service fees. By spring 1991 a few bold institutions were informing depositors that a special fee was being levied to cover the rising federal deposit insurance costs on commercial checking accounts. Most banks, however, recognized the explosiveness of levying a specific charge whereby *consumers* would be billed for the higher insurance fees the Federal Deposit Insurance Corporation started charging following the speculative failures, so instead they wound up taking the money indirectly: by raising service charges, levying new fees and posting high personal loan and credit-card rates while giving unprecedentedly lower interest rates on customers' deposits.[64]

Thus, while Federal Reserve Board chairman Alan Greenspan was lowering interest rates in late 1990 and throughout 1991, *banks,* not *consumers,* were the principal beneficiaries. Although the rates banks *paid* on savings accounts, money market accounts and certificates of deposit might be plummeting into the 4.5 to 6 percent range, the interest they *charged* on unsecured personal loans and on bank credit cards was simultaneously rising to 17.4 percent and 18.9 percent.[65] Appendix C shows how this extraordinary disparity developed and widened in the 1980s. As charted by Bank Rate Monitor, the "spread" between the (low) average yield on one-year bank CDs and the (high) charge on bank credit cards widened from 8.5 percentage points in April 1989 to an extraordinary 12 percentage points in April 1991. By early 1992 the gap was a stunning 14 to 15 percentage points. By sanctioning this unprecedented disparity, federal authorities facilitated a shift of billions of dollars from the pockets of consumers to the profit ledgers of banks and other financial institutions (and to their shareholders). There *was* a larger public-policy rationale: transfusions like these, along with funds strategically deposited by the Federal Reserve, may have kept banks from failing in dangerous numbers. Troubled financial institutions used the time and funds to rebuild and rearrange themselves, and by 1992 many were reporting large profits again. Nevertheless, it was a levy on the citizenry, not least the proverbial middle-class widow in Florida receiving two thirds of her $30,000-a-year income from bank CDs. Lowell Bryan, head of the banking group at McKinsey and Company, the management consultants, acknowledged the economic reality: "Consumers and smaller businesses, which do not have much alternative to banks if they want to borrow, are going to have to pay for banks' bad lending decisions in the past."[66]

Charges by insurance companies were also rising. By 1990–91 bad investments in junk bonds and losses in commercial real estate were a factor, but for automobile insurers—whose rates were particularly controversial—the basic problem of the 1980s had been the soaring costs of litigation, medical care and car repairs, which collectively consumed 86 percent of every premium dollar. As Appendix C shows, the cost of automobile insurance premiums ballooned by nearly 150 percent between 1980 and 1990, far ahead of the inflation rate, yet most companies were making little or no money from auto insurance because claims paid out were rising even faster. There were, of course, horror stories that seemed to document excess: annual auto insurance bills of $3,000 or $4,000 for families in suburban California or Long Island with two cars and two young male drivers under twenty-five. Yet for the most part, while the middle-class squeeze effect of insurance was indisputable, much of its increased cost, in turn, reflected the painful medico-legal vise on the industry.

Which brings us to one of the most critical pressures of the early 1990s: soaring medical-care and health-insurance costs, which in each year after 1980 outpaced the Consumer Price Index. For the entire decade of the 1980s, they were up 118 percent compared with inflation's 71 percent, boosting health care's share of the GNP to 12 percent from 9 percent in 1980 and less than 5 percent in 1947. None of the other major Western economies experienced this kind of medical inflation or explosion, and their health-cost shares of GNP remained much lower—somewhat over 8 percent in Canada and Germany, 6 percent in Britain.

By 1989 and 1990 unhappy Americans were telling pollsters they favored a national health program to bring costs under control. Moreover, because foreign polls also showed citizens of Canada and Germany, in particular, much happier with their systems, these two approaches gained widespread attention as possibilities for the United States to imitate. Americans feared that the U.S. system was failing—not, of course, in its splendid technology but in its expense, its cumbersome uncontrollability, and in how 33 to 39 million Americans, many of them employed and well above poverty levels, had no health insurance in 1991, because their employer didn't offer it or because they couldn't afford it. Millions of others accepted inadequate policies, while others paid almost unbearable costs for comprehensive coverage.

Ultimately the election-year politics of 1992 complicated deliberations over what polls suggested two thirds of Americans wanted: a *national* response to the gathering crisis. Because the federal government wasn't moving, the states, too, began to feel pressure from middle-income voters losing access to health care, from small businesses unable to buy insurance for employees, and from hospitals and other health providers stuck with uncompensated care. Yet few states produced broad blueprints; only the federal government could afford to confront such an expensive nationwide challenge.

Republicans hostile to any national program pointed to survey data showing that the groups most concerned about health care were Democratic: blacks, Hispanics, the poor, the uninsured. Yet aspects of health care were also a middle-class headache. Two thirds of the roughly 35 million Americans uninsured in the early 1990s were employed or from a family in which someone worked. But for the four fifths of Americans with insurance, the problem lay in reduced benefits and rising personal outlays. According to one survey, the percentage of health benefit costs picked up by employers declined from 80 percent in 1980 to 69 percent by the end of the decade, thereby increasing the employee share.[67] The result was to inflate costs for the average employee and family. Hay/Higgins and Company, the benefits consultants, estimated that the typical corporate employee with family coverage was paying more than $1,300 a year from his or her pocket for health insurance, up from $150 in 1980.[68]

For nervous Middle Americans, mostly insured but worried about high premiums and uncovered illnesses, the objective was comprehensive coverage at the lower prices available elsewhere, which required reducing some of the U.S. health-care costs already at 12 percent of GNP and projected to reach 15 percent in 2000. Experts looking for a federal-level solution could point out several contributing U.S. costs that were better managed elsewhere. One was high pay for doctors, whose average earnings had climbed by 79 percent from $89,900 in 1981 to $155,800 in 1989, well above either inflation or the income gain of the average family.[69] By contrast, physicians' fees in Canada, capped by the government, brought them incomes about one-third lower than those in the United States—an average of roughly $100,000 in 1990, according to unofficial estimates.[70] As for Germany, since 1986 total spending for office-based physicians had not been permitted to rise faster than the average wage, German doctors also made less than their U.S. counterparts in 1989—$107,200 a year versus $155,800. This was about four times the average German wage, down from a six-to-one ratio in 1986, whereas doctors in the United States made 6.7 times the average U.S. wage in 1988, according to the American Medical Association.[71]

A second inflationary factor was the American legal system's liability explosion, which obliged doctors to pay large sums ($20,000 or $25,000 a year) for malpractice insurance and simultaneously encouraged them to provide expensive or possibly unnecessary treatments, which, after all, could be billed to insurers. North of the border, medical lawsuits were rare because Canadian lawyers had to work for a fee rather than a share in malpractice awards and patients could not sue for punitive damages.[72] Malpractice premiums were very low in Germany by U.S. standards because Germans very rarely sue.[73]

Over the years the Canadian and German national health care approaches, while different, had both evolved much simpler, more efficient administrative systems, which gave little incentive for medical excess, whereas in the United States, payment and responsibility were so diffused—among patient, doctor, hospital, insurer, employer and often several layers of government—that spending decisions were made by people with little reason to economize. And, of course, this fragmentation and massive staffing of U.S. health administration was also expensive in itself, a bureaucrat's dream. The U.S. General Accounting Office estimated in 1991 that a government-sponsored health plan following the Canadian model would save Americans some $67 billion a year, principally by ending insurance overhead and reducing the procedural costs of reimbursing U.S. hospitals and doctors by America's crazy quilt of public agencies and private insurers. In Germany the country's eleven hundred Sick Funds (insurers) were all financed by the same government-run payroll tax and all supplied with the same government-mandated forms, so that only 5 percent of total health-care costs was consumed by administration versus almost 25 percent for the United States.[74]

Factor number five was the vast U.S. lead in—and voracious consumer appetite for—the most advanced medical technology. "We are to medical-care technologies what the French are to wines," observed Robert Blendon, chairman of Harvard's health policy department.[75] Namely, the greatest experts, the biggest exporters and the proudest consumers. This, too, worked to build inflation into the system, although the Germans, almost equally technology-oriented, managed to control that aspect as well. Canada stinted on technology.

The cost of drugs was also much higher in the United States than in almost any other country. Appendix C charts the surprising international comparison. Americans paid an average of 54 percent more than Europeans for twenty-five commonly prescribed drugs, according to one study, and some individual prices were worse: a month's supply of Eldepryl, the Parkinson's disease medication, cost $240 in the United States and just $28 in Italy.[76] One cause of the disparity, economists said, was that European governments typically used their mass purchasing power to bargain drug prices with pharmaceutical firms, letting them recover their manufacturing and distribution costs but very little of their overall research outlay. The U.S. government, however, was allowing foreign and domestic drug companies to set their own prices in the American market, enabling them to recover a disproportionate share of their *worldwide* research at the expense of American consumers.

In late 1991 the U.S. Senate's Special Committee on Aging noted that even while U.S. health-care costs were growing at two to three times the inflation rate, prescription drug costs were rising 10 to 15 percent faster than health-care costs.* So favored, the drug industry was America's most profitable, earning 13.6 percent on industrywide revenues in 1990 while Fortune 500 companies averaged 4.1 percent.[77] The special committee's chairman, Senator David Pryor of Arkansas, unmistakably angered by the findings, raised the prospect most worrisome to the drug industry: substantial new price regulation.

Taken together, these various health-cost inflators were part of a U.S. system better for those adequately insured than any other in the world—and better also for its component doctors, manufacturers and administrators. Yet for many median- or average-income American families, the unavoidable corollary was a growing financial fear of doctors, hospitals, health insurance and prescriptions.

For the 1980s as a whole the cost of these seven private services, about which Americans particularly complained to the Conference Board, more than doubled, while general inflation went up by two thirds, although only a few of the seven had reliable indexes. What's more, it seems beyond debate that the broad Consumer Price Index fell far short of reflecting the cumulative, converging weight of these soaring charges on middle-income families making $40,000 to $75,000 a year, especially in expensive large metropolitan areas. For many, their disposable income after subtracting these costs was shrinking, not growing. Besides, even household incomes that stayed just ahead of

---

*A follow-up report in 1992 by the Families USA Foundation, endorsed by the U.S. Senate special committee, found that prices of the twenty most popular prescription drugs jumped 80 percent on average between 1985 and 1991, about three times the inflation rate.

inflation could be squeezed well below it by the sudden cost of a teenager's auto insurance, a sick relative's medicine, a moderate legal bill or a child at a university with mushrooming tuition. Back in the 1950s or 1960s, middle-class incomes and purchasing power had not been so much at risk for these same services.

The politics of whom to blame was raised only indirectly, even as the 1992 debate over the middle-class squeeze heated up. Democratic administrations from Johnson to Carter had been more responsible for the underlying inflation that began to roll in the 1960s and 1970s, yet in many ways, the inflation of the 1980s and early 1990s was a new variety. *Commodity* prices were not rising very much; it was *service* costs that were. Back in the 1970s, conservatives had come up with a perceptive analysis that identified the expanding size and regulatory role of government—the so-called inflationary state—as a major cause of rising prices. By the early 1990s questions were starting to take shape about the inflationary role of the "deregulatory state" or the "non-regulatory state."

Deregulation in most industries had some favorable effect on consumer prices, but there was not much doubt about its inflationary impact on bank and cable television charges. With respect to banks, polls taken in 1991 and 1992 showed the public favoring *more* regulation. Likewise for cable television. And in the entertainment area, state consumer officials were beginning to call for regulation of the fees charged by ticket services. As for colleges, collusive Ivy League "price-fixing" helped double tuition during the 1980s until the government secured a consent decree in 1991. Lawyers, too, effectively doubled their rates, although large corporations began to follow angry judges in rejecting attorneys' billings and forcing reductions, and by the decade's end, legislators in Washington and the states were pursuing ways to crack down on trial lawyers, outrageous verdicts and the broad problem of the "litigation explosion." As for the soaring costs of insurance, worsened in some instances by some insurance companies' speculative or business practices, these were at least abetted by regulatory gaps—insurers were regulated only at the state level, and there often weakly. In 1991 the House of Representatives held hearings on establishing some partial federal regulatory role.

Soaring health costs, however, were probably the area of the greatest regulatory vacuum during the 1980s—and the greatest target of regulatory discussion during the 1990s. Doctor's fees, already regulated in almost every other major nation, moved further in that direction in 1991, when federal authorities rewrote what doctors could charge and be reimbursed for under Medicare, increasing allowable fees for family physicians but curbing them for some specialists. In 1992 the American College of Physicians broke with most other doctors' organizations and endorsed a national cap on health-care spending, including limits on doctor and hospital fees. The biggest change, that of assembling some sort of national health program, was merely debated during the presidential election campaign; enactment remained in the future. Yet even private groups like Blue Cross and Blue Shield were talking about the inevitability of an increased federal regulatory role.* Calls for greater regulation of the galloping prices of prescription drugs mounted following the critical 1991 report of the U.S. Senate Special Committee.

Government regulation had begun the 1980s in disrepute for spurring inflation, but by the early nineties the rising service-cost ingredients of the middle-class squeeze were laying the framework for another shift. In a variety of situations, some economic regulation by some level of the government was starting to look like the best way—or even the only way—for Middle America to squeeze back.

Imperiled Benefits, Pensions and Retirement

If wage and salary gains for earners in the $20,000–$40,000 range lagged during the 1970s and early 1980s, as they clearly did, one reason was the simultaneous increase in employee benefits. During the 1980s, in fact, nominal benefits, unadjusted for inflation, grew faster than wages and salaries, as the table below shows:

To an extent, it was deceptive. Much of the surge in benefits represented the exploding payments made by employers for employee health insurance. That was important coverage; without insurance, unexpected health costs could be a disaster for an employee. At the same time, however, the increasing expenses companies had to bear for health insurance payments minimized employee wage gains, on an overall basis keeping them at or below inflation. Then, by the end of the eighties, it was clear that companies, unwilling to let their profits

---

*In 1992 a survey by The New York Times reported that a growing number of states, convinced that the free-market model of unchecked competition was failing to curb the growth of health costs, were adopting new laws and regulations to control the construction of hospitals and nursing homes and the purchase of costly medical equipment. Many also started convening groups of doctors, consumers, hospital executives, insurers and employers to negotiate the allocation of health-care resources ("States Are Moving to Re-regulation on Health Costs," New York Times, May 11, 1992).

Table 7. Comparative Increases During the 1980s:
Anemic Paychecks, Healthy Benefits

Year	Benefits	Wages and Salaries
1981	12.1%	8.8%
1982	7.2	6.3
1983	7.4	4.9
1984	6.5	4.2
1985	3.5	4.1
1986	3.4	3.2
1987	3.4	3.3
1988	6.9	4.1
1989	6.1	4.1
1990	6.6	4.0
1991	6.2	3.7

Source: Bureau of Labor Statistics, Employment Cost Index (Scott Burns, *Dallas News,* April 29, 1990), with a BLS update for 1991.

suffer, were reducing employee benefits and shrinking their rosters of full-time employees. The benefits tide of the 1970s had reversed and started to ebb. International Survey Research, a Chicago consulting company, after measurements of employees at twenty-eight companies, found sharply fewer willing to rate their employer's benefits as either good or very good. Overall satisfaction with company tuition-refund plans dropped from 87 percent in 1982–83 to 32 percent in 1989–90. For life insurance the satisfaction decline was from 92 percent to 36 percent, for dental plans from 83 percent to 38 percent, for medical plans from 87 percent to 45 percent, for pension plans from 75 percent to 37 percent, and for disability insurance from 86 percent to 47 percent.[78]

Part of the disquiet, as we have seen, was that employers were asking employees to pay a higher and higher share of their benefits, especially health coverage, which added yet another untabulated offset to nominal income. The second blow to Middle America came as more companies reduced their full-time core work force in order to reduce long-term liability for benefits like health insurance, profit sharing and pensions. "The whole idea of reducing your core work force has developed in parallel with the growth of employee benefit costs," said Frank Cassell, professor of management at Northwestern University. "You sort your labor market into two parts. One gets good benefits and has continuity of employment. The secondary work force . . . get no pensions and no benefits."[79] In California, Robert McDonough, chairman of Remedy Temp, a thriving new personnel agency, posited a new business creed for the 1990s: the company with the fewest permanent workers would win.[80]

As the relatively benefit-less "contingent work force" grew in the 1980s, the number of part-timers grew by 19 percent, from 16.4 million persons to 20 million. In 1990, over 4 million of these indicated that they would rather have full-time jobs; by early 1992, 6 million were saying so. The number of self-employed grew almost as quickly, rising by 18 percent to more than 10 million in 1990, many of them thinly disguised part-timers. Still another telling indicator lay in the 1.4 million persons working for "temp" firms—"personnel supply services," in the stilted language of the Bureau of Labor Statistics. Between 1980 and 1990, their numbers had soared by 151 percent.[81] Each of these categories had significant percentages of unemployment or underemployment, but, for purposes of federal data, none of the individuals counted as unemployed.

Most part-time workers were ineligible for unemployment insurance, poorly paid (with a 1987 median hourly wage of $4.42 versus a full-timer's median of $7.43) and unlikely to get health insurance or pension coverage. According to one calculus, only 22 percent of part-time workers received health insurance and only 26 percent had employer-supplied pension coverage.[82] During the early-1990s recession, the number of part-timers saying they would prefer full-time work rose rapidly. For many, part-time work was becoming subemployment— often at real expense to living standards.

Unemployment benefits themselves shrank as a safety net during the 1980s. Federal legislation encouraged states to tighten eligibility for benefits, which they did. Consequently, as the recession began, the percentage of workers receiving benefits fell dramatically below the levels of previous downturns. According to one study, less than 38 percent of U.S. unemployed workers received benefits in 1990 as compared with 75 percent in the 1974–75 recession.[83]

Other benefits were being reduced, too. As we have seen, in 1991 the Bush administration proposed to cut federal aid benefits to the middle class, not merely by increasing Medicare premium charges to those retirees with six-figure incomes but also by cutting school-lunch subsidies and by eliminating the eligibility of students from median-income families for federal college tuition aid.

Private retirement benefits were also weakening. As the 1990s began, firms across the United States were reducing benefits, terminating pension plans and failing to start new ones either because of financial pressures or because federal rules governing retirement programs were becoming increasingly expensive and complex to interpret. In 1989, according to the Association for Private Pension and Welfare Plans, about 15,856 defined-benefit pension plans were shut down, up 37 percent from 1988, while only 5,461 plans were created, a 67 percent drop. "Retiring with pension is becoming the exception, not the rule," a Kemper Financial Services publication indicated, citing Census Bureau figures that showed a significant decline in the percentage of workers covered by pension plans—from 55.7 percent in 1979 to 49 percent in 1990.[84] In previous decades since World War II, that coverage had been rising, so the decline was striking. Appendix C details these changes, including the sharp 1975–88 ebb in the percentage of U.S. workers with pensions that were federally insured. Keith Kilty, an Ohio State University professor researching retirement planning, went so far as to predict that "by the year 2000, people probably won't be able to retire at all," given the strains on the system. He predicted a steady increase in the age at which people retire, beginning in the early 1990s.[85]

Many employees still sure of a private pension had reason to doubt that health insurance coverage would come with it. Personal finance columnist Jane Bryant Quinn told her readers that "when you retire, your blanket (health) plan may be buried wherever the boss's promises go to die." Although some 25 million workers and spouses forty and up enjoyed lifetime company-paid health insurance, or believed they did, the odds were that many companies would be forced by future cost and profit pressures to alter or drop these promises, which had no legal backstop.[86]

In short, still another part of the American dream was at risk. Back in the 1970s, while median family income stagnated, and in the early 1980s, while hourly wages failed to keep up with inflation, employee benefits were a growth sector, even if runaway health costs gobbled up much of the increase. By the early 1990s, however, employee and retirement benefits, now diminishing, were no longer an exception to the tightening noose; they were shrinking, too.

Changing Households, Rising Life-style Pressures and Declining Leisure

In addition to the other aspects of the middle-class squeeze visible by the early 1990s, many counted the erosion of family life and the increasing costs imposed on the new "average" two-earner household with a working wife as well as husband. Families getting their extra income through a second earner paid for that help with added strains in dollars, emotional stress and lost leisure, little or none of it included as an offset to real income—and women lost the most.

The wage pressure was real enough. Husbands' inflation-adjusted salaries declined in 80 percent of married-couple households between 1979 and 1986, according to one estimate, and only a dramatic (18 percent) increase in the number of hours worked by wives kept a majority of these household incomes from falling behind the cost of living.[87] Many fell behind anyway. Traditional families, with just the husband working, on average lost even more ground.

In reality, though, the traditional U.S. family of the suburban white picket fence and mother-at-home 1950s stereotype wasn't really traditional at all—most eighteenth- and nineteenth-century wives had worked, albeit often at onerous household or farm chores rather than as part of the outside work force, so that America's mid-century families were a brief aberration. "After the war, all of our competitor nations were devastated," explained Martha Farnsworth Riche, an editor at *American Demographics* magazine. "Up until the 1960s, we had an unnatural competitive advantage and were making, in terms of real earnings, much more than we should have been. For the one and only time in our history, an ordinary guy with a high school degree could afford to have a non-working wife."[88] The 1970s, and still more the 1980s, were the painful economic transition that brought the aberration to an end.

The result was a slow reshaping of middle-class culture. More than before, families shattered in divorce, children returned home after graduating from college without jobs or unable to maintain a household of their own; and unrelated individuals grouped to share housing they could not otherwise afford. Divorce often dropped wives out of the middle class, and young people from solid suburban families found it hard to maintain middle-class status once they were on their own. Downward mobility was everywhere. Working divorced women with children could often keep their middle-class status and purchasing power only by moonlighting at a second job. The Bureau of Labor Statistics found in a late 1980s sampling that the number of women with two or more jobs had soared from 2.2 percent of 28.9 million working women in 1970 to 5.9 percent of the 52.8 million at work in May 1989.[89]

Even the two-earner family that held on to its middle-class status paid a stiff price, which is the concern of this subchapter. Princeton

University's Rebecca Blank, who studied two-income couples, noted that for many wives, going to work or returning to it could be a difficult decision "taking into consideration both what she will have to pay for child care and the increased expense the family is likely to incur for such things as more meals eaten out, assistance in the home or yard maintenance."[90] For a wife who might earn $18,000 a year, those costs—plus additional travel expenses, clothes and the like—might reach $6,000 to $8,000, yet government per capita and family income statistics would gather in the full $18,000, grossly overstating economic reality. According to one study cited by the Joint Economic Committee of Congress, the additional expenditures and taxes offset between one third and one half of the additional earnings of a second earner.[91]

Arranging child care was the largest of the nontax costs. It hit the poor hardest, with some families paying 15 to 25 percent of their income for care, but middle-class families paid about 6 percent.[92] Moreover, child-care expenses were rising faster than inflation, reaching an average of $49 per week in mid-1987, up 17 percent in thirty-two months relative to a CPI increase of just 10 percent.[93] By 1990 costs were higher still, especially in cities like Boston, where care averaged $5,664 a year; New York ($4,956); and Washington, D.C. ($4,548). Ogden, Utah, turned in the lowest figure—$1,992 a year.[94] In the major metropolitan areas, the maximum allowable child-care tax credit available to the middle class—$480 per child—constituted negligible relief. Many working women considered such a small credit insulting compared with the businessman's deductible lunches and hotel rooms.

Meanwhile, fewer could afford a home. In late 1989 Ira Gribin, president of the National Association of Realtors, summed up the new residential economics:

> There has been a definite trend over the past eight years. What is beginning to happen is that only the wealthiest families can afford housing. People with low incomes are being forced to move farther and farther from work and are having to drive one to two hours. This has begun to cause problems in families.[95]

In 1989 a Harvard University study suggested that the plummeting ratio of homeownership for households in the twenty-five- to twenty-nine-year-old group threatened "to produce a permanent underclass of disadvantaged renters and to jeopardize the long-term financial security of future generations."[96] The Census Bureau's own publication *Home Ownership Trends in the 1980s* reported that just 63.9 percent of households owned their own home in 1989, down from 65.6 percent in 1980.[97] Then in a 1991 report entitled *Who Can Afford to Buy a House?* the Census Bureau provided the unhappy answer: 57 percent of all households couldn't afford a median-priced house in their market with a conventional thirty-year fixed mortgage, and 48 percent couldn't swing even a modestly priced home (defined as one cheaper than 75 percent of the homes in that market)—including, of course, many lucky enough to already occupy a median or modest dwelling. Young families were particularly unable to buy, but even 37 percent of married couples could not afford a median home.[98]

California prices, in particular, were so high relative to incomes that by 1990 households of two or more unmarried individuals accounted for 12 percent of all statewide home sales, twice the rate of 1986. "The surge in the number of nontraditional households buying homes over the past five years was sparked by the state's continuing affordability crisis," said the president of the California Association of Realtors. "Affordability pressure has forced some unmarried individuals to form nontraditional households to make homeownership possible."[99] In and around New York City, a similar pressure could be seen; many of the middle class could not afford houses; working-class families could not afford apartments. Nationally, housing economist Michael Sumichrast complained that "it requires two members of families to buy a typical house, but even then it's sometimes impossible. We are approaching more European-type income-price house relationships, which is terrible, absolutely terrible."[100]

In parts of the nation the decline in housing prices starting at the end of the 1980s and continuing in the early 1990s eased this predicament—as did lower mortgage interest rates. But lower-middle- and middle-income Americans, in general, were still broadly priced out of the single-family home market, and not just by the price of housing itself. Legal, financial and government fees had grown so much that whereas back in 1952, it took a factory worker just one day to pay the closing costs on a new house in Levittown, then costing $10,000, the 1989 closing costs, broadly construed, on that same Levittown home, by then selling at roughly $100,000, would have required a number of weeks of work.[101]

In New England, although per capita income soared during the 1980s, housing costs rose even faster. In 1989, 40 percent of all renters were paying rents that were at least 30 percent or more of their household incomes. "People's incomes were consumed by the basics of shelter, which led to a deterioration in overall spendable income," according to Gary Ciminero, chief economist of Rhode Island's Fleet Financial Group.[101A]

Besides two-earner family expenses and the cost of housing, an increasing number of families was also burdened by the cost of providing for elderly parents—to say nothing of fears that health care and pension trends could increase this parental dependency. By 1991 Census Bureau analysts were suggesting that over the next three decades the number of dependent *elders*—aging relatives who need intermittent or even constant care—could wind up surpassing the number of dependent *children*.[102] Indeed, an internal survey by IBM found that the proportion of its employees with elderly dependents had doubled from 8 percent in 1986 to 16 percent in 1991.[103]

The toll on families was high. Pollyannas could burble about the enjoyment and benefits of new technology and products ranging from personal computers to videocassettes and microwavable "gourmet" meals, but for households below the top tier, these were often overshadowed by more pressing basic situations like unaffordable housing, escalating taxes, deteriorating services, undereducated children, declining leisure and eroding purchasing power. Not only was a record percentage of Americans working by the early 1990s, but they were working longer hours. Between 1979 and 1987, the average U.S. worker put in 95 more hours a year to make up for the decline in real wages, with the result that he or she was working 5.9 percent more hours at an hourly wage 3.3 percent less than in 1979.[104] By 1987 manufacturing workers in the United States spent more hours on the job each year than did their peers in Germany, France or Britain.

Though men were conscious of losing ground—of staying ahead of inflation only because of their wives' earnings—the larger leisure-time burden fell on women. Harvard economist Juliet Schor, attempting to calculate the impact of work both at home and at the job, estimated that, between 1973 and 1985, hours spent working rose from 40.6 to 48.8 while leisure time dropped from 26.2 hours to 17.7.[105] The decline in leisure particularly affected women, whose tasks at home did not ease much even after they took jobs, although cooking-time was reduced by new easily prepared foods and by eating out.

By the early 1990s, as companies thinned their ranks of employees, they were also starting to curb vacations and personal leave, and to demand more hours of work from those who remained. Vacations became use-them-or-lose-them propositions year to year, company picnics were disappearing, frequent-flier miles were becoming company property, personal days were shrinking and so were company outlays for conferences, staff training and personal development. Some companies were quietly extending workweeks for little or no extra pay, asking traveling employees to spend weekends away from home to get cheaper airline fares by staying over a Saturday, and requiring employees to accept one or two connecting flights instead of nonstop travel where that saved money.[106] Just before Labor Day, 1991, the *Chicago Tribune* reported that the length of an average American vacation had peaked in the mid-1980s and was shrinking fast, having fallen by almost one third.[107] Appendix C charts the decline.

In 1990 surveys began recording unprecedented frustration, especially among women. That year, Yankelovich, Clancy and Shulman, a market research firm, reported 80 percent saying they would quit their jobs or reduce their workload if they didn't need the money, a massive increase from just 39 percent a year earlier.[108] In Los Angeles and Orange counties, California, local survey-takers found 40 percent of fathers and 80 percent of mothers haunted by anxiety about spending too little time with their children and wishing they could quit their jobs.[109] Then in 1991 a study by the Americans' Use of Time Project at the University of Maryland determined that 61 percent of Americans, regardless of marital status, education or geographic location, were willing to sacrifice one or even two days' pay each week to have those days off. "We are at a point in history where, to most Americans, the value of time is reaching parity with the value of money," said project director John Robinson.[110]

As the quality of life seemed to deteriorate, more and more frustrated middle-class Americans were saying they wanted to get off the merry-go-round. For most, however, there was no getting off.

By the early 1990s, then, middle-class Americans found themselves beset on all sides. Government services were costing more in taxes and delivering less, forcing new outlays. Private services, in turn, usually involved soaring costs, rarely or reluctantly regulated by politicians loyal to the marketplace and to upper-bracket contributors. Employee benefits were eroding, and voters worried that future pensions were in greater jeopardy than corporate or government officialdom would admit.

As we saw in Chapter 5, rising taxes had turned nominal Middle American income gains into stagnation. The effect on households of unavoidable costs and fees surging far beyond the increase in the Consumer Price Index, conjoined with declining employee benefits, made that stagnation into something worse. Much of the great American middle class was losing ground—and knew it. For the median family of 1990, to send a child to a four-year private college cost 43 percent of annual income versus 30 percent back in 1970. To buy an average new car took 47 percent of that income in 1990, up from 35 percent in 1979.[111] In 1989 the mortgage payment on a median-priced family home required 33 percent of the median income of entry-level buyers in the twenty-five to twenty-nine age group, up from 21 percent back in 1969. To more and more Americans, the assurances of the 1980s seemed to have been betrayed.

Survey after survey showed that people were starting to sense that the so-called middle-class squeeze was really much more: a sign of America's declining position in the global economy, posing a real threat to their own futures and their children's. How they would respond—and whom they would blame—were also becoming important. As we will now explore in Part Three, fears of declining net worth and future economic jeopardy were in the air. Middle-class radicalization and the politics of frustration were gathering force.

THE POLITICS OF ECONOMIC FRUSTRATION

C H A P T E R 7

Economic Polarization, Shrinking Assets and the Implications of Middle-Class Decline

The 1973 period marked the beginning of the decline of the American standard of living. The Reagan years interrupted that trend by borrowing and spending, which led to the retrenchment that has deepened the current slump.

—Allen Sinai, chief economist of the Boston Company, 1992

And in the '80s a funny thing happened to the middle class, meaning, roughly, those who inhabit the middle of the income-distribution curve. If a middle-class life-style is defined by home ownership, vacations in Orlando and college for the kids, then a middle-size income was shrinking to the level of an inadequate pittance. While the price of housing and tuition went shooting through the roof, the median household income remained stuck where it has been ever since the late '70s, at about $30,000 a year. The curious result being that if you want to be middle class in the old-fashioned suburban sense, you need to be pretty near rich.

—Barbara Ehrenreich, author, 1992

. . . an imbalance between rich and poor is the oldest and most fatal ailment of republics.

—Plutarch, first century A.D.

A major deterioration in any nation's middle class is a profound cultural and political event—and by the early 1990s, as we have seen, the economic and psychological pressures building on Middle America were beginning to produce not only restiveness but occasional radical election results. Defenders of the policies of the 1980s insisted that middle-class decline was a myth, that, at worst, prosperity was simply changing gears, and that the silicon-chip economy of the twenty-first century would lead its American pioneers to unprecedented affluence. Yet the economic erosion of 1990 and 1991 provided an unsettling counterpoint—household net worth in the United States suffered its sharpest loss since the 1930s, while even in high-tech citadels from Massachusetts to California businessmen feared that America's entrepreneurial zenith had passed, that middle-class decline might be secular and long-term, not brief and cyclical.

As we will see in this chapter, such worries went beyond either the immediate job losses of the recession or the tax- and inflation-linked inroads on purchasing power discussed in Part Two. There was an equally unnerving erosion of assets, especially home values, and Americans also worried about their provisions for the future—pensions, annuities and insurance policies. If too many streets were no longer safe, neither were hard-won levels of home equity, the wherewithal to retire or even middle-class status itself. In Part Two, we looked at inroads on disposable and after-tax incomes; in Part Three, we will look at the larger threat to the middle class of economic polarization, weakening safety nets, endangered assets and fears that the next generation might not live as well as their parents—and then weigh the political and cultural effects and implications.

These fears have always been the stuff of political upheaval, especially when the rich get richer while the average person loses ground without quite understanding why—and also when the nation involved has just experienced its zenith of broad-based success. The more exhilarating the peak, the more alarming the valley. After the middle-class triumph of Holland's golden seventeenth century, the social stratification and economic decay of the eighteenth century eventually led to revolution. Similarly, after Britain's transformation from the mid-nineteenth-century middle-class workshop of the world to the extravagance of the Edwardian era, rising class politics produced the Labour party.

More recently, when such countries as Argentina, Uruguay, Australia and New Zealand lost the great agricultural export prosperity that had put them among the world's richest nations from 1900 to 1929 ("rich as an Argentine" was a cliché in London and Paris), frustrated voters grasped at social welfare schemes—often promoted with populist rhetoric—to maintain their living standards. In the 1930s the German middle and lower-middle classes, devastated by defeat in World War I and then by the inflation of the 1920s, turned to the populist far right under Nazism.

Closer to home for most Americans, Canadian voters reacted to the 1990–92 recession and their own middle-class squeeze by embracing the socialist New Democratic party in provincial elections from Ontario to Saskatchewan and British Columbia. Pundits started wondering whether the rise of the new populist conservative Reform party based in oil-rich Alberta might even mean the end of Canada's governing Conservative party. Though the politics of economic frustration varies from nation to nation, a pattern recurs where a middle-class standard of living is under pressure. In Chapter 9, I will look at how this started to happen in the United States as the 1990s began.

No comparable squeeze on the middle class could have taken place in the postwar quarter century when the interests of Middle America dominated the political agenda and the lessons of the 1920s and 1930s were still remembered. *De-polarization* had been the postwar vogue: as the middle grew stronger, those farther down could begin to rise, although the difficulty of achieving these hopes became increasingly apparent in the late 1960s. By the late 1970s or early 1980s, income and wealth began to polarize in the United States and most other major financial powers for the reasons we have seen in earlier chapters: a rightward shift in politics, accompanying upheavals in technology, and industrial and financial deregulation that favored people with capital, skills and education. Billionaires and centimillionaires flourished and multiplied under Reagan, as did cutting-edge portions of the middle class, especially those in finance, the professions, high technology and communications. At the opposite pole, as we have also seen, many of the working poor and substantial segments of the middle class were losing ground, especially those on overpaid Midwest production lines or overinflated corporate staffs, or otherwise propped up by the last fading artificial advantages that had favored the postwar U.S. economy for more than a generation after 1945. Fearful voters were beginning to wonder where it would end.

The Downscaling of Middle America?

The critical political question, rarely confronted by elected officials, was whether America was really in economic decline in the 1990s—and how much? Some of the evidence could be dismissed as merely short-term. Bankruptcies multiplied in the best-manicured areas of New York, New Jersey and Connecticut. Companies that made stretch limousines—the quintessential 1980s ego symbol—began to go out of business in 1990, and the New York Debutante Cotillion presented only half as many young women in December 1990 as in December 1989.[1] Such symptoms often reflect no more than the business cycle, and the *Forbes* and *Fortune* lists of America's richest men and women continued to show that most of the great fortunes were increasing.

Below the median income, however, Darwinian economic effects had already convinced some dispassionate marketing strategists to give some of their business and retail clients blunt new advice: *Go downscale*. The extremes, panhandlers and the homeless, might lack purchasing power, but "downscale" America—households with unskilled breadwinners and incomes circa 1991 below $25,000 a year—was a large market predicted to get larger despite upturns in the business cycle. Management Horizons, a retail consulting firm, projected that the number of households with annual incomes of $15,000 or less, as calculated in 1984 dollars (some $22,000 in 1991 dollars), would expand to 36 percent of the U.S. total in the year 2000, up from 31.2 percent in 1970 and about 34 percent in 1991.[2] Retail chains like Lerner's and catalog merchants like Fingerhut were already building high sales from nonaffluent consumers, and in late 1990 food retailers followed suit, as chains like McDonald's, Hardee's and Red Lobster posted new bargain meals. Harris Rusitzky, president of the National Restaurant Association, acknowledged "considerable evidence that customers now want a more casual, less structured, less expensive dining-out experience. To a great extent, casualization will be manifest in the down-scaling of existing restaurants."[3] He meant that eating out would be getting cheaper.

Whether in rural areas, manufacturing centers or service-industry suburbs, the downward pressure on the ordinary family's purchasing power was a fact of the early 1990s. All too frequently, job opportunities and incomes were shrinking. By 1988, well before the downturn, the U.S. General Accounting Office was even reporting a resurgence of small sweatshops—shops and factories that employed workers at low wages for long hours under poor conditions.[4] By January 1991, as the recession bit, 11 percent of Illinoisans, right in the heart of Middle America, were receiving some form of state assistance, and welfare recipients reached their highest number since the Great Depression.[5] Official national measurements of work-force unemployment remained in the neighborhood of 7 percent, but when underemployment was added, the total exceeded 12 percent.

Many of those affected were—or *had been*—in the middle class. When the Illinois Department of Revenue published data on the distribution of income for 1989 and appended similar statistics for 1980, the *Chicago Tribune* and First National Bank of Chicago published rough inflation-adjusted comparisons, and the polarization was stunning. Even before the recession of the early 1990s, the decline in well-paid manufacturing jobs had devastated middle-range incomes, while a surge in unearned income and sharp growth in highly paid professional and financial-services jobs bolstered gains at the top. "There was real growth in per-return dollars in the 1980s, but those figures lie," explained Diane Swonk, regional economist for the First National Bank of Chicago. "You didn't get growth in the bulk of the population. The bulk of people were getting poorer, while the rich were getting richer."[6] The number of million-dollar-a-year households in Illinois rose sixfold, from 920 to 5,860. However, the proportion of reportable earnings going to "middle Illinois" plummeted.

The shock was the erosion of the group making $50,000 to $100,000 in constant 1989 dollars. Back in 1980 those in the comparable income range ($32,876 to $65,750) had been 17.2 percent of the total; by 1989 that had fallen to 13.7 percent. The small upper tier, by contrast, boomed. The 4.2 percent of Illinoisans with adjusted gross incomes over $50,000 had mustered 19 percent of the state's reported income in 1980, but by 1989 the smaller 3.4 percent of all taxpayers making over $100,000 controlled a startling 29.9 percent of all reported Illinois income. Because a $50,000 income in 1980 equaled roughly $80,000 in 1989, the two groups were reasonably comparable in scope, yet the top 3.4 percent enjoyed a much larger share of state income than the top 4.2 percent had just nine years earlier.

This was polarization with a vengeance—the widening split between the 1 percent or 2 percent of increasingly wealthy haves and a growing bottom third of have-nots, as the great in-between postwar middle class quietly eroded. Mid–Corn Belt Illinois was no center of financial, social or communications glitterati; it was the Land of Lincoln, proudly so proclaimed by its own license plates, the site of cities like Peoria, America's colloquial synonym for middle-class culture, and of Chicago, Carl Sandburg's blue-collar "hog butcher" to the world. If polarization could drain the middle class there, it could do so anywhere. The downscaling of Middle America was real.

Polarization and the Upper-Middle Class: A Metaphor for America?

Yet Peoria, with its old-line economy, was not necessarily the right yardstick. Conservatives insisted that any significant decline in the middle class really reflected the number of middle-class earners crossing the $100,000-a-year line, where true affluence supposedly began. Magazine publisher Malcolm Forbes, Jr., excited by Census data showing that one American family in twenty-five had a 1990 income over $100,000, predicted that by the late 1990s, as the high-technology economy grew, one family in ten could rise to a comparable income. That, he thought, would make them allies of the Forbes 400: "Karl Marx would be proven right about the political power of the rich, but in a way he never would have believed possible—because there will be so many of them."[7] Most of those who anticipated this upward mobility expected it to relieve popular economic frustration. But some took a contrary perspective.

Social thinker Charles Murray hypothesized a nation in which the most prosperous 10 percent (or more) of Americans would cluster in privileged enclaves, leaving the public-service world of inadequate schools, unsafe streets, uncollected garbage and gridlocked transportation to the lower and middle classes—and taking their tax dollars with them. "The Left has been complaining for years that the rich have too much power," said Murray. "They ain't seen nothing yet."[8] Others who agreed that the top 10 percent of Americans would continue to gain while average families were forced downscale were more hopeful that mobility and new values could keep the economy and society vibrant. Yet there was something wrong with these glib assumptions about a pampered top tenth or fortunate fifth: decay and declining opportunity were even beginning to lap at the top 4 percent of families already making over $100,000.

In California's Silicon Valley, a survey in late 1991 by the *Los Angeles Times* found a pervasive worry, transcending the immediate recession. The big electronics firms weren't growing much, and many midsize companies were faltering; middle managers had few prospects for dramatic advancement, while intense competition was making successful start-up companies rare. As a result, "it is now clear to all but the most blindly ambitious that the vision of entrepreneurial riches is mostly myth."[9] Between April 1989 and April 1992 Silicon Valley lost about 6 percent of its electronics jobs—although that was a relatively minor loss compared with the steeper decline in electronics jobs in the Boston and Dallas areas.

Following the 1990 census, a study by the California governor's office of planning and research found that the "most remarkable" change was that rich "counties like San Mateo [adjacent to Silicon Valley] and Marin, and cities like Beverly Hills, Rancho Palos Verdes and San Marino, showed no gain and even population loss during the decade," mostly because potential residents could not afford these locations; that was true even of suburban children who had grown up there.[10] Instead, population was increasing in cheap, distant, end-of-the-freeway tract homes and in poor urban neighborhoods, where "much of the growth comes from immigrants doubling up or more in existing dwellings." Thousands of families, the report found, were housed, often illegally, in what had been residential garages.

Twenty-five hundred miles to the east in East Brunswick, New Jersey, at the crossroads of America's great pharmaceutical and medical-equipment corporations, the twelfth annual conference of the New Jersey Data Center agreed that the boom had ended. Houses would be less grand. "The upscale outer-suburb life style will fade," said Rutgers University demographer James Hughes. "The 80s consumer would pay anything to save time. Now people will drive to outlet stores to save money."[11]

The new high-technology economy was not proving to be an immediate boon to the ordinary householder any more than capitalism's previous breakthrough periods—the nineteenth-century Industrial Revolution and the great expansion of commerce in the sixteenth century following the Renaissance—had been.* Part of the problem was that the United States, even as it invented and launched the silicon chip, was also the seat of huge automobile, steel, machinery, textile and electronics industries, all of which had declined rapidly following the overseas spread of computer technology, robotics and other innovations that helped many nations with low wage scales develop advanced production facilities and outsell American producers. This globalization, in turn, obliged American firms to squeeze their workers, first blue-collar, then white-collar. Rising productivity no longer brought employees wage increases. By 1991–92, after serious corporate layoffs and the unsuccessful United Autoworkers' strike against Caterpillar, labor relations experts like Harley Shaiken at the University of California suggested that competitive pressures were striking at long-held American assumptions:

We've always seen aggressive managements in many industries. What's different now is that a number of companies who for most of the

---

*Both the period of the Renaissance and the rise of capitalism and the period of the Industrial Revolution were eras in which those who had capital, skills and education gained, often greatly, but ordinary people generally lost ground. The great economic historian Fernand Braudel has noted that during the two centuries of capitalist excitement from 1450 to 1650, the "progress made by the upper reaches of the economy and the increase in economic potential were paid for by the hardship of the mass of the people whose numbers were increasing as fast or faster than production" (Fernand Braudel, *The Perspective of the World, Civilization & Capitalism 15th–18th Century,* p. 87). And moving ahead to the earlier years of the Industrial Revolution in Britain, Braudel concluded: "I am inclined to agree with the earliest historians who studied the question, that there was indeed a deterioration in the well-being of the British masses, a decline in real wages, for farm labourers as well as for workers in factories or transport" (Braudel, op. cit., p. 614).

last 40 years operated on the basis of a certain social contract are rede-
fining the terms of that contract. It isn't just a back-alley machine shop
with 200 workers going after its union. It's AT&T violating seniority
rules. It's Caterpillar threatening to replace its work force. . . . Public
companies that would have shunned these tactics a decade ago are now
using them.[12]

If European peasants, artisans and small farmers in the mid-six-
teenth century and British manufacturing workers of 1825 saw that no
matter how hard they worked, they could not live as well as their
fathers, the same fear was overtaking tens of millions of young Americans of the 1990s, for whom yesteryear's high-paying factory and, to
a lesser extent, corporate white-collar jobs were just a memory. Employment in the new high-tech industries, by contrast, depended more
on education and therefore helped polarize wages and rewards.

Inadequate U.S. education was part of the threat. In 1990, 31 percent of men between the ages of thirty-four and forty-five had completed four years of college; in the younger twenty-five- to thirty-
our-year-old group, only 25 percent had done so, as college was
becoming less affordable.[13] Meanwhile, only 20 percent or so of Americans, according to Harvard's Robert Reich, had the training and skills
to compete in the tougher international economy of the postindustrial
era. Trade rivals like Japan and Germany, by contrast, were providing
35 to 40 percent of their populations with competitive technical and
educational skills. America's less well-equipped work force might not
be able to support a strong enough economy to maintain an economic
elite of 10 percent high-earners.* The elite might be much smaller.

Few debates went more to the heart of the economic future. One
prominent study prepared by the Hudson Institute for the U.S. Labor
Department assured policymakers that the new computer-chip economy would generate a dramatic "upskilling" of available jobs, thereby
increasing highly paid positions. The liberal Economic Policy Institute
replied that upskilling and occupational changes would come even
more slowly in the 1990s than in the 1980s.[14] In 1992 the Census
Bureau released a survey, supporting the Hudson Institute findings,
that argued that nearly three fifths of the 6 million jobs created between 1987 and 1989 were in high-paying, not low-paying, industries.
The deception, critics insisted, was that many of the jobs created in
"high-paying" industries like finance were actually low-paying back-
office positions. Skeptics also questioned the future contribution of

*Rising U.S. illiteracy was also a broader harbinger of a class society, but it was not usually
a middle-class problem. Inadequate education, however, often was.

U.S. exports, cautioning that while some were sophisticated—airplanes, entertainment products, drugs and medical technology—others were merely commodities that might as easily have been shipped from a low-wage Third World nation: soybeans, wheat, coal and unprocessed timber.

By late 1991 and 1992, corporations were being forced to break their "social contract" with upper-level as well as lower-level employees. As I discussed in the previous chapter, more and more managers saw their jobs and benefits at risk as company after company reduced its permanent work force in order to cut benefit costs with more part-timers or to "outsource" production and jobs to low-wage Mexico or Taiwan. Corporate chiefs, many of whom enjoyed record compensation, declared that their U.S.-based employees had to make do with less. "Wages overseas will come up, but one way or another, the gap will have to close," said Robert E. Mercer, chairman of the Goodyear Tire and Rubber Company. And the chief economist at General Electric, Walter Joelson, added: "Let's talk about the differences in living standards rather than wages. What in the Bible says we should have a better living standard than others? We have to give a bit of it back."[15]

If the top 1 percent was not much at risk, substantial parts of the upper-middle class were. Record numbers of stunned advertising managers, accountants and aerospace engineers found themselves on unemployment lines. Silicon chips would have to create a lot of new, highly paid jobs to make up for the millions of low, middle and even upper managerial positions eliminated as General Motors, Du Pont and 3M and multitudes of lesser firms reduced large and expensive staffs.

There was another problem, for even if new economic forces did increase the end-of-the-century ratio of American households with incomes over $100,000 in constant 1990 dollars from 4 percent to 10 percent, other circumstances were eroding that supposed income's real economic meaning—and had been doing so throughout the 1980s. Many ostensibly prosperous persons and families crossing the $100,000 line were on a treadmill, not an elevator.

Consider the hypothetical Jones family of Riverside, California, or Oceanside, New York. In 1980 Mr. Jones earned $40,000 a year while his wife had a half-time job that paid $10,000. By 1990, his salary had climbed to $65,000 while she drew $35,000 for going back to work full time. That put the Joneses into the magic $100,000-a-year category. Although inflation came to 60 to 70 percent for the decade, this left at least a $15,000 real gain, or it appeared to.

The real world of the middle class, however, made the actual result very different. The Joneses' federal income tax would have climbed from roughly $5,500 to about $9,000. Their combined FICA, or Social Security, burden would have risen from about $2,100 to about $6,000. Their state and local taxes—income, sales and property—probably doubled from $5,000 to $10,000. However, parts of the sales and property tax increases were also in the CPI (and would be factored into yearly inflation adjustments), so the remaining state and local tax increase can be set at $3,500. By this calculus, then, increased taxes would have eaten up roughly $10,000 of the after-inflation gain. In addition, Mrs. Jones's added expenses for going back to work full time drained off another $2,000 or so. Then there's the higher cost of child care or college expenses, neither of which had much weight in the CPI inflation calculus. If we assume that the Jones family had either small children or collegians, then because tuition roughly doubled during the 1980s and day-care costs were not far behind, either burden could easily have increased by over $2,500 during the decade.

So much for the nominal gain. Already, $14,500 is gone, with nothing to show for it—and no adjustment has yet been made for health care; automobile insurance; lawyers' fees; water bills; federal, state and local government fees; cable television charges; prescription drug costs; and other important areas where the burden on middle-class families far outran the CPI. For many families like the Joneses, it's possible that the whole $15,000 to $20,000 of after-inflation extra income disappeared without any notable gain in living standard.

Yet it was individuals or families like these, doubling incomes from $50,000 in 1980 to $100,000 in 1990 or from $55,000 to $110,000, who pushed 4 percent of all households above the Census Bureau's $100,000 frontier versus a little over 1 percent a decade earlier. But if most of these gains were unreal, then the significance of $100,000-a-year households expanding from 1 percent to 4 percent of the population was also largely illusory. One angry California taxpayer expressed the frustration: "Earning $100,000 doesn't make you wealthy in Southern California. I have a lot of friends in the same tax bracket, and they'll tell you that they are barely getting by. The last thing we need is to get hit with a rich man's tax."[16] The average-income family, of course, was worse off, because as income brackets dropped toward the median, nominal gains got smaller. Slackening public services aggravated the problem, and as later sections of this chapter will show, a parallel decline in assets and net worth provided an even more disquieting signal.

By the early 1990s, social scientists and pollsters perceived a related change: that so many years of stagnant incomes had begun to affect the middle-class psyche. Earlier psychologies rooted in unprecedented U.S. affluence—in which homeownership, upward mobility and high levels of consumer spending were assumed to be American birthrights—were breaking down in favor of a new one. Young householders, in particular, while still pursuing the good life, were beginning to pick their purchases to simulate affluence, not to achieve it.[17] A suburban home with two reasonably new cars in the garage might be unachievable—as it had not been for their fathers and mothers in 1954 or 1963—yet a chic alternative (and more akin to the tastes of stratified urban Europe) could be achieved by concentrating money on stylish clothing, compact disc players and sophisticated wine and food.

Economically, then, even large portions of the upper-middle class were not secure. To call them new rich was silly. Only two and a half million people in America's top 1 percent of households, with annual incomes ranging upward from $250,000 and net worth typically well above a million dollars, were clearly on the winning side of economic polarization. The clearest winners of all were those ranging from 100,000 decamillionaires to billion-dollar households to which ordinary bills were no great bother. Yet for seemingly prosperous Americans in the top tenth of the population but short of the top 1 percent, the nineties brought surprising economic uncertainty. White-collar suburbs and high-tech centers seemed almost as nervous as Peoria.

Debt, Eroding Home Prices and Declining Middle-Class Net Worth

The record buildup of debt and speculation during the Reagan years, combined with the wicked rise and fall in home prices, provided an ominous accompaniment to the polarization of income. By 1992, things were just as bad or worse on the net-worth side of the ledger. We have seen how between 1983 and 1989 the top 1 percent of Americans increased their share of the nation's total wealth from 31 percent to 37 percent, a level unmatched since the 1920s. For many middle-income families, however, the economic changes of the Reagan years wound up depressing their net worth.

Household debt soared during the 1980s, mirroring the devil-may-care attitudes of Washington and Wall Street. For investors, debt became "leverage," and often worked to enlarge wealth. Many middle-income households, however, borrowed not to invest but to pay for a house or college or simply to stay afloat, and the debt they took on during the 1980s became a major offset to nominal gains in income and assets.

According to the Federal Reserve Board, American households as a whole increased their combined home mortgage and consumer debt almost threefold during the 1980s—from $1.3 trillion in late 1980 to just under $3.4 trillion at the end of 1990.[18] This was about 50 percent faster than the rate at which consumers' income grew. In 1991, the average household owed about $35,000 and paid interest of about $3,500 per year, almost 18 percent of its disposable income.[19]

But economists disagreed over what the new indebtedness meant— for families and for the nation as a whole. Optimists said that households could easily service higher payments because assets had increased even faster than debt. Worriers said that federal statistics based on averages camouflaged critical differences between the rich, the middle-class and the poor. The rich—the familiar top 1 percent of Americans—had borrowed enormous sums to invest and speculate with, but for the most part (real estate developers and builders were a troubled exception), their net worths, fattening with the stock market, had expanded far more than their debt. They could pay their notes.

For the bottom 80 percent of the population, though, debt ratios appear to have risen sharply even while incomes and assets were relatively stagnant, suggesting that a lot of their borrowing was to make up for declines in wages or purchasing power. Prominent proponents of this interpretation, such as Robert Pollin, author of a study entitled *Deeper in Debt,* were often sharp critics of Reaganism.[20] Nevertheless, considerable evidence supported their arguments. Even during the ostensible prosperity of the late 1980s, the nation's savings rate had fallen, partly because so many families had no margin to save. Then during the 1990–91 recession, foreclosures and bankruptcies increased, reaching an all-time record of nearly one million in 1991. Federal bankruptcy courts expanded and bankruptcy law became a growth industry. Tens of millions of Americans, many in the middle class, obviously had been borrowing to stay afloat.

Broad government data don't show how much more of its disposable income the typical middle- or upper-middle-class family was spending on debt service in 1990 or 1991 relative to 1980 or 1981. One credible private estimate was that in 1990 *overall* U.S. household debt service consumed 14 percent of disposable income, up only a little from 13 percent at the start of the 1980s, when interest rates were sky-high, but well above the 11.5 percent of 1987.[21] As for a typical two-earner family with an income that rose from $30,000 in 1980 to $50,000 in 1990, it's possible that the cost of debt service climbed from 15 to 16 percent of disposable income to 18 percent. As we have seen, the share of U.S. personal income spent on a combination of debt service, taxes, Social Security and health insurance soared—up from 33 percent in 1980 to 40 percent in 1990 (see the chart on page 94). For the average family, debt service was one of the Four Horsemen of slowly declining purchasing power.

Debt's impact on net worth, however, was even more damaging. According to the Census Bureau, the typical household's net worth, which had been $37,000 in 1984, actually *fell* slightly over the next four years, based on a national sample of twenty-four thousand households, which the bureau acknowledged involved very few wealthy families.[22] The latter had done much better. The Forbes 400 richest Americans almost doubled their net worth from $125 billion to $220 billion during these same four years.[23]

This divergence of net worth between the top 1 percent and the stagnant middle worsened as the overstretched economy slid into the 1990–92 recession. Depressed by soaring bankruptcies and plummeting home values, real household net worth—assets minus liabilities—sank by 5.8 percent in 1990, the biggest decline since the Federal Reserve Board started keeping records in the early 1950s.[24] As we shall see, much of the slide hit ordinary families, especially in the value of their homes. The circumstances of the rich varied. Yet three quarters of those in the Forbes 400 continued to gain from 1990 to 1991, with their combined net worth rising another $15 billion.[25]

In troubled New England one survey for local banks found that among a sample of one thousand regional professional and managerial households in the thirty-five- to fifty-four-year-old age bracket and with an average income of $55,000, fully 53 percent were at or near a negative-equity position in 1992. After a buying binge in the 1980s, the cash liquidation value of their assets, including real estate, was near or below their total outstanding debt. Nationally, the "nebbies"—negative-equity baby boomers—were estimated to constitute 20 to 30 percent of their age bracket.[25A]

The wealth that different groups added during the 1980s depended on the types of assets they held. The rich, from billionaires down to the approximately 100,000 decamillionaires, derived most of their wealth from business ownership and financial investments. If we start with the Forbes 400, add some 1,200 to 1,500 other Americans with net worths of over $100 million, and then add the decamillionaires, whose members ballooned from 30,000 in 1982 to 100,000 by the end of the 1980s, this entire group may well have increased its net worth by $1.5 to $2.5 trillion. The remainder of top 1 percent America—another 900,000 families—probably added an average of $800,000 per household, for a total of $700 billion. Overall, one can plausibly conclude that the top 1 percent might have garnered some $3 trillion of the $7 trillion of new net worth added by households during the 1980s. This overall $7 trillion increment, it should be underscored, was in *nominal* dollars; using inflation-adjusted 1982 dollars, the expansion of U.S. household net worth was only $3 trillion—up from $10 trillion in 1982 to $13 trillion in 1989. Furthermore, it's entirely plausible to assume that the top 1 percent got some 40 to 50 percent of the increase in household net worth because these families already had roughly 31 percent of the existing wealth, and, more specifically, they held about half of the individually owned corporate stock, two thirds of the bonds, an even higher percentage of the municipal bonds, and roughly 45 percent of the nonresidential real estate!* What was going up during the 1980s was mostly what they owned.

Ordinary Americans, by contrast, had most of their assets in less-favored real estate—in their houses, farms or small commercial properties. According to the Census Bureau, 43 percent of collective U.S. net worth in 1988 came from homeowners' equity.[26] Right up to the 95th percentile, the solid middle class was home-dependent because only the top 1 percent or 2 percent of U.S. households had most of their net worth in financial assets like stocks and bonds. Even for taxpayers with net worths of $100,000 to $200,000, most of whose incomes would have been in the top fifth, homes were all-important.

The consequence was that the disinflationary 1980s worked *for* the wealthiest households that held financial assets and *against* the net worth of the middle and upper-middle classes that was so dependent on personal residences. In 1982, when Washington responded to inflation with higher interest rates, Murray Weidenbaum, chairman of the President's Council of Economic Advisers, predicted that disinflation would bring "a major redistribution of wealth," at the expense of the American homeowner.[27] Which is exactly what happened. Home prices soared in a few locales during the 1980s—Hawaii, California, New England and the New York–Washington megalopolis (regions where demand was bolstered by large concentrations of financial and profes-

---

*Indeed, the Federal Reserve Board estimate, released in 1992, that the top 1 percent of Americans increased their share of the nation's wealth from 31 percent in 1983 to 37 percent in 1989 suggests that they must have collected at least 50 percent of the new wealth created during this period.

sional workers). Nationally, though, the Census Bureau later estimated that the median value of owner-occupied homes rose only modestly from $47,200 in 1980 to $79,100 in 1990, about 5 percent after inflation—and the true increase for *preexisting* homes was even less, possibly a decline, because the nation's housing stock was enlarged and improved during the 1980s by many high-priced new houses with central air conditioning and other amenities.[28] In the 1970s, by contrast, the median value of the owner-occupied housing had increased 39 percent even after adjustment for inflation.

In the hardest-hit places—Oil Patch cities like Houston or Baton Rouge or Farm Belt centers like Omaha—home prices were virtually the same in 1990 as they had been back in 1980, which meant huge after-inflation declines for the owners. In constant dollars, local net worths sank. Yet even in more typical metropolitan areas like Cincinnati, Milwaukee and St. Louis the fact that housing prices added 20 percent or 30 percent in nominal dollars faded to real 25 percent to 30 percent losses for homeowners after inflation. In Milwaukee, where television producers had set the location of *Happy Days,* the nostalgia-for-the-1950s television show, the *Milwaukee Journal* sorted data from the 1990 federal housing census into a vivid front-page portrait of "a punishing decade" for Wisconsin homeowners. Expressed in real 1991 dollars, the 1980 statewide median home value had been $87,000 and fell to $65,900 by 1990, a decline of 25 percent. In metropolitan Milwaukee, the decline was slightly higher.[29] Nothing of this sort had happened since the 1930s. Roughly half of America's major metropolitan areas chalked up at least 15 percent inflation-adjusted drops in home values.*

Nor were principal residences the only personal real estate losing ground. According to the business-backed Conference Board, the total value of farmland in the United States fell from $712 billion in 1980 to $392 billion in 1986, although part of that loss was recovered later in the decade.[30] In mid-1991, the U.S. vacation-home market was so weak that in Nantucket, Massachusetts, where 82 percent of the island's homes were vacation residences, prices had fallen 35 percent in 1989, slipped 11 percent further in 1990 and were continuing to drop in 1991. In the overbuilt resort of Hilton Head, South Carolina, the price of two-bedroom condominiums dropped from $90,000 in 1986 to $40,000 in 1991.[31]

Increased debt not only drained the average family income but

---

*Moreover, even in areas where housing prices nominally doubled, the increase after inflation was only 30 percent. In a sale by someone who had bought in 1980, capital gains taxes, fees and real estate broker commissions would eat up most of that.

reduced equity in the family home. Even as the inflation-adjusted value of homes declined—which during the mid-1980s happened mainly in the oil and farm states and Rust Belt but then from 1989 to 1992 concentrated in California, Florida and the Northeast—expanding mortgages and home-equity loans also reduced net worth. From the mid-eighties to 1990, home values in the United States rose by roughly $1 trillion, but because home-mortgage debt (including home-equity loans) increased even faster, homeowner equity actually *declined.* The Census Bureau reported that the average homeowner had $43,070 of equity in 1988, down from $46,106 in 1984.[32] In 1989 and 1990, the mortgage-debt surge further accelerated, as the hard-pressed middle class channeled its borrowing through second mortgages and home-equity loans, which were among the few loans on which interest payments still qualified for federal tax deductibility in the 1990s.

For the average family's net worth, the declining home values, combined with stepped-up use of second mortgages and home-equity loans, often meant a significant write-down. For 1990, alone, the Mortgage Bankers Association reported a stunning 15.7 percent drop in the equity that Americans held in their homes, the sharpest one-year decline since record-keeping began in 1945.[33] Mortgage debt as a percentage of total home value jumped to 57.6 percent in 1990, up from 50.5 percent in 1990 and just 36.7 percent in 1980.

Automobile values, another major component of net worth for median- and average-income families, also sagged. By early 1992, as the devastation of the U.S. automobile industry became clear, industry analysts explained that one of the reasons was the excessive debt on existing cars:

> All of a sudden, 60% of the cars that have been financed over the last few years were under water (they actually had negative equity in them). So when people walked into a dealership thinking they had a car to trade in, in fact they still owed several thousand dollars on the car that was sitting outside. They were unable to buy the car because they had a balance sheet problem. They didn't have the values and assets they thought they did.[34]

Facing this kind of undertow, real household net worth declined sharply in 1990 and then stabilized in 1991. And fears of what else might be involved were also real. The average family's deposits in the thousands of savings and loan associations that fell into insolvency during the 1980s had been protected, but the commercial bank failures of the 1990s raised new questions about the adequacy of federal deposit insurance. In some midsize failures, like New York's Freedom National Bank, accounts over $100,000 were not fully covered. Credit unions were another potential problem; in 1991, more than 150,000 Rhode Islanders had their savings immobilized in a credit union collapse.

Collapses and bankruptcies of insurance firms were also a worry, although they remained on a small scale. As a rule, when an insurance company failed, policyholders were covered for the losses up to $100,000 for policy values and up to $300,000 for death benefits by the individual state-operated funds of the National Organization of Life and Health Guaranty Associations.[35] In the early 1990s, however, as failure overtook major insurance companies like Mutual Benefit Life and Executive Life, skeptics noted that one or two major collapses could wipe out the thinly financed state guaranty associations. In Louisiana, where forty-seven insurance firms, mostly small, collapsed between 1986 and 1991, tens of thousands of people lost annuities or found themselves with unpayable claims. The New Orleans *Times-Picayune* worried that the state's private insurance system might collapse.[36]

While the shambles in Louisiana was unique, experts identified three other acknowledged vulnerabilities in the insurance safety net. The first affected the 3 to 4 million Americans who, willingly or by employer arrangement, drew their retirement benefits in the form of annuities from insurance companies. Howard Weizmann, executive director of the Association of Private Pension and Welfare Plans, called retirement annuities "the Achilles heel of the private retirement system" because, unlike defined benefit pensions, they were not covered by the federal Pension Benefit Guarantee Corporation.[37] A second problem area, insurers agreed, lay with title insurance—the virtually unregulated segment of the industry that provided protection to U.S. real estate owners by guaranteeing their titles to the property. As claims soared in the early 1990s, both Wall Street analysts and the Federal National Mortgage Association became concerned about the adequacy of the title insurers' reserves.[38] With the failure of a major title company, worriers argued, millions of homeowners and lenders would be vulnerable until they found another title insurer, and the real estate industry could be snarled. A third weakness lay in health insurance coverage. When Blue Cross and Blue Shield of West Virginia failed in October 1990, it left fifty thousand policyholders with $42 million in unpaid medical bills.

Retirement pensions, in turn, were another "asset" that voters worried about. As we have seen in Chapter 6, steadily fewer Americans were covered by the private pension system, and many of those who thought they were covered had reason for concern. During the 1980s, scores of major corporate pension funds had been tapped—most of the time legally—by corporate raiders or by a nervous management in need of money. In other instances, financially troubled corporations had simply stopped making payments to their pension funds, knowing that the Pension Benefit Guarantee Corporation, the Washington-based federal safety net, was obliged to pay defined-benefit pensions to retirees after their companies or plans had failed. By 1991, PBGC had taken over payment of 125,000 individual pensions, up from 28,000 in 1980. In November of that year, however, nervous PBGC officials announced that the nation's fifty largest underfunded corporate pension plans alone had a potential shortfall of $21.5 billion, up 50 percent from the year before.[39] Because the PBGC was already in the red, executive director James Lockhart worried that "unless we find a way to stop the growth of our deficit, the specter of ever-increasing premiums and ultimately an S&L-type bail-out looms over our future."[40] "People are already losing benefits," Lockhart said in 1992. "We see some sad stories" of retirees whose pension checks are halved after the PBGC takes over and can offer only a maximum annual pension of about $28,000.[40A]

Public-employee pensions also stirred some concern. Experts testifying before a joint hearing of the House Select Committee on Aging and the Joint Economic Committee in late 1991 warned that millions of Americans might never collect the pensions owed them because economically strapped state and local governments were raiding public-employee pension funds. In California that year, the governor and legislature sought to take $1.6 billion from the state workers' pension fund to apply to the huge budget deficit, and in Illinois $21 million was transferred out of the state pension fund to help meet the deficit despite the state comptroller's insistence that state pension funds were underfunded by $10 billion. One expert told the hearings that six major pension funds—teachers' plans in West Virginia, Oklahoma, Maine and Washington, and state employee plans in Maine and Massachusetts—were "in such bad shape that assets were insufficient to meet benefit payments for current retirees."[41]

Despite the FICA tax increases of the 1980s, many workers doubted the future solvency of the federal Social Security system. In late 1991 Dorcas Hardy, Social Security commissioner during the Reagan era, published a book entitled *Social Insecurity,* in which she called the system "a ticking time bomb. In the next century the United States will face a potentially devastating crisis: the retirement checks that should be sent to benefit millions of Americans will not be there." Her concern echoed that of Daniel P. Moynihan and other U.S. senators. "The Treasury," Hardy said, "siphons the money off to pay for current operations, and in exchange it gives Social Security an IOU. When the IOU comes due, there will be no money in the Treasury to pay it off, so one way or another, at that point Congress will have to raise revenue" from taxes or bonds.[42] Other former senior Social Security officials criticized Hardy for making unnecessarily alarming statements, but she was voicing fears widely shared by the public. The nation's pension system, like the single-family home, showed signs of becoming a weak link in the American Dream.

In the 1930s homes and other assets lost 30 to 45 percent of their value across much of the United States and household net worth plunged.* Many families had no safety net, and New Deal programs and agencies like Social Security, the Federal Deposit Insurance Corporation and federally insured mortgages were established to create one. The early 1990s stirred some new concerns. But there were also differences. In the early 1930s, Hoover's hands-off Republican administration did not decide which groups would be protected and which would not as the economy unraveled. Sixty years later, the Bush administration would manage the implosion in behalf of America's financial assets holders.

The Imploding Debt-and-Speculative Bubble of 1989–92 and Its Effects on Polarization and Wealth Distribution

The Reagan administration's controversial budget director, David Stockman, gone from Washington to Wall Street before the debt-and-speculative bubble finally popped in the late 1980s, later described it as "a once-in-50-year flood-type of cycle that happened because a generation that had learned all the lessons from the last great correction finally left the financial system. That's about where we were in the 80s. We were due for a final era of excess."[43]

After the great collapses of 1893 and 1929, conservative presidents Cleveland and Hoover let the speculative breakdowns play themselves

---

*One landmark study by Robert Williams, a UCLA professor, showed Los Angeles home prices declining steadily from 1925 to 1940, slipping from a median $7,660 to $4,200 ("Unlike Stocks, Home Prices Rarely Collapse," *Los Angeles Times,* August 28, 1988).

out. So many financial institutions failed in 1893 that U.S. bank deposits shrank by almost one third. There were enormous losses in the stock market and in speculative railroad bonds. Almost forty years later, Republican Secretary of the Treasury Andrew Mellon made his famous but impolitic remark about letting weak companies, financial institutions, farmers and investors go under and be replaced by strong ones. In neither downturn was federal deposit insurance available to prevent panics and protect depositors. As for the Federal Reserve Board, it did not yet exist in the 1890s, and although it did exist during the crisis of 1930–33, its governors declined to assume a countercyclical role.

The late 1980s and 1990s were different. After the 508-point stock market crash of October 1987 the Reagan and then the Bush administrations, along with the Republican-controlled Federal Reserve Board, sought to head off a major economic downturn and control the limited implosion that slowly developed. With the help of the ill-fated Federal Savings and Loan Insurance Corporation (FSLIC) and the Federal Deposit Insurance Corporation (FDIC), the economy did not collapse as it had in the earlier downturns, despite the S&L debacle and the sharp drop in real estate prices. But what was also unusual was that the post-1987 financial implosion was generally managed in behalf of the same classes and economic strata that had enjoyed and profited from the pre-1987 boom.

One reason, beyond general party loyalties, was that many powerful executive branch officials, including Bush and his close friend James Baker were Texans from a financial culture where bank failures, real estate collapses and bankruptcies were not abstract but involved familiar faces—friends, relatives, political allies and campaign contributors. From leveraged-buyout architect Henry Kravis to real estate developer Trammell Crow, many leading 1980s speculators were also allies and campaign contributors. The chairman of the Federal Reserve Board, Alan Greenspan, was not just an economist but a New York money manager and consultant who had written a testimonial letter for Charles Keating, who was later to be convicted in the S&L scandal. Greenspan said that Lincoln Savings and Loan, Keating's flagship, was as sound as seventeen other "thriving" thrifts, sixteen of which wound up bankrupt.[44] Unlike Andrew Mellon, none of these high officials believed in letting the overextended speculators and developers go under in the name of a cleansing, rehabilitating financial Darwinism.

Consequently, as events unfolded after 1987, from the October

Crash through the 1988–89 S&L debacle to the 1990–92 crisis of junk bonds, real estate, banking and insurance, key Washington decisions were made with great concern for financial markets, banks, speculators and highly leveraged transactions, having the taxpaying middle class pay to bail these interests out. The results upheld the redistribution of the 1980s.

The most blatant example was the mammoth cost of sorting out the large portion of the savings and loan industry that had taken advantage of deregulation to speculate in everything from real estate to art and junk bonds, leading to numerous failures, sometimes through what amounted to open looting by owners. The initial stage of Washington's negligence—the excesses of deregulation, inept supervision and political protectiveness toward wrongdoers—was essentially bipartisan. It was the next stage, the costly financial mismanagement of the bailout, largely by the executive branch, that had a profound impact on the distribution of U.S. wealth and income.

In 1988, as the magnitude of the breakdown was becoming obvious to those directly involved, the Reagan administration's first approach was further privatization: groups of almost insolvent or insolvent S&Ls were assembled for sale to private buyers (corporate and individual) at low prices made even more attractive by huge tax breaks and subsidies. Thus the government's books didn't show a payout from the FSLIC insurance fund. The General Accounting Office later estimated that these hastily given tax breaks cost the government $8.5 billion (federal regulators ultimately sought the return of some of the money and commitments given in several of the major late-1988 deals).[45] This, however, was a prelude. A much larger burden fell on the public when the Bush administration, wanting to minimize immediate costs and afraid to alarm voters, decided to finance the bailout with federal bonds, issued off-budget by a quasi-governmental corporation, to be paid off over thirty years. Experts set the ultimate cost to taxpayers at between $300 billion and $500 billion—$1,200 to $2,000 for each American alive in 1990—and economists from Stanford University contended that over those forty years, total outlays might reach $1.3 trillion, with $900 billion representing interest payments alone.[46]

The overall U.S. economy also suffered, although estimates varied widely. The Congressional Budget Office, using a computer model designed to simulate the effects on the national income of the capital resources lost in the bailout, figured the overall loss for the years between 1980 and 2000 at about $484 billion, with the highest annual impact in the early 1990s—about $40 billion a year. As of early 1992, according to *The New York Times,* that was roughly equivalent to the output lost up to that point in the 1990–92 recession![47]

Ralph Nader's Public Citizen group argued that instead of issuing bonds several hundred billion dollars' worth of taxes should be levied over the next five to ten years on those who had been participants in the 1980s speculative bubble. Public Citizen praised a proposal that included an additional 7.5 percent tax on unearned income—interest, dividends and capital gains.[48] Other critics generally urged surcharges on individual and corporate income. Publisher William Randolph Hearst called for a 25 percent surtax on the profits of every bank or S&L that sold junk bonds or made bad loans until taxpayers were repaid for the cost of the bailout.[49] Self-styled populist Jim Hightower, chairman of the Financial Democracy Campaign, proposed surcharges on incomes above $540,000 a year and taxes on large currency trades. "The wealthy folks, those who had the party and made the mess in the 1980s, should pay for it in the 1990s," said Hightower, characterizing the administration's program as a "class transfer" of wealth from the middle class to the rich.[50] At the very least, the bailout spared investors who had moved deals and funds through high-flying S&Ls during the 1980s from paying for the costs of the breakdown. The generality of taxpayers would pay instead.

Then in 1991 it became clear that commercial banks also needed to be rescued—and with kindred considerations at stake: would investors and financial elites pay, or would taxpayers as a whole? That spring, Treasury Secretary Nicholas Brady had asked Congress for a package of $70 billion in taxpayer-backed loans to the Federal Deposit Insurance Corporation, denying that another bailout was under way because the bankers had pledged to repay the money when they were healthy again. Others thought the cost would be much higher. Congress reluctantly voted the funds, although skeptics suggested that instead of opening up yet another line of public credit, it would be cheaper to let some of the big banks fail and have the government reimburse depositors only up to $100,000 for each account. That, however, would have involved major losses by banks' stockholders, bondholders, creditors and large depositors.

Meanwhile the federal government was abetting a second, less obvious rescue of financial institutions, with the result that their profits—except in a few incurable cases—rose substantially.* Chairman Greenspan moved Federal Reserve Board deposits to needy institu-

---

*The prices of bank stocks also soared in 1991, rewarding shareholders.

tions, including Lincoln Savings and Loan. As identified by conservative financial columnist Warren Brookes, the Fed made huge "overnight" loans reaching nearly $100 million to Lincoln, just as it was about to fail, keeping the wolf away from the door for four months "to allow all those depositors with accounts of more than $100,000 to get out 'whole' from the Lincoln mess without losing a dime."[51] Otherwise, large deposits made in search of high rates would not have been covered because federal deposit insurance stopped at $100,000.

In Chapter 6 we saw how banks imposed new charges and fees on depositors and checking-account holders without objection from regulators, permitting them to charge customers indirectly for the sharply rising cost of federal deposit insurance, in effect billing the cost of their earlier speculative practices to the public. Next, and far more significant, as the Federal Reserve Board relentlessly cut interest rates, letting banks reduce what they paid depositors and holders of checking accounts, regulators allowed the banks, many of them hard-pressed, to keep charging borrowers sky-high rates for credit-card interest and personal loans. Appendix C shows what dropped and what didn't. The spread was one of the largest and most profitable on record; commercial banks that ended 1991 paying depositors 4½ percent on their short-term money were charging ordinary borrowers three to four times as much.

Angered by the gap, Democrats on the House Banking Committee introduced legislation to require the nation's credit-card issuers, including banks, to "share the wealth" with borrowers by reducing their charges.[52] In late 1991 the Senate actually passed legislation to cap credit-card interest-rate charges, but then backed off when the stock market appeared to tremble. There were other implications for wealth distribution that went far beyond bank profits. As Chairman Greenspan eased interest rates, helping speculators and banks as well as small businessmen and would-be home buyers, a few economists, such as John Williams of American Business Econometrics, calculated a net drag on the economy as huge numbers of Americans, especially middle-class retirees, would suffer as interest payments tumbled. At the beginning of 1990, interest had represented 15 percent of U.S. personal income. In the next two years that percentage took its biggest slide since World War II.[53] Williams calculated that the four-point decline in short-term interest rates between autumn 1989 and autumn 1991 had caused a $34-billion-a-year drop in household interest income—a dangerous contraction—while interest payments by households fell by only $4 billion a year.[54] A significant chunk of the $30 billion net household loss was going from the pockets of Florida widows and retired Iowa farmers to financial institutions.*

As a result, there was little change in the distribution of wealth and income during the 1990s, despite the weakness of the economy and the financial and real estate crises. In 1991 the largest number of Americans since the Great Depression were receiving public assistance, average-family net worth was sliding and troubled state and local governments were raising taxes on everything from homes to potato chips to speeding tickets. Yet in 1992 the stock market was setting new highs, federal tax rates on the rich remained close to their post-1932 lows and bank stocks were climbing again, a sharp contrast with 1893–96 and 1929–33. Those crises, however, had not been managed by an activist government in behalf of the same financial elites that had created the bubble.

The Decline of Young America and the Trend to Wealth by Inheritance

For young Americans, those under thirty or thirty-five, two decades of polarization had brought a special, though widely unappreciated, irony: not only were they (and those younger) in danger of being the first generation of Americans to suffer a lower standard of living than their parents, but they would be the first generation to receive—or not receive—much of their economic opportunity from family inheritance, not personal achievement.

By the early 1990s it had become a cottage industry for journalists to show how young Americans were losing ground. Hardly any could buy a home. Many could not even afford to marry. Young men with only a high school education, who could have gone into steel plants or auto factories—and earned blue-collar middle-class wages—back when postwar America enjoyed the economic hegemony won at Bastogne and Iwo Jima, now faced what Brookings Institution economist Gary Burtless called "a future of lousy jobs." Only the skilled 25 percent, the college-educated, had middle-class opportunities. Huge numbers of others found themselves caught up in what some called the K-Mart Economy—low-paid employment in retail stores, discount centers, back offices and fast-food emporia.

---

*When the Federal Reserve Board's interest-rate reductions finally brought serious declines in mortgage interest rates in late 1991 and early 1992, the benefit to ordinary households increased, but Williams and some other economists contended that the near-term effects on overall household income were still negative.

Some of the statistics were extraordinary. Back in 1950 the average thirty-year-old man would have added 58 percent more pay by the time he reached forty, and in 1960 his successor would have added 44 percent more over those same ten years. By contrast, the thirty-year-old of 1977 had gained only 21 percent more by 1987.[55] In terms of real purchasing power, the earnings of a typical thirty-year-old high school graduate of 1991 bought about 20 percent less than the earnings of his counterpart of 1973, when the great postwar expansion came to an end. Research by the Children's Defense Fund and the Center for Labor Market Studies at Northeastern University developed an even more stark analysis. The average earnings, in 1986 dollars, of families headed by someone under thirty dropped from $19,243 in 1973 to $13,607 in 1987, a decline of nearly 30 percent. The drop was even larger—36 percent—for young families with children; and young families headed by high school dropouts lost nearly 52 percent. During the early years of the Great Depression, by comparison, the loss of purchasing power by Americans was roughly 27 percent.[56]

Meanwhile, persons between the ages of forty-five and seventy-five controlled the overwhelming bulk of America's household net worth, the proceeds of both the postwar era and the 1980s heyday. Future opportunities were expected to be thinner. Frank Levy and Richard C. Michel, in their book *The Economic Future of American Families,* projected that the baby-boom generation at middle age would have only half of the real net worth their parents had at that same stage.[57] With the American economy losing its power, their younger brothers and sisters would fall even further behind.

But not uniformly. For those who were twenty, thirty and thirty-five years old in the 1990s, achievement and inheritance were beginning to reverse their traditional economic roles. Some $8 trillion to $10 trillion in net worth was in the hands of Americans over fifty, and as it began to pass to the next generation—largely baby boomers—in the 1990s, the pattern of opportunity and success in the United States would be transformed. Economist Robert Avery of Cornell University, a leading student of the phenomenon, predicted that "we will soon be seeing the largest transfer of income in the history of the world. The passing of the extraordinary wealth created in America in the past five decades will speed up in the 1990s, as those alive and working during those years reach their 70s and 80s."[58]

Inheritance, then, was about to become a critical component of the younger generation's future, something America had never before experienced. Edward Wolff, a New York economist studying the pattern, contended that "if it weren't for gifts and inheritances, most baby boomers would never be able to accumulate any real wealth." Indeed, the process had already begun. In 1973, 56 percent of the total wealth held by persons aged thirty-five to thirty-nine was given them by their parents. By 1986 the figure for thirty-five- to thirty-nine-year-old baby boomers had risen to 86 percent.[59] Higher ratios were still to come, and according to economists, inheritances would peak between 1997 and 2011, with each year's volume equaling roughly 6 percent of GNP.[60]

If these predictions came true, baby boomers would be the most polarized and stratified generation in U.S. history. Economist Wolff projected that if inheritance followed the approximate lines of U.S. wealth concentration in the 1990s, then the wealth going to the top 1 percent would average $3 million, that going to the richest 5 percent (the 95th to 99th percentiles) would average $900,000. Thereafter, the 90th to 94th percentiles would average about $400,000, the 85th to 89th percentiles $200,000, and the 80th to 84th percentiles $100,000. Those in the middle fifth (40th to 59th percentiles) would receive $49,000. For those further down, inheritances would be negligible.[61] Among the upper few percentages, inheritance taxes would take a significant chunk, but the overall pattern would be unmistakable: inherited wealth would create a hereditary caste; class lines would harden.

For all these reasons—from the downscaling of Middle America to the declining net worth of the average family and the chances of hereditary stratification—economic polarization was becoming a reality in the 1990s. So doubts about the economic future and its fairness grew, and politics began to seethe. But as concern among ordinary families rose, history offered some disturbing precedents: the United States wasn't unique; other great economic powers had been there before—and the lessons they taught were disturbing.

The Late-Twentieth-Century United States and the Historical Symptoms of Middle-Class Decline

The cities [Greek city-states] that were formerly great, have most of them become insignificant; and such as are at present powerful, were weak in olden time. I shall therefore discourse equally of both, convinced that human happiness never continues long in one state.

—Herodotus, fifth century B.C.

A number of influential Japanese writers and commentators were exchange students in the U.S. in 1950s. Many were greatly impressed by this high-point of American power. Many, too, have been appalled by America's social and sexual revolutions of the 1960s, its war-torn and oil-shocked 1970s, and its economic excesses during the 1980s. They see American decline, as Edward Gibbon viewed Roman decline, as a long process of unhappy change. Americans may not see it.

—*Japan Times,* 1992

I think America is at a crossroads and Americans know it. I think that Americans know we are winning the Cold War and losing the competitive war. I think they know that we are defeating the Soviet empire, but that we are losing the domestic struggle against the drugs, crime, ignorance and welfare. They know we are losing the world market to Germany, Japan and Korea. They know we are losing faith in our constitutional system, that they do not see it working. They do not see their leaders being effective. They do not see the structures their Founding Fathers gave them producing results. And so they are almost in agony.

—U.S. House Republican whip Newt Gingrich, 1992

While many ordinary Americans found their eroding circumstances economically painful and politically frustrating, they were hardly unique. Nor was the larger decline overtaking the United States unique. Holland and Britain had also fallen from their middle-class zeniths when manufacturing, trade, nationalism and bourgeois spirit gave way to "financialization"—the cumulating influence of finance, government debt, unearned income, *rentiers,* overseas investment, domestic economic polarization and social stratification.

Excessive preoccupation with finance and tolerance of debt are apparently typical of great economic powers in their late stages. They foreshadow economic decline, but often accompany new heights of cultural sophistication, in part because the hurly-burly expansion of the middle class and its values are receding. Yet these slow transitions involve real economic cost to the average person or family, and political restiveness reflects that.

This chapter will consider what happened to the middle classes and ordinary folk in three nations that succeeded one another as the dominant economic powers of modern Europe: the Britain of Queen Victoria and King Edward VII, Holland of the seventeenth and early eighteenth centuries, and imperial Spain of the sixteenth and early seventeenth centuries. Spain's precedents are less direct, but still worth some attention. All three provide a context in which to contemplate the United States at the end of the twentieth century.

The warning to Americans is pointed. Holland and Britain experienced a crisis of values and circumstances similar to what seems to be happening again in the United States. Just as the rise of the Dutch and British middle classes was inseparable from their countries' emergence as great powers, the onset of polarization and declining purchasing power for ordinary families in each country signaled a broad national decline.

To be sure, more was involved than the wider distribution of prosperity that accompanied manufacturing and was slowly lost by a shift to finance. Burdensome taxation was another frequent sign of decline. So was cosmopolitanism, and the way in which prolonged free-trade doctrine and retention of a costly global military role—so-called imperial overstretch—have also seemed to accompany the ebb of great powers' broadest prosperity. At early stages these trends had been helpful, but at late stages they have hurt the average citizen and family. In Chapter 10, we will look at how the United States might best learn from these lessons of the past, but first let us see what happened to the Dutch and British middle classes as their national economies rose and fell.

The Crucial Role of Manufacturing, Commerce and "the Middling Sort"

Some American economists of the 1980s and 1990s felt that the United States no longer needed some of its old manufacturing industries—steel, textiles, even consumer electronics—any more than it needed new ships to rebuild the almost vanished American merchant marine. These were the productive assets of another era. If other countries could produce such things better and more cheaply, then let them, the argument went. National boundaries were losing economic meaning. The United States, for its part, would thrive on finance, services and high-value-added manufactures. Besides, although the American economy was in transition, manufacturing circa 1990 still accounted for about the same share (23 percent) of the Gross National Product that it had ten to fifteen years earlier. Talk about the de-industrialization of America was misleading; large elements of manufacturing—pharmaceuticals, for example—had never been more profitable for shareholders.

What manufacturing in the United States no longer held out, however, was the opportunity for blue-collar workers to achieve middle-class status that had been so important from the 1940s to the mid-1970s. Not only did the average hourly wage in manufacturing fall during the 1980s, from $8.49 to $8.14 in constant 1982 dollars, but from Pittsburgh and Buffalo west to Missouri and Wisconsin, huge chunks of industrial America—a region quickly nicknamed the Rust Belt—had become graveyards of vocational mobility. Between 1985 and 1990, Flint, Michigan, whose dying automobile industry sparked a popular movie lampooning General Motors chairman Roger Smith, lost 30 percent of its automotive jobs and 20 percent of its manufacturing jobs.[1] In metropolitan Pittsburgh, the largest employer was health services, with over 100,000 workers by 1991, who earned far less than steelworkers, of whom only 25,000 remained. Local wits called Pittsburgh the Incredible Shrinking City because of its 12.8 percent population drop in the 1980s.[2] The longer-term decline was worse; between 1950 and 1990, 306,926 residents had departed, leaving only 369,879 behind. As we shall see, what happened to Flint, Pittsburgh and other American industrial cities resembled the fate of Enkhuizen, Leiden and the Zaan when Holland's fishing, textile and shipbuilding industries slumped in the eighteenth century, and then the woes of Teesmouth, Lancashire, South Wales and Clydeside as British steel, textiles, coal and shipbuilding declined after World War I.

Yet the overall story of how U.S. manufacturing was losing its earlier ability to support a blue-collar middle class was more complex. Jobs lost to foreign competition in heavily unionized, highly paid industries like steel, autos and machinery were not being replaced simply by low-wage service jobs at McDonald's and K-Mart. Sometimes they were, but not *necessarily*. Between 1980 and 1990, manufacturing employment in the United States dropped by only 6 percent—from 20.3 million to 19.1 million. More to the point, manufacturing work was shifting from unionized heavy industry to nonunionized light industry, and many of the new manufacturing jobs—in computerboard assembly, beverage bottling or grocery manufacturing, for example—didn't pay as well as the old ones. Often that wage reduction was the difference between middle-class status and ex-middle-class status. The worst-paying jobs of all were in the sweatshops that reappeared during the 1980s, many employing the growing number of legal and illegal immigrants entering the United States and willing to take positions shunned by even laid-off native workers. The wages of the unskilled, in particular, eroded as immigration boosted the foreign-born share of the U.S. work force from 6.9 percent in 1980 to 9.3 percent in 1988.[3]

The net effect on one relatively successful Middle American city can be seen in Fort Wayne, Indiana.[4] After 28,000 jobs vanished in the early 1980s, one third of them because a large International Harvester plant closed, the Fort Wayne area rallied to add 57,000 new positions later in the decade, winning a place on *Inc.* magazine's 1989 list of places where job and economic growth was highest. Insurance and other services were part of the resurgence, but so were new poorly paid manufacturing jobs, because once Harvester shut down, there was nothing left to keep a floor under manufacturing wages. Declining wages, in other words, fueled local recovery. Thomas Guthrie, director of Purdue University's Community Research Institute, acknowledged that "in part, we've traded high-paying union jobs in and around Fort Wayne for relatively low-paying non-union jobs farther out" in surrounding rural areas.[5] Lower wages made such companies competitive internationally, but millions of Americans dropped out of middle-class ranks. This was the slippage so vivid in the 1980–89 Illinois income and tax data examined on pages 170–71.

More than income was lost with high-value-added manufacturing. Historically, national populations tend to be at their most spirited as they shape the industries that briefly move their countries ahead of the rest of the world—the revolutionary Dutch of the early seventeenth century, expelling Spanish overlords while gathering world trade into Amsterdam; the British of the mid-nineteenth century, already leading the Industrial Revolution, amazing the world with the technology on display at the famous 1851 Crystal Palace Exhibition; and mid-twentieth-century Americans, building the world's largest and richest middle class on their massive post–World War II manufacturing supremacy. Finance cannot nurture a comparable class, because only a small elite portion of any national population—Dutch, British or American—can share in the profits of bourse, merchant bank and countinghouse. Manufacturing, transportation and trade supremacies, by contrast, provide a broader national prosperity in which the ordinary person can man the production lines, mines, mills, wheels, mainsails and nets. Once this stage of economic development yields to the next, with its sharper divisions from capital, skills and education, great middle-class societies lose something vital and unique, just what worriers believed was happening again to the United States in the late twentieth century.

History's lessons are instructive, even the lesson of great-power Spain, with its limited manufacturing and its small middle class, that such a prosperity is not sustainable. When Spain began receiving growing quantities of gold from the New World after 1492, textiles and ceramics, the iron of Vizcaya, the blades of Toledo, were all examples of Spanish manufacturing success, albeit limited. Visitors to such cities in northern Spain as Burgos and Medina del Campo described them in the early 1500s as dominated by merchants, artisans and financiers.[6] A bourgeoisie was in the making.

Yet by the mid-1550s, the effect of ever-growing supplies of gold, the disdain for trade on the part of Spain's military and aristocratic *hidalgo* tradition, and the anti-individualist Counter-Reformation attack on Protestantism all came together to squelch industry, the bourgeois spirit and the incipient middle class. Laws overtly stigmatized pursuit of trade and manufacturing: why stoop to manufacture when Holland, London, Milan and Flanders were willing to do so for Spanish gold? Guilds were disbanded, the incipient industrial and mercantile centers lost half or more of their populations by the century's end. By the early 1600s, as it became clear that Spain's lassitude and polarization between rich and poor would soon leave her vulnerable when the gold and silver of Mexico and Peru ran out, the economic wise men of the *arbitrista* movement identified the danger brought on by the lack of a manufacturing economy and a bourgeoisie: Spain "has come to be an extreme contrast of rich and poor, and there is no means of adjusting them to one another. Our condition is one in which we have rich who look at ease, or poor who beg, and we lack people of the middling sort, whom neither wealth nor poverty prevents from pursuing the rightful kind of business enjoined by natural law."[7]

The emergent country that proved what mercantile spirits could achieve was Holland circa 1600, even then in the process of winning its independence from Spain. In contrast to aristocratic Spain, puritan Holland was dominated by artisans and merchants—the *brede midden-stand*—with a strong sense of its own destiny as a class and nation:

> They stamped indelibly the persona of their class on Dutch society. Their cautious, prudent, self-satisfied, unostentatious faces stare out of the canvases of Rembrandt or Hals, giving little away of their uncon-scious drives, but speaking eloquently of the sobriety and dedication of their lives. The comely facades of their great houses along the Keizers-gracht and Heerengracht of Amsterdam, dignified, restrained, so unem-phatic in their elegance, bespeak the integrity of generations of bourgeois endeavour—that amalgam of hard work, calculated risk, guarded self-indulgence, all without panache or ostentation or flamboyance, which became the hallmarks of the Dutch character.[8]

Until 1620 or so, the Dutch thrived mostly on seafaring and the booming commerce of Amsterdam. By mid-century, however, they had used their technical sophistication and control of vital raw com-modities to build successful industries ranging from textiles to tobacco, sugar, distilling, Delftware, diamonds and shipbuilding. Supported by Holland's bourgeois virtues, trading preeminence and credit, Dutch manufactures soon dominated a number of European markets. Visi-tors to Holland circa 1680 were struck by Dutch innovations, ranging from multiple-blade timber saws to Leeuwenhoek's microscope and grinding machines for processing coffee, chocolate, mustard and li-queurs.[9] Yet by some point in the early to mid-eighteenth century—Dutch historians disagree just when—Holland had lost its cultural, industrial and technological momentum.

We have no need of a compendium, but by roughly 1750, although Holland still had its sea trade, the country's high-value-added exports had shriveled: Leiden's textiles slumped, so did Gouda's pipe industry, and Delftware was swept from the drawing rooms of Europe.[10] The Dutch industrialists and technicians, who were to the seventeenth cen-tury what Scots engineers would be to the nineteenth, faded from prominence.

Finance, as we shall see, rose in its place, bringing economic and social polarization—the erosion of the *brede middenstand* and prudent, unostentatious Calvinism. Historians call the mid-eighteenth century Holland's Periwig Era because of its stratifying wealth and rising social pretensions. French clothes, paintings, wines and culture had become fashionable in the late seventeenth century, and historian Fernand Braudel interpreted the spread of the French language as another way for the emerging elites to stand aloof from the common people.[11] By 1764, James Boswell could write from Utrecht that: "Most of their principal towns are sadly decayed, and instead of finding every mortal employed, you meet with multitudes of poor creatures who are starving in idleness. Utrecht is remarkably ruined. There are whole lanes of wretches who have no other subsistence than potatoes, gin and stuff which they call tea and coffee; and what is worst of all, I believe they are so habituated to this life that they would not take work if it should be offered to them . . . you see, then, that things are very different here from what most people in England imagine. Were Sir William Temple to revisit these Provinces, he would scarcely believe the amazing alteration which they have undergone." Fourteen years later, the Dutch newspaper *De Borger* ventured an analysis of Holland much like those of the Spanish *arbitristas* one hundred seventy-five years earlier: "the body of the Commonwealth would shortly consist of little more than rentiers and beggars—the two kinds of people who are the least useful to the country."[12] In both Spain and Holland, the ordinary people were left with nothing from their country's zenith.

Britain, too, achieved its peak of worldwide supremacy and comparative affluence on a wave of middle-class economic and political emergence conjoined with manufacturing and the Industrial Revolution. Middle-class political consciousness, which dated back to the late 1700s, finally triumphed in the 1830s and 1840s with the democratization of parliamentary constituencies and the repeal of the corn laws, which protected the agricultural interests of the British aristocracy.[13] The term "middle class" came into actual use around 1812, quickly developing larger implications—both in the narrow sense as a shorthand for the emerging commercial and manufacturing classes and in the far grander context of the middle class as the emerging repository of Britain's new liberal individualism and commercial spirit. Thomas Macaulay, the principal historian of the age, described it as "that brave, honest and stout-hearted class, which is as anxious for the maintenance of order and the security of property, as it is hostile to corruption and oppression."[14]

The extent to which such florid language dripped with politics is important, because by the 1850s and 1860s the British middle class was the sort of touchstone that Middle America would become a century later. Though aristocrats still dominated the cabinets of Liberal and Conservative prime ministers alike, the rise of the middle class was the true measure of Britain's greatness, and elements of the Liberal party were already beginning to theorize about rule by a democratic majority.[15] In short, the Britain that became the "workshop of the world" in the 1840s and 1850s—and by 1860 controlled 40 to 45 percent of the world's industry, two fifths of its trade in manufactures and one third of its merchant ships—was a nation in which a rising middle class was bursting its old bonds, just as the burghers of Holland had been some two centuries earlier and the citizens of the postwar United States would be a century later.

It was reasonably clear that British national self-confidence and Britain's share of world manufactures probably peaked more or less together around 1870. The pattern of later decline was not so neat; great supremacies are not lost quickly. Concern about foreign competition began to gnaw at national optimism in the 1870s, especially after the downturn of 1873, but the average Briton's standard of living continued to improve. Gains were still occurring in the 1890s, even after fifteen years in which British industrial production grew by an average of only 1.5 percent annually, much less than that of the United States (which now led Britain in manufacturing) or Germany (which was catching up). Nevertheless, the 1890s were the decade in which some deterioration came into the open as Britons began to see their great industries—steel, coal, even machine tools and engineering—losing ground to American and German competition, and by the mid-1890s, popular writers in Britain were tapping growing popular anxieties with books entitled *Made in Germany* and *The American Invaders*.[16] If it all sounds familiar to Americans of the 1990s, it should.

As the twentieth century dawned the dilemma had become clearer: British finance and overseas investment had never been so strong, with implications we will pursue later in this chapter, but British manufacturing was flagging. Joseph Chamberlain, the prophetic colonial secretary, warned in 1903 that "in the course of another generation, this will be much less an industrial country inhabited by a race of skillful artisans than a distributive country with a smaller population consisting of rich consumers on the one hand and people engaged in the work of distribution."[17] The gap between the rich and the ordinary folk was growing, which Chamberlain thought inauspicious, because the living standards of the average family had finally started to decline even as the dividends, interest income and life-styles of the rich continued to expand.

For the Victorian equivalent of the median-income family, historians seem to agree that erosion began around the turn of the century, when manufacturing began to slide. G.D.H. Cole, in his famous chronicle of *The British Common People, 1746–1946,* concludes:

> There can be no doubt that the standard was falling. Between the later 'nineties, when the cost of living began to rise, and about 1910, when the great labour unrest set in, home consumption of wheat per head of population remained stationary, and home consumption of both meat and sugar declined. There was a great fall in the consumption of both beer and spirits; but it does not appear that this was offset by a rise in the consumption of food. According to Mr. G.H. Wood's calculations, average real wage-rates were 4 per cent lower in 1910 than they had been in 1896; and even in 1914 the purchasing power of 1896 had not been regained. Between 1899 and 1913 real wages had actually declined by about 10 per cent. Wages were reckoned as having constituted in 1880 about 41 or 42 per cent of the national income: in 1913 they were only 35 or 36 per cent. Doubtless, some part of this decrease was due to the increased numbers of salary-earners and professionals; but even so there is a large fall left unaccounted for.[18]

Sampling in London revealed a fall of 6 percent in real wages between 1900–1901 and 1911–12, while other surveys confirmed this deterioration.[19] As manufacturing declined, British industrial workers, whose wages in 1860 or 1870 had exceeded those on the Continent, were slipping for reasons similar to those confronting U.S. manufacturing employees in the Rust Belt of the 1980s: increasing competition from overseas competitors whose workers were paid less and whose plants were newer. Moreover, the die seems to have been cast. British manufacturing boomed again during World War I, boosting worker incomes and living standards, but then more ground was lost from 1920 to 1924–25 as postwar economic reality sent British heavy industry into another retreat.

For a generation, ordinary working-class Britons experienced the decline earlier visited upon the Spanish and Dutch. On the other hand, the middle classes, which, by including clerks and shopkeepers, accounted for some 25 to 30 percent of the population of Britain just before World War I, continued to gain in the 1900–1914 era. The upper-middle class fared very well, and the lower-middle class held its own, although economists began to take note of what would squeeze Middle America three generations later—the unique burden of middle-class expenditure, with its relatively heavy outlays for insurance, schools, health care, home purchase and the like.[20] The middle class did not come under severe pressure until the end of the 1930s and the war years, when Britain, having fought one draining conflict and now embroiled in another, neared the end of its financial resources.

Nevertheless, in an irony we shall revisit in Chapter 10's look ahead at America's possible pathways, the rich-poor divisions of the Edwardian era radicalized British politics, making the socialist Labour party the official opposition, and then later in the 1920s, Labour became the government. Social welfare expenditures climbed, as did taxes and a mild redistribution of income, and from the mid-1920s on, the working class found its living standards improving, especially in the 1930s as consumer prices declined, wages more or less held even and the welfare state began to take firm hold. Prosperous Britons, conversely, found *their* income tax burdens climbing to help the bottom two thirds of the population. Between 1913 and 1937 the total effect of income redistribution by government was to raise the incomes of the working classes by 8 to 14 percent and *reduce* those of the upper and middle classes by 10 to 15 percent.[21] Parenthetically, social historians differentiate between the lower-middle and middle classes, who did better or held steady in the between-the-war years because of both relatively low taxes and continued availability of domestic servants, and the upper- and upper-middle-income groups, who were losing ground.[22] Britain's decline was catching up with them.

For Jaguar- and Daimler-driving Britons, moreover, worse was still to come. Taxes rose in the late 1930s as the United Kingdom rearmed against Hitler and the welfare state bit even deeper. Then, as World War II cut British global economic clout and investment income to the bone, the real, pretax income of the wealthiest 100,000 plunged by 64 percent between 1938 and 1949 while real pretax income for the largely upper-middle-class top 500,000 Britons fell by 37 percent.[23] And that was *pretax*; the Treasury's higher levies aggravated the relative decline.

To upper-bracket Americans of the 1990s these precedents were only partially relevant, because mid-century socialism in Britain and elsewhere was on a rare historic roll. By the late 1940s, indeed, welfarism, socialism and redistribution of income had partially reversed the polarization of the Edwardian years even though heavy manufacturing would never recover its old prosperity. As we have seen, British workers were better off, with higher incomes; elements of the lower-middle class were, too. But for the upper-middle class, the 2 percent or 3 percent of British families in the professional and managerial classes who had lived so well in 1910 on £1,500 or £2,000 a year, when such families generally had a cook, a parlor maid and one or two other servants, when meals were a groaning board of joints and roasts, and holidays were excursions to Nice, Tuscany or Montreux, the economic circumstances of 1945–49 were an extraordinary comedown. British finances had been shattered by the war; senior officials hung on details of the latest dollar loan from Washington. Facing punitive taxes, some dukes and earls held on to their family castles by personally conducting guided tours for gawking coveys of tourists from Paducah and Burbank, but for the average London solicitor, Edinburgh bank manager or Coventry works director, the late 1940s were unpleasant in a way that went far beyond crimped income.

Few Britons care to remember, but although World War II ended in August 1945, food rationing for British families didn't end until 1954. Worse still, in peacetime 1948, food allowances had fallen *below* the wartime average.[24] The average adult male's weekly allowance was 13 ounces of meat, 1½ ounces of cheese, 6 ounces of butter and margarine, 1 ounce of cooking fat, 8 ounces of sugar, 2 pints of milk and 1 egg. Doctors reported that poor diets were lowering resistance to infection, especially among older citizens. In pursuit of new and cheap protein sources, the government brought in huge quantities of *snoek*, a tasteless fish no one wanted to eat, from the waters off South Africa. *Vogue* magazine published recipes for cauliflower soup and stuffed marrows. Going out, even to the Savoy Grill, was no solution, as one contemporary chronicle recalls:

> In restaurants, bread was made one of the maximum number of three dishes allowed at any one meal. Served as bread and cheese, or as the ground floor of Welsh rarebit or sardines on toast, it didn't count as a separate dish. But any customer who now demanded bread with his soup would find, by the end of the meal, that he had forfeited his right to a pudding.[25]

The lavish tables at which Edwardians stuffed themselves were only a memory. Fresh fruit was a luxury often unavailable in the nation that just forty years earlier had been Europe's best provisioned. Air Vice Marshal "Pathfinder" Bennett, a war hero, won new fame by flying in peaches from France. Even the royal family was constrained—when Princess Elizabeth got married, it was announced she would be given

100 ration coupons for her wedding, but rationing would apply. British tourists, yesteryear's "milords," traveled abroad in no style worth mentioning—if they traveled at all—because only a small amount of money could be taken out of the country, which needed every shilling for foreign exchange. The decline of upper- and upper-middle-class Britain in the long generation between 1914 and the late 1940s was a painful and extraordinary one. Even in the late 1980s, when Britain had a boom of sorts under Margaret Thatcher, British per capita incomes had fallen behind Italy's, whereas in 1910, the average Briton had been roughly twice as well off as the average Italian. As things turned out, the ebb of manufacturing and of ordinary British living standards that was shrugged off during the 1900–1914 period had been a signal to heed.

Debt, Rentiers and the Pitfalls of Financialization

A significant part of what overtook each of these nations was the emergence of finance, debt and an investor or rentier class within their respective societies, as the bourgeois emphasis on manufacturing and trade diminished. In many respects, of course, sharp finance is an asset. Highly developed financial services have been a strategic advantage to major powers, as well as a useful national economic cushion when manufacturing industries began to decline. Yet the drawback lay in how investment, speculation and brokerage, at a certain point, worked to polarize incomes and wealth at the expense of what had been—at least in Holland and Britain—aggressive societies of entrepreneurs, tinkerers and engineers. Because a similar pattern of booming finance while old manufacturing industries declined was apparent in the United States of the 1980s and 1990s, it's useful to review the process of "financialization" and its effect on the ebb of the former great economic powers—even atypical Spain.

In a sense, Spain was the ultimate hollowed-out economy—a financial shell once the flood of New World gold and silver in the sixteenth century undercut any manufacturing potential. The leader of Spain's *arbitrista* economic critics, González de Cellorigo, looked back from the next century with a regretful perception that Spain's gold had not been "true wealth" because it increased only its stock of precious metals, not its productive agricultural or industrial capacity. "Money is not true wealth," de Cellorigo said, and Spain's was being unproductively invested—"dissipated on thin air—on papers, contracts, *censos* and letters of exchange, on cash, and silver and gold instead of being expended on things that yield profits and attract riches from outside to augment the riches within."[26]

More specifically, the huge wealth brought by the treasure fleets was fatal for embryonic Spanish industry; it eroded belief in hard work and manual labor while also forcing up prices, making local labor and goods expensive. Cheap foreign products poured in, convincing Spaniards that so long as the gold lasted, other nations would produce their needs. In addition, the willingness of European bankers to lend money against the arrival of the galleons at Seville made Spain's already wasteful Hapsburg rulers even more so. The result, by the 1540s, was that Charles V had borrowed from the bankers of Genoa, Germany and Antwerp by mortgaging large chunks of *future* Spanish revenues. Innovative debt instruments proliferated, another poor augury. The Crown also began to raise money by selling, on a mammoth scale, bonds or annuities called *juros,* which paid about 7 percent a year. Financial practices like these, besides demanding huge shares of the national revenues and diverting money that might have been invested in more solid enterprise, also created an influential and apparently pernicious creditor class:

> Juros were bought by foreign and native bankers, by merchants and nobles, and by anyone with a little money to spare. The result was the growth of a powerful rentier class in Castile, investing its money not in trade or industry but in profitable Government bonds, and living contentedly on its annuities. If ever a suggestion was made, as it was in 1552, that the Government should undertake a gradual redemption of the juros, there was an immediate outcry from all holders of juros, who saw no safe alternative for their investments except in the purchase of land, the price of which would rise sharply if the juros were redeemed.[27]

To put the perils of debt financing in perspective, at the death of King Philip II in 1598, interest payments on the government's debt took two thirds of Spain's yearly revenues. Spanish elites had come to look to investment in juros and place-holding in the bureaucracies of the Catholic Church, the Royal Court and the government to secure the incomes they haughtily disdained to earn from commerce. Together with the hunger for titles of nobility (which included exemption from most taxes), these attitudes led the bourgeoisie to throw in with the unproductive upper class. Narrow monetary wealth, irresponsible finance and an indolent rentier class were important in the decline that was taking hold in Spain one hundred to one hundred fifty years after Columbus's voyages.

The extraordinary thing was that Calvinist Holland, through a different evolution, reached a somewhat similar stage within two centuries. The ability of the thrifty, puritanical Dutch to save large sums of money and lend them at low interest rates had been central to the country's rapid emergence as the seventeenth-century center of world commerce. By the end of that century, however, after two or three generations of prosperity, finance was taking on a different social role. Traders were complaining that whereas the town regents had previously been active merchants, they were no longer active, "but derived their income from houses, lands and money at interest."[28] Rentier influence steadily intensified, and by the mid-eighteenth century, when Dutch manufacturing, fishing and engineering were losing headway, Dutch banking, finance and the Amsterdam stock market were booming, aggravating social and economic polarization. "Seventy years ago," wrote one foreign observer in 1771, "the wealthiest businessmen [in Amsterdam] did not have gardens or country houses comparable to those their brokers own today. The worst thing is not the building and immense expense of maintaining these fairy-tale palaces, or rather bottomless pits, it is that the distraction and negligence occasioned by this luxury often causes prejudice to business and trade."[29] Moreover, not only was Dutch capital forsaking industry and commerce, switching to government finance, stocks and credit operations, but it was increasingly looking to overseas rather than domestic investments.

No other eighteenth-century nation matched the Dutch as international lenders. British authorities estimated that in 1737 Dutch investors held about 22.7 percent of the British public debt, and a 1762 estimate put the proportion at 25 percent. Meanwhile, Hollanders were estimated to hold about a third of the stock in both the Bank of England and the East India Company.[30] This huge foreign investment sparked controversy, however, because critics were outraged at how so much money was being invested abroad rather than at home to relieve Holland's decay and unemployment. True, the interest and dividends that flowed back to Holland were large, but they went mostly to the rich and increased economic polarization. Fernand Braudel, criticizing the "perversion of capital," noted that Holland's small financial elite had so much to invest, even as ordinary Dutchmen starved, that by the late eighteenth century they were drawn into increasingly risky loans, producing bubbles and panics. The money men themselves recognized how they had drawn apart from the rest of Holland. Finally, after sporadic tax and food riots, Holland faced the angry but unsuccessful Batavian Revolution of 1780, when mobs decried *les richards* in a foretaste of the French Revolution a decade later.[31]

Britain, too, saw the emergence of a substantial rentier class as it reached its global trade and manufacturing zenith in the 1870s. The sums put Dutch finance in the shade. Since the end of the Napoleonic wars in 1815, Britain's annual foreign investment had ballooned from £6 million to £75 million, for a grand total of £700 million in 1875, and the resultant annual flow of dividends and interest back into Britain exceeded £50 million, also a huge sum for those days. According to one chronicle, "by 1871 Britain contained 170,000 'persons of rank and property' without visible occupation—almost all of them women, or rather 'ladies'; a surprising number of them unmarried ladies. Stocks and shares, including shares in family firms formed into 'private companies' for this purpose, were a convenient way of providing for widows, daughters and other relatives who could not—and no longer needed to—be associated with the management of property and enterprise."[32]

Even more to the point, banks and investment firms had prospered and multiplied, with additional stock exchanges to supplement London's having been organized in Liverpool, Manchester and Glasgow during the 1840s. Through the 1890s, the rise of finance was not generally criticized as being at the expense of other parts of the British economy. But then, as the new century opened, such worries found increasing voice.

In a split that would foreshadow the late-twentieth-century United States, ordinary families dependent on manufacturing employment were seeing their purchasing power decline, while Britain's turn-of-the-century rich enjoyed a surge in income from business profits and interest—up 55 percent between 1899 and 1913, according to income tax authorities.[33] Revealingly, while "accumulation of capital out of profits became swift beyond all precedent," according to historian G.D.H. Cole, relatively little of that flowed into *British* industry. Instead, in the manner of the Dutch, most was invested in overseas portions of the empire or in foreign countries where interest rates were higher or where greater profits could be realized by taking advantage of cheaper labor. What fattened finance, however, often had the simultaneous effect of helping countries that competed with British industry. From a total of £700 million in 1875, British overseas investments soared to £1 billion in 1900, £3 billion in 1907 and £4 billion by 1914.[34] By 1913 overseas holdings were bringing the British investing classes a net annual return of about £200 million a year—a huge sum, which exceeded the annual budget of the British government, and which was only minimally taxed.

Despite the limitations of early-twentieth-century economic statistics, a small minority of British economists and politicians sensed a dangerous imbalance. Even back in 1865, Matthew Arnold had suggested what must have seemed farfetched at the time—"an imminent danger of England losing immeasureably in all ways, declining into a sort of greater Holland."[35] Colonial Secretary Joseph Chamberlain, in words that now seem prophetic, warned that Britain could not survive as merely "a hoarder of invested securities" if it was not also the "creator of new wealth." In 1904, to a meeting of bankers in the City of London, he said that "granted you are the clearing house of the world," but

> are you entirely beyond anxiety as to the permanence of your great position. . . . Banking is not the creator of our prosperity, but is the creation of it. It is not the cause of our wealth, but it is the consequence of our wealth; and if the industrial energy and development which has been going on for so many years in this country were to be hindered or relaxed, then finance, and all that finance means, will follow trade to the countries which are more successful than ourselves.[36]

Financialization, however, also meant that—from their own perspective—bankers, insurers and financiers had good reason to fear that protection of declining home manufacturing industries could bring foreign retaliation against Britain's profitable shipping, investments and financial services. And they *were* profitable. Even after the economic blows of the 1914–18 war, while British heavy industry sank further during the 1920s, the City of London managed to hold its place as the center of world finance. What's more, British international investments actually earned more than ever before, as did financial and insurance services, which seemed to disprove Chamberlain's fears. Then, however, the devastating economic effects of World War II tragically confirmed the forecast that finance would be a thin reed. The £175 million Britain had earned from overseas investments in 1938 slumped to £73 million in 1940. The postwar annual figures nominally returned to prewar levels, but adjusted for inflation they were much lower—and Britain also staggered under the weight of $13 billion of new external liabilities. Financial supremacy followed economic and manufacturing supremacy to the United States, and we have seen how hard times caught up with middle- and upper-middle-class Britons, although the City of London—like Amsterdam—still maintained an important world role.

The purpose of these quick summaries is to illustrate, particularly with reference to Holland and Britain, a progression all too visible in the United States of the 1990s. The later-stage financialization of the world's leading economic powers has generally accompanied the decline of domestic industry and led to the growth of a rentier class, the erosion of economic patriotism, the rise of rich-poor polarization and the economic stagnation (or worse) of the average citizen or family. If the examples I have given in this chapter seem repetitive, they are meant to underscore that the problem is repetitive—and the extent to which the same trends and circumstances were recurring in the United States in the 1980s and 1990s makes the Dutch and British lessons especially cautionary.

We have seen that, much as in turn-of-the-century Britain, heavy industry in the United States has receded significantly, eliminating jobs that provided high wages for many ordinary breadwinners. Simultaneously, burgeoning U.S. financial services—the business of insurance companies, credit managers, stockbrokers, shipping agents and investment bankers—sold well enough in global markets to offset a fair portion of the U.S. trade deficit in manufactured goods. The service and investment sectors were king, even though by 1990 foreigners took almost as much from the United States in interest and dividends as Americans earned overseas. A decade earlier, the U.S. earnings edge had been lopsided.

By some calculations, the rising percentage of U.S. investments directed overseas cost many American jobs. Economists Norman Glickman of Rutgers University and Douglas Woodward of the University of South Carolina estimated the loss at 2.7 million positions in the United States between 1977 and 1986.[37] By reducing domestic employment, these overseas investments also worsened economic polarization in the United States—and according to a National Bureau of Economic Research study, the increase in the trade deficit during the 1980s brought the same effect.

Whatever was happening to manufacturing workers, the earnings of American financiers had never been higher. At their peak in the late 1980s, the highest-earning individuals in the U.S. financial community, as cataloged each year by *Financial World* magazine, counted levels of income and wealth far exceeding those of the Dutch financiers of the Periwig period and Britain's Edwardian moneymen.* These riches were further confirmation of rising economic polarization. The same

---

*The financial community's fees, incomes and wealth during this period are discussed at some length in Chapter 6 of *The Politics of Rich and Poor*.

mergers, leveraged buyouts and other restructurings of American industry, devastating for so many blue- and white-collar workers, were
manna for Wall Street and its attendant law firms, proxy solicitors and
accountants. And like Spain, Holland and Britain, each in turn, the
United States of the early 1990s was home to a disproportionate financial and rentier class. Between the mid-1970s and the late 1980s, the
percentage of U.S. national income categorizable as unearned—interest, dividends and rents, rather than wages and salaries—grew from 14
percent to 20 percent. New financial and debt instruments proliferated
by the hundreds, producing zoological acronyms like LIONS (Lehman
Investment Opportunity Notes), CATS (Certificates of Accrual on
Treasury Certificates), OPPOSSMS (Options to Purchase or Sell Spec-
ified Mortgage-backed Securities) and LYNX (Liquid Yield Note Exchanges).* In a controversial statement to the Japanese Diet, Prime
Minister Kiichi Miyazawa, while admitting that Japan shared the
problem of excessive financialization, argued that during the 1980s the
United States had become so caught up in Wall Street speculation and
easy money that it neglected manufacturing and stopped producing
engineers.†

Rising indebtedness was another troubling sign. As with previous
great powers, economic complexity, debt and speculation fed on each
other in the United States of the 1980s. Conservatives replaced liberals
as the principal excuse-makers for federal debt and deficits. In 1992 the
Bush administration acknowledged that federal deficits of $200 billion
to $400 billion a year were inevitable at least through 1997; meanwhile,
government debt had expanded so much that net federal interest payments came to $195 billion a year, swallowing 15 percent of the total
budget—up from just $17 billion and 7 percent in 1973.

That 15 percent was well under the two thirds of the yearly budget
that Spanish debt service required by the 1590s, but, like Spanish 7

---

*The prize for the new financing instrument with the most amusing acronym, however, went
to sale-and-leaseback obligations—SLOBs.

†Miyazawa's statement, distorted in some reports, was actually quite reasonable: "Over the
last 10 years," he said, "it seems that America has reached the point that the mindset to
produce things and create value has loosened sharply. Many people getting out of college
have gone to Wall Street for very high salaries, with the result that the number of engineers
who produce goods has gone down quickly." Miyazawa then criticized the "money market"
because of its junk bonds, leveraged buyouts and large loans that require big interest
payments. "These things, which nobody thought could last long, have gone on for 10 years,"
Miyazawa continued. "And I have thought for a long time that the work ethic is lacking as
far as that area is concerned" ("Miyazawa: Work Ethic Flags in U.S.," *Washington Post*,
February 4, 1992).

percent juros, Washington's huge interest outlays represented a transfer to rentiers of money that could have been used for investment in industry and infrastructure. By 1989–90, interest payments to Americans alone had grown so large—about 15 percent of personal income—that when short-term interest rates plummeted, the decline in household income caused by slumping interest payments significantly affected U.S. purchasing power. At the same time, observers made the point that besides draining industry and abetting private indebtedness, the federal government's huge outlays for servicing U.S. long-term debt at high interest rates represented a thinly hidden transfer of wealth.[38] George Will, the conservative columnist, stated the case with particular flair:

> To pay the interest component of the 1988 budget will require a sum ($210 billion) equal to approximately half of all the personal income-tax receipts. This represents, as Sen. Pat Moynihan has said, a transfer of wealth from labor to capital unprecedented in American history.
>
> Tax revenues are being collected from average Americans (the median income of a family of four is slightly under $30,000) and given to the buyers of U.S. government bonds—buyers in Beverly Hills, Lake Forest, Shaker Heights and Grosse Pointe, and Tokyo and Riyadh.[39]

This, of course, is another way in which great-power "financialization" has been a burden on ordinary families. History, alas, suggests that the whole process, while destructive, also has an air of inevitability.

Taxes and Middle-Class Decline

If high public debt and interest payments to a rentier class have often been a signal of great-power decline, unfair or oppressive taxes are another signal. When taxes are high in emerging great powers, reasonable balance and fairness usually have been observed. The United States, for example, had imposed high taxes on the rich in the decade before World War II and during the two golden decades after 1945. Holland, during its emergence as a great power, required Europe's highest taxes to finance its revolution against Spain. The tax policy of a declining power, however, often displays characteristics different from those of the policy of happier periods. Some of the tax trends in the United States of the 1980s and early 1990s, such as California's sales levy on snack foods rather than on luxuries, burgeoning state and local fees and charges, and the layers of federal taxation that wound up making middle-class marginal rates higher than those of the rich, were omens, although mild next to earlier European excesses.

Hapsburg Spain levied a tax called the *servicio,* imposed by local authorities on a list of taxpayers or ratepayers from which the *hidalgos,* or noblemen, were exempted. This kind of charge put the burden of paying for government on the peasantry and what there was of a middle class, inducing wealthy businessmen to abandon their enterprise and buy "hidalgo" status in order to escape taxation.⁴⁰ The declining Holland of the mid-eighteenth century imposed Europe's highest taxes, mostly consumption taxes that fell disproportionately on the poor and sat lightly on the rich, whose growing wealth was provocative. One historian noted that Dutch resentment of "patrician opulence . . . gathered momentum through the mid-18th Century and kindled an increasing number of [tax] riots and disturbances."⁴¹

By contrast, the British were lightly taxed as their nation's relative decline began in the 1880s and 1890s, so taxes were not an obvious culprit. But taxes rose sharply later, so that for an upper-middle-class family with £10,000 a year, the share taken by income tax escalated from 8 percent in 1913–14 to 39 percent in 1937–38.⁴² Then from 1938 to 1949, as we have seen, the tax burdens of upper-class and upper-middle-class Britons escalated again, not just because of Britain's growing debt burden, but also because the income tax became a vehicle for deliberate downward redistribution of income. Taxes clearly made Britain's postwar decline worse.

Taxes in the early-1990s United States were in between: lower than those of most other major nations, but of greater overall weight than those of Britain circa 1925. More to the point, for ordinary Americans taxes were starting to show some resemblance to the Spanish and Dutch precedents. The danger sign, however, lay less in the total U.S. tax burden than in the inequities of its arrangement and distribution.

Free Trade, Immigration, Cosmopolitan Culture and "Imperial Overstretch" Military Policy

The eras in which great economic powers have been dominated by assertive middle classes have been provincial rather than sophisticated. Cosmopolitan internationalism has come at a later stage when economic vitality is past its peak.

The golden eras of Holland, Britain and the United States were marked by bourgeois patriotism and provincialism, whereas their decline as manufacturing and ordinary-family income stagnated seems to have been characterized by recurrent attitudes: a diminishing concern for fading national industries, rising transnational values, support for minimal restraint on immigration, willingness to sell critical technology overseas and an eagerness of domestic capital to invest in rival foreign economies. "Cosmopolitanism" is as good a collective label as any. Yet another variety of globalism typical of such eras is what Paul Kennedy called "imperial overstretch"—the tendency of great-power elites to cling to an expensive international military or peacekeeping role that a weakening economy can no longer afford.

Far from being abstractions, these great-power circumstances affect average families as well as nations. Take great-power commitment to some variety of free trade and adherence to the theory that in the optimal world economy, restraints on trade should be avoided so that each nation might do what it does best. For great powers at the crest of the world economy, the rationale is simple: free trade is commercial self-interest. Restraints on imports into Spain circa 1550, Holland circa 1650 and Britain circa 1870 were relatively few, because in trade terms, these nations saw the world as their commercial oyster. One cocky Spaniard of the sixteenth century even wrote:

> Let London manufacture those fine fabrics of hers to her heart's content; Holland her chambrays; Florence her cloth; the Indies their beaver and vicuna; Milan her brocades; Italy and Flanders their linens . . . so long as our capital can enjoy them: the only thing it proves is that all nations train journeymen for Madrid and that Madrid is the queen of parliaments, for all the world serves her and she serves nobody.[43]

At roughly the same point in Britain's heyday, economist William Jevons expressed a similar enthusiasm, naming "Chicago and Odessa our granaries, Canada and the Baltic our timber forests . . . Spain and France our vineyards."[44] In turn, much of the world bought British manufactures. We can be sure that a seventeenth-century Dutchman or two wrote enthusiastically about how their vessels carried the tar and pitch of Sweden, the beaver pelts of New Amsterdam and the coffee of Java, just as Americans of the 1950s and 1960s gloried in a world at their beck and call.

Within a generation or two of these enthusiasms, however, each of these great powers saw its manufacturing competitiveness weaken as factories began to age, technologies lagged and aggressive protectionist or mercantilist practices by commercial rivals took their toll. Moreover, capital needed for domestic industry was diverted because the nation's financial or rentier sector preferred more profitable overseas investments. Nor could mature great economic powers enact or implement plans for national manufacturing renewal, because they could not mobilize divided interest groups. As many domestic manufacturing industries lose their earlier advantage, free trade and national self-interest diverge.

Spain's manufacturing industry, as we have seen, was sacrificed early, so that foreign imports became a necessity. Holland, however, illustrates the usual evolution. Sometime in the early 1700s, Dutch manufacturing and technology began to slip, in part because of Dutch investors' moving their capital elsewhere, but also because of rising European protectionism. Textiles—the greatest of Dutch industries—"were at the heart of mercantile policy in all countries," save free-trading Holland. England and France first imposed heavy duties on Dutch cloths in the late 1600s, followed by Russia, Prussia, Denmark, Norway and Spain in the early 1700s, ensuring the decline of Holland's textile industry.[45] Yet increased Dutch dependence on international shipping and finance ruled out serious countermeasures to protect embattled manufactures. Holland had no alternative to maintaining free markets, yet by a certain point that commitment was partly a trap.

Britain's experience is also relevant. Exports had started to slip in the 1870s, and in 1885 the Conservative government of Lord Salisbury appointed a commission to report on the "Depression of Trade and Industry," because of concern over losing domestic and overseas markets, especially to German competition.[46] In fact, apprehension was overdue, because continental Europe's brief mid-century flirtation with free trade had ended. France raised tariffs in 1872 and 1882, Germany in 1879 and Russia in 1883 and 1887. In the burgeoning United States, steep duties were pushed higher in the 1890s.[47] In addition, by the turn of the century, the former "workshop of the world" had lost much of its earlier lead in science and technology to Germany and the United States. Moreover, some of what Britain sold to maintain high export volume was partly counterproductive. Much export growth was in coal, which was not just raw material but a commodity critical to foreign industry. Two other major exports—ships and machinery—also helped nurture rivals in trade and manufacturing.

By 1903 Conservative prime minister Arthur J. Balfour was worried enough to propose a mild agenda of protection and imperial preference.* He told the House of Commons that the free-trade circumstances of the 1850s no longer existed: "We have seen, to begin with, a tariff wall steadily raised against us in every one of the great countries with whom we desire to deal. We have seen . . . an enormous growth of the trust system working behind tariffs."[48] The result, he claimed, allowed foreign producers to dump goods in Britain, reducing the profits of British industry and crippling its ability to undertake needed modernization. His solution—which Americans would also find themselves debating in the 1980s and 1990s—was to establish a framework for imposing retaliatory tariffs on countries that erected protective walls against British goods.

But Balfour failed, and his government lost the next general election in 1906. Many economists and rival politicians simply rejected his analyses, preferring to take comfort in free-trade theory, in Britain's past commercial glories and in claims that since the economy was continuing to grow, it was not in trouble. However, a central constraint, as in Holland two centuries earlier, was that shipping and financial services had become so important to Britain's international earnings that these sectors opposed risking foreign retaliation by protecting aging manufacturing industries. So no action was taken. For Britain, too, free trade had gone from being a strength to being something of a trap.

In the late twentieth century the United States was following suit. Old heavy industries were in decline in the Rust Belt and elsewhere. Handicapped by inferior scientific and mathematical education (as late-nineteenth-century Britain was weak relative to Germany), the United States was losing ground to Japan in technology. Neomercantilism, industrial strategies and export subsidies were routine practices on the part of U.S. trade rivals—continental European as well as Asian. Yet the Reagan and Bush administrations, which leaned toward free trade, generally opposed efforts to wield conditional access to the U.S. market as a retaliatory club against foreign neomercantilism.

As had earlier happened in Britain, free traders insisted that U.S. weaknesses had been exaggerated, citing the high U.S. exports of 1988–91.† Nor was there any real willingness to protect old-line manu-

---

*These paragraphs draw heavily on Aaron Friedman's excellent book *The Weary Titan: Britain and the Experience of Relative Decline, 1895–1905.*

†In another perverse coincidence, just as Britain enlarged its early-twentieth-century exports by shipping huge quantities of coal, the United States of the 1980s and 1990s achieved high export levels partly through shipments of coal, wheat, soybeans, timber and paper pulp. Neither pattern promoted long-term high-value-added industry growth.

facturing industry—automobiles, textiles or machine tools—on the part of internationally minded trade, insurance and financial sectors, on which the United States, like prior maturing powers, had come to depend for strong worldwide earnings and profits. Protectionism was implausible, given this dependence, but significant chunks of blue-collar Middle America paid the price as old-line industry eroded.

There are other ways in which internationalism can mean neglect of parochial interests. Each of the great nations at which we have been looking experienced rapid internationalization of its outlook during its zenith and thereafter. Besides opening up much of America, sixteenth-century Spain was also ruling a Hapsburg empire that extended beyond the Iberian Peninsula to Flanders, Germany, Austria and Italy. Increasingly, Madrid came to look to the worldly financiers of Genoa, Augsburg and Antwerp; Spain's upper classes bought large quantities of foreign goods, and by the mid-seventeenth century even Spain's once-Castilian army had become largely one of mercenaries.

The Dutch republic provides a more apt example. At first militantly puritan and nationalistic, shaped by its bitter religious, commercial and political revolution against Spain, early-seventeenth-century Holland scorned French wines and luxury goods. The increasingly polarized and sophisticated Holland of a century later cherished them. French art and the French language, as we have seen, became fashionable. The Dutch traded all over the world, and, in turn, people from almost everywhere came to make their fortunes in Amsterdam. Some were poor—like the soldiers and sailors drawn from virtually everywhere in Europe, and the low-wage German workers known as the *Hollandgänger*—but many were more prosperous or even rich: the French Protestant Huguenots, who came after the revocation of the Edict of Nantes in 1685, Flemish refugees from Hapsburg Antwerp, Sephardic Jews from Spain and Portugal. Braudel notes that by 1650 no less than one third of Amsterdam's population was foreign-born or of foreign extraction. So it was not surprising, during the 1700s, as Dutch investors and financiers sent their ships to Surinam and Java, invested in huge chunks of British government debt, and wooed borrowers—from the Prince of Mecklenburg-Strelitz to the Empress of all the Russias—that the monied classes were in no hurry to rebuild the decaying towns and industries described so vividly by Boswell. Grand international exposures do not whet concern for the low and middle order of one's own nation.

Britain's traditional antipathy to France also faded in the late nineteenth century, as the entente cordiale took shape, and then the Ed-wardian era acquired an increasingly cosmopolitan taste for things French—not least richly sauced food and the balmy winter tempera-tures of Nice or Menton. One chronicler, noting the conspicuous con-sumption of the Edwardian period, pointed out that these were the years when international luxury hotels redrew the profiles of Biarritz, Cannes, Monte Carlo and Marienbad.[49] The Edwardians certainly had the cash. By 1914 Britain's investments overseas represented 43 percent of the *world* total, an unprecedented share, so that investment firms like Rothschilds, Barings and Hambros were not just merchant bank-ers but global powers. Middle-class investors from Tiptree to Tooting thrilled to the profits of Argentine railroads, Canadian gold mines, and Ceylonese tea plantations. Like the mobile or migratory rich who had flocked to Amsterdam two centuries earlier, foreign millionaires found themselves purchasing British estates or London town houses. Like mid-eighteenth-century Holland, Edwardian England was for the wealthy, not a country in which opinion molders worried about the declining purchasing power or prospects of the ordinary British family.

The same was true of the United States of the 1980s. Under Ronald Reagan, the nation attracted many categories of foreigners: political refugees from Latin America and Asia; poor people looking for jobs, mostly from below the border; investors looking for high interest rates; and an upper-bracket minority who partied from the Hamptons to Palm Springs and bought expensive luxury goods and homes in Hawaii and California, Florida and New York. As we have seen, the global chic of market economics, low taxes and deregulation turned conservatives into the most enthusiastic internationalists. In general, free-trade advocates also applauded easy immigration, both legal and illegal, which furnished cheap labor for America's harvests and factories, Irish nannies for Boston, Hispanic and Asian restaurant and household workers for almost every major metropolitan area. For job-seeking Americans with median skills, they might be competitors who depressed wages. For prosperous landowners, factory owners and householders, cheap immi-grant labor was a godsend.

A further measure of immigration's interaction with U.S. cosmopol-itan capitalism was that in 1990 Congress and the president agreed to extraordinary legislation establishing a yearly allotment of permanent residence visas for the families of those who would invest at least $1 million in enterprises that create ten or more new jobs. International investment from nonresidents was also a source of wealth to Ameri-cans. Foreigners' purchases of homes and commercial property in

California, New York and elsewhere tended to boost real estate prices in the late 1980s while paying major commission dollars to U.S. brokers. Moreover, so much money was involved in selling small and large corporations to foreign investors that one newsmagazine observed in 1987 that "the buying of America has virtually turned into an industry of its own."[50] And Japanese investors were also a mainstay of the U.S. bond market.

Downsides abounded. In Hawaii Japanese purchasers pushed the price of houses so high that local residents could no longer afford them. In Washington, D.C., three dozen of the fifty largest foreign multinational corporations had established some form of corporate office by 1991, often because they had bought or established U.S. subsidiaries, and the accelerating influence of foreign lobbyists in the U.S. political process became an issue in Congress and especially in the 1992 presidential race. American multinational corporations also looked overseas, setting up scores of offices in London, Tokyo, Paris, Geneva and Brussels; many were caught up in a transnationalism that de-emphasized commitment to U.S. employees and reduced dependence on the U.S. market for earnings. Prior to the opening of the 1992 World's Fair in Seville, Spain, the U.S. commissioner, Frederick Bush, acknowledged that U.S. companies didn't want to participate and identify themselves as "American." Firms like Time-Warner, CNN and Du Pont, he said, "considered themselves global and transnational and didn't want to be pegged as an American company."[51] Meanwhile, in the automobile industry, production of models and parts was so dispersed around the world that even U.S. government agencies could not agree between themselves on which models were domestic and which were foreign. In 1991–92 the purchase by U.S. investors of *foreign* rather than American stocks and bonds set record after record. As had earlier been the case in Holland and Britain, this cosmopolitanism was no asset to the ordinary American family, which often saw consumer prices rise, public policies shift, manufacturing plants relocate and job opportunities shrivel with a relentlessness that produced a sense of helplessness and frustration.

The third variety of international involvement, a burden on Spain, Holland, Britain and, by the late twentieth century, the United States, was the inevitable overcommitment of declining great economic powers to the sort of military might they could truly afford only at earlier, wealthier stages. In each case, more important national needs were sacrificed.

Spain's military overextension was almost a caricature. Even with gold from the Americas, the wars of the 1540s and 1550s forced the

Spanish Crown to declare itself bankrupt in 1557, and a little less than a century later, as the gold shipments slackened, Spain finally bled to death economically from financing its campaigns in the Thirty Years War that raged across Europe. Paul Kennedy's vivid descriptions in *The Rise and Fall of the Great Powers* hardly require repetition here: Spain spent far beyond its means, even as those means were drying up.

However, even the initially pragmatic Dutch, after less than a century of independence, indulged imperial overstretch in the War of the Spanish Succession (1689–1713) by undertaking a disproportionate military commitment in Flanders and the Iberian Peninsula. The strain broke Holland as a naval power and forced Dutch interest rates up to 9 percent, the highest since independence. The Dutch national debt, just 30 million guilders in 1688, had quintupled to 148 million by 1713, at the end of the war.[52]

The British, in turn, began their tour in the global sun with restraint. Just as their taxes were low in the mid-nineteenth century, so were their military outlays, representing some 2 to 3 percent of GNP. The Crimean War of 1854 had not been widely popular; London kept out of the wars and confrontations on the European continent; and the Liberal governments of the period often displayed anti-imperial tendencies. Britain's national debt fell almost steadily from the finish of the Crimean War to the 1890s. But by the end of the nineteenth century, imperialist sentiment, military outlays and Conservative governments flourished together, culminating in the Boer War of 1899–1902, which increased Britain's debt by 25 percent and precipitated a financial crisis—the first of three, each worse than its predecessor, that would follow Britain's twentieth-century conflicts.

As in Spain, the debt by which Britain ruined itself was largely war-related. World War I saw Britain's national debt expand tenfold, forcing the British to liquidate one fifth to one quarter of their overseas investments, while borrowing £1 billion from the United States and exchanging the status of global creditor for that of debtor. Yet London could not give up its empire, on which the sun still did not set and in which British troops paraded from Bermuda to Bombay while the Royal Navy steamed from Scapa Flow to Singapore.

Then as World War II loomed on Britain's global horizon, the share of GNP spent on defense rose from 5.5 percent in 1937 to 12.5 percent in 1939 and then took over the wartime economy.[53] Once again, national debt rose, more overseas assets were liquidated, and, as we have seen, British economic prowess was reduced to a shadow of yesteryear's.

The historical moral is simple: Excessive global pride or peacekeeping is fiscally self-destructive. Those great economic powers whom the gods would humble, they first line up on the parade grounds of imperial overstretch, although the process seems as much inevitable as voluntary. Great powers do have international responsibilities. And if trade follows the flag, so does ego. Moreover, even when economic resources start running too low to support previous military and policing commitments, fading great powers invariably find themselves involved in military-diplomatic commitments to uphold cherished roles—be they in India, Egypt, Korea or the North Atlantic Treaty Organization.

When the United States was defeated in Vietnam, some historians drew a parallel to Britain's turn-of-the-century embarrassment in the Boer War. But in retrospect, the U.S. disarray after Vietnam was much worse in terms of lost prestige, public frustration, increased debt and inflation. The last quickly caused the oil-producing nations to decide that *they* needed a price increase, making inflation worse. In this sense, the end of the post-1945 era and the stagnation of the 1970s began in the rice paddies of Indochina. What came out of the velds of the Transvaal was minor by comparison.

Yet imperial overstretch is partly psychological, and because Americans were uncomfortable with the lowered world respect that followed U.S. defeat in Vietnam, they rallied to Ronald Reagan's promise in 1980 to rebuild American military strength and prestige. They applauded the series of successful invasions and punitive actions against Third World dictators launched by the Reagan and Bush administrations: Grenada (1983), Tripoli (1986), Panama (1989) and the Persian Gulf (1990–91). Each expedition was followed by 70 to 85 percent support in opinion polls, boosting presidential ratings and diverting attention from less popular domestic and economic policies. But by the early 1990s the huge U.S. federal budget deficit suggested that the military buildup of the 1980s had done serious fiscal damage—though it also contributed to the devastation of the rival Soviet Union, which came undone in 1990–92 partly because its leadership had devoted an even more crippling level of resources to the military.

Reagan entered the White House in 1981 with a federal budget deficit of $74 billion and a total national debt of $1 trillion. By 1992 the budget deficit had quadrupled to roughly $300 billion a year and the total national debt had quadrupled to nearly $4 trillion. Formerly the world's leading creditor, the United States had borrowed enough money overseas—shades of 1914–45 Britain—to become the world's leading debtor, although careful computations suggested that talk of a $700 billion or $800 billion indebtedness was exaggerated. Because of these pressures, as the Bush administration moved closer to war in the Persian Gulf, it responded to congressional demands that other military allies—in particular the kings, emirs and sheikhs of the Gulf, plus the rich Germans and Japanese—share the financial burden. They did, but while fighting in the Gulf the Bush administration neglected the recession at home, and the public's persisting conclusion that the United States was still militarily overextended became an important political complaint in 1991–92. Commitments and expenditures abroad were needed at home, not abroad. Candidates in the primaries of both parties used a battle cry that had not been heard since 1940: Stop dissipating our resources elsewhere; take care of "America first."

Unfortunately, even this concern has its historical counterparts. American defense strategists of the 1990s can usefully recall that in the 1620s Castile, well past its peak, saw that it could no longer afford to bear the principal burden of financing Spain's soldiery—the crack troops whose "Castilian steel" remains a cliché for strength—and the king's chief minister asked the separate parliaments of Aragón, Valencia and Catalonia to share the burden of men and money in a Union of Arms. Aragón and Valencia partially complied; Catalonia scoffed.[54]

British attempts at military burden-sharing began in 1897, when it was suggested that the colonies—principally Canada, Australia and New Zealand—might contribute more to the navy. But by 1902, after the financial stress of the Boer War, the British government called representatives of the colonies and dominions to London to discuss formal naval burden-sharing arrangements, greeting them with charts showing how the average British taxpayer paid 15 shillings a year to support the Royal Navy, the average Australian or New Zealander just a few shillings, and the average Canadian absolutely nothing.[55] Australia, in particular, increased its contribution, but Canada opted for its own small navy. Like Madrid three hundred years earlier (and Washington ninety years later), London wanted to divide the economic burden, but not the strategic control. Unwillingness to divide decision-making is an important reason that imperial overstretch—and its pressure on declining nations and their populations—prevents financial solutions until it is too late.

By the late twentieth century, U.S. opinion-molders had embraced internationalism and cosmopolitanism, and sophisticated Americans had become enthusiastic internationalists. For the economic top 10 percent, that orientation clearly paid off. But as the end of the century drew near, polls showed that the average American believed that "internationalism" was one reason that for them the American Dream was fading.

. . .

In this chapter I have tried to show that within a broad framework, repetition of certain national transitions and failures has marked the decline of great economic powers—and reduced the prospects for ordinary families. In Chapter 10 I shall come back, briefly, to what these historical precedents suggest the United States should do in the 1990s and beyond. But, first, it is appropriate to return to politics—to the signals of economic frustration that were building as the 1990s got under way.

CHAPTER 9

The Politics of
Middle-Class Frustration

Historically, the idea of a broad middle class living in relative comfort—with meat on the table, a car, money in the bank—was a wild fantasy. For most Americans, it did not become reality until the end of the Second World War triggered the swiftest, broadest rise in living standards any society has ever known. But what happens if the fears of more and more of us turn out to be true? What if the middle class discovers it cannot pass a good life on to its children? . . . That kind of realization, I think, can throw our political stability into real jeopardy.

—Columnist Jeff Greenfield, 1991

For the first decade since before World War II, middle-class Americans worked harder, spent less time with their children and spent more on health care, education, housing and taxes. We saw the absolute destruction of the middle class and an explosion in poverty. Only the very wealthy did better in a decade in which Americans literally thought their country was coming apart.

—Democratic presidential nominee Bill Clinton, 1992

The problem is a government and mainstream political parties that don't address the legitimate grievances of the middle class. Until these grievances are addressed, these white working-class and middle-class voters will turn to demogogues who offer simple explanations and simple solutions.

—Lance Hill, executive director of the Louisiana Coalition Against Nazism and Racism, 1991

There was nothing surprising about the spasms of middle-class political radicalism that occurred in 1990–92 as the United States slid into the economic slump that followed the debt-and-speculative orgy of the 1980s. Populism, as we have seen, is never far from the surface of U.S. politics, and signals that had been largely ignored in the elections of November 1990—from the success of independent Socialist Bernard Sanders in his bid for Congress from Vermont to the upset U.S. Senate victory of radical Paul Wellstone in Minnesota—were followed by even more striking results in 1991. Democrat Harris Wofford stunned observers of that year's special Senate election in Pennsylvania by molding issues like national health insurance, fairer taxes, protection for U.S. industries and disdain for Washington into a so-called middle-class populism and achieving that rarest of political successes—an upset *landslide. The Philadelphia Inquirer,* with its daily circulation of a million, had helped shape local restiveness with a preelection series of eight front-page articles describing how the middle class was being hurt by Washington policies that favored the rich. The other big shock came in Louisiana, where former American Nazi David Duke beat the incumbent Republican governor in an open primary, then went on to win two fifths of the statewide total and a surprising 60 percent of the white-middle-class vote, following a campaign in which he presented himself as their political hope. Together, the two results made the political establishment fearful that 1992 was about to bring another of America's periodic rounds of frustration politics—and it was, culminating in Clinton's victory and the 62 percent of the vote cast for populist candidates and change in Washington.

In the United States and Europe alike, popular fear of downward mobility has been one of history's proven sources of political radicalism, both cultural and economic. As we have seen, polarization and anger among ordinary citizens of previous great economic powers who saw themselves losing ground led to food and tax riots and finally revolution in eighteenth-century Holland, and then, in early-twentieth-century Britain, to rapid gains for the Labour party, with its blueprints for class warfare, socialism and the expansion of the welfare state. In both of America's earlier capitalist-conservative boom periods, the Gilded Age and the Roaring Twenties, mild forms of the politics of economic frustration arose even during the optimistic years, and then stronger versions emerged once the debt-and-speculative bubble burst. Partial radicalization of the middle class played a role in both post-boom reactions.

While it is to these frustration politics that we now turn, a second lesson of American history is that corrective mechanisms have worked; the political mainstream *has* adjusted, sometimes unhappily. In 1992, of course, the pressure on the major parties to cope with popular alienation was particularly intensified by the independent challenge of Ross Perot. Yet, over the years, one critical key to the success of the U.S. political system has been its ability—except during the unique Civil War of 1861–65—to control radicalism by absorbing it and/or defusing it in the great watershed realignments we have already discussed in Chapter 3. In these pivotal elections, change-minded or reformist politicians absorbed the messages of splinter candidacies and public discontent, captured the presidency and gave their successive parties a new generation of White House control. In most of the upheavals, specifically in 1824–28, 1892–96, 1932–36 and 1968–72, spasms of radicalism briefly unnerved political moderates, but each time moderate change prevailed, although sometimes it was a close thing.

Against this backdrop, fears expressed before and after the 1992 election that U.S. political stability might break down were also nothing new. Similar predictions had been made in the mid-1890s, early 1930s and late 1960s, always wrongly. True, several of the warnings offered in 1991 came from men to whom the 1930s were a personal memory. William L. Shirer, whose Berlin diaries recorded Adolf Hitler's rise to power, called the politics represented by David Duke in Louisiana a "serious threat to our society," analogizing his appeal to Hitler's.[1] Columnist Max Lerner suggested that, like Weimar Germany, "America today has social and cultural vulnerabilities open for exploiting. Where we hurt most is in the fears, anxieties and rages of our middle class. It has been collecting injustices and letting them fester inwardly since the 1960s. The 90s may prove to be the decade when the explosive angers break out openly and play havoc with party loyalties."[2] As we will see, other serious observers saw fascist and anti-Semitic overtones not just in Duke but in Patrick Buchanan's strong primary challenge to Bush. The brief Democratic primary success of Jerry Brown, with his vitriolic attacks on the corruption of the U.S. political system, followed by Perot's stunning spring emergence and unexpected November strength, held up yet another mirror. And Perot, too, was charged with fascism and authoritarianism. No sooner had one practitioner of frustration or outsider politics subsided than another took his place. If Clinton sounded more radical in 1992 than Franklin D. Roosevelt had in 1932, it was no coincidence.

Prior U.S. Capitalist Heydays and Middle American Frustration Politics

Indeed, the political response of the frustrated middle class in the 1990s recalled previous Middle American responses to earlier boom-and-bust cycles. As we have seen, even before the financial crashes of 1893 and 1929, huge numbers of Americans were being squeezed from farms or jobs by upheavals in technology and shifts in the global economy, which accelerate during boom times.* Then the financial crashes brought much wider pain, and each time this pain produced angry politics.

The excesses of the Gilded Age coincided with a slow and relentless deflation that brutally shrank the agricultural sector after farmers had borrowed to expand during the Civil War decade. We have seen how after 1873, as agricultural income declined and as farms were foreclosed or turned back to prairie, the financial system recycled the credit withdrawn from tillers of the soil to expand railroads and manufacturing, creating huge new wealth for their owners—larger fortunes, indeed, than any the world had ever seen before.

For farmers and dependent small-town merchants and professional men, it was an unbearable policy, a moral outrage. They came to hate the bankers in Wall Street and London, the "robber baron" operators of the great whiskey, leather, beef and tobacco trusts, the railroad owners in Minneapolis, Chicago and Kansas City who charged such high rates for their freight and the politicians who represented these various interests in Washington and state capitals. Because much of this anger was justified, the Granger and Greenback movements of the 1870s and 1880s and the great Populist protest of the 1890s have received a generally sympathetic nod from history. Not coincidentally, many of the measures the Populists proposed—from the progressive income tax to direct election of U.S. senators and popular initiative and referendum at the state level—became law in the progressive reform years from 1900 to 1914.

But Populist frustration involved more than a courageous yeomanry gathering at church suppers and giant open-air rallies to fight for economic justice. When the interests of so many ordinary people are trampled and their entreaties ignored, they turn angry, bitter—and radical. Genealogists seeking the ancestry of political alienation in the early 1990s will find forebears in the late nineteenth century.

The original Populist economics were radical enough that the party's 1892 platform proclaimed that "a vast conspiracy against mankind has been organized on two continents," and William Jennings Bryan's platform in 1896 attacked international moneylenders. A few Populist leaders like Mary Ellen Lease attacked the influence of Jewish bankers and British gold, although Seymour Martin Lipset in his book *The Politics of Unreason* allows that most major Populist leaders made no anti-Semitic references.[3] Part of the reason, however, was that

*See Chapter 4.

anti-Catholicism and concern about immigration were the more typical and familiar response of the largely Protestant population to hard times. As job fears intensified after the Panic of 1893, the American Protective Association, which claimed 2.5 million members, repeatedly raised allegations that Catholics were taking over politics and getting unfair preference in civil service exams. This was a forerunner of the concern over racial quotas and job and college preferences for blacks that would throb in the first years of the 1990s. Even absurd claims that Pope Leo XIII had instructed American Catholics to kill all heretics were taken seriously, and in September 1893 the mayor of Toledo, Ohio, kept the national guard on duty for a week to protect local Protestants against a Catholic murder plot.[4] The American Protective Association was by no means beyond the respectable pale; powerful in California and the Midwest, it was closely connected with the Republican party in the 1894 election. Two years later, however, the GOP was looking for Eastern industrial-state Catholic votes against Bryan and avoided the group.

Most middle-class voters had distrusted Bryan, but once his defeat in 1896 calmed their fears of hayseeds, anarchists and backwoods economists, many well-established Americans felt freer to develop their own parallel indictment of the Gilded Age, laissez-faire and the growth of the great trusts. Historian Richard Hofstadter described the new mood: "The great capitalist entrepreneur, hitherto heroic, lost much of his glamour. He was condemned as an exploiter of labor and an extorter from the consumer, pilloried as an unfair competitor and exposed as a corrupter of political life."[5]

By the first decade of the new century the movement had a name: *Progressivism*. And as one of its leaders, Kansas journalist William Allen White, admitted, he and his allies had originally looked down on the Populists and other "agrarian movements [that] too often appealed to the ne'er-do-wells, the misfits—farmers who had failed, lawyers and doctors who were not orthodox, teachers who could not make the grade, and neurotics full of hates and ebullient, evanescent enthusiasms."[6] Within a few years, however, White would admit that Progressives "caught the Populists in swimming and stole all their clothing except the frayed underdrawers of free silver." And in 1912, when he surveyed the ranks of those who supported Theodore Roosevelt's Progressive third-party bid for the presidency, he described the reformist constituency as "in the main and in its heart of hearts *petit bourgeois*: a movement of little businessmen, professional men, well-to-do farmers, skilled artisans from the upper-brackets of organized labor . . . the successful middle-class country-town citizens, the farmer whose barn was painted, the well-paid railroad engineer and the country editor."[7]

The result, according to Hofstadter, was that after 1900 "populism and progressivism merge." In partially absorbing radicalism, the middle class subdued it—and with far-reaching legislative success, even though Roosevelt lost his 1912 bid to establish progressivism as a political force that would displace or capture the Republican party. From trust-busting to popular election of U.S. senators, much of the old Populist platform found its way into the statute books.

To better understand middle-class frustration in the 1990s, it is fair to recall early-twentieth-century progressivism as the middle-class response to the kindred excesses of the first Gilded Age. Delayed and separately channeled by middle-class cultural incompatibility with rustic Bryanism, progressivism was nevertheless a related response to the disruptions of Darwinian economics, unbridled capitalism and the gaudy conspicuous consumption of nouveaux riches whose colossal fortunes overshadowed and aroused the gentry and professional classes, all phenomena that repeated themselves in the 1980s. Hofstadter and other historians described progressivism circa 1910 as partly the response of a "displaced elite"—the anger of the old Northern Protestant middle and upper-middle classes, from shopkeeper to gentry, at the upheaval that had diminished their influence in favor of robber barons, Wall Street speculators, labor leaders and Catholic big-city machine bosses with their immigrant flocks. As we shall see, this is what the politics of middle-class frustration have often involved: a mixture of cultural conservatism, apprehension about economic status, nativism and anger at the new rich.

The capitalist-conservative heyday of the 1920s, in turn, also produced a backlash even during the boom itself. As early as 1924, maverick GOP senator Robert La Follette of Wisconsin ran for president on a third-party ticket, claiming that 1920s prosperity excluded groups ranging from Midwest dairy farmers to Pacific lumber-mill workers and national railway workers' unions. Beyond broad boom-era support in some areas for the Ku Klux Klan, which was then less controversial than it would soon become, the electorate's flirtation with political extremism did not become serious until well *after* the 1929 Crash—not until 1934 and 1935, after two years of the Roosevelt administration had still not cured the worst economic slump anyone could remember.

With the Depression still unfolding, the election of 1932 had been reasonably sedate, although the Communist and Socialist vote tripled to nearly one million. Some observers suggested that voters were still numb. Not so by 1934, when socialist Upton Sinclair got 38 percent of the vote running as the Democratic nominee for governor of California, and partly socialist factions or third parties dominated state politics in Washington, North Dakota, Wisconsin and Minnesota. While William Dudley Pelley's Silver Shirts were a small Nazi-like group, as was the Black Legion, which a grand jury in Michigan refused to indict for fascist conspiracy because its leaders were so unintelligent, the largest radical movements of the time combined components of left *and* right, as well as elements of both populism and middle-class radicalism.[8] These were the Share-the-Wealth movement of Louisiana U.S. senator Huey Long and the National Union for Social Justice, organized and run by Father Charles Coughlin, the Michigan-based Catholic radio priest, both of which somewhat foreshadowed Duke and Buchanan in 1991–92.

Both traded on the deepening frustration with the moderate politics of Franklin D. Roosevelt as the Depression continued, and because Long and Coughlin together had the political support of millions heading toward the 1936 elections, Roosevelt shifted his tax and economic policies leftward in 1935 to head them off, but that is getting ahead of our story. Long, who had risen during the 1920s to become Louisiana's governor, thereafter moving to the U.S. Senate in 1932, was a fierce populist who rejected that label and lineage because of its leftover bumpkin implications. As governor he had an extraordinary record—if one overlooked his dictatorial manner and open corruption—of giving children free textbooks, building roads and schools, and restructuring state taxes so that corporations and utilities had to pay. One way or another, his whole career foreshadowed what he finally proposed in 1934 and 1935: his revolutionary scheme for sharing the nation's wealth through a minimum wage of $2,500 a year, an end to unemployment, a gift of $4,000 for every family from the confiscation of millionaires' wealth and college educations at federal expense for every boy who had the abilities.

Huey Long had begun his career in Washington as a supporter of FDR, but he had changed his mind by 1933, calling the new president an enemy of the poor. By 1934 he had launched his Share-the-Wealth organization, started a regular national weekly radio program and established a newspaper, the *American Progress,* through which he attacked Wall Street and its power, harangued against how much the rich spent on yachts and even discussed plots by Standard Oil to kill him. His enemies were characterized as "high-brow Brain Trusters, low-brow eastern politicians, top-hatted . . . cigar-smoking Wall Streeters" allied in their commitment to bilking the common man.[9] When asked if he intended to be a candidate against Roosevelt in 1936, he said, "If events appear to be what they are now and circumstances are what they appear to be, it's almost certain that I will be a candidate."[10]

White House strategists were more than worried. In February 1935 Long claimed to have more than 27,000 Share-the-Wealth clubs, plus the names of almost 8 million members on file. When the Democratic National Committee commissioned a private opinion poll to measure his appeal as a potential third-party candidate, it found that he might draw 3 or 4 million votes, 7 to 9 percent of the total, and, in the words of party chairman James A. Farley, "might have the balance of power in the 1936 election."[11]

Father Coughlin, much less important, was another 1932 Roosevelt supporter who had turned against the administration as the Depression persisted and he saw the president courting establishment interests. In the autumn of 1934 he founded the National Union for Social Justice to press for a guaranteed annual wage and government ownership and control of U.S. banks. Although Coughlin, like Long, shunned the populist label, his speeches had an unmistakable populist flavoring. One chronicler notes that he denounced rich and well-educated Easterners, "the luxury of Park Avenue and Westchester" against "widows, orphans and inarticulate farmers," and "Wall Street attorneys, the erudition of Harvard, of Yale, of Princeton, of Columbia," directed against servant girls, laborers, farmers.[12] Coughlin claimed 5 million members for the National Union, and a Gallup Poll suggested that 7 percent would vote for a Coughlin-favored candidate in the 1936 presidential election.

Franklin Delano Roosevelt didn't wait to find out. His close adviser Raymond Moley later recalled that the president began discussing ways of trying to steal "Long's thunder" by making a "counteroffer" to the voters. This he did in June 1935 by asking Congress to pass the Wealth Tax Act, with its soak-the-rich income levies, new inheritance tax, increased estate- and gift-tax levies and new graduated tax on corporate incomes. In his message to Congress, Roosevelt stole some of Long's thunder and declared, "Our revenue laws have operated in many ways to the unfair advantage of the few, and they have done little to prevent an unjust concentration of wealth and economic power."[13] Along with other legislation like the Social Security Act, the Public

Utility Holding Company Act and the Farm Mortgage Moratorium Act, the Wealth Tax Act was the centerpiece of the Second New Deal—Roosevelt's shift to the left in preparation for a 1936 election in which he would be opposed by Long on a third-party ticket, attacking Roosevelt as the lapdog of the Mellons and Morgans.

It never happened, because in September 1935, only months after the Second New Deal was completed, Long was assassinated in the state capitol in Baton Rouge. His followers were devastated. As one half-admiring journalist wrote years later of his funeral, "one hundred thousand people trekked to Baton Rouge to pay their respects. Funeral trains left New Orleans every half hour, and cars backed up for miles waiting to cross the Mississippi River by ferry."[14] Without Long, and with Roosevelt having turned to the left, Father Coughlin and other, lesser figures turned increasingly shrill and anti-Semitic, falling from the heights of their broader 1934–35 appeal.

Even so, Roosevelt took no chances. In his 1936 annual message to Congress he welcomed "the hatred of entrenched greed," later telling a campaign rally, "I should like to have it said of my first Administration that in it the forces of selfishness and of lust for power met their match. I should like to have it said of my second Administration that in it, these forces met their master."[15] Some of Roosevelt's rallies turned these sentiments into something uncommon in U.S. politics— open class warfare:

As the 1936 campaign got underway, the note of class conflict sometimes reached a high pitch. At an excited night meeting at Forbes Field in Pittsburgh, a stern-faced Danton, State Senator Warren Roberts, spat out the names of the Republican oligarchs: Mellon, Grundy, Pew, Rockefeller. The crowd greeted each name with a resounding "boo." "You could almost hear the swish of the guillotine blade," wrote one reporter afterwards. Then came Governor George Earle, their handsome Mirabeau, and he too churned up the crowd against the enemies of their class. "There are the Mellons, who have grown fabulously wealthy from the toil of men of iron and steel . . . Grundy, whose sweatshop operators have been the shame and disgrace of Pennsylvania for a generation; Pew, who strives to build a political and economic empire with himself as dictator; the duPonts, whose dollars were earned with the blood of American soldiers; Morgan, financier of war." As he sounded each name, the crowd interrupted him with a chorus of jeers against the business leaders. Then the gates opened at a far corner of the park; a motor-cycle convoy put-putted its way into the field, followed by an open car in which rode

Franklin Delano Roosevelt, grinning and waving his hat, and the crowd, whipped to a frenzy, roared its welcome to their champion.[16]

The 1936 elections were a great Democratic success and cemented realignment. Roosevelt had absorbed the vital part of Long's message. Coughlin's presidential candidate, North Dakota congressman William Lemke, running as an independent, could manage only 2 percent of the total vote. Coughlin's radio programs continued, but the possibility of a major national radical movement ended in 1935.

Just as the 1991–92 rhetoric of Buchanan and Duke would mix an anti-elite and populist message in a confusing package that also included nationalism, anti-immigrant sentiment and economic appeals to the middle class, historians disagree on what Long and Coughlin represented—lower-class populism, fascism or a blurred middle-class radical response to economic upheaval. Arthur Schlesinger, Jr., identified the adherents of Long and Coughlin as coming "mostly . . . from the old lower-middle classes, now in an unprecedented stage of frustration and fear."[17] Seymour Martin Lipset and Earl Raab, while pointing out the basically populist antecedents of Long's low-income Louisiana electorate, argued that both men enjoyed a considerable middle-class following as their national movement swelled during the peak years of discontent in 1934–35.[18] Periods of economic frustration commonly produce this kind of ideological confusion; indeed, it's to be counted on.

Perhaps the best analysis of the hybrid forces involved was Alan Brinkley's in his 1982 book, *Voices of Protest.* Long and Coughlin, he pointed out, declined to call themselves populists, despite their similar depiction of foes as scheming financiers or sybaritic plutocrats, first because they preferred to avoid a linkage with past electoral failure, but also because they preferred to shun some of Populism's economic radicalisms so as to enlarge their middle-class appeal. Whereas the Populists had often criticized local merchants and bankers, Long and Coughlin often romanticized them, upholding their role against the threat of giant corporations, militant labor unions, remote bureaucrats and international bankers. Duke and Buchanan would read from somewhat similar scripts sixty years later. In 1935 *The New Republic* had been surprised, Brinkley points out, that Long and Coughlin seemed to be rallying the "lower middle class," "small businessmen and professionals," in a "militant and honorable protest."[19] Because of its relevance again almost sixty years later, his explanation is worth quoting in full:

The term "middle class" is a vague one, to be sure; and if the conventional, popular image of the American bourgeoisie were to be the standard, few Long and Coughlin supporters would qualify. They were not usually men and women who lived in neat suburban bungalows or who worked at comfortable, white-collar jobs. More often they lived precariously and somewhat shabbily. Their membership in the middle class was less a result of their level of material comfort than of a certain social outlook. They were, they believed, people who had risen above the lowest levels of society, who had acquired a stake, however modest, in their community, who were protecting hard-won badges of status and carefully guarded, if modest, financial achievements. Others may have suffered more in absolute terms from the 1930s economy, but those on the fringes of the middle class confronted an especially agonizing form of loss. Having gained a foothold in the world of bourgeois respectability, they stood in danger of being plunged back into what they viewed as an abyss of powerlessness and dependence. It was that fear that made the middle class, even more than those who were truly rootless and indigent, a politically volatile group.[20]

The New Deal and World War II rescued these worried Americans, so that they or their children would march in the broad, triumphant middle-class parade of the 1950s and 1960s. But the next decade brought back kindred concerns, making the hybrid radicalism of the early to mid-1930s—what some academicians have called "extremism of the center"—a psychological and political precedent for the anger that flared again in Middle America at intervals of economic stress from the mid-1970s down to the 1990s.

The New Wave of Middle American Radicalism, 1973–1981

The Republican presidential majority that was created in the 1968–72 period, stealing the third-party thunder of George Wallace much as FDR had stolen that of Huey Long, once again affirmed the success of the system. As in previous U.S. political realignments, the "center" had radicalized, shifted, and was settling. But within two years, the OPEC oil shock of 1973 and Nixon's resignation over Watergate would leave the direction of U.S. politics and economics in doubt once more. George Wallace's political insurgency of 1964–72 had drawn largely on national (and especially Southern) racial and cultural frustration. From 1973 on, a third factor became increasingly important—economics had now joined culture and race.

Not surprisingly, the first forced resignation of a president of the United States in 1974 and the stagflation of 1973–74 sent the American political fever chart rising. George Wallace, until he was shot in 1972, had warned about a radicalization of the middle class. By late 1974, in the trough of that year's recession, polls gave new weight to that prospect. Back in the mid-1970s, I briefly collaborated with Patrick Caddell—who had been George McGovern's pollster in 1972 and would be Jimmy Carter's in 1976 and 1980—on some research into middle-class radicalism. Caddell believed that America was caught up in a new wave of frustration politics, and in late 1974, with Watergate a fresh scar on the nation's psyche and unemployment climbing toward a post-Depression high, he conducted a survey based on two-and-a-half-hour, in-depth interviews designed to drag to the surface political beliefs and pathologies overlooked by more superficial samplings.

The results were fascinating. Back in 1972 Caddell had found 18 percent of those queried willing to back George Wallace for president—9 percent really wanted him in the Oval Office and the other 9 percent were willing to cast a protest vote. By late 1974, however, Caddell found fully 18 percent eager to put Wallace in the White House, while another 17 percent were willing to cast a protest vote for him. That came to 35 percent, twice Wallace's 1972 strength and nearly triple his actual 1968 third-party presidential vote. Voter ideology was churning, the Democratic polltaker pointed out, as a growing number of people simultaneously favored radical socialist economic positions while backing a hard-line, even authoritarian position on social issues. "The people smack in the middle—the people who are the least ideological—are the most volatile," he said. Forty-one percent agreed that "the true American way of life is disappearing so fast we may have to use force to save it." He concluded that "the middle class is coming unhinged. 'Center extremism' is correct" as a description.[21]

That was at the low point of the recession. But another analyst, University of Michigan sociologist Donald Warren, argued more broadly that the convulsions of the 1960s and early 1970s had turned 20 to 30 percent of the electorate into what he called "Middle American radicals"—men and women whose ideology fitted neither liberal nor conservative prescriptions but mixed economic apprehension with indignant social conservatism and suspicion of rich and poor alike:

For many white Americans, the rejection of the blacks and poor is only one part of a larger rejection of the government and the rich. Preliminary data from a national cross-section probability sampling of 1690 white Americans indicate that 30 percent of the population thought that the blacks had too much political power; 63 percent said that about the rich. Approximately 30 percent said that poor blacks were getting more than their fair share of government aid; 56 percent said the same thing about the rich. Eighteen percent said that blacks have a better chance than whites to get fair treatment from courts, while 42 percent said that about the rich. In other words, hostility toward the rich is extensive; it may equal, or even exceed, hostility toward blacks.[22]

By this analysis, racial tensions were partly fueled by a larger frustration. What Caddell and Warren were talking about in the 1970s, besides its continuity with elements of the Long and Coughlin movements of the 1930s, also foreshadowed dynamics that would operate again in the early 1990s. Indeed, David Duke's roots in the American Nazi movement, although he disavowed them in 1991 and 1992, suggest a further perspective: The "center extremist" analysis of a radicalized Middle America had also described—in much more inflammatory circumstances—the surprising support base of Adolf Hitler's National Socialist German Workers' party. According to the sociologist Harold Lasswell in the 1930s and Seymour Martin Lipset in the 1960s and 1970s, the core of national socialism was a frustrated and radicalized lower-middle and middle class. The Nazi party arose not out of the traditional political right but out of the breakdown of what had in the 1920s been the middle-class parties of the political *center*.[23] Nazism, from this perspective, was middle-class radicalization at its extreme.

In the less provocative context of the United States, the trauma of 1973–75 had left enough disillusionment that by 1980, as the Carter administration was overtaken by further embarrassments ranging from double-digit inflation to Iran's seizure of the U.S. embassy staff as hostages, confidence in government slumped and another round of radicalism stirred on the periphery of Middle American politics. Harold Covington, leader of the U.S. Nazi party, got over 40 percent of the vote in the May 1980 Republican primary for attorney general of North Carolina; Thomas Metzger, leader of the state Ku Klux Klan, won the Democratic nomination for Congress in the June primary in the suburban 43rd Congressional District of California; and former Nazi party member Gerald Carlson, who quit to found the National Christian Democratic Union, won the Republican primary in the suburban 15th District of Michigan, and then scored heavily in the general election as well. In both California and Michigan, party officials expressed concern that the radical votes were cast deliberately, and that the more publicity Metzger and Carlson got, the more support they would get.[24]

It turned out not to matter, though, because in a sense the most important "radical" success in 1980 came at the White House level: the election of an "outsider conservative" Republican president—Ronald Reagan—whose appeal reinvigorated the basic coalition that had put Richard Nixon in office twelve years earlier by promising a new prosperity, a new patriotism and a new U.S. global eminence. Middle American radicalism thereupon waited to see if the promise would be fulfilled.

David Duke, Patrick Buchanan, Jerry Brown, Ross Perot and the Return of Middle American Radicalism in the 1990s

By the early 1990s the acid eating into America's confidence measured how much those hopes were fading. There had been some disturbing evidence in 1988; by 1991–92 there was much more. Senior Japanese officials were publicly scoffing at the United States, and opinion polls found that a 63 percent majority of Americans described the United States as in decline. The American Dream was collapsing in a cross fire of shrunken home values, eroding real family incomes and shaky pensions. And so politics, the inescapable mirror, began producing another round of Middle American radicalism. Autumn 1990 brought several unexpected election results, and then in 1991, when Duke surprised in Louisiana and liberal Democrat Wofford won Pennsylvania's Senate race on a platform of middle-class populism, Democratic strategist Robert Beckel identified the feelings to which they had successfully appealed: frustration and fear.[25]

It was Wofford's success, ironically, that persuaded right-wing populist commentator Buchanan to oppose Bush in the 1992 Republican primaries. Then Duke quickly followed suit. Middle American radicalism would have a national forum. Buchanan's Irish Catholic father had listened to Father Coughlin back in the 1930s, and some journalists perceived a recurring isolationist and anti-Semitic thread: the Louisiana neo-fascist and the feisty Irish rightist were tapping into old currents.*

*Democratic Senator Tom Harkin of Iowa, whose Irish father also listened to Coughlin, was, despite his liberalism, the other 1992 presidential candidate who joined the conservative Buchanan in populism, class warfare, trade protectionism, neo-isolationism and likening Bush to Britain's King George III.

Indeed, one can identify common ingredients that reach from Buchanan and Duke back through the 1930s and in some cases to the 1890s: middle-class economic apprehensions and status fears, concern that other groups are getting unfair job preferences, overtones of anti-Semitism and nativism, opposition to excessive immigration, economic nationalism and distrust of foreign bankers and diplomats, explicit isolationist or America First psychologies, hostility to various groups—Wall Street, Washington, big labor or big business—and the intensifying of the desire of voters for more "direct democracy" in order to bypass entrenched interest groups. Brown and Perot also voiced some of these viewpoints while avoiding the pitfalls of anti-Semitism, nativism, racism or isolationism. Candidates drawing heavily—rather than marginally—on such themes have generated significant political bow waves only in periods of high economic fear, notably the busts following the three booms that this book has been examining.

Yet despite this continuity with previous periods of fear for the American Dream, the malaise of the 1990s also involved important differences. In sharp contrast with its situation in the 1890s and 1930s, the United States was past its global economic peak, losing ground in ways that threatened purchasing power and standards of living for many Americans. These threats produced an international focus largely missing in the 1930s or 1890s, specifically fear of Japan and the emergence of the Japanese as 1992 political bogeymen for Americans, although concern that U.S. manufacturing jobs were moving to Mexico was also a factor. Still another difference lay in the greater importance of racial fears, which had been a part of the post-1968 Republican presidential coalition. Duke and then, more prominently, Buchanan spoke to both racial and international apprehensions; Brown and Perot confined themselves to the economic concerns about Japan and Mexico.

Let us stipulate: ethnic, racial and religious tensions in the United States have typically accompanied hard times as individuals and groups worry about lost jobs, declining incomes and competition for scarce rewards. So the rise of racial quotas as an issue among white votes in the early 1990s in several ways echoed the 1890s. On one hand, it bore some resemblance to the fear among Northern Protestants in the mid-1890s of job preferences going to Catholics with the help of big-city political machines. In the South, however, the intergroup tension in the 1890s was racial, and at the state level, conservatives often used race to defeat populist challenges, sometimes by mobilizing blocks of subservient black voters to defeat white populists, but sometimes by using racial animosities to break up tentative black-white populist coalitions.

Some analysts believed that national frustration would produce similar effects in the 1990s—that economic progressivism or populism would fail because conservatives would employ racial politics to suppress it. According to this argument, the Republicans, after building their presidential coalition around racial tensions, would continue to inflame them, helped by Democratic insensitivity to middle-class concerns on taxes, crime and the welfare system. There was some basis for these assumptions because the 1968–72 realignment had left the Democrats with 90 to 95 percent of the black vote and a liberal social philosophy disliked by parts of Middle America for seeming to "pander" to blacks at the expense of white interests. After 1968, presidential voting across much of the South had indeed polarized along racial lines. Moreover, the 1988 Bush campaign had sought to tap racial tensions with its emphasis on Willie Horton, the black murderer who raped a white woman while he was on furlough from prison, and then again in its 1991 attempt to elevate racial quotas into a major national issue.

Despite these tactics, the racial basis of voting was frequently exaggerated, as shown by Democrat Clinton's ability to subordinate old tensions in a 1992 victory that combined a majority of the black vote with a close division of the white vote. Many critics of the GOP did not fully understand how earlier Democratic loyalties in the South and Northern ethnic areas had broken down over two generations for a wide range of reasons, far beyond race. When the Democrats had a winning message again, racial tensions would not stop them. In 1969, in *The Emerging Republican Majority,* I laid out the history of the forces combining to pull the South and border states into the Republican presidential coalition. The first momentum came in 1952, when most of the segregationist Dixiecrats who had voted for Strom Thurmond's States Rights presidential ticket in 1948 realigned to support Republican Dwight Eisenhower. Parenthetically, Eisenhower didn't give them any racial concessions; on the contrary, he lost some support in the Deep South in 1956 after he sent federal troops into Little Rock, Arkansas, to uphold the school desegregation mandated in 1953 by the U.S. Supreme Court. However, Dixiecrat voting, highest in the plantation South and affluent suburbs, was motivated by economics as well as by race, so that once historic ties to the Democratic party of the Confederacy had been broken, these constituencies had broad socioeconomic reasons to vote Republican. Southerners followed suit again in 1956—despite Eisenhower's enforcement of desegregation—so that the GOP incumbent, besides carrying Texas, Tennessee, Florida and Virginia, also won Louisiana and came surprisingly close in Arkansas and North Carolina.

By the 1960s, then, Southern white Democratic presidential loyalties had been fading for over a decade and were all but gone in high- and upper-middle-income areas. Yet, with the civil rights revolution at its peak, some Republicans foolishly gambled in 1964 that they could hasten Southern realignment by opposing civil rights—the basis of the disastrous presidential campaign of Arizona senator Barry Goldwater, who lost every state in the nation except for the Deep South tier of South Carolina, Georgia, Alabama, Mississippi and Louisiana. Four years later, with Alabama governor Wallace bolting the Democratic party to run as a pro-segregation independent, the Republicans under Richard Nixon had wisely fallen back to a pro–civil rights posture waiting for regional third-party activity to exhaust itself so that disillusioned white Democrats would be drawn to the GOP by a broad range of cultural issues. This meant that in 1968 Nixon carried essentially the states of the Outer South; the rest would wait.

I discussed these pro-Republican forces in detail in my 1969 book, and as they converged so massively in Richard Nixon's 1972 Southern sweep, they included not just race but also small-town and rural values, patriotism, doubts about welfare, religious traditionalism and a hostility toward bureaucrats, judges, intellectuals and the news media.* No one doubted, for example, that the South was the most hawkish part of the United States in supporting the war in Vietnam—on the day George Wallace was shot in Maryland in 1972, he had been attacking liberals for starting the war and then not letting America win. Moreover, in the early 1970s several books were published on the rapid emergence of white fundamentalist and evangelical Protestants, many of them Southerners, as a key swing vote that threatened the Democratic party's future.[26] Race was a catalyst of Dixie realignment, but by no means its only one, there were many others.

What *The Emerging Republican Majority* had shown, in a nutshell, was that the Democratic presidential coalition was collapsing because it reflected obsolescent and unsustainable Civil War loyalties. Back in 1960, counties in the fifteen or so Southern and border states still voted

---

*Published in 1969, *The Emerging Republican Majority* predicted that the South would turn into a mainstay of a Republican presidential cycle and explained the dynamics involved. *Newsweek* described the book as "the political bible of the Nixon Era," and it had a substantial effect on GOP strategy.

largely as they had fought in 1861–65, an allegiance that made decreasing sense as the presidential Democratic party turned away from its old values and became the party of Harvard, Harlem and Hollywood. Cultural upheaval in the United States of the 1960s was simply too intense to permit a national party committed to left-liberal elites and their values to retain small-town, rural and suburban presidential voters of moderate to conservative outlook who were Democrats largely because a century earlier their families had worn Confederate gray. For this reason, I predicted that the Republicans would first win the relatively moderate Outer South and then would win the racially tense Deep South or Contingent South once these states acquiesced in the civil rights revolution and stopped supporting sectional third-party protest candidates.

That is what happened by 1972, but power shifts invariably breed controversy, and some liberal critics of the Republican party found malevolent depths in the Southern realignment, calling it racist. The irony was that Richard Nixon, while opposing busing for racial balance, permissive jurisprudence and weak handling of crime and riots, was a Quaker with a strong civil rights record. As president, he proposed—somewhat naively—a family-assistance (guaranteed-income) plan for the poor, successfully launched the federal food stamp program and submitted an early version, refused in Congress, of a national health insurance program. He even endorsed affirmative action proposals—the so-called Philadelphia plan—that paved the way for racial hiring quotas. To other critics, not just the GOP but the U.S. electorate as a whole was "racist." Historically, though, the old Civil War Democratic presidential coalition was simply unsustainable by the mid-1960s. Its collapse empowered a cultural and economic conservatism that benefited from some obvious racial cleavages, but categorically racial interpretations were unwarranted, at least at the time.

In the 1980s, however, the politics of maintaining the Republican coalition became more strident. Back in 1970, not only did Richard Nixon remember his Quaker upbringing and the 20 to 30 percent of the black vote he received in the 1960 presidential election, but the memory of the 1964 Goldwater debacle was still strong and cautionary while an egalitarian commitment remained a powerful force in U.S. culture. After Ronald Reagan's inauguration, as we have seen, a new climate began to unfold. Goldwater's defeat in 1964 had been avenged by the election in 1980 of a GOP president almost as conservative; once avenged, Goldwater's loss was no longer a chastening memory. Egalitarian thinking was also in retreat; survival-of-the-fittest economic conservatism and use-your-own-bootstraps antiwelfarist ideology were first cousins. As the apparent boom of the eighties got under way, Republicans believed themselves to be building a realignment and new national majority in which blacks didn't matter much save for a small but growing minority of conservative black businessmen and entrepreneurs. Voters also reflected the new ideology and restated it bluntly enough to inquiring pollsters: the Democrats were too soft on crime, welfare and racial quotas and paid too much attention to blacks. GOP political postures were reinforced accordingly.

Yet too little attention was being paid to important countercurrents. Despite the racial tensions and polarization apparent in the Deep South and in many big cities, national opinion polls showed Americans distinctly more liberal on racial issues than they had been twenty or twenty-five years earlier. By 1989, when David Dinkins became New York City's first black mayor, most of the other big U.S. cities had already broken this barrier. That year also saw the victory of the nation's first elected black governor—Douglas Wilder of Virginia. Then in 1990, Harvey Gantt, a black former mayor of Charlotte, drew 47 percent in North Carolina's Senate race against conservative Republican stalwart Jesse Helms. Incumbent Helms ran TV commercials unfairly linking Gantt to racial quotas, but Gantt *had,* in fact, participated in a broadcasting license application involving a minority preference. Also to the point, had Gantt opposed Helms back in 1972, he would have been lucky to get 36 percent or 38 percent of the vote. In 1990, however, the onetime Charlotte mayor ran well enough in some normally Republican-leaning suburbs to help the Democrats *gain* seats in the North Carolina House of Representatives, and when that House met in January 1991, it elected its first black Speaker. These events hardly symbolized a powerful new backlash against blacks.

Such perceptions were widespread, though, and partially in response, the Bush administration decided to attack the so-called Civil Rights Act of 1991 as a Democratic attempt to enact a system of racial quotas. Bush himself made this charge on several occasions. Aware of how much voters disliked quotas, some commentators proclaimed that Bush had found a way to override Democratic attempts to dabble in class warfare or economic populism. The middle class, they said, would vote according to racial, not economic, resentments. But there were complications even within the Republican coalition. Suburban and upper-income moderate voters, unhappy with the president's racial tactics, were pressuring him to stop, while critics on Bush's right, such as Duke and Buchanan, charged him with appeasement of racial disorder and insincerity in his anti-quota position. Conservative cohesion was crumbling.

Then in late 1991, after Duke's defeat of Republican governor Roemer in Louisiana's open primary, pundits and civil rights leaders unleashed a new criticism. The Bush administration, they charged, had helped create the harsh atmosphere in which an ex-Nazi could succeed. Some moderate Republicans agreed. Bush thereupon quickly agreed to a civil rights bill very much like the one he had earlier opposed, rejecting conservative complaints that the bipartisan compromise still accepted racial quotas.

His decision was a two-edged sword. Blacks were minimally reassured, but both Buchanan and Duke accused the president of betraying low- and middle-income whites. Indeed, following his surprising February GOP primary showing in New Hampshire, Buchanan made a powerful speech to the national Conservative Political Action Conference: upper-class Republicans couldn't be trusted, he said, because they were willing to let ordinary families bear the brunt of minority preferences. It was the "sons of Middle America," in the factories, front offices and fire departments, who were being betrayed on racial quotas by the "Exeter-Yale GOP club . . . the scions of Yale and Harvard . . . the Walker's Point GOP." Such bitter, class-based attacks from the populist right struck at the core of what some described as a White House strategy of administering racial preferences while publicly deploring them and dabbling in covert racial incitement to distract less affluent white voters from economic dissatisfactions. That kind of straddle was unworkable against a serious opposition on the right that demanded anti-quota actions, not just words, even while liberals belabored Bush's inconsistency from the other direction.

Exactly this, however, was part of what Buchanan and Duke briefly represented: significant right-wing insurgency against a Republican president and ruling GOP establishment for the first time since the 1970s. By spring, independent presidential candidate Perot, a former Republican, attacked from yet another direction, this one centrist and critical of Bush's inattention to the cities and lack of a domestic policy as well as his reliance on racial tactics like the Willie Horton ad. Middle American radicalism was back, but in a new role. *Frustrated voters were now ready to question the tactics, loyalties and failures of establishment conservatism, and thus begin fragmenting the right.* Populist dissatisfaction with elite conservative performance would make some cultural and racial issues *divisive* instead of *expansive* for the aging

Republican coalition. Several Rupublicans complained that Bush was hobbled on the quotas issue; the Democrats would only need to quote Pat Buchanan. Moreover, populist voters—not least George Wallace supporters and their heirs, who had been pulled into the Republican coalition by Nixon and then Reagan—were starting to demand government activism, which they doubted could ever come from establishment Republicanism. Voter dissatisfaction with the weak economy and seeming White House inattention to domestic policy was pervasive. Thus, when Los Angeles burst into flames in late April, White House strategists were stunned: instead of profiting from rising racial tension, George Bush lost support for appearing indecisive and trying to blame the chaos on the programs of a Democratic administration that had left office in 1969!

Simply put, liberalism circa 1992 had been out of power too long to be an effective straw man and conservatives had been in power too long to shift responsibility. Voters were anxious over economic and social problems—including unemployment and urban breakdown—that had worsened during three successive Republican presidencies after 1980. Liberals might share blame—indeed, most Americans thought they did—but voter opposition to the status quo necessarily created problems for the party with twelve years in the White House. Moreover, whether in 1860, the 1890s, 1932 or 1968, voters blamed the party in the White House when the national social fabric was torn by riots and other expressions of discontent, and they did again in 1992. Assumptions by Bush strategists that racial tensions and family "values" would still rescue them on Election Day staggered under three separate challenges—from right-wing populists who charged them with deceiving Middle America on behalf of the Exeter-Yale GOP Club, from centrists who said the nation could not afford a domestic policy premised on negativism, and from Democrat Clinton, who took advantage of the failure of both conservative economics and liberal social theory to start building a biracial coalition around a new centrist politics.

The Democratic nominee himself used reasonably strong populist language about taking the country back for middle-class and working-class Americans, words and images that helped him win a large percentage of the disillusioned and outsider electorate. However, the full-fledged frustration candidates had played a pivotal role—and also an extraordinary role because there were so many of them. In different ways and degrees, Duke, Buchanan, Brown and Perot were successive heirs in 1991–92 to what Caddell and Warren had called center extremism and Middle American radicalism. In the end, Duke faded with little lasting effect save to help embarrass Bush into abandoning the racial-quotas issue. Buchanan and Brown both played important catalytic roles, and the 37 percent that Buchanan drew against Bush in the New Hampshire primary *did* turn out to forecast the president's November defeat. No elected Republican president since William Howard Taft—not even Herbert Hoover—had been forced to spend almost a month actively campaigning against a challenger for renomination, and many of the 30 to 35 percent of GOP voters who supported Buchanan in February and March primaries hardened their further opposition to Bush. Buchanan's pollster, in fact, soon turned up taking surveys for Ross Perot.

The Texas billionaire, of course, was the most powerful voice of 1992 frustration politics, attacking Washington's scandals, foreign lobbyists and special interests, exhorting citizens to preserve their children's future and demanding that the United States take care of American interests and American jobs and worry less about the rest of the world. His was a more centrist and less ideological message than that of the others—several pundits likened Perot to a national Roto-Rooter-man —and it proved so powerful that in May and June national surveys showed him pulling ahead of both Bush and Clinton, the strongest independent showing ever recorded. When he dropped out of the race in July—following sharp personal attacks orchestrated by the Bush White House—the fight between the Republicans and Democrats for Perot supporters, as we shall see, became the key to the election, with Clinton the principal beneficiary. Although Perot reentered the race in October to promote his economic message and institutionalize his support for some future purpose, his most important effect on the 1992 political outcome was to damage Bush and divert a large chunk of the Republican coalition, something Clinton had been too weak to achieve during the April, May, and June period when Perot was at his peak. More than any other aroused voices of 1991–92, Perot enlarged the "frustration electorate" to the detriment of the crumbling Republican coalition.

And so in large measure, history appeared to repeat itself. Once again, the forces of Middle American radicalism, unable to carry the day in their own right, were obliged to imprint the valid portions of their agendas, platforms and demand for change on mainstream politics. This was what had happened during the Progressive and New Deal eras, and Democrats assumed that the new Clinton administration, elected on the rhetoric of populism and progressivism, would be similarly energized. But although 1992 appeared to follow this familiar pattern, there were potentially significant differences.

The Election of 1992 and the Prospect of Middle-Class Renewal

A Democratic candidate then (in 1992) must link the idea of America's larger role in the post-cold-war world with the U.S. economic crisis, which must be considered as the crisis of the middle class. These crises—of the U.S. economy and the middle class—must be seen as one and the same. Any drift in the message away from this central linkage will almost certainly prove to be self-defeating. The indispensable element for national action remains a strong purposeful, energetic presidency.

—*The New Republic,* 1990

For some time, it has been clear that U.S. national security interests must include the development of policies that will increase our economic strength and domestic stability. Now, I believe a new definition of national security that recalls the vision of 1947—and augments it with more forceful economic and domestic policy components—is urgently needed. Indeed, I suspect that no foreign challenge of the 1990s will affect America's security as much as what we do, or fail to do, at home on a range of economic and social issues.

—Peter G. Peterson, chairman of the Council on Foreign Relations, 1991

If there is not a substantial reversal of this [federal budget deficit] trend, you will see a third party in 1996, and it will be a broadly based third party.

—Republican U.S. senator Warren Rudman, October 1992

November 3, 1992, was a sunny day in Washington, bright with optimism, and long before it was over, the capital was caught up in reports of a huge Election Day turnout and a Democratic landslide in the making.

By the next morning, Democrats were speaking of a political watershed, but without saying exactly what this watershed would be. However, in the last weeks of the campaign, it had become clear what any watershed would have to involve: nothing less than the economic renewal of the United States and its worried middle class. As the race ended, George Bush and Bill Clinton were each promising middle-class

Americans not to raise their taxes or cut their entitlement programs while warning that the other candidate could not be trusted. Never before were such commitments so central to a presidential campaign. In the watershed election of 1968 the promises of the winning Republicans were largely cultural—to curb crime, restore order and uphold patriotism; in 1992, however, the critical pledges were economic: *that the federal government would not further jeopardize the already endangered middle-class standard of living by taking more money from ordinary Americans' wallets.* National politics, in short, was parading onto a new battlefield.

Clinton had helped draw the lines in the late October presidential debates. Pressed on his tax intentions, he reiterated that he planned "to raise marginal income (tax rates) on family incomes above $200,000 from 31 to 36 percent," but added a new commitment: that "if the money does not come in there to pay for these [spending] programs, we will cut other government spending or we will slow down the phase-in of the programs. I am not going to raise taxes on the middle class to pay for these programs." Then on *Meet the Press* on October 25, the moderator pressured Clinton campaign chairman Mickey Kantor: "Yesterday, the campaign spokesman for your campaign defined the middle class as $50,000. Bill Clinton had said previously that he wouldn't raise taxes on anyone making less than $200,000—any family. Can we expect that people making between $50,000 and $200,000 are eligible for taxation?" Kantor took the bait: "He is only going to raise taxes marginally on those folks making $200,000 a year or more. . . . There will be no taxes on the middle class."[1]

These were not promises to be taken lightly. Bush's widely criticized breach of his own 1988 promise of "Read my lips—no new taxes" had established a new guideline for the 1990s: breaking a tax pledge to the embattled middle class could be dangerous, even fatal. Failing to restore middle-class economic health and confidence could be just as dangerous. The new challenge of American politics was in place.

A Democratic Middle-Class Watershed?

The Democratic strategists who crowded the microphones on the day after the election had reason to be pleased: The 1992 results could be interpreted as a Democratic watershed. Turnout had surged from 50 percent in 1988 to 55 percent, significant because increases in voter participation have frequently characterized turning points in U.S. electoral history. Furthermore, the 1968–88 Republican presidential coalition had collapsed in 1992, just as the earlier GOP coalition had in 1932 after the Roaring Twenties slid into the depressed thirties. The parallel economic circumstances that marked the 1980s, the 1920s and the Gilded Age, which I outlined in *The Politics of Rich and Poor,* yielded another political shift. Though George Bush tried to deny even a partial resemblance between the early 1990s and the early 1930s, the electorate did not.

One comparison is particularly apt. Each of the three major presidential realignments of the Republican-Democratic rivalry since the 1850s started with an electoral "big bang" in which the party in power lost 16 to 18 percentage points of voter support, the extreme magnitude of rejection. Between 1856 and 1860, the ruling Democrats plummeted from 45 percent of the total vote to 29 percent, and the Civil War Republican coalition took its place. Then between 1928 and 1932, support for the ruling Republicans collapsed from 58 percent to 40 percent, putting the New Deal Democratic coalition in office. Then between 1964 and 1968 the Democrats dropped from 61 percent of the total presidential vote to just 43 percent, and the Nixon-Reagan GOP coalition controlled the White House for twenty of the next twenty-four years.* By this yardstick, the 16-point drop in Republican support between Bush's 54 percent in 1988 and his 38 percent debacle in 1992 also qualified as a "big bang." The important geographical differences from previous presidential voting patterns visible in 1992 supported the same conclusion.

The erosion of GOP ideological appeal in the late 1980s and early 1990s also suggested a change whose causes went far beyond the personal weaknesses of George Bush. Breakdowns could be seen in all three of the major issue sectors—foreign affairs, economics and domestic policy—that had promoted GOP presidential success in 1968 to 1988. The Cold War had underscored competencies in dealing with the Soviet Union, keeping America strong and protecting national security, and the GOP was the beneficiary. The collapse of Russia, however, dropped foreign policy so far down the list that fewer than 10 percent of voters gave it major priority. For the average American, Washington's new international emphasis was to safeguard U.S. jobs and industries. The most important foreign policy priority was to have less of it. Returning the national focus to domestic affairs was a shift that favored Democrats.

*The only other comparable loss of support for the party in the White House came in the three-way Wilson–Taft–Theodore Roosevelt race of 1912. The unusual 1896 watershed did not involve this kind of change.

The reversal in economics was devastating. Economic policy hadn't been a critical GOP issue in 1968–72, but by the mid-1980s Reagan made taxes, prosperity and economic management work for the GOP, hiding the party's traditional vulnerability on these issues in a boom financed by debt. By 1992, however, after the financial bailouts and the speculative implosion, the long downturn and tax policy controversies, the old Republican albatross was back. In domestic affairs, we have seen how much of the critical GOP momentum in the Nixon and Reagan years had come from social issues: rising crime, judicial permissiveness, the death penalty, riots and racial tension, welfare, pornography, campus radicalism, busing, quotas, patriotism, parades and support for the flag. Religious themes and appeals were closely related. Not only did these points, too, lose importance next to 1992 dislocations in the economy, but a new set of domestic and cultural issues were emerging for the 1990s: health care, education, urban problems, the environment, economic fairness, abortion and what could be called a "women's" array of concerns, including day care, parental leave, equal pay, the feminization of poverty, the glass ceiling in employment, women's political empowerment and sexual harassment. Issues like these favored the Democrats, affirming that electoral watersheds usually overlap with new domestic-policy agendas.

Another such sign came from the 1988–92 breakdown of presidential GOP voting in suburbia. The greater the local distress, the greater the loss. From Long Island to Los Angeles, through metropolitan Philadelphia and the "collar counties" of Chicago, postelection analysis confirmed a stark new reality: suburbia now held a majority of the U.S. population, but the Republicans no longer held a majority of suburbia. The polls showed that Clinton led among suburban voters by about five points nationally, the Democrats' first edge since Lyndon Johnson's 1964 landslide. Those suburban victories had proved transient; the gains of 1992 had more social, economic and demographic depth, although it was premature to say that suburbia had a Democratic future.

A further demographic change could be seen in the increasing political role of women and minorities visible in 1992. The political culture of the 1980s, one could argue, had a definite male or aggressive coloration—getting tough on crime, whipping inflation, curbing government, regaining world respect, idealizing Darwinian economics, de-emphasizing welfare and the safety net, and reversing defeat in Vietnam, the Panama Canal treaties and the 1979 hostage-taking of the U.S. embassy staff in Iran by a decade of gunboat diplomacy from Grenada to

Tripoli and Panama. White males liked it and went almost two to one for Ronald Reagan in 1984; women split more evenly. The "gender gap" of the 1980s, then, was pro-Republican because it reflected male ideological enthusiasm and female ambivalence. The 1990s began with signs of a very different political culture. White males, many of them under economic pressure, had less command, while women and minorities enjoyed more influence as the broader national emphasis shifted from gunboat diplomacy and Darwinian economics toward more concern with domestic problems, national and household budgets, pressures on families, repair of the safety net, and more concerns for those who lost ground during the 1980s. The new gender gap, which helped Democrats in 1992 because women were lopsidedly in favor of new-agenda politics and men were divided, also supported the thesis of a sea change.

While all these changes encouraged the Democrats, the central caution remained: the favorable trends could dissipate quickly if the new administration failed to revitalize and sustain the economy—and the lessons of history and of past great powers were more cautionary than encouraging.

The Lessons of Great-Power History

As we have seen, the magnitude of frustration voting in 1992 reflected how middle-class Americans worried not just about recession but about the signs of a *larger* decline: stagnant incomes and loss of the economic cushion the United States had gained in World War II, the troubling emergence of the United States as a lower-wage manufacturing nation, and speculation that the next generation's standard of living might fall.

When candidate Clinton blamed part of the U.S. decline on lack of a national economic strategy, Republicans grumbled about the Democrats running America down, contending that things were not that bad. Ironically, when one compares the circumstances of the United States with those of previous economic powers as they began to decline—seventeenth-century Spain, eighteenth-century Holland and turn-of-the-century Britain—*both* sides had a point.

Overall, America clearly *was* slipping. Despite GOP denials, the late 1980s and early 1990s revealed serious and continuing declines: real hourly wages were in a steady downtrend, infrastructure was wearing out, car-jackings and drive-by shootings were increasing, public debt was expanding and U.S. air and naval bases were being dismantled around the world, just as the legions of the Roman and British empires had departed in their day. Yet if Democrats were correct in framing the broad facts of America's ebb—a tide the general public, too, felt and feared—optimists also had a case. Unlike Holland and Britain in their heydays, the United States was not a relatively small maritime power lacking great natural resources or a large domestic market and thereby vulnerable. On the contrary, because of its size, resources and the possibility of a larger North American economic union, the United States had no reason to expect the Dutch and British fate, provided its policymakers learned from earlier downturns that imperial overreach, mushrooming debt and increased emphasis on finance, money and the interests of rentiers rather than on manufacturing were more than a source of great-power decline. These circumstances were also clues to possible remedies.

Understanding is not enough, though. Indeed, Clinton and Perot between them raised many of the needed perspectives in the 1992 campaign, and some Spaniards, Dutchmen and Britons, debating their nations' predicaments, had also understood what was going wrong. We have seen in Chapter 8 how, as Spanish gold shipments from the New World were about to decline, the early-seventeenth-century economic reformers known as *arbitristas* explained that Spain was destroying itself through excessive bureaucracy and debt, overreliance on importing gold and indifference to manufacturing and the middle class. One prime minister, the Count-Duke of Olivares, proposed a plausible reform agenda, only to see it overwhelmed by the Thirty Years War. Many in Holland circa 1750 could see that financial speculation and a preference for overseas investment had subordinated concern about decaying Dutch manufacturing and growing poverty; no Dutch government, however, implemented any remedy. Even before Britain's economy peaked relative to the rest of the world, Matthew Arnold had warned of the danger of becoming a second Holland, and by the 1890s, books worrying about the German and U.S. challenges had become best-sellers. In 1903, as we have seen, Prime Minister A. J. Balfour put the case for helping British manufacturing before Parliament and the electorate, only to see it rejected.

As the results of the U.S. presidential election of 1992 sank in, the question for the new decade and the upcoming century was whether the United States could go beyond a vague debate to concrete remedial action. Despite America's greater size and broader renewal opportunities, it did suffer from many of the same weaknesses that had eventually crippled earlier great economic powers. The dangers deserved attention.

Take the process of financialization, with its favoritism to upper-bracket elites and financial interests. This had proceeded apace in the late 1980s and early 1990s, as the salaries of corporate CEOs soared from 30 times that of the average worker in 1980 to 130 to 140 times as much in 1991 while real hourly wages declined, and the income of investment firms' set records while unprecedented numbers of ordinary Americans fell back on public assistance. But the most crippling corollary of financialization has always been the expansion of debt and government deficits. Although profligacy in modern public finance has so far typically involved left-liberal politicians and their constituencies, a variation occurs in leading economic powers as they move past their zenith: then conservatives, too, discover the convenience of government debt in helping them maintain a military presence around the world, in letting policymakers borrow instead of raising taxes on the rich, and in sustaining a large rentier class dependent on safe, profitable returns on investments. Moreover, as debt serves these functions, old political and moral restraints break down: ignoring the inevitable risks becomes easier.

Loose financial practices, in turn, create entrenched dependents and constituencies. The Hapsburgs drowned Spain in debt, but in 1622, when the government proposed to cap the interest on bonds at 5 percent, the rentiers and foreign bankers who had grown accustomed to much higher rates balked and proposed to let some other class bear the consequences.[2] After Holland increased its public debt sixfold in the wars of the early eighteenth century, holding and trading debt instruments became a financial life-style for wealthy Dutchmen, even though by the 1760s and 1770s many Dutch financiers were sure that the country's speculative bubble would soon burst.

The financialization of early-twentieth-century Britain, in turn, proceeded rapidly even as the nation slipped in manufacturing and technology. That the national debt had expanded tenfold during the Great War didn't seem to matter during the go-go years of the 1920s. London remained the capital of international finance, but further borrowing would soon end that, because after the national debt tripled again to £25 billion during World War II, Britain found itself dependent on U.S. monetary support. The general economic recovery of the 1950s and 1960s helped, but by the time of the next currency devaluation in 1967, one economic historian described the extraordinary transformation: In fifty years, the capitalist superpower of 1914 had become "the ward of the other developed countries of the non-Communist world. They constituted a creditors' club exercising the same watchful con-

252 □ KEVIN PHILLIPS

cern over the British economy that the Aid Consortia exercised over those of India, Indonesia or Turkey."³

As Americans, too, would discover by the late 1980s, the early stages of major chronic indebtedness are more numbing than energizing. Former U.S. commerce secretary Peter Peterson, who in 1991 described America's passivity toward rising domestic and foreign debt as "pathological," invoked Britain's precedent. Even in the 1950s and 1960s, said Peterson, "most Britons did not seem too sensitive to the crushing burden—either on their pockets or on their consciences. Their regret seemed a trifle perfunctory, their concern superficial, and their appreciation of the scale and urgency with which the creditors required repayment very vague indeed."⁴ Late-twentieth-century American attitudes were surprisingly similar, abetted by the profitability of debt, leverage and speculation to the financial community.

Meanwhile, the overindulgence of financial elites and investors by the political right is often countered by the left's overenlargement of the welfare state. In rich countries starting to fade, politicians have often turned to welfare statism and expanded public payrolls to avoid or cushion working-class or middle-class income losses. Consider the European-settled nations of the Southern Hemisphere—Australia, New Zealand, Argentina and Uruguay—that quickly grew rich at the turn of the century from producing grain and meat. As their relative wealth faded in the 1920s and 1930s, they embraced welfare-state solutions: cradle-to-grave security, family allowances, bloated government payrolls and high pensions. So, too, had the great economic powers: government and church payrolls maintained a veritable welfare state in seventeenth-century Spain, likewise swollen provincial and municipal payrolls in eighteenth-century Holland, and, no one can ignore the mid-twentieth-century British welfare state. While such policies can mitigate unfairness, they do not result in long-term revitalization. The challenge for middle-class renewal is to curb the several sources of excessive debt: the abuses sponsored by financial elites, interest groups and welfare statists alike.

In all these respects, historical precedents offer little encouragement. The extent to which Washington of the early 1990s was an "iron triangle" of lobbies and influence wielders was matched in many state capitals, and the documentation was weighty: inch-and-a-half-thick directories of Washington representatives listing fourteen thousand names, cynical surveys ranking the fifty states by their ratios of lobbyists to elected legislators. Kindred buildups had been a stifling presence before. Four hundred years earlier the flow of New World gold to Spain helped Madrid's population grow from 4,000 in 1530 to 100,000 a century later, luring bankers and moneymen from all parts of Europe, supporting a huge Hapsburg court and a massive church establishment in which every religious order and faction imaginable was represented. By 1611 the government was ordering the great nobles to leave Madrid and return home, according to one historian, in hopes of reducing the ranks of parasites, but the attempt failed.[5]

Mancur Olson, the contemporary U.S. historian who has linked the sclerosis of great nations to high interest-group ratios, explains the decline of twentieth-century Britain by its much larger number of associations than any other country except the United States and a network of interest groups so powerful that it gave rise to the term "establishment."[6] The United States of the 1990s, in turn, probably ranked as the greatest interest-group concentration in world history—and in Washington some of the most influential agents represented foreign masters. None of the previous great economic powers had been able to clear out the sclerosis of entrenched elites and interest groups; the United States, with its populist traditions, would have to be the first.

A related challenge lay in America's entrenched and complex geographic subdivisions from states down to counties, municipalities and even water districts and special tax districts. Like the Hapsburg empire, the United Provinces of the Netherlands and the United Kingdom of Great Britain and Ireland, the United States got an explosive boost from the way its territories, markets and population came together—even the names reveal the geographic fusion processes that have helped each great economic power to its zenith. The problem, however, is that as great powers have matured and then begun to decline, once-vital geographic boundaries have calcified into regional interest groups and expensive duplicative bureaucracies. Here, too, the precedents are glum, but the opportunities of a North American economic union could give the United States a rare re-energizing.

There are other areas where late twentieth-century U.S. policymakers may learn from history, not least the accumulating political demands of 1991–92 to replace yesteryear's internationalism with a narrower set of U.S. interests and a greater emphasis on domestic problems. Beyond the overt nationalists like Buchanan, Harkin and Perot, even Paul Tsongas, whose demands for sacrifice in his brief 1992 presidential campaign endeared him to the upper-middle-class intelligentsia, bragged about buying an American automobile "because I think like an economic patriot"—and he struck a chord by proclaiming that "the Cold War is over—Japan and Germany won."[7]

In 1991, Peter Peterson, chairman of both the Council on Foreign

Relations and the Institute for International Economics, wrote a paper entitled *Rethinking America's Security: The Primacy of the Domestic Agenda,* and its demand for emphasizing domestic affairs was promptly endorsed by the bipartisan American Assembly. William G. Hyland, editor of *Foreign Affairs,* the nation's best-known foreign policy journal, had broken the ice a few months earlier by declaring, "What is desperately needed is a psychological turn inward. . . . We need to start selectively disengaging abroad to save resources."[8] The editor of another journal was even more blunt: "A new isolationism focused on domestic reform and intent on strictly evaluating our foreign commitments has much to commend itself to the American people."[9]

Ohio professor Alfred Eckes, former chairman of the International Trade Commission under Ronald Reagan, pointed out that since World War II U.S. policymakers had relentlessly subordinated domestic economic considerations, jobs and even industries to please allies and advance diplomatic and military objectives. Even with the Cold War over, Eckes said, "Officials in Washington continue to play the old game of trading access to the U.S. market for cooperation on non-trade issues." The United States, he said, could no longer afford that.[10]

The plans announced by Clinton in 1992 to emphasize rebuilding the U.S. infrastructure and high-value-added, high-wage jobs also drew on what history said about the past failures of declining economic powers. The Republicans, argued Democratic theorists, had favored investors and investment too much for their own sake, witness George Bush's repeated calls for reduction of the capital gains tax on virtually every kind of asset, not just new ones but also old assets bought years ago. New York governor Mario Cuomo, campaigning for Clinton, charged that in the Reagan-Bush era, too many investors had put their money in Taiwan, junk bonds or BMWs instead of in Ohio, Pennsylvania or other parts of the United States.

The nation's need for investment had become a cliché, but government statistics showed that the top 1 percent of Americans—the investing class by any definition—had already formed huge sums of capital during the 1980s boom. Stock prices had soared, but so did the price of French Impressionist paintings, English antique furniture, classic automobiles, rare Burgundies, seaside mansions and Park Avenue triplexes for the rich, as well as the similar but less costly items demanded by $150,000- or $250,000-a-year doctors, lawyers and corporate vice presidents. Speculation and lavish consumption flourished, but too little was ultimately invested in ways that would rebuild Middle America's fading high-wage jobs base. Lobster salad tasted better, Ferraris were more fun, junk bonds paid higher interest, plants in Tijuana returned more dividends than those in Terre Haute and paper entrepreneurialism produced the quickest capital gains. What was missing wasn't capital but its productive investment in the national interest— and the wise men of the previous great economic powers could have cited chapter and verse about that, too.

The Democrats proposed guidelines. Wealth, in general, would be taxed more, and long-term investments would be treated better than short-term investments; so would funds invested in high-technology start-ups. Multinational companies would be more closely scrutinized; foreign multinationals operating in the United States would face higher taxes, while U.S. multinationals would no longer get tax breaks for moving jobs overseas. "Trickle-down" Republican economics, which Clinton derided, would be replaced by more investment in public infrastructure, from schools to transportation, and more investment in people through increased outlays for health insurance, education and job retraining.

Greater controversy surrounded a national industrial policy to promote the high-technology sector. The lack of statist traditions made the United States more like Britain and Holland, which could not manage such strategies and transformations, and less like Japan or Germany. Moreover, there was a second roadblock: the enormous role and power of interest groups and the likelihood they would warp any national strategy to suit their own purposes. A more limited national-interest and competitiveness agenda should have been pursued a decade earlier; by the 1990s, strategic coordination and decision-making still made sense, but interest groups, political considerations and bailouts for politically favored groups were sure to figure more prominently in the outcome.*

The most important strategy of all was obscure—how to reduce the U.S. budget deficit and high level of international indebtedness. Neither blueprint, Democratic or Republican, had been taken seriously by economists during the 1992 presidential election. Only the independent Perot had spoken to that predicament. And perhaps more than any other circumstance of America's global decline during the previous

*In 1984 I published a book entitled *Staying on Top: The Business Case for a National Industrial Strategy*, which argued for what was then a relatively limited competitiveness agenda. Eight years later the likelihood of distortion by interest groups seemed much higher, an argument I set forth in the July/August 1992 *Harvard Business Review*.

two decades, it hung like a sword over U.S. prospects for renewed economic growth—and over the new Democratic administration's prospects for consolidating a true watershed.

Economic Decline, Middle-Class Renewal and the Future of the Party System

Economic decline sours voters, curdles the public psychology and changes political systems. It is a tale that has been told since Greece and Rome, and most recently in the Great Britain of the first half of the twentieth century which, as its people lost their confidence, exchanged the politics of optimism that had characterized the nineteenth-century party system of Liberals versus Conservatives for what soon became class-conscious competition between capitalist Conservatives and socialist Labourites.

Democrats quickly claimed that the 1992 presidential election in the United States, by drawing frustration politics into the two-party system, represented a renewal of the same populist-progressive traditions that had marked the previous upheavals of the industrial era in the administrations of Theodore Roosevelt and Woodrow Wilson and then Franklin D. Roosevelt. Nineteen ninety-two was, they claimed, another such moment. But under the unusual circumstances of the 1990s, that possibility remained as much a question as an answer.

Not only does economic decline curdle voter psychology, it consumes politicians and national leaders, as it had from Rome down to a between-the-wars Britain managed by little-remembered prime ministers who could not stop the tide. The same could be true of the United States since the war in Vietnam and its haunting theme song, "Bye-Bye Miss American Pie." Presidents Lyndon Johnson, Richard Nixon, Gerald Ford, Jimmy Carter and George Bush were all defeated for reelection or forced to step down before completing two terms. Only Ronald Reagan, apostle of "America is back," the debt-laden shadow empire of the 1980s, managed two terms before reality set in again.

The careful historian will note that the U.S. political system has survived such problems before. From 1876 to 1892, none in a series of weak presidents, almost all single-termers, could win a majority rather than plurality of the popular vote. Politics did not regain a firm base until the Democratic fusion with the Populists in 1896. Before that there were the ineffective pre–Civil War presidencies of 1840–60, six men in twenty years, none of whom served more than a single term, partly because the party system was breaking down as the Civil War approached.

That the unsuccessful or thwarted presidencies since the 1960s pointed to another larger upheaval—and not toward a simple watershed replacement of Republicans with Democrats—also seemed conceivable in 1992, a possibility dramatized by the extraordinary independent candidacy of Ross Perot, who in May and June achieved the hitherto unimaginable: national polls showed him passing the presumptive Democratic and Republican presidential nominees even before he entered the race. Several commentators noted in June that by a number of important yardsticks, Perot's third-party candidacy stood to be the most broadly based since John C. Fremont won 33 percent for the fledgling Republican party in the election of 1856. At its peak, Perot's movement was stronger than Fremont's in the polls, and in contrast to previous third-party contenders, his support was not just in one angry region, cultural group or among an ideological fringe, it was *national*. His appeal was not to a periphery with peripheral issues but to the angry, radicalizing middle—the people whose frustrations and circumstances we have been examining. In June, private polls gave Perot a stunning 60 percent backing in Orange County, California, famous as the archetype of heavily Republican high-tech suburbia.

The formerly Republican billionaire businessman's decision to leave the contest in July, with a partial nod to Clinton, sent his supporters flooding into the Democratic nominee's column and gave the Arkansas governor a lead over Bush that he never lost. That was Perot's principal near-term effect: to help realign Republican and Independent voters in Clinton's direction. Even when he returned to the race in October, ultimately pulling more or less evenly from Bush and Clinton, his overall effect was twofold; first, to attack Bush on grounds of both economic failure and personal integrity, partly neutralizing the incumbent's attacks on Clinton; and, second, to provide an alternative ballot choice to anti-Bush Republicans and independents, especially in the suburbs, where a huge 20–25 percent vote for Perot did its greatest— and fatal—damage to the Republican presidential coalition.

Nevertheless, if Perot had simply wanted to beat Bush, whom he regarded as having failed the American people, he would not have reentered, for Bush was about to lose. The importance of his reentry was that by winning one or two of the three presidential debates, he regained much of the reputation he had lost after July's withdrawal. And by doing so, he was able to win 19 percent of the vote on Election Day, not the best showing by a third-party nominee since 1856, as might have been possible earlier, but the best since 1912, when Theodore Roosevelt tried to reclaim the White House on the third-party Progressive ticket—and TR was an ex-president at the time.

The major third-party candidates have generally seen the valid part of their critique absorbed by one of the two major parties, except in the 1850s, when that was not possible. In July 1992 Clinton seemed to have absorbed the Perot constituency at little relative cost; by November 1992 that was no longer true. Perot's message and constituency would have to be preempted by actions and achievements in the cause around which Perot had based his candidacy: restoration of the American Dream, serious reduction of the deficit that hung over America's children, reduction of interest-group control in Washington and adoption of a national strategy to rebuild manufacturing and the larger U.S. economy.

Many Americans thought Perot suffered from egotism and more than a hint of paranoia, but polls showed that three quarters of voters were glad that he had run. Perhaps more important, as Election Day closed in on a weary electorate, late-October Time/CNN polls showed that 63 percent of Americans favored the formation of "a third political party that would run candidates for president, Congress and state offices against the Democratic and Republican candidates." Even in June, at Perot's zenith, a lower 59 percent had thought so, and the October support included 62 percent of Republicans, 76 percent of Independents and 58 percent of Democrats. While some looked to Perot, others were talking about third parties and new centrist movements. The existing party system was weaker, much further removed from its Civil War roots, than when Theodore Roosevelt had tried to breach it in 1912.

Much of the burden of upholding the nation's two-party tradition and making economic and political renewal work was on Bill Clinton and the Democrats, despite their own encrustation with interest groups, but that was just one part of the equation. From the frontier vitality of Jacksonian Democracy in 1828 to the electoral revolution of 1992, ordinary Americans—whether they be called yeomanry, the "middling sort" or twentieth-century middle class—have made the U.S. system of politics and government one of the world's most effective. It is they who have made democracy work. As we have seen in Chapter 3, the United States has successfully used watershed elections to manage economic and cultural upheavals that have torn other nations apart. Swing voters have made national politics a reliable process of renewal by repeatedly turning against unpopular elites and rebuilding what historians have called the "vital center." The 1990s, however, looked as if they might be different.

Despite the validity of ordinary Americans' economic concerns, there were signs that the middle class, which had come to rage against "special interest groups," could become the biggest economic interest group of them all. In previous eras, expanding income, increasing national wealth and greater opportunity and mobility had underpinned the ability of the great mass of the population to be a force for national renewal. However, it had now begun to seem that middle-class decline and frustration could no longer be rectified in this manner. And although voters knew that federal budget deficits would make some economic sacrifices necessary, they also knew that reducing or taxing middle-class entitlement programs—from Medicare to Social Security and even children's eligibility for college loans—would further diminish what were for many already-eroding incomes or living standards. Politicians would have to generate an agenda of shared sacrifice and renewal that rested more heavily on those who had made so much money from the speculations and abuses of the 1980s before the general public would accept retrenchment.

The United States was not alone in watching its politics and economics of the 1990s turn away from the speculative and ideological excesses of the prior decade. Even as George Bush lost the presidency, the conservative leaders of most of the other G-7 governments were also worrying about upcoming elections and the difficulty of survival with their job ratings in the 20s and 30s. New tides were coming in Britain, Canada, Germany, Japan and elsewhere, not just in Washington. But the United States *was* alone in the trauma of a great power sliding from its increasingly distant zenith. What was at stake in the revitalization of the United States economy and the middle class was nothing less than the remaining belief—and perhaps now more the hope—in American exceptionalism.

Notes

Chapter 1

1. For example, the U.S. Census Bureau in 1992 reported a decline in the percentage of persons with "middle" incomes from 71.2 percent in 1969 to 63.3 percent in 1989 ("U.S. Says Middle Class Shrinking," *New York Times*, February 22, 1992). The University of Michigan's Panel Study of Income Dynamics found a 15-point shrinkage from 1978 to 1989 ("America's Middle-Class Meltdown," *Washington Post*, December 1, 1991).
2. "U.S. Underestimated Job Losses," *Los Angeles Times*, February 2, 1992.
3. "Kids Count," Survey Release and Data Sheet, Annie Casey Foundation, Greenwich, Connecticut, January 1992.
4. "Index of Social Ills Shows U.S. Woes," *Chicago Tribune*, January 14, 1992.
5. "U.S. Society Called in Decline," *Chicago Tribune*, February 23, 1992.
6. "New Suburbs," *Wall Street Journal*, March 26, 1987.
7. "Backlash Hits Growth-Loving Moreno Valley," *Los Angeles Times*, January 13, 1992.
8. Frank S. Levy and Richard C. Michel, *The Economic Future of American Families: Income and Wealth Trends* (Washington, D.C.: Urban Institute Press, 1991), p. 101.
9. "Study Finds Income Growth Rate of Two-Parent Families Declined in 1980s," *Washington Post*, January 17, 1992.
10. "Rich Get Richer, the Middle Class Poorer," *Philadelphia Inquirer*, December 12, 1991.
11. "The Incredible Shrinking Middle Class," *American Demographics*, May 1992, pp. 34-38.
12. "Rich-Poor Gap Is Widening," Associated Press, *Boston Globe*, December 3, 1990.
13. Cader, Rainwater and Smeeding, *American Economic Review*, May 1989.
14. "Consumers Draw Down Value in Their Homes," *Wall Street Journal*, August 5, 1991.
15. "The Other Suburbia," *Newsweek*, June 26, 1989, pp. 22–24.
16. "Jobless, Their Affluence Ebbs Away," *Boston Globe*, December 30, 1990.

17. "Once Welfare Meant Someone Else," *New York Times,* March 11, 1991.

18. "Tough Times Hit Home for Those Who Lose Theirs," *Los Angeles Times,* January 28, 1992.

19. "Suburban Homeless Seek Shelter," *Chicago Tribune,* February 5, 1992.

20. "Country Club Helps Members Find Work," *Los Angeles Times,* May 18, 1991.

21. "Signs of Distress Are Rising in the Suburbs," *Philadelphia Inquirer,* March 22, 1992.

22. Ibid.

23. "Welfare Line No Longer Just for Hardcore Poor," *Chicago Tribune,* January 19, 1992.

24. "Recession Impacting Family," Rocky Mountain Poll release, March 12, 1992.

25. "New Poor Swelling State's Welfare Rolls," *Dallas News,* February 9, 1992.

26. "Reality of Homeless Teens Sinks In," *Chicago Tribune,* October 9, 1990.

27. "Hunger Rears Head in Affluent Suburbs," *Denver Post,* March 10, 1991.

28. "Record Numbers of Americans Enlist in Food Stamp Program," *Boston Globe,* February 2, 1992.

29. "Food Pantries on the Rise in Affluent Areas," *Boston Globe,* July 12, 1991.

30. "School Lunch Numbers Testify to Hard Times," *Washington Post,* December 14, 1991.

31. Patricia Calhoun Bibby, "Is the Yuppie Era of Buying Spent?" *Louisville Courier-Journal,* February 24, 1991.

32. "U.S. Workforce Gets Bludgeoned," *Philadelphia Inquirer,* December 7, 1991.

33. "Bye-Bye America's Pie," *Washington Post,* February 11, 1992.

34. "U.S. Workers on Job Longer for Less Pay," *Christian Science Monitor,* May 15, 1992.

35. "Graduates Facing Worst Prospects in Last Two Decades," *New York Times,* May 12, 1992.

36. See Katherine S. Newman, *Falling from Grace* (New York: Free Press, 1988).

37. Frederick Lewis Allen, *The Big Change: 1900–1950* (New York: Bantam Books, 1961), p. 127.

38. Ibid., p. 128.

39. Ibid., p. 184.

40. "The New Rich," *Fortune,* January 1952, p. 62.

41. Ibid., p. 184.

42. Ibid., pp. 185–86.

43. Ibid., p. 183.

44. Simon Schama, *The Embarrassment of Riches* (Berkeley: University of California Press, 1988), p. 4.

45. Ibid., p. 323.

46. C. R. Boxer, *The Dutch Seaborne Empire, 1600–1800* (London: Pelican Books, 1988), p. xxiii.

47. F. Crouzet, *The Victorian Economy*, quoted in Paul Kennedy, *Rise and Fall of the Great Powers* (New York: Random House, 1987), p. 151.
48. E. J. Hobsbawn, *The Pelican Economic History of Britain: From 1750 to the Present Day: Industry and Empire*, Vol. 3 (Baltimore, Md.: Penguin Books, 1968), p. 154, Appendix 10.
49. Abbé Coyer, *Nouvelles Observations sur l'Angleterre* (1779), p. 15.
50. "The New Rich," p. 62.
51. Allen, op. cit. p. 204.
52. Allen, op. cit., p. 187.
53. Various speeches by Joseph Chamberlain in Aaron L. Friedberg, *The Weary Titan: Britain and the Experience of Relative Decline, 1985–1905* (Princeton, N.J.: Princeton University Press, 1988), p. 75.
54. Ibid., p. 72.
55. Walter Russell Mead, "Why the Roller-Coaster Only Goes One Way: Down," *Los Angeles Times*, April 14, 1991.
56. Donald H. Straszheim, *Merrill Lynch First Quarter 1991 Economic Analysis*, p. 14.
57. "Not Getting Ahead," *New York Times*, December 16, 1990, Section 4, p. 1.
58. "Downward Mobility Is Stalking Baby Boomers," *Business Week*, January 29, 1991, p. 22.
59. "Consumer Spending: From Spur to Drag," *Wall Street Journal*, January 21, 1991.
60. "Hours of Work Up," *Christian Science Monitor*, August 31, 1990.
61. Katherine Newman, "Falling from Grace" (New York: Free Press, 1988), p. 21.
62. "America's Middle-Class Meltdown," *Washington Post*, December 1, 1991.
63. Shares of pretax adjusted family income from Congressional Budget Office tax simulation model, House Ways and Means Committee 1992 Green Book, p. 1521.
64. Denny Braun, *The Rich Get Richer* (Chicago: Nelson-Hall, 1990), p. 246.
65. Ibid., p. 249.
66. Benjamin Friedman, *Day of Reckoning* (New York: Random House, 1988), p. 38.
67. Barry Siegel, "Crises of Pessimism Part of U.S. History," *Los Angeles Times*, April 4, 1982, p. 10.
68. Ibid.
69. In 1975, close to the peak of U.S. economic confidence, the Gallup Poll, in its last question of this sort, found 72 percent of Americans putting themselves into the middle class (release, July 21, 1975).
70. Frank Levy, *Dollars and Dreams: The Changing American Income Distribution* (Russell Sage Foundation, 1987), p. 206.
71. Levy and Michel, op. cit., p. 54.

Chapter 2

1. "Rich-Poor Gap Is Widening in Western Nations," *Boston Globe*, December 3, 1990.
2. "Cardboard Citizens," *Financial Times*, April 30, 1991.
3. "Thatcher's Poll Tax," *Philadelphia Inquirer*, April 24, 1988.
4. "Fight Over British Tax Shift Imperils Thatcher Ideology," *New York Times*, April 23, 1990.
5. "By-election Jolts British Conservatives," *Washington Post*, March 9, 1991.
6. "Canada Decides to Introduce New Sales Tax," *Wall Street Journal*, April 25, 1989.
7. "Mulroney Could Pay Dearly for Canada's New Tax," Reuters, *Boston Globe*, December 16, 1990.
8. "Canada Bites the Budget Bullet," *Washington Times*, February 14, 1991.
9. Gallup Poll Canada, October 1991.
10. "Rich Man, Poor Man in Japan," *New York Times*, December 26, 1988.
11. Statement of Senator Daniel P. Moynihan to U.S. Senate Finance Committee, December 13, 1991.
12. "An End to the 80% Tax," *U.S. News & World Report*, March 9, 1992, p. 70.
13. 1991 Handbook, Advisory Commission on Intergovernmental Relations, pp. 122–30.
14. Ibid.
15. "Some Worry Plan to Cut Tax Credits May Spur New Backlash," *Los Angeles Times*, April 24, 1990.
16. David Broder, "Who's the Fairest of Them All," *Washington Post*, February 13, 1991.
17. *Tax Features*, November 1990, p. 5.
18. "Once-Proud British Rail System," *Chicago Tribune*, May 12, 1991.
19. "Triumph of Capitalism Rings False," London *Observer* / Cleveland *Plain Dealer*, December 31, 1989.
20. "Suburbs Staggered by Cuomo Budget Cuts," *New York Times*, February 6, 1991.
21. "Budget Cuts Begin to Hit Where It Hurts," *Los Angeles Times*, September 30, 1991.
22. Warren Brookes, "The New Deficit Dynamic," *Washington Times*, December 3, 1990.
23. "Law and Economics: A New Order in the Court?" *Business Week*, November 16, 1987, p. 93.
24. Statement by the President, July 3, 1987, the White House Press Office.
25. "Study Assails Values of the New Right," *Los Angeles Times*, January 25, 1985.
26. Bob Kuttner, "The Fraying of America's Communal Thread," *Boston Globe*, March 8, 1985.
27. "Conservative One-Worlders," *Wall Street Journal*, April 3, 1989.

28. E. J. Dionne, "Economic Inequality Becoming the Norm," *Washington Post,* May 13, 1990, p. 1.
29. Benjamin DeMott, "The Myth of Classlessness," *New York Times,* October 10, 1990.
30. Ibid.
31. Kuttner, op. cit.
32. "Books on Greed Worry Wall Street," *New York Times,* February 12, 1990.
33. "The Cutting Edge: Wealth Issues, Tax Fairness Themes and Populist Public Opinion," *American Political Report,* May 24, 1991.
34. "Rich Man, Poor Man in Japan."

Chapter 3

1. See, in particular, Margaret Canavan, *Populism* (New York: Harcourt Brace Jovanovich, 1981).
2. Interview, National Conference of State Legislatures, September 10, 1992.
3. NBC/Wall Street Journal poll, April 11–14, 1992.
4. *Washington Post,* July 8, 1992, p. 1.
5. "California Budget Agreement Forged," *Investors Daily,* July 23, 1991.
6. "A Brewing Revolt Against the Rich," *Fortune,* December 17, 1990, p. 90.
7. "Democrats Coalescing on 1992 Strategy," *Washington Post,* July 26, 1991.
8. Washington Outlook, *Business Week,* October 7, 1991, p. 45.
9. "The Greening of Corporate Executives," *Dallas News,* November 10, 1991.
10. "Roper's the Public Pulse," Research Supplement, June 1991, p. 4.
11. "On the Eve of '92: Fault Lines in the Electorate," Times-Mirror Center for People and the Press, December 4, 1991.
12. William Safire, *The New Language of Politics* (New York: Collier Books, 1972), p. 387.
13. *Third Barnhart Dictionary of New English* (New York: H. W. Wilson Co., 1990).
14. Lawrence Goodwyn, *The Populist Moment* (New York: Oxford University Press, 1978), p. 281.
15. Fingerhut-Granados Opinion Research, "Post-Election Poll Shows Mondale Could Have Won Vote of Reagan Democrats with Populist Economic Appeal," November 8, 1984, p. 2.
16. Ibid., p. 3.
17. Kevin Phillips, *The Politics of Rich and Poor* (New York: Random House, 1990), p. 29.
18. "The Electronic Election," *Boston Globe,* November 13, 1988, p. B12.
19. "To Broaden Political Base, Dukakis Must Keep Running," *Christian Science Monitor,* November 14, 1988.
20. "Liberalism Reconstructed," *The Commonwealth Report,* April 1989, p. 1.

21. Ibid.
22. "Democrats Coalescing on 1992 Strategy."
23. "Wofford Pulls Even with Thornburgh in Pennsylvania," *Wall Street Journal,* October 31, 1991.
24. "U.S. Report Says Voters Feel Shut Out of Political Process," *Financial Times,* June 11, 1991.
25. Mancur Olson, *The Rise and Decline of Nations* (New Haven, Conn.: Yale University Press, 1982).

Chapter 4

1. "Millionaires," *The Nation,* January 18, 1928, p. 57.
2. Ibid.
3. Geoffrey Perrett, *America in the Twenties* (New York: Touchstone Books, 1982), pp. 321–22.
4. Stuart Chase, *Prosperity: Fact and Myth* (New York: Charles Boni Paper Books, 1929), p. 116.
5. Charles F. Holt, "Who Benefitted from the Prosperity of the Twenties?" *Explorations in Economic History,* 14, July 1977, pp. 277–89.
6. William Greider, *Secrets of the Temple: How the Federal Reserve Runs the Country* (New York: Simon and Schuster, 1987), p. 692.
7. Ibid., p. 245.
8. U.S. Census Bureau, *The Statistical History of the United States* (New York: Basic Books, 1976), p. 1112.
9. "Sensitive Issues Reportedly Kept Poverty Study Quiet for Months," *Boston Globe,* May 13, 1991.
10. "Economists Question Accuracy and Value of U.S. Statistics," *Washington Post,* July 5, 1990.
11. Ibid.
12. Ibid.
13. "Did Economy Trip on False Statistics?" *Charlotte Observer,* June 5, 1991.
14. "U.S. Jobless Figures Fail to Add Hidden Unemployed," *Los Angeles Times,* April 11, 1991.
15. "Official Decries Gap Between Rich and Poor," *Los Angeles Times,* October 30, 1991.
16. "U.S. Underestimated Job Losses, State Finds," *Los Angeles Times,* February 3, 1992.
17. "Jobless Figures Don't Add Up," *Philadelphia Inquirer,* July 5, 1992.
18. "Inflation May Be Worse Than Data Show," *Wall Street Journal,* May 10, 1990.
19. "How Accurately Does the Government Measure the Pinch of Inflation?" *New York Times,* April 7, 1991.
20. Ibid.

Chapter 5

1. "The Ides of Taxes Are Upon Us," *Washington Times,* April 12, 1992.
2. Release, February 5, 1991.
3. The data on the different effective state tax rates on middle-class and rich families comes from *A Far Cry from Fair,* Citizens for Tax Justice, April 1991.
4. Ibid., p. 12.
5. "Unpopularity Tax," *Forbes,* June 24, 1991, p. 88.
6. "High-Taxes New Yorkers Face Milking," Associated Press, *Washington Times,* September 19, 1991.
7. Brad Sherman, revised statement of March 22, 1991, p. 3.
7A. "They're Not Called Taxes, But Fees to Rise," *Los Angeles Times,* August 31, 1992.
8. "Making Tax Code Family-Friendly," *Miami Herald,* June 2, 1991.
9. Ibid.
10. *The Tax Fairness Index,* Progressive Policy Institute Report, July 1990, p. 4.
11. Unpublished data from the Urban Institute.
12. "The New Rich," *Fortune,* January 1952, p. 63.
13. Robert Shapiro, "Invest," *The New Republic,* December 23, 1991, p. 17.
14. "How Hefty a Tax for Millionaires?" *Washington Times,* January 22, 1991.
15. Ben J. Wattenberg, ed., *The Statistical History of the United States* (New York: Basic Books, 1976), p. 1112.
16. "States and Cities Fight Recession with New Taxes," *New York Times,* July 27, 1991.
17. " 'Soak the Rich' Fallacy," *Christian Science Monitor,* May 10, 1991.
18. Release, February 5, 1991.
19. Ibid., pp. 20, 51.
20. "States Take Up New Burdens," *New York Times,* May 21, 1990.
21. "Cuomo: U.S. Must Alter Course," *Christian Science Monitor,* August 12, 1991.
22. Neil Peirce, "Hard-Hit States Pass Bill Down the Line," *Philadelphia Inquirer,* April 22, 1991.
23. "Cries for Help Go Unheeded," *Los Angeles Times,* February 4, 1991.
24. "The Natives Are Restless," *Forbes,* April 16, 1990.
25. Jon Margolis, "Government Closest to the People," *Chicago Tribune,* July 23, 1991.
26. *A Far Cry from Fair,* Citizens for Tax Justice, April 1991, p. 11.
27. "Tax Charade Hits Rural Areas," *Des Moines Register,* June 11, 1989.
28. "Hidden Taxes Set to Deluge New Yorkers," *New York Times,* May 22, 1990.
29. "Are State Courts Becoming Tax Collectors?" *California Journal,* September 1991, p. 425.
30. Ibid.

31. "Mapping Options as Court Takes Up Prop. 13," *Los Angeles Times,* October 27, 1991.
32. "Business Fees Replace Overt Tax Hikes," *Human Events,* May 23, 1992, p. 15.
33. "Higher and Higher," *Dallas News,* October 1, 1991.
34. "State's Water Rate under Attack," *Boston Globe,* February 8, 1992.
35. "The Natives Are Restless."
36. "As Realty Taxes Go Up, Up," *New York Times,* February 4, 1991.
37. "Poor Towns Taxed More to Get Less," *Chicago Tribune,* July 22, 1990.
38. "Beyond the Property Tax," *U.S. News & World Report,* August 6, 1990, p. 39.
39. "Red Tape Kills an American Dream," *Los Angeles Times,* July 8, 1991.
40. "Who's That Taxing at Your Door," *Chicago Tribune,* May 7, 1991.
41. "Beyond the Property Tax," p. 40.
42. "Nationline," *USA Today,* August 13, 1991.
43. "Legacy of Anti-Tax Fervor: Levies, But with a Purpose," *New York Times,* November 27, 1990.
44. "Not a Big Tilt in Tax Policy," *New York Times,* October 27, 1990.
45. "Budget Pact Creates New Bubble," *Investor's Daily,* November 27, 1990.
46. "Budget Tricks and Treats," *Washington Times,* October 31, 1990.
47. "Budget Deadlock Is Not about Whether to Tax the Wealthy But How to Do It," *Wall Street Journal,* October 24, 1990.
48. "Bush Considers Taxing Worker Health Benefits," *Chicago Tribune,* April 26, 1991.
49. Steven D. Gold, "A New Twist for State Tax Policy in 1991," *State Legislatures Magazine,* December 1991.
50. Ibid.
51. "Business Fees Replace Overt Tax Hikes," p. 15.
52. "Unpopularity Tax," *Forbes,* June 24, 1991, pp. 88–89.
53. "Colleges Fear Proposed Tax on Students," *Los Angeles Times,* June 2, 1990.
54. "For Travelers, It Seems Nothing Is Certain Except Taxes," *Wall Street Journal,* March 14, 1991.

Chapter 6

1. "Cries for Help Go Unheeded," *Los Angeles Times,* February 4, 1991.
2. "Eighties Leave States and Cities in Need," *New York Times,* December 30, 1990.
3. "Suburbs Staggered by Cuomo Budget Cuts," *New York Times,* February 6, 1991.
4. "An Era of Abundance Ends in Nassau County," *New York Times,* December 16, 1991.
5. "New Cuts Sap Feeble School Districts," *New York Times,* April 11, 1991.

6. "Recession Leaving State Governments More Efficient," *New York Times,* April 22, 1992.

7. "Governors Say States Face Increasing Pinch," *Boston Globe,* April 22, 1992.

8. Henry J. Aaron, "Why States, Cities Are in Such a Sorry State," *Boston Globe,* June 23, 1991.

9. "Fat Paychecks Got States and Cities Deep in Hock," *Business Week,* September 23, 1991, p. 26.

10. "As Libraries Face Cuts, Supporters Plan a Protest," *New York Times,* July 8, 1991.

11. "Many Public Libraries Suffer Major Blows," *Wall Street Journal,* February 13, 1991.

12. "Study: U.S. Ranks Low in Spending on Schools," *Chicago Tribune,* April 9, 1991.

13. Interview with American Federation of Teachers, June 1992.

14. "Gains at Private Primary Schools," *USA Today,* December 28, 1991.

15. Jane Bryant Quinn, "Squeezed by Tighter Budgets," *Chicago Tribune,* April 15, 1991.

16. "Cal State System Crippled," *Los Angeles Times,* October 11, 1991.

16A. "At U Conn, Costs Squeeze Its Students," *New York Times,* August 16, 1992.

17. Quinn, op. cit.

18. "Are College Costs Out of Line," *Investor's Daily,* Nov. 12, 1991.

19. "Bush Seeks Limits on U.S. Aid to Students," *Chicago Tribune,* May 29, 1991.

20. "Dallas Students Protest Teacher Layoffs," *Philadelphia Inquirer,* September 4, 1991.

21. "Millionaires' Tax Urged for Student Loan Fund," *New York Times,* July 31, 1991.

22. "Rich Tactic for the Poor," *Los Angeles Times,* July 20, 1991.

23. "Budget Cuts Ravage Hospital Care," *New York Times,* October 22, 1991.

24. "State Mental Health System Deterioration," *Chicago Tribune,* November 18, 1991.

25. "An Investment in America," *Boston Globe,* February 7, 1990.

26. "Economists Warn of Third Deficit," *Dallas News,* September 28, 1989.

27. "Shoddy Infrastructure Gets Scant Attention," *Boston Globe,* April 11, 1990.

28. "Infrastructure Poses Trillion-Dollar Problem," Cleveland *Plain Dealer,* June 4, 1989.

29. "States Pay Bigger Share for Highways, Bridges," *Los Angeles Times,* April 17, 1990.

30. "Federal Cuts Derailing Mass Transit," *Christian Science Monitor,* April 8, 1991.

31. Ibid.

32. See, respectively, Fred Barnes, "Planes, Migraines and Automobiles,"

Business Month, August 1990, and "Shoddy Infrastructure Gets Scant Attention," *Boston Globe,* April 11, 1990.

33. Barnes, op. cit.

34. "Stuck in Traffic," *California Journal,* August 1991.

35. "Taming the L.A. Traffic Monster," *Christian Science Monitor,* November 28, 1990.

36. Ibid.

37. "The Public Fat Cats," *Wall Street Journal,* December 28, 1990.

38. "Rising Costs Force Towns to Share Various Services," *New York Times,* July 15, 1991.

39. "School Fundraisers: Rich Areas Prosper, Poor Suffer," *Los Angeles Times,* June 17, 1991.

40. "Many Are Buying Their Own Security," *Philadelphia Inquirer,* June 23, 1991.

41. Ibid.

42. "Legacy of Anti-Tax Fervor," *New York Times,* November 27, 1990.

43. Milton Goldin, *Ronald Reagan and the Commercialization of Giving* (Tarrytown, N.Y., 1990), pp. 31–33.

44. "U.S. Charities See Increase in Gifts," *Boston Globe,* December 16, 1990.

45. "Look Who's Being Tightfisted," *Business Week,* November 5, 1990, p. 29.

46. Ibid.

47. Ibid.

48. "Pul-eeze! Will Somebody Help Me?" *Time,* February ?, 1987, pp. 48–56.

49. Ibid., pp. 49, 52.

50. Ibid., p. 55.

51. "Poultry, Yes, Hospital Care, No, Consumers Say," *Birmingham News,* June 10, 1990.

52. Jane Bryant Quinn, "The Middle Class Melt," *Newsweek,* December 17, 1990.

53. Ibid.

54. "Lower Tuition Becomes an Enticement," *Boston Globe,* January 13, 1992.

55. "Big Chill on Campus," *Time,* February 3, 1992, p. 61.

56. Ibid., p. 63.

57. "Cost of Cable Service Up 56%," *Washington Post,* July 19, 1991.

58. "Cable on Defensive," *Los Angeles Times,* November 23, 1991.

59. "Ticket Flap: What Price Convenience?" *Los Angeles Times,* May 10, 1991.

60. "It's Slippery at the Top," *Forbes,* September 30, 1991, pp. 113–22.

61. Ibid.

62. "High Attorneys' Fees Are Coming under Attack," *Philadelphia Inquirer,* September 9, 1990.

63. "Activists Want to Pry Open Lawyers' World," *Wall Street Journal,* August 31, 1990.

64. "Banks Revise Fee Structures," *Wall Street Journal,* May 13, 1991.

65. "Interest on Deposits Falls," *New York Times*, April 19, 1991.
66. Ibid.
67. "Ills of the Nation's Health Care System," *Wall Street Journal*, June 24, 1991.
68. "Soaring Medical Costs," *Business Week*, October 28, 1991, p. 24.
69. "Doctors' Pay Up 73% in Three Years," *Des Moines Register*, May 5, 1991.
70. This was the usual estimate Canadians gave to the U.S. press in 1991–92.
71. "Successful System Focuses on Controlling Doctors' Costs," *Boston Globe*, May 13, 1991.
72. "In Canada, a Government System That Provides Health Care for All," *New York Times*, April 30, 1991.
73. "Successful System."
74. "Germans' Health Care Model," *Boston Globe*, May 5, 1991.
75. "Why Health Care Costs Are Tough to Cure," *USA Today*, March 11, 1991.
76. "Why Drugs Cost More in the U.S.," *New York Times*, May 24, 1991.
77. "Drug Costs under Fire," *USA Today*, September 25, 1991.
78. "Are Soaring Medical Costs Sinking Employee Morale?" *Investor's Daily*, June 21, 1991.
79. "Part-time Work a Full-time Chore," *Chicago Tribune*, March 31, 1991.
80. "The New Bragging Rights," *California Business*, July/August, 1991, p. 61.
81. "Part-time Work a Full-time Chore."
82. Chris Tilly, *Short Hours, Short Shrift* (Washington, D.C.: Economic Policy Institute, 1990), p. 3.
83. "Unprepared for Recession," Economic Policy Institute, March 1992, press release, p. 1.
84. "Beware: Pensions Are an Endangered Species," Reuters New Service, *Los Angeles Times*, July 30, 1990.
85. "Retirement Prospects Grow Bleaker for Many as Job Scene Changes," *Wall Street Journal*, August 26, 1987.
86. Jane Bryant Quinn, "Lost: Another Health Benefit," *Newsweek*, June 17, 1991.
87. Stephen Rose and David Fesenfest, *Family Income Changes in the 1980s* (Washington, D.C.: Economic Policy Institute, 1990), p. 17.
88. "The American Family Isn't Mom, Dad and the Kids Anymore," *Atlanta Constitution*, November 13, 1988.
89. "For Many Women, One Job Isn't Enough," *New York Times*, February 15, 1990.
90. "Two Income Couples Earn More," *Investor's Daily*, November 18, 1988.
91. *Families on a Treadmill in Staff Study of the Joint Economic Committee*, January 13, 1992, p. 18.
92. "Child Care Costs Hit Poor Hardest," *Boston Globe*, August 15, 1990.
93. "Census Report Shows a Rise in Child Care," *New York Times*, August 16, 1990.

94. "Options Help Lower Child Care Costs," *Chicago Tribune,* February 4, 1991.

95. "Home Ownership Dream Fading for Middle Class," *Chicago Tribune,* October 3, 1989.

96. "Home Ownership for Young Buyers Dropping," Associated Press, *Birmingham News,* June 25, 1989.

97. "Americans Less Likely to Own Homes Now," *Investor's Daily,* December 21, 1990.

98. "Foundations of Homeownership Crack," *Wall Street Journal,* June 14, 1991.

99. "Homebuying by Unmarrieds Surges in State," *Los Angeles Times,* January 10, 1991.

100. "Foundations of Home Ownership Crack."

101. "America: What Went Wrong," *Philadelphia Inquirer,* October 20, 1991.

101A. "Boom Decade Rang Faintly," *Boston Globe,* April 19, 1992.

102. "Baby Boom Faces Care of Aging Relatives," *Wall Street Journal,* September 26, 1991.

103. Ibid.

104. "Hours of Work Up, Hourly Pay Down," August 31, 1990.

105. "Shift of Women into Labor Market," *Baltimore Sun,* September 11, 1988.

106. "When It Comes to Cutbacks, Little Things Now Mean a Lot," *Philadelphia Inquirer,* September 6, 1991.

107. "The New 'In' Vacation: Shorter, Closer to Home," *Chicago Tribune,* September 1, 1991.

108. "Stagnant Pay: A Delayed Impact," *New York Times,* June 18, 1991.

109. "Two-Career Families Face Dilemma," *Los Angeles Times,* August 12, 1990.

110. "Americans Would Take Cut in Income to Gain More Leisure Time, Survey Says," *Christian Science Monitor,* June 20, 1991.

111. "Stagnant Pay: A Delayed Impact."

Chapter 7

1. "What's a Deb to Do?" *New York Times,* December 16, 1990.

2. "Looking Downscale Without Looking Down," *Business Week,* October 8, 1990, p. 62.

3. "Restaurants Go Downscale to Draw Families," *Investor's Daily,* December 11, 1990.

4. "Sweatshops Are Found Resurging and Spreading," *New York Times,* September 4, 1988.

5. "Welfare Rolls in Illinois Largest Since Depression," *Chicago Tribune,* February 28, 1991.

6. "1980s Gravy Train Left Most Behind," *Chicago Tribune,* May 12, 1991.

7. "Tremendous Trend," *Forbes,* September 2, 1991, p. 23.
8. Ibid.
9. "Dream of Striking It Rich Fading in Silicon Valley," *Los Angeles Times,* September 9, 1991.
10. "California Population Surprise," *Washington Post,* December 17, 1991.
11. "Lavish Homes Seen Losing Luster in New Jersey," *New York Times,* October 9, 1991.
12. "Jobs Vanish and May Not Return," *Los Angeles Times,* November 28, 1991.
13. Robert Reich, "The Unprepared American," *Christian Science Monitor,* April 11, 1991.
14. Lawrence Mishel and Rudy Texeira, "The Myth of the Coming Labor Shortage" (Washington, D.C.: Economic Policy Institute, 1991).
15. "Narrowing a Wage Gap," *New York Times,* June 26, 1987.
16. "California Is No. 1 in Taxes on Rich," *Los Angeles Times,* July 25, 1991, p. D4.
17. "Americans Are Just Simulating the Good Life," *San Francisco Chronicle,* June 18, 1991.
18. "85% of All Households in Hock," *Investor's Daily,* April 22, 1991.
19. "An Excess of Plastic," *Forbes,* February 4, 1991, p. 52.
20. Robert Pollin, *Deeper in Debt: The Changing Financial Conditions of U.S. Households* (Washington, D.C.: Economic Policy Institute, 1990).
21. These are the estimates of Susan Sterne of Economic Analysis Associates Inc. of Stowe, Vermont.
22. "Wealth of U.S. Households Stayed Flat," *Wall Street Journal,* January 11, 1991.
23. "The Richest People in America," *Forbes,* October 21, 1991, p. 145.
24. "Even with Less Consumers May Spend More," *Business Week,* July 29, 1991, p. 20.
25. "The Richest People in America," p. 145.
25A. Mortimer Zuckerman, "Washington's Nasty Addiction," *U.S. News & World Report,* May 4, 1992, p. 100.
26. "Wealth of U.S. Households Stayed Flat."
27. William Greider, *Secrets of the Temple: How the Federal Reserve Runs the Country* (New York: Simon and Schuster, 1987), p. 591.
28. "The 1980s Surge in Home Prices Was Mostly a Mirage," *Business Week,* September 23, 1991.
29. "Eighties Pounded State Renters, Homeowners," *Milwaukee Journal,* September 14, 1991.
30. Phillips, *Politics of Rich and Poor,* p. 194.
31. "Vacation-House Sales Slow to a Standstill in Some Parts of U.S.," *Wall Street Journal,* June 21, 1991.
32. "Wealth of U.S. Households Stayed Flat."
33. "Consumers Draw Down Value in Their Homes," *Wall Street Journal,* August 5, 1991.

34. "1992 Roundtable," *Barron's*, January 20, 1992, p. 15.

35. "Winning Bid for Exec Comes at a Key Moment," *Los Angeles Times*, October 25, 1991.

36. "Firms' Failures Leave Lives in Ruin," *New Orleans Times-Picayune*, October 27, 1991.

37. Howard C. Weizmann, "Safe Annuities or Federalized Annuities," *Wall Street Journal*, October 24, 1991.

38. "Title Insurers' Reserves Stir Worry," *New York Times*, November 9, 1991.

39. "Shortfall Doubles for the Country's Top Pension Plans," *Washington Times*, November 26, 1991.

40. "Retire or Bust," *Newsweek*, November 25, 1991, p. 50.

40A. "Private Pension Funds in Peril," *Washington Times*, July 29, 1992.

41. "Warning Given on Public Employee Pensions," *Philadelphia Inquirer*, November 21, 1991.

42. "Social Security Faces Crisis, Former Official Warns in Book," *Miami Herald*, January 5, 1992.

43. "Stockman: The Economy Is Now Out of the Woods," *Philadelphia Inquirer*, July 14, 1991.

44. Public Citizen, *Who Robbed America?* (New York: Random House, 1990).

45. "RTC May Try to Redo Some Costly Deals," *Chicago Tribune*, July 22, 1990.

46. "Taxpayers' Nightmare," *San Francisco Examiner*, June 16, 1991.

47. Peter Passell, "Economic Scene," *New York Times*, February 12, 1992.

48. *Who Robbed America?* p. 149.

49. "Taxpayers' Nightmare."

50. "Changes Sought in S&L Bail-out," *Chicago Tribune*, July 31, 1991.

51. "Fed's Fat Cat Insurance," *Washington Times*, October 20, 1991.

52. "Bank Rates Hit," *Washington Times*, October 9, 1991.

53. "Economic Diary," *Business Week*, September 16, 1991.

54. "Economic Scene," *New York Times*, June 5, 1991.

55. "Earning Plight of Baby Boomers," *New York Times*, September 21, 1988.

56. "Many Young Families Face '30s Living Standards," *Portland Oregonian*, April 1, 1990.

57. "Downward Mobility Is Stalking Baby Boomers," *Business Week*, January 28, 1991.

58. "A Generation's Vast Wealth Is Baby-Boomer Windfall," *Philadelphia Inquirer*, May 26, 1991.

59. Ibid.

60. "The Windfall Awaiting the New Inheritors," *Fortune*, May 7, 1990, p. 72.

61. "Generation to Inherit Uneven Riches," *Boston Globe*, October 6, 1991.

Chapter 8

1. Report of Genesee Economic Area Revitalization (GEAR), 1990, p. 7.
2. "Pittsburgh Shakes Off Rust," *Los Angeles Times,* October 9, 1991.
3. "Imports, Immigrants Hurt the Unskilled," *Christian Science Monitor,* September 6, 1991.
4. This paragraph is based on the survey "Rust Belt's Recession Cushion" published by the *Los Angeles Times* on January 7, 1991. A kindred examination of much more distressed Peoria, Illinois, was published by *The New York Times* on November 17, 1991.
5. "Rust Belt's Recession Cushion."
6. J. H. Elliott, *Imperial Spain 1469–1716* (New York: Mentor Books, 1966), pp. 194–95.
7. González de Cellorigo, quoted in ibid., pp. 306–7.
8. C. R. Boxer, *The Dutch Seaborne Empire, 1600–1800* (London: Penguin Books, 1965), p. xxiii.
9. Jonathan I. Israel, *Dutch Primacy in World Trade, 1585–1740* (Oxford: Clarendon Paperbacks, 1991), p. 357.
10. Ibid., p. 402.
11. Fernand Braudel, *The Perspective of the World, Civilization and Capitalism 15th–18th Centuries,* p. 197.
12. Boxer, op. cit., p. 328.
13. Asa Briggs, "Middle Class Consciousness in British Politics, 1780–1846," *Past and Present,* Vol. I (1956), pp. 65–74.
14. Ibid.
15. Samuel H. Beer, *British Politics in the Collectivist Age* (New York: Knopf, 1961), p. 45.
16. Aaron L. Friedberg, *The Weary Titan* (Princeton: Princeton University Press, 1988), pp. 38–40.
17. Ibid., p. 75.
18. G.D.H. Cole and Raymond Postgate, eds., *The British Common People, 1746–1946* (London: Methuen & Co./University Paperbacks, 1961), p. 497.
19. John Stevenson, *British Society, 1914–45* (London: Penguin Books), p. 38.
20. E. J. Hobsbawm, *The Pelican Economic History of Britain: From 1750 to the Present Day: Industry and Empire,* Vol. 3 (Baltimore, Md.: Penguin Books, 1968), p. 273.
21. Stevenson, op. cit, p. 119.
22. Ibid., pp. 130–31.
23. Ibid., p. 123.
24. Michael Sissons and Philip French, *Age of Austerity* (London: Penguin Books, 1964), p. 38.
25. Ibid., p. 42.
26. Elliott, op. cit., p. 313.
27. Ibid., p. 204.

276 □ NOTES

28. Boxer, op. cit., pp. 34–35.
29. Braudel, op. cit., p. 197.
30. Boxer, op. cit.
31. Braudel, op. cit., pp. 274–75.
32. Hobsbawm, op. cit., p. 119.
33. Cole and Postgate, op. cit., p. 498.
34. Ibid.
35. Joseph S. Nye, Jr., "Before Fall," *New Republic,* February 13, 1989, p. 37.
36. Charles W. Boyd, ed., *Mr. Chamberlain's Speeches* (London: Constable, 1914), Vol. 2, pp. 535–36.
37. "Democratic Campaign Issue: Jobs," *Washington Times,* July 5, 1991.
38. Economists from Japan's Nomura Institute and elsewhere made this point in several international publications.
39. George F. Will, "What Dukakis Should Be Saying," *Washington Post,* September 15, 1988.
40. Elliott, op. cit., pp. 200–201.
41. Simon Schama, *The Embarrassment of Riches: An Interpretation of Dutch Culture in the Golden Age* (New York: Knopf/University of California Press, 1988), p. 166.
42. Stevenson, op. cit., p. 124.
43. Roger Milliken, "Power, Wealth and Protectionism," speech delivered to National Conference of Christians and Jews, New York, December 6, 1985.
44. Paul Kennedy, *The Rise and Fall of the Great Powers* (New York: Random House, 1987), pp. 151–52.
45. Boxer, op. cit., pp. 324–25.
46. Friedberg, op. cit., p. 39.
47. Ibid., p. 64.
48. Ibid., p. 63.
49. Hobsbawm, op. cit., p. 166.
50. "For Sale: America," *Time,* September 14, 1987, p. 53.
51. John B. Judis, "Show and Tell," *New Republic,* January 20, 1992, p. 15.
52. Boxer, op. cit., p. 118.
53. Kennedy, op cit., p. 319.
54. Elliott, op. cit., pp. 326–29.
55. Friedberg, op. cit., pp. 116–18.

Chapter 9

1. Christopher Matthews, "From One Who Warned of Hitler," *Washington Times,* November 12, 1991.
2. Max Lerner, "Enduring Qualities of Evil," *Washington Times,* November 24, 1991.
3. Seymour Martin Lipset and Earl Raab, *The Politics of Unreason* (New York: Harper Torchbooks, 1970), p. 95.

4. Ibid., p. 80.
5. Richard Hofstadter, *Social Darwinism in American Thought* (Boston: Beacon Press, 1955), p. 119.
6. Richard Hofstadter, *The Age of Reform* (New York: Knopf, 1955), p. 132.
7. Ibid.
8. Lipset and Raab, op. cit., p. 167.
9. Ibid., p. 190.
10. Ibid., p. 169.
11. James A. Farley, *Behind the Ballots* (New York: Harcourt Brace, 1938), p. 250.
12. Lipset and Raab, op. cit., p. 169.
13. Richard B. Morris, ed., *Encyclopedia of American History* (New York: Harper & Row, 1976), pp. 417–18.
14. Ken Bode, "Hero or Demagogue?" *New Republic,* March 3, 1986, p. 37.
15. *Papers of Franklin D. Roosevelt,* 1938. Vol. 5, pp. 69–69.
16. William Leuchtenburg, *Franklin D. Roosevelt and the New Deal* (New York: Harper & Row, 1963), pp. 53–54.
17. Arthur M. Schlesinger, Jr., *The Politics of Upheaval* (Boston: Houghton Mifflin, 1960), p. 68.
18. Lipset and Raab, op. cit., pp. 176, 194.
19. Alan Brinkley, *Voices of Protest* (New York: Knopf, 1982), p. 198.
20. Ibid.
21. This paragraph was largely taken, with some rephrasing, from p. 198 of my book *Post-Conservative America,* published by Random House in 1982.
22. Eugene Litwak, Nancy Hooyman and Donald Warren, "Ideological Complexity and Middle American Rationality," *Public Opinion Quarterly,* Fall 1973, p. 320.
23. See Seymour M. Lipset, *Political Man* (New York: Anchor Books, 1963), pp. 131–73.
24. See "KKK Leader's Race Stirs Dismay," *Los Angeles Times* (May 29, 1980), and "White Supremacist's Vote-Getting Talent Stuns His GOP Detractors," *Washington Post* (November 15, 1980).
25. "Angry Voters Send Message," *Washington Times,* November 14, 1991.
26. See, in particular, Lowell Streiker and Gerald S. Strober, *Religion and the New Majority,* 1972.
27. NBC/Wall Street Journal poll, April 1992.
28. "On the Eve of '92: Fault Lines in the Electorate," Times-Mirror Center for People and the Press, Washington, D.C., December 1991, pp. 2–3.

Chapter 10

1. "Clinton's Stand on Middle-Class Tax Hike," *Human Events,* November 7, 1992, p. 3.

2. "Imperial Spain," p. 311.
3. Peter Peterson, "Rethinking America's Security: The Primacy of the Domestic Agenda," privately printed, May 11, 1991.
4. Ibid., p. 7.
5. "Imperial Spain," p. 311.
6. Mancur Olson, *The Rise and Decline of Nations* (New Haven, Conn.: Yale University Press, 1980), pp. 77–80.
7. Bob Kuttner, "Tsongas' Plea for Economic Patriots," *Boston Globe,* June 7, 1991.
8. "Shift to Domestic Concerns Urged," *Washington Post,* July 19, 1991.
9. "Time for a New Isolationism," *Christian Science Monitor,* June 18, 1990.
10. Alfred Eckes, "Trading American Interests," *Foreign Affairs,* Fall 1992, pp. 135–54.

The Converging Income Shares of the Middle Quintile and the Top 1 Percent of the U.S. Population

Shares of Pretax Adjusted Family Income (AFI)

(In percent)

All families (by income group)	1977	1980	1985	1988	1989
Lowest quintile	4.7	4.3	3.7	3.5	3.6
Second quintile	10.8	10.5	9.5	9.1	9.2
Middle quintile	16.3	16.0	15.1	14.6	14.7
Fourth quintile	22.9	22.9	22.2	21.7	21.7
81 to 90 percent	15.6	15.7	15.7	15.3	15.4
91 to 95 percent	10.1	10.1	10.4	10.1	10.3
96 to 99 percent	11.6	11.7	12.4	12.6	12.7
Top 1 percent	8.3	9.2	11.6	13.4	13.0
Overall	100.0	100.0	100.0	100.0	100.0
Highest quintile	45.6	46.7	50.1	51.4	**51.4**
Top 10 percent	30.0	31.0	34.4	36.1	36.0
Top 5 percent	19.9	20.9	24.0	26.0	25.7

Note: Table reads for boldface figure that 51.4 percent of all adjusted pretax family income in 1989 belonged to families in the fifth or highest quintile. Quintiles are weighted by persons.

Source: Congressional Budget Office tax simulation model, cited in U.S. House Ways and Means Committee 1992 Green Book. p. 1521.

Important Changes in the Tax Burden

The Declining Importance of the Personal Exemption

Federal Income Tax Personal Exemption, as a Percent
of U.S. Individual Income

Source: The Urban Institute

The Rising Social Security (FICA) Tax

Year	Tax Rate	Tax Base	Max Payment
1980	5.80%	$25,900	$1,502
1981	6.65%	$29,700	$1,975
1982	6.70%	$32,400	$2,170
1983	6.70%	$35,700	$2,391
1984	7.00%	$37,800	$2,646
1985	7.05%	$39,000	$2,749
1986	7.15%	$42,000	$3,003
1987	7.15%	$43,800	$3,131
1988	7.51%	$45,000	$3,379
1989	7.51%	$48,000	$3,604
1990	7.65%	$51,300	$3,924

Source: Social Security Administration

Tax Changes and the Benefit to the Top 1% and Top 5% (1977–1989)

Total Federal Effective Tax Rates for All Families

All families (by income group)	1977	1980	1985	1988	1989	Percent change 1977–1989
Lowest quintile	9.3	8.1	10.3	9.3	9.3	0.1
Second quintile	15.4	15.6	15.8	15.9	15.7	1.4
Middle quintile	19.5	19.8	19.1	19.8	19.4	-.4
Fourth quintile	21.8	22.9	21.7	22.4	22.0	.7
81 to 90 percent	24.0	25.3	23.4	24.6	24.2	.9
91 to 95 percent	25.2	26.3	24.2	26.0	25.6	1.5
96 to 99 percent	27.0	27.9	24.3	26.5	26.2	-2.9
Top 1 percent	35.5	31.7	24.9	26.9	26.7	-24.7
Overall	22.8	23.3	21.7	22.9	22.6	-.7
Highest quintile	27.2	27.5	24.1	26.0	25.6	-5.8
Top 10 percent	28.8	28.6	24.5	26.5	26.2	-9.0
Top 5 percent	30.6	29.6	24.6	26.7	26.5	-13.5

Note: Table reads for boldface figure that, for the lowest 20 percent of income of the population in 1977, total Federal taxes were 9.3 percent of income. Quintiles are weighted by families.

Source: Congressional Budget Office (CBO) tax simulation model, cited in 1992 Green Book of House Ways and Means Committee, p. 1510

The Rising Burden of Real Estate Taxes

Property tax revenue outpaces inflation in New Jersey

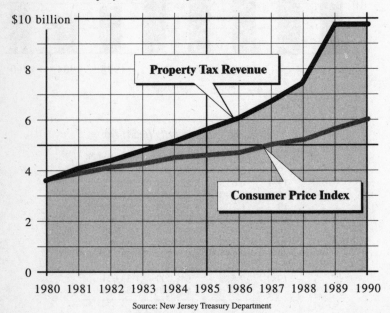

Source: New Jersey Treasury Department

The Rising Burden of Real Estate Taxes (continued)

The Ten U.S. Counties with the Highest Per Capita Property Taxes (1990)

County	Property Tax Revenue Per Person	Property Tax As Share of Total County Revenue
Fairfax, Va.	$1,185	74%
Prince William, Va.	770	67%
Montgomery, Md.	627	42%
Henrico, Va.	623	43%
Baltimore, Md.	502	44%
Anne Arundel, Md.	459	37%
Prince George's, Md.	395	42%
Mecklenburg, N.C.	376	57%
Westchester, N.Y.	356	30%
Onondaga, N.Y.	313	36%

Source: *City & State newspaper, U.S. News and World Report*

The Soaring Cost of Services and the Weakening Health and Pension Safety Net

The Inflation in Health Costs

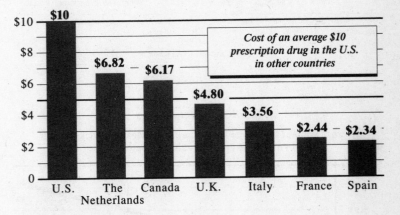

Cost of an average $10 prescription drug in the U.S. in other countries

Source: 1989 Annual Survey of Farmindustria, Italian Pharmaceutical Association

Doctors' income

Source: American Medical Association

Prices and Profits for 20 Prescription Drugs

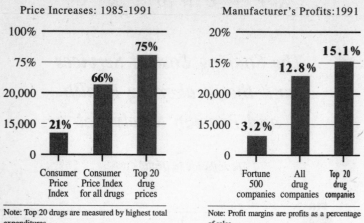

Price Increases: 1985-1991

Note: Top 20 drugs are measured by highest total expenditures.

Manufacturer's Profits: 1991

Note: Profit margins are profits as a percentage of sales

Source: Families USA Foundation

Health Care Contributions

Average Annual Employee Contribution for Health Care Coverage and Percent of Plans Requiring Contributions

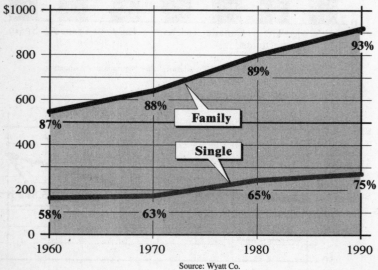

Source: Wyatt Co.

The Rising Cost of Attending College

Average Annual Increases in Tuition and Fees at Four-Year Colleges
(in percentage change from previous year)

Source: College Board

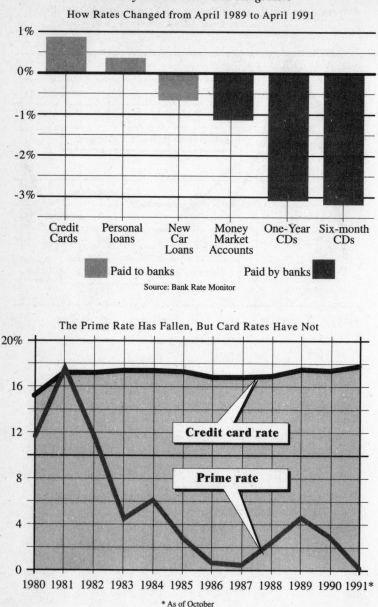

Banks Pay Less Interest—and Charge More

How Rates Changed from April 1989 to April 1991

Paid to banks   Paid by banks

Source: Bank Rate Monitor

The Prime Rate Has Fallen, But Card Rates Have Not

Credit card rate

Prime rate

* As of October

Source: Bancard Holders of America

Soaring Cable Television Charges

U.S. Cable Rates

Average Basic Monthly Service Charge per Subscriber

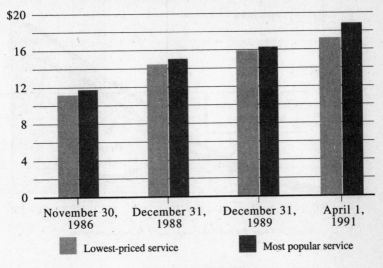

Source: General Accounting Office

Soaring Cable Rates in Los Angeles

*Since cable deregulation went into effect in January 1987,
average basic cable TV rates among the fourteen cable TV franchises
in the city of Los Angeles have jumped 107%*

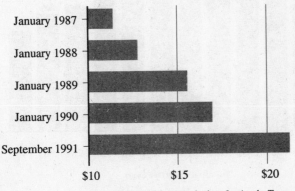

Source: Office of Telecommunications, *Los Angeles Times*

Surging Automobile Premiums

Accelerating Costs since 1980

1980=100%

Claims paid out by insurers

Premiums charged

Source: *U.S. News & World Report*, Basic data: A.M. Best Company, Inc.

Shrinking Vacations

Vacation Length
Average number of nights

Source: U.S. Travel Data Center

Declining Pension Coverage and Safety

In the 1980s, employers by the thousands terminated pension plans, cut back on their contributions, or claimed pension fund assets.

Corporate Pension Contributions Shrinking

$60 Billion
58
56
54
52
50

1980 1981 1982 1983 1984 1985 1986 1987

Source: Pension and Welfare Benefit Administration

Pension Terminations on the Rise

12 Plans Ended in Thousands
10
8
4
2
0

1975 1977 1979 1981 1983 1985 1987 1989

Source: Pension Benefit Guaranty Corp.

Companies Reclaim Assets from Pensions
Since 1980, thousands of employers have taken $21 billion in pension assets from retirement plans.

$25 Billions
20
15
10
5
0

1980 1981 1982 1983 1984 1985 1986 1987 1988 1989 1990

Source: Pension Benefit Guaranty Corp., Newhouse News Service

Declining Pension Coverage and Safety (continued)

Workers and Pensions
*While the number of workers is growing,
the number of those with pensions is not*

Total workers — 93.0

Workers with guaranteed pensions — 27.8

Sources: *Philadelphia Inquirer*, Bureau of Labor Statistics

Less Coverage
*Percentage of private-sector workers,
16 and older, covered by pensions*

*Note: Figures after 1988 are estimates.

Sources: David E. Bloom of Columbia University and Richard B. Freeman
of Harvard University, *The New York Times*

Index

Federal Deposit Insurance Corporation
(FDIC), 148, 185, 186, 188
federal government, 131
aid programs of, 47, 52, 64
breach of social contract of, 50–55
debt and deficits of, xxiii, 26, 36, 44,
88, 130, 137, 210, 220, 251, 255, 258,
259
funding strategies of, 111
limitation of, 34, 35, 62, 72
popular opinion of, xvii–xviii
reductions in aid from, 36, 54, 116–17,
132, 140, 156, 259
rich and powerful favored by, xvii–xviii
transfer-payment programs of, 52
see also United States; *specific
administrations*
Federalists, 41–42, 64
Federal Reserve Board, xix, xx, 23, 91,
178, 179, 180n, 186, 188–89, 190n
Federal Savings and Loan Insurance
Corporation (FSLIC), 186, 187
fees and charges, 42, 45, 46, 47, 49, 52,
53, 94, 96, 105, 106, 118–19, 120–22,
127, 130, 162, 176
Ferguson, Fred, 127
FICA, *see* Social Security
financialization, 193–94, 204–11, 251–52
financial services and institutions, 96,
185–90, 209
see also banks
Financial World, 209
Flint, Mich., 195
Florida, 46, 47, 104, 118, 126, 134
food stamps, 10, 11, 240
Forbes, 146, 169
Forbes, Malcolm, Jr., 171–72
Forbes 400, 24n, 179
Ford, Gerald, 256
foreclosures, 178
Foreign Affairs, 254
foreign interests, 54
foreign investments, 17
foreign trade, 25, 31
Fortune, 56, 62, 169
Fort Wayne, Ind., 196
France, 36
free market, xx, xxi–xxii, 33, 37, 40, 50,
52–54, 194, 213–17
Fremont, John C., 257
Friedman, Benjamin, 26, 35
frustration politics, 63, 168–69, 223–44,
256, 259

G-7 nations, xxiii, 36, 37, 259
Gantt, Harvey, 241
General Motors, 11
Gephardt, Richard, xi, 77, 85
Germany, 36, 37, 174, 255, 259
CEOs in, 63
health care in, 149, 150, 151
Germany, Nazi, 168
Germany, Weimar, 225
Gibbon, Edward, 193
Gibson, Ted, 99
Gifford, Walter S., 142n
Gilded Age, 34, 35–36, 61, 69, 72, 73, 78,
80, 87, 89–93, 224, 226, 227, 228,
247
elements of, 35
Gingrich, Newt, 193
Gladstone, William E., 17
Glickman, Norman, 209
globalism, 50, 53–54, 173, 212–21
Gold, Steven, 126
Goldberg, Fred, 47
Goldberg, Jackie, 140
Goldin, Claudia, xix
Goldwater, Barry, 67, 239, 240
Goodwyn, Lawrence, 69
Government at the Crossroads, 139
Gramm-Rudman Act (1985), 44,
79
Great Britain, 36, 37, 56, 86, 134, 136,
199–204, 206, 224, 256, 259
Conservative party of, 37, 38, 40–41,
256
debt of, 219, 220, 251–52
decline of, 253
Edwardian era of, 21, 168, 194, 202,
203, 209, 217
financialization of, 251
food rationing in, 203
foreign investments of, 217
free trade and, 40–41, 214–15
Industrial Revolution in, 173n
Labour party of, xx, 38, 168, 202, 224,
256
Liberal Democratic party of, 38
Liberal party of, 200, 219, 256
manufacturing in, 195
middle class in, 199–203, 204
public services in, 51
redistribution of income in, 202–3,
212
taxes in, 37–38, 40–41, 50
welfare in, 202, 224, 252

ABOUT THE AUTHOR

KEVIN PHILLIPS was chief political analyst for the 1968 Republican presidential campaign and later served as assistant to the attorney general. Since 1971 he has been the editor-publisher of *The American Political Report*. Phillips is a contributing columnist to the *Los Angeles Times*, a member of the political strategists' panel of *The Wall Street Journal*, and a regular commentator for National Public Radio. He served as a commentator for CBS Television at the 1984, 1988 and 1992 Republican and Democratic presidential conventions. He is also a periodic contributor to the Op-ed page of *The New York Times* and the Outlook section of *The Washington Post*.

Phillips's first book, *The Emerging Republican Majority*, was described by *Newsweek* as "the political bible of the Nixon Era." It predicted the coming conservative era in U.S. national politics.